MW00831587

Enemies of the Cross

Enemies of the Cross

Suffering, Truth, and Mysticism in the Early Reformation

VINCENT EVENER

OXFORD
UNIVERSITY PRESS

OXFORD

UNIVERSITY PRESS

Oxford University Press is a department of the University of Oxford. It furthers
the University's objective of excellence in research, scholarship, and education
by publishing worldwide. Oxford is a registered trade mark of Oxford University
Press in the UK and certain other countries.

Published in the United States of America by Oxford University Press
198 Madison Avenue, New York, NY 10016, United States of America.

© Oxford University Press 2021

Library of Congress Cataloging-in-Publication Data
Names: Evener, Vincent, author.
Title: Enemies of the cross : suffering, truth, and mysticism
in the early Reformation / by Vincent Evener.
Description: New York, NY, United States of America :
Oxford University Press, 2021. | Includes bibliographical references and index.
Identifiers: LCCN 2020024998 (print) | LCCN 2020024999 (ebook) |
ISBN 9780190073183 (hb) | ISBN 9780190073213 (oso) |
ISBN 9780190073206 (epub) | ISBN 9780190073190 (updf)
Subjects: LCSH: Reformation. | Theology, Doctrinal—History.
Classification: LCC BR307 .E84 2021 (print) |
LCC BR307 (ebook) | DDC 270.6—dc23
LC record available at https://lccn.loc.gov/2020024998
LC ebook record available at https://lccn.loc.gov/2020024999

1 3 5 7 9 8 6 4 2

Printed by Integrated Books International, United States of America

For my grandparents, Helen May (Wright) Bonsall (1933–2014)
and Gerald Eugene Bonsall (1930–2004)

Contents

Contents

Acknowledgments

We accumulate debts to countless others every day of our lives, and the gifts we receive from those others, known and unknown to us, shape and enrich our existence. A set of acknowledgments for even so humble an accomplishment as a scholarly book can scarcely recognize all those who have contributed to the realization of the venture. This book began as a doctoral dissertation at the University of Chicago Divinity School, where Susan E. Schreiner was my *Doktormutter*. A devoted and inspiring teacher, Susan stimulated my interest in Reformation history and theology, and she sent me forth on intellectual adventures that I could not have imagined when I began graduate studies. She has influenced the ensuing book through direct guidance and through her scholarship. I also owe a deep debt of gratitude to Ronald K. Rittgers, who agreed to serve as an outside reader on the dissertation committee after only a brief email exchange and one personal meeting. Like Susan, Ron lives out the conviction that each generation of scholars must cultivate the next. Ron has remained an adviser and an ally, and I am particularly grateful for his invitation to work together on an edited volume, *Protestants and Mysticism in Reformation Europe* (Brill, 2019). It was a joy to work on that book, and I learned much from the expert contributors that has shaped my continued interpretation of the texts and themes discussed in this book. As this book took shape at the dissertation stage, I also benefited from the advice of Willemien Otten, and more broadly, from the conversation and encouragement of faculty and fellow students at the Divinity School.

Funding for research and writing was provided by a fellowship from the Martin Marty Center for the Advanced Study of Religion, where I participated in a fellows' seminar led by Michael Sells. A grant from the Rolf und Ursula Schneider Stiftung allowed me to study three months at the extraordinary Herzog August Bibliothek; thanks are due to Jill Bepler and the entire library staff. With the support of a Fulbright grant, I spent nearly a year at the *Sächsische Landesbibliothek—Staats- und Universitätsbibliothek*, Dresden; again, thanks are due to the library staff. In Dresden, Hans-Peter Hasse extended a warm welcome to me and my wife; he not only assisted me in the painstaking work of deciphering Andreas Karlstadt's marginal annotations to Tauler's sermons, but he also helped connect me to scholars, libraries, and conferences throughout Germany. I had the opportunity to complete a paleography seminar in Göttingen under the direction of Ulrich Bubenheimer, and I received a friendly welcome there from Alejandro Zorzin and others with the Karlstadt Edition, an important project directed by Thomas Kaufmann. I have since enjoyed and benefited from correspondence with both Drs. Bubenheimer and Zorzin.

Since completing my graduate studies, I have been able to revise and conclude this book while serving on the faculty of the Lutheran Theological Seminary at Gettysburg, which in 2017 became United Lutheran Seminary. I am grateful to many colleagues for the warm reception that my family received in Gettysburg in 2015. Trying times have followed for the seminary, but throughout, I have been inspired by my colleagues' dedication to scholarship, education, and the church. Direct assistance on this project was provided by fellow Chicago alum Eric Crump, who read and provided feedback on an earlier version of the manuscript, and of course by the library staff. Most recently, library director Evan Boyd and his staff have handled a flurry of requests—sometimes for rather obscure material—with kindness and efficiency.

I am thankful to Theo Calderara, religion editor for Oxford University Press, for his willingness to publish this book in the *Oxford Studies in Historical Theology* series, to the editorial board of the series, and to the anonymous reviewers who provided me with much useful feedback. The competitive nature of the academic field is well-known; the work of anonymous reviewers is a reminder that there is far more collegiality and shared commitment to learning than we sometimes realize. My thanks are also due to Travis Ables, who compiled the index on rather short notice.

I have recently been reminded of just how much others support us as we try to render our own gifts to the world. A serious bicycle accident put me on crutches just a few weeks before this manuscript was due. My brother-in-law, Dietrich Koch, drove three hours and helped move my office upstairs so that I could work; my father-in-law, Gary Koch, flew from across the country to help keep the household afloat; concerned notes came from friends across the country; we have received more food than our refrigerator and pantry can hold. Thanks to this generosity, I am able to sit comfortably behind my computer, read and reflect on sixteenth-century texts, and fumble for expressions of gratitude.

No one contributed more to this book than my wife, Philippa, and the two sons we welcomed to the world while work was in progress—Casper and Felix. Philippa was a learned resource for exploring ideas and interpretations large and small; at the same time, she, Casper, and Felix have constantly kept before my eyes the world outside the book, the world that the book seeks to serve as a contribution to knowledge. This book was undertaken out of the love of learning, but also out of the conviction that learning is a responsibility we have to the societies in which we live, to future generations, and to the world around us. With the responsibility to learn comes the responsibility and the satisfaction of acting in fidelity to truth. For all the struggle and transition that marks the academic world in the present moment, I know that scholars will continue to represent these values to a needy world. I conclude this book in the hope that my children will live in a world where teaching and learning are respected and where knowledge is not a source of fear.

I dedicated my dissertation to my mother, Judy Mae Evener (1952–2012), who died two years before its conclusion; shortly after I completed graduate studies, I lost my grandmother. This book is dedicated to my grandparents, who were among my first teachers. They knew little of Martin Luther, but their lives embodied his belief that God puts us on earth to serve others: "Creatures are only the hands, channels, and means through which God bestows all blessings."[1]

Vincent Evener, September 5, 2019

Introduction

For many live as enemies of the cross of Christ; I have often told you of them, and now I tell you even with tears. Their end is destruction; their god is the belly; and their glory is in their shame; their minds are set on earthly things. But our citizenship is in heaven, and it is from there that we are expecting a Savior, the Lord Jesus Christ.

—Philippians 3:18–20 (NRSV)

[The true church] must always be tried and persecuted. In contrast, other religions and faiths are invented anew each day from human beings' own imagination, without divine testimony or revelation. Thus, they have this character: they arouse no persecution or resistance, but . . . they shun and flee the cross and are accepted by the world only because they give peace, rest, good days, honor and goods, and serve the stomach. The devil leaves such [religions], his servants, in peace.

—Martin Luther, Sermon for the 4th Sunday after Epiphany, January 31, 1546[1]

The whole Christian people is becoming a whore with its adulation of man. It is adulation of man . . . when fear of their lords and princes leads men to deny God's word and his holy name completely for the sake of their pathetic food and of their stomachs; St Paul would call them . . . beasts ruled by their stomachs, saying that their God is their stomach. . . . The devil is a really wily rascal, always luring men with food and security, for he knows that fleshy men are fond of that. And so for the sake of it they are forced to deny God. Isn't that a ghastly, pathetic lack of faith [*vnglaube*]. For if you do not believe that God is mighty enough, when you risk or abandon your wealth and bodily food and even your life for the sake of God, to give you different food and more than before, how will you ever be able to believe that he can give you eternal life? It is a truly childlike belief

Enemies of the Cross. Vincent Evener, Oxford University Press (2021). © Oxford University Press.
DOI: 10.1093/oso/9780190073183.001.0001.

[*ein rechter kynderglaub*] that God will give us our food, but to trust
that he will give us eternal life is a supernatural belief, beyond all
human reason.

—Thomas Müntzer, Letter to the Christians of Sangerhausen,
c. July 13, 1524[2]

As European Christianity splintered in the sixteenth century, each side
claimed to possess the essential truths necessary for salvation, while
denying that their opponents possessed these truths. Theologians and
pastors were involved in a multifaceted project: not only did they need to
define the sources of truth—scripture, tradition, and direct divine experience were all possibilities[3]—but they also needed to teach Christians how
to distinguish between truth and falsehood, how to shape their thoughts,
beliefs, worship, devotion, and lives after the former, and how to avoid as
much as possible any taint of the latter. Truth needed to persuade and to
transform Christians, to claim and shape mind and heart, and to inspire and
inform self-discipline, including in the face of suffering that threatened to
unmoor religious commitments.[4] In his 1539 treatise, *On the Councils and
the Church*, Martin Luther (1483–1546) identified the "cross and suffering"
as one of seven marks of the true church,[5] and in one of Luther's last sermons
before his death on February 18, 1546, the reformer went so far as to say that
the endurance of suffering and persecution distinguished the true Christian
church from all "other religions and faiths." Among the latter, Luther
grouped not only Judaism, Islam, and paganism, but also his intra-Christian
competitors. Like all non-Christian faiths, Catholic, Reformed, and radical
Christianity were, in Luther's view, dreamed up by human reason and imagination for the purposes of wish fulfillment.[6] Invoking Philippians 3:18–20
with his reference to "serving the stomach," Luther divided the world into
two groups—friends and enemies of the cross of Christ. Similar logic could
be turned against Luther, however: in a 1524 letter, the radical preacher
Thomas Müntzer (c. 1489–1525) encouraged Christians facing persecution
to welcome the deprivation of basic necessities. How else could they learn to
trust in God's promises? Müntzer's message about God's promises, the need
for faith in those promises, and the pedagogical value of trials resonated
with central themes in Luther's teaching. Nonetheless, by the time of this
letter, Müntzer had identified Luther as the most wily "enemy of the cross."

In his view, Luther taught an outward religion of ease under the guise of humility and suffering.

The present book seeks the roots of such arguments and polemic in the earliest days of the Reformation, in Luther's efforts to define and defend his understanding of Christian doctrine and life vis-à-vis Catholic opponents, and in the debate between Luther and his most significant early intra-Reformation critics, Müntzer and Andreas Bodenstein von Karlstadt (1486–1541). A sustained focus on Luther, Karlstadt, and Müntzer in the period between 1517 and 1525 will allow us to witness how divergent views on the connection between suffering, truth, and salvation emerged from engagement with shared sources, including especially those forms of late-medieval mysticism that sought union with God through an experience of the soul's annihilation unto nothingness, inspired by the controversial Dominican Meister Eckhart (c. 1260–1327/1328).[7]

It is well known that Luther was a catalyst for Protestant and radical interest in post-Eckhartian mysticism:[8] he praised Eckhart's disciple Johannes Tauler (c. 1300–1361) and published the anonymous *German Theology*, a fourteenth- or fifteenth-century text from the Eckhartian stream.[9] Until recently, however, scholars have usually emphasized Luther's discontinuity with medieval mystical authors; many have argued and still argue that Luther found in the mystics primarily confirmation of views already won from the Bible or Augustine.[10] Meanwhile, reformers like Karlstadt and Müntzer have been depicted as champions of "old" mystical concepts against the "new" or more-biblical theology of Luther.[11] This book examines the three reformers' competing development of a shared tradition in the service of equally shared assumptions concerning both the necessity of spiritual suffering in order to receive divine truth and the inevitability of visible suffering for true Christians. It attends to the "mystical roots" of Luther's essential teachings concerning salvation and the recognition of theological truth,[12] and even more to how Luther used mystical ideas and vocabulary to make those teachings persuasive—to convince Christians of their truth content, to teach them how to assess their own experiences, and to teach them how to navigate a world filled with false teachers and false Christians.[13] I show that Karlstadt and Müntzer were equally involved in this creative theological and pastoral work, unfolding teachings rooted in Eckhartian mysticism around themes of true and false suffering to meet the hopes and anxieties of a new age.[14] While acknowledging the influence of other strands of theological tradition, including mystical authors outside the Eckhartian fold, I focus on the post-Eckhartian tradition because scholarship has yet to show how and why reformers took up its bold and profound teachings on union through annihilation: briefly stated, reformers assumed that human thoughts and desires independent from the divine source of truth and life were dangerous and deceptive.

The present book also argues that the use of mysticism to define experiences necessary for all *true* Christians inevitably forced the question of how these true Christians, on the basis of union with God, were to relate to imperfect institutions and false Christians. The much-discussed democratization of mysticism in the Reformation was joined with a delimitation—mystical teachings helped identify the false—and together this democratization and delimitation had enormous social-political implications, stirring dissent that could be differently channeled depending on one's understanding of union with God.[15]

Andreas Bodenstein von Karlstadt was Luther's colleague on the theological faculty of the University of Wittenberg. Thomas Müntzer was a priest who came to Wittenberg in late 1517 and who studied there until 1519. Karlstadt and Müntzer shared in Luther's enthusiasm for mystical literature from the post-Eckhartian tradition. Within a few years, however, and partly because they drew different conclusions from Eckhartian sources, the three reformers developed competing theologies and visions for the reform of individual and community.[16] They defined union with God differently, and as a consequence, advanced divergent visions of how Christians were to live both as sufferers and social-political actors—two roles that were intertwined. At the same time, each maintained a kindred view of human sinfulness as springing from self-assertion—in the form of self-trust (Luther), self-will (Karlstadt), or pleasure seeking (Müntzer)—that had to be crushed by God's contrary work of salvation. Salvation had to be suffered, and then lived out in a world hostile to God's truth and God's children. Reformers' views were shaped and expressed by rich German and Latin terms—*leiden, passio, pati*—that simultaneously referenced pain, anguish, and passivity.

In historical hindsight, Luther usually appears as the winner of a two-way contest pitting him against some "radicals" who emerged from his camp;[17] in truth, this was a three-way contest whose outcome was not obvious in the moment.[18] Karlstadt and Müntzer gathered their own circles of followers— men like Martin Reinhart, Gerhard Westerburg, Simon Haferitz, and Georg Amandus, whose names are little known today—and their goals appeared realizable to at least some of their contemporaries. Yet Müntzer and his vision met disaster after he aligned with the rebels in the Peasants' War of 1524–1525; he took the field with an army of thousands that was slaughtered at Frankenhausen, and he was captured and executed shortly thereafter, on May 27, 1525. Karlstadt was unwilling either to endorse rebellion in the name of the Gospel or to toe the line of conformity to Luther's teachings; consequently, he found himself without a community of supporters in 1525. Forced to seek refuge with Luther in Wittenberg, Karlstadt subsequently wandered for several years before finding a home in the Swiss Reformed church in 1530. Karlstadt died in Basel in 1541 while ministering to victims of the plague. Luther, meanwhile, remained at the forefront of a movement that came to be called "Lutheranism," his teachings prized by generation after generation following his death in 1546. Much of what Luther learned about suffering and salvation from the Eckhartian mystical tradition, and then refined in debate with Karlstadt and Müntzer, became an enduring part of Lutheran spirituality and doctrine. The influence of Müntzer and Karlstadt was significant in some circles—both influenced Anabaptists and spiritualists, and Karlstadt also had some influence in the Reformed tradition—but more diffuse in the long run.[19] Karlstadt did find readers among some later seventeenth-century Lutheran Pietists interested in inner experience and ethical renewal as an antidote to the academic subtlety, confessional controversy, and stultifying preoccupation with doctrinal rectitude that they perceived as dominant in their own age.[20]

It is not surprising that Luther and his early followers claimed to suffer according to the example of Christ; they were not only rejected and condemned by the Roman ecclesial hierarchy, but also threatened by political authorities who defended the "old faith," including the Holy Roman Emperor himself.[21] Neither is it surprising that Karlstadt, Müntzer, and their followers made the same claim upon Christ-like suffering when they were maligned and excluded from Luther's inner circle, which enjoyed the backing of the Ernestine Saxon princes. Passionate devotion to the suffering humanity of Christ was a prominent feature of late-medieval Christian piety and the "imitation of Christ" was embraced as a pious practice both within and beyond the walls of the cloister—as evidenced by the wide circulation of Thomas à Kempis's (d. 1471) manual on the topic. Christians also remembered saintly feats of renunciation and endurance in the face of suffering, torture, and martyrdom, marking such feats on festival days and venerating the relics of the saints themselves.[22] Luther himself was an Augustinian friar steeped in teachings and practices of self-mortification and the cultivation of contrition—a deep, inward sorrow for sin mounting even to self-hatred. Finally, the strife of the Reformation quickly brought on mortal danger, as Christians made martyrs of Christians.[23] Both Luther and Karlstadt lived under the threat of imperial execution after 1522. Karlstadt was expelled from Ernestine Saxony in September 1524, and he subsequently found himself distrusted by all sides as the Peasants' War progressed around Rothenburg ob der Tauber; from 1525 to 1530, he lived near Wittenberg as an impoverished farmer and peddler, under surveillance and threatened with arrest. For his part, Müntzer fled or was kicked out of town after town throughout his reforming career, and he paid with his life for seeing God's hand in the Peasants' War.

Yet there were martyrs on all sides, just as there was suffering, poverty, disease, old age, and spiritual anguish on all sides. The claim that suffering and cross-bearing identified one's own camp as the true church required dismissing the self-evident suffering of others as "false." The central claim of this book is that Luther, Karlstadt, and Müntzer, in their respective claiming and dismissing of the cross, drew upon and clashed within a shared paradigm of the Christian as sufferer: they agreed that fallen, self-assertive human beings had to suffer to become *receptive* to true doctrine, faith, and life, *preceptive* about the truth or falsehood of doctrines, teachers, and their own experiences, and *active* in the world in ways pleasing to God. The true experience of God and God's work brought suffering both spiritual and visible for fallen human beings; the true doctrine proclaimed this suffering; and true Christians were remade by the divinely worked mortification or even annihilation of their fallen self-will to discern whether and where God's message was being heard and obeyed. Conversely, false suffering in the reformers' (shared) view fell into three broad types: unwanted suffering allowed or sent by God to punish wicked adherents to falsehood, who in turn suffered without hope or patience; unexpected suffering that was embraced with feigned patience for the sake of human applause or reward from God; and self-chosen suffering, undertaken likewise for human applause or divine reward. Only one type of false suffering was, in fact, true, unwanted suffering; at other times, "enemies of God" adopted an appearance of suffering to conceal underlying self-assertion,[24] removing from suffering its essential passivity. Behind such diagnoses of false suffering loomed the Eckhartian insistence that the highest works and sufferings on behalf of God had to be free of the exercise of self-will. As Bernard McGinn has shown, the Eckhartian tradition was centrally concerned with the critique of literal forms of the imitation of Christ, then widely practiced; the mystic had to break through to a true spiritual imitation devoid of self-will.[25] Reformers found this critique of self-chosen suffering in Tauler, and they learned it well.

While the quote from Luther's sermon at the beginning of this introduction shows the reformer upholding suffering and persecution as unambiguous, visible, and historical markers of the true church,[26] the same passage makes clear that the root of false religion lay in human desire for earthly comfort. Karlstadt and Müntzer would have agreed. The passage quoted from Müntzer seeks to expose the distrust of God—that is, the unbelief—he saw behind anxiety about physical needs in the face of persecution. For all three reformers studied here, true Christian suffering began with the realization that salvation, however desirable in and of itself, did not come in the way that human beings expected or wanted, namely, through offering something to God worthy of eternal reward. Salvation required a painful separation from fallen, inborn desires and even the best resources of human reason.[27] Variously but unanimously, Luther, Karlstadt, and Müntzer endorsed the view, inspired especially by the Eckhartian mystics, that human beings must realize the truth of their own "nothingness" before God in order to be born into true faith and to become instruments for God's work in the world. Each understood nothingness, faith, union, and instrumentality differently— indeed, the theme of faith became most central for Karlstadt precisely as he distanced himself from Luther in 1524–1525, whereas previously he tended to group faith with other "virtues"[28]—but these terms established the boundaries within and the poles around which the debate over true and false suffering occurred.

The goal was to shape Christians both individually and in their corporate conduct. Luther, Karlstadt, and Müntzer wanted Christians to interpret and respond to their own suffering, whether spiritual or corporeal, in new ways reflecting what they regarded as newly rediscovered divine truth. Christians also had to be equipped to interpret others' suffering whenever such suffering—like the monks' ascetic achievements—was presented as a sign of true teaching or the true church. Finally, Christians needed to be told when and how to suffer for the goal of reform, and to be taught how to respond to oppression and persecution as political beings, as members of a Christian *polis*. Medieval mysticism, despite its primary locus in the cloister or cloister-like settings, was seldom the apolitical phenomenon that modern interpreters imagine;[29] nonetheless, the reformers' adoption of concepts of annihilation and union as applicable to all true believers—with the corresponding delimitation that those who had not experienced these things were false Christians—had profound consequences that ranged from the pastoral to the political.

The definition of union became crucial here: Luther redefined union with God to mean union with Christ through faith in the Word, which addresses Christians from outside of themselves (*extra nos*) and directs them to what Christ has already done for them.[30] Born into a profound trust in the personal relevance of Christ's redemptive work for them (*pro nobis*), Christians were to accept suffering in its many forms, from disease to persecution, as God's work under a contrary. Karlstadt, conversely, conceived of union as a sinking into the divine will and a return to human beings' (pre-)created unity with God;[31] thus, he stood in unmistakable continuity with the Eckhartian mystical tradition, although with one pivotal caveat—he did not regard such union as achievable in earthly life, and his writings do not describe even a temporary experience of union. Sinking into God's will was for Karlstadt and his followers an ongoing practice and an ever-demanding end; grace made progress toward union possible, but it all required a long process of learning extending beyond death into a reimagined, evangelical purgatory.[32] Thus, the Christian imperfectly united with the divine will was to patiently yield to that will whenever it required suffering, and even more, to spend his or her days in constant self-accusation for sin defined (as in the *German Theology*) as any willing in separation from God's will. As we will see in chapters 1 and 3, Karlstadt readily received from Tauler and likely also Henry Suso (c. 1300–1366) the teaching that God had foreordained all suffering from eternity, in order to teach Christians to return to their origin.

Müntzer, finally, saw union with God as God's possession of and direct communication with souls—not according to their precreated state but according to God's created order.[33] He also saw such a union as attainable for the elect who responded to the Spirit's stirring. The spiritual tribulation in which true faith was born was temporary—a terrifying but passing encounter with one's unbelief. On the other side of the stormy waters, the elect became instruments for the execution of God's hatred of the ungodly. Whereas Karlstadt regarded the persecution suffered by the true church as a providential spur to self-accusation, Müntzer argued that true faith rejected any passive acceptance of persecution and martyrdom at the hands of the ungodly. The faithful would manifest instead courage to suffer for resistance to ungodly clerics and rulers, and they would willingly join forces in the effort to overthrow those ecclesial and political powers who denied God's direct revelation in souls in order to secure their own comfort and power. Teachings about union and suffering thus shaped the most consequential debates of the early Reformation—and revolutionary consequences followed from Müntzer's model, in which union was attained or at least attainable rather than delayed (as for Karlstadt) or redefined (Luther). The democratization and delimitation of mystical teachings as definitive of true rather than false Christianity thus inspired dissent of differing varieties—from the demand to cling to faith and truth in defiance of persecution to the demand to overthrow the persecutors.

Classical scholarship on the Reformation focused primarily on describing the theology, doctrine, and debates of leading reformers, and studies of this nature continue to abound. By the 1980s, however, attention had turned to the circulation and reception of ideas.[34] More recently still, scholars have addressed how the Reformation gave impetus and energy to the formation of strong but competing political entities. Scholars have examined the mechanisms of ecclesial discipline and addressed the question of how clergy resisted or supported authorities' efforts to discipline populations.[35] This book seeks to bridge gaps in this world of scholarship, attending to soteriology and epistemology—and mystical sources of the same—while asking how reformers sought to make their teachings convincing and transformative. Theology and doctrine were pursued for the purposes of disciplining thought and mind, and discipline was pursued for the purpose of aligning believers' thinking and living with truth.[36] Scholars have devoted extensive attention to the formal mechanisms of discipline—from consistories and visitations to catechisms and sermons[37]— but the strategies employed to equip Christians for discernment and self-discipline are little understood.[38] The study of attitudes toward suffering can be especially illuminating here; no other experience so threatens to undermine disciplined adherence to a set of beliefs and practices.

There has been a recent, detailed study examining attitudes toward suffering in the sixteenth century—Ronald K. Rittgers's *The Reformation of Suffering*. Rittgers's primary interest is in the ministry of consolation, and he addresses questions of continuity and change vis-à-vis the Middle Ages.[39] He focuses on Luther and the "Wittenberg circle," while also taking a comparative view,[40] and he highlights the influence among Lutherans of Luther's theology of the cross, which was intended as a lens for interpreting all experience, including suffering.[41] His central argument is that there was a reformation of suffering because Lutheran soteriology "decoupled suffering and salvation";

suffering might prove and deepen faith, but patient suffering could no longer be offered to God as penance or merit. Correct suffering and consolation became according to Rittgers "the most important litmus test of confessional loyalty, for it was in suffering, as nowhere else, that people's deepest religious convictions were revealed." Rittgers offers the concern for consolation among Lutheran clergymen and a broader flowering of verbal consolation among some classes of Lutheran laity—particularly urban classes with requisite education—as a counterweight to prevailing scholarly emphases on both the clergy's disciplinary role as subject to temporal authority and the failure of the Wittenberg Reformation to Christianize populations.[42] Rittgers's more recent essay in *Church History* argues that consolation was as important as discipline as a clerical goal and lay practice in the broader Age of Reform (c. 1050–c. 1650).[43]

Although also concerned with teachings about suffering, the present book examines different sources with different goals,[44] offering sustained attention to Karlstadt and Müntzer in addition to Luther and pursuing the three reformers' competing development of Eckhartian mystical themes. Above all, I aim to show that suffering was aligned with truth as precondition for and consequence of the reception of truth from God. This alignment with truth was powerful consolation;[45] nevertheless, in the ensuing chapters we will find Luther, Karlstadt, and Müntzer summoning Christians to suffer more and more willingly, rather than simply consoling the suffering. Equally important, we will see that reformers regarded only true suffering as ultimately consolable—suffering for falsehood was but a foretaste of hell—and that they were deeply wary of false consolation.[46] I am less concerned with reformers' efforts to console than with their efforts to convince Christians of the truth of their doctrines and to equip them mentally and emotionally for discernment. I see consolation itself as fundamentally a disciplinary endeavor,[47] and I will proceed with a broad definition of discipline as the effort to inculcate mental, emotional, and practical dispositions. Consolation itself disciplines and seeks to maintain discipline.

In most accounts of the divide between Luther, Karlstadt, and Müntzer, center stage is occupied by their competing views of the relationship between the outer Word (scripture and preaching) and sacraments, on the hand, and inward experience and revelation, on the other.[48] Luther insisted that God reveals truth and gives salvation—killing and making alive again—only through external means, whereas Karlstadt and Müntzer expected unmediated divine communication within the soul.[49] Luther argued that authoritative doctrine was based on scripture alone, while accepting that the Spirit was necessary for right understanding; Karlstadt and Müntzer looked to inner illumination, and Müntzer especially relativized scripture, seeing it as a witness to inner experience but not as necessary to the receipt of salvation and truth.[50] These differences will appear prominently in this book, but we will approach the discussion from a different direction, asking how suffering and truth were connected in the debates. Each reformer regarded his teaching as the product and message of true suffering: for Luther, only Christians who recognized through suffering the nothingness of their inner resources and outer works for salvation could or would receive faith in and through the outer Word and sacraments; only Christians emptied of self-trust (albeit incompletely) could read or hear scripture with understanding of the distinction of Law and Gospel. The law itself worked suffering for humans' fallen, self-trusting nature. For Karlstadt, salvation required sinking into God's will through love of God and self-accusation; here, knowledge of God and hatred of oneself grew ever stronger through inner illumination and the study of scripture working hand-in-hand. Müntzer went further in his internalization of salvific processes, insisting that the doctrine of scripture alone—no less than Roman ritualism—seduced the elect into an easy calming of inner trials through outward means. Elect souls needed to be swept clean by enduring the destruction of their desire for and fear of creatures, and by realizing and breaking through their deep unbelief, so that God could again possess and rule them according to the created order. In turn, these possessed souls used scripture as the witness to inner experience and revelation it was intended to be. Neither Karlstadt nor Müntzer accepted that the Christian could abide with an opposition of law and gospel; although the law convicted human beings of sin, the message of the gospel included God's promise to write the law on the hearts of believers.

Susan Schreiner has shown how the quest for certitude shaped profoundly religious thought and debate in the early modern era; reformers participated in a yearning for experiential knowledge inherited from the late medieval period—and they inherited an equation of epistemological immediacy with certainty—but they gave new direction to this yearning through seeking certitude of salvation and doctrine. The Holy Spirit, associated in the Middle Ages primarily with the infusion of charity, came to serve Catholics, Protestants, and radicals alike as the guarantor of these two certitudes.[51] In the realm of doctrine, the Spirit became an exegetical trump card after the collapse of early reformers' optimism that their supposed return to scripture would yield unified teaching and practice;[52] Catholics pointed to the Spirit's guidance of popes and councils throughout history, while Protestants and radicals looked to the Spirit to guarantee either correct exegesis or—in the case of Müntzer and other "spiritualists"—divine revelation apart from scripture.[53] Importantly, Schreiner underlines the early modern era's pervasive anxiety about the deceptiveness of appearances and about the source of experience: theologians looked for divine truth to claim the person from outside, even as they worried that Satan might do the claiming instead.[54] Beliefs and feelings were readily manipulated by the circulators of falsehood. The pervasive anxiety about deceitful appearances, teachings, and experiences described by Schreiner forms the background for the present study, which shows how the contrariety of divine salvation and truth to human reason and affect became for the reformers the decisive criterion for thought and teaching, and how this assumption defined efforts to remake the Christian as believer, knower, and actor *coram deo et hominibus*.

Despite the deep differences between Luther, Karlstadt, and Müntzer, the three reformers agreed in rejecting the authority both of Roman clergy to mediate salvation through the sacraments and of popes and councils to define true doctrine. They also agreed in repudiating the medieval scholastic assumption that reason could productively investigate theological questions, even if it needed to be supplemented by faith in revelation. For the reformers, fallen reason only worked deceit in matters of salvation; reason aligned with fallen desire and the devil, and it needed to be crushed by God's self-revelation. Unsettling questions followed from these views: If reason could not be trusted except as subordinate to scripture, how was one to judge between competing interpretations of scripture and competing claims to inspired reading? How was one to discern the truth or falsehood of spiritual experiences?[55] What forms of participation in reform, or resistance to oppression, were appropriate? The answers to these questions were supposed to come directly from God by means of scripture or inward revelation—but was the sinful recipient capable of honest reception and application? Here, suffering came to the rescue, buttressing the authority of Luther's appeal to scripture, Müntzer's appeal to inner experience, and Karlstadt's reliance on illumined scriptural study. Because Luther, Karlstadt, and Müntzer diagnosed the fundamental human ailment as self-assertion concealed and defended by fallen reason, they instructed Christians to find truth in doctrines and experiences that were contrary to their desires and expectations. Careful discernment was necessary, however, for even suffering could be used or mimicked for false ends.

Reformers learned to use and analyze suffering in this way—distinguishing between true and false suffering—in part through reading the mystical tradition, especially the post-Eckhartian strand. They needed to describe a saving encounter with God, and to equip Christians to evaluate teachings, teachers, and their own experiences. Eckhartian mystical literature, through its preoccupation with the problem of self-will and the solution of suffering—which demanded surrender of the self-will to God's will (*Gelassenheit*)—nourished a paradigm of the Christian as sufferer, thus structuring the reformers' key teachings on salvation; Eckhartian mysticism also provided vital concepts and terms used by Luther, Karlstadt, and Müntzer to teach Christians to apply that paradigm of suffering to their own lives.

In addition to this main argument, this book makes several further arguments concerning the reception of Eckhartian mysticism: first, that Luther's theology and theological expression were profoundly shaped by the encounter with Eckhartian mysticism beginning in 1515;[56] second, that Luther, Karlstadt, and Müntzer developed a shared mystical inheritance in competing directions; and third, that the democratization of mysticism involved also a delimitation that scholars have little discussed: mysticism helped identify false Christians. Finally, fourth, I argue that existing paradigms concerning the relationship of mysticism to dissent do not square with the evidence found in Luther, Karlstadt, and Müntzer; rather, the use of mysticism to bring all true Christians into new intimacy with God inevitably promised to sow dissent and discord. However, the form and expression of dissent could vary widely depending on how the Christians' union or intimacy with God was described. I have described already the relevant differences between Luther (who saw union as a faith bond), Karlstadt (who saw union as gradual sinking into God's will), and Müntzer (who saw union as being possessed by God). In using the term mysticism, I am guided by Bernard McGinn's broad hermeneutic that identifies a "mystical element" in Christianity consisting of "that part of its belief and practices that concerns the preparation for, the consciousness of, and the reaction to what can be described as the immediate or direct presence of God."[57] My focus, however, will be on the reception of distinct Eckhartian motifs in the Reformation era, not on whether the individuals studied here ought to be called mystics or proponents of mystical theology.

Through the mid-1960s, scholars of Reformation history and theology usually assumed a fundamental opposition between mysticism and Protestantism; in so doing, they depicted mysticism as a monolithic tradition, fundamentally medieval and Roman Catholic, which taught elite practitioners to retreat from the world, to ascend to God by ascetic and contemplative works, and to achieve "ontological union" with God unmediated by Christ, the spoken Word, or the sacraments.[58] In 1966, however, papers offered by Heiko Oberman, Erwin Iserloh, and Bengt Hägglund at the Third International Congress on Luther Research in Helsinki, Finland, signaled a new willingness to examine Luther's substantial debts to the mystical tradition and even to apply the moniker "mystical" to aspects of Luther's theology; this effort was "influenced by the ecumenical movement and also by a growing interest in situating Luther within his late medieval context, which was now viewed less monolithically."[59] Forms of medieval mysticism centered on the Incarnate Christ, the sacraments, or divine descent revealed a rich tradition not bound by narrow Protestant stereotypes. Post-Congress, many scholars continued to hold that Luther did not learn anything new from his reading of mystical authors; instead, they argued, he primarily found confirmation of insights won previously and elsewhere, and he found language helpful for the expression of his views.[60] On the other end of the spectrum, scholars like Bengt Hoffman, Reinhard Schwarz, and Alois Haas described Luther's theology as mystical more or less *in toto*.[61]

An important question is whether Luther's insistence on the mediacy of the spoken Word and the sacraments sets his understanding of faith and union with Christ outside the bounds of mysticism. McGinn's heuristic is broad, and he acknowledges that "immediacy describes the actual mystical encounter itself, not the preparation for it, nor its communication in speech or in writing."[62] In his volume on *Mysticism in the Reformation*, moreover, McGinn affirms the necessity of "Protestant mysticism" as a category for interpreting early modern Christianity, and he depicts Johann Arndt as an evangelical mystic, although union for Arndt begins with baptism.[63] However one may assess Arndt or other later Lutherans, it is vital to remember that some medieval mystics encountered God in the context of the sacraments or through other forms of mediation—including the mediation of visions and voices.[64] Again, my purpose here is not to insist on the moniker "mystical" for Luther; but a falsely narrow conception of mysticism must not be allowed to hamper inquiry into Luther's relationship to the mystical tradition.

Recent work by Berndt Hamm and Volker Leppin has insisted on Luther's deep rootedness in mystical traditions, including the Eckhartian. Hamm has argued that Luther may be understood as "the founder of an evangelical mysticism and as someone at home in a Protestant mystical spirituality"— "Luther's mature theology . . . not only has a mystical side or dimension to it, and not only receives traditional mystical themes, images, and concepts, but also reveals mystical traits in its compositional entirety."[65] Hamm rejects definitions of mysticism that exclude "evangelical approaches to mysticism" a priori—namely, by insisting that mystical union involves a human ascent to ontic union with the uncreated Godhead, as in Dionysius. Seeking a definition grounded in "sources within the Western Christian tradition that disciplined historians can broadly describe as mystical," Hamm proposes that "where a mystical relationship of God to humanity is invoked, it always has to do with the personal, direct, and holistic experience of a blessed nearness to God that reaches its goal through an inner union with God."[66] For Hamm, Luther participated in and extended a late-medieval democratization of mysticism. This democratization involved the spread and use of mystical literature outside the cloister (laicization), and it corresponded to a thematic shift in mystical texts of the fifteenth century, "by [which] time the majority of mystical texts aimed not for the limits of ecstasy or for exceptional experiences but for a simple love of Christ, which yields to the way of the cross in everyday life, and there experiences innermost connection to the incarnate God."[67] Luther's democratization involved the insistence that union with Christ was the starting point and foundation of every believers' life.[68] Luther also transformed the mystical inheritance around the loci of Word and faith, offering a new immediacy to the Word without either moral preconditions for the believer or clerical mediation.[69] Luther's view of "the union of the soul to the Godhead" involved "fractures"—"in sinners' deep experience of *Anfechtung*, in the reality of the crucified Christ's passion, in the hiddenness of God's presence under the opposite form of terrifying divine distance, and in the binding of the communion of God to word and faith"—and Luther did not allow "the innermost soul to gain immediate mystical contact with the hidden secrets of God." All the same, this fracturing represented not a repudiation of mysticism but "an extension and transformation of mysticism" that offered every Christian soul "intimate union" with God through "the indwelling of Christ's Spirit and in the *raptus* of faith."[70]

In a series of detailed essays and a recent book intended for broader audiences, Volker Leppin has traced the "mystical roots" of Luther's core teachings on law and gospel, justification, the priesthood of all believers,[71] and sola scriptura.[72] Leppin's *Die fremde Reformation* focuses especially on Luther's realization of human beings' complete dependence on grace and Christ for salvation—the "*Grundmelodie* of the later doctrine of justification."[73] According to Leppin, Luther democratized and radicalized the monastic and mystical ideal of immediacy, finding no anthropologically significant resource in the soul.[74] Crucial to Leppin's analysis is the understanding that Luther's mature Reformation theology developed only gradually,[75] despite the reformer's own *ex post facto* reconstructions coalescing long developments into stories of sudden breakthrough.[76] The *95 Theses* were an intra-medieval event in which Luther pitted one strand of the tradition against another, aligning himself with Tauler and his views on contrition.[77] Luther ultimately transformed the mystical inheritance through a Word-theological refraction; the emptying of the inner self of salvific resources involved a turning outward to Word and sacrament.[78] Meanwhile, the Reformation became a political event in which Luther aligned with the territorial princes and rejected forces contrary to that consolidation.[79] Against competing uses of the mystical tradition on the part of Müntzer and Karlstadt, Luther expressed suspicion about mystical vocabulary and rejected any Christianity unmoored from the external means of grace.[80]

Leppin argues that Luther, Karlstadt, and Müntzer can be understood as accomplishing three competing "transformations" of the mystical tradition. The present study adopts a similar perspective but offers several significant critiques and expansions. First, as mentioned, I underline that the democratization of mysticism—also emphasized by Hamm and numerous others[81]—involved delimitation; mysticism joined to Reformation doctrines of salvation was turned into a hammer for the identification of false Christians. Second, Leppin sees the radicals' transformation of mysticism primarily in their turn to the reformation of society: Karlstadt deemphasized externals, while seeking to "reshape society completely on the basis of personal piety." Müntzer joined mysticism to Chiliasm, seeing the chosen as instructed by God's Inner Word and driven by the Spirit to establish God's kingdom.[82] I will argue that both radicals, and especially Müntzer, transformed the mystical inheritance in areas of fundamental soteriology and epistemology. Müntzer radically altered Tauler's teachings about God's emptying and refilling of the soul through ideas about election and faith foreign to the mystic.[83] The case of Karlstadt shows us, third, that there is need for concepts other than "transformation" to account for reformers' reception of mysticism: Karlstadt maintained Eckhartian terms for the description of union with God (e.g., sinking into God's will), and his view of the means to union (e.g., surrender to suffering) had strong resonance with Tauler and the *German Theology*, but he relocated and revalued union as part of Christian life.[84]

Fourth, I argue that we should not see the mystical presence in Luther's thought and teaching as something that was subsumed and controlled within a political Reformation. Not only Müntzer and Karlstadt, but Luther himself used his mystical inheritance to make Christians into dissenting ecclesial-political actors. This was as true before the Peasants' War as after. The dissent required by Luther's view of *unio mystica* as a faith bond through the Word was nonetheless of a different character than the dissent taught by Müntzer or Karlstadt. While Luther insisted that true Christians must endure persecution for the Word, this was not simply a counsel of conformity; Luther demanded a hard clinging to truth despite suffering and loss, empowered by intense trust that God works under contraries. On the positive side, Luther called Christians to active participation in the God-given structures of society, impelled by trust in God's blessing—indeed by the Spirit of Christ within—despite the mundane nature of such daily toil and the pervasiveness of sin in society.

Recognition that Luther had a genuine conception of dissent even through the Peasants' War—however unsatisfying the conception may be from modern perspectives—points to the need for new formulations of the relationship of mysticism and dissent in the Reformation era. Significant efforts to theorize this connection have been made by both Steven E. Ozment and Hans-Jürgen Goertz. Ozment recognized the dissenting force latent in mystical practice, experience, and theory: even if mysticism "does not issue in dissent, reform, or revolutionary activity," he wrote, "it uniquely drives home the prerequisite for such, viz. an understanding of the penultimate character of all worldly authority and power. In the mystical traditions, quietism is no less negative a judgment on established power than violent revolution. Mystical salvation is the discovery of the final power and authority of the Self within one's own self."[85] Examining radical uses of the *German Theology* as well as the life and writings of several radical reformers, Ozment argued that radical reformers appropriated medieval mysticism to "redefine the nature of religious truth and authority" over and against the "uncompromising claims of Rome and Wittenberg"; the radicals affirmed "the priority—if not the sovereignty—of individual experience and insight in religious matters."[86] Such a dissenting use of mystical anthropology is indeed present in Müntzer's works from the *Prague Manifesto* forward;[87] nevertheless, the analysis in chapter 5 will show that Müntzer's first concern in reading and using the Eckhartian mystics was a soteriological one, shaped by the conviction that salvation and truth were contrary to fallen reason and desire. The same can be said for Luther, whose dissenting use of mysticism was not recognized by Ozment.[88] Democratization of mystical concepts allowed every Christian to experience union; the question was, how was union to be defined? Could the revolutionary impulses latent in mysticism be contained?

Focusing primarily on Müntzer, Hans-Jürgen Goertz's investigations in the 1960s and 1970s referred to an "externalization of mysticism"—the process of rooting out the "world" that Müntzer at first applied to souls was subsequently projected onto the social plane.[89] More recently, Goertz has argued that Müntzer's reception of mysticism was oriented by anti-clericalism toward the change of objective religious and economic conditions, and that Müntzer's apocalypticism helped him extend his concern for inner processes "into the universal sphere"—an extension that was nonetheless a "logical development" of the "mystical outlook" not a break from it.[90] Leppin, as we've seen, argues similarly that apocalypticism made Müntzer's mysticism revolutionary. The argument in the ensuing pages is that the use of mystical concepts to define the true believer, and hence to distinguish true believers from false, inevitably created the pressing question of how those true Christians united to God were to relate to everyone else: mysticism was no longer an elite pursuit but the sine qua non of Christian identity. There were indeed added ingredients—ranging from apocalyptic perspectives to political considerations—that encouraged Müntzer to turn mystical ideas in a revolutionary direction and restrained Luther and Karlstadt from the same; but the reformers' use of mysticism was, in and of itself and from the get go, an effort to shape Christians as ecclesial-political actors.

By focusing on the connection of suffering and truth, themes of true and false suffering, and the reception of Eckhartian motifs around these loci, the present book offers a new perspective on the theology and reform program of each figure studied. A word about prior assessments of Müntzer and Karlstadt is in order here. Whereas scholarship before the 1970s usually saw Karlstadt and Müntzer as disciples of Luther whose personal failings or intellectual inadequacy caused them to stray from the master into unrestrained "legalism" or "spiritualism,"[91] more recent perspectives usually describe them as original thinkers who, like Luther, did their theological work through study of medieval traditions. Detailed studies of their reception of medieval traditions have yielded much insight, but the tendency to press Karlstadt and Müntzer, along with their respective theologies, into received "types" has hampered understanding[92] and, in Müntzer's case, obscured his deep engagement with themes of promise and faith from Luther.[93] Karlstadt's theology is frequently described as "Augustinian" or "mystical,"[94] while the debate over whether Müntzer was an "apocalyptic," "mystical," or "revolutionary" figure continues to cast a shadow.[95] What is needed now is to see how Karlstadt and Müntzer used inherited traditions to forge theologies equally as creative as Luther's, responding both positively and negatively to Luther and meeting the challenge that the Wittenberg reformation set for itself: dividing the European Christian world into true and false Christianities, and equipping Christians to deal with the difference.

Chapter 1 describes how suffering and union with God were connected in late-medieval Eckhartian mysticism. Reformers were influenced by accents unique to this mysticism, including the daring conception of union with God through annihilation of the self, the critique of self-chosen suffering that left the self-will intact, and the demand to yield to God's will even in the experience of seeming forsakenness (*resignatio ad infernum*). Through a comparison of surviving, handwritten marginal annotations left by Luther and Karlstadt in their respective volumes of Tauler's *Sermons*, chapter 1 demonstrates the reformers' shared interest in the nothingness of the soul, the experience of being reduced to nothing, and the status of the reduced soul as God's instrument. Chapter 1 also discusses the *German Theology*, showing how this text from the Eckhartian stream used the willingness to be reduced to nothing and to endure a hard Christ-life as the key markers of true rather than false forms of union or friendship with God; this preoccupation with truth and falsehood made the *German Theology* especially useful to sixteenth-century reformers. Anonymous, printed marginalia in a 1520 edition of the *German Theology* represent a view of Christian salvation and life similar to the one later developed by Karlstadt—a view that defined sin as claiming for the partial self the life and works imparted to the soul by God, the whole, and that saw *Gelassenheit* as the solution to this *Annehmlichkeit*. The rich inheritance of mysticism in the Reformation would not be constrained by Luther's redefinition of union with God as a faith-bond through trust in the Word *extra nos*. Karlstadt may not have written the marginalia, but he may have learned from them.

In chapter 2, I turn to Luther's criticisms of indulgences and of scholastic theology in 1517 and 1518, and I argue that Luther engaged in a two-front struggle against cross-shirking: interpreting all suffering as a punishment for sin that should be endured willingly by the contrite, Luther on the one hand worried that Christians were taught and encouraged to appropriate the benefit of others' suffering—especially through indulgences and relics—rather than suffering themselves. On the other hand, Luther criticized those whose vigorous self-mortification and apparently patient suffering merely concealed an unwillingness to endure the humiliation and reduction of their own moral and intellectual resources for earning salvation. Crucially, Luther at this time was reorienting the doctrine of salvation around the themes of divine promise and human trust in the Word *extra nos*—moved by grace alone, Christians needed to recognize the nothingness of their mental and moral efforts toward salvation, abandon self-trust, and trust in God's promise incarnate in Christ and spoken in the words of forgiveness on account of Christ. This was a salutary despair of the self, taught by suffering, that won assurance of salvation. Luther criticized scholastic theology and theologians for using reason to construct a theology that reflected and buttressed self-assertion and distrust of God, and he offered suffering as a crucible that would separate true and false theologians and doctrines. The teacher who did not offend reason and pride was an enemy of the cross. Luther's message divided the Christian world—beginning with its theologians and teachers—in terms of true and false rather than in terms of earnest and lukewarm. True Christians needed to discern and trust that God works under contraries of suffering.

With these beginnings, Luther found a ready ally in his colleague Karlstadt—despite the personal rivalry and the substantial theological differences that existed between the two already in 1517. Chapter 3 analyzes some of the many vernacular pamphlets (*Flugschriften*) produced by Luther and Karlstadt between 1519 and 1521 to teach and win over less-educated clergy and the "common person." We will see that this literature was replete with mystical motifs, and both reformers developed a paradigm of annihilation and union, while attributing all agency to God. Nevertheless, their views were distinct: Luther focused on the annihilation of self-trust and union with God through faith, while Karlstadt underlined the need to judge the self and "sink" into the divine will. Both recognized the incompleteness of annihilation and union—Luther seeing a coincidence of full union with Christ through faith and despair of the self; Karlstadt depicting a gradual process of growth in love-rich knowledge of God's will and hatred of self. Above all, chapter 3 shows how the Wittenberg reform message was presented as a summons to the cross away from a supposedly corrupted doctrine that put human ideas in the place of divine teachings and flattered self-will. By undergoing the mortification of their own reason and will, however, and receiving salvation on God's terms, Christians were promised new capacity to see God at work underneath suffering and through the lowly. The reformers' use of mysticism was political from the get-go. Brief examination of Luther's *Wartburg Postil*, authored in exile in late 1521, will show how teachings about the reduction of the sinner unto nothingness and the need for despair of the self were prominent in Luther's program for evangelical preaching; the *Postil* preserved (transformed) Eckhartian motifs in the Lutheran preaching tradition.

Chapters 4 and 5 focus on Karlstadt and Müntzer, respectively, showing how each developed unique views on salvation, spirituality, and reform out of the shared well of Eckhartian mysticism. Karlstadt focused on God's pedagogy of Christians through inward illumination, scriptural study, and eternally ordained suffering. *Gelassenheit* became a hard practice of constant self-accusation, oriented toward the goal of sinking into God's will and returning to the soul's (pre-)created existence. Reform proceeded in the same manner on the communal level, incessantly but gradually, through illumined scriptural study and self-examination. Müntzer, conversely, concluded that God would retake possession of elect souls who responded to God's inward stirring: elect souls needed to confront their inward unbelief, detach themselves from fear of and desire for creatures, and not let themselves be deceived and satisfied by easy externals, whether in the form of Wittenberg's scripture and faith or Rome's ritual and tradition. For Müntzer, the unbelief that elect Christians needed to break through was no mere anxiety about salvation, but fundamental doubt about the truth of Christianity vis-à-vis other religions. By giving themselves over to God's inward work, elect souls returned to the created order of things and became instruments for the execution of God's will on the ecclesial-political plane. Müntzer's core theological loci were promise and faith, but he gave each term different content than Luther, relating God's promise to the possession of souls and the transformation of the ecclesial-political order, and faith to the courage—possible only for pure, possessed souls—to execute God's will without fear of creaturely opposition.

In chapter 6, finally, we will see how the reformers' competing views of suffering, salvation, and union clashed in the debate over violent revolution surrounding the Peasants' War. As discussed earlier, each reformer counseled a different response to oppression and persecution, rooted in their respective paradigms of annihilation and union. Each divided true and false teachers and Christians according to suffering and the readiness to suffer, while dismissing opponents' suffering as feigned, self-imposed, misappropriated, or simply endured on behalf of falsehood. Democratized but delimited, transformed and relocated, mystical ideas became a hammer that people were to use to test their own experiences and to figure out the right side and the right course of action in a troubled world, filled with enemies of the cross of Christ.

1

"No one comes to the living truth except through the way of his nothingness"

Mysticism at the Margins of Christendom

Late-medieval mystical literature bequeathed to the sixteenth century a rich and specialized vocabulary for describing the inner reaches of the soul and the soul's experiences, including spiritual suffering. In the vernacular litera- ture produced by Meister Eckhart and his disciples, central terms included *Grund* (ground), *Abgrund* (abyss), *Gelassenheit* (yieldedness), *vernichten/ Vernichtung* (annihilate/annihilation), *entwerden/Entwerdung* (divest/di- vestment), *Nichts* (nothing or nothingness), *geistliche Armut* (poverty of spirit), and *Demut* or *Demütigkeit* (humility).[1] Reformers read mystical authors from other strands of the medieval tradition—both Luther and Karlstadt read Bernard of Clairvaux (d. 1153), for instance[2]—but the post- Eckhartian tradition attained particular influence and prominence due in part to Luther's repeated endorsements of Johannes Tauler and his *Sermons*.[3] Luther also published an anonymous text from the post-Eckhartian tradi- tion, first in a partial version in 1516, then in a complete edition in 1518, claiming that it had taught him more about "God, Christ, man, and what all things are" than any book apart from the Bible or Augustine's works. Offered as proof that "German theologians" were not "disseminating novelties," this anonymous text was dubbed *A German Theology* in a 1518 edition.[4] From at least 1519, Karlstadt's work reflected sustained study of the *German Theology* and Tauler, as well as acquaintance with another Eckhart disciple, Henry Suso (1295–1366), by far the most widely read mystical author in the late- medieval period.[5] Thomas Müntzer may have studied Tauler and Suso even before he came to Wittenberg in 1517; if that is the case, his interests can only have been encouraged as he began to move in Wittenberg theological circles.[6]

This chapter describes how Eckhart and the Eckhartian tradition connected suffering with the goal of mystical life, union with God, and it

Enemies of the Cross. Vincent Evener, Oxford University Press (2021). © Oxford University Press.
DOI: 10.1093/oso/9780190073183.001.0001.

begins to explore the reformers' reception of mystical ideas and terms by analyzing and comparing marginal annotations that Luther and Karlstadt left in
their respective copies of Tauler's *Sermons*.[7] Although a full study of these
handwritten notes lies beyond the scope of the present project, we can see in
both Luther's and Karlstadt's annotations an interest in Tauler's descriptions
of human nothingness and of the spiritual experience of being "reduced"
to nothing—that is, brought to a painful recognition of one's nothingness.
Related themes also attracted the reformers' attention, especially Tauler's
counsel to yield to God's will in all suffering, his caution about self-chosen
sufferings that left the human will intact, and his teaching that persons united
to God could suffer without suffering—indeed, suffer joyfully—by having no
will but God's. Reformers readily received the idea that human beings were
to be instruments of God in both works and suffering. I will argue in subsequent chapters that these themes became an enduring part of each reformer's
thought, pedagogy, and reform program. Notably, Luther underlined the
nothingness of human worth and works before God—and hence the sinner's
complete dependence on Christ—in the postil collections that he penned
during his stay at the Wartburg in 1521 and 1522. These postils laid the
foundation for an evangelical preaching program, and they continued to be
widely used into the seventeenth century; only Luther's later *House Postils*
(1544) enjoyed wider circulation.[8] Karlstadt's interest in the soul's experience
of annihilation and in *Gelassenheit* bore fruit, in turn, in his view of Christian
salvation and life as oriented toward complete self-abnegation and sinking
into the divine will. For his part, Müntzer read Tauler's *Sermons* in the same
edition used by Luther and Karlstadt (Augsburg 1508), although Müntzer's
volume is regrettably lost.[9] We will see Müntzer's rich reception of themes
of annihilation and nothingness when we come to a detailed study of his
works in chapter 5; Müntzer's conclusion that elect souls could be emptied
of attachments to creatures and become again the possession of God alone—
this was a restoration of the created order in the here and now—had major
consequences for his view of Christians' proper social and political action, as
did Karlstadt's more modest assumption that the union taught by the mystics
could be achieved only after death.

The present chapter will conclude with a discussion of the *German
Theology*, and of how this text served reformers (first Luther, then Karlstadt)
as they claimed and described true suffering and worked to expose false
suffering. Here, we will again encounter marginalia—in this instance, a series of printed annotations that appeared in the 1520 edition of the *German*

Theology.[10] The annotations are of particular historical significance, because they were reproduced in Johann Arndt's 1597 edition of the text, which was often reprinted in the seventeenth century.[11] Although Martin Brecht has attributed the annotations to Luther,[12] they in fact promote a spirituality and vision for reform that resonates seamlessly with Karlstadt's mature teachings of 1523–1525. Again and again, the annotations highlight the *German Theology*'s definition of sin as any human willing in contradiction to God, and they commend the *German Theology*'s solution, the surrender of the human will to God's will through the embrace of a hard "Christ-life." This was Karlstadt's reform program in a nutshell, although we cannot say for certain that he wrote the marginalia; indeed, Karlstadt's study of the *German Theology* may have been shaped by them.

Alongside Tauler and the *German Theology*, the reformers read other sources, including the Bible and the church fathers. For our purposes, it will be important to see how Luther and Karlstadt were influenced by Augustine of Hippo (d. 430) as they read the Eckhartian mystics.[13] Both Luther and Karlstadt read Augustine's later, anti-Pelagian writings alongside mystical literature in decisive years of their respective theological development: Luther beginning in 1515, Karlstadt beginning in early 1517. From Augustine, Luther and Karlstadt learned that the human will was bound to sin, that salvation could only be received from God, by grace according to predestination, and that God's law at first only convicted sinners of sin—telling them what they must do in order to achieve salvation, but giving them no power to accomplish this moral obedience. Thus, the law drove sinners to grace and Christ. Luther and Karlstadt accepted that Tauler's message was in harmony with Augustine's,[14] and they read Tauler as describing the profound spiritual anguish involved in the experience of being moved to salvation by God. The influence of Augustine on Müntzer was less obvious, at least insofar as the interpretation of suffering was concerned; for Müntzer, the elect needed to discover and then break through their hidden unbelief, so that their fear and love would be directed to God as their possessor rather than creatures. This faith-centered view was forged through Müntzer's exchange with Luther and his circle, as well as through the study of mysticism and other sources.

As a subtitle for this chapter, I have chosen "mysticism at the margins of Christendom." My purpose is both to highlight my use of marginalia (written and printed) and to emphasize the location of Luther, Karlstadt, and Müntzer at the margins of the Western European church in the late 1510s. Their challenges to official church doctrine and the practice of scholastic theology inevitably provoked the rebuttal, "Are you the only one and the first one to have the right opinion?"[15] They responded by contending that spiritual suffering opened the Christian to the truth of scripture, and that reason, academic training, and church office could only heap up deception in the service of human pride, if the self-will of the theologian remained unbroken. In the face of questions about their competence to challenge church doctrine and authority, these reformers pointed out that God's truth-bearers always and inevitably suffer ridicule or worse from the worldly wise and the powerful. Truth is always found and sounded by sufferers from the margins.

Eckhart, Suso, and Tauler: Wittenberg's Mystical Library

In this section, I describe the teachings of Eckhart, Suso, and Tauler that are central to the present study, and I discuss details of the reception of Tauler in Wittenberg, including how reformers read Tauler in conjunction with Augustine.

Meister Eckhart

Meister Eckhart was a brilliant and daring mystical thinker—so daring, in fact, that many of his teachings were condemned in March 1329, more than a year after his death. He developed and promulgated a view of mystical union in which the soul experienced its fused identity with God; this teaching, along with its implications for understanding human suffering, was mediated to sixteenth-century reformers through Eckhart's disciples and helped shaped the reformers' soteriology and public teaching, although the reformers were far removed from Eckhart in many of their fundamental convictions and goals. Eckhart was both a scholastic theologian and a Dominican preacher; reformers rejected scholastic theology and monastic life in turn. Bernard McGinn has shown that a cleft between scholastic and mystical theology opened up after the controversy surrounding Eckhart.[16] In the world of Dominican mysticism, specifically, Suso turned his back on his scholastic training and practice, while Tauler had no advanced academic theological training and was frequently critical of scholastic masters and doctors.[17] In their own critique of scholastic theology, Luther, Karlstadt, and Müntzer each reflected Tauler's epistemological principle that truth must be passively received by the detached, yielded, and humble soul—the soul that had put its discursive reasoning and debating to rest.[18]

Born around 1260, Eckhart entered the Dominican order and there attained to the pinnacle of the academic world; he became only the second person after Thomas Aquinas (d. 1274) to be appointed twice to the order's chair of theology in Paris. At the same time, much of Eckhart's life was devoted to the spiritual formation and pastoral care of religious women, including Dominican nuns and Beguines. A proponent of the complete harmony of philosophy and theology, Eckhart developed in his academic work and vernacular preaching a spectacularly new conception of God and the soul's relationship to God, centered on the possibility of an indistinct union of the soul and God in the "ground"—a supra-Trinitarian locus, where God's ground and the soul's ground are one. Eckhart's conception was intellect-centered: God, whose nature is "to know" rather than "to be," is received by the human intellect, which is itself the ground and the complete image of God.[19]

Eckhart's teaching cannot be understood without attention to his concept of analogy. Through the concept of analogy, he asserted not merely the identity of the soul with God, but also the complete dependence of the soul upon God—that is, that the soul's true existence is only in God.[20] For our purpose of understanding the sixteenth-century reformers, the relationship of identity to dependence is especially critical. In one discussion, Eckhart began with the philosophical truth that when one thing is produced by another (the "principle"), the thing produced is "of another nature and thus not the principle itself." Nonetheless, "as it is in the principle, [the produced thing] is not other in nature or supposit." Accordingly, the just man "*insofar as* he preexists in Divine Justice . . . 'is not yet begotten nor Begotten Justice, but is Unbegotten Justice itself.'" Human beings in their actual existence—their "total existential reality"—are distinct from God, but formally identical with God as their principle.[21]

This conception of analogy was bound up with Eckhart's metaphysics and doctrine of creation. Eckhart understood God as ceaselessly "boiling over and out" (*bullitio/ebullitio*)—that is, from the Father or ground into the Trinity, and from the Trinity into creation.[22] God creates ceaselessly and in God's self. Creatures in turn have both a "virtual existence" in God as their "essential cause"—that is, they are "in God as in the First Cause in an intellectual way and in the mind of the Maker"—and a "formal existence in the natural world." The creature is nothing in itself, because the latter, "formal"

existence is entirely dependent and receptive in relation to the virtual existence in God. Bernard McGinn explains:

> Unlike Thomas Aquinas, for whom formal existence was essential for giving
> creatures a reality of their own, Eckhart's attention focuses on the virtual,
> true, that is, the "principial" existence of things in God. . . . Poised between
> two forms of nothingness, the *nihil* by way of eminence that is God,[23] and
> the *nihil* that marks the defect of creatures, Eckhart's mystical message is an
> invitation to the soul to give up the nothingness of its created self in order to
> become one with the divine Nothing that is also all things.[24]

For Eckhart, intellect is the ground of human identity with God because
intellect is the likeness not merely of an idea in God, but of God as whole.
Intellect is "not other than the Only-Begotten Image," the Word, and is related immediately to God "by formal emanation, not creation." The intellect
is able to know God without the mediation of any images, and this knowing
is itself indistinct union with God. Only intellect "provides access to the
ground," and it does not rest until it finds the ground. For Eckhart, the intellect is an "uncreated something" in the soul, but as McGinn explains, only
"insofar as it is intellect, . . . that is as virtual being, not as formal being in the
world. . . . The uncreated something is not and cannot be a part of any-thing.
It is another term for *grunt*."[25]

Along with the concepts of analogy, divine *bullitio* and *ebullitio*, intellect, and ground Eckhart also developed a refined doctrine of the imitation of Christ. For Eckhart, the Christian attains sonship with Christ, and
hence union with God in the ground, through the imitation of Christ. True
imitation, however, is not a matter of external exercises or of the "details
of moral observance" but of "total self denial" in God and God's will. In
one sermon, Eckhart argued that the Christian must undergo physical
and spiritual death like Christ. Physical death meant "accepting willingly
what suffering God may send us," while spiritual death entailed "absolute
abandonment to God's will, even if this should involve annihilation, or
consignment to hell." Eckhart counseled, "You should let God do what he
will with you . . . just as if you did not exist. God's power should be as absolute in all that you are as it is within his own uncreated nature." Eckhart
accordingly rejected self-chosen sufferings—that is, the self-imposed asceticism that often marked the imitation of Christ as it was practiced in
the later Middle Ages. To choose one's suffering, Eckhart argued, would

be to seek physical death in a way that destroys spiritual death; moreover, to claim any suffering as "mine," however unintentionally, would be to remain mired in distinction from God.[26] In his *Book of Divine Consolation*, Eckhart advised the believer to remember that all human suffering is God's will, and even more that, because of the indistinct identity of the soul with God in the ground, to suffer patiently is to suffer in God.[27] If human beings suffer in conformity to the divine will, their suffering becomes "suffering without suffering" and God "suffers with us," although in an incomparably higher way.[28]

These points relate again to Eckhart's teaching on intellect. The intellect is a receptive power, according to Eckhart; it is "no-thing in itself, but rather the capacity to know all." The intellect must become "empty and free of all created forms and all attachment to forms in order to receive God." In this "detachment" there is a surrender of "individual consciousness . . . in the true self-awareness that is God," as well as an annihilation of the "created will," even in its attachment to good works. Detachment compels God to love and fill the soul. McGinn explains, "Absolute self-emptying forces God to fill the vacuum in the soul because it is really nothing else but his own emptiness." Here, the false Ego ("I") of formal existence is replaced by the "transcendental I"—the "I" as it exists virtually in God.[29] Loss of self and detachment from works, however, does not mean that a person no longer acts externally and on behalf of others. Instead, one boils over in God the Trinity, acting from the ground in "which God and human are one, in which the Word is ever being born in the soul." Eckhart called such action "living without a why."[30]

Henry Suso

Despite the posthumous condemnation of some of his teachings, Eckhart exercised far-reaching influence in the world of late-medieval mysticism, particularly through the mediation of Henry Suso. Born in Constance around 1295, Suso entered the local cloister at thirteen. He encountered and was profoundly influenced by Eckhart during studies in philosophy and theology at Strassburg (c. 1319–1321) and then Cologne (c. 1323–1327). Suso's first writing, *The Little Book of Truth* (c. 1329), was a defense of Eckhart's teaching, after Suso himself had come under fire. Despite the controversy, Suso was able to become prior of the convent in Constance for at least four years, 1330–1334, if not longer. He did not pursue an academic career, but "turned wholeheartedly to the life of inner devotion and spiritual guidance of others, especially women." Through his literary works and correspondence, Suso gathered disciples both male and female; one of his closest disciples was Elsbeth Stagel, a Dominican nun who compiled the materials that Suso himself later incorporated into his quasi-autobiographical *Life of the Servant*. In 1348, Suso was transferred from Constance to Ulm, where he remained until his death on January 25, 1366. In Ulm, Suso produced *The Exemplar*, a compilation of four vernacular works: *The Life of the Servant*, the *Little Book of Eternal Wisdom*, the *Little Book of Truth*, and a selection of his correspondence entitled the *Little Book of Letters*.[31]

Surviving manuscripts attest to Suso's wide influence: fifteen partial or complete manuscripts of the *Exemplar* are extant, along with more than 232 of the *Little Book of Wisdom* and 43 of the *Life*. Suso also unfolded the *Little Book of Wisdom* into a larger Latin work, the *Horologium Sapientiae*, which proved even more popular than the earlier vernacular treatise. Only Thomas à Kempis's *Imitation of Christ* survives in more copies.[32] Printed vernacular editions of the *Exemplar* were produced in Augsburg in 1482 (published by Anton Sorg) and again in 1512 (by Hans Othmar),[33] the latter bearing a long title explaining that the book

> contains many good spiritual teachings concerning how a person, when he has turned from God to creatures, should turn back to his first origin where God is; and how he should keep himself in *Gelassenheit* with respect to himself and all creatures, and die to all joy, desire, lust, and pleasure of this world and his own body; [and how he should] keep God before his eyes, seek him, and love him above all things; [and how he should] regard his suffering and keep himself obediently conformed [to Christ] in true humilty [*sich selb vnderwürflich in rechter demu[o]t geleichfo[e]rmiklich halten*], in doing and yielding, in love and suffering; and many other precious teachings, which are especially helpful and useful for a person beginning to turn back to God.[34]

Suso moderated Eckhart's most daring teaching. While Eckhart had insisted on the soul's true identity with God in its virtual existence, Suso argued that the soul's identity with God was a temporary *experience* of the united soul, during which the soul and God remained absolutely ontologically distinct as creature and creator.[35] Suso also differed from Eckhart insofar as Suso's mysticism depended upon and was expressed through accounts of rich visionary experience, which were captured in detailed illustrations in some manuscripts. For his part, Eckhart worried that visions were often, if not always, "dangerous and delusory" rather than truly divine in origin.[36]

For our purposes, Suso merits attention especially because of the direct connection he made between suffering and union with God: for Suso, the imitation of Christ's passion is the gateway to union with God. Suso admitted some role to a literal imitation of Christ. The "servant of eternal Wisdom" described in The Life of the Servant undergoes twenty-two years of gruesome self-punishment: "For a long time he wore a hairshirt and an iron chain until he bled like a fountain and had to give it up," the Life tells us. The servant also had an undergarment of hair fashioned for his lower body, furnished with 150 nails that would dig into his skin while he slept; to keep himself from adjusting or removing the garment or scratching the lice that infested it, he first fashioned a device to bind his arms painfully and then had a pair of gloves outfitted with tacks. Thus, when the sleeping servant "tried to use his hands to help himself, he would run the pointed tacks into his chest and scratch himself." The result was festering wounds "on the skin of his arms and around his heart," but the servant would take up the practice again as soon as he recovered. He continued the practice for sixteen years, until instructed by a vision that "God no longer wanted this of him." Yet there was still more self-mortification to come; the Life continues, "more important than all his other practices was his idea and desire to bear on his body some sign of his heartfelt sympathy for the intense sufferings of his crucified Lord." Thus, the servant made a small wooden cross and hammered thirty nails through it, wearing this cross between his shoulders for eight years. He then added seven needles to "[bear] in praise of the deep sorrow of the pure Mother of God." Initially unable to endure the additional pain, he filed the needles down, but "he soon regretted his unmanly cowardice, and so he sharpened them all with a file and put it back upon himself. It rubbed his back open where his bones were, making him bloody and torn." For a while, he used his fist to "drive the nails into his flesh" two or sometimes three times a day.[37] In all this, it is important to underline that while the servant described in the Life cannot be divorced from Suso himself, the servant also cannot be identified simply with Suso—the biographical details do not line up, and the Life aims at transmitting mystical teachings, not autobiographical rectitude in a modern sense.

More bloody details could be related, but the key turn in the Life comes when the servant leaves behind such brutal self-mortification:

After the servant had led a life filled with the exterior penitential exercises that have been in part described here from his eighteenth to his fortieth year, his whole physical being had been so devastated that the only choice open to him was to die or to give up such exercises. And so he gave them up. And God made it clear to him that such severity and all these different practices together were nothing more than a good beginning and a breaking of the undisciplined man within him.[38]

The servant then receives a vision of a young man who tells him to leave behind the "lower school" of self-mortification, in order to enter into the "advanced school" of "complete and perfect detachment from oneself (*volkomnú gelassenheit sin selbs*)." In this advanced school, the young man says:

A person becomes so utterly nothing [*ein mensch stand in so[e]licher entwordenheit*], no matter how God treats him, either through himself or through other creatures, in joy or sorrow, that he strives continually to be in the state of going away from his "self," to the extent that human frailty allows, and he aims alone at God's praise and honor, just as dear Christ did with regard to his heavenly Father.[39]

The servant thus comes to realize that his "self" has remained through his *self-inflicted* penance, and that he "still [is] not detached enough to accept adversity coming from outside [*ungelassen ze enpfahene fro[e]md widerwertikeit*]."[40] Subsequent chapters of the *Life* tell of many sufferings coming from others, training the servant in the advanced school of complete detachment.

In final analysis, Suso treats the "literal *imitatio passionis* as an initiatory, and even questionable stage" in the mystical journey. For Suso, just like his teacher Eckhart, true imitation of Christ's passion is not finally about outward exercises of self-mortification, but about a complete denial of the self. As McGinn summarizes:

Breaking through Christ's suffering humanity to attain the Son's being in the naked Trinitarian Godhead (i.e. being freed of the forms of creatures, reformed in Christ, and transformed in the Godhead) expresses the essence of Suso's mysticism. . . . Suso's program of mystical transformation is clearly passion-centered, but in a way that stresses the internalization of the meaning of the cross more than the bloody exterior *imitatio passionis* that the Dominican is often cited for. Like his teacher Eckhart, conversion and inwardness, silence and self-knowledge, detachment and letting go, are the essential practices for finding God.[41]

Scholars have done little to explore the reformers' possible reception of Suso, but a few traces of the Suso volume in Karlstadt's works are known. First, an image of the cross on Karlstadt's polemical broadsheet of 1519, the "Wagons,"[42] closely resembles a woodcut by Hans Schäuflein in the Suso edition; Karlstadt's decision to produce a pedagogical image with captions may have found inspiration in Schäuflein's numerous annotated woodcuts, and indeed, one caption from the Schäuflein woodcut appears directly in Karlstadt's image—"bear suffering patiently [*Trag leiden gedulticlich*]." The same cross image in the Suso volume bears other captions that remind of Karlstadt's view of suffering as divine pedagogy intended to produce conformity of the human will with God—"Oh Lord, teach me that I can suffer according to your most-beloved will" and "Receive suffering willingly."[43] A second indication that Karlstadt read Suso appears in the reformer's 1523 treatise on *Gelassenheit*, where he seems to have incorporated a passage about yielding five levels of being from Suso's *Little Book of Eternal Truth*.[44] Of all the Suso books, the *Little Book of Eternal Truth* was most likely to have attracted Karlstadt's positive reception: Karlstadt repudiated key aspects of Suso's piety on display in other texts, such as asceticism that undermines the body and regard for Mary and the saints as intercessors; but the *Little Book of Eternal Truth* is a brief, unadorned reflection on the distinction between true and false *Gelassenheit*, and is replete with themes central to Karlstadt's two major treatises of spring 1523, including the relationship of divine unity and multiplicity, the origin of sin in "possessiveness" of self (*vnrechter angesechner aigenschaft*), the nothingness of human beings and all creatures apart from God, union with God as sinking into God's will, and finally, the teaching that a truly yielded person, dying to self, willingly accepts all suffering as springing from God's will.[45] Karlstadt seldom wrote about dreams and visions, so important to Suso, yet he expressed his openness to divine communication through these means in a letter to Müntzer from December 1522.[46] Müntzer, in turn, may have learned a great deal from Suso—Müntzer strongly insisted on both ascetic self-discipline and the acceptance of God's communication through dreams and visions,[47] which were to be judged according to a higher image-less revelation and according to scripture. We know, however, only that Müntzer read Suso; direct literary evidence of dependence has yet to be uncovered.

Johannes Tauler

Johannes Tauler's influence in Wittenberg theological circles was more direct than Eckhart's and more widespread than Suso's. Luther, Karlstadt, and Müntzer all studied Tauler's *Sermons*, and concrete evidence shows that Luther and Karlstadt accepted Tauler as a model for preaching.[48] Müntzer's fellow pastor and reformer in Allstedt, Simon Haferitz, also borrowed extensively from Tauler for the printed text of an early 1524 sermon, published as *A Sermon on the Feast of the Three Holy Kings*; the sermon interweaves significant motifs from Müntzer—election, the *Ankunft* of faith, false versus true faith, the hostility of *Schriftgelehrten* to spiritual trials and the mortification of lusts—with long excerpts from Tauler, and it may well have been Müntzer who introduced Haferitz to Tauler.[49]

Tauler was born into a well-to-do family in Straßburg around the year 1300, and like his contemporary Suso, he joined the Dominican Order as a young teenager, possibly at fourteen. He was trained by the order to preach but did not seek an academic degree, and he regularly associated academic theology with useless, vain disputation—a theme that endeared him to early sixteenth-century reformers. Nonetheless, no one shaped Tauler's thought and teaching more than Eckhart,[50] whom he probably knew personally from the latter's long occupation in Straßburg.[51] Like Suso, Tauler was compelled to modify Eckhart's teachings, seeking to express them in terms acceptable to ecclesial authorities. Tauler preached often to nuns and beguines—sometimes also to urban classes[52]—and his sermons established his reputation as a *Lebmeister*, a master of concrete, spiritual guidance. Some eighty sermons were compiled already in Tauler's own lifetime,[53] and the collection then circulated in varied manuscript forms in German cloisters of the fourteenth and fifteenth centuries. The sermons were first printed, along with some pseudonymous material, in Leipzig in 1498 and again in Augsburg in 1508.

Tauler's teaching was centered, like Eckhart's, on the concept of the ground as the locus of "fused identity" with God. Within this framework, however, Tauler made innovations and modifications vis-à-vis Eckhart. He referred to the abyss (*abgrunt*) as well as the ground (*grunt*) of the soul, using the fusion of the human and divine abysses to describe identity with God, and he avoided the scandal that dogged Eckhart in part by teaching that the soul's ground or abyss was created and in part by emphasizing that the ground was the *imago Trinitatis*. As McGinn notes, Tauler thus avoided "Eckhartian expressions that suggest[ed] a ground beyond the persons of the Trinity." More important for our present discussion, Tauler also depicted entry into the ground as occurring through "love and seeking," not intellect.[54] He disdained the academic dispute between Franciscans and Dominicans over whether love or intellect was more important for the journey to God.[55]

Tauler's most critical innovation vis-à-vis Eckhart was the concept of the *gemuet*,[56] which McGinn translates as an "essential inclination" (i.e., toward God). For Tauler, the *gemuet* was a part of the soul that was higher than and the source of all other faculties, including reason, will, and love. Tauler described the *gemuet* as eternal: it ceaselessly "beholds, loves, and enjoys God" and indeed "knows itself as God in God, and yet it is created." In technical terms, as McGinn explains, the *gemuet* "beholds its virtual existence in God, although in actual existence it remains something created." The *gemuet* is ineradicable per Tauler's teaching and remains even in hell.[57]

Tauler's sermons exhort the would-be "friend of God" to turn away (*abkehren*) from outward creaturely attachments, to turn inward (*einkehren*), and finally, through an "essential turn" (*weselich ker*), to turn into the ground or abyss.[58] This process involved both ascetic discipline and growth in self-knowledge, leading to recognition of one's two-fold nothingness as a creature entirely dependent on God and a sinful being.[59] One had to become empty (*ledig* or *leer*) of desire for and dependence upon outward creatures and goods, of self-will, and finally of the self entirely. The empty soul then waited for God passively and yielded (*gelass*) in her ground,[60] and God was compelled by God's nature to fill the empty space.[61] Taking a critical stance toward what he perceived as the usual ascetic and meditative practice, Tauler emphasized that *unio mystica* was unattainable by any human-initiated exercise. The work of emptying as well as the work of filling belonged to God or the Holy Spirit.[62]

Tauler's understanding of the passivity, receptivity, and emptiness necessary to receive God in the abyss or ground of the soul defined his constant exhortation to patient suffering as the way to union with God. The friend of God according to Tauler bears suffering—itself a universal, inescapable human experience[63]—"for God's sake" after the example of Christ. Such patient endurance is to take up the cross of Christ, and through this cross-bearing, one attains detachment from creatures and the self (*Ablösung* or *Entwerdung* or *Nacktwerden*).[64] Suffering teaches human beings' two-fold human nothingness.[65] Thus, the process of coming to self-knowledge involves great spiritual anguish, and Tauler's sermons are replete with references to "many kinds of affliction including sorrow, bitterness, fear, sadness, suffering, pain, and trepidation."[66] These are terms of spiritual suffering, revealing Tauler's rejection of an overly "fleshy" or outward imitation of Christ—a rejection he shared with Eckhart and Suso.[67] To focus on one's outward deeds and sufferings was for Tauler to wander in externals, forsaking the necessary turn within. As McGinn summarizes:

> The key to understanding the constant yet developing role of Christ in the path to God is to grasp the difference between meditation on the events of Christ's life as an external model and internalization of Christ's own essential intention, so that we *become* Christ, both in suffering the alienation he experienced at Gethsemane and on the cross, and in participating in the inner life of the Trinitarian processions that he as Son of God incarnate always enjoys.[68]

The end of cross-bearing for Tauler was not freedom from suffering, but a "God-suffering" that transformed the person's relationship to all other suffering. As Alois M. Haas argues, God-suffering "signals the readiness of human beings to receive God there, where God wants to give himself. God-suffering is an inner freedom, a holding-still and waiting for God's work within, so that finally God is present as pure working [*ein luter würcken*] in the person, who has become a pure suffering [*ein luter liden*]." Like Eckhart with his concept of "suffering in God," Tauler presents the possibility of "suffering without suffering," because all suffering is endured in union with the divine. Union is the ultimate "receptivity [*Empfindlichkeit*]" to all suffering in God.[69]

Tauler's repeated insistence that union with God could not be attained by any human activity, but that the soul had to wait for and suffer God's work, made his work attractive to the early reformers. At the same time, Tauler's underlying position regarding the value of human exertion and activity toward self-knowledge and union was nuanced, and this nuance complicated the reformers' reception of Tauler. In one of his more detailed marginal remarks to the *Sermons*, Karlstadt responded to and rejected lines that seemed to espouse a dangerous Pelagianism or at least semi-Pelagianism.[70]

Richard Kieckhefer summarizes the apparent ambiguity in Tauler, which has been a subject of discussion among modern scholars:

> Repeatedly Tauler insisted that one should become wholly passive, and allow God to act within oneself. But just as clearly he condemned "false inactivity" and "inner idleness," and he acknowledged that, alongside passivity, some kind of active human effort was not only permissible but requisite.[71]

Scholars have attempted various resolutions to the seeming tension in Tauler's *Sermons*. Steven Ozment argued that, although Tauler often "insists on the need for human preparation before God does his work in the soul . . . [and] fill[s] the void that man has created," such preparation is finally to be attributed to God's own work in the ground of the soul.[72] Gösta Wrede asserted that the passivity described by Tauler applies only to moments of ecstatic union with God, whereas activity defines an "ongoing condition of one's soul, or one's day-to-day effort for sanctification." Such earnest moral activity is to occur both before and after union.[73] Kieckhefer evaluated the arguments of both Ozment and Wrede, and acknowledged especially the weight of material behind Ozment's.[74] Kieckhefer's own analysis, however, yielded a resolution nearer to Tauler's own nuances. Put briefly, "passivity is not merely a fact but a demand." Passivity does not only describe human existence as God's instrument or the moment of ecstatic union with God, but a "stance" that hearers are enjoined to seek

> by acknowledging God's work within one's soul, and abstaining from claims of personal accomplishment; by attaining a stage of spiritual development in which, at least for intermittent intervals, one abandons discursive prayer and all other artificial "works," and deliberately commits oneself to God in contemplation; and by aligning one's will with God's, especially in those moments of suffering when such alignment is particularly difficult. . . . In every area of religious life, Tauler recognizes first of all a *de facto* dependence of man upon God's will, and secondly a need for man to become perfected by submission to that dependence.[75]

Tauler does not say, finally, that grace is irresistible. The human being for Tauler can interfere with grace through prideful attempts to cooperate with God's work in the soul or to claim that work for the self.[76]

Tauler in Wittenberg

Tauler's *Sermons* were much read in Wittenberg theological circles in the 1510s. Likely, Johannes Lang introduced the *Sermons* to Luther, his brother in the Augustinian Order, and Luther's marginal notations appear in Lang's volume, alongside glosses made by Lang himself and Justus Jonas.[77] Luther himself subsequently recommended Tauler to George Spalatin, court chaplain to Frederick the Wise, and he gave an edition of the *Sermons* to the former-Wittenberg student Martin Glaser in 1529—a fact that calls into question any simplistic assumptions concerning Luther's turn from the mystics after the clash with Karlstadt and Müntzer. Luther's direct or indirect influence may have led to Karlstadt's purchase of the *Sermons* in 1517. Christian Döring, a goldsmith and bookseller in Wittenberg, provided copies of Tauler's *Sermons* to Wittenberg's readers, and he may have read the *Sermons* himself. When Luther asked Melanchthon to procure the 1521 Basel edition and send it to the Wartburg, he directed Melanchthon to Döring.[78]

Luther cited and praised Tauler in lectures and numerous printed works from 1516 through 1522,[79] including in his 1516 introduction to the *German Theology*, his *Explanations to the 95 Theses*, and his Wartburg postil. This praise undoubtedly created interest in the *Sermons*. Müntzer may have turned to Tauler in response to Luther's praise, as Schwarz supposes,[80] or on Karlstadt's recommendation; but there is also evidence that Müntzer studied Tauler and Suso before coming to Wittenberg in the fall of 1517.[81] While Müntzer may have introduced Tauler to Simon Haferitz, the latter was also a student in Wittenberg (matriculation, March 1522) and could have learned of Tauler from others. In any case, Müntzer and Haferitz, like Karlstadt, read Tauler with different results than Luther, setting the stage for a debate in which each side shared ideas and vocabulary borrowed from the same mystical sources.

Reading Tauler with Augustine

Luther and Karlstadt read Tauler in conjunction with Augustine of Hippo's works, in particular Augustine's later, anti-Pelagian writings. The late-medieval reception of Augustine was ubiquitous but complex and diverse. Although some scholars like Gregory of Rimini and Thomas Bradwardine enlisted the later Augustine against a perceived new Pelagianism, Augustine's anti-Pelagian writings did not hold the field in the university or the Augustinian Order. A renaissance of Augustinian scholarship in the order primarily sought to receive the "religio Augustini"—that is, Augustine as a model for professional religious life. Pseudo-Augustinian works circulated widely in the vernacular; yet these works were not consistently anti-Pelagian—rather the reverse—and they offered Augustine primarily as a model of piety.[82] Of enduring significance for Reformation history is the fact that Luther, Karlstadt, and a host of others turned directly to the church father,[83] and gave particular attention to the later, anti-Pelagian works.

Luther studied Augustine early on in his academic career,[84] and he gradually gained knowledge of the anti-Pelagian writings during his first lectures on the Psalter from 1513 to 1515. Only in 1515, however, did Luther obtain the 8th Volume of the Amerbach edition of Augustine's works, which contained key anti-Pelagian works like *The Spirit and the Letter*.[85] When Luther picked up Tauler in 1515–1516, he was lecturing on Romans with the exegetical aid of *The Spirit and the Letter* and other anti-Pelagian writings.[86] Luther cited the *Spirit and the Letter* directly twenty-seven times in his *Lectures on Romans*.[87]

In January 1517, Karlstadt purchased a copy of Augustine's works in order to halt Luther in his increasingly thorough critique of scholasticism and the soteriological teachings of scholastic masters. Instead, Karlstadt was convinced of the bondage of the human will to sin and of the necessity of rescue by grace alone, and consequently of the doctrine of predestination.[88] On April 26, 1517, Karlstadt purchased a copy of Tauler's *Sermons*, and on the same day he posted 152 theses on "nature, law, and grace" largely derived from Augustine's writings on the door of the castle church in Wittenberg. From the summer semester of 1517 through 1519, Karlstadt lectured on Augustine's *The Spirit and the Letter*, even as he was reading Tauler's *Sermons* and using them in his preaching.[89]

Over the final two decades of his life, Augustine was engaged in an intense debate over sin and salvation with the British monk Pelagius and with his followers, including Julian of Eclanum. The position of Pelagius and the Pelagians was that God's grace consisted of the law and the human capacity to obey the law. Human society after Adam and Eve's transgression had fallen into the grips of ignorance and bad habits, and individuals became hardened in this sin over the course of their life. As a remedy, God gave the law and then a perfect exposition of the law through Christ, and it remained for Christians to will a life of hard obedience to the law. Human beings do not begin their lives with inherited corruption and guilt.[90] In response, Augustine argued that inherited corruption was evidenced by humans' inability to obey the law out of genuine, inward delight for its commands and prohibitions. God's law reveals this sinfulness—indeed, God's prohibitions increase the desire to sin—but only the Holy Spirit apart from the law gives Christians the ability to obey truly. The law convinces sick sinners of their illness, and thus drives them to the doctor, Christ, and to grace, on which salvation depends.

Along with medieval mystical teachings and motifs, these arguments helped Luther and Karlstadt develop a rich image of the Christian as a passive sufferer of God's work. Karlstadt's account of salvation and Christian life also gave central place to Augustine's teaching that the Spirit must make believers inwardly obedient to God's will by writing God's law upon their hearts. In his published works from 1519 onward, Karlstadt described rebirth and constant self-accusation (that is, for the incompleteness of one's rebirth) as two sides of the same process of sinking into God's will—the latter motif learned from Tauler, Suso, and the *German Theology*.[91] Initially Karlstadt, like Luther, avidly accepted predestination as the unavoidable implication of Augustine's teachings on the bondage of the will—more avidly perhaps than Augustine himself.[92] Karlstadt, however, worried that such a position made God responsible for evil, and he eventually followed the *German Theology* in arguing that sin, beginning with the devil's sin, involved a refusal to accept passive dependence upon God: angels and human beings receive life and goodness, will and rationality from God, and they fall when they claim these as possessions of the self; sin is the assertion of I, me, and mine.

Thomas Müntzer apparently purchased and read Augustine's works after attending the Leipzig Disputation in 1519, where Luther and Karlstadt invoked the fifth-century bishop to defend their arguments against John Eck; but Müntzer may not have read the anti-Pelagian writings that so impressed Luther and Karlstadt.[93] In a 1520 letter, Müntzer reported that he had "re-read" Augustine's collected works through the sixth volume;[94] if his first reading also did not go beyond the sixth volume, Müntzer did not encounter the anti-Pelagian works directly. Nonetheless, in 1521, when Müntzer set out to depict Johann Silvius Egranus as an inverter of true theology, he put in Egranus's mouth an attack on the "Martinians" for their acceptance of the old Augustine.[95] Müntzer evidently understood Luther's soteriology as a justified attack on "new Pelagians" like Egranus; and there is substantial evidence that Müntzer accepted doctrines of the bondage of the will, predestination, and salvation by grace alone at this time.[96] In late 1524, conversely, when Müntzer attacked Luther in the *Highly-Provoked Vindication and Refutation*, he described Luther's denial of free will as a fantasy learned from "*your* Augustine." Müntzer, like Karlstadt, seems to have been troubled by the implication that God was responsible for evil.[97] That said, neither Müntzer's 1524 derision nor his 1521 defense of the Martinians reveals a marked, direct influence of Augustine upon Müntzer. Ironically, Müntzer's own teachings on the law come closest to Augustine's in the *Highly-Provoked Vindication*, where Müntzer argues that the law reveals to sinners the true depth of their sinfulness and that Christians united with Christ are given power to fulfill the law; but such Augustinian views may well have been mediated to Müntzer by other sources, including Karlstadt. Müntzer's doctrine of Christian suffering, grounded in his unique argument that the elect are tossed about and must weather inward unbelief, found its sources elsewhere, and is inexplicable apart from Müntzer's study of Eckhartian mysticism and the Bible, as well as his exchange with Luther, the clear source for his faith-centrism.

A brief, closer examination of Augustine's arguments in *The Spirit and the Letter* will allow us to see better how Luther and Karlstadt, especially, brought Tauler's discussions of spiritual suffering and *reductio ad nihilum* together with Augustine's teachings on the bondage of the will and the "alien" work of the law. Writing in late 412 or early 413, Augustine argues in the *Spirit and the Letter* that all righteousness or "progress in tending toward it" is a gift of God; without the aid of grace through the Holy Spirit, the human will cannot attain or make progress toward righteousness. Righteousness is not merely a matter of doing good deeds and avoiding evil deeds, as Pelagius assumed, but of willing the good completely, that is, having a will entirely in conformity with God's will, loving God above all things, and loving all things as a means to serve God. After the fall, however, human beings become inherently "curved in upon themselves": they love themselves above all things and love God only as an instrument to fulfill the desires of the self, and they cannot change this (dis)orientation of desire and will by their own natural powers. To adapt Augustine's famous illustration from the *Confessions*, a person who wants to steal pears from his neighbor's tree might choose not to do so, but he cannot choose not to want to do so. Thus, Augustine argues, when Pelagius concedes that salvation is a gift of God insofar as God "created human beings with free choice" and gave the commandments to "remove[] ignorance" regarding good and evil, such arguments reflect and encourage a hardening in self-love. Fallen human beings falsely presume to be saved by resisting their wicked desire, when in fact, the desire itself is damnable. In order to become righteous, human beings require not only the capacity to choose and good instruction, but also "the Holy Spirit so that there arises in their minds a delight in and a love for that highest and immutable good that is God." Without the aid of grace, "free choice is capable only of sinning"—no matter how well the sinner is instructed.[98]

Augustine's central point in *The Spirit and the Letter* is that knowledge of the good and of the law does not allow a person to become righteous, unless the Holy Spirit also gives love of the law: "That teaching from which we receive the commandment to live in continence and rectitude is the letter that kills [2 Cor. 3:6], unless the life-giving Spirit is present." The Ten Commandments kill unless the Spirit makes Christians who can fulfill them from a genuinely good inward disposition. Although God commands, "You shall not desire (Ex. 20:17)," fallen human beings can only desire evil unless the Holy Spirit "substitut[es] good desire for evil desire." By itself, the law only "increases the evil desire by its prohibition."[99] Augustine admits that outward obedience to the law is possible "without the help of the spirit of grace," but he argues that this obedience springs only from "fear of punishment, not out of a love of righteousness," and leads further to a damnable pride in the appearance of good works. Augustine points to Paul's accusation of "the Jews" in Romans 2:17–29, arguing, "God did not see in their will what human beings saw in their action;[100] rather, they were held guilty as a result of what God knew that they preferred to do, if only they could have done so with impunity."[101]

For Augustine, the fact that the law increases evil desire, and brings about sin and pride even where it is obeyed, ironically confers upon the law its essential revelatory power.[102] The law convicts human beings of their need for a doctor. Interpreting Romans 5:20–21, Augustine writes:

> [H]uman beings had to be shown the foulness of their disease; against their sinfulness the holy and good commandment was of no use. It increased sinfulness rather than lessened it when the law entered in so that sin might abound. Then, when they had in that way been found guilty and were put to shame human beings would see that they needed God not only as a teacher, but as a helper who would direct their journeys . . . In what follows [Romans 6:3–11], the apostle pointed out that the same medicine was mystically revealed in the suffering and resurrection of Christ.[103]

Augustine explains here that the "end of our old life and the beginning of our new life" comes not from the "letter of the law," but from "faith in Jesus Christ." Grace gives knowledge of God and righteousness to sinners who have neither—thus the gift depends on no human merit whatsoever.[104] The righteousness of God described in Romans 3:21 is

> not that by which God is righteous, but that with which he clothes a human being when he justifies a sinner. . . . The law bears witness [to this], because by commanding and threatening and yet justifying no one it indicates clearly enough that human beings are justified by the gift of God through the assistance of the Holy Spirit. . . . That is, the believer is not helped by the law, since God shows human beings their weakness through the law in order that they might take refuge in his mercy through faith and be healed. Scripture said of his wisdom that it bears on its tongue the law and mercy, the law, that is, by which he makes the proud guilty, but mercy by which he justifies those who have been humbled.[105]

Faith here means the belief that grace heals the weak will, so that Christians can "fulfill what the law of works commands."[106] Thus, Augustine's position was that God gives Christians meritorious works on account of their faith, itself a gift of grace, that God makes the unrighteous righteous. Conversely, Luther argued that that God saves those who trust—who have faith as a gift of grace—in God's promise of redemption and in Christ's work, rather than in their own works. Nevertheless, the passages cited here were behind Luther's recollection in 1545 that he had found the doctrine of the "passive righteousness of God" in Augustine. Luther also found or confirmed other building blocks for his mature soteriology in *The Spirit and the Letter*, including teachings about the bondage of the will to evil; the sinfulness of human beings' innate inward disposition, whether or not this disposition finds expression in works; the associated danger of pride in apparent good works;[107] and the role of the law to increase sin and convict and humble sinners, driving them to grace and Christ. Luther later discerned crucial differences between his own soteriology and Augustine's; as mentioned Augustine lodged salvation in the merits of holiness, given by the Spirit *sola gratia*,[108] whereas the mature Luther contended that God gives salvation for faith defined as trust in God's promise of salvation without any prerequisite of holiness and merit.[109] Luther thus found sinful pride in any reliance upon one's own holiness, even if one emphasized—like the later Augustine—the priority of grace to this holiness. Luther's defined doctrine of the mediacy of Word and Sacrament also set him apart from Augustine, who speaks of God working through diverse internal and external movements—for instance in his *Confessions*.

Karlstadt too both learned from Augustine and departed from the bishop of Hippo in key respects. Like Luther, Karlstadt upheld the bondage of the will and taught that the law reveals human beings' innate sinfulness, convicting sinners of their self-focus and convincing them of their need for grace. More than Luther, Karlstadt echoed Augustine's primary teaching that sinners must be brought by grace into loving conformity with the divine will; for Luther, such growth in love and conformity follows justification by faith and must not be regarded as a grounds for justification. Karlstadt, in terms reminiscent of the *Spirit and the Letter*, regularly described the renewal that belongs to faith as God's circumcision of the heart,[110] the Spirit writing the law upon believers' hearts,[111] the restoration of the *imago dei* within,[112] and growth in burning desire for God.[113] All that said, Karlstadt like Luther and his Wittenberg allies underlined the life-long perdurance of sin. Karlstadt taught Christians to grow in faith—defined as knowledge of God and God's will—through self-accusation and self-denial, and he had no place for a concept of merit, even if merits were understood as God's gift. Like Luther, albeit with different emphases and goals, Karlstadt regarded Augustine as speaking in harmony with Tauler and the *German Theology* when it came to matters of human nothingness and the spiritual suffering that teaches sinful people about their nothingness.[114] Put better, Augustine and Tauler were thought to have identified the same core scriptural teachings.

"The Way of Nothingness": Luther and Karlstadt Read Tauler

In order to carry out a rich and detailed comparison of Karlstadt's and Luther's reception of Tauler, I focus here on their annotations to a selection of the mystic's sermons—namely, Sermons 4, 13–14, and 51–54 (treated here in reverse order) according to the numbering of the 1508 Augsburg edition. These specific sermons have been selected because both reformers left illuminating marginal remarks in them.[115] I will then describe Luther's detailed remarks to two sermons that Karlstadt annotated only sparsely, Numbers 41 and 45. Although they usually treat Luther and Karlstadt separately, previous studies have amply demonstrated their common interest in Tauler's teachings about the suffering and passivity that mark the path to blessedness.[116] Yet Luther and Karlstadt were also aware of and influenced by the larger paradigm within which Tauler's teachings on suffering and passivity were situated. For Tauler, rightly received suffering contributes to the annihilation of the human in all of his or her creaturely attachments and distinct selfhood. This annihilation is the precursor to union with God and is simultaneously a revelation of the soul's "nothingness": the soul is nothing because it cannot exist apart from God, and because it is turned from God's everything to the nothing of sin.[117] The soul also cannot attain blessedness (union) through activity, however seemingly pious. Pious working and thinking (i.e., the use of discursive reasoning) are exercises of will. When reduced to nothing, the soul becomes an empty space in which God works. This is the state of God-suffering, in which all other suffering can become joyful suffering or suffering without suffering.[118] Such concepts found willing reception among the reformers, who accepted that the receipt of salvation on God's terms—however desirable or joyful in and of itself—is always painful to fallen nature.

Sermons 51–54

Martin Luther left only one remark to Sermon 51, but it is very significant. It reads, "Note this, because the whole of scripture, every figure and all nature teaches this."[119] The remark was a response to Tauler's teaching that human beings must suffer the condemnation of divine judgment and a "dark, distant hope of liberation," both associated with the Old Testament, before they receive the "peace and joy in the Holy Spirit" associated with the New Testament.[120] They must "become united" with the Old Testament and "humbly bend under the powerful hand of God," willingly suffering "inwardly and outwardly," even if the suffering is undeserved. Salvation does not come in the way human beings would want or think, and they must adopt a stance of humble fear during any experience of comfort, inward or outward. Tauler writes, "For the person cannot enter into the kingdom of heaven through this—that is, through pleasure, joy, and the desire of temporal things. He should and must enter through bitter pain and sharp, manifold suffering, and through no other way."[121] These lines resonate with Luther's 95th thesis that Christians should "be confident of entering into heaven through many tribulations rather than through the false security of peace."[122] Tauler rejects frequent confession to escape a "biting conscience." Yielding toward the divine judgment and will (*Gelassenheit*) is the essential confession. Every attempt to escape from the experience of God's judgment through outward exercises, including hearing many sermons, reveals a refusal to yield and wait for God. Indeed, if one does not experience the birth of God (that is, the New Testament) within, one must humbly suffer this deprivation and wait for God. In turn, the person who yields to God in suffering receives help to endure all suffering through God: "You must yield yourself and suffer in truth. If we did that, God would uphold us in all things and all suffering . . . and help us endure and suffer through him. If we submitted ourselves boldly to God doubtless no suffering would be unbearable (*vnleidelich*)."[123]

For Tauler, the recognition of human nothingness enabled *Gelassenheit* before the divine will and patient waiting for God in all suffering; but suffering itself was also God's pedagogical tool to convince human beings of their nothingness. These themes received potent expression, and telling responses from the reformers, in Sermon 53. Here, Karlstadt repeatedly highlighted the theme of *reductio ad nihilum*—the word "nothing" appears ten times in his marginal remarks—while both Karlstadt and Luther responded positively to Tauler's rejection of an external, fleshy cross-bearing in favor of an inward subjection to God's work.

In Sermon 53, Tauler repudiates the debate between the "great doctors and teachers" over whether "knowing or love is greater and nobler," along with the question of the relative merits of Mary and Martha. He interprets Christ's commendation of Mary to mean that "one thing is necessary . . . that you know your own nothingness."[124] To learn this one thing is to choose and obtain with Mary "the best part," indeed the whole; but many confess their nothingness from reason alone, in order to be esteemed by others. Such persons, Tauler says, ultimately deceive themselves and others. Karlstadt followed these remarks with short notes.[125] Tauler's text then proceeds to explicate human nothingness in terms of the vulnerability and insufficiency of the outer person in nature; here, Karlstadt highlighted in the margin the mystic's pithy remark, "God has set all things against human beings." The reformer highlighted as well a citation of Romans 7:14 with which Tauler underlines the wretchedness of the human inclination to sin, that is, that human beings sin even against their will.[126] With a full sentence in the margin, Karlstadt summarized Tauler's decisive point that the outward and spiritual sufferings of humanity are graciously ordained by God in order to drive a person to recognition of his nothingness.[127] Tauler advises his hearers that whenever they are reproached and despised by others—especially by the wise—they should "sink into [their] ground and [their] nothingness. . . . Let all the devils in hell and heaven and earth with every creature assail you. It all will serve you wondrously. Sink only into your nothingness. The best part will come to you." Karlstadt wrote in the margin here "ground and nothing" and "the devils pursue to nothingness."[128]

Tauler interposes now a possible plea by a would-be pious person who contemplates Christ's passion daily; and he exhorts his hearers in response to think of God not as a mere human being, but as the powerful God who made everything and can unmake everything with a word—the God who is super-essential and above thought, and who nonetheless became nothing for his creatures. Tauler writes:

Shame yourself you mortal person, that you regard honor and judgment and pride, and humble yourself under the cross, from wherever it comes, whether from without or within. Set your prideful mind [gemu[o]t] under his thorn of crowns and follow the crucified God with a humbled [vndergeworfem] mind in true despising [verklainung] of yourself in every way, outwardly and inwardly.

Karlstadt here drew a large cross.[129]

Tauler teaches that because God "became nothing so completely and was condemned by his creatures and was crucified and died," we also should suffer patiently after his image; however, most people only think on Christ's suffering with "dead, blind love" rather than exercising themselves in Christ's suffering—a contemplation that bears "living fruit."[130] Luther responded to Tauler's exhortation to a "living" contemplation of Christ's passion with the words, "Note, to have the passion of Christ in memory: literally it profits nothing / spiritually it is life."[131] Meanwhile, Karlstadt wrote in Latin, "this [is] contemplation of the passion of Christ,"[132] to Tauler's ensuing description of life-encompassing self-abasement:

You should make yourself think that the earth unduly bears you on her back, rather than swallowing you. And think that many thousands are in hell, who perhaps never have acted so unjustly as you, and if God had given them as much light and done as much good for them as he has done for you, they would be unlike you. Nevertheless, God has spared and preserved you and eternally damned them. You should think about this often and much, and you should not be able to take a drop of water with freedom and impudent thirstiness, but only with humble fear. Use all things according to the necessity of your weakness [*kranckhait*] and not for satisfaction.[133]

Tauler lambasts those who presume to soar above heaven with their reason, but never realize their own nothingness. These "may well come to rational truth, but to living truth—to where the truth is—no one comes there except through the way of his nothingness."[134] Karlstadt wrote "nicht" once more here and in Latin, "living truth."

The ensuing discussion and Karlstadt's response is intriguing in relation to both Karlstadt's biography and his corresponding belief that the Christian— as God's instrument—might be moved to break with his past, his received vocation, and ecclesial norms. Tauler warns that the worldly wise will wish in the end that they had never learned their high things, but had worked in the field and "earned their bread with sweat." Karlstadt wrote out the relevant Biblical passage from Genesis 3:19, and he commented, among further marginal remarks on this page, "Nothingness subjects the person to God and all creatures."[135]

Karlstadt's profound and also personal interest in the human confession of nothingness is displayed once again in reference to Sermon 54, where Tauler describes "the way to true blessedness" as "a true pure humility," a "complete denial" of self "in spirit and nature." In this humility, says the *Lebmeister*, one "truly holds nothing of himself, or of all that he has done and still can do. If there is much good, that is entirely God's and not the person's." Karlstadt's marginal remarks include, "the way to heaven," "the gifts of God do not belong to human beings (citing *The Spirit and the Letter*)," "the ground of humility," and the first-person, "hold nothing of myself [*von mir selbs nicht halden*]."[136] This last gloss parallels his ensuing response, "von guten werken halden," to Tauler's critique of the presumption in self-chosen but seemingly pious works.[137] Tauler's teaching to regard the self as nothing was read as an affirmation of Augustine's theology of grace, in which good works are themselves gifts of grace, and on just this point, Karlstadt referenced this passage of Tauler in his lectures on *The Spirit and the Letter*.[138] The first-person remark—"von mir selbs nicht halde"—shows, moreover, that Tauler's teaching resonated with Karlstadt personally; as Hans-Peter Hasse argues, the impulse to regard the self as nothing seems to underlie Karlstadt's reticence to claim a special role for himself in the Reformation—contrary to Luther's and Müntzer's rather ambitious claims.[139] On an empty page at the back of his Tauler volume, Karlstadt inscribed Augustine's dictum, "Ubi non ego, ibi felicius ego"—"where I am not, there I am happier"—a citation from *de continentia*.[140] Karlstadt discerned a harmony between Augustine and Tauler, and discerned that his own academic and ecclesial efforts were but a damnable effort to be something. His public summons to self-hatred was rooted in an experience of the same, stirred by reading Augustine and Tauler.[141]

In Sermon 54, Tauler traces the problem of presumption to the human will, concluding that "all true blessedness lies only in true *Gelassenheit* . . . born from the true ground of abasement [*klainhait*], for there the self-will of the person is lost."[142] Luther was an attentive reader here. In response to Tauler's diagnosis that the problem lay in the will, Luther writes,

> that is, [in] affect, because it is not evil to have knowledge and [hear] good things preached, but to be affected [*affici*] by them, to trust in and be pleased with and altogether to have some kind of affection [*affectum*] in these things: this is arrogance and perdition to the soul. . . . Therefore it is necessary that affect be stripped and deprived of all our own wisdom and justice and depend upon God alone and think itself *nothing*.[143]

Crucially, Luther understands self-will in terms of self-trust—that is, trust in human wisdom or works. Luther's ensuing response to Tauler's three-fold anthropology[144] then invokes the concept of faith, of trust in God, as that which is born out of regarding the self and its wisdom and works as nothing. The reformer provides a table as follows (Table 1.1):

Steven Ozment identified in this schemata Luther's rejection of the soteriological significance of the concept of "synteresis." While Luther remains open to the concept of a highest or deepest part of the soul, Ozment explains, it is not any resource of that anthropological structure that brings salvation, but only its trust in God.[145] For our purposes, the essential point is that Luther's key theological term, faith, depends here on the recognition of human nothingness.

Table 1.1 Luther responds to Tauler's anthropology

The human	sensual rational spiritual	relies upon	sense reason faith	which the Apostle seems to call	carnal animal spiritual	which belong to	worldly people philosophers and heretics true Christians

Sermons 13 and 14

The interconnected 13th and 14th sermons of Tauler were of special significance to the reformers' reception of the mystic. Both Luther and Karlstadt
were taken by a story in Sermon 13 about a woman whose vision of God
resulted in indescribable suffering, because she realized her sinfulness and
distance from God. Luther later referenced the story in his *Explanations
of the 95 Theses* and his *Asterisci Lutheri adversus Obeliscos Eckii*, while
Karlstadt referred to it via a handwritten note in a copy of his printed lecture text, the *Epitome . . . on the justification of the impious*—presumably the
copy from which he lectured.[146] In Sermon 13, Tauler describes the strife of
the inner person or spirit, which always seeks God, against the outer person
or flesh, and how "God hunts both [spirit and nature] with his grace." All
those "hunted by the spirit of God are God's chosen children," Tauler says, although they experience "great bitter suffering." Only when a person discovers
God seeking within can his or her soul die "in spirit and nature" and receive
Christ.[147] Tauler declares that "one should humbly enter into [trials] with
thankfulness and pray joyfully for suffering," for in the discovery of such suffering there is certitude of the presence of grace. In the margin, Karlstadt
noted that trials are a "sign of grace."[148]

According to Tauler, the experience of spiritual trials—of being hunted—
brings about an "immeasurable cry" within, a "groundless sigh . . . far
above all nature," uttered by the Holy Spirit (per Rom. 8:26). Thus, the
Spirit prepares the soul's ground more than any human effort ever could.
Although God seems to disregard the sigh, the apparent disregard serves a
good end: the person becomes more yielded, just as the Canaanite women
in Matthew 15 (the pericope for the sermon) yielded when Christ initially
rejected her pleading. On these points, Karlstadt writes "the cry is hope and
desire" and "pure cry," and he provides in Latin the citation to Romans 8:26,
"the spirit itself intercedes with sighs." He also uses the term "renunciation
[*abnegatio*]" to gloss Tauler's description of the soul's growth in yieldedness
as a consequence of God's seeming refusal to heed its cry.[149]

Tauler recounts that Jesus denied the Canaanite woman not only help but
even "natural human being [*wesen*]" by comparing her to a dog. The mystic
praises the woman's response because she "obediently and mildly" yielded
to God's hunting and hunted herself "much deeper than he had hunted her."
She "went hunted into the ground, and still more she pressed into the abyss
and said humbly, 'No dear lord, not a hound but much less, only a small

little hound.'"[150] This was a "drowning and annihilation [*versincken vnd vernichten*] of herself," in which "she remained in a true, solid trust in our Lord Jesus Christ." The woman illustrates for Tauler a "true breaking into [*einschlag*] the ground of truth, . . . into the true ground of God." Karlstadt's responses here are detailed and revealing. He describes Tauler's "ground of truth" as the human confession, "In truth I am nothing,"[151] and he adds several pregnant glosses—"the way of salvation," "he will abandon himself to the will of God," "concerning [human] nothingness," "abnegation," and "vernichten"—to Tauler's ensuing statement:

> Beloved children, this would be the true, right, godly way to eternal truth. If a person could in this way be obediently and meekly yielded and com-posed in all his suffering and tumult, whether from within or without, and could thus be yielded humbly and completely to the will of God in love and suffering, even unto death without making any complaint. This way leads the person truly into God the Lord, indeed without any inter-mediary. For these people think and love a deep annihilation [*grundtloß vernichten*][152] of themselves from God and all God's creatures, and in ad-dition they annihilate themselves completely [*vernicht[e]n sy sich selbs zu[o] grunt*] before God and all creatures. And they remain at all times yieldedly [*gelassentlich*], obediently, and willingly in wretchedness, truly and steadfastly remaining in the ground of truth, persevering in right, true certainty.[153]

Tauler's exhortations to the renunciation of self-will through a confession of human nothingness, and to yielding to the divine will, found a receptive reader in Karlstadt. Tauler argues here that the person who is truly united to God receives, like the Canaanite woman, whatever she asks of God (see Matt. 15:28), because her will is in complete conformity with God's. Tauler paraphrases Christ's response to the women as follows: "You have always and every hour gone out from your own [self] in spirit and in nature. Therefore you must at the same time enter into me without any intermediary, and be-come one with me from grace as I am from nature." Karlstadt glossed these lines several times, including with a repetition of Tauler's phrase about departing from the self in spirit and nature.[154]

The account of the pious woman's vision that so impressed Karlstadt and Luther was offered by Tauler as an example of total self-denial. Tauler describes a woman—still alive at the time of his preaching, he says—who "may well be equal in virtue" to the Canaanite woman of Matthew 15. According to Tauler, this woman had been raptured four years previously into a vision of God, the Virgin Mother, and all the saints. The experience was not joyous, however, for she saw herself "in an inexpressible distance from God and his beloved mother and all his saints." Her spirit was struck by "inexpressible painful torment" and "hellish bitter pain," and she thought she would perish. Indeed, her pain was like that of the souls in hell, who suffer above all "because they know they are distant and separated from God" and will remain so for eternity. She turned "humbly" to the virgin and the saints for intercession, but they were too enraptured in God to hear her cry. She turned next "in a human way to the holy, bitter suffering and painful death of our Lord Jesus Christ," but here she only learned what was necessary, namely to plead with God alone. Tauler adopts the voice of the pleading woman as follows (I include Karlstadt's underlining):

> "O Lord my eternal God, since no one wants to help me, loving God consider that I am your <u>poor creature and you are the eternal God, Lord, and creator of me</u> and all creatures; therefore eternal father, I fall humbly into <u>your just judgment, according to your will, even if you want me to be eternally in this</u> <u>hellish, terrible pain, so that I yield myself humbly into your beloved will in time and in eternity.</u>" . . . Now as soon as she devoted herself humbly [*sich demu[e]tglich ergab*] and completely to the eternal God, yielded in eternity, she was <u>raptured far above any intermediary and immediately</u> enclosed <u>in the loving abyss</u> of divinity.[155]

Karlstadt followed the story here with numerous marginalia and other marks in the text, in black and in red ink (reflecting multiple readings of the passage). Several remarks pick up on Tauler's critique of the worship of saints. Above all, Karlstadt responds to the core message: that a person needs to surrender self-will completely to God's will, accepting without second thought even the worst suffering, eternal separation from God.[156] Karlstadt also reacted here to Tauler's critique of self-invented and self-imposed mortifications as a path to God.[157]

Luther left no remarks to this passage, despite his later citation of it, but he did respond to Tauler's related depiction of the return to God in Sermon 14. The relevant section follows a discussion of hindrances to the soul's return, which obstruct two types of persons: those who "have their lust and satisfaction in creatures and in the outer senses," and the "Pharisees," who outwardly appear to serve God but who are driven by self-will, self-love, and self-seeking.[158] Tauler explains that a Pharisaic spiritual stance comes from the lust of the "natural light" to find "eternal life" by its own means. In order to return to her "origin" and "true light," a person must accomplish "a true denial of self and pure, complete, image-less [blosse] love and regard for God." In this state, Tauler continues:

> One regards nothing of the self in anything, but desires and seeks the honor and glory of God without any intermediary. One accepts everything from God and from no one else—be it love or suffering, sour or sweet, he carries that all back without any hesitation or reversal into the divine free will of God, from which it comes. This is the true, right way to the highest perfection, and in this way the friends of God and the false, possessed grounds separate themselves. For the latter twist all things back to themselves, and always regard themselves and their nature in the gifts of God, and [they] do not always carry the same grace purely back to God with love and with a pure, free renunciation and with thankfulness, in a complete denial of themselves in spirit and in nature, both within and without.[159]

Luther completes the idea that those who are possessed in the ground do not refer the gifts of God back to God as follows: "i.e. that from these persons would come about what is pleasing to God or [what God] wishes, rather than what they themselves wish, that is to say either glory, consolation, or trust."[160]

For Tauler, true and false friends of God are distinguished by their response to and experience of suffering. True friends flee to God and suffer "obediently through his will." Consequently, "God becomes so inward and beloved to them, that suffering isn't suffering; rather it is great joy and jubilation to suffer through God's will." False friends, conversely, are dismayed by suffering.[161] As we will see, Luther underlined the inability of the unfaithful to face suffering and death with confidence. Conversely, one is reminded of Karlstadt's esteem for lay piety when Tauler claims that the "common, worldly person" is better off in suffering than those in exalted spiritual positions, who are like the Pharisees, bishops, and scribes who rejected Christ. The common people "consider themselves sinners and stand constantly in a humble fear of God."[162]

Sermon 4

Both Luther and Karlstadt read Tauler with interest in what the mystic had to say about the purposes of suffering and the appropriate response to suffering, that is, about how suffering rightly borne unites human beings to God and allows them to suffer without suffering, in acceptance of the divine will. These interests are evident in their respective marginalia to Tauler's Fourth Sermon, which describes the suffering that must accompany the turning of the soul from creatures and into its ground, and thus exhorts hearers to receive suffering from God in joy and gratitude. Tauler cautions against the self-imposition of suffering—an exercise that might strengthen rather than break self-will. Both Luther and Karlstadt incorporated a similar critique of self-imposed suffering into their later writings; they could endorse moderate self-mortification only as works flowing from grace, or as the self-discipline of an instrument of God. Müntzer, conversely, attributes an agency of preparation or response—in the form of self-mortification and separation from creaturely desires—to the elect who desire to hear God's inward voice; his perspective resonates more with Suso.[163]

Sermon 4 offers an allegorical exegesis of three types of myrrh as three types of bitterness marking the turn from creatures into the self and into the soul's ground.[164] The first myrrh according to Tauler is the bitterness that accompanies the killing of lust for creaturely things. Here, there are two lengthy marginal notes by Luther. First, where Tauler concedes that the fulfillment of earthly necessities unavoidably creates pleasure but admonishes that this pleasure must not be permitted to penetrate the soul's interior, Luther offers a stern endorsement. Such pleasure is not to be desired and sought, Luther writes, but "endured" and "suffered": "I should prefer to die in affect than to enjoy such pleasure."[165] Second, where Tauler cautions against taking pleasure in the company of good people, Luther remarks, "Note this. What must be rooted out is not so much sweetness of the flesh from affect, but [sweetness] of the spirit such as devotions, affections, consolations and the company of good people."[166] The deceptive sweetness of apparently good spiritual works and experiences receives special emphasis from Luther; thus, Luther here affirmed Tauler's caution about misplaced pleasure, even as his own views of sin were being reoriented around the matter of misplaced trust. For his part, Karlstadt responded with biblical citations to Tauler's declaration that everything that "has possessed the person with lust must be expelled . . . and become as bitter to you as the lust was [strong]"; Karlstadt penned in the margin parts of both Titus 2:11–12, which emphasizes turning from "impiety and worldly desires," and Colossians 3:9–10, where Karlstadt latched onto the phrase, "putting off the old person with his acts and putting on the new one."[167] Part of rebirth is becoming bitter toward oneself.

Tauler's description of the second kind of myrrh, which "far exceeds" the first, also elicited responses from the reformers. Tauler describes this myrrh as God-sent suffering, whether inner or outer, which ought to be accepted "in love from the ground where God gives it." The greatest and least sufferings given by God are, according to Tauler, "from the ground of his inexpressible love" and represent "the highest and best gift that he can give you." The smallest pain in one's finger is intended by God from eternity. Here, Karlstadt penned, "God has loved suffering from eternity." He also underlined, drew a hand, and wrote out a biblical verse, Job 13:3, beside Tauler's statement, "Shall I not then open my inner eyes and thank my God that his eternal plan is completed in me. Should that be suffering to me?" The Job passage, "even if he should kill me, I shall hope in him,"[168] was later invoked by Karlstadt in his *Missive on the Highest Virtue Gelassenheit* of 1520. In his reading of Sermon 4, Karlstadt subsequently underlined the notion that God "prepares" the soul for true joy and peace through trials—a peace anchored in God during and despite trials.[169] For his part, Luther offered a lengthy definition of the second myrrh.[170]

The *Lebmeister* Tauler was concerned with an appropriate response to God-sent suffering. He counsels his hearers not to complain to God about suffering, but to say, "I have deserved it." Whether "deserved or undeserved," suffering is from God and the appropriate response is to "give thanks and suffer and yield yourself." Luther here noted the "beautiful commendation of patience." Karlstadt left underlining and highlighted the foolish complaint of the misguided before God, "It goes badly for me."[171]

Tauler criticized not only impatience before unwanted suffering, but also the self-imposition of suffering. No less than impatience, self-imposed suffering sprung from self-will and boundedness to images, according to Tauler; the self-mortifiers think they please God, but God only reward's God's work, not self-imposed burdens.[172] In the margin here, Luther described the self-imposition of suffering as "the most secret superstition of the superstitious"; and he glossed Tauler's critical statement that people "build on their own precepts [*auff sa[e]tz*]" with the remark, "Just as once the children of Israel sacrificed in the groves and the hills rather than in the temple." Thus, Luther noted the possible deceptiveness of works, especially works of apparent suffering and self-mortification; such deception became a central concern within his mature soteriology and spirituality: idolatry always looks like pious devotion. Luther also summarized Tauler's reference to Augustine, writing: "Whatever you have of merit, prevenient grace gives. God crowns nothing in us besides his gifts."[173] Karlstadt responded in a similar way, with the notes, "One's own myrrhs do not please [God]," and "God does not crown yours but his."[174] Augustine's teaching on merit was thus related to the good work that God does through suffering, if human beings don't make suffering into their own work.

The third and final myrrh described by Tauler was a God-sent spiritual suffering, more bitter still than the second myrrh. Tauler calls it an "inner tumult [gedrenge] and darkness," advising that one must learn to perceive it and give oneself up to it,

> for whomever will perceive it and give himself to it [sich dar ein lassen], this inner work consumes flesh and blood and nature and transforms the colors much more than great outward exercises. For God comes with terrifying trials and in astonishing things and strange ways, which no one knows except the one who experiences them. People have astonishing suffering under these trials—indeed, such a myrrh that one can scarcely deal with it. But God knows well what God wants to do with it. If one does not perceive this, however, that is so harmful that no one can lament it [enough]. In what inconceivable love God gives this myrrh no heart can grasp. This myrrh we should use for our own good.[175]

Luther defined the third myrrh here as "suspension of grace and spirit," and to Tauler's remark about the harm of failing to see that God intends good with this myrrh, he wrote, "Nota bene."[176] With somewhat more detail he remarked on Tauler's ensuing criticism of the effort to understand and master suffering with the natural powers of reason and sense.[177] In addition to several smaller glosses, Luther describes why such people ultimately suffer so greatly, namely "because they do not rise in God, just as Job said, 'The lord gave, the lord took away.'"[178]

Luther's Remarks to Sermons 41 and 45

Karlstadt left only a few remarks to Sermon 41, and none to Sermon 45, but no other sermons elicited more detailed and fascinating remarks from

Luther. Sermon 45 takes as its pericope Luke 5:1–8, where Jesus teaches from Simon Peter's boat and then instructs Peter to take the boat into the deep and cast the nets in the water. Tauler allegorically interprets the boat as the inward person and his thoughts (*menschen gemu[e]t inwennig vn[d] sein meinung*), which must be led out into the stormy sea of the world. Here, the soul or "heart" is carried to and fro in joy and suffering. Bound to the world by love and opinion, it worries about clothing and adornment, while forgetting itself and judgment. If it is not to "perish or drown" in this sea, the *gemu[e]t* must be led away from all that is not God. According to Tauler, the nets in the bible passage symbolize human thought and judgment, which should be "thrown out [*auswerfen*] in holy contemplation and with great effort reflect upon all matters which can entice or incline it to holy devotion: the worthy life and suffering and the holy, virtuous way of life of our Lord." In this first turn, there is joy which "breaks out in jubilation" as "love goes through all one's power and sense."[179] This work of joyous contemplation, however, is only the beginning and the lowest "grade," according to Tauler. In order to become "outwardly and inwardly a yielded person, the person whom Dionysius calls a God-formed person," the ship must be led further into the deep. This means leaving behind anything the lower powers of the soul can grasp, including "all holy thoughts, images, and joy and jubilation. . . . What was given to him by God [now] seems to him entirely a coarse thing and is driven out, so that it no longer pleases him, nor can he remain with it." The separation is not yet complete, however, and the soul in this state is torn "between two directions and is in great pain and tribulation."[180]

Luther provided here a detailed table regarding the tribulations of the soul sent by God. According to this depiction, which expands considerably on Tauler's text, God first takes away temporal goods, so that human beings will learn to trust in and enjoy spiritual goods. God then takes away spiritual goods, so that human beings will learn to trust in and enjoy God in God's self—a relationship Luther describes as faith. At every stage of God's removal of goods, there is resistance even from the seemingly pious, whose renunciation of worldly goods and apparent outward suffering conceals their enjoyment of spiritual goods. Suffering is sunk into the core of the doctrine of faith as expressed here, and God's painful alien work cannot be separated from the proper work of faith. The table may be rendered as follows:

See therefore the order of divine providence.
　　First [God] gives natural goods to all, but in these

the impious are delighted, and—leaving the creator behind—they establish their end in his gifts and trust in these.

the pious are seized into God and use these things for God's sake.

Second [God] takes away those goods, either in effect or affect, that he should give better and spiritual things. And this is a great sorrow, especially [for] those who loved and enjoyed them.

But indeed, in these [spiritual] things others are silent and seek their own glory and reward, and trust in them just as the former in temporal things. Therefore God, wishing that they be converted purely (*nude*) into himself, takes these [spiritual] things from them, that he might give better things (i.e. himself). And in such privation how much greater is the sorrow concerning which he [Tauler] speaks.

And thus God always presses us to ascend from the imperfect to the imperfect, until we grasp God himself, and he always destroys and carries away the prior, that he might confer the following. In such work, however, how greatly are we dumb, un-resigned, querulous and impatient, *because we don't believe in him.*

Indeed, God in this way works by a so secret counsel, that no one feels himself to move or to wish, but only to have been moved (i.e. only after the work of God is completed can it be understood that God did this). . . . When indeed God works, then it appears entirely contrary to God's works, as Isaiah [28:21] [says], "His alien work, that he might work his own work." And therefore our foolishness so greatly impedes God working in us. For when he does not work according to our sense, we think all things are ruined and desperate. And thus we flee and we seek others, just as once the people of Israel fled into the desert.[181]

As we have seen, the idolatry of the Israelites was previously invoked by Luther in his marginal remarks to Sermon 4, where he equated the self-imposition of suffering to idolatry. Here, Luther summarizes how a person is carried by God away from the enjoyment of first temporal and then spiritual goods, finally reaching true trust in God. This suffering is unavoidable because human nature always misjudges the works of God. Indeed, it cannot sense God's works until after they are complete. Nature wants to receive salvation according to its understanding. If the most refined expression of this self-deceit is the self-imposition of suffering, Luther concludes, only a true suffering of God's work, unto faith, will finally free the human from idolatrous worship of the self.

In his marginal remarks to Sermon 41, Luther continued to highlight the lack of awareness on the part of the human being undergoing God's work—a claim that was central to Luther's theology of the cross, which holds that God always works in ways offensive to human reason and will. In Sermon 41, Tauler exegetes Luke 15: 8–9, the parable in which a woman loses a penny and lights a lantern to look for it. Tauler explains that the woman represents divinity, the light deified humanity, and the penny the soul, which to be a proper penny must have the proper weight, material, and image. Formed in the image of God, the penny (soul) has unfathomable weight, while its material is the "in-sunk divinity [*eingesenckt gothait*]." However, if God is to enclose and sink the soul in *Gottheit*, the soul must follow a "nearer and shorter way, which is far above the way that the outer person can seek and above every exercise of the outer person, be it in a suffering or working way."[182] Luther writes, "that is, to suffer only in body and in natural goods. But to suffer in spiritual goods is a most excellent virtue, as in faith, hope, love, thus in dryness, faintheartedness."[183] Luther here values the perception of a lack of faith, hope, and love—a spiritual suffering that yields an increase of the trust in God described in his remark to Sermon 45.

Tauler explains in Sermon 41 that the way to receptivity to God is exemplified by the woman who lights the lantern, which ignites divine love in the soul. He continues:

> Beloved children, you don't know what love is.[184] You think that love means that you have great feeling and sweetness and lust. No. That isn't love, that isn't its essence. Love means that one has a burning in absence and deprivation [*beraubung*] and in being forsaken [*ainem verlassen*]; that there is a state of ceaseless torment, in which one abides in true yieldedness. . . . Children that is love. And that, what you imagine [i.e., that love is], is a lighting of this lantern.[185]

Here, Luther's remarks expand on Tauler by providing an

> example from carnal love, which is greatest when it suffers and performs hardships and difficulties on account of the love object, not however when it enjoys the love object in sweetness and favors. Because that sweetness is the fruit and recompense of love rather than love itself; thus it must be feared that many devoted ones here receive their wages in whole or in part. Whoever abounds in serving God in spiritual consolations: they need [these

consolations] most greatly and are rather eager when they are present but rather sluggish when they are absent.[186]

Where Tauler writes that love has "a burning in absence and deprivation and in being forsaken," Luther defines forsakenness—just as he defined the third myrrh of Sermon 4—as "dereliction by God through the suspension of grace." God leaves the soul without spiritual experience precisely to increase its spiritual capacity. Luther also responds to Tauler's commendation of a response of "level-headed yieldedness [*in gleicher gelassenhait*]" with a Latin translation, "aequabile vel aequamini." Great perturbation in the face of trials is, for Tauler and Luther alike, evidence that one is grounded in the goodness or badness of experience, whether inward or outward, rather than in love of God (Tauler) or faith (Luther). This line of thought introduced a difficult paradox into Luther's mature theology, in which human nature lacks the impregnable fortress of Tauler's ground, as well as the capacity to make a beginning on the way to God. For Luther, Christians must endure the apparent deprivation of spiritual resources—faith, hope, and love—precisely through the resources they cannot feel, above all through faith. Practically, the mature Luther advises such spiritual sufferers to attend to the Word *extra nos*, rather than to the lack in the self; but only faith clings to the Word. Thus, in Sermon 45, we find Luther remarking on Tauler's discussion of the trials of the soul, "Whoever does not remain in faith perishes. They wish rather to know and to see, what will happen and how. And thus they impede God, that he does not work in them."[187]

For Tauler, the person suffering in the in-between state described here must simply remain within herself, anchored in God, and "suffer through it and not seek anything else." Many seek teachers to tell them how to escape these spiritual trials, Tauler cautions, yet such trials can be stilled in only one of two ways: either by the birth of God in the waiting soul, or by the birth of a creature that prevents the divine birth.[188] While Luther shows here no reaction to the "birth of God or creature" theme, the theme of God's annihilation of the soul provokes his longest marginal remark in the *Sermons*. The first part reads as follows:[189]

And if we know that God does not work in us, unless he first destroys us and our things (i.e. through the cross and passions), we are therefore stupid that we should wish so greatly to take up sufferings which we choose or which we see and read to have happened in others. And thus we dictate to God the manner and we are prepared to teach him, what and how he should teach us. And we do not stand naked in pure faith, although God wishes either not to work in us, or to work without our knowing and understanding of that which he does, so that salvation should be faith and pure will. Just as the craftsman does not work with his material according to the form that the material itself has, shows, or exhibits in itself, nor according to that which the material itself is able to seek outside of itself by its own prior capacity: here indeed accidental form happens. But he [the craftsman] directly destroys that substantial form, so that he might introduce another [form] completely different from the prior [form]. Thus God, who teaches, "Just as clay in the hand of the potter, thus you in my hand," directly acts against our plan [*propositum*], hope, and intention, and dissipates all our counsel [*consilium*] by a contrary work, and condemns every thought of the people and declares his counsel, which nevertheless satisfies incomparably more abundantly than ours—than if he had yielded to our counsel. When this happens, disbelievers and sons of distrust, seeing that deep within the contrary to their sense happens, do not put up with the counsel of God, but rather think this to be from the devil. And thus they depart into the counsel of the impious in that they believe their counsel and intention to be from God and everything contrary from the devil. On the contrary, our every intention [is] from the devil and the contrary from God, just as he says, "Be favorable with your adversary along the way."[190] Therefore the whole of salvation is resignation of the will in all things, as he [Tauler] teaches here, whether in spiritual or in temporal [things]. And pure faith in God.[191]

These were Luther's most extensive remarks in his Tauler volume, evidencing a deep engagement with the mystic. The decisive analogy is that of the human being to dirt or clay, to matter whose existing form must be destroyed, so that a new form may be given by its maker. In fact, for Luther, the human being was analogous less to raw material than to material that had been put to bad uses and needed to be melted down or pulverized and repurposed. The human being was sinful and self-deceived material that denied its passive nature and the nothingness of its thoughts and desires. Thus, to become what God the maker willed, human beings had to suffer a painful frustration and annihilation of their every "plan, hope, and intention"; only God could give the clay a pleasing form. In Luther's responses to Tauler, suffering appears as God's pedagogical tool to reveal to human beings—through the removal of visible and especially spiritual gifts—their need for exclusive trust in God, and to train them in that trust. Luther realized, however, that the recipient of this pedagogy nearly always misinterpreted God's action as an expression of wrath; Luther's marginal remarks implied that the only way out of this dilemma was through complete annihilation of human resources for understanding and pleasing God, so that reason and will could no longer object to God. Luther came to emphasize that God's work of annihilation of self-trust was completed only through the sinner's death and resurrection. Here, Luther upheld spiritual suffering as unavoidably part of the receipt of salvation: sinful beings do not want salvation on God's terms, but must suffer to hear and learn that they are enemies of God in their fallen nature. Tauler helped Luther understand, and explain, this experience, which in turn allowed the believer to endure all suffering as willed by God.

I argue in the ensuing chapters that this paradigm of *reductio ad nihilum* represents a framework within which the theologies of Luther, Karlstadt, and Müntzer were elaborated. To speak of a framework or paradigm is to speak of fundamental assumptions and convictions, which can be shared even by bitterly opposed parties. The story of the mutual alienation of our three subjects (with their followers) from one another is a story of the gradual development of antagonisms out of, and often in defense of, shared commitments. It is worth underlining that I am not claiming that Tauler was the sole source of these ideas; he was one source among many.[192] Karlstadt and Luther both read Tauler's message as harmonious with Augustine's, particularly with the African father's teachings on the bondage of the will and prevenient grace, the alien work of the law, and God's creation of all justice and good works in the person. Other sources from the post-Eckhartian mystical tradition also came into play: Karlstadt and Müntzer read Suso, and Luther, Karlstadt, and Müntzer read the *German Theology*, to which we now turn.

The *German Theology*: Mysticism, Dissent, and Suffering

Near the end of 1516, Luther obtained a partial manuscript of an anonymous and untitled mystical work.[193] He published the text with a short preface noting its similarity to Tauler's works, under the title, *A spiritual, noble little book on the right distinction and understanding of the old and the new person, Adam's child and God's child, and how Adam should die in us and Christ rise.*[194] In 1518, Luther obtained and published a complete copy of the work. This book was printed nine times before 1520; the polemical title, *A German*

Theology, underlined that true theology had continued to be expressed in the German language, even as Latin scholastic theologians went astray.[195] In his 1518 preface, Luther claimed, "Next to the Bible and Saint Augustine no other book has come to my attention from which I have learned—and desired to learn—more concerning God, Christ, man, and what all things are." According to Luther, the *German Theology* disproved the reproach of "the highly learned" that "Wittenberg theologians" were "disseminating novelties."[196]

Luther's was not alone in using paratexts to influence readers' reception of the *German Theology*: a 1520 edition published in Wittenberg by Rhau-Grunenberg featured some 180 printed vernacular marginalia. Added by an anonymous author, the annotations highlighted the *German Theology's* demand for complete renunciation of self and the endurance of a hard "Christ-life" against the opposition of self-will and *Annehmlichkeit*—the sin of claiming God's good gifts, beginning with existence itself, as one's own. Although the text of the *German Theology* itself does not include the substantive term, *Gelassenheit*, several marginal annotations alert the reader to discussions of the concept. Scarcely explicable as the work of Luther,[197] the marginalia correspond closely to Karlstadt's mature soteriology, spirituality, and reform program. Karlstadt published his *Missive on the Highest Virtue of Gelassenheit* with Rhau-Grunenberg just two weeks after the press produced the annotated *German Theology*, raising suspicion of his authorship. Nevertheless, the annotations may also have influenced Karlstadt, for the correspondence to his teaching and program is clearest when the annotated *German Theology* is compared to his major works of 1523, rather than the contemporary *Missive*.

Only a few studies have seriously addressed the early reformers' reception and use of the *German Theology*: most significantly, Ozment argued that Luther found in the *German Theology* first (in 1516) a compelling description of the "way to salvation" and later (in 1518) a tool to "blunt the charge of innovation"; however, according to Ozment, Luther was not interested in the text's mystical teachings concerning anthropology, ontology, and union with God. Conversely, Thomas Müntzer, like the other radicals who followed in his wake, was interested primarily in a mystical anthropology that allowed for God's direct instruction of souls.[198] This interpretive line traces too narrowly the boundaries of both reformers' interests: as we have seen, Luther was drawn to themes of self-denial and *reductio ad nihilum*, which were at the core of the *German Theology's* teachings about sin and union, while

Müntzer unfolded detailed teachings surrounding the possession of the soul by creatures or God, the soul's experience of "being emptied," and the necessity of accepting the bitter Christ with the sweet. Scholars of Karlstadt, meanwhile, have questioned whether the *German Theology* exercised a major influence upon the reformer, despite his explicit recommendation of the text in his 1523 treatise on *Gelassenheit*; the absence of the term *Gelassenheit* from the *German Theology* raises suspicion that Karlstadt's greater debt was to Tauler, who used the term often, not the Frankfurter.[199] However, the 1520 marginalia explicitly pointed readers to discussions of *Gelassenheit*; even if Karlstadt neither wrote nor knew the marginalia, this fact suggests that contemporary readers would have understood the Frankfurter to be describing *Gelassenheit* in relevant passages. Broadly, ideas about *Annehmlichkeit* as the root and essence of sin and about *Gelassenheit* as the solution connect Karlstadt to the *German Theology* itself and to the 1520 marginalia. This is not to say that kindred themes are not found throughout Tauler, but verbal resonances and direct connections between Karlstadt and the *German Theology* should not be overlooked either. Likely, both Tauler and the *German Theology* were significant for Karlstadt, alongside Augustine.

For our purposes, it is most important to realize how the *German Theology* used the opposition of God's will to human willing and reason—thus, suffering—as *the* key criteria for determining the verity of spiritual experience and Christian life. As one of the 1520 annotations put it, "God's will and human will are against one another."[200] Thus, the *German Theology* offered a vocabulary and a playbook for dividing the world into friends and enemies of the cross. The text could give this guidance because its original author had been concerned to unmask what he regarded as false claims to union with God—claims that allegedly sprang from the "false light" of nature or reason and that were cloaked in airs of pious annihilation.[201] Luther, Karlstadt, and Müntzer all accepted the connection of suffering and self-denial to the reception of truth. Further key themes of the *German Theology*, however, were received most explicitly by Karlstadt and Müntzer: both accepted a Neo-Platonic framework, centered on the relation between whole and part, and Karlstadt's works in 1523 and after especially resonate with the *German Theology* in this respect. Müntzer's later work also shows his interest in the notion of deification, although not necessarily his dependence on the *German Theology* for his formulation of the concept: Müntzer's hope for deification required forms of direct divine instruction and political action alien to the medieval treatise. For Karlstadt and Luther, the perdurance of sin in the faithful always remained a crucial doctrinal point—Karlstadt is a theologian of self-accusation more than a theologian of deification.

By the time Luther received the *German Theology*, a brief prologue had been added to the original;[202] this prologue framed the text, describing it as something of a manual for the right discernment of truth in an era of uncertainty. The prologue claims that the author (called the "Frankfurter" by scholars)[203] "teaches many wonderful tenets of divine truth and especially how, where, and whereby one might discern those who are in truth God's righteous friends and the unrighteous, false, free spirits who harm the holy church."[204] In fact, the Frankfurter was concerned throughout his text with the so-called heresy of the free spirit, condemned at the Council of Vienne in 1312. According to opponents, "free spirits" claimed to have reached deification and thus freedom from suffering and sin; they accordingly declared themselves above all "orders" (i.e., ecclesial and secular law), the exercise of virtues, the teachings of scripture, and the sacramental mediation of the church. Free spirits were said to believe that everything they did was good because of their identity with God, achieved through the soul's annihilation; they could engage in sexual license or commit the most egregious of crimes with a clean conscience. The Frankfurter reports the claim of a "free spirit" that he could kill ten persons with as little guilt as if he had killed a single dog.[205] The Frankfurter's text was centered on concepts of deification and union with God, and he was, accordingly, compelled to protect his teachings from any possible association with the free spirit heresy and to instruct readers about how to avoid this seductive path.[206] To these ends, the Frankfurter married suffering and truth, teaching that during earthly life, union with God does not remake a person into the likeness of the resurrected Christ, free from suffering, but only into the likeness of the crucified.[207]

Several themes structure and animate the *German Theology*.[208] First, the text relies on a Neo-Platonic opposition of the perfect, unchangeable, immoveable divine being to partial creatures, which have their being in and are moved by the perfect, and which cannot know or experience the perfect "on the basis of . . . creatureliness, createdness, and I-relatedness." The theme of reduction to nothingness is prominent immediately, as the author's exposition proceeds from a citation of I Corinthians 13:10, "When the complete comes, one reduces to nothing [*vornichtiget*] the incomplete and the partial."[209] Second, the *German Theology* describes sin as a turning from the perfect source and as the appropriation for the self of the being, will, and goodness that can only be received from God. The personal pronouns "I, me, and mine" spring from the action of claiming for the self (the verb used is *sich annehmen*) what belongs to God.[210] Sin is the assertion of human independence in knowing, willing, and doing the good, whereas in the perfect person, all knowing, willing, and loving is God's knowing, willing, and loving within a human dwelling, as it was in Christ.[211]

Turning from God (*abkehren*) and appropriation (*annehmen*) are equated by the Frankfurter with disobedience, the old man, and Adam,[212] and any willing apart from the eternal will is described as sin, whether it involves seemingly pious action or suffering,[213] because it claims for the creaturely will an independent existence apart from the divine. Presumption combined with deception—or better, presumptuous self-deception—is the root problem of human sin: the sinner wants to claim being and willing for himself and imagines that this is possible.[214] The Frankfurter regards the exercise of the created will apart from God as sin because the purpose of the created will—and indeed of all creation—is that God's will become effective through it.[215] God requires creatures "so that the divine will may take shape through them, acquiring its own work."[216] The Frankfurter teaches readers to yield their created will to the eternal will, so that sinful selfhood is annihilated.[217]

A third animating theme of the *German Theology* is that such yielding brings a present experience of the incarnation and deification. As God in Christ became human and the human person divine, God becomes human (*vermenscht*) in the yielded individual and the individual is deified (*vergottet*).[218] Human agency lies in permission and yielding, indeed in suffering:

> In this return and betterment, I can or may or should do nothing at all except a pure suffering, so that God alone acts and works and I suffer God and God's work and will. And because I do not want to suffer this, but rather [want] I, me, and mine, that hinders God, so that God may not work alone and without hindrance. Therefore my fall and turning [*abker*] remain unbettered. See, appropriation for the self [*annemen*] does all this.[219]

The desired end is to become God's instrument: "I would like to be to the eternal good just as the hand is to the person."[220]

Another major leitmotif in the *German Theology* is the soul's fluctuation between the true light and the false light—an opposition that is equivalent to the opposition between whole and part, Christ and Adam.[221] Illumination by the true light is not only a matter of receiving knowledge, but represents the complete state of the person who through yielding and the rejection of appropriation allows divine knowledge and love to become manifest in the soul. This person lives in complete obedience to God, without fear of punishment or hell or desire for reward. Such indifference is "true spiritual poverty" according to the Frankfurter, but human beings, he warns, shirk the experience and the guidance of the true light because it involves bitterness.[222] Salvation requires the annihilation of self-hood in the confession that one is unworthy of good or suffering—even of hell itself. Yet God does not permanently abandon the soul to an experience of bitter hell, but also gives foretastes of heaven. The soul has no control over the coming and going of either state, and it is carried back and forth between heaven and hell throughout life. Crucially, both experiences secure the *viator* from deception. They are "two good, certain ways for the human being in time" and one "can be as certain in hell as in heaven." To be in neither state is grave danger, for one is then caught up in creatures rather than divinity.[223]

Such arguments were directed against the free spirits' alleged belief that they could live a life in which they experienced only "heaven," not hell. Their claim to transcend suffering revealed for the Frankfurter their starting point in a self-willed refusal to suffer, to give up their separate willing in order to be the workshop of God's will. Against such spirits, the Frankfurter argued that the deified have intense spiritual suffering, lasting until death, because they abide in a realm driven by the rejection of God.[224] The resulting "divine sorrow" is the suffering of God in the human soul, in the face of whatever is against God.[225] Bodily suffering and material deprivation are also not eliminated here, but they are borne by the God-yielded and God-manifesting person in love, joy, and inner peace, for such suffering has its origins in God's will.[226] For the Frankfurter, finally, just as for Luther, Karlstadt, and Müntzer, Christ's suffering shows that true Christian life is dear to God and bitter to fallen nature, hence simulteoulsy sweet and bitter to the human experiencing it:

> One should note, believe, and know that no life on this earth is as noble, good, and dear to God as the life of Christ but that it is at the same time most bitter to human nature and the self. The opposite kind of life, the careless, free life, is the most sweet and most pleasant to nature, the self, and the I. . . . Although Christ's life is the most bitter of all, it is paradoxically the dearest.[227]

Natural reason or the false light cannot discern this good life correctly, but sees only the bitter:

> Since the life of Christ is most bitter to all natural life, to the self, and to the I—for in the true life of Christ the self and the I and the natural life are surrendered, lost, and given up for dead—natural man shudders as he faces it and he regards it as evil and unjust and foolish. Natural man therefore adopts a life that appears to him pleasant and enjoyable and in his blindness he maintains and imagines that this life is the best possible. Now to the natural man no life is as comfortable and enjoyable as a free, careless life. So natural man holds on to it and extracts pleasures from his self, his selfhood, his own kind of peace, his own doings, and all that belongs to the self. This happens most of all where high natural reasoning holds sway, for it climbs so high in its own light and in itself that it fancies itself to be the eternal true light and passes itself off as precisely that. But this high and learned natural reason deceives itself and pulls with it in the same deceit others who do not know any better and are also inclined in that direction.[228]

Following the example of Tauler and Suso, the Frankfurter here shuffled off Eckhart's marriage of scholastic theology and mysticism in favor of a critique of academic learning as a self-directed and self-seeking exercise.[229] The reformers each listened, in their own ways.

For the Frankfurter, whatever appears best and true to unredeemed, pleasure-seeking persons is entirely false, and only what appears worst is pleasing to God.[230] The highest end attainable in earthly life, the Christ life, is marked by the deepest suffering of God and creatures:

> Whoever wants to suffer God, must suffer everything—that is, God and himself and all creatures, nothing excepted. And whoever wants to be obedient, yielded and submissive to God, must be yielded, obedient and submissive to all things in a suffering way, and not in a doing way,[231] and this all while silently remaining in the ground of his soul and in a heavenly, hidden suffering, bearing and suffering everything, and in all this neither making nor desiring help, excuse, contradiction or revenge, but speaking always in a loving, humble, and true pity, "Father forgive them, for they do not know what they do." See, this would be a good way to and a preparation for the best and final end that the human being may reach in time, that is the bodily life of Christ.[232]

The Frankfurter admitted that the free spirits were not easily recognized. They cloaked themselves in a pretense of the highest spiritual sanctity, in the complete annihilation of the self. In order to aid discernment, the Frankfurter delineated the fruits of the free spirit;[233] yet discernment for the Frankfurter ultimately required the transformation of the discerner—a claim we will see repeated by reformers. Here, one must suffer the recognition of his own nothingness, "that the person in himself and his things is nothing and has and can accomplish and is suited for nothing but sin and vice and evil." Such "true spiritual poverty" or "humility" makes one ready, in turn, to suffer offense, serve all creatures, and respect outward order.[234] The union of the humble with God does not result in the leisure and inactivity embraced by the free spirits; instead, union means that the created will is "melded [with] and become[s] nothing" in the eternal will, which thereafter "alone wills, does, and omits" everything in the person. Union means "to be purely, simply, and completely one and simple [*einfeltig*] with the one, simple, eternal will of God or indeed to be without will." The inner person remains thus sunken into God, even as God lets the outer person be moved to and fro in works and suffering.[235] The free spirits want according to the Frankfurter to bypass the life of the crucified Christ for that of the resurrected Christ[236] and thus to avoid all suffering, all being moved as recipients and instruments of God. The Frankfurter counters that one must first go through and suffer what Christ suffered, namely death and "whatever else belongs to it."[237] Again, the culprit is identified as the "false light," which wants to claim God's eternal characteristics as its own.[238]

The "false light" is richly described in the *German Theology*. It is crucial to note that the false light, for the Frankfurter, both deceives and is deceived.[239] The Frankfurer applies to the false light many names and descriptions: it is "pure nature," and as such it "loves and seeks itself and its own in all things and that which to nature and itself is most self-indulgent and the most pleasant." The false light is caught up in the self and particularity, and hence it cannot be instructed about the "one true Good, which is neither this nor that particularity." The false light is indeed the devil, for it imagines itself to be God, and like the devil, it cannot be "converted or instructed." The false light, finally, is the anti-Christ (*endechrist*). It is not enough to illuminate the false light or to redirect the nature of the person; instead, the false light of nature must be destroyed and replaced by the true light. The Frankfurter teaches that a person is secured from deceit only insofar as the true light shines within him—that is, only insofar as God becomes human within him, meaning that he experiences the Christ-life within and will manifest the same outwardly. This life is said to be recognized by the suffering it inflicts against nature and the false light, which inherently flee the cross. The Frankfurter writes, "In short, the false, deceived light flees everything that is against nature or difficult for nature."[240] Suffering, truth, and salvation are married here and arrayed against the enemy of deception springing from Satan and the false light—nature turned from God into *Annehmlichkeit*.

The frequent reissuing of the *German Theology* in the first few years after its publication reflected demand on the part of readers sympathetic to the Wittenberg Reformation; the text was not immediately forgotten as Luther and his allies began to produce more of their own writings after 1518. There was as yet no intra-Reformation dissent from Wittenberg teachings; the text was instead part of Wittenberg's dissent from scholastic methods and Roman authority and doctrine. Theologians, pastors, and lay readers undoubtedly read the text in varied ways, but the incompatibility of interpretations did not yet appear in the full light of day.

In light of the reformers' responses to Tauler, and of the arguments that we will follow in ensuing chapters, we can conclude that the *German Theology* resonated with and served the reformers' theological commitments and reform goals for several reasons—because the text located human sinfulness in self-assertion that was cloaked in piety and deceived reason (the "false light"), because it depicted salvation and union as the suffering of God's work, and because it offered spiritual suffering and visible cross-bearing as the key verifiers of truth. The Frankfurter wanted to unmask deceit, and he claimed that the way to truth led not through a scholastic assertion of reason, but through a passive acceptance of God's will and being; likewise, he argued that truth was manifested not in self-directed ascetic exercises, but in suffering whatever afflictions God willed, including the wrath of a sinful world.

Already in 1520, however, with the appearance of the aforementioned annotated edition, we see that there was room for competing interpretations and ideals to emerge within this broad paradigm. The 1520 annotations do not haphazardly summarize the text—they largely neglect the theme of deification[241]—but they evidence a deliberate, considered intervention in the contemporary theological controversy. In so doing, they bring to the fore motifs that defined not Luther's but Karlstadt's spirituality, proposing *Gelassenheit* as the foundation of Christian existence and the solution to self-will (*Annehmlichkeit*). I do not argue here that Karlstadt wrote the annotations; this would mean that he annotated a text associated with his rival, glossing not only the *German Theology* itself but Luther's preface. At the same time, it is far more likely that Karlstadt wrote the annotations than it is that Luther did, and the correspondence with Karlstadt's later works is very strong and direct. Karlstadt may well have composed his major treatises of 1523 with the aid of the annotated edition. For present purposes, we want to see in the marginalia only how diverse views of salvation and Christian life began to develop out of and around shared commitments to passivity and suffering as the means to and evidence of Christian truth. The resonance of the marginalia and corresponding text with key themes from Karlstadt's mature writings (to be discussed in chapter 4) makes this point.

Far more than any other theme, the marginal annotations point readers to discussions of the nature of sin, several times using the short phrase, "What sin is [*Was su[e]nd sey*]," that Karlstadt later used in the title of his 1523 treatise on God's will, *On the Multiplicity of the Simple, Singular Will of God [and] What Sin is*. Karlstadt also, and more significantly, adopted the definitions of sin that were glossed with this note, both in *On the Multiplicitly* and, more explicitly, in his related treatise, *What is Meant [by the phrase], "Yield Yourself," and What the Word Gelassenheit Means, and Where in Scripture it is Found.* The first appearance of the annotation, "What sin is," in the 1520 *German Theology* glosses a description of sin as occurring when "the creature turns [*sich . . . abkert*] from the unchangeable . . . [and] whole to the partial and incomplete—and above all to itself. . . . The creature claims as its own [*sich an nympt*] something good, such as being, life, knowledge, ability." Another annotation condenses the meaning of the text with the phrase, "*Annemlickeyt* of nature." Thus, while the Frankfurter used a reflexive verb (*sich annehmen*), the annotator supplied the substantive *Annehmlichkeit*, just as elsewhere the annotator supplied the substantive *Gelassenheit* where the verb form *sich gelassen* was used.[242] While this initial definition of sin certainly found resonance in Karlstadt's 1523 writings, the reformer explicitly adopted the next definition glossed by the phrase "Was sunde sey"; here, the *German Theology* says that sin is "nothing other than that the creature wills other than God or against God."[243] A gloss in a later section reads, "Whatever is against the one will [of God], that is sin."[244]

The printed annotations also highlight the *German Theology*'s equation of *Annhemlichkeit* to disobedience—the disobedience of Adam, who must be reduced to nothing in every person, versus the obedience of Christ, whose human nature was but a "house or dwelling of God." This line of thinking appears prominently in Karlstadt's 1523 treatises. The short note, "disobedience," glosses a passage explaining that disobedience occurs when "the person thinks something of himself [*von ym selber etwas haltet*]"—a passage reminiscent of the advice from Tauler that Karlstadt had glossed. One of many annotations to the *German Theology*'s extended discussion of disobedience points again to an answer for the question, "What is sin?"[245]

Along with the *German Theology*'s definition of sin, the annotator wanted to direct readers to the solution of *Gelassenheit*. The annotator accepted the *German Theology*'s equation of *Gelassenheit* to biblical ideals of humility and spiritual poverty. A key passage in the main text describes how the human soul must descend into hell like Christ, namely by confessing itself unworthy of any good or even of any suffering, including hell itself. The annotation reads, "Deep [*hohe*] humility and *Gelassenheit*." The reader is exhorted by annotations to "yield all creatures [and] hang in God's hand"; and the reader is promised that by so doing, he will have true contrition even in the lack of contrition [*vnrewe*], as well as "peace in tribulation," "joy in difficulty," and "patience in impatience."[246] Anchored by unity with the divine will, the yielded person readily accepts spiritual experiences of heaven or hell, and seeks only the will of God, out of love of God, in outward works and trials.

Crucial to the *German Theology*'s argument, as we've seen, was the claim that such yielding is contrary to what nature and the "false light" desire, and that the resulting life of suffering is avoided by all those whose self-will remains intact. The 1520 annotations also pick up the motif of the bitterness of the Christ-life as edifying for evangelical readers.[247] At the beginning of chapter 16, for example, the gloss reads, "[There is] no more bitter life than Christian life, and thus [it is] the best." The original text here, recalling the opening citation of I Corinthians 13:10, explains how the sinner's knowledge and love of partial things will "come to nothing [*zu nicht wirt*]" when knowledge and hence love of the whole comes. Two annotations here, "knowledge brings love with itself" and "knowledge happens in faith," remind of Karlstadt's later definition of faith as knowledge that produces love. At the conclusion of the ensuing chapter, then, the Frankfurter's discussion of the need to surrender all things (per Matt. 16:24 and related texts) is glossed, "Gelassenheit of all things makes Christians. To cling to partial things [*stucken*] makes fake saints."[248]

Gelassenheit is thus commended by the annotations as a complete surrender of the self and self-will resulting in union with God. In one section, a first gloss explains that "God's children are ruled by God alone through *Gelassenheit*," while the next gloss exhorts, "Be purely and completely without yourself."[249] In just over twenty lines of text at the beginning of chapter 24, five glosses call attention to the *German Theology*'s description of "spiritual poverty" and "spiritual humility" as the recognition that "the person in himself and his things is nothing." One gloss reads, "Hatred of himself [*Vorachtung seynn selbst*]"—the core exercise that Karlstadt came to commend.[250] Finally, the gloss, "One should yield all things spiritually," introduces chapter 25, where the *German Theology* describes union with God as becoming united "with the eternal, simple will of God" or even "without will." Here the text expresses the concept—used by Karlstadt—of the created will flowing or melting into the divine will and thus becoming nothing.[251] Telling glosses later explain that sin is not an exercise of free will but of self-will, and (as noted) that "God's will and human will are opposed to one another."[252] From all this, one might well suppose that Karlstadt created the marginalia, and his work in so doing bore fruit especially in his major 1523 works; the particular motifs highlighted from or added to the text point especially to Karlstadt. Yet caution is due in approaching a source such as marginalia, and the possibility that Karlstadt was influenced by the marginalia, rather than the author of them, remains.

Concluding Remarks

Luther, Karlstadt, and Müntzer were all indebted to the Eckhartian mystical tradition and shared a commitment to the mobilization of its ideas and texts to depict the right way to salvation—and by extension, the right program for ecclesial reform. This shared inheritance helped shape both the reformers' initial alliances and their subsequent divisions. In this chapter, I have shown the responsiveness of Luther and Karlstadt to the theme of annihilation unto nothingness in Tauler. For the reformers, the nothingness of human beings referred to their bondage to sin (a doctrine learned partly from Augustine), to their inability to offer God holiness and works worthy of salvation, and fundamentally, to their status as beings created for God's use and ownership. With regard to the last point, we should recall Luther's description of the human as clay in the hands of God—as matter whose old (sinful) form had to be destroyed, so that new form could be given. Each reformer gave a unique bent to this paradigm, and stark differences between their views became apparent by 1522. Luther's turn was centered on trust: on the need for sinners to first be emptied of self-trust through the alien work of the law and then given the gift of trust in God's promises. For Karlstadt, conversely, the human being was enabled by grace to renounce and accuse the self as part of a process of sinking into the divine will. Müntzer, finally, argued already in the *Prague Manifesto* of 1520 that human beings were created to be possessed by God and to possess creatures in turn; however, sinners give themselves over to be possessed by creatures through fear and love.

All three reformers learned from the Eckhartian mystics that God's action for human salvation meant profound, annihilating suffering for fallen human nature and the self-centered ego, and that the attainment of an exclusive relationship with God (defined by Luther primarily in terms of trust, Karlstadt primarily in terms of love, and Müntzer in terms of possession and fear) could only occur on God's terms, against fallen affect and despite so many subtle evasions of reason. Drawing on the mystical themes of *Gottleiden* and *reductio ad nihilum*, each argued that salvation had to be suffered and lived out in suffering. Spiritual suffering, including that worked by the law, leveled the self-assertion that made perception of truth impossible; spiritual and visible suffering assured faithful sufferers of their possession of truth; outward suffering gave reliable, visible evidence of truth, if only for those with eyes to see—all this in a world filled with deception, divided between true and false forms of Christianity, friends and enemies of the cross. As for the *German Theology*, the marriage of suffering and truth used by the Frankfurter to combat supposed free spirits made the text useful in another age that was more broadly concerned with self-assertion cloaked in piety; the 1520 annotations, conversely, revealed already how the relevant teachings on sin, suffering, and yielding might be developed in ways that Luther did not forsee or desire when he introduced the text.

2

"I will choose what they ridicule"

The Theme of Suffering in Martin Luther's First Theological Protests

> But who will be the judge of these two, in order that we know which one to listen to? Behold, Isaiah, chapter 66 says, "I will choose what they ridicule."
>
> —Martin Luther, *Explanations of the Ninety-Five Theses* (1518)[1]

When Martin Luther challenged the sale of indulgences in 1517, he claimed to have one goal: to save Christians from teachings and practices that, although backed by ecclesial authority, jeopardized their eternal salvation.[2] Luther blamed much on allegedly unscrupulous indulgence preachers who would say anything to sell their wares, but he knew the sale and theory of indulgences had been enshrined by papal decree and backed by leading theologians of the preceding centuries.[3] Luther's critique of indulgences was part of a broader attack on medieval scholastic theology.[4] In early 1517, Luther and colleagues at the University of Wittenberg, including Nicholas von Amsdorf and Andreas Bodenstein von Karlstadt, had set about replacing the study of scholastic theology with the study of the Bible and the church fathers.[5] Luther charged that scholastic theologians used reason and its pagan champion Aristotle to twist and ignore the clear meaning of scripture—all in the service of exalting humans' pride in their innate mental and moral capacities.[6]

Through his *95 Theses* in the fall of 1517 and another set of theses that he defended at a meeting of his order in Heidelberg in April 1518, Luther burst onto the scene as a significant public figure, known throughout the Holy Roman Empire and beyond. The *95 Theses* attacked the "power and efficacy of indulgences," and received further elaboration in a long and revealing document, the *Explanations of the 95 Theses*, authored by Luther in early 1518.

Enemies of the Cross. Vincent Evener, Oxford University Press (2021). © Oxford University Press.
DOI: 10.1093/oso/9780190073183.001.0001.

(The *Explanations* were forwarded to the pope in early summer 1518 and published that August.) The *Heidelberg Disputation* took up the broader question of whether human works and obedience to God's law could earn salvation. Luther criticized in particular teachings about salvation advanced by William of Ockham and Gabriel Biel, who championed the dictum, "If you do what is within you, God will not deny his grace."[7] The *Explanations* and the *Heidelberg Disputation* were authored within a few months of one another, and both relied at crucial moments on the opposition between the "theology of the cross" and the "theology of glory" to address the most fundamental truth questions raised by Luther's protest: If the clerical hierarchy and the theological tradition were not reliable (i.e., true to scripture), how were theologians and clergy to know and teach right doctrine at all, and how were Christian people in turn to distinguish between true and false doctrines and teachers?

My purpose in this chapter is to show how Luther's thought and public message in 1517–1518 revolved around suffering as necessary to the perception of truth and the receipt of salvation by grace through faith in Christ. The suffering in question was spiritual, but it could be provoked by outward trials and even others' hatred—by anything that taught sinners their sinfulness and nothingness *coram deo*. For Luther, such suffering attended God's gift of faith as well as the Christian's lifelong struggle to cling to faith against the guile of fallen reason and the inborn desire to be something before God, earning salvation as a reward. Luther's doctrine of faith was unfolded within a paradigm of the Christian as sufferer: God's alien work needed to check the human presumption to earn salvation rather than receive it by grace through faith; the believing Christian, in turn, was set in opposition to the world, suffering spite and violence from those who rejected God's truth and gift, the pain of God's alien work, and the passivity of receiving rather than claiming salvation. As we will see, this message of suffering attracted Andreas Bodenstein von Karlstadt and Thomas Müntzer, who were inspired—like Luther—by the Eckhartian mystical understanding of union with God through *reductio ad nihilum*.

Luther's understanding of and message about suffering will be illuminated in this chapter by reading the *95 Theses* and their *Explanations* alongside the *Heidelberg Disputation*. Despite the differences between these two sets of theses—they treat different topics with different audiences and goals in view—they attacked the same allegedly false understanding of salvation, albeit on opposite flanks. For Luther, this false understanding of salvation involved a refusal to suffer God's painful work for human salvation. With the 95 *Theses* and *Explanations*, Luther complained that the doctrine and sale of indulgences encouraged Christians to appropriate the benefits of others' suffering rather than patiently enduring contrition (divinely worked sorrow for sin), self-accusation, and visible suffering themselves. In the *Heidelberg Disputation*, Luther criticized "theologians of glory" for failing to understand that all truly good Christian works are suffering—that is, they are done only by God in and through a human instrument, in a manner contrary to the expectations of fallen reason and desire. The *Heidelberg Disputation* unmistakably employs Eckhartian motifs surrounding *Anfechtungen*, annihilation unto nothingness, union with God, *Gelassenheit*, and "suffering without suffering" to describe how God gives salvation in a manner that crushes human pride and remakes the human recipient into an instrument of God; the new person as divine instrument is depicted as ready and able to endure further divine work through suffering, to grow in despair of the self, and thus to receive Christ's presence in that empty space through faith. Luther also attacked self-driven mortifications that concealed the exercise of pride.

Luther's distinction between theologies and theologians of glory and theologies and theologians of the cross represented a decisive move in his understanding of and message about suffering. Luther's argument was that God always reveals God's self and works in human beings "under contraries"—that is, in a manner offensive to fallen reason and will, and thus in a manner that inflicts suffering for the Old Adam. Any theologian or teacher who proclaimed otherwise and exalted human pride was, Luther charged, a theologian of glory—and one of those "enemies of the cross of Christ" described by Paul in Philippians 3:18. True doctrine was distinguished from false based on whether Christians were taught to endure spiritual and visible trials in the hopes that God would reduce them to nothing and use them as God's instrument, united to Christ by faith. Medieval Christianity readily identified earnest Christians as those who were willing—unlike the lukewarm—to endure contrition and trials with patience. Now, suffering and the readiness to suffer were used to divide true and false doctrine, true and false Christians, friends and enemies of the cross. Mystical doctrines were democratized and transformed as part of the life of faith,[8] but also turned into a hammer for criticism of the misguided—namely, the theologians and preachers of indulgences who offered an easy avoidance of suffering, and the theologians of the *via moderna* who imagined an ascent to God by reason and will. That said, in order to distinguish friends and enemies of the cross in a world where everyone suffered, Luther and his allies also needed to define true versus false suffering.

Suffering and Salvation in the Indulgence Controversy, 1517–1518

In order to discuss Luther's argument in the 95 *Theses* and *Explanations*, we must briefly review, first, the historical development of the doctrine of penance and indulgences, and second, Luther's own theological development up to 1517.

Penance and Indulgences

Early Christians believed that baptism conferred forgiveness for sins. Yet this belief raised a question of great consequence: Could the person who committed a serious sin after baptism—especially apostasy in the face of persecution—regain God's forgiveness? Rigorists argued that anyone who thus forfeited the forgiveness conferred in baptism could never regain it. Opting against this notion, bishops developed procedures through which the lapsed could regain God's favor and readmission to the church and the Lord's Supper. Such procedures were severe and public. Penitents had to engage in long abstinence and prayer and to humble themselves before church leaders and the entire congregation; forgiveness (absolution) was conferred after the performance of these acts of penance.[9] Clerics based their authority to absolve the penitent on the "power of the keys" given to Peter in Matthew 16:19.[10]

From the 600s C.E., the circulation and influence of Irish penitential manuals throughout Western Europe led to an expansion and routinization of the practice of penance. Christians now had to confess and do penance for a broader range of sins, but the process was a more private affair between the penitent and the priestly confessor, and the satisfactions imposed were more standardized and hence more predictable. The order of confession, satisfaction, and absolution became "an accepted, frequent, and essential part" of Christian life.[11]

Only in the eleventh century did scholastic inquiry make available conceptual tools for the full articulation of a theology of penance—an account of how and why confession, satisfaction, and absolution obtained divine forgiveness for postbaptismal sin. Anselm of Canterbury introduced in *Cur Deus Homo?* (c. 1100), his attempt to find a rational explanation for the incarnation of Christ, the critical distinction between the guilt (*culpa*) and the punishment or penalty (*poena*) due to sin. For Anselm, human sin involved violation of the single "honor" that God demanded from rational beings, namely the subjection of their will to God's will. Because of this offense, God was due not only repayment of that honor, without which an offender would "remain in a state of guilt," but also "restitution" or repayment "in proportion to the insult which he [the sinner] has inflicted."[12] Anselm's point was that, while humanity was responsible for sin and thus needed to face the penalty or render satisfaction proportionate to the offended party's majesty, only God could accomplish the latter and save humanity from the penalty—hence God became human. The alternative was "either penalty or satisfaction" and applied to salvation history in general.

Twelfth-century scholastics put Anselm's distinction of guilt and penalty to different use, namely to explain the workings of the sacraments of baptism and penance for the individual sinner. Per scholastic teachings, a person inherited both guilt and punishment simply by their birth into fallen humanity. These baleful inheritances were wiped away by baptism, but those who survived long after baptism inevitably committed new sins and incurred new burdens of guilt and penalty. After all, baptism did not eliminate "concupiscence," an inherent inclination to sin that was itself a punishment of original sin. Death in a state of guilt meant damnation according to the church; thus, Christians were taught to seek the sacrament of penance frequently. In the sacrament, guilt was forgiven through confession and absolution, while punishment was transmuted from eternal punishment (hell) into temporal satisfaction. This temporal satisfaction had to be completed either on earth or, if earthly satisfactions proved insufficient, through much greater suffering in purgatory. A crucial change in praxis preceded these theological arguments: in the eleventh century, clerics concerned about the severity of penance changed the traditional order of confession, satisfaction, and absolution, and it became customary instead to absolve the penitent immediately following confession, with the expectation that he or she subsequently would complete or attempt to complete the imposed satisfaction. To fail to do so would lengthen one's stay in purgatory.[13] Unlike hell, purgatory was believed to be a *temporal* realm of the afterlife; purgatory would cease to exist after its work was no longer needed.

Eleventh- and twelfth-century developments surrounding penance and purgatory responded to the needs of lay Christians, who in the church's view inevitably sinned through the entanglements of marriage and economic life. Purgatory was a middle realm in the geography of the afterlife, where those who were "neither saints nor unrepentant sinners" could pay any penalty for sin that remained at their death. Reflecting the growth of urban, middling classes involved in sometimes-compromising economic exchange, the church now distinguished between "mortal" sins, which incurred damnable guilt, and merely "venial" sins.[14]

At the same time, in the flourishing schools and monasteries of this period, there was rising interest in the inward motives for external acts and in the feelings of sorrow for sin and love of God that the penitent brought—or failed to bring—to confession. Such interests could lead in the later Middle Ages to either an intensification of penance via the "internalization and individualization" of requirements, or to a new externalization and reduction of penitential rigor based upon awareness of the failures of the inward person.[15] In either case, the critical innovation was the notion, shared even by bitter rivals like Bernard of Clairvaux (d. 1153) and Peter Abelard (d. 1142), that human salvation depended on a loving response to divine love. According to Berndt Hamm, "the whole weight [in the practice of penance] now falls on the change of direction of the inner will, on the intention to love and the pangs of remorse, not, as in earlier days, on the acts of penance."[16]

This internalized conception inevitably raised questions about the purpose and necessity of the external acts of confession, absolution, and satisfaction.[17] Scholars delineate between three medieval schools of thought regarding the relationship of inner sorrow to auricular confession and priestly absolution; each school endured into the sixteenth century. First, a "contritionist school" associated with Peter Lombard (d. 1160) argued that penitent Christians were forgiven by God for genuine sorrow, while priestly absolution only "declared" a forgiveness that had already occurred.[18] Against this position was the moderate "attritionist school" associated with Thomas Aquinas (d. 1274), which defended the necessity of the priestly words of absolution. Attritionists held that the priest's pronouncement of God's forgiveness truly conveyed that forgiveness, and that priestly absolution could even, in rare cases, transform a mere fear of punishment (called "attrition") into contrition. A third school, the "absolutionist school" associated with Duns Scotus (d. 1308), asserted that most Christians reached contrition only through this latter possibility, that is, the priest's absolution changed their mere attrition into contrition, the "true essence of the sacrament."[19] In the late medieval period, Johannes Geiler (d. 1510), a renowned preacher in Strasbourg, embraced the contritionist position while teaching that human beings could achieve contrition by their own natural powers (*ex puris naturalibus*). At the other extreme, Johannes von Paltz, who was a member of the Erfurt cloister when Luther entered in 1505, proceeded from his pessimistic view of human nature to embrace forms of absolutionist thought. For Paltz, the sacrament was necessary to compensate for the inability of human beings to achieve, even with the aid of grace, anything but attrition.[20] Between these two extremes, however, it was attritionism that prevailed among most confessors on the eve of the Reformation. Attritionism demanded human effort to try to attain true contrition, while also providing sacramental aid to confer forgiveness on the merely attrite.[21]

Thus, the fifteenth- and early sixteenth-century church incorporated a marked diversity of both interior and exterior avenues for the practice of penance and for religious life more broadly. The circulation of ascetic and mystical literature outside the cloister helped sustain currents of thought and devotion centered on the love of God and binding this love to the achievement or experience of true contrition in penance. Such literature often described contrition and satisfaction as the experience of "suffering with the suffering Christ, emulation of the way of the cross, and conformity with him in his passion," just as the image of the crucified Christ in art and literature was understood to provoke human contrition.[22] At the same time, an emphasis on the external rite was nourished by the perception of many that human contrition and satisfaction were always inadequate to meet the divine demand.[23]

A dynamic push-and-pull between rigor and laxity in penance shaped the character of the religion offered to the laity on the eve of the Reformation. Efforts to emphasize the enormity of the penalties due to sin, the pain of enduring those penalties in purgatory, and the need for genuine inward contrition often responded to perceived laxity in the imposition of satisfaction. Laypeople also worried about undue lenience: as historian John Bossy has described it, pious Christians engaged in a range of practices, including "pilgrimages, processions, endowments, and especially [obtaining] indulgences," to "make up the difference between what they believed they owed and what they had been required to pay."[24] Many practices attacked by sixteenth-century reformers as the product of clerical deceit originated in part in the church's responsiveness to the "wishes and needs" of the laity—although the church in turn had a hand in instilling those wishes and needs in the first place. Bernd Moeller has argued that in the late-medieval period "as never before," the laity became "not only a participant, but a molder of religious life within the Church." Underneath this lay self-assertion, how-ever, Moeller detected an "oppressive uncertainty about salvation."[25]

Steven Ozment described the same underlying fear in scholarship be-ginning in the 1970s, but he emphasized the top-down imposition of anxiety by clerics.[26] On this basis, Ozment argued that the appeal of the Reformation to sixteenth-century burghers lay in its offer of unburdening from the individual anxiety and social burdens (e.g., clerical privileges or the draining of local wealth through the sale of indulgences) surrounding penitential religion.[27] Ozment's thesis has been assailed both for its one-sided account of the clerical control and lay experience of late-medieval confession, and for its identification of "un-burdening" as the core of the appeal of the Reformation.[28] Yet the thesis also continues to exert influ-ence, for instance, through Carter Lindberg's popular textbook.[29] Ronald K. Rittgers has recently argued for the "great explanatory appeal" of the thesis, if it is properly corrected. According to Rittgers, while reformers un-doubtedly shaped lay memory of the confessional in a negative direction—a point Ozment overlooked—it is implausible to assume that they "created [a] sense of discontentment *ex nihilo*." Instead, reformers "construct[ed] the spiritually burdened burgher . . . [out of] the inherent tensions of the sacrament of penance—that is, the common insistence that penitents live between hope and fear—and the likelihood of at least occasional harsh confessions. Luther found a way to escape these tensions and 'burdens' . . .; one should not underestimate the appeal of promised certainty to those who have been told there was none." Rittgers reminds us that evangelical burghers attacked not just auricular confession, but the whole surrounding "penitential mentality."[30]

Thus, when Luther's *95 Theses* took up the question, "What should Christians be taught?" he spoke within a complicated religious world, in which some clergy and laity held to the rigor of constant confession and sat-isfaction, while others relied on the mechanisms available to rescue "low achievers." What Luther eventually offered was a certitude of salvation through faith in Christ *extra nos*.[31] This message contained relief from salva-tion anxiety for those who felt tormented by clerical demands or their own expectations, but it also was presented as the summons to a deep self-denying relationship to Christ for those who yearned for models of piety hitherto inaccessible to the ordinary laity. Faith, in Luther's view, came through and with a more profound suffering and a more thorough annihilation of self than most medieval imitators of Christ had upheld. Like the Eckhartian mystics before him, Luther criticized active forms of the imitation of Christ and the saints, including exercises that sought to cultivate inner sorrow, for merely hardening self-assertion and self-will. Unlike Tauler or the *German Theology*,[32] however, Luther allowed for no ambiguity surrounding human participation in the process: there was only pure suffering out of which came despair of self, assurance of the promise, and a life of cross-bearing that expressed and strengthened one's trust in the God incarnate in Jesus Christ. Here, surrender to God's will, endurance of the depths of the cross, and even suffering in God (through faith in Christ) could be found in the most banal daily tasks of the humblest of laypersons, if they patiently and faithfully accepted their God-given lot.

It was on this front that Luther, in the fall of 1517, emerged on the public scene railing against indulgences and other practices that permitted Christians to appropriate vicariously the fruits of others' suffering instead of suffering themselves. Luther called the rigorous and the lax to true suffering; to heed the call, the rigorous had to give up their false, self-imposed, self-assertive suffering in favor of true suffering; the lax had to give up their reliance on others' suffering and on outward rituals to hear the outward Word that truly gripped the inner person. In the end, all true believers could have a certainty denied to rigorous and lax practice alike in the Middle Ages.

Even if they could not claim certainty, late-medieval Christians could increase their security through the purchase of indulgences. Indulgences were integral to the church's penitential system in the late Middle Ages. As mentioned, by confessing and receiving absolution, Christians received forgiveness of the guilt of sin, while the penalty—eternal punishment—was transmuted into a temporal punishment, to be paid in earthly life or in purgatory. Indulgences, in their initial theoretical development, were understood to free penitents from certain penalties imposed by the church's penitential canons, such as fasting, vigils, prayers, pilgrimages, and so forth. During the first crusade (1096–1099), however, and on an increasing number of occasions thereafter, the church offered "plenary indulgences" conferring remission of every penalty for recipients' sins, including purgatorial penalties. By the thirteenth century, scholastic theologians developed the notion of a "treasury of merits." They argued that Christ's passion and death had won superabundant merit—more merit than was necessary to redeem all of humankind—and that this surplus, along with the surplus merits of the saints, constituted a treasury from which the pope could make withdrawals and distributions for the benefit of the faithful. Pope Clement VI's bull *Unigenitus* enshrined this interpretation in 1343, while in 1476, Sixtus IV declared that indulgences could be purchased for the benefit of the deceased, to relieve their suffering in purgatory. Indulgences were often given in return for pious acts—especially the viewing of relics—but the practice of giving indulgences in return for alms is what came to be maligned by critics as the sale of indulgences.[33]

Indulgences were not, however, the only means through which believers had access to the intercession of the church and the saints for the reduction of their suffering. Church teachings described the mass as an unbloody repetition of Christ's sacrifice and claimed that the merits resulting from this repetition could be applied for the benefit of both the living and the dead in purgatory. Accordingly, wealthy Christians endowed masses to be said on behalf of themselves and loved ones. Luther and other reformers later criticized these teachings and practices relentlessly, long after indulgences receded from the center of the sixteenth-century debate. Penitential and purgatorial sufferings were also not the only kinds of suffering that ecclesial and saintly intercession could help. Christians also could pray to Christ or the saints to prevent or remove corporeal and material sufferings, from illness to crop failures. Relics were believed to hold miraculous powers to prevent or cure worldly ills; relics were either objects that had touched the body of Christ or a saint or a remnant of the holy body itself. Equal or greater miraculous power was attributed to the consecrated host, especially after the Fourth Lateran Council (1215) described its transformation in substance into the body of Christ.[34]

Luther's Early Theological Development

In authoring and issuing the *95 Theses*, Luther was driven by new theological insights that he reached gradually between 1505, when he joined an observant order of the Hermits of St. Augustine, and 1518. During these years, Luther received the doctorate and was appointed to the theology faculty at Wittenberg (October 1512), delivering his first lectures on the Psalms between 1513 and 1515, followed by a critical series of lectures on the New Testament epistles of *Romans, Galatians*, and *Hebrews* (1515–1517). For much of the twentieth century, Luther scholars sought to find in Luther's early lectures evidence of a single, decisive theological breakthrough—the so-called tower experience (*Turmerlebnis*) described by Luther in the 1545 preface to his Latin works[35]—when he passed whole cloth from adherence to the old theology to recognition of the new. The best scholarship now recognizes that Luther's mature theology and doctrine consisted of many key pieces, or building blocks, which Luther discovered and arranged over a period of several years of engagement with an array of sources,[36] including the Bible, Augustine, scholastic figures (especially those from the *via moderna*),[37] Bernard of Clairvaux, his confessor Johann von Staupitz, and the post-Eckhartian mystics.[38]

As Berndt Hamm has argued, Luther's early spiritual trials during his cloister years in Erfurt and Wittenberg (1505–1511) contributed greatly to his theological development;[39] these trials were produced by the complex of teachings and practices regarding late-medieval penance we have just reviewed, as well as by broader late medieval teachings about salvation. Influenced by Augustine, medieval theologians held (with considerable diversity in details) that faith was an intellectual assent to the teachings of the church. This "un-formed" faith did not save the believer but represented only the beginning of the Christian life. Such faith had to be "formed" by love, which was poured or infused into the believer by grace.[40] Through the cooperation of their will with this infusion of love, believers progressed in inherent holiness and earned "merit" before God. Underlying these arguments was the foundational conviction—later rejected by Luther—that the human being had to become intrinsically holy to be saved.[41]

Medieval theologians debated over whether any human contribution could precede the first infusion of divine grace into the believer. In mature formulations, Aquinas followed Augustine's teaching that human beings could not will the good or begin to love God truly—that is, as an end rather than a means to other, creaturely ends—until prevenient grace reoriented human desire away from the enjoyment of creatures to the enjoyment of God and God's law.[42] William of Ockham (d. c. 1347) advanced the contrary view, later taken up by Gabriel Biel (d. 1495), that human beings could love God above all things and their neighbor as themselves through their own natural powers (*ex puris naturalibus*) of will and reason, fulfilling God's law according to the "substance of the act" if not the "intention of the lawgiver." While strict anti-Pelagians like Gregory of Rimini (d.

1358) and Thomas Bradwardine (d. 1349) countered that human moral capacity was fundamentally distorted by the sin inherited from Adam and Eve and thus unable to will or accomplish any good—that is, any obedience to God's law not founded on fear of punishment or self-love—before the infusion of grace, Ockham and later Biel argued that human moral capacity was only weakened by inherited sin and that human beings were obligated with this weakened capacity to meet the demands of a covenant established by God. Under this covenant, God promised to give grace, remit the sin, and complete the healing of anyone who "does what is within him."[43] Gregory of Rimini was a learned Augustinian, but his position was by no means the official position of the Augustinian Order;[44] and Luther himself was trained in the theology of Biel and Ockham. Ultimately, Luther rejected not just the possibility of meritorious achievement before grace (Biel and Ockham), but the assumption of all camps that salvation required inherent holiness.

According to Hamm, from his earliest days in the cloister, Luther wrestled both personally and theologically with the tensions in late-medieval piety between the nearness of divine wrath and the nearness of divine mercy, the striving for perfection and the awareness of sin.[45] In fact, the Augustinian order deliberately sought to heighten these tensions, emphasizing both the human inability to merit anything truly (condignly) before God and God's demand for complete inward perfection in love of God. The Augustinian friar was not supposed to be "satisfied with an observance of good works," but to strive instead for "perfection in purity of conscience, selfless love of God and renunciation-full cross-bearing [Kreuzesnachfolge], which accomplishes the hardest things from inner willingness and joy." The pinnacle of this spirituality was the resignatio ad infernum: in conformity with Christ, the Christian so completely overcomes self-love that she or he would willingly be damned, if such were God's will.[46]

Luther was profoundly shaken by his inability to attain this inward holiness, coming in his cloister years to the crucial conviction that all his striving for salvation amounted to nothing before God and that his soul had no capacity to ascend to God. Generalizing from his own experience to the condition of humanity, he concluded that after the fall, human beings can offer God only "sin and absolute unworthiness."[47] As a young professor lecturing on the Psalter from 1513 to 1515, Luther expressed a "humility theology," the idea that God gives grace to those who humble themselves and confess their inability to earn salvation.[48] Soon after, and possibly even before the end of these lectures on the Psalter, Luther concluded that humility itself was the gift of grace.[49]

Scholarly discussion of Luther's theological development after 1513 has focused intensively on the relationship between the concepts of humility and faith: Luther's decisive turn came when he concluded that salvation depended not on humility—not even on humility as a gift of grace—but on faith that was received by hearing the Word, which directed sinners away from their own resources (*extra nos*) to Christ's redemptive work on their behalf (*pro me*). The timing of this turn is much debated, in part because Luther's early lectures joined the terms humility and faith in complicated and sometimes ambiguous ways. The questions are, when did the decoupling of humility and faith occur,[50] and did humility thereafter remain a significant theme for Luther?[51] Some have argued that the 95 *Theses* and *Heidelberg Disputation* continue to express Luther's humility theology,[52] not his doctrine of justification by faith received through hearing the Word proclaimed. More recently, the 95 *Theses* have been analyzed compellingly as the production of a transitional period. Volker Leppin sees the 95 *Theses* as containing both new insights into justification by faith that Luther learned from his study of Romans alongside more-dominant conceptions of inward penance learned from Johannes Tauler and the *German Theology*.[53] Conversely, Berndt Hamm argues that the Reformation character of the theses is evident precisely in the absence of clear expressions of Luther's mature doctrine: Luther had already separated penance and justification, painful sorrow for sin and joyous confidence in the promise of Christ *extra nos*, and in the theses he focused only on the "horizontal plane." According to Hamm, Luther now "defines anew 'true sorrow': no longer, as in the medieval tradition, as a quality of the human soul necessary for salvation and also not as part of faith [as Luther had argued in his first lectures on the Psalter], but rather as the dark backside of faith . . . and the consequence of faith."[54]

The disentangling of humility and faith was clearly a decisive conceptual achievement for Luther, and one that made possible the proclamation of faith as joyous confidence that the work accomplished by Christ applies to oneself. That said, this chapter and the ensuing chapters will show that humility wrought by suffering—whether from hearing the law or from other trials—remained for Luther central to the reception, experience, and verification of faith. Humility as despair of self was a precondition for faith and a result of faith, as Hamm observes. Still more, it was an experience that verified that one's confidence was securely directed *extra nos*; humility was a despair of self that no longer had to be despair of salvation, because salvation no longer depended on the self. As a theme of proclaimed doctrine (e.g., in the Wartburg postils[55]), the demand for humility was proof that evangelical teaching did not serve self-assertion like scholastic teaching, but announced the complete emptiness of human wisdom and moral capacity prior to the gift of revealed truth and faith. It must be underlined, finally, that the question of what role humility plays in Luther's teaching and preaching after 1517/18 requires attention to the audience and purpose of his utterances: Luther as preacher and teacher sought to humble those confident in their moral accomplishments or complacent in sinning, just as he sought to console those already cast down. In the clash with Karlstadt and Müntzer, he vigorously denied that true suffering or humble passivity could be found apart from his understanding of faith.

My analysis in the remainder of this chapter focuses on how the 95 *Theses*, particularly as unfolded in the *Explanations*, and the *Heidelberg Disputation* reflect Luther's movement from a contrition-centered to a faith-centered soteriology. Above all, we need to examine Luther's focus on self-trust rather than self-love as the essence of the sinfulness that gets in the way of human salvation;[56] it was this particular understanding of sinful self-assertion that governed Luther's reception and development of the Eckhartian tradition—self-trust needed to be annihilated; union with God became union with Christ through faith. For Luther, human beings want to earn salvation themselves and to make their own way through life, avoiding suffering or choosing the time and place of (false, self-inflicted) suffering for their own ends. God promises to care for God's creatures in all things temporal and eternal, but human beings do not trust that promise, as evidenced by their fear of true suffering, death, and damnation. Luther concludes that human beings must stand before God with full trust—indeed "peace of conscience"—otherwise they call God a "liar"; but they are unable to find cause for such confidence in themselves, only cause for contrition. Accordingly, peace of conscience can only be given through a word spoken to sinners, directing them to Christ rather than themselves.[57] Despair of self and consolation remain joined, however, for faith as trust in God's promise of salvation cannot begin, endure, or be certain without despair of self.

The 95 Theses and Explanations

The reaction to Luther's October 1517 theses concerning indulgences was not immediate.[58] They were printed in their original Latin in Nuremberg, Leipzig, and Basel already in December 1517; in January 1518, they were translated and began to circulate in German, although circulation of the translation was limited.[59] By February of 1518, the papacy was in contact with Luther's superiors in the Augustinian order, asking them to advise their subordinate against teaching his new doctrine. Luther had composed his *Explanations* by February of 1518, although publication did not occur until August of that year. Luther himself claimed that the *95 Theses* were a provisional work, intended only for a limited, academic audience. Nonetheless, Ernst Kähler is doubtless correct to describe the *Theses* as a manifesto, "artfully constructed and, in their [declamatory] style, calculated to effect."[60] Thus, Luther repeats the phrase, "Christians must be taught [*Docendi sunt Christiani*]." The *Theses* mount to a dramatic conclusion in the 94th and 95th theses, which assert that Christians should find their confidence in suffering: "Christians should be exhorted [*Exhortandi sunt Christiani*] to be diligent in following Christ, their head, through penalties, death, and hell; and thus be confident of entering into heaven through many tribulations rather than through the false security of peace."[61] "Penalties, death, and hell" encompassed for Luther a wide range of sufferings, beginning with a deep inward sorrow for sin and self-hatred that he believed would both transform Christians' understanding of and response to the suffering of natural evils and human violence, and impel Christians to self-giving service of God and neighbor. In this chapter, we will explore especially how Luther joined sorrow for sin and self-hatred to what became his core theological concept, faith defined as trust.

Here, we will approach Luther's *95 Theses* primarily through his later *Explanations*, which increasingly locate salvation in faith rather than contrition.[62] The *Explanations* were long and complicated, and they were neither directed toward nor received by a broad audience—yet they reveal a great deal about Luther's thought and vision for reform at a decisive moment in his theological, professional, and personal journey. For our purposes, they show his readiness to distinguish between true and false teachers and teaching according to the criterion of friendship versus hostility to the cross. I focus in the ensuing discussion on a few selected theses and accompanying explanations. In Theses 1–7, the trajectory of Luther's argument in the *Explanations* carries the reader from the idea that salvation is received through God-given contrition to the assertion of salvation by faith; while analyzing these theses, we will also glance at the discussions of purgatory and *Anfechtung* found in Theses 14–19. In the explanation to Thesis 58, then, we will see how Luther claims assurance of doctrinal truth despite his wholesale condemnation of scholastic theology and the radicalness of his emerging soteriology; here he relies on the assumption that the proclamation of truth invites suffering and ridicule. To conclude, we will look at Luther's complicated use of the notions of "sweetness" and "bitterness" to describe the experience and life of faith, versus following one's nature, and at Luther's depiction of "true and evangelical preaching." This is a discussion of Theses 62–64 and 75 and the accompanying explanations.

Theses 1–7

The *95 Theses* begin with the assertion, "When our Lord and Master Jesus Christ said, 'Repent' [Matthew 4:17], he willed the entire life of believers to be one of repentance." Kähler notes that this first thesis establishes "with great systematic power . . . the beginning from which everything further follows."[63] In his 1518 explanation, Luther describes how sinners must be completely transformed by hatred of sin and self; indeed, "hatred of oneself should involve one's whole life."[64] Luther cites a range of Biblical verses, including Matthew 10: 34, 38, and 39 ("I have not come to bring peace, but a sword"; "He who does not take his cross and follow me, is not worthy of me"; and "He who hates his soul in this life, preserves it for eternal life")—all of which were often referenced by Karlstadt. Bearing the cross here is *odium* or *horror sui* because of sin.[65]

The penance Christ commands cannot be "sacramental penance," Luther argues in his second thesis and explanation, because the sacrament cannot be done all the time as Christ demands. Neither does Christ command "mortification of the passions of the flesh," but an internal sorrow that relativizes the external sacrament. Luther writes, "Sacramental penance is only external and presupposes inward penance without which it has no value. But inward penance can exist without the sacramental." Sacramental penance could be a mere appearance, but internal penance, which Luther here calls "evangelical," "is not able to be unless true and sincere." Consistent with the medieval contritionist school, Luther argues that a "contrite and humble heart," offered unceasingly to God, attains everything necessary for salvation—"even without indulgence letters," Luther adds in Thesis 36.[66]

Following upon this internalization, however, Luther declares in Thesis 3 that "inner repentance is worthless unless it produces various outward mortifications of the flesh"; the explanation references and broadly defines fasting ("all chastenings of the flesh"), prayer ("every pursuit of the soul"), and alms ("every service toward one's neighbor"). While these three satisfactions pertain to "sacramental penance" in so far as the church prescribes the "time and manner" of their execution, Luther insists that they belong more importantly to "evangelical penance" as means by which the contrite strive against "concupiscence of the flesh," pride, and temptations to injustice toward others. "Therefore all mortifications which the conscience-stricken man brings upon himself are the fruit of inner penance," Luther says, "whether they be vigils, work, privation, study, prayers, [or] abstinence from sex and pleasures, insofar as they minister to the spirit." Luther here attributes to the work of the Holy Spirit a "groaning of the heart" which produces good works.[67] God acts in the sinner's contrition, and Christians are instruments of God in their subordination of the flesh and spiritual pride, and in their service to God and neighbor. This view of divine agency and human instrumentality remains prevalent in Luther's corpus.

Thesis 4 contends that the penalties (*poenae*) belonging to evangelical penance remain until death for the true Christian. This thesis, especially helpful for understanding Theses 94 and 95, reads, "The penalty of sin remains as long as the hatred of self, that is, true inner repentance, until our entrance into the kingdom of heaven." Luther's explanation extends his account of Christians' repentance and the "cross of Christ" beyond the "voluntary afflictions" mentioned in Thesis 3 to include all "temptations of the devil, the world, and the flesh, and more especially . . . persecutions and sufferings."[68] No person who is driven by genuine, inward contrition—no person who regards his actual sinful state—would seek to be excused from these assaults. Instead, repentance must last until "the body of sin is destroyed and the inveterate first Adam, along with its image, perishes, and the new Adam is perfected in the image of God." This death and rebirth of Adamic nature happens only through the actual perishing of the body, for "sin remains until death, although it diminishes daily through the renewing of the mind." Crucial for Luther is that, regardless of the progress Christians make in overcoming their sinfulness, no one escapes the penalty of death and what is worse, "the fear of death, which is surely the punishment of punishments and is worse than death in many cases, to say nothing of the fear of judgment and hell, the qualms of conscience, etc."[69] The fear of death and eternal damnation proved definitively for Luther that the old Adam never dies until death itself, for "what man is there who has no fear of death, judgment, and hell?"[70]

With this discussion of the fear of death, Luther confronts the problem of trust. In Thesis 14 he argues, "Imperfect piety or love on the part of the dying person necessarily brings with it great fear; and the smaller the love, the greater the fear." Conversely, if a person had perfect love of God, he would not fear death, judgment, or hell (see I John 4:18). Of critical importance is how Luther binds together love, faith, and trust. His focus on trust controls his definition of faith and love and his conception of sin and redemption. "The reason for dread and fear [of death] is distrust," Luther argues, "and . . . the reason for assurance . . . is faith." Thus, "the person who dies with an imperfect faith necessarily fears and trembles," for "all fear and trembling arises from distrust, every feeling of assurance arises from faith in God. Faith, however, arises out of love, since the person must be like the one in whom he puts his trust." Thus, the "old, carnal" person is defined by Luther not in terms of misguided loves (per Augustine) but in terms of "error, concupiscence, wrath, fear, apprehension, despair, evil conscience, horror of death, etc.," that is, of failures of trust. The conscience *coram deo* makes the person old or new.[71]

The truly contrite Christian wants to be punished, Luther argues—and not only by the penitential canons, but by all God-given penalties (*poenae*), that is, all the burdens and sufferings involved in human life. Thesis 5 places all *poenae* except the canons beyond the papal power to remit.[72] Luther delineates five "kinds of punishment which faithful believers can suffer." The first is eternal damnation, a punishment that only God may remit through "remission of guilt." The second is purgatory, which also is beyond "the power of the pope or of any man."[73] Luther continued to affirm the existence of purgatory, but he rejected the idea that its purpose was the satisfaction of penalties. Rather, "hell, purgatory, and heaven seem to differ the same as despair, fear, and assurance of salvation" (Thesis 16); the work of purgatory, however and wherever it happened, allowed souls to grow from imperfect to perfect *trust* of God.[74] Here, Luther cited Tauler as teaching about the endurance of purgatorial punishment here and now, while offering the autographical lines:

> I myself "knew a man" [II Cor. 12:2] who claimed that he had often suffered these punishments, in fact over a very brief period of time. Yet they were so great and so much like hell that no tongue could adequately express them,

no pen could describe them, and one who had not experienced them could not believe them. And so great were they that, if they had been sustained or had lasted for half an hour, even for one tenth of an hour, he would have perished completely and all his bones would have been reduced to ashes. At such a time God seems terribly angry, and with him the whole creation. At such a time there is no flight, no comfort, within or without, but all things accuse. At such time as that the Psalmist mourns, "I am cut off from thy sight" [Cf. Ps. 31:22], or at least he does not dare to say, "O Lord, . . . do not chasten me in thy wrath" [Ps. 6:1]. In this moment (strange to say) the soul cannot believe that it can ever be redeemed other than that the punishment is not yet completely felt. Yet the soul is eternal and is not able to think of itself as being temporal. All that remains is the stark-naked desire for help and a terrible groaning, but it does not know where to turn for help. In this instance the person is stretched out with Christ so that all his bones may be counted, and every corner of the soul is filled with the greatest bitterness, dread, trembling, and sorrow in such a manner that all these last forever.[75]

Luther describes here a spiritual purgatory that feels like hell ("in such a manner that all these last forever"), in which the torment has the specific content of terror. This was a description of *Anfechtung* shaped by the Psalter—monks sang the whole Psalter each week—but it also echoed the Eckhartian view of a passive *imitatio passionis*, this immediately following a note that Tauler taught "more solid and sincere theology than is found in all the scholastic teachers."[76]

The third punishment listed by Luther is the "voluntary and evangelical punishment which is put into effect by spiritual penance," as I Corinthians 11:31 teaches, "If we were to judge ourselves, surely we should not be judged by the Lord." Luther here refers to the pious activities described in Thesis 3, calling these "the cross and mortification of sufferings." The passage reveals much about Luther's conception of pious works: fasting, praying, and giving alms are all "sufferings," the outward deeds of Christians who are inwardly moved by God. The description of these deeds as "voluntary" refers to a will driven by the Holy Spirit. Luther upholds the pope's ability to impetrate before God for the removal of other sufferings, but contends that impetration for the removal of these sufferings would be blasphemy. Indeed, the pope should ask for this punishment to be imposed or "announce that is has been imposed." "Otherwise, Luther says, the pope "would invalidate the cross of Christ [I Cor. 1:17] and unite the remnants of the Canaanites with his own sons and daughters, and he would not utterly destroy the enemies of God, that is, sins."[77]

The fourth punishment according to Luther is "God's correction and scourging," that is, all the sufferings of disease and human violence, including "sickness, cares, plagues, and fevers . . . wars, insurrections, earthquakes, fires, murders, thefts, as well as the Turks, Tartars, and other infidels"—all of which are endured even by the innocent. Luther argues that these corrections belong to all true children of God. They cannot be remitted, nor should the pope or anyone wish or believe them to be remitted. Regarding bodily illness, Luther concedes that "through the prayers of the church some such punishments could be lifted from the weak." More tellingly, he adds that without a doubt "the rod of God can be removed, not by the power of the keys, but by tears and prayers, and by imposition of more punishments rather than by their remission." He cites the case of the Ninevites, who "humbly scourged themselves by their penances and thereby managed to avert the rod of destruction intended for them."[78] Luther finally concedes to the pope the power to remit only in relation to the fifth punishment, canonical punishments imposed by the church.[79] He also counsels that believers need not be anxious about the sufficiency of "canonical or priestly punishment"—that is, to reduce purgatorial punishment. "One does quite enough by means of the third and fourth punishment," he explains. "God is nearly always satisfied with a contrite heart and with punishment of the third type."[80] For Luther, believers who purchased the remission of punishment were lazy and negligent, and preachers who encouraged them to do so only guided them away from contrition and toward damnation. Luther's first theses and explanations place the punishments of purgatory beyond earthly, clerical grasp—thus undermining a key appeal of the indulgence trade.

It is noteworthy that Luther in the first of the 95 Theses and Explanations operates primarily with a distinction between earnest and negligent Christians, not a distinction between true and false Christians—the lax are deceived by lies about indulgences, but not by a church that fundamentally mistakes sin for holiness, the devil's doctrine for God's. Nevertheless, the matter of truth and falsehood looms just in the background—on the one hand, because the absence of contrition in the sinner reflects an absence of true self-knowledge; on the other hand, because Luther places the final blame on scholastic doctors rather than unscrupulous preachers. Soon he will openly blame the pope.[81] Ultimately, Luther sees no value in the remission of penalties. Earnest Christians experience a painful, divinely worked hatred of sin and the self, which issues forth in the "evangelical cross" of "voluntary" fasting, prayer, and alms-giving, under the impulsion of the Holy Spirit, as well as in the willing, Spirit-driven endurance of all other divine *poenae* for sin, including disease and human violence. According to Luther, the "evangelical penance" that takes up the cross of Christ endures so long as there is sin within a person to hate—that is, until death itself. Luther's centering on trust in God's promises surfaces as he offers his chief evidence for the life-long perdurance of sin: namely the fear of death and damnation from which not even the holiest saints were free. Sin is most evident in distrust of God; salvation requires destruction of trust in the self in favor of trust in God.

Thus, Luther learned to see the rite of confession not as a priestly announcement of God's forgiveness of sins for the contrite sinner—the traditional contritionist view, reflected in Theses 6 and 7—but as a divinely given remedy for divinely created anxiety over sin, a remedy that could be received only through trust. Luther writes in explanation to Thesis 7:

> When God begins to justify a man, he first of all condemns him; . . . and the one to whom he wishes to give life, he kills. . . . He does this, however, when he destroys man and when he humbles and terrifies him into the knowledge of himself and his sins. . . . Thus sinners are turned to hell and their faces are filled with shame. . . . However, in this consternation is the beginning of salvation . . . [and] God works a strange work in order that he may work his own work. This is true contrition and humility of spirit, the sacrifice most pleasing to God. Here is the sacrificial victim cut into pieces and the skin drawn and kindled for the burnt offering. . . . Actually man knows so little about his justification [through this experience] that he believes he is very near condemnation, and he looks upon this, not as infusion of grace but as a diffusion of the wrath of God upon him. Blessed is he, however, if he endures this trial, for just when he thinks he has been consumed, he shall arise as the morning star.[82]

God's inward work for Luther drives Christians outward from themselves. If sinners rely only on their own strength, "sadness will finally be turned into despair," which is the state of hell. Sinners must find peace from divinely worked contrition by fleeing to the church for absolution.[83]

Here, Luther brings the concept of faith explicitly to the fore—faith in the priestly power to absolve.[84] Luther addresses two conflicting assumptions in his argument: first, that a person in order to be saved must be terrified by sin;

and second, that he or she must also have "peace of heart" or "peace of conscience," having heard God's promise. Luther argues that the peace of trust in God's promise of forgiveness can, in fact, abide along with anguish over sin—for the peace comes in faith rather than in experience, which is unreliable. He writes:

> To be sure, the person who is absolved must guard himself very carefully from any doubt that God has remitted his sins, in order that he may find peace of heart. For if he is uncertain of the anguish of his conscience (as it must always be if it is a true sorrow), yet he is constrained to abide by the judgment of another, not at all on account of the prelate himself or his power, but on account of the word of Christ who cannot lie when he says, "Whatever you loose on earth" [Matt. 16:19]. For faith born of this word will bring peace of conscience . . . Whoever seeks peace in another way, for example, inwardly through experience, certainly seems to tempt God and desires to have peace in fact, rather than in faith. For you will have peace only as long as you believe in the word of that one who promised, "Whatever you loose, etc." Christ is our peace, but only through faith. But if anyone does not believe this word, even though he be pardoned a million times by the pope himself, even though he confess before the whole world, he shall never know inner peace.[85]

In Luther's conception, the grace of the remission of guilt comes first under the form of wrath. This divine manner of working under contraries is necessary because of the depth of human sinfulness—human beings usually concede their guilt for sinful acts, but cannot see their fundamental turning from God—but it creates a dangerous possibility that those who experience God's work will distrust God and interpret God as wrathful. In the face of this danger, Luther now argues, the outward sacrament finds its purpose, giving assurance to those who trust God's promise. Luther admits that "even if the remission of guilt takes place through the infusion of grace before the remission of the priest, this infusion is of such a nature and is so hidden under the form of wrath that one is more uncertain of grace when it is present than when it is absent."[86] The person is relieved of this uncertainty through "the judgment of the priest," or rather faith in the promise of Matthew 16:19. Without this certitude of faith, there is in fact no remission according to Luther, because "there is not yet remission for us."[87] Luther's struggle to find an explanation of the external rite—an old problem of contritionism—finds resolution here through the doctrine of faith. The human relationship to God is thus concentrated on the issue of trust; and suffering subsequently finds new meaning for Luther not only as divine punishment for sin—although it remains that—but also as a trial intended to reveal distrust (unbelief) and strengthen trust (faith).

Contrition and humility are not displaced from Luther's view, but transformed into the distrust of self inherent in faith. Luther in the *Explanations* argues first that contrition or the lack thereof determines one's receptivity toward *poenae*—that is, whether one accepts God-sent *poenae* in the "evangelical cross" or scourging (the 3rd and 4th types described earlier), or seeks to remove *poenae* through indulgences.[88] He then proceeds to describe the removal of *poenae* as the goal of fear and distrust, and in his long explanation to Thesis 7, he argues that terror concerning sin—itself a penalty and wrought by penalties—compels the sinner to turn to the external word of absolution; through this turn, faith in the Word anchors the sufferer. Thus, just as the Eckhartian mystical tradition described a suffering without suffering possible through union with the divine will, Luther described a suffering without suffering possible through trust in God's promise. Faith trumping self-will enabled Luther's evangelical version of *Gelassenheit*, whereas Tauler described a sinking into precreated freedom from self-will. Luther cites Tauler's *Anfechtungen* as he seeks—also with autobiographical reference—to illuminate the spiritual experience of hell and purgatory. For Luther, this hell or purgatory consists above all of terror and anxiety, the opposite of joyous confidence in God. Meanwhile, just as Tauler worried that self-imposed suffering might conceal self-will, Luther worried that self-chosen *poenae* reflected and concealed distrust:[89]

> When a man through the remission of guilt . . . has found peace through the acceptance of faith in absolution, every punishment is to him as no punishment at all. For anxiety of conscience makes the punishment harmful, but cheerfulness of conscience makes punishment desirable. And we see that this understanding which people have concerning the power of the keys is adequate when they seek and receive absolution in simple faith. But certain intellectuals, by their contritions, works, and confessions, endeavor to find peace for themselves but do nothing more than go from restlessness to restlessness because they trust in themselves and their works, while, if they feel torment of conscience, they should believe in Christ who says, "Whatever you shall loose, etc."[90]

Teaching people that they may "have their sins cancelled by their contritions and satisfactions" only contributes to "torment of conscience," Luther complains. Instead, "the people must first be taught faith in Christ, the gracious bestower of remission. Then they must be persuaded to despair of their own contrition and satisfaction so that, when they have been strengthened by confidence and joy of heart over the compassion of Christ, they finally may despise sin cheerfully, become contrite, and make satisfaction."[91] Here, faith is to be taught before contrition; it is the desperate who turn to faith nonetheless, and who are enabled subsequently to despair of self without despairing of salvation.

Luther laments that Christians had been taught to "place their confidence" in the pope, rather than "in the word of Christ who gives the promise to the pope." "It is not," he argues, "because the pope grants it that you have anything, but you have it because you believe that you receive it. . . . Therefore by faith we are justified, and by faith also we receive peace, not by works, penance, or confessions."[92] The sacrament confers no grace except to one who already believes and is thus "just and worthy. . . . Therefore it is not the sacrament, but faith in the sacrament, that justifies." The priest only "points out" God's forgiveness for the pacification of conscience.[93] The joy of faith is that it keeps despair of self from becoming despair of salvation, even as the former remains a painful experience constantly inflicted by the penalties of life. Luther takes the mystical teaching that God empties the soul and reduces sinners to nothing to its most radical possible conclusion—the soul is so emptied that it cannot even claim humility as a possession; only naked, God-given trust in God is present.[94]

Thesis 58

Already in the spring of 1518, Luther had experienced the reproach he would spend the rest of his life meeting: "Are you alone wise?" On what basis was his theology and exegesis to be preferred to the understanding of the ecclesial hierarchy, tradition, and scholastic doctors?[95] In the explanation to Thesis 58—one of the longest in the *Explanations*[96]—Luther responded to these challenges with an intellectual and rhetorical move that in the coming years would play an instrumental role in both pulling together, and tearing apart, the Wittenberg reform movement. He described God's manner of giving salvation as entirely contrary to the expectations of fallen reason and will; thus, he argued, true theologians and preachers must be annihilated in their own self-assertion and in turn proclaim a message directed against human pride;

inevitably, true teachers and their flock are despised by the wise and even persecuted.

The occasion for these assertions was Luther's long discussion of the "treasures of the church," which had begun in Thesis 56, "The treasures of the church, out of which the pope distributes indulgences, are not sufficiently discussed or known among Christians." In Thesis 58, Luther denies that these treasures are the merits of Christ or the saints, because "even without the pope, [these merits] always work grace for the inner man, and the cross, death, and hell for the outer man."[97] The saints, moreover, could not accumulate surplus merit according to Luther, for "no saint has adequately fulfilled God's commandments in this life" and even "in their most perfect work, that is, through death, martyrdom, and suffering, [they] do no more than is required . . . and scarcely that."[98] Even if a treasury of merits existed, the argument continues, the church would dispense them cheaply to remit punishments, "for the remission of punishment is the cheapest gift the church possesses and deserves to be presented to the most worthless people. . . . [T]he punishments of the martyrs and saints should be instead an example for us in bearing punishments."[99] Humility and faith bear punishments gladly, as due chastisement. Thus, Luther contends, the merits of Christ and the saints serve the faithful, not "sluggards."[100]

Luther was challenging the scholastic understanding of the "treasury of merits" affirmed in Clement VI's *Unigenitus* (1343), and his *Explanations* took up the inevitable rebuke: "Did . . . St. Thomas err . . .? Does . . . the pope err along with the whole church, which is of the same opinion? . . . [A]re you the only one and the first one to have the right opinion?"[101] Luther responded first by appealing to previous doubters and by asserting that he was, in fact, in agreement with the pope and the church. Nevertheless, he adds, regardless of what scholastic doctors or canonists have said, "it is only right to give preference to the truth first, and then the authority of the pope and the church." Scholars' regard for Aristotle had yielded only "confusing opinions, doubts, and errors," Luther charges; just as God deceived the wayward Israelites through the mouths of prophets (Ezekiel 14), so God had given God's new people, who had forsaken Christ, over to error propounded by supposedly "great and holy men."[102]

How was one to discern the true from the false teacher? Luther's answer was that Christians should look for ridiculed teachers whose doctrine aroused the spite of the prideful. True teaching offended in its demand for self-abasement and suffering before God and human beings. Luther reiterates here that the merits of Christ are given along with the "grace of contrition" without the pope and without and prior to indulgences. These merits accomplish a two-fold work. The "proper work" (*opus proprium*) brings "grace, righteousness, truth, patience, and gentleness in the spirit of a man who has been predestined," for "the righteousness of Christ and his merit justifies and remits sins."[103] The "alien work" (*opus alienum*), however, effects whatever is contrary to human desire and reason, including

> the cross, labor, all kinds of punishment, finally death and hell in the flesh, to the end that the body of sin is destroyed [Rom. 6:6], our members which are upon earth are mortified [Col. 3:5], and sinners are turned into hell. For whoever is baptized in Christ and is renewed shall be prepared for punishments, crosses, and deaths, to the end that "he shall be accounted as a sheep for the slaughter and shall be slain all the day long" [Ps. 44:22]. . . . Just so must we become conformed to the image of the Son of God [Rom. 8:29], so that whoever does not take up his own cross and follow him, is not worthy of him [Matt. 10:38], even if he were filled with all kinds of indulgences.[104]

At this point, Luther invokes a distinction between deceptive scholastic theology and a "theology of the cross," which recognizes that God always works in ways contrary to human reason and desire—thus in ways that inflict suffering. God reveals this manner of working on the cross by coming not as a ruler but as a crucified redeemer.[105] Luther describes "punishments, crosses, and death" as God's most sacred relics,[106] thus declaring in no uncertain terms that God's grace and power were accessible in suffering and not in what relics usually offered, relief from suffering. Luther writes:

> From this you can see how, ever since the scholastic theology—the deceiving theology (for that is the meaning of the word in Greek)—began, the theology of the cross has been abrogated, and everything has been turned upside down. A theologian of the cross (that is, one who speaks of the crucified and hidden God), teaches that punishments, crosses, and death are the most precious treasury and the most sacred relics which the Lord of this theology himself has consecrated and blessed, not alone by the touch of his most holy flesh but also by the embrace of his exceedingly holy divine will, and he has left these relics here to be kissed, sought after, and embraced. Indeed fortunate and blessed is he who is considered by God to

be worthy that these treasures of the relics of Christ would be given to him; rather, who understands that they are given to him. For to whom are they not offered. As St. James says, "Count it all joy, my brethren, when you meet various trials" [Jas. 1:2]. For not all have this grace and glory to receive these treasures, but only the most elect of the children of God.[107]

Scholastic theology regards Christ's treasure as the remission of *poenae*, whereas the true treasure is the imposition of *poenae*. By fashioning theology according to fallen human reason and will, scholastic theologians in Luther's view had completely inverted truth. Their theology of glory failed to regard "the crucified and hidden God alone [I Cor. 2:2]"; that is, by seeking God outside of God's self-revelation on the cross, they found divine majesty revealed in visible things, but they failed to see God's true power hidden under suffering. They failed to grasp that God's work for human redemption always occurs in a manner offensive to reason and will; human beings do not ascend to God, as they would like to do, by the exercise of reason and will, but God descends to those whose rational and emotional expectations are crushed by suffering. From Aristotle, the theologian of glory "learns that God is the highest good" and the object of the human willing, while punishments are "things . . . most evil and worthy of hate." But the theologian of the cross "defines the treasury of Christ as impositions and obligations of punishments, things which are best and most worthy of love." The theologian of glory, then, is greeted by human applause, while "the people do not consider the theologian of the cross worthy of consideration, but finally even persecute him."[108]

Luther thus sets up a fundamental opposition between two theologies and theologians, and he poses the question: "Who will be the judge of these two, in order that we may know which one to listen to?" In answer, he cites Isaiah 66:4, "I will choose what they ridicule," and I Corinthians 1:27, "God chose what is weak in the world to shame the strong."[109] A doctrine that is pleasing to fallen nature or sensible to fallen reason—or that frees the Christian from self-condemnation and teaches him to flee suffering—can only be false, while the true doctrine that proclaims God's majesty hidden in weakness and the cross enables Christians to suffer joyfully, to kiss, seek, and embrace suffering in all its spiritual, corporeal, material, and social manifestations.

Luther's invocation of relics in this context reflected the historical connection between relics and indulgences. Not only did Christians look to relics for the alleviation of earthly ills, but indulgences were often granted for the veneration of relics at places and times designated by the church. Luther's discussion, however, undercuts either use of relics; his point is that true relics do not remove suffering (whether earthly ills or purgatorial punishment) but *are* suffering itself, if the sufferer understands the purpose and value of her suffering. For Luther, material relics threatened to draw Christians away from true suffering even when these relics were the objects of hard and distant pilgrimages—that is, even when the healing or indulgences were hard won. The *Explanations* maligned such pilgrimages as self-assertive false trials that left behind the salutary burdens imposed by God. Against such cross-shirking masquerading as cross-bearing, Luther emphasized the accessibility of the true relics of Christ to all Christians in all times and places, seeking to infuse mundane life with cross-bearing driven by sorrow for sin, distrust of the self, and trust of God.[110] He writes:

> Many make pilgrimages to Rome and to other holy places to see the robe of Christ, the bones of the martyrs, and the places and remains of the saints, which we certainly do not condemn. But we lament the fact that we do not at the same time recognize the true relics, namely, the sufferings and crosses, which have sanctified the bones and relics of the martyrs and made them worthy of such great veneration. And by not recognizing these true relics we not only do not receive them when they are offered at home, but even reject them with all our might and chase from place to place, while with the greatest thirst and constant tears we should beg God that such precious relics of Christ, which are the most sacred of all, should be given to us, as it were, a gift for the elect children of God . . . [S]o holy are these relics and so precious these treasures, that while others could be preserved on earth or most honorably in vessels of gold, silver, precious stones, and silk, these can only be preserved in heavenly, living, rational, immortal, pure, and holy vessels, that is, in the hearts of the faithful which are incomparably more precious than every piece of gold and every precious stone. But nowadays the common people lack the faith by which they might cultivate reverence for relics of this kind to the point where even some popes have become authors and leaders not only in condemning these relics, but even persecuting those who seek them.[111]

Here, Luther identified even "some popes" as enemies of the cross—indeed, as persecutors of the cross-bearers for the sake of defending a system that commended extreme self-chosen crosses (long pilgrimages), despised the trusting acceptance of daily crosses, and remitted earthly and postmortem suffering in exchange for money. Thus, lay Christians were taught to despise the due penalties for their sin rather than to learn despair of self and trust in God. From the supposed vicar of Christ on down, the whole church became averse to the cross.

Theses 62–64, 75

In Theses 62–64, Luther describes the experience of salvation and the human relationship to God in terms reminiscent of the mystical tradition—with references to the relationship of bride and bridegroom, the experience of sweetness and bitterness, and most important for our purposes, the contrast between human seeking to be something and needing to be reduced to nothing. Luther asserts in Thesis 62 that the gospel is the "true treasure of the church."[112] For Luther, the gospel here is the message that salvation is not earned, but passively received by grace through faith in Christ. The gospel is a word of grace, comfort, joy, and peace—"a voice of the bridegroom to the bride." This word lifts the despair wrought in the conscience by the law, which is a word of destruction, wrath, and sadness—"a voice of the judge to the defendant." Following Augustine, Luther argues that the law convicts a person of sin, but does not remove it, and that human powers also cannot remove sin. The result of hearing the voice of the law, accordingly, is a "sinful" or "evil" and "troubled" conscience. The gospel addresses this bad conscience as the "sweetest messenger" of Christ alone, who "fulfills the law for you, whom God has made to be your righteousness, sanctification, wisdom, and redemption, for all those who believe in him." With these words, says Luther, the conscience is freed from terror before God's *poenae*; it "comes to life again, shouts for joy while leaping about full of confidence, and no longer fears death, the types of punishments associated with death, or hell. Therefore those who are still afraid of punishments have not yet heard Christ or the voice of the gospel, but only the voice of Moses." The gospel teaches that the fulfillment of the law requires not works but grace and faith in "all we receive from Christ and partake of in him."[113] Crucially, Luther disregards here Augustine's primary teaching, that grace makes Christians able to fulfill the law, and argues instead that grace confers trust (i.e., faith) in Christ's fulfillment of the law. This trust or faith also involves the courage to trust God precisely when that trust is hardest, in the face of sin and in the final and most extreme penalty of death, which carries the threat of eternal damnation. In Luther's view, Christian death is the experience of God working under a contrary to give eternal life; thus, even here, the Christian has sweetness in bitterness.

While Thesis 62 declares the gospel to be the treasure of the church, Thesis 63 adds, "But this treasure [the gospel] is naturally most odious, for it makes the first to be last." Luther explains that "the gospel destroys those things which exist, it confounds the strong, it confounds the wise and *reduces them to nothingness*, to weakness, to foolishness, because it teaches humility and a cross. . . . Let all those whose pleasure is in earthly things and in their own doing shrink back before this rule of the cross." The gospel is hated, Luther says, by "those who desire to be *something*, . . . to be wise and mighty in their own eyes and before men, and who consider themselves to be 'the first.'" But "the treasure of indulgences," Thesis 64 adds, is naturally most acceptable, for it makes the last to be first."[114] Still, Christ's word is a "sweet word" that "makes a man surrender his will to Christ."[115]

Luther charges here that theologians and church leaders fail to grasp the gospel because of their pride and self-exaltation; and he goes on to explain that the common throng is misled by a kindred regard for the apparently lofty, for position and pomp: "the simple people are used to evaluating the Word of God only in proportion to the gestures and pomp which are used in preaching it." The occasion for this remark was Luther's report of a rumor among the people that the St. Peter's indulgence would absolve a man for violating the Virgin (see Thesis 74). While stating his doubt that anyone had taught such a thing, Luther nonetheless blames the rumor on the trivialization of sins inherent in extolling the power of indulgences. He counters that "true and evangelical preaching is to magnify the sins as much as possible in order that man may develop fear of God and proper repentance." Luther asks, "What is the benefit of sounding off with so many exaggerations, in the interests of that most worthless remission of punishments, in order to extol indulgences, while hardly mumbling in the interests of that most salutary wisdom of the cross?"[116]

Summary
Luther's *Explanations* built on the framework of the *95 Theses* to argue that Christians must embrace rather than seek release from God-sent *poenae*. Throughout the *Explanations*, Luther's views on contrition are shaped by and organized around the locus of trust rather than love as defining the human relationship to God. Luther describes sin as an inborn, fundamental distrust of God, evident in every person's fear of death, and he ultimately concludes

that Christians, to be saved, must despair of self but not of salvation; they must learn their sinfulness in great suffering but abide in faith. Faith here enables *Gelassenheit*, indeed it is itself a sort of yielding to God's manner of giving salvation rather than following the desire of the self to earn it. The experience of suffering as condemnation of sin—whether through hearing the law or feeling the law's condemnation in want, disease, and death—drives Christians outside themselves to the promise of forgiveness on account of Christ; in turn, they can bear suffering joyfully and even suffer without suffering because suffering contributes to the effacement of self-assertion defined as self-trust. Having been reduced to nothing, Christians bear all *poenae* through the faith that unites them to God through Christ; for the self-driven, however, the appearance of holy works and suffering merely veils self-trust.

In the *Explanations*, Luther describes the Gospel not only as the sweet "voice of the bridegroom to the bride"—recalling Song of Songs and Bernard's famous mystical exegesis of that text—but also as, simultaneously, a voice that is "most odious" to human beings, to the bride herself. Human beings want to move themselves and trust themselves, to be something rather than nothing; human beings want to act for salvation, not suffer it. Luther understood indulgences to offer an easy way to salvation; but the deception of indulgences, in his view, sprung from the same sources as the deception of the most active and ascetic works-righteousness. Both manifested a desire to be self-moved, both left self-trust intact, and both were supported by the machinations of fallen reason, which allied itself with Aristotle in the universities. The discernment of truth required suffering—suffering as a hatred and distrust of self that human nature cannot attain or even want through its own powers; and suffering in joyful, trusting submission to all the *poenae* of life. This evangelical *Gelassenheit* did not require *resignatio ad infernum*, however, but sprung from confidence that God did not intend the damnation of the believer.

Luther's discussion of the theology of the cross in Thesis 58 makes a decisive turn, using the embrace of suffering to distinguish not between earnest and lukewarm Christians, but between true and false doctrine, and true and false teachers. Christians "had to be taught" this doctrine of suffering lest they fall victim to an array of rationally and affectively pleasing temptations contrary to Christ's cross. Such hostility to the cross took a variety of forms, including an esteem for pomp and authority; the appropriation of others' suffering through relics, indulgences, and endowed masses;

and the self-exaltation that hid—from human eyes, at least—underneath apparent mortifications and renunciations.

The Heidelberg Disputation

Luther penned his *Explanations* and his famous *Heidelberg Disputation* around the same time, and the content of the two works—both of which reflect upon the theology of the cross—is closely related. In the *Heidelberg Disputation*, Luther shifts his attack on church doctrine, away from the doctrine that taught lay people to appropriate others' suffering through external means like indulgences and relics, to the doctrine, beloved to the monastic audience of the *Heidelberg Disputation*, that taught Christians to seek salvation through works of self-denial and self-mortification. Luther derides such works as shallow, external, and self-exalting. Meanwhile, he attributes the teaching of works righteousness no less than the teaching of indulgences to the intrusion of fallen human desire and reason into theology. Humans want to be something before God, and reason tells them that they are something. For centuries, Luther argues, scholastic theology had devised ways for human beings to deny their nothingness before God, claiming that Christians could cooperate with God to become holy and earn salvation; as a consequence, Christendom was mired in a deceit that drove its most earnest members—Luther's audience included—into an abyss of pride cloaked underneath self-mortification. As in the *Explanations*, the theology of the cross comes to the rescue for Luther by revealing the paradigm for God's interaction with humanity—under the contrary of suffering.

The Heidelberg disputation occurred during the triennial meeting of the general chapter of the Saxon reform congregation of Augustinian eremites. Scholars do not know if the disputation was occasioned by the controversy over the *95 Theses* or if it was planned for some time to debate the broader campaign in Wittenberg against scholastic theology—a campaign that implicated Luther's own teachers in his order. Luther's theses did not address indulgences. In a sign of the perceived significance of the disputation, however, the order sought and obtained permission to hold it in the university— in the *Schola Artistarum*, with the regalia of the Arts Faculty present. Seizing the opportunity to reach a broader public, Luther added 12 philosophical theses to his 28 theological theses.[117] We will be concerned here with the latter, which pose the question of "whether the person by his own power can achieve justice before God or whether he, if he attempts such, incurs mortal sin."[118]

Like the 95 Theses, the Heidelberg Disputation is not a series of disconnected theses, but a structured whole: the Disputation proceeds from discussion of the law of God in the first thesis to the love of God in the twenty-eighth and final thesis.[119] Both of these pillars, in the words of Jos Vercruysse, "direct attention especially to God, that is to say, how he works through the law (it is powerless in reference to justification) and in his creating and justifying love." Vercruysse correctly emphasizes the paraenetic quality of the disputation; it reads as a sermon and exhortation "to seek grace in the crucified Christ." Vercruysse summarizes:

> The first part [Theses 1–12], which considers the works of the person, leads him to the fear of God's judgment over his works. The second part [Theses 13–18], which speaks of the will and the ability of the person, brings him into doubt regarding his ability. The discussions of the theology of glory, the theology of the cross, and the person who is rightly taught by God [Theses 19–24] aim at complete self-abandonment and devotion to the crucified Christ. Only the frightened, doubting, yielded friend of the cross, who has been reduced to nothing, is rightly prepared to receive the grace of justification. Where there is nothing, God's love can enter and create. The harmonious ascent to God by means of an unbroken analogy embedded in nature is fundamentally a terrible self-deception and self-aggrandizement. The way must be radically reversed. God descends, demolishes our arrogance by his alien work, and builds us up anew with gracious mercy by his proper work. Thus, the question posed at the beginning, how the person attains God's justice, receives its answer at the end [Theses 25–28]: only through God's gracious and creating love.[120]

The problems of self-trust and self-deceit in matters of salvation dominate the Heidelberg Disputation. Relying on their fallen will and reason, human beings according to Luther imagine they can attain salvation by working hard in obedience to God's law or even the natural law. Their human works appear good, while divine works "always seem unattractive and evil";[121] but only God's work saves. As Vercruysse's just-cited summary makes clear, Luther draws upon mystical themes of annihilation and union to argue that God must crush human pretense, emptying the human of self-love and self-trust in order to create the space in which God can work. Describing the alien work of

the law (per Isa. 28:21) to reduce human beings to recognition of their nothingness, Luther writes:

> The Lord humbles and frightens us by means of the law and the sight of our
> sins so that we seem in the eyes of men, as in our own, as nothing, foolish,
> and wicked, for we are in truth that. Insofar as we acknowledge and confess
> this, there is no form or beauty in us, but our life is hidden in God (i.e. in
> the bare confidence in his mercy) [sed vivimus in abscondito Dei (id est,
> in nuda fiducia misericordiae eius)], finding in ourselves nothing but sin,
> foolishness, death, and hell.[122]

The word rendered here as "confidence," *fiducia*, also means "trust" or "faith."
To explain faith, Luther invokes the mystical experience of annihilation; and
union human beings are brought to self-hatred and "stripped" of their own
resources, standing naked with only trust in God left. These themes reflect
Luther's reading of Tauler, especially.

The necessity of self-accusation for sin is a major theme of the *Heidelberg
Disputation*. Luther's primary purpose is to convince his hearers that seemingly good works must be the objects of the accusation, not carried out with
the pretense to earn salvation by "doing what is within oneself." "Free will,
after the fall, exists in name only, and as long as it does what it is able to do,
it commits a moral sin," Luther writes in Thesis 13.[123] The only truly good
works are done by God through human beings, whom God wields in God's
hand like a "rusty and rough hatchet." Even these divine works are "de-
formed" by human sinfulness.[124] In Theses 14 and 15, Luther contends that
post-fall, free will "has power to do good only in a passive capacity, but it
always can do evil in an active capacity. Nor could free will endure in a state
of innocence, much less do good, in an active capacity, but only in its passive
capacity."[125] The terminology is scholastic, but the view that human beings
were created to be passive recipients of the divine will and work also has resonance with the *German Theology*, in particular. In any case, for Luther, to
be reduced to nothingness and instrumentality is not merely to suffer a temporary remedy for sin, but to be graciously returned to the status that God
intended all along.

One might describe the progression of the *Heidelberg Disputation* in terms
of digging ever deeper below the surface. Luther begins on the surface, with
works and their appearance before God and human beings, noting that God
sees beneath the surface. He digs deeper then into the source of good works,

which is not the assertion of human intellectual and moral capacity but passivity before the divine, in despair of self and trust in God. Finally, he hits noetic bedrock. How does one come to this essential knowledge? The most famous theses (19–24) address this question:

> [19] That person does not deserve to be called a theologian who looks upon the invisible things of God as though they were clearly perceptible in those things which have actually happened [Rom. 1:20]. [20] He deserves to be called a theologian, however, who comprehends the visible and manifest things of God seen through suffering and the cross. [21] A theologian of glory calls evil good and good evil. A theologian of the cross calls the thing what it actually is. [22] The wisdom which sees the invisible things of God in works as perceived by man is completely puffed up, blinded, and hardened. [23] The law brings the wrath of God, kills, reviles, accuses, judges, and condemns everything that is not in Christ [Rom. 4:15]. [24] Yet that wisdom is not of itself evil, nor is the law to be evaded; but without the theology of the cross man misuses the best in the worst manner.[126]

Thesis 19 references the invisible things of God, meaning all those positive traits medieval theologians associated with the divine whenever they debated which name of God was highest, whether "virtue, godliness, wisdom, justice, goodness, and so forth." As Heinrich Bornkamm points out, Luther does not deny such knowledge of God exists, which would have contradicted Romans 1:20, but that such knowledge is right theology, meaning salvific and not self-exalting theology. When Moses requested a vision of God, Luther recalls, God told him, "My back parts [*posteriora*] you will see" (Ex. 33:23).[127] Luther reads this passage through the lens of the doctrine of incarnation, writing that "the 'back' and visible things of God are placed in opposition to the invisible, namely, his human nature, weakness, foolishness." The incarnation is not just a singular historical event, but also a part and a revelation of God's unchanging manner of acting toward sinful humanity. In creation, God gave knowledge of God's invisible being through created things, but it was misused by human beings for their own exaltation, both in knowing and willing. They presumed to comprehend God and presumed to be able to earn merit and salvation before God from their own goodness and striving. Luther concludes, "Because men misused the knowledge of God through works, God wished to be recognized again in suffering, and to condemn wisdom concerning invisible things by means of wisdom concerning visible things, so that those who did not honor God as manifested in his works should honor him as he is hidden in suffering [*absconditus in passionibus*]."[128] God is hidden both above revelation—in God's invisible power, wisdom, goodness, and so forth—and in revelation, under the weakness and folly of the cross.[129] Whatever can be known about the God hidden but accessible through creation does not save, only what can be known on the cross through suffering.[130] Luther's plea is not merely for a Christ-centered theology and soteriology but for a cross-centered theology and soteriology: "true theology and recognition of God are in the crucified Christ."[131]

Luther's theological and soteriological centering on the paradox of the cross was intended to condemn what he regarded as a Pelagian takeover of the theology of the medieval schools.[132] This takeover had succeeded, in his eyes, because it dressed itself in reason, while flattering human self-assertion and presumption. Luther dismisses his opponents here as those who reject the two-fold way of the cross—of self-condemnation and passivity *coram deo*, and work and suffering as an instrument of God *coram hominibus*. Theologians are either friends or enemies of the cross:

> He who does not know Christ [i.e. who does not begin with the Incarnate God on the cross] does not know God hidden in suffering. Therefore, he prefers works to suffering, glory to the cross, strength to weakness, wisdom to folly, and, in general, good to evil. These are the people whom the apostle calls "enemies of the cross of Christ" [Phil. 3:18], for they hate the cross and suffering and love works and the glory of works. Thus they call the good of the cross evil and the evil of a deed good. God can be found only in suffering and the cross . . . Therefore the friends of the cross say that the cross is good and works are evil, for through the cross works are destroyed and the Old Adam, who is especially edified by works, is crucified. It is impossible for a person not to be puffed up by his good works unless he has first been deflated and destroyed by suffering and evil until he knows that he is worthless and that his works are not his but God's.[133]

As in the *Explanations*, Luther does not convey a nuanced and variegated view of scholasticism, church history, or his present—rather he divides history and the present into truth and falsehood. There are two theologies and two kinds of theologian, and the question is, "Who will judge between the two?" One should believe, Luther teaches, only a message that denies to human beings any innate resources for the attainment of salvific knowledge of God and salvation; this message deflates and destroys hearers, teaching them that they are worthless—indeed, nothing. Understanding this message transforms Christians' attitude toward all suffering;[134] the Christian understands that God uses suffering to subdue human pride, and that truly good works—whether of self-denial or of self-giving—are in fact so many sufferings of God's work. Christians are instruments moved by God.

Luther once again employs mystical themes of annihilation and nothingness in his discussion in Thesis 24 of how the theologian of glory and the theologian of the cross use differently the death-dealing "wisdom" of the law. Luther describes how God's work of annihilation empties sufferers of themselves and brings them to a state of indifference concerning what God chooses to do with them as God's instruments. The reference to *Gelassenheit* is clear; where Tauler commended *Gelassenheit* in response to the experience of God-forsakenness, Luther glossed, "aequabile vel aequamini."[135] In the *Heidelberg Disputation*, Augustine's anti-Pelagian interpretation of Paul is interpreted with the aid of mystical terminology:

[H]e who has not been brought low, *reduced to nothing* through the cross and suffering, takes credit for works and wisdom and does not give credit to God. He thus misuses and defiles the gifts of God. He, however, who has been *emptied* [Phil. 2:7] through suffering no longer works but knows that God works all things in him. For this reason, whether man does works or not, it is all the same to him. He neither boasts if he does good works, nor is he disturbed if God does not do good works through him. He knows that it is sufficient if he suffers and is brought low by the cross in order to *be annihilated all the more*. It is this that Christ says in John 3 [:7], "You must be born anew." To be born anew, one must consequently first die and then be raised up with the Son of Man. To die, I say, means to feel death at hand.[136]

This passage is highly significant, coming at the culmination of Luther's discussion of right knowing and leading into his four final theses, which oppose works-righteousness to God's righteousness, created in the sinner through God-given faith in Christ. Luther declares at the conclusion to his discussion of Thesis 25 that through faith one does works as "Christ's action or instrument [*operatio seu instrumentum*]."[137] Thesis 26 invokes the possibility of union with God in terms of Christ dwelling in believers through faith,[138] holding, "through faith Christ is in us, indeed, one with us. Christ is just and has fulfilled all the commands of God, wherefore we also fulfill everything through him since he was made ours through faith."[139]

For Luther, faith recasts human life after the image of the crucified savior, with its profound offense to human pride—to fallen reason and affect. The love of God received through faith and the presence of Christ in the believer is here an alien force that sets believers against themselves and the world. This love of God cannot spring from nature but must be the result of God's direct work. For the love of God, in Luther's perspective, is not merely above human love, but contrary to it. The final thesis reads, "The love of God does not find, but creates, that which is pleasing to it. The love of man comes into being through that which is pleasing to it." While human love, according to Aristotle, seeks unity with what appears lovable and good to the self, "the love of God living in human beings loves sinners, evil persons, fools, and weaklings in order to make them righteous, good, wise, and strong." Human love "avoids sinners and evil persons," but Christ's love is "the love of the cross, born of the cross, which turns in the direction where it does not find good which it may enjoy, but where it may confer good upon the bad and needy person."[140] God's creative love is extended to wherever God finds nothing—or rather, God's love is bestowed where God has reduced to nothing fallen and self-assertive nature. Those born out of this "love of the cross" are transformed to endure acting and suffering as God's instruments in service to the lowly and afflicted.

Concluding Remarks

By 1517, Luther was convinced that the theology of the universities had fatally misunderstood God's manner of working in and upon human beings for their salvation; consequently, the church was proffering doctrines that endangered Christian souls. The cause of this misunderstanding of salvation was human pride—more specifically, the human desire to be something before God and to offer something to God. This pride was nourished and supported by fallen reason, which readily assumed that an exchange of temporal merit and eternal reward could define the economy of salvation. Against such rational pride, God's true work (according to Luther) inflicted suffering, reducing human self-trust to nothingness and planting trust in Christ in the place of that annihilated self-trust. The teachings of the post-Eckhartian mystics about *Anfechtung*, spiritual annihilation unto nothingness, union with God, *Gelassenheit*, "suffering God," "suffering without suffering," and the problem of self-inflicted suffering, which leaves self-will intact, all helped Luther understand and explain the experience of God's work through Christ, faith, and the cross for human salvation. Luther's depiction of the Christian as an empty vessel for Christ's indwelling and use likewise reminds of the Eckhartian tradition. For Luther, however, any surrender to or union with God's will had to happen through faith's relationship to Christ, not through an inward turn and sinking into precreated unity.

Luther countered scholastic theologians' alleged misunderstanding of suffering and *poenae* and what he saw as Christians' consequent refusal to accept God's work through suffering from two angles in 1517–1518. In the *95 Theses* and *Explanations*, he worried that church doctrine encouraged Christians to shirk salutary contrition and trials by appropriating the merits of those who had suffered such things, namely, Christ and the saints. With the *Heidelberg Disputation*, conversely, Luther attacked the most strenuous pursuit of salvation in order to unmask the presumption and self-assertion that in his view lay beneath even monastic exercises of self-denial. In both instances, Luther trained his sights on scholastic theology above all, the errors of which were epitomized for Luther in the phrase, "If you do what is within you, God will not withhold grace." Luther countered that Christians are not saved by doing what is within them, but by suffering what God does in and through them.

A line was crossed as Luther distinguished between theologians of glory and theologians of the cross. For Luther, right doctrine summoned Christians to the experience of being reduced by God to nothing, to true humility and self-accusation; in turn, the Spirit united believers to Christ by faith and sent them forth as God's instruments, ready to suffer natural evil and human violence with trust in God's care. The Old Adam was not entirely rooted out of the sinner, but the realization of its presence reduced the Christian all the more. For Luther, any other doctrine preserving any vestige of human agency was nothing but pride masquerading under false humility and lying reason. Alongside his distinction between two types of theologian, Luther's distinction between "friends" and "enemies" of the cross encapsulates the divisiveness of his entry onto the stage of Christian history. If those who failed to teach suffering rightly were "enemies of the cross," Luther could not help but conclude that they were not Christian teachers at all, not representatives of the true church. Luther and his followers were about to declare a division in Christian history and in the living world of Christendom between the true church and the false church, true doctrine and false doctrine, true Christians

and false Christians. The true church was to be marked by a right proclamation and a faithful endurance of suffering. The false church would have to be
exposed, in turn, in any of its pretensions to holy suffering.

Looking ahead to the coming chapters, two final points should be emphasized here: first, although it is extremely important to recognize how Luther's
new soteriology offered an unburdening from the demand placed upon late-
medieval Christians to "work out their salvation in fear and trembling," it is
also important to see how Luther's message in his dramatic 1517 and 1518
disputations took shape as a comprehensive summons of Christians and
Christian theology back to the cross and suffering—to the true suffering
that begins with the recognition of human sinfulness and nothingness, and
the faith transforms all of life from the foot of this cross. Luther proclaimed
joyous trust in Christ to those anxious about salvation, but he knew too that
the right preacher had to afflict the proud. Second, while faith and trust—
not penance or contrition—came to represent the ground of salvation according to Luther, faith's relationship to being-accused and being reduced to
nothing by the law and suffering was inescapable for Luther. Despair of self
was necessary; faith preserved such despair from becoming despair of salvation and taught the Christian to reject self-trust all the more. *Gelassenheit*
was decoupled from *resignatio ad infernum*. The marriage of faith to suffering both inward and outward was no passing moment for the reformer
and represented an important aspect of his rebuke of Karlstadt and Müntzer
in 1524–1525. Karlstadt and Müntzer drank from many of the same wells as
Luther—scripture, Augustine, humanism, Eckhartian mysticism—and like
Luther, they brought mystical ideas and vocabulary surrounding spiritual
trials, annihilation, and union with God or Christ into connection with a
doctrine of faith. Luther would not let his adversaries claim a right understanding of faith or suffering; from Luther's perspective, the misguided theologian and teacher was always and everywhere unbroken in reason and
desire—an enemy of the cross of Christ.

3

"To where should he who hopes in God come, unless into his own nothingness?"

Mystical Concepts, Transformed Perception, and the Wittenberg Call to the Cross up to 1522

Between 1517 and 1522, Martin Luther and his university colleague Andreas Bodenstein von Karlstadt produced a flurry of printed literature that exhorted Christians to return to true doctrine and true suffering, while also teaching them to avoid and unmask false doctrines and false suffering. Both learned to use short, vernacular pamphlets (*Flugschriften*) to win popular support—Luther already with the publication of the *Sermon on Indulgence and Grace* in March 1518,[1] Karlstadt by the second half of 1520.[2] The goal was a Christian teaching and practice shaped according to God's plans rather than human invention.

As we saw in chapter 1, both Luther and Karlstadt were receptive to post-Eckhartian mystical teachings about the reduction or annihilation of human beings to nothingness (*reductio ad nihilum/vernichtung*) through spiritual and visible suffering, and about the status of the Christians thus annihilated as instruments in God's hands. In chapter 2, we saw how these motifs found rich expression in early 1518 in Luther's *Explanations to the 95 Theses* and the *Heidelberg Disputation*, alongside teachings about yielding to God's will (*Gelassenheit*), suffering God, and suffering without suffering. Luther also echoed Tauler's critique of self-chosen suffering and the broader Eckhartian objection to self-willed *imitatio Christi*. The initial controversy over indulgences in 1517–1518 was part of a broader attack on scholastic theology, for which the mystical alternative was enlisted to depict human beings as passive recipients of truth rather than as active strivers through reason. As the controversy unfolded and expanded, Luther and Karlstadt drew upon mystical concepts and terminology to define and defend a comprehensive revision of both the doctrine of salvation and the constitution of authority within the church. Whatever their theological differences,[3] they

Enemies of the Cross. Vincent Evener, Oxford University Press (2021). © Oxford University Press.
DOI: 10.1093/oso/9780190073183.001.0001.

became together the standard bearers for a new paradigm of the Christian as sufferer: both taught that salvation could be received only as a gift from God, and that fallen human nature was fundamentally opposed and blind to the necessity for such passivity. Thus, God had to move the unwilling sinner through suffering and trials, both spiritual and visible, to discover and accept salvation on God's terms. The recipients of salvation, in turn, found themselves in fundamental opposition to the world: they inevitably suffered spite and violence at the hands of all those who remained captive to fallen reason and affect, especially the educated and the powerful. Although working sometimes more in parallel than in conjunction,[4] Karlstadt and Luther were able to regard one another as allies—and to be seen by the public as allies— partly because they shared these convictions; at the same time, there was considerable room for diverse emphases and diverse development within shared assumptions. To name one example at the heart of this book, both Luther and Karlstadt saw Christians as united with God and thus able to bear all suffering as God's will, but Luther emphasized that union occurs through faith in Christ and that willing cross-bearing springs from trust that God works under contraries, while Karlstadt spoke already in 1519 in terms of yielding to and uniting with God's will. This difference informed the two reformers' divergent stances toward lay initiative in ecclesial reform, the reform of the social order, and the appropriate Christian response to oppression and persecution. The same applies when Müntzer is considered: Müntzer did not initiate a mystical revolt against the non-mystical Luther, but like Karlstadt, developed a distinct vision from the same sources.[5]

In the first part of this chapter, I analyze Luther's "sacrament cycle" of 1519—a series of three vernacular tracts in which he addressed penance, baptism, and the Eucharist in succession. My purpose is to show how Luther in 1519 continued to argue against doctrines that taught Christians to rely on others' suffering or that cloaked self-assertion under false suffering. Luther unfolded these concerns into and within a comprehensive doctrine of Christian life and faith in which Christians begin to undergo and submit to the destruction of their old Adam and their self-trust in baptism, while experiencing union with Christ and the saints in the Lord's Supper, so that Christ bears their sin and suffering while they also share in the suffering of Christ and all other Christians.[6] Crucially, Luther argues that Christians are trained for a proper, faithful death by trials endured in their God-given occupations; Luther repudiates the self-chosen trials of pilgrimage and monastic life in favor of the unchosen and oft-despised trials of domestic and

political life, thus beginning to elaborate a doctrine of social-political conduct indebted at least partly to the Taulerian critique of self-chosen trials.
Alongside Luther's sacrament cycle, then, I will also describe Luther's "digression on hope and suffering" in his lectures on the Psalter from 1519–1521
(the *Operationes in Psalmos*); printed separately in vernacular translation,
the digression claimed that Christians have hope in suffering—both in the
loss of temporal goods and the condemnation of any supposed merits for
salvation—because such suffering kills and damns them, that is, divests and
strips them of self-trust and reduces them to nothing, so that hope in God
becomes possible.

In the second part of this chapter, I discuss how themes of true and false
suffering were used in the first piece of visual propaganda issued during the
Reformation—a broadsheet depicting two wagons, one carrying a pious
Christian to the cross and Christ, and thence to heaven, the other carrying
a proud monk-theologian to hell. The image was conceived by Karlstadt to
engage and instruct the "common person" in advance of the Leipzig disputation. Possibly inspired by woodcuts in the 1512 Augsburg edition of Henry
Suso's works,[7] Karlstadt also furnished his "Wagons" with numerous captions
and he published an explanatory treatise; both the annotated image and the
treatise put Augustine at center stage, but Karlstadt introduced Eckhartian
mystical motifs as well. Above all, he used the concept *Gelassenheit* to teach
that Christians should be yielded to God's will in rigorous condemnation
of self and in the acceptance of all suffering as eternally ordained by God;
this yielding was, he claimed, the true cross-bearing enjoined by Christ in
the New Testament.[8] Karlstadt's "wagons" will help us understand how he
responded to the threat of excommunication in his 1520 *Missive on the
Highest Virtue Gelassenheit*, one of his most successful vernacular treatises.

Lastly, then, this chapter analyzes two works that Luther authored while in
hiding at the Wartburg Castle in 1521–1522: a short treatise, *The Magnificat
Put into German and Explained*, and the *Wartburg Postil*, a large collection
of model sermons for the Advent and Christmas seasons. The imprint of
Eckhartian mysticism and other streams of the mystical tradition on Luther's
Magnificat commentary is unmistakable; but scholars have yet to devote any
serious attention to Tauler's influence on the postils through themes of spiritual suffering, the nothingness of human works, and cross-bearing. Here,
I will be content only to point to a few illustrative passages, demonstrating
how the themes of this book became part of an enduring Lutheran preaching
tradition that for centuries looked to Luther's postils.[9]

Throughout this chapter, I call attention especially to Luther's and Karlstadt's shared conclusion that Christians, when they receive truth and salvation through the destruction of their old ways of perceiving, understanding, and acting, obtain in turn a new capacity to see all suffering as God's work. To make this point, both reformers relied upon the concrete metaphor of sight. Likewise, both recognized that *apparent* suffering could conceal underlying self-assertion, just as *real* suffering could unmask that self-assertion—after all, false Christians do not recognize God as a God who works under contraries.

Luther, 1519–1520

In this first section, I discuss in turn Luther's vernacular sacrament cycle of 1519 and the "digression on hope and suffering" (1520) from his lectures on the Psalter.

The Sacrament Cycle (1519)

In the *95 Theses*, the *Explanations to the 95 Theses*, and the *Heidelberg Disputation*, Luther addressed educated, Latin-reading audiences with a plea for a revolution in the instruction of all Christians. Already in 1517, however, Luther also took his case directly to the educated public, clerical and lay alike, with a series of powerful and popular vernacular pamphlets.[10] This project made Luther by far the most printed author of the first half of the sixteenth century.[11] In 1519, Luther wrote and published an important and well-received series of pamphlets on the sacraments of penance, baptism, and the Eucharist.[12] The sacraments structured and framed late-medieval Christian life, from cradle to the grave.[13] Thus, Luther's pamphlets signaled his demand for a complete overhaul of Christian existence, from its ground—now understood as faith in God's forgiveness rather than striving for true love of God—to its expression in community. Rittgers reminds us:

It is important to stress that it was through such vernacular works of devotion that the majority of Germans came to know Luther, not through his university lecture courses and scholarly debates. In the minds of his contemporaries, at least those who were sympathetic to him, Luther was first and foremost a pastor who was deeply committed to the care of souls.[14]

In the late Middle Ages, Christians' daily devotion was supposed to be shaped by penance—by the rendering of satisfaction for sin—but Luther in the sacrament cycle began a reorientation of Christian sacramental life and devotion around baptism. Baptism, Luther argued, signifies and works both forgiveness and the slaying of the old Adam. The gift is sacramentally complete when grasped by faith, yet throughout life Christians must constantly endure God's alien work *sub contrariis* to slay the old Adam—that is, until God's final redemptive but terrifying work, death, finally kills Adam *in toto* and brings the believer to new life. Penance becomes in Luther's revised view a reminder of the forgiving work of baptism—a reminder that helps Christians bear the alien work of baptism with trust in God. Luther also argues that Christians are united to Christ and the saints in the Lord's Supper, attaining others' help to bear their suffering, while growing in their love and readiness to suffer for truth and one another in a hostile world. Luther's sacrament cycle upholds the baptismal vow undertaken by all Christians to undergo the death of their old self through a lifetime of trials. The reformer rejects the claim that monks and clergy undertake higher vows of self-denial (poverty, chastity, and obedience; the so-called counsels of perfection), and argues that the most salutary trials are sent by God to Christians in their divinely appointed vocations, whether in marriage and economic activity, government, or the monastery.[15] True suffering is unchosen, and thus empties the Christian of trust in themselves, allowing them to have faith in God. The sacrament cycle seeks to present the sacraments as God's comfort for Christians afflicted by sin and the dread of judgment[16]—yet humility remains the prerequisite for and result of faith, as well as a life-long exercise. It is a despair of self that does not despair of salvation, but looks to Christ. Faith works to destroy self-trust, making possible joyful yielding to the work of baptism, which is painful for the fallen self.

In his pamphlet on penance, Luther answers the charge that he had rejected the necessity of contrition (*Reue*) and suffering, confession and good works. Everything he had said about penance was, he countered, written for Christians who were "uneasy, erring and terrified" about sin and God's judgment—who were not merely contrite but "too contrite," to the point of doubting God's promise of forgiveness. Those who have not "experienced this tormenting anxiety [*marter*]" do not know to seek consolation, which is the sole purpose of the sacrament of penance; "[o]ne must first soften them up with the terrible judgment of God and cause them to quail, so that they too may learn to sigh, and seek for the comfort of the sacrament."[17] Thus, Christian life is defined not by needing and seeking the removal of punishment (*Pein*), but by needing and seeking assurance of the removal of guilt.[18] Through the sacrament, God alone removes terror before God, "calms and gladdens the conscience," and bestows a "peace to the heart" that cannot be attained by indulgences or works, not even by ascetic feats of "fasting and straining." Truly good works—and truly good suffering—can be done only with confidence in forgiveness.[19]

The sacrament is necessary for salvation, Luther argues, but its efficacy depends upon the recipient's faith in the words of Matthew 16:19, spoken by the priest.[20] Faith trusts God's promise and rejects trust in any human grounds for forgiveness, including contrition, works, and the authority of the priest. To trust in the latter is to "sin against the Holy Spirit" by calling God a liar. Faith, conversely, tears Christians away from themselves. Through faith they "let personal opinions go, and . . . give place to the word of God spoken through the priest." Only the Word is certain.[21] Human contrition is never sufficient, and those who trust in it never find or even truly desire peace; building on sand, they attain "ever greater uneasiness of conscience" and in the end, "despair and eternal damnation." They "will not let God be merciful" but want God to be a judge, because they trust in their ability to satisfy that divine judge.[22]

As Luther here rethinks and reorganizes the sacraments and Christian life around the doctrine of salvation by grace through faith, unbelief defined as distrust of God represents the fundamental human sin; consequently, the core of the Christian relationship to God is at stake in how Christians respond to any and every suffering: Do they trust God as sovereign over suffering and relief from it, or do they complain against God and seek their own way out of trials? Here, Luther writes about the trial of unbelief itself, when a person does not feel peace of conscience; Luther advises that the Christian "should not despair" because of weak faith, but "recognize it as a trial and temptation by . . . which God tests, prods, and drives a person to cry out all the more and plead for such faith." This trial teaches the Christian "that everything depends on the grace of God: the sacrament, the forgiveness, and the faith. Giving up all other hope, despairing of himself, he comes to hope exclusively in the grace of God and cling to it without ceasing."[23] Faith requires and involves despair of self.

The second tract in the sacrament cycle is on baptism and is striking in its persistent eschatological orientation. With its immersion and lifting out, baptism according to Luther is a sign of the Christian's dying to sin and the old self and subsequent resurrection in new life. Due to the depth of human sinfulness, however, the necessary dying is completed only in actual death, and the final resurrection occurs only on the Last Day. Meanwhile, "the life of a Christian, from baptism to the grave, is nothing else than the beginning of a blessed death," even as—underneath the suffering and struggle—the "sign" and "significance" of baptism are already completed, death and resurrection have already been given, and the Christian is "sacramentally altogether pure and guiltless," even while the "flesh" remains sinful.[24] In baptism, the Christian commits to God's work of killing their old self, especially through sufferings. Luther writes:

> In the first place, you give yourself up [*du dich ergibst*] to the sacrament of baptism and to what it signifies. That is, you desire to die, together with your sins, and to be made new at the last day. . . . God accepts this desire at your hands and grants you baptism. From that hour he begins to make you a new person. He pours into you his grace and Holy Spirit, who begins to slay nature and sin, and to prepare you for death and the resurrection of the Last Day. In the second place you pledge yourself to continue in this desire, and to slay your sin more and more as long as you live, even until your dying day. This too God accepts. He trains and tests you all your life long, with many good works and with all kinds of suffering. Thereby he accomplishes what you in baptism have desired. Therefore we read and see how bitterly he has let his saints be tortured, and how much he has let them suffer, in order that, almost slain, they might fulfill the sacrament of baptism, die, and be made new. For when this does not happen, when we do not suffer and are not tested, the evil nature gains the upper hand so that a person invalidates baptism, falls into sin, and remains the same old man he was before.[25]

God uses suffering not merely to break desire for earthly things (as in Augustine or even Tauler), but to condemn and break self-trust and increase trust in God; Christians, in turn, are not actors but recipients of God's work, to which they have surrendered themselves (*sich ergeben*) in baptism. The Spirit works from within, giving trust in the face of sin and moving God's newborn instruments to good works, while trials assail and serve the Spirit's work from without.[26]

Luther proceeds to criticize two alleged errors in regard to baptism— both of which sprung, he believed, from a refusal to acknowledge human beings' innate, lifelong sinfulness and from a desire and presumption to be saved through the exercise of the will rather than the reception of God's sometimes-painful work. Some think, Luther reports, that after baptism, the Christian is made "pure" in nature and left with only an inclination to sin (concupiscence) that can be resisted; others think that the Christian, after baptism, must still earn redemption through rendering works of satisfaction. Against these positions, Luther argues that even after baptism, Christians are so turned from God in their old selves that they can find redemption in only one way: they must "joyfully dare to rely [sich froelich erwegen]" on the promise that God will not hold sin against those who believe in and commit to the work of baptism.[27]

This work of baptism, then, consists of both "forgiveness and the driving out of sins." Faith in forgiveness allows the Christian to receive all suffering and even death itself as the destruction of sin, of the old Adam. Sin makes human beings fear death as "bitter" and "horrible," but "[s]uch is the grace and power of God that sin, which has brought death, is driven out again by its very own work." Thus, "baptism makes all sufferings, and especially death, profitable and helpful . . . [and] there is no shorter way [to righteousness] than through baptism and the work of baptism, which is suffering and death." Those who refuse to walk the path of suffering and death show "that they do not properly intend or know how to become righteous," however great their apparent works.[28]

Thus, for Luther, baptism and the gift of forgiveness enable an embrace of suffering that truly mortifies self-will and self-trust, rather than strengthening these characteristics of the old Adam. Luther argues that this true suffering is to be found in Christians' daily, divinely appointed vocations, rather than in ascetic or penitential feats. Because human beings do not see or do not want to walk the baptismal way of death, Luther explains:

> God instituted many estates [stend] in life in which men are to learn to exercise themselves and suffer. To some he has commanded the estate of matrimony, to others the estate of the clergy, to others the estate of temporal rule, and to all he has commanded that they shall toil and labor to kill the flesh and accustom it to death. Because for all who are baptized, their baptism

has made repose, ease, and prosperity in this life a very poison and a hindrance to its work. For in the easy life no one learns to suffer, to die with gladness, to get rid of sin, and to live in harmony with baptism. Instead there grows only love of this life and horror of eternal life, fear of death and unwillingness to blot out sin. Consider now the lives of men. Many there are who fast, pray, go on pilgrimages, and exercise themselves in such things, thinking thereby only to heap up merit and to sit down in high places of heaven; they no longer learn to slay their evil vices. But fasting and all such exercises should be aimed at holding down the old Adam, the sinful nature, and at accustoming it to do without all that is pleasing for this life, and thus preparing it more and more each day for death, so that the work and the purpose of baptism may be fulfilled.[29]

Luther's reinterpretation of salvation and the sacraments thus already aimed at the complete transformation of Christians as social-political actors, especially in response to the suffering and toil that attended daily life in society. Monks of the day renounced the world and practiced self-mortification to slay their attachment to creaturely things and to themselves, while pious laity imitated monastic rigor within constraints, and expressed extraordinary devotion through pilgrimages; Luther, however, in a radical extension of the Eckhartian counsel that self-chosen suffering cannot slay self-will, wanted Christians to embrace suffering in their current lot and estate, recognizing that God uses suffering to teach them to die. This was a message of total self-denial, transformed by Luther's discovery of promise and trust as the nexus of the human relationship to God, and reflecting deep anxiety about the deceptiveness of pious practices. The laity do not earn great merit through pilgrimages, and those who presume to be saved by taking monastic or clerical vows forget the higher baptismal vow common to all Christians—"to slay sin and to become holy through the work and grace of God, to whom we yield and offer ourselves [*unß dargeben und opfern*], as the clay to the potter [Jer. 18 4–6]."[30] To live as a Christian, then, is to cast oneself upon the promise of baptism and to suffer joyfully and confidently the gradual work of baptism through all kinds of trials, spiritual and visible.

With this understanding of baptism, Luther came to see penance as a reminder of baptism, not a separate sacrament—a conclusion he drew specifically in *On the Babylonian Captivity of the Church* in 1520. Already in *A Sermon on the Blessed Sacrament of the Holy, True Body of Christ*, the third and final part of the 1519 sacrament cycle, Luther declares baptism and the Lord's Supper the "principal sacraments" of the church.[31] His treatment of each theme reminds us again of his reception of Eckhartian mysticism and his paradigm of the Christian as sufferer: just as yielding in trials and trusting in the face of sin belong to baptism, so union with Christ and all the saints belongs to the Lord's Supper. Faith grasps the "internal and spiritual" significance of the "external and visible" sign in the Supper, bringing Christians into the "one spiritual body" of Christ, where they receive as "common property" "all the spiritual possessions of Christ and his saints," along with all their suffering and "all sufferings and sins" of other true Christians, to whom they are bound by mutual love.[32] Thus, Christians struggling against sins of the flesh ("anger, hatred, pride, unchastity, and so forth") are helped by the correction and intercession of Christ and the Christian community;[33] and Christians stand in union with Christ and one another whenever they are assailed by the devil, the world, or a conscience fixated on sin and the threat of death and hell. The sacrament strengthens this union and reminds the Christian of it.[34] Like penance, the Lord's Supper bolsters the faith of those whose life work is trusting in God while dying to themselves; and like the yearning for absolution, the hunger for the Supper is felt only by those who recognize their sin and need. Thus, Christ gave the Supper to the disciples only after saddening them with the announcement of his impending death and terrifying them with the news that one of them would betray him.[35]

According to Luther, God sends affliction upon Christians to drive them to the Lord's Supper—to the memory and the increase of their union with Christ and love for one another:[36]

> Now if one will make the afflictions of Christ and of all Christians his own, defend the truth, oppose unrighteousness, and help bear the needs of the innocent and the sufferings of all Christians, then he will find affliction and adversity enough, over and above that which his evil nature, the world, the devil, and sin daily inflict upon him. And it is even God's will and purpose to set so many hounds upon us and oppress us, and everywhere to prepare bitter herbs for us, so that we may long for this strength and take delight in the holy sacrament, and thus be worthy (that is, desirous) of it.[37]

Those who have truly suffered and been driven by God into union and communion are, in turn, made ready to suffer with and for others. Luther writes:

There are those, indeed, who would gladly share in the profits [of the sacrament and communion] but not in the costs. . . . [T]hey like to hear that in this sacrament the help, fellowship, and support of all the saints are promised and given to them. But they are unwilling in their turn to belong also to this fellowship. They will not help the poor, put up with sinners, care for the sorrowing, suffer with the suffering, intercede for others, defend the truth, and at the risk of life, property, and honor seek the betterment of the church and of all Christians. They are unwilling because they fear the world. They do not want to have to suffer disfavor, harm, shame, or death, although it is God's will that they be thus driven—for the sake of the truth and of their neighbors—to desire the great grace and strength of this sacrament.[38]

God uses suffering to bring Christians into saving union with Christ and other Christians; they die to their self-trust daily through this work of baptism and learn to trust in Christ and one another. They give themselves for others as Christ gave himself for them. Structured by the sacraments and anchored in a relationship of faith in Christ, Christian life as Luther depicts it consists of yielding to suffering and death as God's alien work to annihilate self-trust and create despair of self (if only imperfectly), coming into union with Christ and all Christians, and suffering for and giving oneself to others in a community ceaselessly assailed by the devil, the world, and conscience.

As with the first two tracts on the sacraments, Luther's tract on the Lord's Supper culminates in a discussion of faith as that which is needed to grasp the offered sacramental gift.[39] Faith is exercised by the hiddenness of the loving union conferred through the sacrament. God comes to human beings in and through a visible sign but uses the sacrament to train Christians to leave behind the visible, so that they will be ready for the death that completes their redemption:

[E]verything that is bound to time and sense must fall away, and we must learn to do without them, if we are to come to God. For this reason the mass and this sacrament are a sign by which we train and accustom ourselves to let go of all visible love, help, and comfort, and to trust in the invisible love, help, and support of Christ and his saints. For death takes away all the things that are seen and separates us from men and transient things. To meet it, we must, therefore, have the help of the things that are unseen and eternal. And these are indicated to us in the sacrament and sign, to which we cling by faith until we finally attain to them also with sight and senses.

Thus the sacrament is for us a ford, a bridge, a door, a ship, and a stretcher, by which and in which we pass from this world into eternal life. Therefore everything depends on faith. He who does not believe is like the man who is supposed to cross the sea, but who is so timid that he does not trust the ship; and so he must remain and never be saved . . . . This is the fruit of our dependence on the senses and of our untrained faith, which shrinks from the passage across the Jordan of death; and the devil too has a gruesome hand in it.[40]

If the sacrament cycle describes the consolation of the sacraments, its final point may be summarized thus: death ought to be joyous suffering, because it completes baptism's holy work of suffering by killing completely the old, self-trusting Adam. But to see and to bear God's manner of redemption under contraries, one needs the great grace of faith, by which one dares to surrender self-assertion, reason, and even sense perception, stepping onto a ship steered by only God. Christians obtain a new way of knowing, which refuses to listen to the mind or senses or instinct, even when these powers are at their sharpest, in suffering.

On Hope and Suffering (1520)

Thus far, we have seen that a "mystical element"[41] and direct mystical influence are detectable in Luther's sacrament cycle, particularly in how he describes the experience of salvation as a process of being killed and emptied of self-trust, which in turn opens the Christian up to an experience of union with Christ and the saints in the Lord's Supper. (In the sacrament cycle, Luther assumes that God works all this through the mediation of material elements; but he does not emphasize mediacy with the persistence that will come in the debate with Karlstadt, Müntzer, and Zwingli.) Joyful suffering is here a hallmark of Christian life, and it is possible because of faith's bond with Christ and trust that God works under contraries, even death itself. As Luther produced the sacrament cycle in the last months of 1519, he was also beginning a series of lectures on the Psalter for the second time in his relatively new teaching career. These lectures are known as his *Operationes in Psalmos*; lecturing as the process against him intensified, Luther reached the 22nd Psalm by 1521, until work was interrupted by his summons to Worms.[42] We cannot discuss this very long text at any length,[43] but we must pause to consider

Luther's "digression on hope and suffering," which explicitly engages what Luther calls "mystical theology," while mounting to his famous exclamation, "crux sola est nostra theologia!"—"the cross alone is our theology!" It is noteworthy that Luther's "digression" was translated into the vernacular and printed six times in 1524 and 1525, at the height of the Peasants' War and Luther's literary clash with Karlstadt and Müntzer. The printer Hans Lufft in Wittenberg also produced a vernacular translation of Luther's commentary on the entire Fifth Psalm (in which the digression appears); the title of that tract speaks to its context and purposes: *The Fifth Psalm of David, against the Hypocrites and False Prophets, On Hope and Doubt [Verzweyfellung]*.[44]

Luther's digression on hope and suffering occurred within his exegesis of Psalm 5:12, "Let all who hope in you be glad; they will rejoice eternally."[45] Luther here explicitly criticizes "mystical theology," associating the term not with the Eckhartian mysticism of the ground or with mystics like Bernard of Clairvaux and Jean Gerson, but with Pseudo-Dionysius.[46] For Luther, mystical theology in the manner of Dionysius was a damnable theology that sought union with the uncreated Word, without any mediation by the incarnate and crucified Word.[47] Luther aligned this mystical theology with medieval "scholasticism" as one more expression of human pride, self-assertion, and unwillingness to suffer the annihilation and poverty of spirit described so well by Tauler and the *German Theology*. He cites Tauler in defense of his views, using one strand of the mystical tradition against another.[48]

Luther undertakes his digression on hope, he says, for the benefit of "trembling, weak, and simple consciences."[49] As Luther sees it, the experience of suffering should increase faith, hope, and love, but human beings misunderstand how God works and end up in despair. Luther describes two affective errors destructive to hope: first, the desire for worldly goods; second, seeking "an abundance of good works and righteousness and salvation."[50] Luther is especially concerned with the latter of these two errors, which he regards as more dangerous because more subtle and self-deceptive. Confronted by unavoidable spiritual suffering, self-hatred, and terror of damnation in the face of sins, human beings seek a way out through their own works. This supposed escape reveals that they trust in themselves, rather than in the one sure object of hope and trust, God revealed in Christ.[51] The result of such misdirected trust is despair, which becomes evident especially at death, when the sinner finds nothing among his works in which he can hope.[52] The "just," however, live with equanimity in all goods and sufferings, whether they enjoy earthly benefits or suffer evils, whether they live well or sin. They neither presume in "spiritual goods," nor despair in sin, but cling to God who gives good and takes it away.[53]

Thus, suffering proves the reality of hope—that is, whether its foundation rests on God alone or oneself. Fallen human beings look to earthly prosperity or seemingly good works. God uses suffering to unmask the subtle self-deception of the wicked, bringing those who trust in their own merits into spiritual trials or even manifest sin, "that God might lead them to mercy against God's mercy and free them from sin through sin." The message of the cross is that all of God's work contradicts human reason and appearances.[54] Luther pursues here the claim of Hebrews 11:1 that hope rests in things unseen. If one hopes in, believes, or loves something that is seen or felt, one loves only a "carnal apparition," far removed from God. True faith, hope, and love exist only in relation to the "invisible, insensible, incomprehensible promise, which is revealed to one hearing by the word alone." Here again is the theology of the cross—God hidden in aural revelation, while reason and will strive for experiential confirmation. Faith, hope, and love accordingly represent the "most arduous, most bitter, most hard" way for "our flesh," because the "death [of the flesh] rules in these things."[55] In just this "death," however, true theology and the true theologian are born. While many write about "mystical" and "negative" theology, Luther asserts—invoking categories from Dionysius[56]—they do not write on the basis of the experience of death and hell, which are true negative theology, but only on the basis of their own self-exaltation. Negative theology is not about negating positive terms for God, as Dionysius thought, but about God's negation of the sinful self. Luther writes, "By living, or rather by dying and being damned one becomes a theologian, not by understanding, reading or speculating."[57] Luther later explains this dying and being damned as returning to nothingness, the origin of existence, and he even equates this return to deification;. Exegeting Psalm 115:11, "I said in my stupor, everyone is a liar," Luther writes:

The human being is indeed a human being, until he should become God, who alone is true. By participation in God the person is made true, when he clings to God in true faith and hope, having been reduced to nothing by this tribulation [*redactus hoc excessu in nihilum*]. Where indeed should he who hopes in God come, unless into his own nothingness [*sui nihilum*]? To where should he depart, who departs into nothing, except to him from whence he came? He comes from God and his own nothingness; wherefore whoever returns into nothing returns into God. Nor indeed is he who falls [*cadit*] outside himself and every creature able to fall also outside the hand of God, which embraces everything.[58]

The return to nothingness involves true self-knowledge and is a return to union, as in Eckhartian mysticism. For Luther, however, the annihilating self-knowledge is a recognition of sinfulness and self-trust, making possible union with God through faith in Christ. By becoming nothing, the soul attains union with God who is no-thing, but embraces everything.[59]

The error of those who suppose themselves to be mystical theologians is the presumption to ascend to God by their own intellectual and moral powers. These supposed mystical theologians are lumped together by Luther with the "scholastic theologians" who derive from Romans 5:3–5 ("Tribulation works patience, patience proof, proof hope; hope, however, does not confound") a definition of hope as "the certain expectation of reward coming forth from merits."[60] Such a definition, Luther criticizes, makes hope depend on human merit and thus can only result in "the ruin of all theology, ignorance of Christ and the cross and forgetfulness of God." Hope cannot come from any merits but must proceed from the destruction of all human merit. In turn, humans can bear such destruction only through hope as a gift of grace, infused along with faith.[61] However, the presence of faith, hope, and love is not recognized during trials, but only afterward, according to Luther: "Then indeed a person tastes how sweet the Lord is, and he begins to hunger and thirst to suffer more; this tribulation works greater hope. Wherefore it is necessary that faith, hope, and love are [present] in the beginning of every good work and suffering, and nevertheless that which had laid hidden becomes manifest after the work and suffering." Luther specifically references the teaching of Tauler, described here as a man of God ("homo dei"), and other experienced persons that God is never "more gracious, lovable, and sweet or familiar" than after the "proof [*probationem*] of trials."[62]

Allegorically interpreting the *Song of Songs*, Luther refers to Christ as a bridegroom who "afflicts his bride with pleasure contrary to the flesh, [but] always after the embraces. The embraces, indeed, are death and hell."[63] Suffering brings intimacy with God, through a terrible inward struggle, in which the Christian wrestles against God with no other support than God.[64] For Luther, this is the experience of salvation through death and hell—and true negative theology, which contradicts all self-exalting conceptions of ascent to or union with God, whether advanced in the schools or by false forms of negative or mystical theology. Luther's criticizes the presumption to earn salvation or ascend to union, as well as any claim that one can unite with the "invisible essence" of God apart from the Word and the incarnate Christ. Union is suffered, and it unites the sufferer to Christ and the incarnate Word through faith.

Luther redefines mystical union as an experience through faith that involves suffering and death for the self and its works; the "presence of God" is received under a contrary. In a similar manner, Luther redefines active and passive life. For Luther, the active life is not the useful but insufficient way of Martha versus Mary, but a sinful pursuit of hope through merits that needs to be "mortifie[d] and destroy[ed]" by the passive life. In this "suffering and being damned," the Christian is "conformed to the image and example of Christ"—the true imitation of Christ is received and not a matter of literal imitation, which does not experience forsakenness as Christ experienced.[65] Luther notes that Christ began with the active life, but his work "was completed through suffering, with all his works . . . reduced to nothing"; Christ experienced rejection by human beings and God. Thus, everything must be taken away from Christians, including merits (the "highest gifts of God"), so that they trust in God alone; the highest and hardest trial is "the removal of good works and good conscience in our life."[66] Luther charges his theological opponents with fearing nothing so much as "this cross of our merits." They interpret merits as works, while Paul teaches that merits truly are "tribulations, that is, mortifications and crosses of works." One vernacular edition of Luther's digression on hope and suffering offered the marginal annotation, "Schaden, wen man lyden flücht"—"the harm when one flees suffering."[67]

Thus Luther describes an experience of reduction to nothingness, especially through spiritual trials,[68] that alone can break human beings of their presumption to earn salvation through merits. The Christian thus annihilated and united to the Incarnate through faith becomes an instrument of God. "Stripped [exutus] of his own works" and purified by the suffering of faith, hope, and love, the Christian does good works freely, that is, without seeking reward and "from a spontaneous affect of pleasing God."[69] As in the German Theology, good and good works must not be appropriated by the self:

> Those who work good things in this way, work not for themselves but for God as an instrument; they arrogate nothing to themselves, but are content in God alone, in whom they hope. Those who do not work thus are apes of holy men. . . . Good works happen when God alone completely and entirely

does them in us. . . . Wherefore this should be your rule: where scripture teaches you to do a good work, you should understand that it forbids you to do a good work, because you are not able to do it, but you should sanctify the Sabbath to God; thus you should die and be buried and permit God to work in you. To this end, however, you will never come except through faith, hope, and love, that is, through mortification of yourself and all your works.[70]

Luther continued here to use the scholastic language of virtues, according to which the highest "theological" virtues (faith, hope, and love) were infused into the soul and became its *habitus*. Meritorious works were possible, in this view, because they sprung from infused virtue (*habitus*), particularly love (*caritas*). Luther argues, however, that theological virtues are God's work in the human person through the Word—divine work intimately experienced, but only in passivity and suffering due to human beings' innate self-love and self-trust. Faith, hope, and love are perfected only by "suffering divine work within," although the "works of other virtues" (e.g., prudence, temperance, fortitude, justice) are visible as the "fruits of faith, hope, and love." With respect to faith, hope, and love, it makes no sense to distinguish between an act and the habit from which it springs, for "in these divine virtues . . . there is nothing except suffering, rapture, and movement, by which soul is moved, formed, purged and impregnated by the Word of God." Luther describes how the soul is denuded and raptured—set outside of itself—by hearing God's promise of salvation:[71]

Finally, other virtues are exercised externally in coarse and corporeal things, but these [cardinal virtues are exercised] internally in the pure Word of God, by which the soul is seized and does not seize, that is, is stripped of its tunic and its shoes, of all things and phantasms, and is raptured through the Word (to which it clings, or rather, the Word takes hold of and leads the soul wondrously) "into solitude" (as Hosea 2[:14] says), into invisible things, into its bedroom, into the wine cellar (Song of Songs 2:4). But this being led and being raptured, this stripping wretchedly tortures the soul. It is indeed a steep slope and narrow way to leave behind all visible things, to be drawn out from all senses, to be brought away from accustomed things; finally, this is to die and to descend to hell. Indeed, the soul seems to itself to perish completely, while all things are taken away in which it stood and was occupied, and to which it clung; it touches neither earth nor heaven, feels neither itself nor God, saying (Song of Songs 5:8): Announce to my beloved, "because I am ill with love," as if it should say: I am reduced into nothing, and I know nothing, having entered into darkness and fog I see nothing; I live by faith, hope and love alone, and I am ill (that is, I suffer), "when indeed I am ill, then I am strong" (2 Cor. 12: 10).

To be led here the mystical theologians call "to enter into darkness," "to ascend above being and non being." Truly I do not know whether they understand themselves, if they attribute it [entering into darkness] to actions drawn forth and do not rather believe it to signify the sufferings of the cross, death and hell. The CROSS alone is our theology.[72]

The soul here no longer relies on the rational processing of its own sense perceptions and feelings but comes to understand and experience all things anew through relationship to God through Christ. It cannot rely on created things or itself, or even on the sort of sweet divine presence it hopes to experience, but only on faith alone in the God who works under contraries. Luther sees the soul's being reduced to nothingness or raptured into darkness as a necessary experience, and he criticizes so-called mystical theologians for obscuring the experience with enigmatic terms that finally seek to claim *unio mystica* as a human achievement—thus replacing true spiritual suffering and union with a fantasy. They seek the uncreated Word, while Christians must experience the forsakenness of the incarnate Word to trust in rescue through the incarnate Word.

In the inward works of faith, hope, and love, Luther writes, there is nothing of free will, but only "motion, rapture, and the leading of the Word of God along with a certain continual purgation and renewal of the mind and sense from day to day in the knowledge of God." This suffering and passivity varies in intensity, but "it is always suffering [*semper est passio*]." Luther applies to the human condition *coram deo* telling analogies: the vase that is polished and refined for the master's use; clay in the potter's hand; and the sword which truly moves, yet at another's behest. He thus argues that the will does not cooperate in its willing, "which is motion of the Word of God, mere suffering of the will."[73]

The polemical force of Luther's remarks here—directed against those who presumed to penetrate the mystery of God apart from the incarnate and spoken Word; those who imagined an intrinsic possession of faith, hope, and love; and those who wanted a more-than-instrumental participation of human beings in good works—identified the wellspring of false religion and

mystical theology in the refusal to suffer and be reduced to nothing, the refusal to enter life through death and burial, bearing "this cross of our merits."
Even those who claimed to follow "negative theology" or the "passive life"—
the contemplative way of Mary rather than the active way of Martha—were
hiding behind evasive terminology and claiming suffering, annihilation, and
union as human achievements of ascent to uncreatedness. True negative theology (Luther countered) experiences God's negation of the soul's presumption to self-movement. The legacy of Dionysius in medieval mysticism and
theology was rich and diverse, and Luther did not seek to give Dionysius a
fair shake in these pages; we should not fail to see that Luther himself positively appropriates the image of darkness to describe a life of faith in abnegation of reliance on the visible—on reason and sense perception. Our primary
goal, nonetheless, is to understand what Luther thought he needed to accomplish and how he went about that work. He criticized "mystical theology" as a
theology of obscurantism and pride, but precisely because this theology and
its practitioners, in his view, failed to understand the teachings about annihilation, union, and human instrumentality that Luther had found in Tauler
and the *German Theology* and married to his own, revolutionary argument
that salvation depends upon faith in and through the Word incarnate and
proclaimed. The false theologians imagined a sensible encounter with the
uncreated Word for themselves, the elite, missing the presence of God *sub
contrariis* amid the harder and more common road of faith.

Karlstadt, 1519–1520

We now turn to Karlstadt's public message in 1519 and 1520; in so doing,
we will see that Karlstadt no less than Luther received Eckhartian teachings
about annihilation of the self and union with God and employed these ideas
to marry suffering and truth; all the same, Karlstadt's distinct concerns and
goals are apparent, and his teaching centers on self-accusation and union
with God defined as sinking into God's will.

The Wagons (1519)

Shortly before the 1519 Leipzig Disputation between Luther and Karlstadt,
on the one side, and John Eck, on the other,[74] Karlstadt devised a piece of

visual propaganda to take the Wittenberg message to the broader public. Employing the technical and artistic skills of Lucas Cranach the Elder, he produced in March or April of that year a broadsheet depiction of two wagons, one leading to heaven via Christ and Christ's cross, the other to hell.[75] The choice posed to believers could not have been starker or more grave.[76] Karlstadt filled the image with fifty-three captions, many rhyming, and he promised that a German-language explication of the image and captions would appear soon, so that "each person may well determine what is necessary for every Christian to know" (Text Field 1).[77] Despite the jockeying for position that marked Luther's and Karlstadt's relationship to one another surrounding the Leipzig Disputation, Luther responded with approval to the project, noting in a letter to John Lang the offense that the broadsheet caused among "Leipzig theologians." They reacted, Luther wrote, "with astonishing savagery to Karlstadt's *Wagons*; one tore the image in the pulpit before all the people; another interrogated young people in confession about whether they had laughed over the image, and punished them for it."[78]

In the upper frame of the image, a pious Christian rides a wagon (from right to left) toward heaven, before which stands the image of Christ and the cross. The wagon is led by a smaller cross that reads "save me through your cross" (7) and is pulled by horses on which two figures sit, one representing Augustine, the other Paul.[79] The horses themselves depict fallen nature; they resist the journey and need to be whipped. The front pair tellingly turns aside at the exhortation held by Christ's left hand, "Take up your cross and follow me" (27).[80] The wagon image was inspired by Augustine's description of scripture as a wagon. On the side of the upper wagon, a rhyme—lost in translation here—tells us that "God's scripture is good and holy, and makes sin powerful; brings about transgression, wrath, and death; encloses all people in need; increases desire [i.e., to sin]; leads into disgrace; so that Christ is confessed as the only savior" (6, citing Paul and Augustine). Like Luther, Karlstadt learned from Augustine that God's law exposes sin and condemns Christians in order to lead them to grace and Christ.[81] Unlike Luther, Karlstadt is true to Augustine's understanding of the letter and the Spirit when he underlines in the subsequently published *Interpretation* that God's will received in scripture must be written by the Holy Spirit on human hearts.[82]

The central opposition between the two wagons is between yielding to the divine will and following self-will; a short caption next to the pious Christian recalls the Lord's Prayer, "Let your will happen," while an even shorter caption next to the damnation-bound monk reads, "Self-will" (3, 39). Set above the cross-led, cross-seeking Christian in the upper frame is the rhymed plea, "Lead me away from myself. When I look at myself, I am terrified. How gladly would I be alien to myself, if I rightly knew myself" (5), and numerous other captions in the upper frame commend self-accusation, for example, "I confess my evil, that is my righteousness" (21; also 4, 10, 28).[83] This salutary self-hatred is attributed to grace—"You have moved my conscience and placed it in severe distress [*hart b[e]dre[n]g*]; now be gracious to the one you have made sorrowful [*rewhig*]" (9)—as is the origin and execution of all good will and works (11; also 13, 17).[84] Karlstadt maintains that fallen nature is so completely corrupt that a person sins even against his will (14, citing Rom. 7:14) and has nothing that makes him just before God (19); further, "all good works on earth are praiseworthy and wicked" (23). The cross is the goal of the upper wagon, and it is the crucible that determines whether the Christian is yielded or self-willed, for the relevant captions on the cross enjoin love of God without self-interest, the avoidance of hypocrisy, and the willing endurance of persecution (24–25). The shaft of the cross reads, "Withstand the devil and the world; guard yourself from yourself, so that you remain without woe; always judge your weakness and life, so that you give God due honor" (28), while the foundation of the cross informs the viewer, "from the depth of God's righteous and strong [*starcken*] will comes the cross and the person with his works" (29).[85] As we saw in chapter 1, Karlstadt had glossed Tauler's teaching that all suffering is eternally foreordained by God, and the same view finds expression here. The question is how the Christian enabled by grace will respond. In Karlstadt's image, Christ stands by the cross, holding in his right hand the instruction, "Yield your will and self," and in his left, "take up your cross and follow me" (31, 27). Further captions identify Christ as "our peace" and "salvation," and say, "come, you sinners" (12, 26, 30). One warns, "Through cunning un-*Gelassenheit* [even] preachers of divine truth lie" (20).

In the lower frame, a portly monk-theologian[86] rides a wagon (from left to right) into the gaping jaws of hell; the lead horse is ridden by a figure caricaturing Saint George, and the wheels of the wagon are greased by a demon. The true grease is self-will, which drives this wagon (37, 39; also 45, 50, 52), just as the upper wagon is directed by God's will (18).[87] The majority of captions represent scholastic arguments attributing a role for the human will in salvation (35, 38); some contend that grace must complete what the will begins (32, 43) or the reverse (40), thus introducing a false modesty. One caption reduces God's help to a general grace—the Pelagian error (41)—while others deny the sinfulness of works done without faith or love (42, 46; related is 49). The injunction to earn grace by doing what is within oneself is singled out several times (33, 48), along with the claim that one's own reason and will can produce contrition (34). Scholastic reliance on Aristotle is reproached (47), as is allegedly evasive and selective exegetical argumentation (32). The caption on the lower wagon claims that reason learns through scripture what "is called good and evil" and that the will readily follows this knowledge; thus, the lower wagon represents a direct contrast to the teaching on the upper wagon that scripture increases sin so that Christ is recognized as the only redeemer. While the horses at the front of the upper wagon turn away from the cross, the horses on the lower wagon leap with abandon into hell; eternal suffering awaits those who will not suffer the cross now.

With his promised *Interpretation and Explanation* of the "Wagons," printed in May 1519, Karlstadt directed audiences above all to the image of the cross and the crucified;[88] indeed, the title promises to describe especially the cross "to which our God and Lord calls persons." The *Interpretation* argues at length that the heaven-bound Christian surrenders self and self-will to God's will, and that this *Gelassenheit* involves sorrow and self-accusation for sin, the acceptance of all other suffering as ordained by God, and working in conformity to God's will. "Our cross," Karlstadt begins, "consists of holy suffering and fruitful work, as well as to do and to omit everything as it pleases God. Thus no one should make this cross into an unliving wood or hard stone . . . Also no one should be lazy and neglectful about knowing and learning what his own cross involves."[89] Karlstadt understands suffering as God's pedagogy, and human beings must be diligent students; God prepares suffering and works for Christians from all eternity, and only by dying to self and taking up the cross as Christ enjoined do Christians become fruitful of works.[90] Christians grow into union with the divine will by condemning the self, and Karlstadt calls "judgement" of self the highest "work or exercise." No other work of devotion or mortification pleases God "unless it flows from the painful, anguishing, and oppressive judgment of our own sins and faults."[91] Karlstadt devotes the most ink in his interpretation to the five sayings adorning his cross image, beginning with "love God without [expectation of] reward." The *Interpretation* identifies Augustine as the source of the saying. Karlstadt explains that God is to be loved without seeking spiritual or corporeal reward, and that such love removes creaturely mediators between the soul and God; thus, there is an Augustine-inspired conception of immediacy. This love can only be had by the lowly, however, not by those "who delight to rule with God in eternity" or who expect to inherit a real kingdom. For Karlstadt, the Kingdom of God describes the Christian who presently is "small and despised" and wants "to continually come into genuine nothingness of [himself]."[92] This entering into the nothingness of self Karlstadt relates to obedience. Karlstadt writes, "Obedience is the kingdom of God, which we daily pray for," that is, in the Lord's Prayer.[93] Human nature, however, seeks "its own in all doing and yielding, in bitterness and sweetness." Thus, Christ now has his kingdom in the "chosen" only "in part" and "through the imposition of the cross."[94] The first cross must be self-accusation, or all other bitterness can be misappropriated by fallen nature.

Much like Luther, Karlstadt binds together accusation and hatred of self with living for God. One must believe that God can provide anything for which one asks, "and in order to have no doubt in that, it is necessary to measure your own poverty and incapacity." Here, Karlstadt refers to two eyes of the soul, one which "looks up into God's mercy and might, the other down into our poverty, affliction, misery, tribulation, suffering, sadness, care, need, anxiety, agony and terrible crying out to God." Those who feel the "sickness or smallness" of their faith amid this "affliction" should, Karlstadt advises, cry out, "O Lord help my unbelief" (Mark 9:24), and they should "hope against hope" (Rom. 4:18). The recognition of human failing is itself the gift of grace, and in self-accusation one should "not doubt in [God's] mercy, for to the believing all things are possible (Matthew 9)." Indeed, Christ always punishes lack of faith before he rescues the sinner.[95] For all his unique accents, Karlstadt was not unmoved by Luther's teaching that faith, as the gift of grace, should and can be without doubt—that despair of self should not be despair of salvation but rather the reverse.

The inner and outer (spiritual and visible) trials of the faithful are the subject of the exhortations, found on the cross beam, to guard against *Heuchlerei* (hypocrisy) and willingly endure persecution (25). In the *Interpretation*, Karlstadt describes *Heuchlerei* as the deceptively attractive opposite of *Gelassenheit*. Reflecting teachings of the *German* Theology, the reformer argues that hypocrites (*Heuchler*) find something good in themselves, whether in their doing or their suffering. Consequently, they pursue salvation through works and impose crosses on themselves without the necessary prior self-judgment. To proceed in this way is unyieldedness or presumption (*Annehmlichkeit*),[96] which flows from the assertion of the "the mine and the your" (*mein vnd dein . . . meinheit vnd deinheit / ich und du. Item vnserheit vnd icheit*) and is seldom recognized as sin. To ascribe all one's good works to God, conversely, is to become "yielded and let happen whatever God does with you according to his will. Thus your I, you, and mine decays and the blessed mine arises." Karlstadt here references the remark of Augustine, "where I am not, there I am more happy [*vbi non ego: ibi felicius ego*]" that he had inscribed on the inside cover of his copy of Tauler's sermons.[97] He warns readers against the "most capable theologians," who "teach that the person makes the substance of good works" (Caption 35 of the "Wagons"). The devil lies in wait for those who think they do holy works or fulfill God's commands. God, conversely, allows failings and sins in the chosen so that they do not fall into pride, but regard themselves as "useless and little servants."[98] Like Luther, Karlstadt recognizes both the "sweetness" of apparent good works to "cunning nature" and the anxiety that could result from seeking salvation through works—although Karlstadt explains each of these dangers as a result of separation from the divine will.[99] In judgment of self and fear of God, Karlstadt argues, the right hand of the sinner is nailed to the cross, while the left is nailed to the cross in the patient endurance of outward trials.[100]

In its exhortations to self-condemnation, the acceptance of eternally ordained crosses, and *Gelassenheit* as the solution to *Annehmlichkeit*, Karlstadt's *Interpretation* has strong resonances with the *Heidelberg Disputation* and the digression *On Hope and Suffering*. Karlstadt, meanwhile, offers a distinct but parallel account of union with God, emphasizing primarily growth toward union with the divine will over and against Luther's focus on growth in trust amid and through whatever trials God sends or permits. That said, both reformers saw human beings as fundamentally deceived by the "sweet" notion that they might be something before God and contribute something in exchange for their salvation; both thought this deceit had been advanced and buttressed by a scholastic theology of pride, which appealed to the pagan Aristotle, seeking to avoid necessary abnegation of self; both recognized that pride could also conceal itself underneath apparent humility, patient suffering, and self-imposed mortifications; both saw sin not merely as an act but as deeply sunk into human nature;[101] both saw God's imposition of the cross upon believers as the way God unmasks and breaks human pride, reducing human beings to a recognition of their true nothingness; both saw despair of self as the necessary prerequisite to hope in God. Beginning with self-condemnation given by grace—Karlstadt's *Urteil*, Luther's "cross of our merits"—Christian life was thereafter to be marked by the yielded endurance of unchosen sufferings.[102]

Like Luther in the 95th thesis, Karlstadt in the *Interpretation* and in the whole structure of the "Wagons" appropriates for the cause of reform the message of Paul and Barnabas in *Acts* 22: the kingdom of God is entered only "through trials." Nothing is "more terrifying and dangerous" than "to live without suffering [or] persecution," Karlstadt writes. In fact, because "God whips and punishes all his sons and beloved," Christians should desire God's scourges; yet they should never consider themselves worthy of punishment, because no one is worthy to be God's son. Finally, Karlstadt argues, Christians should embrace willingly not only persecution for the sake of Christ's name, but all suffering, even if it seems undeserved.[103]

For Karlstadt like Luther, suffering was both noetic problem and noetic solution. God's hiddenness under contraries—to use Luther's terminology—is confusing and painful for the Christian who suffers God's work. God seems wrathful. Consistent with his pedagogical understanding of God and of suffering, Karlstadt depicts the human suffering before God as a young child who does not understand his father's beating of him. The punishment seems "alien, step-fatherly, and unfavorable," yet as Isaiah 28:21 teaches, "God does all alien work for the sake of his own work, for vexation, trial, and tribulation give understanding and make us to perceive." Desperation is near to understanding, Karlstadt explains, and "it often happens that the person undergoing God's alien work is near to God and hears God rightly, although he experiences no hearing."[104] Indeed, Karlstadt argues, the experience of distance and separation from God found in the recognition of one's sinfulness is the worst suffering one can experience on earth—an experience of hell that brings one near to doubt about the grace of God. This near-doubt issues forth, however, in a cry for divine rescue that resists despair.[105] One should tremble to be without suffering, for the absence of trials produces pride and evil and marks those entrapped by the concupiscence of their own heart and by the devil. At the same time, the one who endures trials with patience must always turn back to self-condemnation (*Urteil*), lest suffering itself produce pride—a persistent concern for Karlstadt.[106] Here, Karlstadt explains how the gift of love of God opposes innate love of self:

> Love is not within our powers and capability, as many doctors [*cappen*] have written, but rather is a gift of God through the Holy Spirit poured into our hearts. The love of God is contrary to [*hat ein widerarth gege[n]*] our nature, for our nature desires its own [*das yr*] . . . But the love of God seeks not its own and leads the person beyond himself into the divine will [*vber*

sich in gotliche[n] willen], and is so powerful that much water cannot put it out [Song of Songs 8].[107]

Unlike Luther, Karlstadt in 1519 did not usually focus singularly on faith, but described numerous virtues involved in the Christian's relationship to God and Christ as sole redeemer *sola gratia*.[108] Here, he writes that the love of God belongs to every divine gift—to faith, hope, patience, humility, *Gelassenheit*, and *Urteil*.[109] Love of God and hence all virtue requires hatred of the self.[110]

Karlstadt's discussion of the sayings adorning his cross image concludes with an affirmation of predestination as the ground of salvation—a point visually underlined by the placement of the caption about predestination at the foot of the cross. The suffering through which God brings the Christian to knowledge and hatred of self, and knowledge and love of God, is ordained from all eternity, as is the fruitful work that God does in and through Christians.[111]

Outside of the captions surrounding the cross, Karlstadt discussed only a few other figures and sayings from the *Wagons* in his *Interpretation*. He describes the figure in the upper wagon as a "just sinner [*ein gerechten sunder*]" who does penance and takes up the cross with contrition, and against Eck, he denies that the sacrament of penance can take away "pain and punishment." The "sign and substance" of the sacrament rather "exhorts us to the fulfillment of Christian life and divine commands." The sacrament is to foster sorrow and self-accusation for sin.[112] Thus, Karlstadt continues the defense of Luther's *95 Theses* against Eck—the very defense that led to the Leipzig disputation in the first place.

Karlstadt also unfolds at some length the Augustinian point that scripture or the law—he does not consistently distinguish the two—exposes and increases sin and points the sorrowful, repentant Christian to Christ: "Scripture points and leads us into our own emptiness [*wustung*] and says, I am not able [to help you] further; if you don't want to remain unhelped, you must cry out to Christ."[113] As mentioned, for Karlstadt, in line with Augustine, the law ceases to be alien when it is written by God upon the heart.[114] God plants a "good will with fruit and roots" in the soul,[115] but God first terrifies the soul with its sins and lack of contrition, so that it knows its need:

God comes in his movement and pulverizes [the soul], that is, creates sorrow in a storm wind that comes from the fact that sin takes the upper hand and blows through the just sinner [*den gerechten sunder*] so swiftly that his spirit feels no sorrow and falls into the abyss of his nothingness [*abgrund seiner nichtikeit*], saying, "I stand in hell and believe not that God hears my cry." When therefore the soul seeks and finds not, it calls to the redeemer, but he does not answer. Blessed is the one for whom sin, through the law, becomes powerful to such a crushing extent.[116]

Karlstadt explicitly rejects any possibility that human beings can produce contrition or obedience to God's commands by their own natural powers. Instead, the "just sinner" must pray to God for "sorrow" and "suffering," as well as the accomplishment of every suffering and work ordained by God.[117] Even when God creates what God wills within the just sinner and moves him as God wills, the human is a "rusty, stained saw," who "pollutes" the good works that God "does through him." Thus, Karlstadt uses the same imagery for the Christian as a faulty instrument of God that Luther had used in the *Heidelberg Disputation*; for Karlstadt, the chief source of stain or rust was *Annehmlichkeit*, claiming the good done by God through the soul as one's own.[118] Every "good" or "holy" work is both "praiseworthy and punishable," for inevitably the love of God is incomplete even in the fulfillment of divine commands.[119]

Karlstadt uses a mystical anthropology reminiscent of Tauler and the *German Theology* to deride scholastic arguments for a human contribution to meritorious works as "wicked *Annehmlichkeit* and *Ungelassenheit*." Against such fundamental sin, human beings must attribute to God all good done in and through themselves. The removal of such good, in turn, reveals *Annehmlichkeit* and *Ungelassenheit*.[120] Nevertheless, only God can give the yielding and the confession of sins that together constitute a proper response to suffering, including persecution, death, martyrdom, and spiritual trials. Karlstadt finally declares that "unlearned, simple laypeople are of a higher understanding than the learned, confused theologians" with respect to human incapacity to do anything except through God's gifts.[121]

Thus, in 1519, Karlstadt counseled Christians to see suffering as a precious work of God to produce knowledge, judgment, and hatred of the self, on the one hand, and knowledge and love of God, on the other. For Karlstadt, Christian life and discernment began with self-accusation; thereafter, Christians were to yield to all suffering as ordained by God from eternity, and to be instruments in and through which God worked, shunning any claim to the good works done by God in and through the soul. Karlstadt did not follow Luther by relating faith and salvation to trust in God's promises; rather, he was already striving toward the view of complete self-abnegation and "sinking into God" as the all-defining but presently unreachable goal of Christian existence. That said, Karlstadt no less than Luther looked to suffering as that which gave Christians eyes to discern between true and false doctrines and ways of life; spiritual suffering unto annihilation of the self enabled the Christian to recognize God's mercy in God's alien work, and to judge doctrines and ways of life (e.g., monasticism) that concealed self-assertion under humility and self-imposed suffering. Karlstadt was particularly critical of any claim that human reason and will could recognize sin and produce contrition apart from grace.[122] For the passenger on the lower wagon, it was a smooth drive to hell, on well-oiled wheels, pulled by horses who needed no whip. Although Karlstadt's figure was a monk-theologian, the message applied to all: the choice to shun the cross of self-accusation and suffering would meet with no objection from one's nature, the world, or Satan.[123]

Missive on the Highest Virtue Gelassenheit (1520)

On June 15, 1520, Pope Leo X issued the bull *Exsurge Domine*, threatening Luther with excommunication if he did not recant; on September 21, Eck added Karlstadt's name to the bull, acting with papal permission. When the bull reached Wittenberg that October, Karlstadt's struggle to maintain his reverence for the papacy[124] along with his new theological convictions, including the authority of scripture alone, reached a head. Karlstadt presented his *Missive on Gelassenheit* as an explication to his mother, relatives, and friends of why he could not recant, despite their pleading on behalf of his temporal well-being and his duty to the pope. He also had a much larger audience in mind. The *Missive* was printed seven times between October 1520 and 1521,[125] spreading the message that Wittenberg was aligned with patient endurance of the cross and suffering—of God's will in all its contrariness to human will—while Rome was aligned with the shirking of the cross according to the desires of fallen nature. Indeed, the pope and his allies were depicted as demonic, scripturally ignorant persecutors of pious, suffering Christians.

More than in the *Interpretation and Explication*, Karlstadt in the *Missive* echoes Luther's definition of faith as trust in God's promises, received through hearing the Word; Karlstadt also now adopts the position that scripture alone is authoritative in matters of doctrine. Karlstadt's central claim might be called a mystical variant of sola scriptura: scripture as an expression of God's will cuts the believer away from earthly loves and attachments, including friends and family, and from all self-will; the commands of scripture are to be received with obedient *Gelassenheit*, despite the suffering that obedience brings upon the faithful in a hostile world. Eckhartian mystical terminology abounds as Karlstadt describes sinking or drowning in the divine will.

Karlstadt begins with an invocation to God describing his state of "deep anxiety" amid "sorrow, trials, and temptations," and his absence of any recourse but God. He is driven, he says, to God's "true and unchanging word," which promises "comfort" to Christians on the condition of faith: "You desire no more than for me to believe in you, to believe that you are my Creator, my help, my Redeemer from all evil, and my Savior." Faith is here depicted as the product of God's Word, which penetrates the heart—Karlstadt cites Romans 10:17, among many other texts—and gives a renewed life defined by exclusive trust, hope, and love toward God, as well as comfort in tribulation. Karlstadt claims that the threat of temporal harm is "nothing compared to the suffering my spirit must face when they [threaten] to take the word of your promise out of my heart and understanding."[126]

The *Missive* seeks to delineate a proper, Christian response to suffering. The "judgment of the world"—brought home to Karlstadt by his well-intentioned friends and family—counsels avoidance of suffering, and when avoidance fails, it yields to despair.[127] The Christian, however, accepts God's promise of presence even in seeming forsakenness, just as Christ expressed a sense of "abandonment" on the cross ("why have you forsaken me?"), while simultaneously committing his spirit to God ("into your hands I commit my spirit"). Christians look at the same suffering as everyone else, but see it differently. They see suffering through the lens of the remembrance of the passion, and they trust that God has ordained their suffering from eternity—per the caption that Karlstadt, in the "Wagons," placed at the foot of the cross. Karlstadt writes:

> [T]he word of God is true (when it says), "I am with you in sorrow and anguish, in pain and misery." Therefore, Christ in his suffering must ever be before my eyes and go ahead of me. Although God permits me to be beaten and ridiculed, boiled or roasted, broken on a wheel and torn to pieces, I know, nonetheless, that he is my God, that he is in control of my life and

my suffering, and that he is my redeemer.... And although he [God] should kill and murder me (as Job says), I will hope in him none the less.[128]

Karlstadt asks God to "avert his eyes" from those who mock and ridicule him, so that he might declare despite the world's judgment, "I trust in God's promise."[129]

Karlstadt reminds his mother, family, and friends that he must choose temporal death over eternal, just as he must choose the honor and "unerring word" of God in scripture rather than the word of an "unlearned pope."[130] Karlstadt must also resist his family and the "soft" path they recommend, which leads away from scripture:[131]

In this matter I know neither father nor mother. I follow divine Scripture alone—it cannot err; it cannot deceive me. Although I should have to endure shame, derision, poverty, and misery, I shall do so happily. I will willingly divest myself of my archdeaconate and all the goods which I have; renounce father and mother, brothers and sisters; surrender [gelassen] everything in body and soul which draws me away and distances me from divine promises. I know that I must be yielded [gelassen sein], and that I must let go [gelassen muß] of all creatures, and that I must not trust any angel who wishes to teach and bless me other than is delineated in the Bible [Gal. 1:8f.]. Everything which an angel from heaven teaches, other than what is contained in Holy Scripture, is an abomination, dreaded and hateful, worthy of excommunication and banning from God. Why then should I fall for a person who has not studied Holy Scripture much, when he wishes to teach me contrary to that which is written in Holy Scripture?[132]

The concept of yielding in the *Missive* involves, first, obedience to scripture alone as a revelation of God's will, and second, rejection of any attachment to self or creatures contrary to that obedience. According to Karlstadt, scripture is the sword promised by Christ in Matthew 10:34—the sword that separates "children from their parents, wives from their husbands, brothers from sisters, yes, the soul from the body." This same sword "places a person wholly and totally in the divine will [*hencket den menschen gar vnd gantz in gottlichen willen*], in love, hope, and faith, in such a way that neither derision nor need, neither sword nor danger, neither torture nor fire shall separate us from God." Christ is found in scripture "as if in a temple" and in the "yielded person," who becomes a "temple within which his word rings out." Karlstadt adds here that the sword of scripture also will "separate the pope from Christendom," and that the sword "must be accomplished with suffering, blood, and death."[133]

The *Missive* builds toward its conclusion as Karlstadt declares that he must "yield" not only others but himself:

> Yes, not only must I detach from [*gelassen*] you, but from myself as well.
> I must not claim [*nicht annhemen*] my own body and soul. I must wrong
> myself and be irksome and willingly face death. For Christ says, "Whoever
> does not take up his cross and follow me, is not worthy of me" [Lk. 14:27].
> The term cross means suffering, scorn, sneering, mockery, ridicule, death,
> and destruction. Yes, it means descending into the abyss of hell, yet in
> God's pleasure it also means that a kernel of grain must die unto Christ [Jn.
> 12: 24]. Now, since Christ says we must take up the cross and follow him, it
> is necessary that in the end we are fastened to the cross (i.e. to misery and
> pain). . . . . Everything within and around me must be yielded.[134]

Karlstadt accused himself here: he admitted that he did not long for martyrdom and that he would flee death until overtaken, although he was aware that God's will must be fulfilled "even though it may appear to me like bitter and acrid gall and puss."[135] Karlstadt oriented Christian life toward the perfection of union with God's will, but he used the goal to cultivate self-accusation rather than pride; his honesty about himself shaped his doctrine and piety deeply.

Here, as in the *Interpretation*, Karlstadt insists that yielding of the self in *odium sui* must precede any other suffering or work, if the latter are to occur without *Annehmlichkeit*:

> I know that there is no greater virtue on earth and in heaven than
> *Gelassenheit*. Even if someone forsakes all his goods, honor, friends, body
> and soul, even if I should burn in the midst of the flames, if I did not have
> *Gelassenheit*, my suffering would be useless (*undinlich*) to me, i.e. if I did
> not love God and place my trust, comfort, faith, and hope in him, I would
> be like a sounding bell [I Cor. 13:1]. Christ says, "No one has greater love
> than to give his life for his friends" [Jn. 3:1]. I have friends in Christ (whom
> the precious blood of Christ made). On their account I am to suffer (so that
> they might not decrease in God's word). No evil, fire, or death can happen

beneficially [*fruchtbarlich*] without divine love. The reason: Anyone who loves God aright seeks nothing other than God's honor in suffering and works, in sweetness and bitterness. But the one who places himself before his eyes and pursues his own glory, loves himself and not God, and does not serve God in any of his suffering or works. For this reason Paul says [I Cor. 13:2], "Although I believe in miracles so that mountains should move themselves into the sea on my word, but if I have no divine love *and hatred of myself*, my faith would be useless." Christ diligently admonishes us, saying, "Whoever wants to follow me, must deny himself, carry his cross daily, and follow me" [Lk. 9:23]. [Margin: *Gelassenheit* in suffering and works] Is it not a painful matter that I cannot accept [*annemen*] any suffering as if it were my own doing? If I desire to suffer something or carry a cross for God's sake, I must first deny [*vorleuchnen*] and forsake [*vorlassen*] myself. I must totally submerge [*vorsencken*] my own will in God's will and drown my self-will in all things. Hence, I must will as God wills. Therefore he places *Gelassenheit* ahead of works and suffering, even the person himself, saying, Whoever wants to come after me, must deny himself. [Margin: *Gelassenheit der person*] See and hear how works fall away from self-will. If you want to hear of suffering, note what he says about the cross.[136]

What had blinded wayward Christians for generation after generation was nature's desire to claim something for itself, even in suffering. Thus, while suffering and self-accusation were eye opening in Karlstadt's view, the danger of greater deceit and deeper *Annehmlichkeit* loomed, if the sufferer came to regard the cross as an accomplishment and possession of the self.

The only solution, for Karlstadt, was to regard the self as nothing and look to Christ:

Every created thing [*alle creatur*]—be it sweet or sour, sharp or mild—must be drawn out of my eyes. I must have no standing in my own eyes, but Christ alone. He alone is to be in my thoughts and before my eyes. In him and in nothing else, I must stand. Now I must deny all works, my suffering and death, yes, even myself, and must alienate myself from myself; neither mother nor friend, pope or pope's mother must dare make me put him or them before my eyes and cause me to depart from God's word. I would rather suffer tongs, torture, and the most gruesome death. Christ our Lord expressed how *Gelassenheit* ought to be [Lk. 14:33]. He said, "Whoever does not hate his soul, cannot be my disciple." I must develop a tough, serious, and rigorous hatred and envy against myself when I hear the voice of the Lord and note how my soul draws me away and blocks me.[137]

Luther and Karlstadt knew well the noetic problems of suffering for self-focused creatures. God's hard grace might be taken as wrath, just as human responses of apparent yieldedness—like the self-imposition of suffering—might deceive the self and others, concealing the presumption to be something before and earn reward from God. Between the poles of despair and pride, the only safe path was what Luther called the "way of nothingness." God alone set Christians on this safe way, demolishing self-regard, self-will, and self-trust, and redirecting the Christian's gaze from self to Christ—to the revelation of God's intention to save Christians in a manner offensive to human reason and emotion. For Karlstadt in the *Missive*, scripture is the sole place where God reveals God's will, and it serves as God's tool to teach and compel *Gelassenheit*, detaching Christians from regard for others and even their very selves. The goal of Christian existence is sinking into the divine will through complete self-abnegation; thus, Karlstadt alters I Corinthians 13:2 to refer to love of God and hatred of the self.

Luther at the Wartburg, 1521

In late 1520 and early 1521, the process against Luther came to a head. Having already identified the papacy as the anti-Christ, Luther in December 1520 burned the bull threatening his excommunication;[138] he was officially excommunicated on January 3, 1521, and summoned to appear before the Emperor at Worms on March 6. After refusing to recant on April 18, he was spirited away in early May and placed in protective custody at the Wartburg until March 1, 1522, when he returned to Wittenberg to reclaim authority over the reform movement there.[139]

Although Frederick the Wise ultimately did not surrender Luther, the monk turned reformer was nevertheless a vulnerable figure in the years between 1517 and 1522, and the possibility of execution loomed. This reality should not be forgotten as we investigate Luther's marriage of suffering to the reception and expression of true faith and teaching in these years. Likewise, we should not forget the scope of Luther's historical claim that centuries of Christian teaching and scholastic practice had been dead wrong—misguided by a sweet, subtle, and ever prevalent deceit—to the eternal peril of souls. Theology had to find a new starting point, Luther claimed, in God's contrariety to human reason and will; in turn, Christians' understanding and perception of the world had to be transformed to allow them to relate and respond to God and the world in new ways. Luther's return from the Wartburg to Wittenberg was a political move, yielding authority to the prince over and against the town council, in return for the prince's protection of evangelical reform against the emperor. But Luther had already been concerned with shaping Christians in ways that inevitably and thoroughly affected their actions as members of ecclesial and social-political bodies.

At the Wartburg, Luther undertook an ambitious project to shape evangelical preaching and hence, the beliefs, thoughts, perceptions, emotions, and actions of evangelical believers; he devoted particular attention to explaining how God works through suffering to destroy self-trust and give the faith necessary to understand and bear all suffering as God's alien work. Luther's *Postils* abound in references to the "nothingness" of human works; his continued interest in Tauler is evidenced by his request that Melanchthon purchase and send him a copy of the new, Basil edition of Tauler's sermons.[140] The Eckhartian influence—and a broader mystical influence—is even more pronounced in Luther's *The Magnificat Explained*, completed at the Wartburg a few months before Luther undertook the *Postils*.[141] *The Magnificat Explained* represents an extended reflection on how God reduces believers to nothing in order to create new life—and new perception—out of nothing. *The Magnificat Explained* appeared before the public fissure between Luther and Karlstadt in March 1522, and it is illuminating to read it alongside Karlstadt's *Missive*: in these two texts and others (e.g., Luther's excursus on hope and suffering), Luther and Karlstadt were drawing from the same spiritual wells; few contemporaries could have predicted the bitter divide about to ensue.

The Magnificat put into German and Explained

Luther began work on *The Magnificat put into German and Explained* in December 1520, the same month in which he burned the papal bull *Exsurge Domine*, but his progress was interrupted by the summons to Worms. He completed work in May or June of 1521, while in protective custody at the Wartburg, and *The Magnificat Explained* was printed first in August and a total of seven times in 1521.[142] The treatise is no less infused with mystical concepts and vocabulary than Karlstadt's *Missive*; indeed, while Karlstadt primarily explicates *Gelassenheit* and its opposite, *Annehmlichkeit*, Luther joins this opposition to an even broader array of mystical ideas and reorganizes them around the nexus of faith defined as trust. Primarily, Luther directs readers to discern God's work under contraries, building from the fundamental insight that God is always a God who creates *ex nihilo*. Thus, while human beings always look above themselves, God looks only into the depths to save those who are "nothing." To see where and how God works, Christians must undergo a transformation of their perception through the immediate instruction of the Holy Spirit. Luther writes:

> [W]e need to bear in mind that the Blessed Virgin Mary is speaking on the basis of her own experience, in which she was enlightened and instructed by the Holy Spirit. No one can correctly understand God or His Word unless he has received such understanding immediately [*on mittel*] from the Holy Spirit. But no one can receive it from the Holy Spirit without experiencing, proving, and feeling it. In such experience the Holy Spirit instructs us as in His own school, outside of which nothing is learned but empty words and prattle. When the holy virgin experienced what great things God was working in her despite her insignificance, lowliness, poverty, and inferiority, the Holy Spirit taught her this deep insight and wisdom, that God is the kind of Lord who does nothing but exalt those of low degree and put down the mighty from their thrones, in short, break what is whole and make whole what is broken.[143]

From direct experience, Mary learns God's two-fold manner of working [*creatio ex nihilo* and *reductio ad nihilum*]. Luther goes on to explain why this "deep insight and wisdom" cannot be learned otherwise—first, because creatures cannot create from nothing; and second, because sinful human beings will not look at their own nothingness or regard others who seem to be nothing. Luther's teaching is thus grounded in binary oppositions between (1) God's destructive and creative work; (2) divine and human power; and (3) divine and human perception.[144] With regard to God's *reductio ad nihilum*, Luther teaches that God's work through spiritual and visible suffering is salvific within and among the faithful; but God also punishes the wise, mighty, and rich—although they often seem to flourish in human eyes.

On the critical contrast between divine and human vision, Luther writes:

[God's] eyes look only into the depths, not to the heights ... and the farther one is beneath Him, the better He sees him. The eyes of the world and of men, on the contrary, look only above them and are lifted up with pride. ... Everyone strives after that which is above him, honor, power, wealth, knowledge, a life of ease, and whatever is lofty and great. ... On the other hand, no one is willing to look into the depths with their poverty, disgrace, squalor, misery, anguish. From these all turn away their eyes.[145]

Human misperception means that knowledge and an experience of God can only come through suffering—through experiences that reveal the creature's nothingness and God's regard for those who are nothing. Thus, God has "imposed death on us all and laid the cross of Christ together with countless sufferings and afflictions on His beloved children and Christians. ... He even lets us fall into sin, in order that He may look into the depths even more, bring help to many, ... show Himself a true Creator [i.e., one who creates "from nothing"], and thereby make Himself known and worthy of love and praise." Christ, who was "cast ... into the depths" and then most highly exalted, reveals God's manner of saving all God's children, although the "world with its proud eyes" does not want to accept it.[146]

For Luther, Mary's song in Luke 1 flowed from an experience of rapture, in which her soul both recognized its own nothingness and experienced the fullness of God's presence through faith in a "joyful suffering." This paradoxical, mystical experience is, according to Luther, accessible to anyone who will "trust in God with his [or her!] whole heart when he is in the depths and in sore straits." On Luke 1:46, "My soul magnifies [erhebt] God, the Lord," Luther writes:

These words express the strong ardor and exuberant joy with which all her mind and life are inwardly exalted in the Spirit. ... It is as if she said: "My life and all my senses float in the love and praise of God and in lofty pleasures, so that I am no longer mistress of myself ...." This is the experience of all those who are saturated with the divine sweetness and Spirit: they cannot find words to utter what they feel. For to praise the Lord with gladness is not a work of man; it is rather a joyful suffering [frolich leyden] and the work of God alone. It cannot be taught in words but must be learned in one's own experience. ... [The person who has trusted in the depths] will experience the work of God within himself and will thus attain to His sensible sweetness and through it to all knowledge and understanding.[147]

To experience God's "sweetness and Spirit" and hence to praise God is "joyful suffering"—not simply because the experience is received passively, but even more because fallen nature must be compelled by suffering to cling to God as the sole source of rescue, to receive rather than grasp salvation, and to trust that God is at work while enduring the painful contrariety of God's work to fallen nature.

Faith, for Luther, must trust in God even when the soul experiences no spiritual joy or divine presence whatsoever. Indeed, because Luther redefines union with God or the experience of God's presence as something that happens through faith, he concludes that this union or experience can be at its strongest when it is least felt—or not felt at all. The more implausible the promise seems, the greater the trust of the believer. Thus, as Luther recounts Mary's genuine spiritual experiences, he insists that she did not rely upon them:

> [Mary] clings only to God's goodness, which she neither sees nor feels, overlooks the good things she does feel, and neither takes pleasure nor seeks her own enjoyment in it. . . . [Her spirit] exults only in faith and rejoices not in the good things of God that she felt, but only in God, *whom she did not feel* and who is her Salvation, known by her in faith alone. Such are the true lowly, naked, hungry, and God-fearing spirits.[148]

The claim that Mary "did not feel" God appears to contradict Luther's earlier statement that "no one can receive it [understanding of God or the Word] from the Holy Spirit without experiencing, proving, and feeling it." Luther strives here to express the notion that faith grasps the inner reaches of the self while nonetheless clinging only to that which is *extra nos*; faith finds no resources in the empty, nothing self. Furthermore, faith trusts only in the unseen, because things present or promises fulfilled require no trust. Also operative here is Luther's pastoral purpose of teaching Christians how to trust in God and God's promises amid mundane experience, including experiences of suffering and divine absence. The *Magnificat* was to be the song of every Christian in daily life; for this to be possible, the manner of God's presence had to be correctly explained.

Faith's trust in and union with God even in suffering or the lack of spiritual experience is the chief theme of an anthropological excursus that Luther introduces on the basis of Mary's reference to her soul in verse 1:46. Luther here accepts—if only superficially—a three-fold anthropology of spirit, soul, and body, while arguing that all three are either turned "toward evil or the self . . ., or . . . are transformed by faith dwelling in the spirit." His key point is that reason (which operates on the level of soul in this scheme) must be ruled by faith, which finds its home in the spirit.[149] The spirit, however, is not an impregnable anthropological fortress, like the ground or the synteresis in medieval mystical literature;[150] rather, for Luther, the spirit is the locus of the struggle between reason, which wants to earn salvation and rejects suffering, and faith. Luther describes faith as a "brighter light" than reason, but also as "darkness," thus (implicitly) invoking Dionysius and Bonaventure, for whom union with God involved plunging into divine darkness.[151] Yet for Luther, this union means faith: "God dwells in the darkness of faith; for he (the Christian man) believes that which he neither sees nor feels nor comprehends. . . . [T]he spirit has nothing to do with things comprehensible." The battle, finally, is between trust in God and trust in one's self, works, and experiences. Luther warns that a Christian must abide in the depths of his or her soul, in darkness, when "false teachers" come to "lure the spirit out of doors" into the pursuit of holiness by "external works and rules." The reference is to monastic rules, in particular, as Luther goes on to criticize the "manifold sects and orders," each of which wanted to be holier than the others: they have no remaining perception of faith, Luther alleges.[152]

Two kinds of false spirits cannot sing the *Magnificat*, Luther says: those who are "unwilling to suffer oppression and be in the depths" and thus cannot come to God's proper works; and those who (more deceptively) "appropriate" God's gifts as their own and "regard themselves as better than others who have no such things."[153] The first false spirits regard temporal goods, the latter good works and spiritual consolations. The danger here is *Annehmlichkeit*, but Mary avoids it—and teaches the reader how to avoid it—by "regarding herself as unworthy." Consequently, she would have been yielded had God "withdrawn these blessings." Luther continues:

> So little did she lay claim to anything but left all of God's gifts freely in His hands [*Szo gantz und gar hat sie sich der aller nichts angenummen und got seine gutter frey, ledig und eigen gelassen*], being herself no more than a cheerful guest chamber and willing hostess for so great a Guest. Therefore she also kept all these things forever. That is to magnify God alone, to count only Him great and lay claim to nothing [*keynisz dings annemen*]. We see here how strong an incentive she had to fall into sin, so that it is no less a miracle that she refrained from pride and arrogance [*annehmung*] than that

she received the gifts she did. . . . She finds herself the Mother of God . . . and still remains so simple and so yielded [*einfeltig und gelassen*] that she does not think of any poor serving maid as beneath her. . . . What should we do if we possessed such great blessings? . . . . God lets us remain poor and hapless, because we cannot leave His tender gifts undefiled or keep an even mind . . . Mary's heart remains the same at all times; she lets God have His will with her [*lessit got ynn yhr wirckenn nach seinen willen*] and draws from it all only a good comfort, joy, and trust in God.[154]

The passage here relies, just like Karlstadt's *Missive*, on the opposition of *Gelassenheit* and *Annehmlichkeit*; for Luther, the wellspring of *Gelassenheit* is faith, which regards the unseen and the unfelt, and trusts God in the presence or absence of spiritual gifts. Such faith makes a pure lover of God, who no longer regards "das unszer" or "das yhre."[155] Likewise striking is the depiction of Mary as an empty space—a guest chamber—for God's work.

In the *Magnificat Explained*, Luther teaches both how to discern God's proper work underneath God's alien work and how to discern human pride underneath seemingly pious works, including self-imposed suffering and self-claimed humility. The latter concern takes center stage as Luther exegetes *Luke* 1:48, which he translates "He has regarded the nothingness of his handmaiden." He complains that the Vulgate's "humilitas" had usually been translated into German as "humility [*Demut*]," thus implying that Mary had boasted of an inherent quality of herself. "Humility" is indeed "the highest virtue [*die aller hochste tugend*]," Luther declares, using the same phrase Karlstadt had applied to *Gelassenheit* in his *Missive*. Like Karlstadt, Luther here shows his continuity with Tauler's conception of humility as a recognition of human nothingness necessary to sink into union with God.[156] Luther argues that "humility" in its scriptural usage is the state of the humiliated, of those who are "brought to nothing." The humble do not humble themselves or even know they are humble. Humility is rather a "disregarded, despised, and lowly estate, such as that of men who are poor, sick, hungry, thirsty, in prison, suffering, and dying. . . . Those are the depths of which we said . . . that God's eyes look only into them, but men's eyes only to the heights."[157] True humility is "a love and leaning to lowly and despised things," although many give the false appearance of humility while their "roguish eye [*yhr schalckhafftig auge*]" seeks only to be esteemed by others.[158] Both true and false humility are deceived; neither sees itself or correctly assesses God's judgment over the person.[159]

According to Luther, self-denial and self-mortification absent faith merely evidence false humility, underneath which lies the presumption that one is "worthy of salvation." God uses true suffering, over and against false self-imposed suffering, to turn Christians' eyes away from themselves and lofty things. "That is the purpose of the many sufferings, of death, and all manner of afflictions we have to bear on earth," Luther writes; "by means of the trouble and pain they cause us we are to pluck out the evil eye."[160] A self-imposed practice of humility cannot correct spiritual blindness or make one see by faith rather than reason. Luther teaches:

> It is in vain . . . to teach men to be humble by teaching them to set their eyes on lowly things, nor does anyone become proud by setting his eyes on lofty things. Not the things but our eyes must be changed, for we must spend our life here in the midst of things both lowly and lofty. It is our eye that must be plucked out. . . . [W]e should set our hope on His grace, concerned only lest we be not cheerful and contented enough in our low estate and lest our evil [falsch] eye be opened too wide and deceive us by secretly lusting after lofty things and satisfaction with the self, which is the death of humility. What profit is it to the damned that they are humbled to the lowest degree, since they are not willing and content to be where they are? Again, what harm is it to all angels that they are exalted to the highest degree, so long as they do not cling to their station with false desire.[161]

From the knowledge of how God creates *ex nihilo* in every soul "flows love and trust in God, by which we yield ourselves to Him and gladly obey Him."[162] As for Tauler, *Anfechtungen* produce self-knowledge of human nothingness, that is, humility; yet for Luther, the humble soul's discovery of God is a discovery of faith as a presence and work of the Holy Spirit directing the soul's gaze outward. Taulerian humility thus reinterpreted is, furthermore, not a preferred and higher way to salvation but the only way.

Following the progression of the *Magnificat* itself, Luther moves in his exposition of Luke 1:50 from a discussion of how God works in and for individuals to how God works in history, among different groups of people.[163] The two parts of the treatise are integrally related, for only those whose eyes have been changed by faith can see that God does not stand with the wise, the mighty, and the rich, but only with the "poor in spirit," the oppressed, and the impoverished.[164] Luther argues here that God periodically humiliates those who consider themselves something, and he insists that God would rescue the afflicted more readily and more often if their faith were only stronger. Nonetheless, Luther's primary point is that the eyes of faith must see that which is hidden to reasoned processing of sense perception—that God is actually on the side of the lowly, more specifically those "poor in spirit" whose faith and doctrine offends worldly wisdom.[165] Luther declares, "We do not know His proper works and therefore do not know Him, neither His mercy nor His arm. For He must and will be known by faith; hence our sense and our reason must close their eyes. This is the eye that offends us; therefore it must be plucked out and cast from us."[166]

The *Magnificat* commentary was written at the behest of a prince, John Frederick, who expressed anxiety about the passage, "He has brought down the powerful from their thrones"; often classified as a devotional or pastoral writing,[167] the treatise also seeks to caution powerful secular and ecclesial authorities, to inculcate hope and trust in God among the downtrodden (particularly those downtrodden on account of their faith profession), and to enjoin all to accept with yielding their divinely given lot and sufferings as training in faith. It is ironic that the message about accepting one's station found its champion in a man whose entrepreneurial father leased a mine and sent his son to university.[168] In any case, the instruction to yield to God's will in daily work and suffering and to embrace humiliation used mystical terminology—married to and transformed through Luther's revolutionary message about faith as trust—to give political counsel intended expressly for use outside the monastery.

For Luther, the true suffering that mortifies the old Adam was found in daily toil and life in the world, not on the cloister walk or the pilgrim's way. Thus, against much of the medieval tradition, Luther insists in the *Magnificat* commentary that Mary belonged to an impoverished family, albeit one with royal lineage, and that she was a simple milkmaid, who went about her daily work and was willing to be "despised" by others despite the great things that God had done for her.[169] Those who accept God's truth inevitably suffer shame, spite, and ridicule, Luther teaches;[170] they consider themselves worthy of nothing and "are glad to be naked and bare before God and the world."[171]

In relatively short space, then, Luther musters an array of mystical motifs in order to make the case both that faith is given through God's *reductio ad nihilum* and *creatio ex nihilo*, and that this faith transforms Christians' perception of and response to all suffering, allowing them to trust that God is at work under contraries. Luther's teaching applied to Christians' experiences of personal illness, loss, and struggle, but also to their view of God's involvement on the plane of ecclesial and political history—where God allows the wise, mighty, and powerful to afflict the "foolish," the oppressed, and the poor. In addition to the theme of *reductio ad nihilum*, Luther offers extended reflections on "humility" as the state of the "reduced," on the opposition of *Annehmlichkeit* and *Gelassenheit*, and on Mary (and by extension, all true Christians) as an empty space within which God dwells and works. He further equates trusting in God amid or after deep suffering to rapture and saturation with divine sweetness, describing the consequent praise of God as "joyful suffering"; he refers to faith as darkness within which God dwells and through which the believer is united to God; he talks of Mary or the Christian standing bare or naked (*blosse, ledig, nackt*) before the naked goodness of God;[172] and he claims that knowledge of God's manner of working in individuals and history can be gained only by direct experience—an experience that cannot be expressed or understood by those who have not had it. Luther would not have said his goal was to make mystics of ordinary Christians; but mystical motifs served Luther as he worked to teach Christians new ways of experiencing God and being in the world, arguing that salvation comes not through striving to be humble or appease God, but through being reduced to nothing by God. Accepting the Eckhartian caution toward self-imposed trials, Luther taught the Christian to embrace unchosen sufferings that were truly opposed to self-will and self-regard.

The Postils

I cannot offer here a complete study of Luther's Wartburg postils, which are replete with the themes discussed earlier.[173] Instead, I offer only a few references to show how Luther identified God's humiliation or reduction of sinners unto nothingness as a central theme that audiences needed to hear from the pulpit. Preaching was to proclaim the Word that creates faith *ex auditu*, but this very goal required that Christians learn to cease judging God's ways according to human reason and affect, as papal religion had allegedly done. Indeed, Christians needed to see by faith and not reason that true Christianity was found among the small, afflicted, seemingly foolish evangelical camp, rather than among the wise doctors, showy prelates, and powerful rulers aligned with Rome. Mystical teachings about annihilation unto nothingness, humility, and *Gelassenheit* thus found polemical use against "papists"; Luther was introducing preaching as a tool for the division of Christendom, although the primary target of such rhetoric was wayward clerics, monks, and scholastic theologians, rather than "papist" laity. Throughout, we should note, the postils are adamant—far more so than the *Magnificat* commentary—that humility is worked by God through the mediacy of the preached Word.

In the prefatory epistle to his postils, Luther declares that Matthew 23:12, "Whoever humbles himself will be exalted," states [the] "chief point of evangelical doctrine." Luther thus establishes humility as a key theme of the postils, throughout which he clarifies that humility is not a human achievement but a state into which Christians are driven by God, who teaches them the nothingness of their works.[174] In the preface, Luther points to Christ as an "example" of humility and being humiliated: "No one was ever so deeply humbled, no one diminished himself so very much, as Christ did."[175] Here again, Luther echoes the call for a true, passive *imitatio passionis*, centered on the inward self rather than outward exercises, although perhaps spurred by visible suffering. Luther also buttressed his own teaching authority by describing himself as a "despised and condemned person . . . under the pope's ban": "I hope that it is not unfitting for me to deal with this despised, small, insignificant book of the Gospel about the smallest and most despised Child of God and to abandon the high, great, lengthy books of the triple-crowned king at Rome."[176]

As he unfolded a preaching program in this polemical context, then, Luther wanted preachers to inculcate humiliation as a defining experience and humility as a defining state of evangelical Christians over and against the papal teaching of pride and reliance on works. People needed to know why they should believe evangelical doctrine and what evangelical faith felt like— and humility served Luther on both fronts, that is, as proof that the doctrine was divine rather than human and as experiential content of true faith. To make this claim on humility, however, Luther had to answer the objection that his teachings on certitude of salvation through Christ sowed damnable arrogance before God, telling Christians to regard themselves as "equal to the saints." The Roman church taught that salvation required intrinsic holiness. Accordingly, any claim to individual certitude involved a claim to unfailing perfection—a claim to sainthood.[177] Luther answered the objection to his doctrine of humility thus:

If you want to be a Christian, you must let these words be spoken to you, to you, to you, and cling to them and believe without any doubt that it will happen to you just as the words say. You must not consider it arrogance [*vormessenheytt*] that in this you are like the saints, but rather a most necessary humility and despair [*demut und vortzagung*]—not of God's grace but of yourself. . . . It would be arrogance if you wanted to be holy and saved through yourself and your own work, as the apostate papists are now teaching. . . . But when you dare to be holy in faith in Christ and through his coming, that is the true praise and glory of God, by which you confess, love, and praise [God's] work in you, and cast aside, scorn, and condemn yourself with your works, and despair of yourself. That is being a Christian. . . . If you want to be a part of the holy Christian Church and the communion of saints, then you must indeed be holy as the Church is, but not through yourself nor from yourself, but from Christ alone, from whom others are holy too.[178]

Luther here used both the humble acceptance of nothingness and the confident clinging to God's promise—complete despair of the self that rescues from despair of salvation—to draw a line between the evangelical and the "papist" camps. Crucially, Luther set the papists outside the true church, that is, the true community of believers. There was as yet no contest between competing ecclesial structures backed by political authorities; Luther who elsewhere sought to reform allegedly false doctrine here sought primarily to rescue Christians from allegedly false teachers. Still, his rhetoric served the division of Christendom into competing ecclesial bodies and offered criteria of suffering and faith to identify the true church.

Throughout the postils, Luther explains that despair of the self or humility comes only through trials: we learn, for example, that scripture "does not remove adversity, suffering, and death," but rather "foretells nothing but the holy cross . . . [W]hoever has not tasted suffering and dying can know nothing of the comfort of scripture."[179] Elsewhere, Luther declares that human beings cannot recognize the self-directed intentions of their supposed good works except through "much severe suffering, with all kinds of misfortune."[180] Luther prioritizes spiritual suffering—the inward humiliation, usually produced by outward preaching, that brings Christians to despair of their natural resources for earning salvation. Nevertheless, Luther assumes that all suffering can train receptive sufferers to trust in God rather than self.[181] Luther is also insistent that those who preach the way of humility can expect to be reviled and slaughtered like John the Baptist;[182] and he warns that the world makes life so unpleasant for all "godly persons"—the humiliated—that they inevitably "wish, cry out, and call for death and the last Day."[183]

Again and again, Luther returns to the question, "What makes a person a Christian?" and he locates the beginning of Christian existence in a despair of the self, brought on by hearing the message of one's nothingness. For example, in reference to Matthew 11:5, "The poor have the Gospel preached to them," Luther explains that the Gospel "has always been preached to the whole world," but it is received only by "those poor, brokenhearted ones who in the agony of their conscience seek and desire help and consolation"— that is, the "spiritually poor" or the "humble."[184] In his sermon on John 1:19–28, Luther declares that the office of John the Baptist, which is shared by all preachers, is "to humble all the world and proclaim that they are all sinners"—that their "work and life is nothing [*nichts*]." This means "to truly humble and cut out and reduce to nothing [*tzu nichte machen*] the presumption of all people."[185] Luther admonishes:

> Here you must learn well and understand spiritually what the way of the Lord is, how it is prepared, and what prevents Him from finding room in us. The way of the Lord . . . is that He does all things within us, so that all our works are not ours but His, which happens by faith. But the preparation does not consist in you making yourself worthy by praying, fasting, mortifying yourself, and your own works . . . Rather . . . it is a spiritual preparation, consisting in a thoroughgoing knowledge and confession of your being unfit, a sinner, poor, damned, and miserable, with all the works you can do.[186]

Luther here invokes the image of the soul as space that must be cleared, and of the human being as God's instrument, while underlining that these Eckhartian mystical ideals are realized in faith. Faith requires self-knowledge of one's wretchedness and nothingness; as Luther writes elsewhere, "you have to recognize and confess your inability, give up all hope in yourself, and thus humbled on this correct and true basis [*ynn rechtem grund und warheyt gedemutigt*], you can recognize that you are nothing and that you lead a godless, graceless, hopeless life. See, humiliation [*demutigung*] teaches you about grace appearing through the Gospel, and this humility makes you correctly desirous of grace and salvation [*gnadgyrig und heylsuchtig*]."[187]

Luther's descriptions of "humility" resemble Tauler's, but Luther relates humility to faith and sees both as created through the preached Word. To quote from the Sermon on Matthew 21:1–9 (First Sunday of Advent):

> Learn . . . what takes place when God begins to make us godly . . . There is no other beginning than that your King comes to you and begins to work in you . . . The Gospel must be . . . preached and heard. In it you hear and learn how all you do is nothing and that everything you do or begin is sin. Your King must first be in you and rule you. See, here is the beginning of your salvation. You relinquish your works and despair of yourself [*da lessistu fallen deyn werck und vortzagist an dyr selbs*], because you hear and see that all you do is sin and amounts to nothing . . . and you begin to receive your King.[188]

Luther's postils underline that God's humbling or humiliation of sinners is necessary to defeat the deepest human sin, pride understood as the desire to be something before God. In his Gospel sermon for Christmas day, Luther explained how Adam sought to claim God's glory as his own (*yhm selb tzugeeygent*), thus bringing "disgrace" upon himself and all his descendants. No "vice [*laster*]" is more deeply rooted in human nature than the seeking of honor, Luther declares: "no one wants to be nothing" and "from this comes all distress, strife, and war on earth." Christ, however, casts down and reduces to nothing human self-satisfaction and glory.[189] Christians who hear and experience this teaching "know to regard nothing as their own [*sie wissenn, das nichts yhr eygen ist*]," and as a result, they can have peace rather than strife with one another, and peace of heart whether they experience good or evil. In suffering, they do not complain but "stand beautifully yielded [*gelassen*] and willing in God's will."[190]

The postils divide the Christian world into those who have been humiliated and who bear crosses, and those who may put on such appearances but who are not truly Christian. If, as mentioned, Luther's polemic is aimed primarily at authorities, clerical and scholastic, the implications are clear enough for all people choosing sides (or declining to do so). In a sermon for the Sunday after Christmas, Luther adopted Abel and Cain as respective figures for those who are justified by faith and those who rely on works according to reason and who rage against God and true Christians. Scholastic doctrine is explicitly said to be the doctrine of Cain; its adherents are "Cain-saints," who do not have the faith that "makes a person small, even nothing, so that he must despair of all his works and only cling to God's grace." Indeed, with veiled pride, the Cain-saints claim to humble themselves. However, they know nothing of joyful obedience to God's law, but must be driven by a desire for pleasure or fear of punishment. Their reliance on themselves also can only produce anxiety and fear of suffering, and "they are afraid of the leaf of a tree" (Lev. 26:36). Hope in the self only produces despair of salvation. The Cain-saints cannot hear the Spirit in their heart interceding for them (Rom. 8:26) or bearing witness that they are children of God (Rom. 8:16), for such perception is awakened by "temptation and suffering." Luther acknowledges the nature of Cain in everyone: "Because we fear and flee the cross, . . . we never perceive the Spirit and remain under Cain." Indeed, for Luther, everyone is born a Cain and must become an Abel. However, papist doctrine hardens people as Cains who are unwilling to suffer humiliation within and fearful of the temptations and trials that attend earthly life. As the teacher, so the student: the people of Cain are "not Christians, but enemies and destroyers of all Christians and persecutors of the Christian faith."[191]

Concluding Remarks

The intention of Luther and Karlstadt to remake Christians from the ground up, reshaping how they perceived and responded to God's work and acted in ecclesial and political life, energized and animated a torrent of vernacular publication, beginning for Luther already in 1518 and for Karlstadt a year or two later. Both authors filled their publications with mystical motifs, particularly surrounding annihilation, yielding, humility, and union with Christ (Luther) or God's will (Karlstadt), driving home the message that God's manner of conferring salvation and God's will for Christian life contradicted painfully the thoughts and wishes of fallen human beings. In the perception and experience of such contradiction, however, lay the possibility for discerning truth and the truthfulness of one's relationship to God. Luther and Karlstadt expressed distinct views—Luther's centered on the destruction of self-trust so that faith might take root, Karlstadt's on the annihilation of self-will and growth in conformity to the divine will. Nevertheless, a shared paradigm of Christians as sufferers unto the (incomplete) abnegation of any self apart from God allowed for common cause, and sixteenth-century readers familiar with Luther's discussion of arrogance (*Annehmung*) and yielding in his *Magnificat* commentary could hardly have been offended by the opposition of *Gelassenheit* and *Annehmlichkeit* central to Karlstadt's *Missive* or to the annotations in the 1520 *German Theology* (see chapter 1). Luther's emphasis on the role of preaching and hearing in the postils would eventually distinguish his reformation and preaching program from Karlstadt's, but for now, both Luther and Karlstadt appeared as amicable friends of the cross, aligned against self-willed and persecuting papists.

For Luther and Karlstadt, suffering was both a noetic problem and a noetic solution. It was a noetic problem on the level of appearances—on the level of stimuli interpreted by the fallen mind according to fallen desire.[192] The reformers admitted that the godly suffer in ways that reason and affect regard as despicable, while the ungodly triumph or, even more deceptively, are adorned with seemingly holy, patient suffering. They also recognized that God's work through suffering might be misinterpreted by the recipient as pure wrath rather than grace. Accordingly, both sought to show how the Christian's perception was transformed through true suffering—through the suffering that leveled self-confidence or self-will, united the Christian to God, and made him or her into God's instrument. Neither good works nor true suffering flowed from the self, Luther and Karlstadt insisted, but from God's presence in and work through the soul. However holy the papists might appear, they invented or claimed their own works and suffering.

4

"Bring about . . . that I may become to myself like a bitter boil"

Self-Accusation and Sinking into the Divine Will in Karlstadt's Pamphlets, 1522–1524

> It is an indication and sign of God's eternal and constant will to ap-
> pear painful and bitter to our will. A Christian can understand by
> this which of God's wills comes to him. If it appears sweet and mild
> when united with our will, it is harmful to us.[1]

After his refusal to recant at the Diet of Worms in 1521, Luther was declared
an outlaw in the Holy Roman Empire.[2] Frederick the Wise protected his professor by arranging for Luther to be kidnapped as he journeyed home from
the Diet and to be placed in a safe, secret location—the Wartburg Castle.
During Luther's absence, his allies in Wittenberg worked to bring worship
and ecclesial and social life in the town in line with evangelical teachings.[3]
This "Wittenberg movement" was carried forward by figures in the local
church, university, and government; Andreas Bodenstein von Karlstadt,
Philip Melanchthon, Justus Jonas, Nicholas von Amsdorf, and Gabriel
Zwilling all had a hand in teaching evangelical doctrine, introducing reforms
to worship (sometimes without official sanction), and stirring up the support and unrest of citizens, students, and monks. Karlstadt, after initial con-
servatism regarding the pace and the process of reform,[4] moved to the fore
in December 1521 and January 1522 with two dramatic acts: he celebrated
an evangelical version of the mass in the city church on Christmas Day;[5]
and he married Anna von Mochau, becoming the most prominent cleric in
Wittenberg circles to marry up to that point. Equally consequential, Karlstadt
refused to toe the line when Luther returned to Wittenberg in March 1522

Enemies of the Cross. Vincent Evener, Oxford University Press (2021). © Oxford University Press.
DOI: 10.1093/oso/9780190073183.001.0001.

and condemned the Wittenberg movement for its alleged reliance on compulsion and return to works-righteousness.

Scholars have sometimes argued that Karlstadt and Luther at this time were divided mostly by practical positions on the pace of reform; serious theological rifts, the argument goes, emerged only after and in response to personal and strategic differences.[6] As we have seen, however, Karlstadt already upheld union with the divine will as the goal of Christian life, and he regarded *Gelassenheit* and self-accusation as necessary practices that carried Christians to this goal. The whole process was rooted in grace and predestination, and the Christian was oriented by Christ's exhortation to and example of yielding, self-denial, and cross-bearing. These theological and spiritual principles shaped his view of how a Christian community should implement reform: God's will, once rightly discerned in scripture, had to be implemented as much as possible and with as little delay as possible. For his part, Luther did not think God's will in scripture could be set aside for human convenience—although Karlstadt and Müntzer eventually attributed this position to Luther—but Luther married mystical ideas about union and yielding to his understanding of faith as trust in God's work under contraries. Consequently, Luther defined appropriate ecclesial-political action differently than Karlstadt or Müntzer, and he supported a course of reform that subjected currents of popular support to measured academic and princely leadership. This is not to deny that each reformer operated in constrained space, needing some authority to back their reform programs—Luther found the electoral court; Karlstadt the *Rat* and the *Gemeinde*. Müntzer failed in a bid to gain the princes' backing, and he could not maintain the enduring support of civic officials in Allstedt or Mühlhausen; he finally turned to the embittered masses.

From 1522 to 1524, Karlstadt unfolded a unique theology and reform program centered on God's inward pedagogy and on scriptural study. According to Karlstadt, this learning from God produced love of God and intense hatred of the self,[7] while impelling the learner as part of a Christian community to work to bring about God's will in that community—peaceably but accepting whatever suffering resulted from the offense of the spiritually weak or the politically powerful.[8] Karlstadt in these years imbibed still more deeply the teachings of the *German Theology* and Johannes Tauler—acquaintance with Heinrich Suso is also evident—and he produced treatises replete with Eckhartian mystical vocabulary and concepts (*Gelassenheit*; *Annehmlichkeit*; the *Grund*; *Vernichtung*; the effacing of the I, me, and mine). He explicitly commended the *German Theology* as a sort of text-book introduction to the "school of God." At the same time, he never shed a deep pessimism about how far individual human beings or human society could progress in holiness—his spirituality became an exercise in self-hate, striving toward a freedom from self-assertion that could be attained only after long, postmortem learning. Consequently, Karlstadt's ecclesial-political program proved more modest in its aspirations than Thomas Müntzer's. This chapter follows the development of Karlstadt's theology and reform program after the public break with Luther in 1522. Most important for our present purposes, we will see that Karlstadt depicted Luther and his Wittenberg allies as enemies of the cross, who refused to sink into God's will by accusing and denying their own will, and who thus preferred a practical reform program that did not arouse opposition. In many respects, this verdict mirrored the verdict against scholastic theology and so-called papists that Luther and Karlstadt shared.

Karlstadt and the Wittenberg Movement

The aggressive translation of evangelical theology and exegesis into concrete act and reality in Wittenberg began in the Augustinian cloister, spurred by the fiery preaching of Gabriel Zwilling. In October and November 1521, Melanchthon and Jonas also pushed aggressively for reform, even as Karlstadt argued that reform should be orderly, directed by legitimate, local authorities (specifically the *Rat*), and carried out with the broad consent of the *Gemeinde*.[9] Events of December 1521, however, dramatically unsettled the reform scene. First, in multiple incidents on December 3, 4, and 6, students and citizens interrupted masses in the city church and the Franciscan cloister, and they threatened to storm the latter.[10] Soon thereafter, citizens demanded the *Rat*'s concession to a series of reforms, submitting six articles that called "for free preaching, the abolition of various practices concerning the mass [including endowed private masses], communion in both kinds, and the abolition of taverns and whorehouses."[11] Reform henceforth would have to reckon with lay aspiration and self-assertion. A menacing and profane crowd interrupted services in both the parish and castle church on Christmas Eve. Just after Christmas, the arrival of the Zwickau prophets added claims of direct divine inspiration to the mix, further threatening the control over reform by academic, ecclesial, and magisterial officials. The prophets "proclaimed the imminent arrival of one whose spirit surpassed Luther," foretold upheaval in the world, and attacked the baptism of infants.[12]

Karlstadt's Christmas day mass responded to demands of the citizens and the stance of the *Rat* itself, to his own theological and spiritual focus on conformity to God's will, and to exegetical and theological conclusions about the Lord's Supper that he shared with other Wittenberg theologians like Melanchthon and Jonas.[13] It was not the first time that communion was distributed in both kinds in Wittenberg,[14] but Karlstadt's attempt at a truly evangelical rite raised excitement and alarm, especially as it occurred in the city church and as he drew large crowds of up to 2,000 people for subsequent celebrations.[15] On Christmas Day, Karlstadt preached first that faith and not prior sacramental reception made one worthy to receive; this faith was in the promises of forgiveness (associated with the cup) and resurrection (associated with the bread). He celebrated the mass without donning clerical vestments, he spoke the words of institution in the vernacular, and he did not elevate the host, signaling that the mass was not a sacrifice offered by priestly hands to God. He then placed both elements into the hands of the unconfessed. On the next day, Karlstadt traveled to Seegrehna with a flock of supporters, including Melanchthon and Jonas, to be engaged to fifteen-year-old Anna von Mochau. Karlstadt had written in favor of clerical marriage and the dissolution of monastic vows already in the summer of 1521.[16] His marriage to Anna occurred on January 19, 1522. A few days later, on January 24, the *Rat* enacted an order that had been drawn up in consultation with a university committee consisting of Karlstadt, Melanchthon, Jonas, Amsdorf, and Johann Eisermann. The order implemented an evangelical celebration of the mass in the city church, including communion in both kinds, and called for the removal of images and altars.[17] The order also sought to make Wittenberg into a truly Christian city by prohibiting begging by professional religious, students, and all able-bodied persons; creating a common chest to care for the poor who could not work; providing basic education to poor children and orphans, including girls; and banning usury and brothels.[18] When the *Rat* did not act immediately to remove images, citizens carried out iconoclasm at the city church in late January or early February.[19]

Through January 1522, Luther publicly and privately expressed his support for the reforms undertaken in Wittenberg.[20] At the same time, Luther cautioned against the introduction of new outward forms before Christians had been convinced of the falsity of the old,[21] and in December 1521, Luther sent Spalatin his cautionary treatise, *A Sincere Admonition to All Christians to Guard Against Insurrection and Rebellion.*[22] In January, Luther expressed support of Karlstadt's marriage, but in February, Luther wrote to the Elector about "Judases" within the reform camp. He explained that because Satan had failed to stamp out the newly revived Word by outside force, he now stirred up "false brethren" from within—deceivers whose arguments seduced with apparent rationality.[23] Returning to Wittenberg,[24] Luther delivered a series of sermons that both reestablished his personal leadership of the Wittenberg reformation and articulated a coherent stance against the execution of "outward" reforms before the people had been prepared by inward conversion.[25] While insisting that the preservation of true doctrine was absolutely necessary for human salvation and love of one's neighbor, Luther distinguished between "necessary" and "free" forms of worship and life. Private masses could have no place among true Christians, but Christians were free to marry or remain celibate, to use images or disregard them, choosing whatever best served their faith and love of neighbor. However, no form of worship or life—whether necessary or free—was to be imposed on others; such an imposition, Luther argued, would only create new laws, burden consciences, and deceive the newborn faithful into thinking that salvation depended on doing this or that, rather than on faith alone. Those with strong faith must put up with the elevation of the host or the use of images, knowing their salvation lies elsewhere. If they set aside Christian love and compel the weak, the latter will either be scandalized and reject the truth, or regard the new praxis as necessary to salvation. Luther offered himself as an example of the right approach: he had only preached the Word, and let the results follow according to its power and timetable. Reform should proceed through proclamation of the Word, through which the Spirit penetrates hearts and gives faith in Christ alone.[26] After Luther's return to Wittenberg, the mass was again celebrated with many of its traditional forms, although its sacramental character was repudiated. Communion in both kinds remained available for laity who felt themselves prepared. A vernacular liturgy was not introduced by Luther until 1525, however, at which time he deemed that the weak had been spared long enough.[27]

Karlstadt on Images and Prophetic Speech
(January–February 1522)

Just three days after the Wittenberg Ordinance was issued, Karlstadt published what remains one of his best-known tracts, *On the Removal of Images, and that there should be no beggars among Christians.*[28] With this treatise, Karlstadt sought to pressure the *Rat* into the speedy execution of its resolutions in these areas. Karlstadt argues that "divine and infallible Scripture" prohibits both images in churches and begging among the Christian community.[29] God prohibited images because human beings readily accept idols into their heart. Human beings are to worship God as "the one of whom there can be no image"; God is revealed in scripture, which does not create an image in the heart.[30] Karlstadt admitted that a love and fear of images had been instilled in him since his youth, but he did not realize his attachment until he read about it in God's word.[31] When an idol or image takes root in the heart, Karlstadt explains, the heart becomes divided between image-less God and created image, just like the physical space of church and altar is divided between God and the saints.[32] Karlstadt insists that "carnal" images cannot create the internal reality necessary for salvation. Those who promote the worship of images teach the laity only the "physical suffering of Christ," not "why he was hanged"; they teach the humanity of Christ but not the power without which "no one will be saved."[33] Salvation comes through the spiritual teaching of God's Word, per John 6:44, and by grace alone, rather than through carnal images. "No Christian can deny that spiritual prayer is a divine work which God alone effects . . . [and] no image ever can."[34]

Despite this stance, Karlstadt agrees that God, according to scripture, uses some "external admonitions or reminders" to bring people to salvation; he names suffering first and foremost:

> If I should ever want to have external admonitions or reminders, I would seek out those which Scripture suggests and not those which it hates and forbids. Thus I should much rather be subject to trial and anguish with horse and wagon than to come to an image . . . [Images] would be of some use if they were able to admonish us and lead us to God in the spirit of truth. Scripture, however, teaches us that tribulation does teach and admonish externally, causing us to know, call on, and worship God. It says, "Affliction and vexation give understanding," Isa. 28. "You punished me and I was

taught," Jer. 31:18. "God beats us and teaches us as a father his sons," Prov. 3:12; Heb. 12:5. "God wants us to cry to him in the day of our distress," Ps. [86:7][35]

The crux of the divine pedagogy described here is that it separates human beings both from a pseudo-knowledge of God derived from internalized images of created things rather than scripture, and from self-will and attachment to creatures, setting recipients in the knowledge and will of God. Karlstadt underlines the function of scripture as a sword,[36] and he enjoins the laity to learn about God and Christ there. Lay fathers are to teach their children from scripture.

The antipathy between God's word and human nature—and thus the need to mortify or renounce the latter in order to receive the former—likewise forms an important theme in a sermon on *Malachi* that Karlstadt published around the same time as *On the Removal of Images*.[37] Here Karlstadt's chief concern was prophetic speech. Prophetic speech provides the paradigm for the speech of the evangelical preacher, who speaks from a correct discernment of God's word in scripture.[38] The prophet, Karlstadt explains, is one in whom God creates a "new mouth," so that he becomes a divine mouthpiece; his proclamation is from God and not from himself. God must create speech without a human contribution, because God's word is above and contrary to human nature and reason. "God's word is alien to our natural mouth and above all assistance or cooperation of [human] nature," Karlstadt writes; indeed, God's word is "usually opposed and bitter" to nature. Karlstadt describes the prophet as a man for whom "the mouth is only an instrument, just as if God spoke his word through a hand . . . When we speak [God's word], we do no more than a water-rose when water flows through it." According to Karlstadt, those who hear God's word are to be instruments just like the prophet or preacher; they are to translate that word into speech and action, denying their own reason and will and enduring human opposition. "We have no authority to deal with God's word as we want," Karlstadt writes, even though the "pope, cardinals, bishops, priests, and monks appropriate authority to themselves, as if they should or may interpret and explain holy scripture however they want." They add or take away from God's word at will, against express biblical command.[39] Delivered and published before Luther's return to Wittenberg, Karlstadt's sermon on Malachi reflects already a key theme of his response to Luther's stance—God's word cannot be bent to human convenience.

Karlstadt conceives of the true prophet or preacher here as a practitioner of *Gelassenheit* who claims no ownership of the message: they declare that "their teaching is not their own, but God's." A preacher must acknowledge "that he can grasp and retain God's word neither through himself nor through other creatures, but that to know something of scripture stands purely in God's will. If they do that, they are an instrument or hand through which God proclaims his word."[40] God's internal pedagogy thus gives insight into God's will revealed in scripture; the chief characteristic of that will is that it separates human beings from self-will and their own reason, both of which are attached to creatures. Knowledge built on sense perception and fashioned according to human wants is thus set aside in favor of true knowledge of the divine will.

Self-Accusation and Union with God in Karlstadt's Sermon on Purgatory (Late 1522)

The events of spring 1522 demonstrated clearly that theologians and pastors in the Wittenberg circle would be subject to Luther's judgment and authority. Although singled out in the Invocavit sermons along with Karlstadt as teachers of error and inciters of "uproar," Zwilling and Jonas quickly reconciled to Luther. Conversely, Karlstadt maintained public silence, and in an expressly private letter to Hektor Pömer in March, Karlstadt accused Luther of self-contradiction, while expressing hope that God would turn the "good father" Luther from his error.[41] From Luther's perspective, Karlstadt's intentions were unclear but suspect. Karlstadt's preaching activity was restricted by the Elector's intervention,[42] and his publications were suppressed by a newly established board of censors at the University. A pause in Karlstadt's publishing activity lasted from May 1522 until January 1523,[43] when he published a sermon on the afterlife and purgatory he had preached on November 2, 1522, the day for the commemoration of souls.[44] Karlstadt's *Sermon on the State of the Christ-believing Souls, on Abraham's Bosom and the Purgatory of Departed Souls* intervened in an ongoing debate about the doctrine of purgatory in Wittenberg.[45] Late medieval theology and preaching described purgatory as a place where departed souls went to pay any penalty for their sins that remained at death,[46] but such a place made no sense if the necessity of payment was denied. Karlstadt's sermon represented a clear assertion of his own distinct theology and reform program. Grounded

in the teaching that Christians must accept God's inward spiritual pedagogy through self-accusation, self-denial, and turning from creatures,
Karlstadt's view of reform looked for the reordering of communal worship
and life according to the divine will, rightly discerned in scripture by the inwardly guided. The implication was clear: those who follow Luther's seductive arguments, sparing themselves and the "weak," refuse to suffer either the
learning of God's will or the consequences of life in conformity to that will in
a hostile world.

Karlstadt's *Sermon* reinterprets purgatory, arguing that Christians'
learning from God is a purgative experience and process, producing love of
God *and* hatred of self. According to the *Sermon*, this process begins during
earthly life and is completed after death. Departed souls go to a spiritual
purgatory, where they willingly undergo torment worked by ever-growing
knowledge of and incompletely satiated desire for God. In the first part of
the *Sermon*, Karlstadt uses the pericope, "Brothers, I do not want you to be
troubled like those who have no hope" (I Thess. 4:13), to counsel hearers not
to be anxious or seek costly intercessions on behalf of departed loved ones.
He notes as well that departed unbelievers are beyond help. The state of the
dead must be commended to God's will alone, with the prayer, "Your will be
done."[47]

In the second part of his *Sermon*, Karlstadt describes "what the dead
in Christ have, over which we should be joyful"—namely, that they are
transformed (*verwandelt*) into the nature of Christ more than Christians on
earth. Christ in John 6 teaches that those who consume his flesh and blood
will be transformed into his nature and life (*sein natur / art / lebe[n] weyss
vn[d] wesen*); this means, Karlstadt argues, that Christians' fallen nature and
life is "completely and utterly destroyed, and the life of Christ grows in its
place." By dying to themselves and living "for Christ's sake"—that is, con-
suming Christ spiritually—Christians "have the indwelling Spirit of Christ
in their hearts, which enlivens their souls and in the future will enliven also
their body." Human beings must "taste and feed upon Christ in the ground of
their soul," or their life remains "carnal, deceptive, [and] temporal," not "spiritual, true, and eternal." According to Karlstadt, the process of dying to temporal life and being transformed into eternal life—into a life like Christ's and
in communion with Christ—becomes "better and higher" after the death of
the body. There are then no more setbacks, nor lessening of growth.[48]

As Karlstadt's reference to the "ground of the soul" shows, the *Sermon*
substantially incorporates concepts from the Eckhartian mystical tradition.

Accordingly, when Karlstadt introduces his core distinction of three stages of eternal life, he invokes the *German Theology*'s argument that friendship and union with God requires accepting the divine light rather than the false natural light. Christian life here is conceived as a process of growing in knowledge of God and Christ, and the brightness of this knowledge corresponds to nighttime (earthly life), morning (postmortem purgation), and noon (bliss)—an analogy taken from Wessel Gansfort.[49] Karlstadt begins:

> Eternal life consists in this, that they know the true God alone and the sent Jesus Christ. John 17. This knowledge of God happens neither in reason nor in the false natural light, as when the doctors dispute over God, but in the ground of the soul, in the divine un-deceiving light, and it makes the person a friend of God, for it unites the soul to God the Lord, as Christ says, "I call you now my friends, for I have revealed to you the thing[s] which I have heard from my father." John 15.... Thus eternal life is a true knowing [*erkennen*] of God and Christ, which the Spirit alone infuses and teaches when it unites itself with the soul and becomes one thing.[50]

In the first stage during earthly life, God and Christ are known "in darkness and wonder [*wundern*] of the Lord." After death, the faithful departed recognize God as the rising sun. In heaven, God is "seen" as the sun at mid-day.[51] The agent of union is the Holy Spirit, who infuses the soul with love-rich knowledge of Christ and the Father, but only for those who receive knowledge from God rather than exercising discursive reason in the pursuit of partial and outward knowledge. The influence of Tauler and the *German Theology* is evident, yet Karlstadt has now relocated *unio mystica* to the afterlife, rather than confining it to the spiritual elite.

For Karlstadt, the soul on earth is held down by "darkness and hindrance," by the infirmities, vulnerabilities, and sufferings of the flesh. The soul cannot possess the "life of Christ" or the "Christ-formed life" in essence or reality, but "only in burning desire." It wants to seize the "will of Christ," and this burning desire hurts, for it comes with an intense awareness of absence of the desired life with God. Karlstadt writes that there are many more people who want "to die and live with Christ" than there are people who can truly say, "Christ lives in me." These souls feel "trapped in their flesh as in a prison," while they "sigh and yearn for another life without ceasing." For Karlstadt, there is no expectation of full union with God in the here and now; Christian life is defined by self-hatred and painful desire for God. The stronger the desire for heaven, the more intense the pain of exile. Indeed, the departed souls who see God as a morning sun are freed from bodily hindrances only to feel the spiritual "purifying fire" more intensely. Nonetheless, they would not want this flame of their "purgatory" to be cooled at the behest of the living.[52]

Karlstadt's *Sermon* seeks to offer assurance of the happy postmortem fate of the faithful, even as the reformer affirms the reality of continued, painful growth in knowledge and love of God after death. Declaring purgatory an un-scriptural doctrine, Karlstadt argues that only the damned go to the flames; believers are not "tortured through flames" and do not sit in "material fire." Like Lazarus in Luke 16, they rest in Abraham's bosom, "in a state of comfort and justice." Their fate is a reward for enduring God's rod, especially perse-cution for Christ's sake, before the demise of their bodies. Conversely, the damned suffer for eternity because they lived in comfort with the world.[53]

As Karlstadt elaborates on the life of souls departed in Christ, however, it is not the static comfort of the bosom of Abraham that dominates his depic-tion, but the continuing encounter of sinful souls with the burning divine word. Separated souls dispense with the distractions of embodied life, but they remain sinful in themselves, insufficient in their love and knowledge of God. Spoken in the heart or ground of such souls—Karlstadt uses the terms interchangeably—God's word is the same "fiercely spreading and red-glowing fire" that burned Jeremiah "so dry he could no longer bear it." God's word, Karlstadt continues,

> cuts through bone and mark and separates the spirit from the soul when it rises from God in the ground of the soul and the good field, for if it is accepted in faith, what is it other than the fire that Christ has sent, which will burn, Luke 12. It gives birth to longing, love, justice, wisdom, and newness of human beings; should it not then burn, ignite, sweep, and pu-rify? Accordingly, I might call a yearning and a consuming desire for God (which comes from the living word of God) a purgatory, and say that the burning and fiery desire for God consumes all wood, hay, and stubble in souls and purges weakness, rust, and infirmity.[54]

The souls of the departed cannot immediately see God because their eyes are impure, and they may still have works, thoughts, or a will that contain "hay or stubble." They need to grow in faith, love, and righteousness. They suffer because they desire to "see God with a pure eye" but cannot yet do so; thus, the souls "yearn and have bitter desire" for the beatific vision and thereby "stand in *Gelassenheit* and overwhelming tediousness [*geschwinder lanckweyligkait*]."[55]

There is no soaring rapture here, such as Luther attributed to the virgin Mary and to anyone who trusts in God in dire straits. Rather, rapturous union is delayed until the end, leaving earthly and postmortem life, morning and afternoon, to be defined by the practice of self-accusation. Returning to the theme of *reductio ad nihilum*, Karlstadt writes:

> If undoubtedly the fiery and fervent yearning for God is in us as a fire, it brings our own soul, the world, and everything that is worldly into a strenuous hatred and fierce envy and makes our powers, wisdom, desire and work to become as an enemy, whom we fear and always want to flee; and thus this yearning within us is a purgatory, which through envy and hate against our soul judges and reduces to nothing everything that is ours. But this fire is often dampened in our troubled lives and wages a constant war with our flesh; therefore it cannot be so hot as in the souls who have taken off their coat and clothing and sleep from all outwardness, although their heart watches and hears what the Spirit of God speaks and teaches in them. [Song of] Songs 5. And because of this they become a thousand times hotter in their yearning for God than us. Therefore I can call such a painful [*angstliche*] yearning for God in the soul a purgatory, although they are comforted and have a dear divine life.[56]

For Karlstadt, the middle stage of the afterlife becomes, in the tradition of mystical paradox, joyful suffering. Self-hatred and yearning for God are two sides of the same coin: they empty the soul, so that it is free for the Holy Spirit to enter; they plow and "rip open" the soul, so that it can be seeded and watered by God. The seed must fall in the ground and die to become fruitful.[57]

At the end of his sermon, Karlstadt asks about the fate of souls who die with little knowledge of God or Christ, and hence little judgment concerning themselves. Karlstadt concludes that such souls must "study and learn" after death, "if they are otherwise foreseen [*versehen*] to blessedness," and they must come to "know every true judgment or precept that God wants to have known."[58] Karlstadt asserts that the postmortem learning process is more painful for ignorant souls than for souls who struggled through the cross of divine learning, desire for God, and self-hatred on earth. Of the ignorant souls, he writes:

For them, one hour will be more miserable and harder than many years here, because they suffer or do everything without the hindrance of bodily misfortune, suffering, or working. Thus the spirit of sleep or of biting powerlessness [anmechtigkait], which one calls the spiritu[m] co[m] punctionis et extasis, attacks, stabs, and torments them in an incomparably harder way.[59]

A final exhortation admonishes those who do not want to suffer this pain to study and keep God's word diligently here and now.[60]

It was no mere happenstance that Karlstadt returned to public writing with a published sermon on purgatory. The Sermon guides readers into what Karlstadt viewed as true theology and devotion, which were to be centered on the study of God's will in scripture and on the exercise of self-accusation opening the soul up to God's inner pedagogy and love of God's will. The Sermon implicitly charges Luther and his allies with setting human will and the false light above the divine will and the true light. They were not willing, Karlstadt alleged, to suffer the receipt of God's inward pedagogy in detachment from their own reason and outward desires; accordingly, they could neither truly grasp God's will in scripture, nor bear the true cross by ordering their lives according to scripture. As a sword, scripture cuts away love of self and creatures, giving a new knowledge and a new love that is not derived from creatures. To receive knowledge of God and Christ from God is to receive eternal life through purgatory.

Karlstadt's Major Mystical Treatises of 1523: *Annehmlichkeit, Gelassenheit,* and Union

By the beginning of 1523, Karlstadt had turned against the vision of a scholar-led Reformation, and he argued that God's direct, inward pedagogy gives everyone access to the teachings (*Urteilen*) of scripture.[61] Thus, only a divine, inward calling and not academic training qualified a person for leadership in the church. Academic training and university life fostered and hardened pride, encouraging participants to seek glory for themselves. From Karlstadt's perspective, the Wittenberg reformation was tarnished by the same sort of self-exaltation and cross-shirking that had defined medieval scholasticism—riding the wagon to hell in Karlstadt's 1519 image.[62] Within a few months of publishing his *Sermon* on purgatory, Karlstadt issued in the spring of 1523 two of his longest, most detailed discussions of the nature of Christian salvation and life: *The Multiplicity of the Singular, Simple Will of God and What Sin Is* [*Von Mannigfaltigkeit*][63] and *What it Means to Say, "Yield Yourself," and What the Word Gelassenheit Means, and Where it is Found in Scripture* [*Was gesagt ist*].[64] These two treatises reflect Karlstadt's effort to distance his theology and reform program from Luther's, even as they draw from the shared well of Eckhartian mysticism and remain true to the Wittenberg loci of grace, Christ, and scripture alone.[65] At this time, Karlstadt was already making plans to take over the post of vicar in the small village of Orlamünde.

Karlstadt described himself on the cover pages of both *Von Manigfaltigkeit* and *Was gesagt ist* as "a new lay person." Thus, he signaled not merely his rejection of his academic and priestly vocation, but more broadly, a radical abolition of the cleric-lay distinction. Rather than declare everyone a priest, Karlstadt as an ex-priest declares himself "lay"—and more importantly, he then teaches others as a layperson. Behind these moves was Karlstadt's conviction that every person can and must search for God's will in scripture, with discernment, courage, and yielding enabled by and in the face of God's inner pedagogy. Karlstadt continued to use the categories of Eckhartian mysticism to describe the Christian as suffering self-hatred, growth in knowledge of and conformity to the divine will, and all the cross-bearing that came with life in conformity to God's will. Above all, *Von Mannigfaltigkeit* mobilizes concepts from the *German Theology* to answer the question that had preoccupied the annotator of the 1520 edition— What is sin (*Was Sünde sei*)? As argued in chapter 1, Karlstadt's study of the *German Theology* may have been guided by the relevant annotations, or he or a close ally may have produced them.

Von Mannigfaltigkeit

Von Mannigfaltigkeit begins with the statement, "people ask from time to time what sin is," and Karlstadt promises to relate answers from the "best teachers" and to show "through testimony of the Holy Spirit . . . that we should not speak of sin superficially nor treat it as insignificant"—a clear shot across the bow of Luther and his circle. Karlstadt's initial definition of sin is almost a direct quotation of the *German Theology*, referencing lines glossed by the 1520 annotator with the phrase, "What sin is."[66] Karlstadt writes, "Sin is nothing other than disobedience, being of a contrary will, another will, or a separate will [*ein wyder will ander will oder bey will*] which wills contrary to or other than God wills." Karlstadt elaborates by using the language of friendship with God, which as we saw in chapter 1, had been introduced into the *German Theology* primarily by later scribes. "Whoever desires to be a friend of God . . . must do God's will and live in keeping with the divine will."[67] Further definitions of sin just a few pages later likewise pick up on passages from the *German Theology* annotated with the words, "what sin is." Karlstadt renders the relevant definitions, "Sin is nothing other than not to will as God wills," and, "Sin is when the creature turns from the creator, or sin is a turning from the whole to the part. Sin is the disobedience which we show toward God."[68]

According to Karlstadt, Christ reveals to God's friends both the divine will itself and the expectation of union with that will even in suffering and death. Karlstadt describes this union in terms of a sinking or immersion of the created will into the divine.[69] For Karlstadt, a stance of receiving or accepting—underlined by repeated uses of the verb "annehmen"—defines the soul's relationship to God or creatures. The soul is open to and controlled by things outside the self, whether God's will or, through the intervention of self-will, creatures; knowledge and emotion follow the will and take their quality from its direction to God or creatures.[70] The soul's openness reaches to the ground itself. Thus, contrary to the view of the Eckhartian mystics, although tellingly in line with Luther's discussion of soul and spirit in the *Magnificat* commentary, Karlstadt does not conceive of an anthropological structure allowing for untroubled, unassailable union with God in earthly life. For Karlstadt, earthly life is instead defined by growth into union with God's will and the bitter experience of incomplete union. Union is attained only after postmortem purgation. On earth, creatures can still enter the ground—permitted by the will—and elicit the fear and love that should be reserved for God alone.

It is especially important to note Karlstadt's assertion that suffering embraced from a *wyder will*, *ander will*, or *bey will* in no way pleases God; thus, as for Luther, the appearance of suffering *always* marks truth, but the same appearance can *sometimes* conceal falsehood. Karlstadt's caution about appearances has in view monastic and penitential self-mortification: "Should you be self-willed and have a will other than God's, nothing in you is pleasing to God, even though you were to pray yourself to death, hunger and castigate yourself, and have a voice like that of an angel, give alms, be naked, and give your body into the fire to be burned." Christians "accomplish nothing" unless they attack and repent of their self-will.[71]

After defining sin as separation from the divine will, Karlstadt turns to the matter of how God's will is "revealed"[72]—he says through scripture and through the "example or advice of God-fearing persons"[73]—and of "how two wills may be experienced in God." He also notes that "God has an un-fathomable and wondrous will which no one is able to fathom but which is nonetheless always just and good." He complains about the trivialization of sin, of disobedience and self-seeking, which alienate from God, and without naming names, he makes the cutting observation that those who care little about deviation from God's will become enraged whenever someone speaks or acts against their own, refusing any society with the offender and calling him an enemy.[74] They also demand absolute obedience to parents or rulers—a plain reference to Luther—yet they have no regard for their heavenly Father and king, "from whom all fatherhood [and kingship] flows as from an abyss." Such people should know, says Karlstadt, "that they have been removed and ejected from God's eyes simply because of their disobedience from which all sins have sprung." They call others their enemy, but they themselves are ene-mies of God.[75]

In this polemical context, Karlstadt confronts the origin of evil, rooted in his view in the birth of self-will from the divine will. The problem, he writes, is that "we accept [annemen] and love 'the our' more than God," contrary to Matthew 10:37, "Whoever loves his father or mother more than me." We cannot love our own soul or person without the consequence of alienation from God, but such self-love happens "as soon as we think of ourselves in all we do or when we find our soul there." Self-hatred is the way to salvation. Karlstadt cites Luke 14:26:

> Christ said, "Whoever wants to come after me and does not hate father, mother, brother and sister and his own soul, too, which means himself, cannot be my disciple" . . . But one who engages in such self-hate is a dis-ciple [leerjung] of Christ. This hatred is a total dying [absterben] to our self-will. Since Christ compares such hatred of self to a kernel that falls into the ground and dies and then bears fruit, Jn. 12:24, then, if the soul falls and dies to itself completely, it will yield divine fruit which shall remain forever. This is the ingrafting into the good vine which is Christ. Anyone whom the heavenly father implants into his beloved Son lets go of his self-will com-pletely and takes unto himself [nympt an sich] the full life, growth, and fruit

bearing, in line with the nature and quality of Christ [to] whom no creature in heaven or earth [has been] equal and who had thoroughly died to his own will, seeking God's will alone. . . . [In Matthew 12:49, Christ's words amount to saying,] I am a vine and all who remain in me, i.e., who totally die to self-will as I died, and intend and seek God's will alone, are my disciples and my friends and the kernel which not only fell into the ground but also died. Those whose total life is tribulation and cross, and who hate their soul and themselves, are my disciples.[76]

Karlstadt anticipated Luther's likely response here, putting in the mouth of an unnamed objector the words, "I would truly have to despair then," for even Paul confessed that he had not "die[d] to his own will." Karlstadt's counter insists on the necessity of despairing of oneself, a point Luther had underlined constantly in writings up to that point, for example in his *Postils*. Karlstadt explains, "I would very much like you to despair of all creatures and of yourself so that your life be to you as it is to a bedridden sick person . . . He actually feels the cross." Invoking Augustine's favored analogy to describe the work of God's law apart from the Spirit, Karlstadt argues that the sick sinner is thus driven to Christ as the doctor, crying out with Paul, "Who will redeem me from this body of death?" Christ is the "fulfillment of the law, a repayer and vindicator of all deficiencies," and through faith in Christ, there is certitude of salvation: "If we believe in him and that he was sent for us, we are certain and sure that he places our sin upon himself and pays the ransom for which he was sent by the Father." Yet Karlstadt dwells far less than Luther on the certitude of salvation available through trust in Christ, instead underlining the insufficiency of rebirth—defined in terms of surrender of self-will and acceptance of the divine—and the consequent necessity of self-accusation and pleading for Christ's assistance.[77] For Karlstadt (like Luther) the danger of presumption in good works was of central concern, and Karlstadt argues here that God allows Christians' sinful flesh to remain strong so that they avoid the worst presumption or *Annehmlichkeit*, claiming God's goodness and works for the self.[78] There is, then, rich overlap between the views of Karlstadt and Luther, but Karlstadt's focus on self-accusation and sinking into the divine will impelled him to a differing assessment of outward sin, particularly in matters of ritual, over and against Luther's emphasis on trust despite appearances.

Karlstadt traced the trivialization of sin among his infra-Reformation opponents to the belief that God was responsible for evil—a matter that had been debated within Wittenberg theological circles during the earliest years of the Reformation.[79] Karlstadt caricatures the position he intends to criticize as holding that God as omnipotent wills human sinning; thus, "sin is good in God's sight." At stake was Karlstadt's definition of sin—sin cannot be to will apart God, if God wills sin—as well as his spirituality of self-accusation and his argument for ordering worship and life according to the divine will revealed in scripture. Approaching the topic through the form of a scholastic *Quaestio*, Karlstadt has a speaker state first the position that will be repudiated, namely, that there is no distinction between God's "eternal and temporal will or between God's constant [*bestendigem*] and his permissive will [*verhencklichem*]."[80] In short, God directly and actively works sin. In the role of the scholastic master, Karlstadt replies that God "allowed" the fall of Adam because "righteousness is more clearly known in its opposite," but God's permission does not mean that sin is "good in God's sight" or happens "according to [God's] eternal will." Karlstadt offers the distinction that "[sin] is not good as it is or as it happens, but for a different reason." He thus maintains his definition of sin. However, when Karlstadt (in line with scholastic method) turns to answer the original objections, he makes a concession that undermines the entire argument—that is, he argues that God's permissive will is "an effective power [*ein wirkende krafft*],"[81] which "must be fulfilled" or "bring its work into reality." Nonetheless, "everything that creatures do or leave undone through this permissive will is contrary to the eternal, divine will." Karlstadt offers the persecution of Christians as an example, describing the Christian in terms of the *German Theology* as a "deified servant of God."[82] The permissive will, he concludes accordingly, may be called "the hardening will of God" or the "wrathful will," while "the eternal, enduring will may be called a merciful will." Ultimately, the reformer concludes that the distinction between the two wills consists only in the human perception of contradictory effects. God's will is truly one.[83] How a single will can have "two contradictory effects" is beyond reason, Karlstadt admits. He declares, "I will leave [it] to God. . . . I believe whatever I cannot grasp through reason."[84]

Critical to the separation Karlstadt sought to create between his own and Luther's positions was the argument that God's "eternal will is a will contrary to ours, or at least above our own will and nature." Conversely, the "wrathful or permissive will" merely "inclines the human heart to its own affairs," while the permissive will is "after our own heart and adapts to the desires of our nature," as Romans 1:24 says, "God has given them to immorality through the desires of their hearts."[85] These reflections mirror positions expressed in two adjacent annotations in the 1520 *German Theology:* "The person has no free will but rather self-will [*eyn aygen willenn*]" and "God's will and the human will are opposed to one another [*wydder eynander*]."[86] The former remark seeks to locate sin in willing apart from God, without rejecting the Augustinian and Wittenberg doctrine of the bondage of the will. Self-will in Karlstadt's view bound the human to love of self and creatures.

As Karlstadt in *Von Mannigfaltigkeit* airs this subtle, intra-Reformation debate over God's responsibility for evil,[87] he scolds his opponents for their reliance on reason[88]—thus making the very same charge that Wittenberg reformers as a group liked to level against scholastic theology. Karlstadt also complains severely about those who regard disobedience toward God as a small matter compared to dissent from their own learned opinions or dis-obedience toward earthly rulers. Through these paths, Karlstadt arrives at the critical truth-question, "How to discern the merciful and constant will of God?" The plausibility of his views on soteriology and reform—both of which focused on conformity to God's will—hung on the answer to this question. Here, Karlstadt penned the lines quoted at the beginning of this chapter. Human beings must believe and do and "accept [*annehmen*]" what-ever is "painful and bitter" to their nature and will. Whatever is "sweet and mild when united to our will . . . is harmful to us." Thus, the Christian is to pray to become obedient to God as an instrument. Karlstadt formulates such a prayer as follows:[89]

"O Lord, my God, your gracious will be done that I may become your kingdom and you my king; that I become your earth and you my creator who creates justice and mercy in his earth, Jer. 9, that I become in myself small and nothing and you in me great and everything. . . . Bring about that I do not find pleasure in myself but in you alone and that without you I am afraid and feel ill, with a hellish pain driving me to live, work, rest, sleep, suffer, and die for you alone. And that all which is mine—my wisdom, riches, and power—be to me like green poison and yellow pus and that I may become to myself like a bitter boil, so abominable in my own eyes as to desire to flee myself." Whoever does not hold himself as a cross, does not experience God's will; but if he desires that within him his lusts and desires fall away and [if he desires] to become a terrifying enemy to himself, he has a good desire, and shall not cease to pray to God with eternal sighs, that he yield himself, along with all his desires, as something for which he has bitter abomination and which he would gladly spit out. For "the our" must perish and disappear, so God's will in us may happen, rise and rule. As Christ said, "Not as I will, but as you will." And he teaches us to pray, "our father, your will come about."[90]

The passage is replete with Karlstadt's spirituality of self-accusation and conformity to the divine will, expressed through Eckhartian themes about recognizing human nothingness, shedding the "our," and surrendering the self. Through self-hatred as part of *Gelassenheit*, the soul is to become an empty space awaiting divine filling—soil awaiting divine planting. The human will does not choose God's will, but God's will sprouts in the ground of the death of the self-will. The self is a called a "cross," but it is even more something to be crucified. Kindred teachings in the *German Theology* had been glossed with lines like "God's will and human will are opposed," "The life of Christ is opposed to all nature," and "The life of Christ is a cross to nature."[91]

For Karlstadt, assurance of salvation, right willing, and right action rests on the anguish caused by growing in conformity with the divine will over and against all self-will. When Christians pray the Lord's prayer, they pray, "Father, make your will real within us—the eternal and merciful will which is contrary to our will and which drives out the lusts of our own will."[92] This divine work cannot be understood by human intellectual resources, but must be tasted (suffered) in the mortification of human desire: "We cannot discern the eternal will through reason, but through our senses, and we must taste, discover, and confess that God's eternal will does not happen within us without bitterness and the agony of the cross. Thus it is not possible for us to retain our natural desires and will and to receive God's eternal will."[93] Whatever is believed, taught, or carried out by Christians can be evaluated for its conformity to truth according to whether it vexes nature, in which case it represents God's eternal and merciful will, or pleases nature, in which case it was introduced by nature through God's permissive or wrathful will. The merciful will must be created alienly and directly by God, whereas the permissive or wrathful will has a toehold in nature.[94] The eternal will of God demands an exclusive love and fear of God, which takes no comfort in and fears no offence of creatures.[95]

Karlstadt finally distinguishes in a scholastic manner the "temporal" will of God from the wrathful and permissive,[96] and he maps these varied distinctions of the divine wills—or rather, varied perceptions of the singular divine will—onto a distinction between what is known from outside the self and God's truth revealed within. While God's wrathful will binds us to the fear of creatures and God's temporal will institutes signs like circumcision and baptism to point to inward realities, only God's eternal will, given directly within the soul, unites us to God. Karlstadt writes, "God's eternal will is not rooted in any external exercise or physical devotion—all that may be false and deceitful. It does not become true in us until God works his eternal will in human works which means that he brings us to will what God wills and to accomplish the divine work."[97] The renunciation of self-will and sinking into God's will secures the soul against the danger of outward dispersion into multiplicity and deception. Thus the soul is rescued from misdirected *Annehmlichkeit*. Karlstadt writes, in a passage that resonates strongly with descriptions of unio mystica in the *German Theology*:[98]

> The inner being must remain forever and simply in the singular, eternal will of God and must concern itself with it at all times. The external being, by contrast, hovers in its physical motion—now up, now down, now to this side, then to the other. Now it is embittered, then sweet; now it is joyful, then in sorrow; now at work, then at rest; now in life, then in death; now in heaven, then in hell. And although there are thousands of these happenings, they are drawn into a unity, nonetheless. Whenever we merge and are absorbed into the divine will [*gantz . . . in go[e]tlichem willen versmeltz vnnd verloren*], hell becomes heaven for us. The eternal will of God, when accepted with one's whole heart, turns hell into heaven and death into life. It brings about that we desire and want to have God's will alone, and that we hold to and respect God's will alone. In the contrary case, all things become to us like nothing: fire, sword, death, and hell become in our eyes like nothing . . .[99] We are like ships, drifting about in the blustering dangers of the sea, being tossed to and fro without perishing, because all the while we are anchored and the anchor is firmly grounded. So, a person who is without will is not harmed by anything, however evil it may be, as long as we are anchored and the anchor is sunk into God's eternal will. The anchor is to die and to totally abnegate all creatureliness [*absterben vnd gantz entwerden allen creature[n]*] through the faith that is like a mustard seed. The earth or rock on which the anchor is fastened is God's eternal will which brought humankind into being.[100]

Anchoring or sinking into the eternal will of God offers the only stability possible for the vulnerable human creatures Karlstadt describes—creatures who accept all life and knowledge from outside themselves and thus enter into a bondage of love with either God (through inner divine instruction received without self-will) or creatures (through self-willed rational processing of sense perception). Union with God's will, in turn, turns the experience of death and hell into heaven. Karlstadt reflects the Eckhartian heritage in his final goal—not simply conformity with the divine will, but a state of will-lessness.

Yet Karlstadt adopts this exalted language of annihilation of the will and union with God alongside a profound pessimism about human spiritual and moral capacity. Consequently, he argues that rebirth and union in the here and now are experienced only through suffering—through self-hatred and the bearing of crosses. Whereas Luther had redefined union with God around the Christian's faith in Christ *extra nos*, Karlstadt maintained traditional Eckhartian terms for union, while delaying any substantial attainment until the afterlife—indeed, even then union took time—in line with Reformation understandings of the severity and perdurance of sin. There is less of a transformation than a relocation of unio mystica.[101] For Karlstadt, finally, Luther and his cohort went astray because they refused to suffer God's will and work in self-hatred and self-accusation; thus, they trivialized sin and were more concerned about the offense of earthly rulers and parents than the offense of God, the source of all rule and parenthood.

Was gesagt ist

In his treatise on *Gelassenheit* (*Was gesagt ist*), Karlstadt again lambasted the scholars' concern for receiving honor and glory from human beings; no less than the Roman clergy, their attachment to creatures disqualified them from leading the church. All sides failed to recognize "God's glory and our shame, . . . God's something and being . . . [and] our nothingness."[102] The dedicatory epistle to *Was gesagt ist* presents the tract as a response to a series of questions posed to Karlstadt by Jörg Schenck of Schlesingen. Having read the *German Theology*, Schenck inquired about the "meaning and origin" of the terms *gelassen* and *Gelassenheit*,[103] about why Karlstadt had called *Gelassenheit* the "highest virtue" in his *Missive*, and about the seeming contradiction in the Lord's prayer between the phrase, "your will be done," which only the yielded can pray, and the plea, "do not lead us into temptation," which appears to want to preempt the divine will.[104] In response, Karlstadt defines *Gelassenheit* as a separation from creaturely attachments—whether based on love, trust, fear, or another emotion—and from one's own soul. Reflecting a passage from Suso, Karlstadt argues that *Gelassenheit* requires the yielding of every level of human being, from the nature shared with every creature, to reason, and ultimately distinct personality or selfhood. Scripture itself must be yielded, Karlstadt teaches, for it is a created thing.[105] Karlstadt also repeatedly warns about the appropriation (*Annehmlichkeit*) of spiritual gifts,[106] of suffering, and of *Gelassenheit* itself as subtle and deceptive dangers to the yielded life.[107] The goal is a union with God described in terms of spiritual marriage,[108] the return of the soul to its uncreated nothingness,[109] or finally, the sinking of the created will into the divine will.[110] Through this sinking, the self is recast as a Christ-formed self, who does not will in separation from the divine.[111]

If sinking into God's will is the goal and *Gelassenheit* the means, however, the latter defines Christian life not as an attained state but as an exercise in self-accusation and self-hatred:

> I should wish . . . to be nailed to a cruel, shameful cross and to have a holy dread of myself and to become wholly ashamed of my thoughts, desires, and works as of a horrible vice, which I would avoid as one avoids a yellow, pussy boil. To see nothing in my soul and powers but my inability to do good and . . . my capacity for and inclination towards everything evil, punishable, dissolute, and shameful . . . [W]hatever is good and praiseworthy, I ought to carry to its origin, attributing it freely and wholly to the one alone who created and gave it.[112]

Karlstadt's ideal of Christian life involves an ascetic emphasis on daily exercise, and the chief exercise is learning to detest the self—to "know human malady and call increasingly on God's grace." For the Christ-formed ego, anything that diverts him from the "acceptance of God's will" becomes a martyrdom and daily cross.[113] The influence of Eckhartian mysticism is profound—hence the orientation around *Gelassenheit* and union—but just as profound are the consequences of Karlstadt's break with Eckhartian mysticism: namely that he makes union a goal both universally binding and presently unachievable.

The theme of divine pedagogy appears prominently when Karlstadt describes *Gelassenheit* as an experience that "prepares the soul for the study of divine matters." This *Gelassenheit* is not an attained state, but an exercise of self-accusation, which Karlstadt describes as the beginning of Christian life.[114] It makes the soul an "apprentice or disciple" or "student" of Christ. Such *Gelassenheit* is beyond human powers and created by grace alone, Karlstadt underlines.[115]

Wittenberg humanists at this time celebrated the image of the suffering scholar, who renounced material comfort and was willing to endure exile for his pursuit of the truth.[116] Karlstadt directly attacks this ideal in *Was gesagt ist*, describing it as a human accomplishment that merely despises one created thing (wealth) for another (the "wisdom of this world"). One must despise instead all created things for the sake of God or Christ.[117] For Karlstadt, the school of Christ is entirely opposed to nature, reason and will. He states:

> Note, how bitter and harsh the school of Christ is, and what a frightful, pitiable thing it is to our intellect, will, and nature. Note also that Christ was right in saying, "Whoever does not carry his cross and follow me cannot be my disciple," Lk. 14:27. . . . Christ teaches that yieldedness [*gelassenheit*], which surrenders everything, is a daily cross that we must carry without standing still. Rather, we must follow Christ and be where Christ is in will, thought, love, desire, [and] suffering at the right hand of God. And all that is ours must be fused in God's eternal will and *become nothing.*[118]

Karlstadt goes so far as to say that *Gelassenheit* must last eternally—the self-will must be so completely denied that only God's will remains. During earthly life, *Gelassenheit* as daily exercise involves an inner self-hatred and self-denial nourished by encountering another will in scripture and executing that will amid suffering.[119] For Karlstadt, the Wittenberg reformation was failing to lead people into hatred of sin and the removal of ritual and social transgressions abominable to God.[120] Luther approached scripture with an intact self-will, just as the papists had done, and he cloaked disobedience to God under seemingly pious regard for the weak or obedience to parents or earthly rulers. The problem was not the doctrine of salvation by faith, grace, and Christ alone, but Luther's failure to accept that God's work in giving faith, love, and fear of God entailed death to the Christian's self-will—a failure to acknowledge the nothingness of the self and to suffer God's manner of giving salvation. Thus, Karlstadt's verdict against Luther resembled the verdict that he and Luther together—in common if separate dialogue with Eckhartian mysticism—continued to share against scholastic theology and the "papists." To the question of how we might characterize Karlstadt's theology at this point in his career, it is vital to recognize that themes of *Gelassenheit*, union, and rebirth associated with mystical and Augustinian traditions found their place in his works next to strong convictions about the human incapacity to attain—or indeed receive—the goals except in nascence, in the exercise of self-accusation. *Gelassenheit* was less a state than an activity undertaken by the disciple of Christ and student of God's inner pedagogy. Just as for Luther, for Karlstadt apparent good works and holiness remained the prime enemy of salvation, leading would-be Christians to lodge hope in the self rather than God. The holiest lifestyle contrived by human reason was, after all, easier than accepting what God had in mind.[121]

Karlstadt in Orlamünde and in Open Confrontation with Luther, Late 1523–1524

In the summer of 1523, Karlstadt left Wittenberg to assume the pastorate in Orlamünde, a move he had held in view from the time shortly after Luther's return to Wittenberg.[122] He initially lived as a peasant, as "Neighbor Andrew," seeking to earn his own bread.[123] In the December 1523 tract, *Reasons Why Andreas Carlstadt Remained Silent for a Time and On the True, Un-deceitful [unbetrüglicher] Calling* (henceforth, *Reasons*), he references a personal spiritual crisis concerning his authority to teach. Nonetheless, Karlstadt soon found in Orlamünde the opportunity to carry out reform on his own terms— to purify worship according to scripture and to grant the community fuller participation in that worship. Images were removed from the church, and the community adopted an evangelical celebration of the Lord's Supper with communion in both kinds. Karlstadt recited the liturgy in the vernacular and translated psalms for congregational singing. Above all, Karlstadt encouraged the congregation to read scripture for themselves and to debate it publicly. Karlstadt also ended infant baptism, believing that a baptizand should be able to confess his or her faith[124]—a position Müntzer, too, expressed in his December 1523 *Protestation*. In March 1524, however, amid a climate of rising peasant unrest in Saxony, the University of Wittenberg and the All Saints' Chapter recalled Karlstadt. In accordance with the wishes of the Elector, the aim of this move was to bring Karlstadt under tighter control and to separate him from his press at Jena. Karlstadt responded by resigning his posts in Wittenberg.[125]

Luther's visitation to East Thuringia from August 21–25, 1524, brought to a head both the personal animosity between Karlstadt and Luther, and the broader clash at play between the course of reform at Orlamünde, which empowered the laity and the local government via the *Rat*, and Luther's vision of reform directed by scholars and prince (the *Landesherr*). Secretly attending a sermon given by Luther at Jena on the 22nd, Karlstadt felt himself unfairly associated with Müntzer and rebellion. He insisted through messengers on a personal meeting with Luther, which became heated and ended with Luther challenging Karlstadt to publish his opinion. After the meeting, Luther reluctantly traveled to Orlamünde, on the invitation of the *Rat*, and found there a self-assertive community willing to challenge his own interpretation of scripture. According to a partisan but plausible account, Luther left Orlamünde enraged;[126] shortly thereafter, on September 18, 1524, Karlstadt was expelled from electoral Saxony, along with his allies Martin Reinhart and Gerhard Westerburg. In 1525, Anna Karlstadt was expelled for refusing to baptize the couple's son.[127]

The period from late 1523 to the end of 1524 was one of remarkable theological creativity and publishing productivity for Karlsadt. He produced many treatises on the Lord's Supper,[128] while also continuing to address underlying questions surrounding sin and salvation, especially the matter of human responsibility for evil and good. In the remainder of this chapter, my purpose is only to show how Karlstadt, over and against Luther, aligned his own theology, spirituality, and reform program with true suffering—with readiness to endure both bitter self-hatred and self-accusation in order learn and unite with God's will, and the hatred and persecution of others in order to obey God's will. To this end, I discuss first Karlstadt's understanding of the calling and vocation of ministers—a topic he had addressed in the published sermon on Malachi—and second, his continued debate with Luther over to what extent reforms of worship and communal life should be delayed or moderated out of "regard for the weak." I then turn, third, to the teachings that Karlstadt developed on faith and salvation just before events cut short his independent theological publication. Finally, fourth, I discuss the place of mystical motifs and ideas about suffering in one of Karlstadt's treatises on the Lord's Supper.

Suffering and True Calling

After his major tracts on God's will and *Gelassenheit* in the spring of 1523, Karlstadt did not publish again until December, when *Reasons* came off the presses.[129] Presenting himself as a minister duly called by the Orlamünders,[130] Karlstadt reports in this treatise that some in the congregation had accused him of laziness and leaving the "better work of teaching" in favor of "outward bodily labor." Karlstadt intends to convince these brothers with sufficient reasons and scriptural testimony that "no external testimony (such as writing and preaching the truth) can take place without some risk and without grave temptation of the Spirit of God."[131] Karlstadt also addresses a broader audience, seeking to justify his long literary silence. He notes that he cannot respond to the enemies who surround him and God's "Israel" (i.e., Orlamünde) without "rankness," which is to the detriment of the growth of Christian love.[132] Even more, he argues, no one should preach, write, or testify unless he discerns with certitude God's "will and command" through an inward call. A human call is insufficient and possibly "nothing" before God or even "against God." One may offend God as the prophets of Jeremiah 23, who ran without being sent. One should not and cannot testify to Christ until God's Spirit gives that testimony.[133] Karlstadt accepted the authority of congregations to call their own ministers. Consequently, he now imposed on congregations the necessity of discerning the divine, inward call of candidates. Such discernment was to be sought through prayer for God's inward guidance and if necessary, through lots. Above all, Karlstadt insists that the people must not follow their own "will and intention," which are prone to deception. He assures his readers that God will point earnest and inspired seekers to true "shepherds who have suffered or tasted the spirit of Christ."[134] Inward suffering in the receipt of God's pedagogy qualifies the minister as someone ready to proclaim God's word and will rather than human will.

Karlstadt confesses that he does not feel God's inward call[135]—thus he is personally unqualified to teach—but he then adds another cause for silence that would have left every pulpit empty: "God's word is pure and upright, and only those who are upright and pure—not the unclean—are to handle it." Paul himself did not claim such purity, Karlstadt notes. Precisely through this line of thought, however, Karlstadt finds a divine warrant to teach publicly. He lays aside the question of inward inspiration and argues that teaching is a God-sent cross, which must be endured according to God's will rather than one's own. This cross is not an experience that is completed, so that one teaches because of purity attained through suffering. It is a cross of both daily self-accusation and the endurance of others' hatred, which inevitably follows the proclamation of truth. Because God's word is "pure like silver that has been refined seven times" (Ps. 12:6), those who handle it "ought to be swept clean seven times" and must endure a "seven-fold purgatory."[136] Karlstadt writes:

> You know that we must daily bear our cross of hatred and envy of our own soul, and those who lay it aside for a moment destroy themselves. For Christ says, "Whoever finds his soul in this world loses it. And whoever does not carry his cross and follow me is not my disciple." Accordingly, I ought to hate my soul unceasingly and carry my cross continuously to follow Christ, especially when I want to proclaim God's spotless word. I have nothing myself, and it is God's doing and not mine.[137]

These lines deepen the image of the right preacher described by Karlstadt in the sermon on Malachi through Karlstadt's understanding (derived from the *German Theology*, Tauler, and Suso) of self-accusation and cross-bearing as the cure for evil forms of *Annehmlichkeit*. Crucially, Karlstadt recognizes the ideal is unattainable—the mouthpiece for God's word and wisdom inevitably claims wisdom and honor for itself. With reference to himself he writes:

> But the soul gloats whenever the word is praised as if it were its own and thinks itself better. For this I ought to hate it profoundly. But I feel nothing within me except will and desire. Would that the love of my soul had become ice-cold and that it were scattered like ashes. Would that envy and fierce hatred had taken its place. Would that I could handle God's word as I should—without finding my soul. Yet how far from me is the power and resolve to do what God demands and what I would like to do.[138]

The confession here was personal, yet the issues involved were universal.

Karlstadt finds a "remedy" to this quandary in the declaration, "God's will shall be done, and I will obey him"—his teaching and preaching will be an exercise of sinking into God's will. He adds that, if he "goes forth" by teaching, preaching, and publishing, the insults of the "godless Philistines and Moabites" will consume as a "hot purgatory" his "evil lusts and *Ungelassenheit*" and make up for the insufficiency of his own self-accusation and *Gelassenheit*.[139] Briefly stated, Karlstadt chooses to accept his lot, recognizing that self-accusation and the accusations of others can protect him from misdirected *Annehmlichkeit*. He must yield his self-will to God's will— the latter revealed in biblical teachings on the diversity of gifts, which are to be shared for the benefit of others (I Cor. 12:4) and in the parable of the talents (Luke 19). It is noteworthy and characteristic that Karlstadt extends this logic to the lay life of work and family. God has appointed all who understand God's word as "priests," he writes. Fathers are priests to their families, neighbors to their neighbors, and "we must slay or set aside our thoughts, our cares and fears, along with all better intentions, to realize God's will."[140]

Suffering and the Reform of Worship and Life

Karlstadt's formulation here that it is "better to do what God's will intends and to confess the flaws in our works than to relax God's commandments on account of such flaws,"[141] expresses in a nutshell his stance on the matter of images and ritual reforms. In his view, Luther and his allies sought flexibility from God's commands, rather than confessing their own failure and yielding themselves. The Wittenberg reformation thus wrought neither self-accusation nor obedience—both components of *Gelassenheit*—but only self-will.

Karlstadt explicitly addressed the implementation of reform in a January 1524 treatise, *The Understanding of Paul's Words, "I desired to be an outcast [Verbannter] from Christ for my brothers," Rom. [9:3],*[142] and in *Whether We Should Go Slowly and Avoid Offending the Weak in Matters Pertaining to God's Will*, printed in November 1524.[143] Although the latter treatise is better known to modern readers, the former offers more insight into the themes of this chapter. In *Paul's Words*, Karlstadt confronts the same question as in *Whether We Should Go Slowly*, but through the lens of Paul's statement in Romans 9:3.[144] Karlstadt rejects the interpretation of Romans 9:3 to mean that Paul would choose to be banned, reviled, or accursed by Christ rather than "consent" to the "perishing" of his brothers. Through such an interpretation, Karlstadt alleges, the "entire world" wants to draw the "binding conclusion" that a Christian "should esteem and use brotherly love so highly that one should rather do or permit something against God than provoke or anger his brother";[145] indeed, the "world" claims that a Christian, for love of his neighbor, ought to let stand stumbling blocks to that neighbor's salvation.[146] Paul's desire, however, must be in union with and not "against Christ's will." Paul suffers great anguish, Karlstadt explains, because his Jewish brethren for whom Christ was sent "do not want to know and accept Christ." The suffering Paul describes is thus a "co-suffering [*mit-leiden*]" with Christ and indeed the highest and most bitter Christian cross, born of and borne in witnessing the rejection of God's redemptive mercy. This is the purest possible cross, Karlstadt declares, flowing from love of God and neighbor.[147] Karlstadt's discussion here recalls the insistence of the *German Theology*—against the supposed claim of free spirits to live without suffering, like the resurrected Christ—that the deified suffer greatly and throughout their lives to witness the sinfulness of others.[148]

What Paul truly says in Romans 9:3, Karlstadt argues, is that he would rather be "hung up" as an offering—this is the right definition of "outcast" (*Verbannter* or *Anathema*) in the passage, Karlstadt contends—than to witness the evil of his brethren. Paul's willingness to suffer follows the example of Christ and is aimed at rescuing his brethren from darkness and *Widerwille* before God. Like Christ, Paul would gladly bear the penalty due his brethren. By no means does Paul want to be cut off from God and Christ per the "common" understanding of a *Verbannter* or *Anathema*. Such a desire "would mean not to follow after Christ and offer his own soul for his brother, as Christ commanded, but to depart from the way of Christ. It would mean also to seek not the cross of Christ, but one's self; not to die [*absterben*] in the Father's will, but in the will of the flesh."[149] It is impossible to suffer for others or to suffer for good ends at all except through suffering conformity to God's will, setting aside self-will. Karlstadt writes, "Whoever has Christ's Spirit is of Christ and can neither with words, nor with thoughts, nor with deeds be without or against Christ, for the Spirit drives him ... [H]e cannot do otherwise, so long as he *suffers* the work of the Spirit of Christ."[150]

In sum, Karlstadt sought to unmask the insistence upon "regard for the weak" as an excuse to lay down the cross and to seek easy days with others rather than enduring what God teaches in scripture and demands in practice—indeed, what love of one's neighbor in conformity with and out of the divine will demands.[151] From a shared inheritance of Eckhartian mysticism, Karlstadt had drawn a different conclusion than Luther: reform required sinking into and then acting out of the divine will, and these two actions were to be done with constant self-accusation. *Gelassenheit* was an exercise of striving for complete renunciation of self and self-will; Gelassenheit was not, as Luther continued to invoke the concept, mere trust in God's work under contraries, including sin. Karlstadt divided Orlamünde and Wittenberg between friends and enemies of the cross; Luther would respond in kind.

Suffering and Faith

On themes of sin and salvation, Karlstadt's thought and teaching developed substantially through 1524, as he intentionally deepened the rift between himself and Wittenberg. Karlstadt rejected any implication that God was responsible for evil,[152] and his understanding of divine pedagogy led him to the conclusion that faith became saving and unbelief damning only when God was lovingly embraced or malevolently rejected with full knowledge.[153] Thus, Karlstadt lodged salvation in faith, but defined faith as knowledge that produces love.[154] Karlstadt denounced the notion that true, saving faith comes as soon as the Word is heard, and he insisted that only long suffering extending into the afterlife prepared the soul to receive—or possibly to reject—divine truth. This suffering represented God's movement of the soul, either through outward *Anfechtungen* or directly—that is, through the "created and the uncreated wind."[155] Operating within the *German Theology's* neo-Platonic framework of God as a singular whole and creatures as partial, Karlstadt argued that human beings either could follow the true light, recognize the good "powers" in their soul as from God, and give these powers over to God in faith, love, and fear; or follow the false light and thereby become vulnerable to love and fear of creatures.[156] The devil and sinful human beings after him fall because they regard their will and the virtues of their soul as their own possession and sufficient for salvation.[157] They will not yield themselves or suffer God's work, but remain in *Annehmlichkeit* with respect to the powers of the soul.[158] Against the false light and self-will, however, saving faith is born when God speaks truth directly into the heart.[159] Thus, Karlstadt focused with new intensity on the Reformation theme of faith precisely as he reached his furthest point of departure from Wittenberg views; faith and the anthropology of the *German Theology* were joined, each understood in relation to the other. Through this work, Karlstadt charted a middle course between affirming the complete bondage of the will and returning to what he regarded as Roman works-righteousness.[160] Concerning the rejection of divine truth by the devil and all "sons of the devil," Karlstadt writes:

> The devil regarded himself and his high creaturely powers, with which God created him, and wanted neither to stretch out nor to elevate them in order to desire to suffer God's spiritual work any longer [*wolt sie nit erstrecken noch vffheben zu[o] begeren Gottes geystliche werck / ferner zu[o] leyde[n]*]; rather he believed that his own powers were sufficient for him to attain

blessedness, and thus he chose his creaturely nature more than God and set darkness in the place of light.[161]

By 1524, Karlstadt traced damnation to hatred of divine truth on the part of those who do not want to be passive or suffer before God, or acknowledge that all goodness in them is from God.[162] When Christ declares that "whoever does not believe is damned" (John 3:18), he refers according to Karlstadt to the person who "despises and hates the clearly-known truth . . . and hates it eternally without remorse and sorrow." In the end, the recognition of truth becomes eternal suffering for such a soul, "bitterer and sourer than bile, vinegar, or wormwood," because this soul refuses to suffer truth in the "middle time," the time allotted by God for souls' learning and growth.[163]

Karlstadt's reflections on sin, faith, and free will left a critical question unanswered—namely, why anyone would reject God once God the whole had been fully revealed to him or her through the pedagogy of the inner Word. Who would or could choose not to love the supremely lovable source of all life? Who would or could choose damnation in full knowledge of the alternative and the consequences? These unanswered questions aside, for our purposes it is crucial that Karlstadt locates ultimate deception and damnation in the refusal to suffer divine pedagogy and the renunciation of self-will; in the language of the *German Theology*, this was a refusal to yield one's partial existence to God as the whole who is the source of life and all good.

The Lord's Supper

In the debate over the Lord's Supper, finally, Karlstadt's wrote from the conviction that only God's inward spiritual instruction allows for the proper understanding and use of outward words, signs, and experiences. Thus, he argued that true reception of the sacrament and assurance of forgiveness requires a "passionate remembrance" of Christ's suffering and death. In *On the Anti-Christian Abuse of the Lord's Bread and Cup*,[164] Karlstadt complains that Christians have been led to seek forgiveness of sins in the sacrament, stilling anxiety for sin with an easily won but merely temporal "peace" and "comfort"—with a false faith that "imagines something [to be] as it wants to have it."[165] In Karlstadt's exegesis, however, I Corinthians 11:26 ("As often as you eat from this bread and drink from this cup, you shall proclaim the death of the lord until he comes") commands Christians first to remember

Christ's body and blood in "the ground of their heart," and only then to proclaim the body and blood in the physical act of partaking.[166] This memory
of Christ's body and blood in the ground or heart belongs to justifying faith,
for it is "a burning and love-rich knowledge [*kunst oder erkantnuß*]," which
attends not to the physical sacrifice but to the "cause [*Ursache*]" of that sacrifice, the redemption from sin.[167] Such knowledge can only be a direct gift of
the Spirit,[168] and it transforms the recipient into the "life and death of Christ,"
now truly known. This means that the remembering Christian wills in conformity with Christ's will.[169] Those who recall with passion that Christ died
in their stead—out of "great love" and "incomparable obedience" to God, although he was fully innocent—will be joyous at the very mention of Christ's
name, eager to fulfill Christ's will, "eternally" ashamed of any deed contrary
to Christ, and terrified that their sin had to be redeemed by the death of God's
innocent son.[170]

Concluding Remarks

Beginning in earnest with his sermon on purgatory in late 1522, Karlstadt
intentionally distanced himself from Luther's soteriology and reform program. In so doing, he made extensive use of vocabulary and concepts from
the shared well of Eckhartian mysticism; but while Luther transformed
Gelassenheit into an evangelical ideal of trusting in and submitting to God's
work under contraries, for Karlstadt *Gelassenheit* was a practice of striving
toward the total renunciation of the self as constituted by the will. The goal
was to reduce the self-will to nothingness, returning to the precreated and
pristine created state in which the only will was God's. This was union with
God for Karlstadt, whereas for Luther union with Christ was secured by the
wedding ring of faith—by trust in Christ *extra nos* and *sub contrariis*. All that
said, Karlstadt shared Luther's pessimism about human moral achievement
and the danger of even seemingly good works in the clenches of human pride;
consequently, Karlstadt could imagine the realization of the goal of sinking
into the divine will only in the postmortem life of souls. Souls must suffer
and be moved by the Spirit for far longer than the span of earthly life. For
Luther death was the final trial of trust and God's final destruction of the Old
Adam; for Karlstadt death was a graduation from elementary school and the
beginning of a deeper, harder, and simultaneously more love-rich learning in
the school of Christ. To prepare oneself for this graduation, present Christian

life was to be marked by daily self-accusation and willing acceptance of whatever suffering might come for striving to obey God's will.

Karlstadt more than Luther insisted on remaking worship and corporate life according to scripture, and he sought to cultivate lay Christians who would study scripture without the interference of their own wills. Self-accusation and consolation were both necessary for Karlstadt, but he clearly deemed himself and his contemporaries more in need of the former. Karlstadt claimed the true cross and suffering for his version of reform, and he lambasted Luther and his allies for rejecting the same. Like Rome, Wittenberg had become a camp filled with enemies of the cross, driven by the hope of an easy forgiveness conferred from outside and an easy obedience without mortification of self-will or risk of human opposition and spite. Still, Karlstadt's delay of union with God until the afterlife moderated his idealism with respect to ecclesial and social reform, at least vis-à-vis Müntzer, whom we will discuss in the next chapter. For Karlstadt, the right approach was to recognize, lament, and struggle against human failing, individual and communal, before God's law; Christians needed to reject the temptation to bend God's law rather than struggle with their own and their neighbors' disobedience.

Karlstadt concludes *On the anti-Christian Abuse* with the assertion that he does not bring "such new things into light" frivolously or in order to gain fame, but because he fears God who will be his judge. He would rather remain silent "for the sake of fear"—that is, the fear of men. "I know," he writes, "that I will suffer slander and persecution on this account, especially from those who want to be regarded as good, evangelical people." The proponents of an easy, external, and human-contrived faith bathe themselves in the light of the gospel, and those who expose and challenge them will have to suffer. In 1524, Karlstadt was convinced that truth had not yet found its willing sufferers. The final line of *On the anti-Christian Abuse* declares that the true gospel of Christ "in many hundred years still has not been rightly preached by anyone."[171] The fear of suffering silences God's Word within and without. Fallen, self-assertive human beings do not want to hear about the suffering necessary for salvation—about the opposition of God's will to all human reason and desire, about the need for complete renunciation of the self. Would-be speakers of this hard word tremble to utter it.

5

The "Bitter Side of Faith"

Suffering and Thomas Müntzer's Critique of the Wittenberg *Solas*, 1517–1524

Thomas Müntzer was already an ordained priest and a critic of indulgences before he came to Wittenberg as a student in the fall of 1517; he studied in Wittenberg through 1519, establishing contacts with numerous leading reformers, including Andreas Karlstadt, Philip Melanchthon, and Franz Günther. In Jüterbog in April 1519 and then for a more extended period in Zwickau in 1520–1521, he preached the Gospel as a self-professed "Martinian" in regular contact with Wittenberg. Luther may have recommended Müntzer for the preaching post in Zwickau, and he certainly approved of the appointment.[1] Journeying to Prague in the fall of 1521, Müntzer introduced himself as an "Emulus Martini."[2] Extant sources reveal that for a time around 1519–1521, Müntzer avidly grounded salvation in faith, grace, Christ, and predestination alone. He shared with Luther and Karlstadt a keen interest in Eckhartian mystical literature, and he may have studied Tauler together with Karlstadt in Wittenberg.[3] As the discussion here will show, he discerned in Luther and others in the Wittenberg circle a shared conviction that human beings must suffer the complete destruction of their intellectual and moral presumptions in order to receive truth and salvation from God. Out of and around this very message, however, he turned critical of Wittenberg teachings, complaining that Luther and his allies failed to teach Christians to strive against their lusts or to confront genuine spiritual trials; they thus left souls in the grips of creaturely attachments, possessed by creatures rather than God, closed off to inward divine revelation, and deluded by an easy false faith. Müntzer believed that God moved elect souls to salvation through terrible spiritual consternation; on the other side of the consternation lay true faith and fear of God rather than creatures. He charged that Wittenberg's *solas* hindered the arrival (*Ankunft*) of true faith by offering easy, outward relief from this necessary spiritual suffering; Wittenberg doctrine simply

Enemies of the Cross. Vincent Evener, Oxford University Press (2021). © Oxford University Press.
DOI: 10.1093/oso/9780190073183.001.0001.

replaced the easy externalism of Roman ritualism with the more deceptive externalism of scripture alone.

This chapter examines Müntzer's theological development up to the publication of his critique of the *solas* (faith, Christ, and scripture alone) in his treatises *Protestation or Proposition* and *On Counterfeit Faith* in late 1523–early 1524. We will proceed chronologically, allowing us to witness the development of Müntzer's unique view out of shared sources and commitments. In the two treatises, we will see that although Müntzer understood the purpose of the *solas*—namely, to exclude saints, human rituals, and human-produced works from the economy of salvation—he focused on their effects for souls possessed by creatures through lust and fear and attacked their alleged grounding in a partial view of Christ and scripture. Thus, he argued that scripture alone could not impart genuine faith; rather, it could only testify to faith received directly in the ground of the soul. Likewise, it did not suffice for Christ alone to suffer, but all Christians had to suffer through the experience of forsakenness like Christ. Faith, finally, did not save without works because faith was itself a work of God endured by receptive human beings.[4]

Müntzer unfolded a perspective that drew from both Eckhartian mysticism—the soul must be emptied of creaturely attachments so that God can fill the empty space—and Luther. Müntzer's teachings were consistently oriented toward faith in God's promises; indeed, he focused on faith more singularly than Karlstadt, who tended to group faith with other virtues and *Gelassenheit*. Like Luther, he demanded that faith and doctrine be certain.[5] Nonetheless, Müntzer gave the concepts of promise and faith unique content: he saw the trial of unbelief that every believer must face not as a matter of self-trust or self-will, but as a matter of fundamental doubt concerning whether Christianity or some other religion was true. He saw the promise grasped by faith, in turn, as a promise of God's direct presence within and instruction of souls. Ultimately, he expected God to establish a church led by the faithful who received direct inward revelation as well as visions and dreams. Müntzer set himself up as a prophet—as an experienced believer who had broken through unbelief to true faith, and who thus was receptive to and could properly discern valid visions and dreams.

After the Peasants' War of 1524–1525, Luther and his allies made a concerted effort to depict Müntzer as the arch-leader of peasant rebels across the Empire.[6] Centuries later, Müntzer's supposed "fanaticism" became a virtue in the eyes of Marxist thinkers and historians, who held up Müntzer as a leader of "early bourgeois revolution." Such was the image of Müntzer propagated in East Germany, at least until the government sought to reappropriate Luther's legacy on the 500th anniversary of the Wittenberg reformer's birth in 1983.[7] Meanwhile, non-Marxist historians working primarily in West Germany and the United States pursued the religious and theological bases of Müntzer's turn to revolution, while debating for much of the twentieth century whether Müntzer was best understood as a "disciple of Luther" who went astray, or as an independent figure steeped in medieval mysticism or apocalypticism.[8] The evidence and analysis presented in this chapter will show that none of these interpretations does justice to the interplay of dependence and independence in Müntzer's relationship to Luther or the Wittenberg movement more broadly. Sources from 1519 and 1520 reveal his genuine indebtedness to Luther, a sense of common cause, and shared assumptions and sources; but Müntzer read widely and thought independently. He was, moreover, a figure in constant motion, whose core commitments developed in dialogue with ever-new experiences as a preacher, pastor, and champion of reform.[9] Günter Vogler has helpfully argued that Müntzer should be viewed as someone who developed a "competing theology" vis-à-vis Wittenberg, in a moment that seemed more open-ended than it truly was.[10] Here, we will witness the development of a competing theology out of shared Eckhartian sources and a shared paradigm of the Christian as sufferer. Thus, we will avoid positing stark discontinuities where neither Müntzer nor contemporaries could have seen them.[11] I will show that Müntzer transformed the inheritance of Eckhartian mysticism not only through apocalypticism, as scholars have noted,[12] but through the Wittenberg loci of promise and faith; Eckhartian mysticism, in turn, shaped how he understood and applied Wittenberg loci in his everchanging contexts.

The only way to view Müntzer with fresh eyes today is to return to the sources and to ask new questions; accordingly, this chapter follows Müntzer's journey from his initial contacts with Wittenberg theological circles to his express criticisms of *sola scriptura*, *sola fides*, and *solus Christus* at the end of 1523. The question is: How did Müntzer employ mystically infused themes of suffering and the cross (long recognized as central to his work) in order to differentiate himself from a movement, the Wittenberg reformation, that had used the same broad themes and drawn from the same mystical wells to differentiate itself from scholastic theology and Roman Christianity?

Müntzer to 1519: Connections to Wittenberg and Eckhartian Mysticism

Details regarding Thomas Müntzer's early life are elusive.[13] Likely he was born between 1488 and 1491. His hometown was Stolberg in the Harz Mountains, and his family came from the upper layer of *Bürger* society, actively pursuing wealth and education and participating in local governance. Throughout his relatively short life, Müntzer's travels were determined in part by family connections to merchants and goldsmiths in the Harz and surrounding regions. Müntzer appears to have matriculated at the Universities of Leipzig (in 1506) and Frankfurt an der Oder (in 1512). At some point, Müntzer received a Bachelor and Master of Arts and a Bachelor of the Bible. It is not known precisely when and where he attained these degrees, although he was a Master by 1514.[14] He was a priest in Halberstadt before receiving a prebend at St. Michael's in Braunschweig on May 6, 1514.[15]

In Braunschweig, Müntzer associated with a circle of reform-minded laity centered on the merchant Hans Pelt, to whom Müntzer may have been related by marriage. Intriguing but scant evidence suggests that Müntzer and other members of this circle were attracted to mystical teachings and ideals of martyrdom—thus seeking identification with Christ in love and suffering. Müntzer may have adopted a critical stance toward ecclesial authorities and tradition already by 1515. One correspondent called him a "castigator of unrighteousness."[16] Evidence from mid-1517 reveals that Müntzer was critical of indulgences even before Luther's famous theses.[17] Later opponents claimed that Müntzer was "expelled" from Braunschweig.[18] The Braunschweig reform circle, including seemingly Müntzer himself, was impressed by Martin Luther when he burst onto the public scene in late 1517 and early 1518. In a June 1521 letter, Pelt describes the strong devotion to "Martin" among his associates, as well as his own avid acquisition of Luther's works.[19] During his time in Braunschweig, Müntzer also formed a friendship with the future Wittenberg reformer Johann Agricola, who came to the city no later than 1514.[20]

Müntzer relocated to Wittenberg in late 1517. He may have been drawn there by publicity surrounding Luther's protest against indulgences, or he may have arrived shortly before the *95 Theses* were made public. Müntzer studied and lived in Wittenberg through at least early 1519, after which he spent three months in Orlamünde and a few days in Jüterbog, preaching during Easter (April 24–26, 1519) to the great offense of local Franciscans.[21]

Müntzer may then have returned to Wittenberg and remained until November 1519; if so, this accords with evidence for Müntzer's presence at the Leipzig Disputation (June 27–July 15, 1519). Some 200 students traveled with Luther and Karlstadt to that event. Müntzer possibly also witnessed the disputation in which Melanchthon attained his *baccalaureus biblicus* on September 9, 1519.[22]

Humanism with its ideal of returning *ad fontes*—to scripture and the church fathers—was ascendant at the University of Wittenberg,[23] and Müntzer attended lectures on Jerome given by the humanist John Rhagius Aesticampianus. These lectures exposed Müntzer to the humanist ideal of an ascetic scholar—a scholar who mortifies his lusts and renounces marriage in order to focus energy on learning, and who is willing to suffer exile and wandering for the sake of truth.[24] Müntzer was not a "disciple of Luther" in these years; rather, he engaged a broad and diverse intellectual community, forming significant contacts with Karlstadt as well as Melanchthon, Günther, and Nicholas Hausmann. He knew Agricola already from his Braunschweig days. He may not have met Luther until the Leipzig Disputation.

Karlstadt may have provided Müntzer with a brief appointment in Orlamünde in the winter of 1518–1519. An enigmatic note left behind by Martin Glaser (d. 1553) claims that Müntzer read Tauler's *Sermons* in Orlamünde together with a female cook, who was regarded as a holy woman by some people in Leipzig. Glaser made this note in his own volume of Tauler, a gift from Luther in 1529(!), remarking that Müntzer had misunderstood and thus been seduced by Tauler's teachings on the Spirit and the ground of the soul; Glaser asserts that Müntzer subsequently led Karlstadt into error. Because Glaser resided in Wittenberg from 1505/1506–1518, Ulrich Bubenheimer has proposed that his account may contain a kernel of historical truth—namely, a shared study of Tauler by Karlstadt and Müntzer—although in Bubenheimer's view it is more likely that Karlstadt influenced Müntzer than the reverse.[25] That said, Müntzer he may have read Tauler's *Sermons* and Henry Suso's works already in 1515–1516.[26] Müntzer's high regard for both visions and intensive ascetic practice could have been connected to his reception of Suso, whether he learned these things from Suso's writings or simply found them reinforced there.

In the lead up to Easter in 1519, Müntzer's friendship with Franz Günther brought him to Jüterbog. Günther was a distinguished student of Luther's and had earned his Bachelor of Scripture by defending Luther's *Disputation against Scholastic Theology* on September 4, 1517. In early 1519, Günther took a preaching post in Jüterbog and promptly provoked controversy with the local Franciscans there, as well as the local abbess. When Günther agreed to suspend his preaching, Müntzer filled this role with vigor. A complaint made by the Franciscan Bernard Dappen to the bishop of Brandenberg about the preaching of the two "Lutherans" gives some insight into what Müntzer proclaimed from the pulpit. He and Günther both repudiated the authority of councils acting contrary to scripture,[27] and Müntzer in particular is said to have preached that the pope's authority was contingent upon the will of the bishops and that the pope must call a council every five years.[28] Müntzer also rejected the canonization of Bonaventure and Aquinas, declaring that their teachings had never converted a single heretic, and he charged that the church's acceptance of scholastic theology had coincided with the corruption of the church and society—the letting of "whores and pimps into the city." Müntzer's critique of scholastic theology as dry and ineffective coincided with mystical, humanist, and Wittenberg currents of reform; his concern with impurity would, when further developed, set him apart from Wittenberg.[29] For now, Müntzer echoed Luther's conclusion that Satanic forces had long deceived Christendom in matters of salvation, finding their toehold in fallen human reason. Reason was the enemy of true theology and doctrine, as Karlstadt also agreed. Dappen relates Müntzer's claim that Aquinas and Bonaventure "relied on natural reasoning, and all such reason is from the devil." Dappen depicts Müntzer as setting faith and the gospel in complete opposition to scholastic theology and self-serving church leaders, who allegedly used theology to conceal the truth. According to Dappen, Müntzer denounced bishops as self-serving tyrants: he complained that bishops no longer visited their subordinates yearly to "examine them in faith" and that priests in turn no longer opposed the bishops' misdeeds. The bishops were "flatterers and seducers of the erring people, calling good evil and evil good." Consequently, the gospel had "lain under a bank for more than 400 years; for its recovery very many still would be compelled to extend their necks," that is, suffer martyrdom.[30]

Around December 1519, Müntzer obtained a post at the Cistercian nunnery in Beuditz. The post offered much-needed financial support and, as Müntzer reported in a January 1, 1520 letter to Günther, precious time to study Augustine, Eusebius, and (Pseudo-)Hegesippus. In the same letter, Müntzer described his inability to attain other desired books as "a bitter cross to me in my Lord Jesus" and as a punishment for preaching without an inward call, possibly in Braunschweig;[31] yet Müntzer professed contentment with his lot and his willingness to be sent wherever it pleased God. Studies of church history soon convinced Müntzer that the church's fall into deception and idolatry had occurred not merely 400 years in the past, but in the time immediately following the death of the apostles.[32] Müntzer thus sought to explain and correct the fall of the church through a deep knowledge of church history; one thing was for certain, the church had accommodated ease and sin and masked its deceit with the best thinking human ingenuity could muster!

Zwickau in 1520–1521: Attacking the Cross-Shirkers on All Sides

In early May 1520, Müntzer took up the preaching post at St. Mary's in Zwickau, as a temporary replacement for Johann Silvius Egranus, a humanist scholar and preacher supportive of reforms along Erasmian lines. Luther may have recommended Müntzer to Egranus at the Leipzig Disputation.[33] Müntzer immediately clashed with local Franciscans, already angered by Egranus's criticism of the cult of St. Anne. In the fall of 1520, however, after Egranus returned to his pulpit and the popular Müntzer relocated to the city's St. Katherine's Church, Müntzer attacked Egranus himself, sensing the latter's lack of sympathy for Wittenberg's soteriology, its exegetical commitments, and its summons of believers to the cross. In both of these conflicts, Müntzer acted in perceived commonality with the Wittenberg reformation movement, whose center he found in the assertion that human beings must suffer painful divine work within—true *conformitas Christi*—in order to receive faith from God and thereafter live a life marked by suffering before human beings.[34] Müntzer's stance in Zwickau is especially illuminated by two surviving sources: a draft of a letter to Martin Luther,[35] dated July 13, 1520, which relates to his controversy with the Franciscans, and a series of "propositions" purporting to represent teachings of Egranus.

The first lines of Müntzer's letter to Luther indicate that the Zwickau Franciscans had made an official complaint about his preaching to their Provincial, and that the town council had instructed Müntzer to seek Luther's advice on the matter. Müntzer's letter assumes common cause with Luther, particularly with respect to Christians' necessary endurance of the suffering of Christ, through which (the letter claims) faith is assured.[36] He proudly describes his denunciation of monks and clergy who, rather than promoting true faith among Christians, offered the people a false assurance of salvation in exchange for material goods. Müntzer did not exonerate the laity from blame, however, for they "had failed hitherto to pray and sigh for shepherds of souls, hence the Lord had justly set blind watchers over the blind sheep." Müntzer thus depicted an exchange in which indolent laity received the false promise and consolation of an easy salvation (sealed here through ritual acts, including last rites), and gave money and goods in return. At the center of the monstrous exchange was a shared regard for ceremonies.[37] Conversely, Müntzer depicts himself as walking the hard path of discipleship, bearing accusations of blasphemy and slander against his person, all the while knowing that the servant is not above the master (John 15). "You are my advocate (*patrocinium*) in the Lord Jesus," he tells Luther. "I beg you not to lend your ears to those who are defaming me."[38]

Müntzer declares his readiness to suffer as an instrument of God alongside Luther in a broad struggle for Christian renewal. He writes, "Graver struggles are ahead of me; I have a manly trust that God intends notable things through your plans and those of all Christians. My cross is not yet complete."[39] Müntzer's model for imitation was not only Christ, however, but also Luther himself. Müntzer asserts that the townspeople want him, if Luther approves, to appeal against his detractors to a future council. He notes that he had declared himself willing to appear before the relevant authorities—in this case, "representatives of the bishop of Naumburg"—to give an account of his faith and to present his sermons for emendation. He seeks Luther's permission to meet his foes in open disputation or through the presses.[40] In short, Müntzer asks Luther's permission to take the same dramatic steps—appeal to a future council, public account, disputation, and publication—that Luther himself had taken from 1518–1520, and that had made the latter into a celebrity and hero of faith. Müntzer later presented himself in Prague as an "imitator of Martin" and he may even have intended to emulate the posting of the 95 Theses with his own Prague Manifesto.[41] The pattern of *Nachfolge Lutheri* continued.

Müntzer promised to "set both [Luther's] ears ringing" with a series of "articles" supposedly preached before the people by the Franciscan Tiburtius of Weissenfels.[42] We can infer at least the contours of Müntzer's position from this list of diametrically opposed teaching. Foundational for Müntzer was the necessity of Christians' inward appropriation of Christ's suffering and concrete imitation of Christ. Müntzer thus charged Tiburtius with teaching that "Christ died once for all, so that he need not die in us; nor should his sacrament be a comfort to us or his example be transformed into imitation. The services of the Mass preserve us from having to suffer in this world."[43] The distinction between Christ as sacrament and Christ as example came from Luther, who insisted that Christ must be received in faith as the sole source of salvation (as sacrament) before his example could be followed without hypocritical presumption to earn one's salvation.[44] Here, Müntzer equates the consolation of receiving Christ not with freedom from suffering but with Christ dying in the Christian and with *imitatio Christi* in the world. Thus, the next five articles accuse Tiburtius and his ilk of softening the true Gospel with human commands, additions, and excuses, including by denying that Christ's injunctions to poverty and "turning the other cheek" were binding upon all Christians. Like Luther, Müntzer rejected a distinction between "counsels of perfection" and commands; all Christians were to adhere to the Sermon on the Mount.[45] The two reformers developed this point differently, however: Müntzer looked for the restoration of a lost created order among true, Spirit-led Christians, to the exclusion of the impure. Luther insisted that Christians must participate in government and economy, understood as original and enduringly good structures of God's creation, out of love for their neighbors, even the impure ones.[46]

Like Luther and Karlstadt, Müntzer in 1520 underlined the necessity of suffering spiritually through the realization of human beings' complete inability to contribute to their salvation; thus, he affirmed a doctrine of salvation by grace alone, directed against supposed "works-righteousness." Along these lines, the seventh reported offensive statement of Tiburtius read, "Predestination is an imaginary thing; it should not be included in faith, so that we base our confidence on it rather than on works; the people should not be cautioned against the latter, but the people of Zwickau, dear to me for 24 years, should continue to burn candles and perform the most virtuous works." Thus, Müntzer joined Luther both by affirming the certitude of true faith as grounded in grace and predestination and by criticizing anxious striving for salvation through ritual works. Conversely, Müntzer likely already had a distinct understanding of how faith related to God's presence in the soul, an understanding that later developed into his assertion that God must possess and fill empty souls—this over and against Luther's teachings concerning Christ's presence through faith and faith's direction of the Christian *extra nos*. The final offensive statement attributed to Tiburtius reads, "Eternal blessedness cannot be predicated of the kingdom of faith within us, since only in the future will it be our homeland; here we are most uncertain about our blessedness."[47] Evident throughout the list of offensive teachings is Müntzer's demand for a true rather than a false assurance, the latter aligned with human machinations seeking freedom from suffering and hard obedience. Müntzer expressed his self-understanding with the claim that he was "inspire[d]" by the Spirit to combat those "anxious to appear as Christians" with the "trumpet of the Word of God."[48]

Müntzer explicitly maligns his Franciscan opponents as "adversaries of the cross" who seek to extinguish the "light of consolation [*lux consolationis*]"[49]—the truth and salvation given to those who suffer like Christ and accept Christ's hard commands rather than seeking to earn salvation and to console themselves with easy rituals (the mass, the burning of candles). Müntzer closes with praise of Luther as "a model and beacon to the friends of God"—a term that was used in the post-Eckhartian tradition for people who had attained intimacy with God, and that was adopted for a loose network of mystical authors and readers in the fourteenth century.[50] Müntzer identifies himself as "Thomas Müntzer, whom you brought to birth by the gospel,"[51] but he later tried to erase this profession of indebtedness to Luther; we do not know when or why. In evaluating the line and the letter, it is important to remember that Müntzer's purpose was to win Luther's support. Numerous lines reflect Müntzer's confidence that he, like Luther, was called and driven by God to a shared struggle. He had been instructed by the city council to seek Luther's advice; it is impossible to tell if he truly deemed himself in need of such advice. All the same, Müntzer's self-confident assurance of divine calling makes it unlikely that he altered his positions to please Luther; he demonstrates a substantial knowledge and reception of Luther's teachings, and a sense that he is chosen to be another Luther, first and foremost by proclaiming certitude of faith and salvation through the way of the cross, offensive to human reason and desire.

Neither a final draft of this letter nor a response from Luther is extant, so we do not know if the correspondence was ever sent, received, or answered. Nonetheless, Müntzer remained in contact with Wittenberg circles. On November 2, Johann Agricola penned a letter to Müntzer that opened, "I have to congratulate you on the situation you are in, being found worthy to bear fierce insults in the name of Christ." Agricola's letter sought to ward off conflict between Müntzer and the recently returned Egranus—albeit for strategic purposes, as Agricola recognized that Egranus had little sympathy for Wittenberg theology.[52] Rejecting this strategic counsel, Müntzer went on the attack,[53] prompting Agricola and even Luther himself to plead for restraint.[54]

Müntzer evidently reacted with anger, although the relevant correspondence is not extant; he earned the scolding rebuke from Agricola, "YOU BREATHE OUT NOTHING BUT SLAUGHTER AND BLOOD!"[55] Müntzer's attack on Egranus was answered by the latter, and circles of their followers entered the fray; when the conflict devolved into a public exchange of polemical poetry, Müntzer was dismissed in April 1521. Egranus had already resigned in December 1520.[56]

Müntzer's assessment of Egranus is revealed by his compilation of "Propositions of that upright man, Dr. Egranus";[57] the exact date and purpose of this writing is unclear, as is the extent to which the propositions were drawn from Egranus's own teachings and the extent to which Müntzer caricatured those teachings. The text contains annotations and additions.[58] It is certain that the propositions represent positions that Müntzer deemed offensive to core Christian truths. The propositions are clearly colored by and couched within polemic—including the sarcastic introduction of Egranus as "upright" and a concluding promise (put in Egranus's mouth) to "defend these axioms against the whole world and especially that ass, Thomas Müntzer."[59] I will treat the text as crafted polemic here, whether or not it was intended or put to public use. The overall effect of the document is to depict Egranus as an effete scholar who placed hope for salvation in human reason and moral effort and who looked to God and Christ for liberation from spiritual and outward suffering.

Similar to the alleged "Articles" of Tiburtius, the "Propositions of Egranus" reveal by statement of the opposite Müntzer's core conviction that Christians must suffer on their way to and from true and certain faith; suffering is necessary because the fundamental human problem is a preference for ease cloaked in the rationalization of minds closed to revelation. Thus, Proposition 1 states, "Christ is not the savior of all the elect, or of those who were under the Law, or of those who lived prior to the Law or outside its jurisdiction"[60]—a view that offended Müntzer as claiming that salvation was possible by human moral effort outside of Christ received as a sacrament. Luther would have agreed with Müntzer, albeit with a different understanding of what it meant to receive Christ as sacrament. Proposition 2 adds, "Christ did not come into the world to teach us to bear our sufferings patiently and so follow in his footsteps, but he suffered so that we might have complete security, free of bitterness [*amaritudine*] of any kind."[61] Peter Matheson notes that this alleged statement contradicts the last of Luther's 95 *Theses*, which held that "Christians should be exhorted" to follow Christ through "penalties, death, and hell; and thus be confident of entering into heaven through many tribulations rather than through the false security of peace."[62] Müntzer may also have discerned in Egranus a reincarnation of the *German Theology's* "free spirits," who wanted to have the heavenly Christ-life without the earthly Christ-life. In any case, Egranus's opposition to the *95 Theses* was further exposed by the notion (Propositions 6a–b) that human beings could manufacture contrition by their own powers, without enduring divine *poenae*, and that having thus won forgiveness they no longer needed to seek further *poenae*. Müntzer took particular offense at the denial of *tentationes*, listing the following among Egranus's teachings: "It is right . . . to reject temptations of one's faith which are not of this world, the temptations of hell etc. These are nothing but fantasies produced by human inclinations" (6b). Egranus is said to have regarded the Eucharist as a mere sign "to commemorate the Passion," rather than as a vehicle conveying forgiveness and the Holy Spirit (4), and also to have held that "the Passion was not so agonising as the loose talk of many folk suggests, and the sole benefit it confers is a disposition to good works. Human death cannot be agonising, either, but is a gentle dissolution of soul and body" (5). However unfair,[63] Müntzer depicts Egranus as teaching that Christ's passion enabled human effort for salvation and conferred an assurance that did not require Christians themselves to suffer like Christ, through the work of the Holy Spirit. The seventh proposition relates the claim that "the only experience of faith we can have in this world is derived from books. This is why neither the layman nor the unlearned—however much they have been put to the test—can make any judgments on matters of faith, but judgments on all such matters pertains to those with mitres but no experience at all." Müntzer soon pushed toward radically democratic horizons from the basic principle expressed here—the principle, shared with Luther, that truth was received in the reduction of intellectual assertion, not through intellectual assertion. Conversely, Luther's insistence on the authority of scripture and the mediacy of the preached Word went hand-in-hand with his desire to cultivate an educated cadre of preachers; in Luther's view, faith equipped all believers for judgment and required such judgment of them, but learning and ordination made the pastor and preacher.

Undergirding Egranus's errors about suffering and salvation, in Müntzer's view, was his humanist exegetical agenda, which sought to explain the unique, literal-historical meaning of each passage.[64] For Müntzer, this was to approach scripture with human understanding, denying the need for interpretation (i.e., allegorical exegesis; 9, 10) and the comparison of passages

(11). Egranus denied according to Müntzer that the Old Testament and the Decalogue applied to Christians (8, 14)—there was no need to instill the fear of God "in men's breasts" (15). For Egranus, Paul's reference to a struggle of flesh and spirit pertained to the Jews, not all people.[65] To Müntzer, this amounted to wish fulfillment: nothing has to be endured to break sinners' creaturely attachments. Indeed, "No one has to believe what his intellect cannot grasp. For man's rational faculties are most ample, and are not surrendered to the obedience of faith; this is completely unnecessary, anyway; indeed, it is the height of folly for something free to be made captive" (17). By not surrendering the intellect to faith, Egranus embraced the outrageous conclusions that God was omnipotent, but "not over our free will" (18), and that Abraham, Zechariah, and Elizabeth were "just in the eyes of the Lord" before the visitation of God (19). Müntzer's sense of common cause with Wittenberg is evident as he recounts Egranus's claim, "The Pelagians, whom the unlearned call heretics, are better Christians than that most unlearned man, Augustine, than that most awkward fellow, Bernard, than all these wandering Martinian men.[66] For they [the Pelagians] preach that man is saved or damned of his own volition. They did not comfort themselves in this world like the Manichaeans" (20).

In a nutshell, Egranus was to be repudiated for the same arrogant self-reliance that Luther and Karlstadt had condemned in the scholastics—for his reliance on human intellect as sufficient to understand God and the way to salvation, and on human will as sufficient to walk the way to heaven. This was self-assertion against suffering and the cross. For Müntzer, however, it was also *eo ipso* rejection of the Spirit-led church, as Propositions 21 and 22 underlined, "Only the apostles had the holy Spirit. It was not necessary for other men, because the Church had been put on a firm enough footing by the labours of the apostles. . . . For a thousand years no man has had the holy Spirit; the Church is not ruled by it either."[67]

In a final proposition, Müntzer had Egranus confess his "lust for money" and his desire to please the powerful (24), exposing the base motives he discerned behind apparently sophisticated cross-shirking. He would later do the same publicly against Luther. In the "Propositions," there is a complicated mixture of agreement with and independence from Luther; there is a shared conviction that faith must be received and manifested in suffering in order to be certain, and there are glimpses of future differences surrounding the nature of *tentationes* and surrounding who it was that should—and would—lead reform of the church. As Helmar Junghans summarizes it, Müntzer's clash with Egranus in Zwickau represented both a first public airing of the differences between Wittenberg and Erasmian principles of religious reform, and the beginning of Müntzer's own alienation from the Wittenbergers.[68]

Prague, 1521: The Trials of the Elect

Released from Zwickau, Müntzer next set his sights on Prague. He first made a short journey to Bohemia, then returned to the area around Zwickau to plan a more ambitious venture.[69] During this planning period, Müntzer corresponded with Nicholaus Hausmann, who had replaced Egranus in Zwickau after serving in Schneeberg from 1519 to 1521. Hausmann had criticized Müntzer for his "immodest" attack on Egranus. Müntzer responded by making a distinction between spiritual and carnal "modesty": "The voice of God [eloqu[i]um Dei] teaches a spiritual modesty, not a carnal one, disclosed by the lampstand of truth to all the elect of God." Spiritual modesty involves the acceptance of God's will, Spirit, and truth, Müntzer argues, and it may produce acts offensive to the world and its vaunted reason, such as when Elijah killed 1,000 followers of Baal. Here was the principle that became decisive for Müntzer as the Peasants' War approached: the elect need not suffer passively at the hands of the ungodly; instead, they should be courageous to suffer out of knowledge of and conformity with God's will—as God's possession and instruments—in active opposition to the ungodly. Along these lines, Müntzer complains that Hausmann had remained silent when Egranus publicly denied the working of the Holy Spirit among Christians, and he reports hearing that Hausmann preferred to please priests and nobles rather than see to the needs of the "common throng." Müntzer lambastes Hausmann's "mendacious pretense of sanctity," which invoked "modesty" to conceal cross-shirking. Hausmann's words and speech should instead "breath forth the entire crucified Christ," for "no disciple who sets himself up above his master will ever be able to preach him."[70] Müntzer presents himself, conversely, as a true disciple of Christ, "desiring nothing else but my own persecution, so that all may profit and be converted through me."[71] He had hoped to meet martyrdom in Bohemia (i.e., during his initial, brief visit), he says:

> I visited Bohemia not for the sake of my own petty glory, not from a burning desire for money, but in the hope of my coming death. By these words I want to prevent the mystery of the cross, as I have preached it, from

being eradicated. If you or my successor Zeidler are intending to root out the tender shoots of the word which I have watered you should be aware that boys and old men will confound you. For it is impossible for the word of God to return void. [Isaiah 55:11] Nor will that same word allow itself to be directed by the teaching authority of men or to be darkened by the head-strong councils of the untested and the effeminate.[72]

Like the letter to Hausmann, Müntzer's so-called *Prague Manifesto* was a document born out of frustration. Müntzer was given a warm reception in Prague in mid-July as an ally of the Wittenberg reformation—as a "Lutheran" according to one chronicle source. He himself paved the way for this reception. In advance of his arrival in the city, he sent a series of theses authored by Melanchthon,[73] offering to defend these theses publicly and writing on the outside of the papers that he was an "an imitator of Martin before the Lord." Müntzer was provided lodging at the *Collegium Corolinum*, probably by Utraquist supporters, and he was given access to some of the city's most important pulpits. But he was immediately at odds with Roman believers and conservative Old Utraquists, and he soon alienated many among the New Utraquists and the Bohemian Brethren—probably because of his elevation of direct instruction by the Spirit above the authority of scripture and the clergy. By October, Müntzer left or was forced out of the *Collegium Corolinum*, taking up residence with individual supporters, and he was no longer wel-comed in any pulpits. The *Prague Manifesto* apparently was a last-ditch effort to turn the tide through appeal to a broader public.[74]

In fact, there were multiple versions of the document directed to mul-tiple publics, and as Friedrich de Boor has shown, it is important to attend to the audience and purpose of each.[75] According to de Boor, a Latin ver-sion, long regarded as the last one written, may well have been the first—an appeal to the powerful and the learned, made in order to regain access to pulpits. The failure of that appeal may then have been behind Müntzer's cre-ation of a short German version on a single sheet of paper; dated November 1, 1521, this version may have been intended for public posting in emulation of Luther's *95 Theses*.[76] More certain still in de Boor's view is that a break with the upper classes inspired the long, polemical German version dated November 25, which does not survive in Müntzer's own hand; this version directly addresses the "arme Volk," contains sharp criticism of clergy and scholars, and explicitly announces the coming of the Anti-Christ and Christ's kingdom after that. The Latin version contains no apocalyptic conclusion, while the single-sheet German version merely warns that the Turks will strike down the Bohemians if they do not heed Müntzer's message.[77]

The short German version contains *in nuce* the most essential themes of the other versions, while offering Müntzer's most detailed remarks on direct divine instruction.[78] My brief review here will focus on this version, showing how Müntzer traced the rejection of divine immediacy to a refusal to suffer both the removal of one's attachments to creatures and the confrontation with one's inner unbelief. Such a view became the core of Müntzer's argument against Luther and his Wittenberg allies, even though both sides saw spiritual suffering—the experience of God's reduction to nothing of human self-assertion—as crucial to the discernment of true versus false faith and certitude. Reflecting a deep appropriation of mystical literature,[79] Müntzer in the *Prague Manifesto* now clearly describes the human relationship to God and creatures as one of possession—that is, the soul is possessed by God or creatures.[80] For Müntzer, God works through suffering to break the soul's clinging to creatures and to then occupy the empty space, so that the soul fears only God. Through the marriage of suffering and truth, Müntzer addressed Bohemiam skepticism regarding the introduction of yet another teaching into the fray.

Müntzer claims authority in the opening lines of the short version by appealing to his unsurpassed "diligence" in seeking "better instruction about the holy and invincible Christian faith." He complains that no monk or priest had ever taught him about "the true exercise of the faith" or "the edifying time of trial [*dye nutzbarliche anfechtungk*] which clarifies faith in the spirit of the fear of God, showing the need for an elect man to have the seven-fold gift of the Holy Spirit [Isaiah 11, which Müntzer connected to Numbers 19:12]." Likewise, "scholars [*gelerten*]" in Müntzer's experience failed to teach "about the order of God implanted in all creatures" or about how to grasp "the whole [of scripture] as a unity of parts." Inexperienced themselves, the would-be leaders of Christendom fed the people "mere" scripture or "stolen" scripture, saying nothing about God's inner Word or work.[81] In other words, the scholars extracted and upheld this or that verse, while denying and concealing the meaning of the whole of scripture concerning God's created order—the *Ordnung Gottes*. For Müntzer, this order involved God's possession of souls and the souls' possession of other creatures in turn; the proper order was reversed by the fall, as humans' lust for created things rendered them subject to those things.[82] Müntzer identities scripture itself as a creature, readily bent to the goals of creaturely desire—above all, the desire for freedom from suffering. Only the inward testimony of the Spirit gives certitude of faith or understanding.[83] Müntzer's argument was similar to Karlstadt's mature position—not developed at this time—in affirming that only an unmediated, inward instruction secured the soul from deceit; knowledge coming from outside the soul was inevitably processed according to self-will. Luther, conversely, would conclude that claims to inward instruction apart from the Word represented the epitome of unbroken pride. The debate thus turned in part on the question of what was required to subvert the pretensions of reason and will to understand God and earn salvation on human terms.

The chaotic, divided religious situation of Bohemia looms behind the *Prague Manifesto*. Müntzer's was conscious of having to meet the charge that he offered just one more "sect." The *Manifesto* notes that "the world (led astray by many sects) has for a long time been yearning desperately for the truth."[84] Scripture was not the solution, but contributed to uncertainty because the clergy offered hungry Christians only the unbroken bread of the "letter" of scripture, not "the true spirit of the fear of God," which alone convinces recipients that they are irrevocably among God's children.[85] As a consequence, Christians became "sissies [*memmen*]," claiming that God no longer speaks but communicates only through books. The clerics' offer of a shallow, letter-based religion rather than a religion of *conformitas Christi* allured with the offer of creaturely comfort, but failed to offer real consolation and invincible faith.[86]

The longer German version of the *Manifesto*, although not in Müntzer's own hand,[87] contains a telling auto-biographical reference to Müntzer's own spiritual trials and anxiety over the possession of true faith: "Like me many other men have complained that, although laboring under genuinely intolerable burdens,[88] they have never once been comforted, or enabled to be confident that in all their desires and deeds they have been led by faith, but had to work their own way through them."[89] While we have no reason to doubt the authenticity of Müntzer's self-depiction, it stands alongside similar self-depictions offered by both Luther and Karlstadt.[90] In recounting their struggles with and triumphs over *Anfechtungen*, the reformers presented themselves not only as models for the would-be saved and competent teachers of the afflicted, but also as spiritual men who had broken through to essential truths, unavailable to the less enduring. By placing their own trials publicly beside Luther's, Karlstadt and Müntzer made a claim to equal authority.

With regard to the experience of doubt, Müntzer wanted a Christianity that could meet not just anxiety about one's own election or salvation, or about the verity of a particular Christian doctrine, but fundamental rejection of the Bible, the church, and the Christian story. This account of *Anfechtungen* was central to the distinct view of annihilation and union that Müntzer developed over-and-against Luther and Karlstadt. Müntzer concluded that all God's elect were stirred by such deep, inward unbelief, and they needed guidance to weather the storm. Indeed, Christian teaching needed to guide not only the elect in their midst, but elect persons stirred by God among Muslims, Jews, and "heathen." He writes:

> Nor is it any surprise to me that all the nations of men deride us Christians, and spew us out, if no one can do better than [to assert]: It is written here, it is written there. . . . If a simple man or an unbeliever were to come into one of our gatherings, and we tried to bowl him over with our chatter he would say, "Are you mad or stupid? What is your scripture to me?" But if we learn the real living word of God we will win over the unbeliever and speak with obvious authority when the secret places of his heart are revealed so that he has to confess humbly that God is in us.[91]

Müntzer claims that the preacher who does not experience "revelations" has no authority to preach. Right preachers have come through spiritual trials and are possessed by God; thus, they can deliver prophesy received from God to prove the verity of their doctrine. Even the devil "believes in the truth of the Christian faith,"[92] he notes, although the devil has no true faith.

Müntzer brings the *Manifesto* to a conclusion by situating Christianity's fall into self-deception historically in the time "after the death of the apostles' pupils," when "the immaculate virginal church became a whore by the adultery of the clergy"—that is, the clergy's preference to be possessed by and serve creatures rather than God. Müntzer also blames "the scholars who always want to sit up top."[93] Müntzer declares that the new church, which will hear God and prophesy, will begin with the chosen in Bohemia, and he summons "every single person to help in the defense of God's word." If the Bohemians will not listen, he warns, God will allow the Turk to strike them down in the next year; thus, as his own view of the true preacher required, Müntzer offers prophesy to prove the verity of doctrine. Müntzer declares himself ready to suffer and die for his teaching and prophesy: "I am ready to suffer for it what Jeremiah had to bear."[94] Müntzer concludes with the stern warning that both he and the Bohemians will have to give an "account" (*Rechenschaft*) of their faith to God (I Pet. 4:1–5).[95] Müntzer's subsequent writings regularly insist that true believers can give *Rechenschaft*—an account of the trials involved in the onset of faith, particularly the struggle with inner unbelief. No one can be certain of their own election and salvation unless they have endured this struggle; no one who has come through the struggle, conversely, will fear to suffer the wrath of human beings.

Wandering and Letters, 1522–1523

By the time of the *Prague Manifesto* in late 1521, major theological rifts separated Müntzer from the Wittenbergers: Müntzer rejected the doctrine of *sola scriptura*, viewing scripture instead as a witness to the inward experience of God had by all the elect, and he demanded the separation of the godly from the godless. For a time, however, Müntzer sought to sway the leading Wittenberg theologians to his version of reform.[96] Seemingly, he regarded the Wittenberg reform movement as a divine intervention in history, while his own God-given purpose was to keep that movement from stopping with the easy appeal to scripture alone. Christians needed to learn about the inner confrontation with fundamental unbelief, to be broken of their desire for creatures, and to be transformed into people who feared only God in all their actions.

The circumstances of Müntzer's departure from Prague are unclear, but he may have been forced to flee sometime in December 1521.[97] He entered thereafter into a period of wandering, impoverished and seeking a position.[98] On March 29, 1522, from an unknown location possibly very near to Wittenberg, Müntzer wrote to Melanchthon.[99] He greeted the latter as an "instrument [*organum*] of Christ" and declared, "your theology I embrace with all my heart for it has snatched many souls of the elect[100] away from the snares of the hunters." Müntzer commended the rejection of clerical celibacy but criticized Melanchthon's alleged teachings on matrimony for leading clerics into a "Satanic brothel."[101] Müntzer envisioned a "coming church" led by clergy who were freed of desires for creaturely things—of "pleasures" that possessed and "tyrannize[d]" over the soul—and thus receptive to receiving God's "true" or "living" Word within; these clergy would lead all the elect to this blessed receptivity to God, separating the godly from the reprobate. Indeed, Christians emptied of lust and possessed by God would produce "elect offspring" in "the fear of God and the spirit of wisdom." To lead to this future, the Wittenbergers needed to give up the shallow and easy understanding of scripture that served and hardened their refusal to mortify their lusts. "We" use scripture to "trample down the world," Müntzer says, expressing common cause through use of the first-person plural, but scripture tells men to seek the truth that "proceeds from the mouth of God and not from books. . . . For unless it arises from the heart it is the word of man, condemning the turn-coat scribes, who rob the holy oracles, Jeremiah 23. The Lord has never spoken to them, yet they usurp his words." Müntzer exhorts, "O most beloved, see to it that you prophesy, otherwise *our* theology will not be worth a cent. . . . God is more willing to speak than you are prepared to listen. We are brim full of desires. This hinders the finger of the living God from piercing his tablets." Clergy gripped by lust for wives and full of pleasure cannot have "living colloquy with God."[102] Müntzer sets his admonition in the context of Revelation 16:4, the pouring out of the third vial: "The outpouring of blood has been accomplished; but their mind is oriented towards flesh and blood. Some are chosen, but their minds cannot be opened" because they are in the grips of creaturely pleasure. Consequently, their works are indistinguishable from those of the reprobate, although the fear of God marks them as elect.[103] Against Luther's argument for sparing the weak,[104] Müntzer argues:

> Our most beloved Martin acts ignorantly because he does not want to offend the little ones; but those little ones today are just like the boys who lived to be a hundred years old and were damned.[105] But the tribulation of Christians is already at the door, why you should consider that it is still to come, I do not know. Dear brothers, leave your dallying, the time has come![106] Do not delay, summer is at the door. Do not make peace with the reprobate, for they impede the mighty working of the word. Do not flatter your princes; otherwise you will live to see your undoing, which may the blessed God forfend.[107]

Müntzer's apocalyptic remarks here aimed at an urgent redirection of evangelical teaching and preaching; clergy were to model and then proclaim the mortification of lusts (i.e., sanctification) necessary to empty souls and make them receptive to the inner Word. There could be no gentle toleration and coexistence with the reprobate—no reformation on the basis of base political calculation. Müntzer also denounced the denial of purgatory as an "abominable error" reflecting ignorance of scripture and "the knowledge of the spirit": "papist" fantasies were to be rejected, but "no one can enter into rest unless the seven grades of reason are opened to the seven spirits." Müntzer offered to prove all his arguments "from the Scriptures, from the order of creation, from experience, and from the clear word of God." Switching from Latin to German, he admonished, "You delicate biblical scholars, do not hang back. I cannot proceed any other way."[108]

The phrase "delicate biblical scholars" reflects Müntzer's understanding of *sola scriptura* as a position imagined by the clergy and embraced by the people in order to avoid the hard path of discipline and inner confrontation with unbelief. The superficial and self-deceptive appeal to sparing the weak likewise excused the responsible parties—ultimately all elect—from necessary struggle on the ecclesial-social plane. The Wittenberg reformation was crashing on the rocks of lust for women and fear of rulers. Easy Roman fantasies and rituals had been discarded, but the more plausible poison of scripture, regard for the weak, obedience to due authority, and "modesty" (as in the letter to Hausmann) revealed a cowardice that might prove fatal.

Only a few surviving sources testify to Müntzer's opinions and experiences for the second half of 1522 and the first half of 1523. In one letter to an unknown critic, Müntzer lambastes the Wittenbergers as self-seeking souls, not possessed by God and unable to carry forward what they started.[109] Just before Easter in 1523, then, Müntzer began an appointment at the St. John's Church in Allstedt, a small town under the electoral Saxon jurisdiction; his nearly seventeen months in the town proved to be the longest respite from wandering in his career. He married, and his wife gave birth to a son.[110] Like Karlstadt in Orlamünde, Müntzer in Allstedt now sought to create a "Gegen-Wittenberg."[111] He published vernacular liturgical works, including songs for congregational use, forcing Luther and his allies to produce competing material.[112] Müntzer's reformed services and sermons at Allstedt proved popular and drew worshippers and hearers from neighboring jurisdictions. Müntzer also found an ally in the town's other preacher, Simon Haferitz.[113] Together with Müntzer and Haferitz, the town council embarked on a course of confrontation on multiple fronts—with the nuns of the Naundorf cloister, the Ernestine princes, Ernest of Mansfeld, and George of Saxony.

When Müntzer wrote to Luther on July 9, 1523, tensions had been mounting for some time. Siegfried Bräuer argues that Luther had already given up on Müntzer as an "ally for the common cause," but Müntzer "seems to have had hope, in spite of all reservations, that the distance from Luther still was bridgeable." The July letter, according to Bräuer, is a defense, explication, and attempt at reconciliation.[114] Occasioned by Luther's objections to his teachings—objections that Müntzer may have learned about through intermediaries or correspondence—Müntzer's letter mostly eschews the scolding and instructing of the Wittenbergers that had marked his earlier correspondence with Melanchthon. The letter works instead to distance Müntzer from his reputation as a disturber of the peace and his association with the "Zwickau prophets." Müntzer opens with exalted praise of Luther's sincerity and devotion to others, denies that he incited any disturbance upon his departure from Zwickau,[115] coldly refuses to defend Storch and Stübner, and responds to Luther's revulsion at the prophets' mystical vocabulary only by saying that he, Müntzer, shuns "profane novelties and pseudo-knowledge" unsupportable by scripture.[116] Still, the letter is not entirely conciliatory: Müntzer expresses wonder at Luther's commendation of Egranus, discerning Luther's motive as political convenience.[117]

The bulk of Müntzer's apology is devoted to the issue of present revelation. Müntzer accepts that visions and voices might be demonic as well as divine; thus, they need to be evaluated through a deeper learning directly "from the mouth of the living God," without the mediation of sense perception. Likewise, Christians can have assurance of the truth of scripture, which is read and heard through the senses, only from this direct divine experience. Inward experience itself is proven true through suffering conformity to the crucified. Müntzer thus charts a course between what he regards as dead Biblicism, on the one side, and unbridled visionary claims, on the other. Just as those who think God never speaks refuse to endure the spiritual trials associated with hearing the divine—the purging of attachment to soul-possessing creatures, or the recognition of hidden unbelief—those who think God always is at hand have not experienced forsakenness. I quote at length:

> The recognition of the divine will, which should fill us with wisdom [sapientia] through Christ, with a spiritual and infallible understanding [intellectu], this knowledge of God [scientia Dei] is to be possessed by all (as the apostle teaches the Colossians [1:9]), so that we may be seen to be taught by the mouth of the living God and may know with complete certainty that the teaching of Christ was not devised by man but comes to us from the living God without any shadow of deception. For Christ himself

wants us to have judgment over his teaching ... No mortal man knows this teaching or knows whether Ch[rist] is mendacious or truthful, unless his will is conformed to the crucified one, unless he, too, has first endured the swells and surges of the waters, which for most of the time are cascading over the heads of the elect from all sides. After a struggle, however, he is rescued again, having cried out hoarsely and learnt to hope against hope [Romans 4:18] and to seek his will alone on the day of visitation that comes after prolonged waiting. Then his feet will be set upon the rock and the Lord who works wonders will appear from afar; at long last authentic testimonies of God [*testimonia Dei credibilia*] will be rendered. But anyone who disdains all this, expecting the Lord to be always at hand, is quite at variance with the entire body of Scripture. Nor should those who boast about Christ be believed unless they have his [S]pirit, Romans 8: That he may testify to their spirit that they are sons of God, Isaiah 8. Moreover, no one is a son of God unless he suffers with him and becomes as a sheep for the slaughter all the day long. Let God not spare himself, but forsake him for a while, until at length he is assured that no created thing can detach him from the living God and the absolutely true testimony of the Scriptures. This assurance [*Is tanta certitudine fretus*] enables him to distinguish by divine revelation between the work of God and that of malignant spirits; here he draws quite legitimately on really genuine appearances and hidden portents, discerning profound mysteries from the mouth of God.[118]

Müntzer pleads, "Dearest of patrons, you know Thomas by name and character. I am not the sort of person to accept ecstasies and visions unless compelled to by God." Appealing to John 16:13, Müntzer argues that the Holy Spirit does teach Christians about the future, but he assures Luther that he accepts visions only with the confirming testimony of scripture. Visions, dreams and voices are to be measured against scriptural testimony. The key to scripture, in turn, is the divine, unassailable *scientia* or *sapientia* won in inward suffering.[119]

In conclusion to the letter, Müntzer expresses his willingness to be corrected by Luther's "superior testimony," and he pleads, "renew your old love."[120] Whatever Müntzer hoped to accomplish with such flattery and pleading, the letter itself opened no doors to new understanding or cooperation: scripture for Müntzer offered secondary confirmation of truth, and those who relied on scripture as the supposed source of truth refused suffering conformity to the crucified. These cross-shirkers could have no true confidence in the verity of Christ's teaching; they could not judge doctrine. For Müntzer, moreover, the *Anfechtungen* that emptied the soul and opened the mind were passing if terrible surges, not (as Luther believed) the constant suffering of self-trusting sinners before sin, death, the devil, and divine law and judgment. Kindred was the quest for certitude of faith and doctrine, and the assumption that self-assertive fallen nature and reason stood in the way, but each reformer gave the self's assertion (desire for creatures versus self-trust) and the self's anxiety (fundamental unbelief versus anxiety about salvation) a different cast and found a different remedy.

Within ten days of penning his attempt to convince Luther of God's plan to occupy human souls, Müntzer's first publication addressed a group of Christians who, in his view, sought to claim God's presence and impulsion without the requisite suffering. In a circular letter to "brothers" in his hometown of Stolberg, Müntzer warned them to avoid "unjustifiable rebellion [*auffrur*]."[121] We know little about the circumstances that provoked the letter, other than the provocation noted by Müntzer himself: "You [Stolbergers] combine vainglory with a failure to study; you are negligent; when you are in your cups you talk a great deal about our mission [*der sache*]; when sober you are a bunch of milksops [*memmen*]."[122] In response, Müntzer does not rule out the possibility of a Christian use of force,[123] as Karlstadt and his Orlamünde community would do later, but he declares that the proper implementation of God's order can be carried out only by those who have first suffered inwardly in order to become God's instruments, conformed to Christ and hence the divine will. Along with Müntzer's "private" letter to Luther and its self-distancing from popular tumult and visionary prophecy,[124] this printed letter to the Stolbergers reveals a concerted effort by Müntzer in mid-1523 to demonstrate that his way of reform was not unruly, capricious, or self-invented. Rather, the inner Word that could not be twisted by fallen desire was to guide the judgment of visions and voices, doctrine and exegesis, and the course of reform. Müntzer's stance toward Wittenberg theology in the Stolberg letter is openly critical, although with the express intention of correction.

The central theme of the Stolberg letter is the necessity of suffering God's inward work before acting in human affairs as a divine instrument for the establishment of God's *Ordnung*.[125] Müntzer begins, "What heights of folly that many of God's elect friends imagine that God will speed to their aid and quickly put Christianity to rights, although no one is really yearning for this or longing to reach poverty in spirit by suffering and endurance, Matthew 5, Luke 6." A person is not worthy to be ruled by God, Müntzer declares, until he has "tasted [*vorsucht*]" poverty of spirit. A central theme in Tauler,[126] poverty of spirit represents here the opposite of self-willed living in pursuit of the "good life." To attain "real, unvarnished poverty of spirit," one "must first (by human reckoning) be forsaken by God . . . [and] leave all creature comforts behind [*sich euβere[n]*]. But as long as the elect cannot bring themselves to show respect for God's work God can do nothing." Like Karlstadt and Luther, Müntzer here ascribes a positive pedagogical value to outward suffering, insofar as it provokes a spiritual reorientation. God, he writes, makes tyrants "rage more and more, Kings 8, so that the countenance of his elect is covered in shame and vice [*laster*] and they are driven to seek the name and glory and honor of God alone, Psalm 82. For the lot or reward of the elect will be identical with that of the damned if they are indolent Luke 12."[127]

In a striking turn, Müntzer has dispensed with the predestinarian views that surfaced in his documents lambasting Tiburtius and Egranus, insisting now that the elect must adopt an appropriate stance before God—readiness to suffer God's work—and engage in the mortification of creaturely attachments. Müntzer argues that joyful participation in God's new kingdom will begin here and now for elect souls who proves receptive; but these souls must first realize the depths of their unbelief, which mounts to hatred of God. Müntzer writes:

> God's true reign is truly and joyfully inaugurated when the elect come to see what God's work reveals to them in the experience of the spirit. Those people who have not tasted the reverse, bitter side of faith do not know this, for they have not believed against belief, or hoped against hope, or met God's love with hate I Corinthians 2.[128]

For Müntzer, people with untried faith cannot hope to implement correct reform, for they do not know "what harms, or profits, the people of Christ." "They do not want to believe" in the reality or sufficiency of God's direct instruction: "That is why the whole world lacks the chief point of salvation [*heuptstu[o]ck der seligkeit*], which is faith, not being able to credit that God would deign to be our schoolteacher, Matthew 23, James 3."[129] Like Luther, then, Müntzer treats faith as the certain expectation of something seemingly impossible—but for Luther, the impossible was salvation by faith without works on account of Christ; for Müntzer, who here reflected a level of kinship with Karlstadt, the impossible was God's direct instruction as a divine pedagogue. At the same time, Müntzer sees the reception of God as a more complete, unambiguous, and hence joyous experience than Karlstadt, who expected human self-will to continue to impede the reception of God's inner Word.

Müntzer described the recognition of unbelief in the Stolberg letter, complaining that this necessary disturbance of the soul's waters was too quickly stilled among Christians by ritual (Rome) or by scripture (Wittenberg). As a result, Christianity produced only "foolish men" who did not know what "move[d]" them to be Christians "rather than pagans, or why the Koran should not be as valid as the gospel. For they cannot refute the opponents from the divine order." The margin here reads, *ratio fidei*, and a reference to 1 Peter 3:15 underlines that true believers must give an account of their bitter trials and faith.[130] As long as they are deceived about faith because of their refusal to suffer God's work within, Müntzer warns, the Stolbergers' bombast will amount to nothing—or worse, to an "unjustifiable rebellion" that even if successful will only heap deceit onto deceit:

> So it is all important that we allow God to rule; that we know for sure that our faith does not deceive us, having genuinely suffered [*erlyden*] the working of the living word and being able to discriminate between the work of God and that of his creatures. As yet the world cannot accept this. We are invested with kingly splendour, with real strength, when we experience the might of God surging through us; but we will be girded around [martyred] as Peter was . . . Only then will the assembly of the elect lay hold on the whole wide world, which will acquire a Christian government that no sack of gunpowder can ever topple. But because our zeal to grow in the spirit of truth does not increase, our soul is not ready to be a throne for God; but he who sits on the throne of abomination will rule over the man who will not let God rule over him.[131]

Until his execution in 1525, Müntzer did not cease to chide all those who, in his view, fled from an inner experience of unbelief—that is, the papists and the Wittenbergers, along with all the laity who eagerly accepted their easy, outward ways to salvation and even those who, seeking direct revelation, claimed to hear the voice of God without requisite discipline.

Müntzer's Criticism of the Wittenberg *Solas* (Faith, Christ, and Scripture Alone), 1523–1524

In a letter to Spalatin on August 3, 1523, Luther reported that he had tried to arrange a meeting with Müntzer to test his teaching.[132] This personal meeting between Luther and Müntzer never occurred, but there is some evidence that Müntzer and Simon Haferitz met with John Lang and George Spalatin in early November 1523, when the electoral retinue stopped for a few days at the Allstedt castle.[133] In December, Müntzer published a substantial statement of his views, under the title *Protestation or Proposition*. This text may represent the "final form" of a confession written for the meeting with Lang. Müntzer's concise *On Counterfeit Faith* was published after the *Protestation* and appears to have been connected—precisely how remains obscure—to a series of eleven questions that Spalatin sent to Müntzer, possibly in connection with the *Lehrgespräch*.[134] These questions seek grounds for certitude of faith and doctrine:

> (1) Which, and what, is truly Christian faith? (2) How is faith born? . . . (6) How can we be sure (*certi*) of our faith? (7) How can, and ought, each individual test his faith? (8) Who are the true followers [*fideles*] of Christ? (9) What are the trials [*in quibus tentationibus*] under which faith is born, bears seed, and grows? (10) How can faith maintain itself under trials and emerge as conqueror? (11) Which faith saves and how?[135]

Such questions invited Müntzer's identification of true, saving faith as that which is born in and endures throughout trials.

The lengthy title of the *Protestation or Proposition* promises a public explication of Müntzer's teachings, especially those dealing with the beginnings of faith and with baptism. Directly addressing readers, Müntzer declares that he preaches "Jesus Christ, he who was crucified, and you and me with him."[136] For Müntzer, the true church consisted only of those who could give account of their receipt of faith through inner tribulation; consequently, the practice of infant baptism—indeed, the necessity of water baptism at all—was placed into question. Some exchange between Müntzer and the Wittenberg camp on this topic preceded publication of the *Protestation*, possibly at Allstedt Castle.[137] As a whole, the *Protestation* is a rebuttal of Wittenberg's faith-, Christ- and scripture-alone formulations, yet a rebuttal carried out partly through ideas shared with Luther, including the deceptiveness of fallen nature, the necessity of certain faith, and the association of certitude and consolation with suffering—because there is only false certitude and consolation in circumstances pleasing to fallen nature. The common source of Eckhartian mysticism looms in the background.

The *Protestation* takes a historical view, an orientation we witnessed already in the Müntzer of the Jüterbog sermons. According to Müntzer, God chose the elect to be "pure wheat" and placed them in "fruitful and profitable soil," but they now find themselves overwhelmed by the weeds, even as their "heartfelt groaning and yearning to follow God's will is the one infallible mark of true apostolic Christianity."[138] The mingling of elect and reprobate in the church followed the introduction of infant baptism. The church began to trust in a symbol more than reality—that is, it trusted in water to create faith—and no longer required a long period of catechism before baptism.[139] To defend infant baptism, *Schriftgelehrten* appeal to John 3:5, "Whoever is not baptized with water and the Holy Spirit will not come into the kingdom of God," but in so doing, they only pluck one piece of scripture out of the whole, interpreting it with the goal of avoiding suffering. Müntzer counters that John 3 can only be understood in light of John 7, which Müntzer renders, "If someone is thirsty, let him come to me and drink. For . . . whoever believes in me, streams of water will flow from his body, living waters." Müntzer interprets the reference to water as a reference to the Holy Spirit given to the Apostles at Pentecost; water refers, further, to "the movement of our spirit in God's." Looking more fully at John, Müntzer argues that John 1 explains this meaning, while John 2 shows that our water turns into wine, meaning, "Our movement begins to long to suffer." John baptizes with water in the third chapter to show that "until there are many waters, and much movement, the voice of the bridegroom cannot be understood." Nicodemus, who comes to Christ in John 3, represents the biblical scholars who focus on material signs, while Christ points them to true water, that is, tribulation and spirit. "There is no other sign than that of Jonah," which means for Müntzer that the elect must suffer and be swallowed up in the confrontation with unbelief.[140]

Müntzer thus criticizes the Wittenberg reformation for supporting outward, infant baptism, supposedly on the basis of "scripture alone," while never asking believers to confront the reality and depth of their false faith through an inward spiritual baptism. Thus, according to Müntzer, Luther's teaching had only deepened the "blindness" of Christendom, replacing a manifestly false faith with a faith that *appeared* to rest on solid ground. "If our eyes are to be opened," he admonishes, "we have to first recognize our blindness, of which the most obvious marks are the counterfeit faith and the hypocritical works which follow from it." Müntzer casts his Wittenberg opponents in the role of the scholars in John 9, who object to Christ, "We know that God speaks through Moses"; Müntzer counters that scripture's "rightness" kills rather than making alive. The purpose of scripture is to deepen the suffering of those who have the beginning of faith. Müntzer often referred to this beginning of faith as the "spirit of fear"; here, he speaks of the "mustard seed" of faith (from Matt. 17:20/Luke 17:6). For Müntzer, being slain means recognizing inner unbelief; hence, the beginning or arrival of faith is experienced first as unbelief. By its killing work—that is, its exposure of unbelief—scripture makes faith to grow so that the believer knows and feels without any doubt that Christianity and no other faith is true. Müntzer writes:

> [Scripture] is written for us ignorant people, so that the holy faith, the mustard seed, should taste bitter as if there were no Scripture at all, bringing about a tremendous, irresistible feeling of consternation [vorwu[e]nderung]. Am I really going to accept Scripture just because the church gives its outward approval, with no further knowledge of how one arrives at faith?[141]

The "heathen" also believe "their gods are pious saints, subject to the highest God," Müntzer says, and Turks "boast of their Mohammed as highly as we of our Christ." Meanwhile, Jewish tradition is more ancient than Christian tradition—Christians invent a new law every day, Müntzer scorns—and Jews excel Christians in their devotion to scripture and moral conduct.[142] There is, in short, no outward, visible cause for preferring Christianity at all.

Especially noteworthy for our purposes is that Müntzer extends this polemical comparison of Christians to their various others (pagans, Muslims, and Jews) beyond matters of tradition and morality to what he took to be the defining stance of faith—the preparedness to suffer. Müntzer argues that Christians' preoccupation with avoiding suffering renders them no better than the followers of other faiths. Like heathens, Christians want saints to whom they can pray for physical and material assistance, for "being such delicate plants, we cannot bear to suffer at all." Christians call upon St. Margaret to avert the pain of childbirth, contrary to the text of Genesis 3:16, and like the Turks, they want a God who is "far too gentle" to allow the crucifixion. Müntzer rails, "Isn't our whole world today party to a similar fantastic, sensual, deceptively attractive way of looking at things, although it still likes to dress up neatly in Holy Scripture. It makes a great song and dance about the faith of the apostles and the prophets, but apparently the only price we need to pay for the faith so bitterly gained by them is to stagger round mad-drunk."[143] A marginal remark here glosses Müntzer's exclamation, "Does it strike you how our whole life rages in open idolatry against the equitable will of God?" with the cue, "this book in the whole says nothing else." Müntzer laments that Christians cannot and will not see their folly, and he lays the blame on the "unreliable [*ungetrewen*]" biblical scholars who had led Christendom from Roman ritualism into an even deeper deceit.[144]

Müntzer's *Protestation* accordingly seeks to unmask the falsehood of the Wittenberg doctrine of faith. He dismisses that doctrine for supposedly requiring a mere intellectual faith, based on the remembrance of Christ's self-sacrifice, rather than present conformity to the crucified through the suffering of God's work within. He had leveled similar charges against Egranus, in the belief that his position was Wittenberg's position. Müntzer now skillfully turns against Luther and his allies core shared commitments (e.g., to faith, certitude, suffering, and passivity *coram deo*) as well as vocabulary and ideas from the Eckhartian mystical tradition (e.g., surrounding the soul's separation from creaturely attachments and God's direct work in its depths). Müntzer's readiness to claim authority over Christian teaching was wedded to a palpable sense of betrayal—a sense that in rejecting him, the "ungetrewen" Wittenbergers had abandoned the very purpose of the reform then underway, the teaching and practice of human receptivity to God over and against a human-invented, self-assertive, and lust-serving faith. Because of the misguided teaching of the *Schriftgelehrten*, Müntzer writes, "we too have become arrogant—just like our opponents—and are inclined promptly to throw to the dogs anyone who does not hold our views in every respect." Müntzer continues:

> The real reason [for the arrogant suppression of dissent] is that many people have no eyes for the work of God. They imagine that all one needs to do to come to the Christian faith [*man kund also leichtlich zum christenglauben kommen*] is think about what CHRIST has said. No, my dear man, what you must do is endure patiently, and learn [*wissen*] how God himself will root out your weeds, thistles and thorns from the rich soil which is your heart. Otherwise nothing good will grow there, only the

raging devil in the guise of light, and showy corn-cockles etc. . . . Even if you have already devoured all the books of the Bible you still must suffer the sharp edge of the plough-share. For you will never have faith unless God himself gives it to you, and instructs you in it. If that is to happen, then at first, my dear biblical scholar, the book will be closed to you, too. For even if you burst in the effort, neither reason nor any created being can open it for you. God has to gird your loins; yes, you must let God, working in you, strip [you] of all the clothing of creaturely origin which you have been wearing, and you must not do what the clever ones do, producing one saying here, another there, without a scrupulous comparison with the whole spirit of Scripture.[145]

Müntzer contends that the scholars use partial exegesis to support and hide their refusal to suffer God's work; they prefer to ascend to God through reason. The scholars say, "Christ has achieved everything on his own," but that is "much, much too short. If you do not see the head in relation to its members, how can you hope to follow in his footsteps? I suppose on a good, warm fur, or on a silk cushion."[146]

Müntzer's attack on the Wittenberg *solas* deliberately divorces the slogans from the frameworks—including Luther's commitment to passivity *coram deo* and the surrender of self-trust—that had governed their initial articulation. For Müntzer, "Christ alone" reflected a partial exegesis in the service of cross-shirking, just as "scripture alone" diverted attention from and encouraged an easy calming of spiritual anguish. The result was the doctrine of "faith alone," that is, faith without works. Luther, of course, had meant that faith saves without works, not that faith produces no works or suffers no divine work. For Müntzer, the addition of "alone" to scripture, Christ, and faith served in each case to strip away the painful aspects of accepting scripture, Christ, and faith. Müntzer recalls Luther's own complaint against indulgences as seeking to remove *poenae* that should be patiently endured, writing:

The Romans distributed indulgences, and remitted penalty and guilt, and are we, straight away, to build on a similar foundation? That would be equivalent to having an old house white-washed and saying it was new. We would be doing the same if we preached a honey-sweet CHRIST, well-pleasing to our murderous nature. Yes, what would we achieve if it didn't have to suffer anything and Christ gave everything gratuitously? Wouldn't

228 ENEMIES OF THE CROSS

we just be blowing the same fanfare as the Turk? He denies the history of CHRIST, our savior; and we wanted to deny it secretly, or rather thievingly; so that we do not need to suffer and can let the wheat and thorns vaunt themselves side by side.[147]

The only way to salvation, Müntzer continues, is "the narrow way, so that a text [alle urteil] is not studied according to outward appearances, but according to the most loving will of God in his living word and tested in crises [anfechtung] of faith of all kinds, as CHRIST says himself . . . Only then does a person realize that his house—he himself . . .—is built on the immoveable rock."[148]

Müntzer's "narrow way" was also, in his terms, a deeper way, seeking to discover that inner experience that certifies the truth of scripture and reveals its meaning and Christ's meaning. As we noted earlier, the beginning of faith in Müntzer's view was the elect person's realization that she or he had no true faith—neither in scripture nor Christ. Only this crisis brought the Christian to the "immoveable" foundation—the living Word within—upon which true faith and responsible exegesis could be built. Müntzer cites the apostle Peter's experience to argue that all Christians must fall and fail in their faith. The experience is purgative: "the apostles and all the prophets could not face the words of God" or experience the power of God "until all the weeds and the temerity of a counterfeit faith had been hoed away." Only after his fall did Peter realize "his temerity," and thereafter, "he became quite resolute."[149] Müntzer writes, "I have to know whether it is God who said this and not the devil; I have to distinguish the work of both of them in the ground of the soul. Otherwise I will let myself be hoodwinked in a way which only catches wind, such as the biblical scholars who have not been put to the test, practice on themselves and others, Matthew 7." The Matthew citation here refers to the statement that Christ taught as one with authority, unlike the Schriftgelehrten, who learned and taught from books. The scribes do not speak with "the power [gewalt] of God," asserting instead that their faith is from scripture alone. Thus, they make faith easy and attractive to fallen reason. "The light of nature has such a high conceit of itself that it fancies that [faith] is so easy to come by."[150]

The reference to the ground here points unmistakably to the Eckhartian tradition, and the dialectic of false or natural light versus true light—joined to a discussion of the bitterness of the true Christ life—reminds of the German Theology in particular. For Müntzer, the "self-opinionated [gutdunckende] light of nature" cloaks itself in the pious trappings of "scripture alone," so that it might cling to the sweet rather than the bitter Christ ("Christ alone") and to an easy faith, separated from works ("faith alone"). The light of nature says, "Yes, there is no doubt about it, you are born to Christian parents, you have never once doubted, and you will continue to stand firm. Yes, yes, I am a good Christian. O, can I come to salvation so easily?" Consequently, the elect are led astray and have "no intention either of embarking on faith or on upright works, for those who champion the gospel at the moment praise faith above all things."[151]

Müntzer's reference to works requires close examination, for he does not claim that works are meritorious of salvation; whenever Müntzer associates works with salvation, he refers to God's inward movement to take possession of the soul, to ascetic self-discipline (separation from creaturely attachments) to prepare the soul to perceive and receive God's movement, and to the activity of the purified believer impelled by God to be God's instrument in a godless world. In the first and the third points—the ones emphasized in the present text—he was not so far removed from Luther or Karlstadt and their shared mystical heritage. "The mark is missed completely," Müntzer declares, "if one preaches that faith and not works have to justify us," for this "immodest [*unbescheidene*]" teaching "does not confront one's nature with the fact that man comes to faith *by the work of God and that this is the first and the main thing for which one must wait*. Otherwise faith is not worth a cent and is a lie from beginning to end, being based on our efforts." The right, evangelical preacher will say "how it feels to be poor in spirit" and will give examples of "tribulations" from the fathers and the Bible, for the "written promises" of God only "reveal how his almighty power has been active in all his elect."[152] Here it is helpful to recall what Müntzer had written already in the anti-Roman context of the *Prague Manifesto*, "They say one can surely flee the anger of God with good works and with costly virtues. From none of these, however, do they learn what it is to experience God, what real faith is, what robust virtue is, what good works are after reconciliation with God [*eintragen zu Gott*]."[153] Even as Müntzer repudiates the Wittenberg reformation, he does not make works prior to and causative of the "reconciliation with God"; although he allows for the necessity of ascetic praxis and a proper response of the elect to God (as in the letter to the Stolbergers), salvation for Müntzer is suffered because it is directed against fallen nature—which lusts after and is possessed by creatures. Like Karlstadt, Müntzer departed from the strictest doctrine of the bondage of the will partly by appropriating mystical teachings about "waiting," along with the broader notion in Tauler and the *German Theology* that one can and must adopt a stance of passivity.[154]

Müntzer laments that few Christians accept God's work in and through them. Instead, "they want to be good evangelical folk by using many vainglorious words," and many adopt evangelical Christianity merely "as a pretext to pursue a loose life."[155] On the other hand, the "honest people" who reject "fleshy enjoyment" and tread the narrow way cannot come to a right end for lack of true teaching. With their right desire they only fall into "a hedge of thorns, that is into heathen ceremonies and rites, into excesses of fasting and praying, [etc.,] and to think that now they have discovered the way."[156] One must not be stilled by works-righteousness, but "gnaw . . . through counterfeit faith and outward works," discovering that "the word, on which true faith depends, . . . springs out of the abyss of the heart." This process means to become "sober, to bid all the lusts farewell and exert oneself to the utmost in the expectation [*mit der hochsten arbeyt wartten*] of a word or promise of this kind from God." Faith must be first-hand, "[f]or a man does not believe because he has heard it from other people," nor does he lose faith when others reject the truth.[157] Thus, Müntzer pairs ascetic self-mortification and waiting for God as necessary responses to the discovery of one's deep-seated unbelief. He writes:

> It is the zealous expectation of the word that is the first step to being a Christian. This expectation must begin by enduring the word patiently, and there must be no confidence at all that we will be forgiven eternally because of our works. Then a person thinks he has no trace of faith. . . . He feels or finds a feeble desire for true faith, which is so faint that he is scarcely and only after great difficulty aware of it. But finally it has to burst out and he cries, "O, what a wretched man I am, what is going on in my heart? My conscience devours the very marrow of my being, my strength, everything that makes me what I am. What on earth am I to do now? I am at my wits' end, and receive no comfort from God or man. For God is plaguing me with my conscience, with my lack of belief, my despair and with blaspheming against him. Outwardly I am visited by sickness, poverty, wretchedness and every manner of distress by the deeds of evil men, etc. And the inward stresses are far greater than the outward ones. What wouldn't I give to be able to believe truly, since everything seems to depend on this. If only I knew what the right way was! Then I'd be ready to run to the ends of the earth to obtain it."[158]

In Müntzer's view, Luther and his allies did not help the elect to understand these stirrings—the consternation produced by the mustard seed of faith within—or prepare them to render the proper response of waiting for and enduring God's work. The Wittenbergers' feigned modesty or humility, expressed in the *solas*, concealed their lust-driven, self-willed preference to remain on the surface of spiritual experience rather than suffer God's work. Consequently, the Wittenbergers failed to provide the certitude of salvation demanded by Luther's own doctrine of salvation or the consolation that they all agreed was a chief task of the minister. The Wittenbergers preferred that people trust in their own learned insights rather than God's power:

> [The] disheartened people come to them (who are the very best there are) saying, "Dear, estimable, honourable, most learned sir" and a lot of similar rubbish. "I am a poor devil at my wits' end. I really have no faith in God or creatures. I feel so bad that I really don't know if I would rather be dead or alive. For God's sake give me some good advice, for I suspect that the devil has got hold of me." Then the learned gentlemen, who are always enormously irritated at having to open their mouths, for one word from them costs many a pretty penny, reply, "Now, now, my good chap; if you won't believe, then go to the devil!" Then the poor creature will answer: "I'm sorry, most learned doctor, I really would like to believe, but unbelief smothers my good intentions [*der unglawbe vordruckt alle mein begir*]. How in the world should I deal with it?" The learned man says: "Well, my dear fellow, you should not be concerning yourself with such lofty matters. Just have simple faith and chase these ideas away. It is pure fantasy. Go back to your own folk and cheer up, then you'll forget your worries." You see, my dear brother, this is the sort of consolation which holds sway in the churches— the only sort! Such consolation has made all serious discipleship abominable in men's eyes.[159]

Müntzer explains that reason is suspicious of spiritual trials, not trusting that God can preserve its sanity. This mistrust is "the first unbelief" and the reason that the "idle" biblical scholars object to Müntzer's teaching as too high for the "poor coarse people."[160]

The final section of the *Protestation*—before three short "appendices"— polemicizes against such "unfaithful false scholars" as the "fattened pigs" whom Christ calls "false prophets." Müntzer maligns the scholars as wholly deceived and unable to preach rightly; they have no experience of God because they refuse to suffer it. Consequently, "they should believe that there are many, many infants at the breast whom God will use to spread his name abroad. For all who do this will, in the eyes of the world, be trodden underfoot like worms as Christ was."[161] Müntzer underlines, finally, the purpose of his writing: "I hope by this initiative to bring about an improvement in the teaching of the evangelical preachers; nor have I any desire to despise our backward and slow Roman brothers." He declares his willingness to be corrected and to stake his life on his teachings, but only in an open hearing before "men of all nations and all faiths."[162]

Counterfeit Faith rehearses many of the same themes as the *Protestation*, reflecting upon Christendom's imaginary faith, which appeals to fallen human nature. Müntzer defines Christian faith as "an assurance [*sicherung*] that one can rely on the word and promise of Christ," while insisting that one becomes "receptive to God's word and work" only through purgative suffering. The elect person who "yearns for and endures the word" seeks "to be found conformable to [Christ] in every respect":

> [I]f anyone is to grasp hold of this word with an upright, unfeigned [*ungetichten*] heart his ears must first be swept free of the droning of all sorrows and lusts. For a man can no more claim that he is a Christian before his cross has made him receptive to God's work and word than a field can produce a heavy crop of wheat until it has been ploughed. The elect friend of God who yearns for and endures the word is no counterfeit [*getichten*] hearer, but a diligent pupil of his master, constantly and ardently watching all that he does, seeking to be found conformable to him in every respect, to the best of his ability.[163]

Müntzer states that Christ is the end of human life, "the true goal of blessedness," and he explains that *conformitas Christi* means to seek the destruction of one's secret unbelief: "Whenever a person hears or sees something pointing him to Christ he takes it as a miraculous indication of how to chase away, do to death, reduce to pulp his unbelief." Scripture thus represents a "two-edged sword" for the elect. Its first purpose is to "to choke us to death, not to vivify us," by showing "how sorely God has tried all his elect from the very beginning, not even sparing his only son." Scripture points the elect to experience. The "self-indulgent biblical scholars" may boast about their faith, presenting themselves as "angels of light," but the falsehood of their faith is revealed by their inability to give an account of its origin (*yrs glaubens ankunfft und rechenschafft geben*).[164]

Like the *Protestation*, *Counterfeit Faith* uses terms of emptying and plowing to describe the divinely worked trials at the beginning of faith. Here, the reception of Eckhartian mysticism is oriented around and gives depth to his definition of faith as a trust in and fear of God that has overcome fundamental unbelief—doubt concerning the truth of Christianity itself—and accepts the unbelievable promise of God's direct presence in the soul. Vis-à-vis Luther, Müntzer consciously adopts language of divine promise and human trust, but he argues that Luther and his Wittenberg scholars trivialize the wondrous nature of the promise, which seems impossible to nature. According to Müntzer, the fallen "light of nature" thinks it has faith. The elect are convinced otherwise only through trials and shame, which open their *ratio* so that they can hear the word rather than the drone of nature. Müntzer calls on Biblical examples, beginning with Abraham. He explains that "God caused Abraham to be miserable and forsaken so that he would put his trust in God alone [*an Gott allein solte sicher sein*], not in any created being." Abraham was "plagued" by God's promise, the fulfillment of which always seemed "very far-fetched indeed to the light of nature." Müntzer asks, "If the light of nature had to be obliterated [*vortilget*] so radically in Abraham, how much more will this be true of us?"[165] In a similar manner, Müntzer argues, Moses could not trust in God's "living promise" prior to the destruction of the light of nature in him through a painful recognition of unbelief:

> Before [Moses] could come to an unfeigned trust in God [*ungeticht sich auff Got verlassen*] his unbelief had to be made quite clear to him. Otherwise he could not have been sure that the devil would not plant himself in his path in the guise of a dog. For Moses might well have taken God for a devil if he had not recognized the distinction between the directness [*einfeltigkayt*] of God and the deviousness [*hinderlist*] of the creatures laid down in the order between God and the creatures. Even should the entire world accept something as God-given the man who is poor in spirit will only be satisfied [*kan es doch den armgeistigen nicht stillen*] if it accords with what he has found after tribulation.[166]

Just as human creatures either give themselves to be God's possession and thus possess subordinate creatures, or reject God and find themselves ruled by creatures, so too they either know the whole through the immediate, simple divinity present within them, or are deceived by false and partial "knowledge" drawn from and imparted by multiple creaturely objects.

The fictitious, partial images with which *Counterfeit Faith* is concerned are those of the merciful God and the sweet Christ, both supported by a partial reading of scripture. Müntzer again wants to expose "scripture alone" and "Christ alone" as claims to no more than a part of scripture or Christ. He scolds contemporary Christians as "untried persons" who rely on "counterfeit faith and a fictitious picture of God's mercy" and dream they "can storm the heavens with the help of a *natural* promise or assurance." Taken in its whole, scripture "both consoles and affrights us." Scripture "purges" the soul, so that it can hear "the living word which brings us to life."[167] Müntzer charges contemporary preachers with extracting from scripture only the sweet Christ, while they set aside the whole Christ. Reflecting a central theme of the *German Theology*, he describes the consequence of this preaching for its "fleshy" hearers: they want to be God-formed—made like God in God's glory and impassibility—but not Christ-formed. Müntzer cites Christ's declaration, "My sheep hear my voice and pay no heed to the voice of strangers" (John 10:27), and he identifies the stranger as "anyone who neglects the way to eternal life, leaves the thorns and thistles standing, and proclaims: 'Believe! Believe!'"[168]

The 12th section of *Counterfeit Faith* represents the logical culmination of Müntzer's exposition of the whole scripture and the whole Christ. It is a mystical culmination, describing union with God in and through the crucified; the foundation for this union is Christ's union with the Father and preservation of the sheep given to him by the Father (John 10:27–30). Christ is "unchanging like the father" and lovingly separates his elect from the damned by making the former "sheep for the slaughter" (Rom. 8:36). While the damned tremble at "being expelled or killed," the elect remember how it is that the "little lamb . . . takes away the sin of the world" (i.e., through the crucifixion) and how none of the "old fathers in the bible" became "one with [God] until he had overcome through his suffering (assigned to him before all time). Thus we are transfigured by the glory of God from splendour to splendour."[169] Müntzer, like Karlstadt in his *Wagons*, underlines God's eternal decree of suffering as a means to bring the elect back into unity; but Müntzer's account of union is quite different from Karlstadt's, both because Müntzer focuses on faith in God's impossible promises rather than sinking into the divine will, and because Müntzer is convinced of the completeness of the union here and now.

Counterfeit Faith concludes with a direct exhortation to the elect, likely added for the purposes of publishing a tract that originally had served another purpose, perhaps in relation to Spalatin's questions. Unlike the *Protestation*, *Counterfeit Faith* does not otherwise directly address or exhort the elect. Here, Müntzer enjoins the elect to read "every word" of Matthew 16, and he offers a summation of both his treatises in parallel to that chapter.[170] The culminating moment is Müntzer's call of the elect to confront unbelief. Around this, his central concern, he developed a spiritual teaching that was uniquely his own vis-à-vis Karlstadt and Luther. Müntzer writes:

> The faith of the damned and of the elect is arrived at very differently. The godless man is only too happy to accept Scripture. He builds a strong faith on the fact that someone has suffered before him. But when it comes to facing the little lamb who opens the book, he has no intention of losing his life [*sele*], or of conforming himself to the lamb, but hopes in his worldly [*synlichen*] way to save his skin with proof-texts. That is all wrong. The scholar cannot grasp the meaning of scripture, although the whole of it has been expounded to him in a human way, and although he may be about to burst apart [with all his knowledge]; he has to wait until the key of David has revealed it to him, until he has been trodden underfoot with all his habitual ways in the wine-press. There he will attain such poverty of spirit as to acknowledge that there is no faith in him at all; only the desire to learn true faith. This, then, is the faith which becomes as small as a mustard seed [margin: Luke 17]. Then man must see how he is to endure the work of God, in order that he may grow from day to day in the knowledge of God. Then man will be taught by God alone, person to person, and not by any created being. Everything known to created being will become bitter gall to him, since its ways are perverse.[171]

Thus, the elect person attains union with God in a direct pedagogical relationship, which opens up the full meaning of scripture, but only through and after being broken in the attempt to approach God through external learning and according to creaturely desire.

As a second appendix to *Counterfeit Faith*, Müntzer published a letter he had written to Hans Zeiß on December 2, 1523. In it, the Allstedt preacher again took up the supposed claim "that only Christ is required to suffer, while we do not need to suffer anything after his genuine suffering for our sin"—an assertion Müntzer derided as "delicacy of spirit" and "unseemly passivity."[172]

Noteworthy is the letter's claim that Luther and his allies had only set "false faith" in the place of "clownish works," thus "poisoning the world" more thoroughly.[173] Like Luther himself, Müntzer occupied a world divided less between earnest and negligent Christians than between true and false ones, the latter blinded by their sweet and seemingly rational deceit.

Concluding Remarks

Thomas Müntzer consistently traced religious error to one source, namely, the preference for an easy, pleasure-filled life that subjected the soul to creatures—to food and drink, to material wealth and comfort, to sex, to godless clergy and rulers. From post-Apostolic times on down, he concluded, Christian clergy did not want to break their own outward-reaching desires to receive God's instruction within, and the laity gladly accepted false means to still the inner consternation experienced by all the elect. Rulers were feared for the harm they could inflict upon the body and material well-being, while the eternal ruler was deprived of the rightful possession of souls. The order of creation was inverted. Early evidence of Müntzer's preaching and teaching from 1519 and 1520 reveals a figure who interpreted the message of the Wittenberg reformation as a call to suffer God's work to annihilate human rational and moral presumption in matters of salvation; Müntzer was expressly predestinarian in his views. He complained about the false consolation offered through an accumulation of ritual works, and he clearly shared Luther's quest for certain faith. The search for certitude and true consolation through the way of suffering remained central to Müntzer's theology, proclamation, and reform efforts throughout his short public career; his letters and writings focused on categories of *Anfechtung*, promise, and faith, even as he came to fill these terms with far different content than Luther. The promise became God's promise to possess elect souls and lead a pure church through inward revelation; the fulfillment of this promise could not be received, however, until souls were emptied of lusts and—even more—until they confronted their fundamental unbelief about the verity of Christianity vis-à-vis other religions. God moved the elect to this deep consternation.

The ideas and terminology of Eckhartian mysticism abound in Müntzer's writings by 1521: Müntzer refers to the ground of the soul, to the abyss out of which faith must grow, to purgation or emptying of attachments, to the true Christ-life rejected by the false light, to *Verwünderung*, to God's possession of the soul, and more.[174] Müntzer transformed these mystical ideas and expressions not only by bringing them into an apocalyptic framework, as some scholars have noted, but also around the nexus of promise and faith. The most central themes of the Wittenberg reformation affected how Müntzer read and used the mystics; the mystics in turn shaped how Müntzer spoke of the promise and faith in his ever-changing contexts.

Müntzer's attack on the one-sidedness of the Wittenberg *solas* was the attack of someone with a deep sense of what Luther was all about: Luther's goal was to teach Christians to despair of their own wisdom and moral capacity, trusting in scripture alone, Christ alone, and faith alone—so that certitude of salvation could be received in the ashes of despair of the self. Müntzer traced the alleged partial interpretation of these loci by Luther and his allies to their desire to avoid a painful confrontation with the true filth of their own and others' creaturely attachments and unbelief. The Wittenbergers' claims to despair of self, humble obedience to scripture alone, pious submission to rulers, and loving regard for the weak all reflected a trivialization of God's promise and a fear of the means to its realization. The Wittenbergers were enemies of the cross; their god was their stomach. Their vaunted faith did not come through plumbing the depths of unbelief. Through a partial and parsed interpretation of scripture, they dispatched with the bitter side of Christ and with the works that must accompany unfeigned faith, namely, patient waiting for and endurance of inner trials, ascetic renunciation of creaturely attachments, and finally, life as God's possession and instrument, as part of the suffering body of Christ—a pure, Spirit-led church—in a world ruled by the ungodly. In Müntzer's view, the Wittenberg reformation had only dispensed with obvious fantasies in favor of more humble, deceptive, and seemingly scriptural ones. Wittenberg's Christianity, however, bloomed from the soil of the same base motivation as Roman Christianity, or for that matter, Judaism, Islam, and paganism—the avoidance of suffering.

6

"The Cross and the Impossibility of Faith"

Suffering and Right Action in a Troubled World, 1524–1525

Luther dismissed Müntzer and Karlstadt as "fanatics" driven by the same demonic spirit. On the one hand, Luther charged, they upheld external actions as necessary to salvation, rather than basing salvation on faith alone. On the other hand, they rejected the divinely appointed externals of scripture, the preached Word and the sacraments, boasting instead of the voice of the Holy Spirit within.[1] Neither man was willing to wait patiently for God's preached Word to effect a true reformation of hearers' hearts; both wanted to shatter the order of church and society with their fists. In Luther's assessment, Karlstadt and Müntzer were dupes and tools of Satan, who wanted to crush the gospel beneath the weight of Mosaic law. By the summer of 1524, amid rising unrest among the lower classes, Luther resolved to write publicly against these supposed "fanatics" and their followers. Luther's arguments continued to bind true suffering to true faith, reflecting his indebtedness both to Augustine's teachings about the work of the law to reveal sin and to mystical teachings about union with God through annihilation. Luther also sought to expose Karlstadt's and Müntzer's apparent sufferings as mere cloaks for their refusal to accept salvation and reformation on God's terms.

Against Luther, Karlstadt and Müntzer both insisted that the message of the gospel included Christ's empowerment of his members to fulfill God's law, inwardly and outwardly, and hence become children of God, as John 1 describes. Nonetheless, the hope of common cause shared for a time between Karlstadt and Müntzer could not withstand the pressure of events. By 1524, Müntzer publicly and unequivocally rejected a passive acceptance of martyrdom, arguing that true faith and the fear of God rather than men would make Christians courageous, ready to risk their necks for the defense of the gospel and the implementation of God's law

Enemies of the Cross. Vincent Evener, Oxford University Press (2021). © Oxford University Press.
DOI: 10.1093/oso/9780190073183.001.0001.

against the ungodly. For Müntzer, the most threatening class of ungodly consisted of those rulers and clerics who wanted to stifle God's inner presence and communication among the elect. Christians, he contended, must not meekly lay their necks on the chopping block and allow these ungodly to triumph—a passivity contrary to the biblical witness about the Spirit-driven faithful. Müntzer regarded the inner trials attending the birth of true faith as a temporary experience, a stage the elect could break through; thereafter, the elect became people taught directly by God and ready to live for God rather than human beings, even to the point of overturning a society structured to serve the pleasures of the powerful. For Müntzer, union with God was fully attainable in the here and now, and it created a class of people separated from creaturely attachments; the key practical question became, how were these divine ones to relate to everyone else?

Karlstadt never accepted a perfection of union in the here and now; for Karlstadt, Christian life was about growth in union, about ever-deeper sinking into the divine will through love of God and hatred of self. His theology and spirituality were different than Müntzer's, and he sought to create a different sort of ecclesial and political actor, committed to the local implementation of right worship and the acceptance of martyrdom, if necessary. Those who have political authority ought to use it for God's purposes; those who do not must accept oppression when it comes as due punishment for sin. Persecution is to be endured as God's pedagogy. Thus, although both Karlstadt and Müntzer continued to describe the soul's annihilation and union with God in terms substantially indebted to Eckhartian mysticism, Karlstadt's delay of union until the afterlife constrained the potential revolutionary implications involved in democratizing and delimiting mysticism: union became a daily practice and goal for individual and society. Luther, meanwhile, redefined union with God—as union with Christ through faith and the Word[2]—in ways that encouraged Christians to accept gradual reform, to participate in and support imperfect ecclesial-political structures, and to endure rather than rebel against oppressors. The three reformers made annihilation and union universal experiences for all true Christians, but their varied understandings of annihilation and union yielded equally varied positions on appropriate ecclesial-political action.[3]

Suffering and the Defense of the Gospel: Müntzer, Luther, and the Princes, 1524

In 1524–1525, Luther treated Karlstadt and Müntzer as serious challengers to his prophetic authority over the definition of true evangelical theology and a right reform program. Both challengers had popular and local magisterial support, in Orlamünde and Allstedt respectively. More troubling still, both had access to printers. Karlstadt's reform efforts in Orlamünde and his publications through late 1524 have already been discussed in chapter 4, so we begin here with a continuation of Müntzer's story.

Through early 1524, the Wittenbergers remained in contact with Müntzer. Meetings of Wittenberg theologians (John Lang, Justus Jonas, et al.) with Müntzer and Haferitz occurred in November 1523 and again in late February or early March 1524. The Wittenbergers' goal was to convince Müntzer to submit to a judgment over his teaching by Luther in Wittenberg.[4] At this time, tensions were mounting between the authorities and preachers in Allstedt and the rulers both of neighboring Albertine Saxony and of Ernestine Saxony itself. In February 1524, George of Albertine Saxony—a loyal Catholic—ordered the use of force to stop subjects from attending worship in Allstedt; the order was carried out against subjects of the cloister at Memleben in May and against residents of Sangerhausen in July. Meanwhile, strife between the Allstedters and the cloister at Naundorf incited Ernestine measures against the course of reform in the town. In the summer of 1523, the Allstedters had ceased to pay tithes to the cloister, preferring to apply the money to care for the poor. The abbess appealed to Frederick the Wise, and the measure was withdrawn through his intervention.[5] On March 24, 1524, however, the cloister's Chapel of St. Mary at Mallerbach was burned to the ground. The abbess again turned to Frederick, who demanded an investigation and action against the guilty. After months of stalling and maneuvering, Hans Zeiß finally made an arrest in June.[6]

By then, Müntzer was fully convinced of the necessity of an armed defense of the gospel against godless rulers and clergy, and he regarded such a defense as entirely in accord with the biblical witness. Müntzer expected George to act against subjects of Ernestine Saxony, and he hoped the Ernestine princes would resist George. Thus, when Duke John and John Frederick spent the night of July 12 in the Allstedt castle, Müntzer seized the opportunity to attempt to sway them to this purpose.[7] On the morning of the 13th, Müntzer delivered to the princes a sermon on Daniel 2. He published the sermon that same month under the title, *Interpretation of the Second Chapter of the Prophet Daniel preached . . . . before the great and revered dukes and rulers of Saxony* (henceforth, *Sermon to the Princes* or *Sermon*), placing the princes in an awkward political position vis-à-vis the Empire.[8] For his part, even before he had seen the *Sermon to the Princes*,[9] Luther had dispatched to the printer his *Letter to the Princes of Saxony concerning the Rebellious Spirit*. Luther gave up his long hesitation to battle Müntzer via the presses after he became convinced of Müntzer's willingness to resort to force to achieve his reforming aims.[10] Both Müntzer's *Sermon* and Luther's *Letter* show how understandings of suffering—true and false, inward and outward—involved and affected reformers' views of right action for ecclesial and political reform.

Müntzer's *Sermon to the Princes* builds to a dramatic appeal to the Ernestine princes to fulfill their God-given responsibility to punish evildoers and protect the godly from the godless. Müntzer exhorts the princes to slay those monks and clergy who "denounce the holy gospel as heresy and yet count themselves the best Christians." Likewise, the wicked rulers who support the godless clergy should be slain, while others among the wicked may be permitted to live, although only at the behest of the godly. Müntzer warns the Ernestine princes that, if they do not carry out their office in this way, as pious "true rulers," God will take the sword from them and give it to the people. The princes have hitherto been deceived by false "rational" arguments, such as that they should offer the weak a "counterfeit clemency [*getichte gu[e]ttigkeit*],"[11] that Old Testament injunctions to cast down idols and slay the wicked do not apply to Christians, and that the office of a ruler per Romans 13 does not extend beyond maintaining "civic order." However, the time of harvest has arrived,[12] and God is already pouring out God's spirit on all flesh, guiding Christians through prophesies, dreams, and visions. Müntzer tells the princes that they must be guided by a "new Daniel," Müntzer himself, who can interpret these revelations. He cautions that not every prophesy is to be accepted, because human beings are prone to deception springing from their nature or from the devil. As in his July 1523 letter to Luther, Müntzer contends that the power of discernment comes only through a higher wisdom conferred by God's direct communication with the soul, without the mediation of sense organs—that is, by God's inner Word revealed in the heart or abyss of the soul. He polemicizes, "To expect visions and to receive them while in tribulation and suffering, is in the true spirit of the apostles, the patriarchs, and the prophets. Hence it is no wonder that Brother Fatted Big and Brother Soft Life reject them, Job 28. But when one has not yet heard the clear word of God in the soul one has to have visions."[13] In order to hear this Word, one must be swept free of creaturely lusts through mortification of the flesh and spiritual trials.[14]

Müntzer imagines true rulers as instruments of God, just as the sword is an instrument in the rulers' hands. For their work, the princes must be prepared by a cross and trials that will strip them of the fear of creatures and establish them in the fear of God.[15] According to Müntzer, Luther rejects true dreams and visions, along with the higher Inner Word that enables discernment, because he rejects the prerequisite mortification and spiritual trials; consequently, Luther's appeals to "simple faith" and "scripture alone" leave Christians in the grips of nature and reason, without God's guidance:

> We need knowledge—not just some windy faith [*wir mu[e]ssen wissen und nit allein in windt gleuben*]—so we can discern what has come to us from God, from the devil, or from nature. For if our natural reason is to be taken captive and made subject to faith, 2 Cor. 10, then it must be brought to the very limits of its own judgment. . . . [T]he more our nature reaches after God the more the operation of the holy spirit recedes . . . The fact is that if man really understood the audacity of natural reason he would certainly resort no more to a stolen Scripture . . . and would instead come to experience the operation of the divine word from the well of his heart, John 4. . . . [Our scholars] mingle nature and grace indiscriminately [*on allen unterscheit*]. They obstruct the passage of the word, Psalm 118 [119], which springs from the abyss of the soul. . . . [The Word] comes down from God on high in a state of deep consternation . . . Now this state of consternation, wondering whether something is the word of God, begins when one is a child of six or seven, as Numbers 19 signifies. . . . [A]nyone who has not become conscious and receptive to this through the living witness of God, Romans 8, may have devoured a hundred thousand Bibles, but he can say nothing about God which has any validity. It should be clear enough from this to anyone, then, how far removed the world still is from faith in Christ. But if a man is to become conscious of the word and of his receptivity to it, then God must free him from his fleshy lusts, and when God's movement invades his heart—to put to death all the pleasures of the flesh—he must make way for God, so that God receives his working [*das er yhm do stadt gebe, das er seine wirckung bekummen mag*]. For a man who behaves like an animal has no ear for what God says in the soul, I Cor. 2. The holy spirit must direct him to consider earnestly the pure and straight-forward

meaning of the law, Psalm 18. Otherwise his heart will be blind and he will dream up for himself a wooden Christ and lead himself astray.[16]

Müntzer's "consternation" (*Verwunderung*) here involves profound uncertainty about whether the inward Word is truly divine; this is the unbelief of one who remains attached to creatures, whether in bestial desire or fear of suffering. Müntzer returns again and again in his *Sermon* to the "fear of men," citing this fear as the reason people reverence scholars who are hostile to the Spirit and the reason rulers hesitate to stand with the gospel. The wisdom of God comes through the fear of God.[17]

Müntzer's attack on reason for its sweet seduction in matters of salvation and his description of true faith as certitude against all doubt (appealing to Rom. 8: 9)[18] together reveal a figure who was bound to Luther by direct indebtedness as well as by shared concerns and sources. For Müntzer, however, certitude lay in the reception of the inner Word by a soul freed of outward lusts—in direct rather than mediated divine knowledge. Certain faith was not, moreover, a faith that freed Christians to serve even in imperfect social structures according to others' needs, but a faith that made the receptive elect into instruments for the execution of God's will against the godless. When Müntzer says that the "biblical scholars" (i.e., Luther and his circle) are not certain of their salvation,[19] the point is that they do not hear the inner Word and hence are unqualified (Müntzer would say, "untried") to lead reform. By scorning the "spirit of Christ," the scholars like the Roman clergy before them had brought Christendom to ruin.[20]

The *Schriftgelehrten* were for Müntzer a type of enemy of God present throughout scripture and history, much as the "false prophets" for Luther.[21] Thus, from Müntzer's perspective, the Wittenbergers were just the latest manifestation of a constant danger. The scholars had rejected Christ in his own lifetime, and after the death of the apostles' students, they turned Christ's passion into a game, repudiating God's Spirit who comes through suffering. In the place of Christ's "true voice" to his sheep and the "pure knowledge of God," the scholars erected "a pretty, fine, golden god of their own making, before which the poor peasants smack their lips."[22] A message of ease always finds ready hearing, Müntzer thought.

Müntzer's *Sermon* repeatedly identifies the "biblical scholars" as the "enemies of the cross of Christ" described in Philippians 3. "I have come to the conclusion," he says, "that the beasts of the belly, Phil. 3, and the pigs, described in Matt. 7[:6] and 2 Peter 2[:22], have trodden the precious stone, Jesus

Christ, completely underfoot, to the best of their ability."[23] Müntzer argues, further, that Philippians 3:20 ("our citizenship is in heaven") confirms the point of Daniel 2:28 that dreams can be interpreted only by those who have "communion [*gemeynschafft*] in heaven." When Nebuchadnezzar demanded that the soothsayers tell him his dream, they responded that this was possible only for the gods, "who have no communion with men on earth." They spoke from reason and without faith in God, "for they were godless flatterers and hypocrites who said what their masters wanted to hear, as is the case today with the biblical scholars who like the choicest morsels at court."[24] In the printed version of his sermon, Müntzer's final plea to the princes reads:

> Rejoice, you true friends of God, that the hearts of the enemies of the cross have fallen into their boots, for they have no choice but to do right, though they never dreamt of doing so.[25] If we fear God, why should we be alarmed by rootless, feckless men . . .? So be bold! He to whom all power is given in heaven and on earth is taking the government into his own hands.[26]

When the princes themselves rejected Müntzer's plea, he interpreted their actions within this paradigm: they were enemies of the cross, unwilling to be detached from the love and fear of creatures, and thus unable to hear God's Word within or fight for a church and society arranged according to God's order.

Luther's published repudiation of Müntzer followed quickly on the heels of the latter's sermon and took aim primarily at Müntzer's *Protestation*. The *Letter* asserted Luther's personal authority over the definition of right teaching, while attacking Müntzer's character and motivation. These personal claims and attacks embodied Luther's foundational soteriological and epistemological conclusions concerning suffering and truth—namely, that spiritual suffering always accompanies the receipt of true faith, as God repudiates any claim for natural human ability in understanding God or attaining salvation; that life in and from faith is always marked by the suffering of persecution and spite from unbelievers; and that faith patiently bears this and all suffering through trust that God works *sub contrariis*. Thus, suffering and the cross visibly and reliably distinguish—if only for those who through faith see God's work *sub contrariis*—true faith from presumption, the true preacher from the false spirit, and right action against evil from mere self-direction and self-assertion against the divine will. Müntzer had described a clash, running throughout history, between cross-shirking scholars and the elect who find the Word within through detachment from the world and spiritual *Verwundering*; in turn, Luther opened his *Letter* to Frederick and John by describing how Satan always and everywhere assails the Word first through force and then, when force fails, through "false spirits and teachings"—false religion cloaked as true. Satan first assailed the ancient church through persecution, then through "heretics and sects right down to the time of the pope . . . the last and greatest Antichrist." These efforts to suppress and distort the Word, however, also paradoxically make it visible to those with seeing eyes of faith: "So we may recognize the Word of God for what it is, things must go on as they always have."[27]

Luther's *Letter* seldom mentions Müntzer by name but refers instead to "Satan" or the "unruly spirit" at Allstedt. In addition, Luther often alternates between the use of "he" and "they" in the same sentence. Bräuer argues that Luther intended to point to Simon Haferitz alongside Müntzer, and that any reference to Karlstadt was indirect and secondary.[28] However that may be, Luther saw himself confronted by a spirit common to Müntzer and Karlstadt, and Luther recognized a personal and theological claim to suffering as definitive of that spirit. This suffering had to be exposed as false. Luther mocks, "Though so far no one has touched *them* either with fist or mouth or pen *he* cries out horribly, complaining *he* must suffer much. *They* dream that they must bear a heavy cross. With such frivolity and without cause the Satan has to lie, though he cannot conceal himself."[29]

Cutting to the quick, Luther dismisses his opponents' claim to the immediate instruction of God as a form of cross-shirking—a refusal to accept without self-assertion clear scriptural doctrine and humble life in the existing God-given social order. He writes:

> I am especially glad that none of ours start a disturbance of this kind. They themselves boast that they do not belong to us, and have learned and received nothing from us. They come from heaven, and hear God himself speaking to them as to angels. What is taught at Wittenberg concerning faith and love and the cross of Christ is an unimportant thing. "You yourself must hear the voice of God," they say, "and suffer the work of God in you and feel how much your talents weigh. The Bible means nothing. It is Bible—Booble—Babel," etc. Were we to say such things of them their cross and sufferings would seem more precious than the sufferings of Christ, and be more highly esteemed and praised, too. In this manner the poor spirit is

eager to suffer and boast of his cross. But they will not suffer anyone to cast
a bit of doubt or counsel caution as to their heavenly voice and work of God.
They want to be believed immediately, with force, without considering that
I have never read or heard of a more arrogant, imperious holy spirit (if such
there be).[30]

Luther declares that he will eschew in his *Letter* any discussion of "their
teaching."[31] Instead, he addresses the princes, he says, because he has "heard
and also gathered from their writings that this same spirit will not let the
matter rest with words . . . [but] instigate revolt without delay."[32] The princes
may discern the evil "spirit of Allstedt" partly through his fear to suffer for
action or confession. The spirit destroys churches, cloisters, and images in
the safety of Electoral Saxony, not in Dresden, Berlin, or Ingolstadt, and he
will not submit with Christian humility to a "testing" of his teaching. He will
not come "into the open before his enemies and opponents," but "avoids this
as the devil avoids the cross," although "in his hiding place he uses the most
fearless language as though he were full of three holy spirits." Luther offers his
own spiritual disposition and practical conduct as a contrast. He relates how
he embarked upon his criticism of the "papists" not with exalted claims to a
"heavenly voice" but in humility and with "trembling and fear." "In the poverty of my spirit," Luther writes, invoking the ideal of an absence of self-will
that he had celebrated in the *Magnificat* commentary, "I accomplished such
things as this world-consuming spirit has never attempted." Müntzer offered
in the *Protestation* only to appear before a "harmless assembly," but Luther in
his humility accepted danger.[33] He recounts:

> At Leipzig I had to take my stand in debate before a very threatening as-
> sembly. I had to appear at Augsburg without safe-conduct before my
> worst enemy. At Worms I had to appear before the Emperor and the whole
> realm, though I already knew well that my safe-conduct was worthless, and
> all kinds of strange wiles and deceit were directed at me. Weak and poor
> though I was there, yet this was the disposition of my heart: If I had known
> that as many devils as there were tiles on the roofs at Worms took aim at me,
> I would still have entered the city on horseback, and this, even though I had
> never heard of a heavenly voice, or of God's talents and works, or of the
> Allstedt spirit. I had to take my stand in closed groups of one, two, or three,
> and meet them wherever and whenever they decided. *My poor and troubled
> spirit has had to stand unshielded as a flower in the field, without being able to*

choose time, person, place, manner, or degree. I had to be ready and willing to give every man an answer, as St. Peter admonishes [I Pet. 3:15].[34]

For Luther, his own "poor spirit" was the Christian spirit, yielded to God and willing to accept whatever suffering might come for true confession, in contrast to the Allstedt spirit. The false spirits, Luther complains, use his victory to take wives and shed papal tyranny, "but they have done no battle for it and risked no bloodshed to attain it. But I have had to attain it for them and, until now, at the risk of my body and my life."[35]

Luther believed himself to be battling a demonic spirit whose intent was to nullify scripture and the preached Word, abolish the two sacraments, and establish works righteousness on a doctrine of free will, dictating the "time, place, and measure for God when he wants to deal with us."[36] This false spirit was driven by self-trust and self-assertion, and it sought works more exalted than Christian works of obedience to the Decalogue flowing from faith. Thus, Luther argued, the false spirit judged doctrine on account of seemingly deficient moral life, whereas the Holy Spirit condemned false teaching but endured weakness of faith and life.[37]

Luther explains that his intention in the *Letter* is to remind and exhort the princes to carry out their God-given "duty to maintain order" per Romans 13. They ought to allow free preaching, but they can and should expel any preacher who wants to fight with force rather than words.[38] Those whose office is to preach the Word must have nothing to do with force: "Our calling is to preach and to suffer, not to strike and defend ourselves with the fist. Christ and his apostles destroyed no churches and broke no images. They won hearts with the Word of God, then churches and images fell of themselves."[39] The evil spirits, Luther charges, refuse to do what a right preacher must—proclaim the Word simply, wait for its effect patiently, and suffer in the meantime the inevitable assaults of the wicked. The spirits' impatience flows from and reflects their arrogant presumption to seize the Holy Spirit, rather than wait for the gifts of faith and love through God's appointed external means. Luther offers once again his own attitude and actions as a normative counterexample. He had never "disturbed a stone, broken a thing, or set fire to a cloister," but his teaching emptied monasteries even in realms whose rulers were "opposed to the gospel." The first and most decisive reformation is the redemption of hearts, out of which extraordinary effects might then appear.[40] Luther closes with an exhortation to the princes to take the danger of the Allstedt spirit seriously, and he expressly aligns genuine preaching and teaching with readiness to suffer for proclamation of the Word rather than internal spiritual possession: "They are not Christians who want to go beyond the Word and to use violence, but who are not instead more ready to suffer all things, even if they boast of being full and overfull with ten holy spirits."[41]

A masterful interweaving of soteriological assumptions and personal assertions and attacks, Luther's *Letter to the Princes* sets the "poor spirit" of Wittenberg—emptied of self-trust, sustained and driven by faith in God's self-revelation—in opposition to the haughty spirit of Allstedt, and clearly also Orlamünde. Luther seeks to undermine Müntzer's and Karlstadt's claims to authority, knowing these claims relied on forms of spiritual suffering and union with God that were supposed to become manifest in outward actions and cross-bearing. Conversely, Luther scarcely acknowledged Müntzer's desire to plumb the painful depths of unbelief; and while Müntzer described faith as courage to change a social order perverted by humans' lust for possession and domination, Luther held to the line that the existing order—however unholy it appeared—was ordained by God to stand between humanity and anarchy. For Luther, persecution for right faith was to be accepted by Christians as a divine trial of faith; God works under contraries. God is usually on the side of the persecuted, but reason can misjudge who truly suffers without self-assertion.

Müntzer's Final Publications, Late July–December 1524: The Impossibility of Faith and the Work of the Law

In July 1524, as mentioned, authorities in Albertine Saxony stepped up their pressure on subjects who travelled to worship in Allstedt. Residents of Sangerhausen were apparently imprisoned,[42] and some turned to Müntzer for advice, receiving among other words the following:

[T]he whole Christian people is becoming a whore with its adulation of man. It is adulation of man . . . when fear of lords and princes leads men to deny God's word and his holy name completely for the sake of their pathetic food and of their stomachs; St. Paul would call them, as he did the Philippians, beasts ruled by their stomachs, saying that their God is their stomach. . . . The devil is a really wily rascal, always luring men with food and security, for he knows that fleshy men are fond of that. . . . [I]f you do not believe that God is mighty enough, when you risk or abandon your wealth and bodily food and even your life for the sake of God, to give you different food and more than before, how will you ever believe that he can give you eternal life? It is a truly childlike belief that God will give us our food, but to trust that he will give us eternal life is a supernatural belief, beyond all human reason.[43]

Some refugees sought cover in Allstedt, but they were informed, apparently on Zeiß's order, that Allstedt would turn them over to their princes.[44] In a sermon on July 24, Müntzer responded by exhorting hearers to form a "covenant [Bund]" in defense of the gospel, after the example of 2 Kings 23:3. Five hundred persons were promptly enrolled.[45]

"Covenants" of some sort had been formed already in various German cities.[46] Along with the grounding of the Allstedt Bund, Müntzer sought the foundation of like covenants in other cities, hoping to bind the groups together.[47] Already on July 19, he and his supporters had turned to Karlstadt and Orlamünde for this purpose, but they were sharply and publicly repudiated—as will be described later in this chapter. In early August, Müntzer's time in Allstedt ran out. Zeiß and other Allstedt authorities yielded to pressure from Duke John, agreeing to dissolve the Bund and send away a printer that Müntzer wanted to establish in Allstedt.[48] Anticipating arrest or expulsion, Müntzer departed secretly in the night of August 7 or 8.[49] From Mühlhausen on August 15, he wrote a letter to the Allstedters (to the Rat and Gemeinde) that praised the willingness to undertake trials and suffering on behalf of the gospel, but rejected any passive suffering that simply allowed godless authorities to have their way. Müntzer recounted his time in Allstedt, describing how he had first rebuked tyrants against the gospel, then rebuked the theologians who "defend[ed] such godless, abandoned men." He had taught that "a Christian should not offer himself up so pitifully to the butcher's block, and that if the big wigs do not stop this, one should take the reins of government away from them." Müntzer underlined his unwillingness to give up his life to the godless—"the fear of God within me will not give way to the insolence of anyone else"—and he criticized the Allstedters' fear of humans, namely Duke John. He could not have remained with such fearful people, he explained, for they could not bear the trials that would come about because of his unrestrained proclamation of the "the righteousness of God." "You wanted to elude the time of trial," Müntzer wrote, "but this is just impossible in an age like ours if we are to do what is right." Right preaching provokes offense, for Christ is a "stone of offense"; yet "this sly, but silly Christian people must be scandalized much more than it ever has been since its origins for the sake of the progress which nothing will be able to stop. So do not think of progress in the complacent terms [*nach yrer ruge*] of the world, but as Job does in chapter 28."[50]

At the behest of John Frederick, Luther undertook a visitation Thuringia in 1524. He was to identify the preachers of "enthusiasm [*Schwärmerei*]," whom the princes would then remove.[51] This visitation led to Luther's dramatic meetings with Karlstadt and the Orlamünders, and to the expulsion of Karlstadt and several allies from Electoral Saxony. Luther also wrote to the authorities of Mühlhausen to warn them about the "false spirit and prophet" and wolf in sheep's clothing, whose only fruit was "murder and uprising and bloodshed."[52] Nonetheless, Müntzer received a friendly reception from at least some residents of that city.[53] Müntzer quickly aligned himself with Heinrich Pfeiffer, and the two clerics were together involved in the drafting and presentation to the town council of eleven articles, which sought to install a new council that would rule with "the fear of God" and according to the word of God. Rich and poor were to be treated with equal justice.[54] On September 27, the existing council succeeded in expelling Müntzer and Pfeiffer, but before their departure, an "eternal *Bund* of God" had been grounded with 219 names enrolled.[55] At this time, Müntzer entrusted his treatise, *A Manifest Exposé of False Faith*, to the future Anabaptist leader Hans Hut; Hut had the book printed in Nuremberg, but its circulation was largely prevented by the city's *Rat*.[56]

Müntzer had begun writing already in July 1524, and he conveyed a version of the text to Duke John at the beginning of August.[57] A sweeping exegesis of Luke 1, the text rehearses arguments we have already discussed at length in chapter 5, explaining how the elect come to true faith through the discovery of their unbelief, and how true believers fear God rather than creatures. The biblical scholars (*Schriftgelehrten*) are indicted for inhibiting the arrival of true faith through clever evasions that allow themselves and their hearers to wallow in creature-directed pleasure and fear. These scholars buttress the authority of temporal rulers who crush or, at the very least, refuse to defend the adherents to truth. Human beings were created to possess creatures and to be possessed by God; but the soul's love of pleasure and fear of creatures makes it the possession of creatures rather than God.

The *Exposé* represents Müntzer's most-detailed discussion of the impossibility of faith for natural, human powers. Like Luther, Müntzer argues that faith involves certain trust in God and that such faith is impossible to reason and nature. However, Müntzer refers the impossibility of faith to imminent transformations—to the deification of the elect who recognize their unbelief and to the transformation of Christian society through the casting down of ungodly rulers and clergy,[58] the separation of the godly from the godless, and the gathering of the elect from all nations. The faithful for Müntzer must and will be prepared to risk their necks in order to fulfill these divine purposes.

Müntzer's text addresses the "poor, scattered Christian people" and promises instruction on "Christian authority [meisterschaft]" in answer to "slanderous books."[59] Nevertheless, Müntzer does not address at length how Christians ought to govern or the appropriate response of Christians to persecuting rulers; rather, he focuses on the authority to teach and on God's rightful Meisterschaft and possession of the soul, unmistakably criticizing Luther's alleged deference to human rather than divine authority. He attacks the entirety of Wittenberg exegesis[60] and doctrine[61] and the right of the Wittenberg theologians to teach; Müntzer dismisses the Wittenbergers as untried men possessed by creaturely lusts rather than God.

Müntzer intended his exegesis of Luke to serve as the hearing before all nations he had requested in the Protestation.[62] In the forward, he stresses his willingness to endure the dangerous assaults of the godless scholars, asserting that "no one else is willing to grasp the rudder of the ship because of the fierce struggle ahead." He also defends his refusal to accept a private hearing before Luther by offering biblical examples in which Christ shunned biblical scholars (John 7 and 18). The Wittenberg "scholars," Müntzer alleges, want exclusive authority to "judge the faith," but they seek "honor and goods" before the education of the "common man."[63]

The first of six sections of the Exposé seek to uncover the "intolerable abomination" that the faithless "set themselves up as preachers of the Christian faith," although they have no experience of faith and no idea "what goes on in the heart of a believer." Their chief error is that "they imagine . . . faith is as easily come by as their self-opinionated blathering suggests." Müntzer reads Luke 1, which recounts Gabriel's announcements of the births of John the Baptist and Jesus, as a lesson in "how the unbelief of all the elect was disclosed." Müntzer explains that Zechariah "did not want to believe because what was promised him seemed so impossible," and Mary herself "wanted confirmation, and an easy access to faith." These two "did not arrive at their faith . . . in a glossy, superficial way," or "go about saying: 'Yes, all I need to do is believe, and God will bring it to pass.'" Instead, they were "seized by the fear of God until the mustard-seed of faith overcame their unbelief, of which they became aware in great fear and trembling." Everyone must "tolerate [*erdulde*]" such a beginning of faith, Müntzer argues, exclaiming, "Oho, that is for our nature an insufferable work, the fear of God at the beginning of faith."[64] An untried faith is always marked, initially, by trembling and the most difficult work of yielding to God's self-revelation, but only this salutary fear gives the Holy Spirit room to work.[65]

Müntzer charges that the scholars, through their appeal to faith and scripture alone, "would like to still [*settigen*] the stormy movement and heart-felt anxiety of the elect, or to attribute it dogmatically to the devil." They tell the poor to search scripture, but "all their words and deeds ensure that the poor man is too worried about getting his food to have time to read." According to the scholars, the poor are to let themselves "be flayed and fleeced by the tyrants." The scholars also use the notion that faith comes from hearing to set themselves between the poor and God, denying God's direct communion. In fact, Müntzer counters, "[i]f someone had never had sight or sound of the Bible at any time in his life he could still hold the one true Christian faith because of the true teaching of the spirit, just like all those who composed the holy Scripture without any books at all." That teaching of the Spirit would give the recipient the fullest assurance that his faith is from God, not the devil or "his own natural reason"; he could then, like all true believers, give an account of his faith "to any who have a . . . genuine faith tried like gold in the fire of the severest, heart-felt anguish."[66]

As in the *Protestation*, Müntzer argues that necessary certitude of both salvation and doctrine can come about only through God's direct work;[67] the *sola fides* and *sola scriptura* doctrines cannot meet and dispel fundamental doubt concerning the truth of scripture and of Christianity itself. It is insufficient to say that scripture is true because "it has been handed down from of old, and . . . accepted by many." Jews, Turks, and "all other peoples" can say the same; neither can Roman appeals to authority show why Christianity is to be preferred to other faiths. Müntzer cites the story of the centurion Cornelius (Acts 10) to predict that Christians will "join harmoniously . . . with all the elect, of every sect and tribe and of every faith," but for this joining to happen Christians must understand "how someone who has been brought up . . . among unbelievers feels," that is, how "the true work and teaching of God" are experienced "apart from books."[68]

Müntzer expressly relates the tribulation associated with the beginning of faith to the impossibility of faith for "a fleshy man." The angel assured Mary that "nothing is impossible for God" because "for our natural reason, it was quite impossible." Müntzer writes:

> Just as happens to all of us at the arrival [*in der ankunfft*] of faith: we must believe that we fleshy, earthly men are to become gods through Christ's becoming man, and thus become God's pupils with him—to be taught by Christ himself, and become divine, yes, and far more—to be totally trans-figured into him so that this earthly life swings up into heaven, Phil. 3[:20]. See what an impossible thing this was to all the godless and to the slow elect, John 10[:33]; Psalm 81 [82:5].[69]

Here, as in the *Sermon to the Princes*, deification is communion with heaven (Phil. 3:20), which is rejected by the "enemies of the cross" (Phil. 3:18–19) who are too "fleshy," that is, controlled by desire for creatures.

Luther taught that the object of faith—that is, Christ's defeat of sin, death, and the devil on behalf of sinners (*pro nobis*)—was impossible for fallen nature to grasp; and that true faith in Christ's redemption found a certitude un-attainable by nature. For Luther, faith meant trust in God's promise of eternal and temporal provision for the faithful, even when God's true work and in-tention had to be discovered under contraries of suffering. Müntzer accepted that faith entailed certitude with respect to an impossible object, but faith for Müntzer had a different, more tangible object—namely the imminent trans-formation of individual and society through God's possession and direction of souls as instruments of the divine will. In the *Exposé*, Müntzer derides Luther as "Brother Soft Life and Father Pussyfoot," charging that Luther cannot bear God's possession of his own or any other soul, because Luther wants to have his "status and riches" together with a "well-tried faith." He and his kind want to serve two masters. Invoking Tauler's principle that creatures must exit the soul before God can enter, Müntzer insists that "anyone who lets such honours and goods take possession of him will in the end be left forever empty by God. . . . This is why powerful, self-willed unbelievers must be torn down from their seats, because they hinder the advancement of the true, holy Christian faith in themselves and in the whole world, just when it is about to burst forth in all its pristine truth."[70]

Just as Herod raged against the births of John and Christ, godless author-ities still rage against "God and all his anointed ones," Müntzer says.[71] This is the "true nature of . . . secular rule." Rulers presume to rule over faith but refuse to endure its beginning and will not allow others to experience faith.

The suffering of the elect at the hands of these rulers serves as both deserved punishment for their fear of creatures, as well as salutary fatherly discipline, for God permits no one to come to faith lightly.[72] The "spirit of the fear of God" leads the elect to wisdom, convincing them that secular tyranny and deafness to God's voice will not endure. Without the "spirit of fear," which Müntzer equates to the Holy Spirit, such a promise could only be regarded by nature as impossible.[73] Thus, the scholars dismiss God's possibilities as impossible, while imposing on Christians something genuinely impossible—service of two masters, of God and "unintelligent rulers who offend against all equity and do not accept the word of God." As a consequence, Mary's prediction that God will "tear the godless from their judgment seats and raise up humble, coarse folk in their place" seems like a "pure fantasy [*mechtig groß schwermerey*]" to "countless people." "They are bound to consider that a ploy like this can never be launched and executed," Müntzer writes. "The world and its scum, the biblical scholars," imagines that God will not elevate the lowly and separate them from the godless until the last day; in the meantime, they say, God "never reveals his judgments," so that "no one can know who is chosen or damned."[74]

In order to serve God without fear of human beings, Müntzer teaches, the elect must respond to God's movement by turning within—one recalls here Tauler's theme of *Einkehren*—just as Zecheriah entered the temple in Luke 1, and they must realize that they themselves are temples, "destined for God from all eternity, and . . . created for this alone: to accept the holy spirit as the schoolmaster of [their] faith and be receptive to all the workings of the holy spirit."[75] Müntzer laments that ordinary Christians do not turn within to find direct communion but rely on the priests and scholars. They are trapped by reverence for learning and titles, or for tradition, and are too preoccupied by the "grim struggle for bread in order to fill the throats of the most godless tyrants." Thus, Müntzer recognizes the political and economic victimization of the peasantry; at the same time, he does not excuse the peasants from blame. All Christians have preferred and received an easy, false religion rather than true Christianity: "All share the guilt for the whole Christian congregation worshipping a dumb God. How has this come to pass? Simply because every peasant wanted a priest, to ensure them an easy time." Indeed, the world still violently opposes a "right priesthood."[76]

There can be no hope of correction, Müntzer argues, until the false "prelates" of Christendom are removed. Meanwhile, the "poor, common folk" must "exercise itself in the recollection of the spirit" and learn to long for a true preacher, a new John the Baptist, "whose faith is solidly based on the experience of his unbelief." Such longing means to put aside satisfaction with scripture alone, believing that God will disclose God's will through direct revelation.[77]

The new Christendom will begin, Müntzer teaches, with those who are ready to be crushed inwardly, to experience tribulation and the recognition of their unbelief. These elect will receive in turn true faith, the fear of God alone, and the courage to confront every human threat. Müntzer does not, then, describe a life-long experience of *Anfechtung* but a temporary experience that produces yielded Christians whose action in the world, however assertive it may appear, implements God's will and revelation. The purified elect are instruments of God and have no more self-will than the arm vis-à-vis the brain. Müntzer's rich language reads:

> If . . . anyone is to be filled with the good things of God which never pass away, then he must submit to long discipline and then be made empty by his suffering and cross so that his measure of faith may be filled up with the highest treasures of Christian wisdom . . . Everyone must receive the knowledge of God, the true Christian faith, not from the stinking breath of the devilish biblical scholars, but from the eternal, powerful word of the father in the son as explained by the holy spirit, so that in his soul he may know its length and width and breadth and depth and height Eph. 3. In short, there is no alternative: men must smash to pieces their stolen, counterfeit Christian faith by going through real agony of heart, painful tribulation, and the consternation [*verwundern*] which inevitably follows. Then a man becomes very small and contemptible in his own eyes; to give the godless the chance to puff themselves up and strut around the elect man must hit the depths. Then he can glorify and magnify God and, *with his heart-felt tribulation behind him*, can rejoice whole-heartedly in God, his savior. Then the great will have to give way to the lowly and be humiliated before the latter.[78]

The last lines here exegete Mary's *Magnificat*. Müntzer bewails that the "poor, rejected peasants" pay no attention to God's use of the "lowly" Mary, Zechariah, and Elizabeth, and God's rejection of "big-wigs" like Herod and Caiaphas. God always works in this way. Nonetheless, "many poor, coarse folk imagine that the big, fat, greasy, chubby-faced types know everything about coming to the Christian faith." The reference to the Wittenbergers is clear:

O, my most dear friends, what sort of knowledge can they have, when they deny that we have any movement of faith, and curse and outlaw anything that goes against them, using the crudest abuse? For they have spent their life in drinking and gorging themselves like animals. From their youth on they have been brought up in the most delicate way; not one bad day have they had throughout their life; nor have they the least desire or intention to put up with one for the sake of the truth or to exact one cent less interest for their money. And such people want to be regarded as judges and protectors of the faith. O, you poor Christian people, as a result of these clumsy dolts, you have become nothing but a chopping-block. How wretchedly you are provided for because of them![79]

What was needed, in Müntzer's view, was the "bitter truth," spoken by "a servant of God . . . full of grace, and endowed with the Spirit of Elijah." This new Elijah, Müntzer predicts, will stir hearers to "sweep the Christian people free of its godless rulers," and he will scold the people for their "unbridled lusts," which hinder them from discovering God's work and learning what is possible. Instead of wasting their time (*verkurtzweylen*) with creaturely desires, the people must submit to the "patient endurance [*langweil*]" of God's work.[80]

Müntzer delineates between true and false preachers based on their preaching and their personal exercise of self-renunciation. He complains that Luther and his scholars had only given "excuses" to "pleasure-loving men" to avoid the renunciation of desire for creatures. Christ "did not despise sinners," they say.[81] In reply, Müntzer argues that lust impedes the Holy Spirit and that an entire lifetime is insufficient to better this consequence of the fall. The preaching of the "beasts of the belly" is "without power," and "[t]he sole and only outcome of their teaching is the freedom of flesh. . . . [T]hey poison the Bible for the holy spirit." Conversely, John the Baptist shows that "all true preachers" are marked by "earnestness, a fruit of the undaunted sobriety by which they aim to set all lusts aside, allowing the powers of the soul to be disclosed [*emplo[e]sset*], so that the abyss of the spirit may emerge through all the powers and the holy spirit can then have his say [*sein einreden thu[o]n*]." A true preacher according to Müntzer must be "wondrously driven to such disclosure [*emplo[e]ssung*] from his very youth in a life of self-denial. Hence John was sanctified in the womb of his mother as an archetype of all preachers."[82] As in the *Prague Manifesto*, Müntzer claims to have possessed extraordinary piety since his youth; he now defines that piety in terms of rigorous self-renunciation, setting up a contrast between himself as a divinely chosen messenger and the Wittenberg scholars. The latter have given no room to the Holy Spirit, and they consequently lack any assurance of their own faith or understanding of the preacher's task:

> [T]he preachers must know who it is that sends them out to the harvest, Mat. 9, John 4, for which, like a strong scythe or sickle, they have been sharpened by God from the beginning of their lives. Not everyone can execute this office, even if he has read every book that has been written! For he must first have the assurance of faith [*die sicherheyt seynes glaubens*] possessed by those who wrote the Scriptures . . . Therefore the completely yielded [*allergelassenste*] person must be awakened by God from the desolation of his heart, break forth and work zealously among the delicate, pleasure-loving types, who are harder than adamant when it comes to accepting the truth. Through an exemplary life, he must reveal to others the cross, which he has recognized since his youth, and cry out into the wretched, desolate, erring hearts of the God-fearing, who are now beginning to watch out for the truth, Luke 12. O, how gladly they would come to true faith, if only they could come across it![83]

With these lines, Müntzer sought to compete with Luther's claim to prophetic authority. Luther referred to what the Word had accomplished amid and through his poverty of spirit—that is, his humble awareness of his nothingness. Müntzer presents himself, conversely, as chosen from the womb and driven by the Holy Spirit from youth to deny himself and seek true teaching; he is a new John the Baptist or Elijah or (as in the *Sermon to the Princes*) a new Daniel.

Müntzer's prophetic self-consciousness was nourished no less than Luther's by a sense of living near the end of time; but while Luther expected the historical struggle of true and false church, Christ and anti-Christ, to find resolution only on the Last Day,[84] Müntzer predicted that the work of "true preachers" would bring about a separation of the godly from the godless. The decisive criterion was whether or not a person could give an account of the trials involved in the arrival of true faith. Müntzer writes, "The time is fast approaching when everyone will have to give an account of how he came to faith. Surely it is this which constitutes a true Christian church, that the godless are separated off from the chosen; for the former have never been saddened by their unbelief or even recognized its existence."[85] The present church is "an old whore," Müntzer explains, and the "weeds" will have to "suffer the winnowing-shovel," although they shout out that the harvest has not yet arrived. After this winnowing, "the gospel will spread even more fully than in the time of the apostles," while "[f]rom many lands and strange nations great numbers of elect will appear who will be far superior to us lazy, negligent Christians."[86]

There are many "heathen" and "Turks," Müntzer asserts, who experience the inward trials of the elect. Indeed, "they are often overcome by grief in a way which transcends all reason and so are assured that they are inclined and destined for eternal life." Müntzer claims to have heard directly from these predestined outsiders that they are offended by the shallow faith and "licentious behavior" of Christians. They do not become Christians because they, like the Christians themselves, find no "true testimony to faith."[87] Neither the clergy nor the rulers of Christendom show true faith. For his part, Müntzer says, he prefers "giving the most elementary instruction to heathens, Turks and Jews about God and his ordering of things: to give an account of the dominion given to us and that of God over us."[88]

Müntzer argues that the scholars of the New Testament rejected Christ because he was "a contemptible person" who had the audacity to chide their pleasure-seeking; in the same way, the godless still slander anyone who assails "their pretenses, their pomp, their false, slick wisdom." Müntzer here expresses his own theology of the cross, according to which God's work is hidden from the sight of fallen reason and will; but for Müntzer, it is creaturely pleasure that blinds human beings, whereas Luther blamed self-trust in matters of salvation. According to Müntzer, the "eternal word" had usually been hidden in history within the souls of elect Christians outcast by others:

> O, how often the eternal word has concealed itself in chosen men, in our Christian Nazareth, that is to say among the burgeoning elect, who flourish and burgeon sweetly in the wisdom of the cross, though every pussy-footing pleasure-lover has regarded them as mad and idiotic. That is the wicked way of the world: at that which should really better it, the world takes the greatest offense.[89]

Preferring to wallow in pleasure, human beings do not want to accept the "wisdom of the cross." The way is too hard, and the promised destination seems unbelievable. Thus, like Mary, "we are terrified by God's greeting when

God wants us to become gods through his son becoming man, that is, when he tests our faith like gold in the fire." Müntzer concludes:

> Just as Mary's natural reason led her to be skeptical of the angel, so we distrust upright preachers who explain and expound the cross and the impossibility of faith, so that we can understand it; although the true kingdom of David is where Christ rules from the cross and we are crucified with him. And what is the house of Jacob but your soul that has been emptied by the crushing of your loins, by the doing away of your lusts. There the power of the almighty brings to birth in our suffering the impossible work of God, by the overshadowing of the sacred old covenant, which is completely transfigured by the light of the world, the true genuine son of God, Jesus Christ.[90]

The cross thus makes possible a real deification and union with God that empowers the elect to act with certitude in the world, sweeping away godless overlords and establishing a pure church separated from those who cannot give an account of their faith.

The deeply exegetical *Manifest Exposé* did not represent a direct answer to Luther's *Letter to the Princes*, but Müntzer soon provided this answer with his *Highly-Provoked Vindication and Refutation of the Unspiritual, Soft-living Flesh at Wittenberg*.[91] Müntzer dedicates the tract "to his Eminence, the first-born prince and almighty lord, Jesus Christ," and to Christ's "grieving and only bride, the poor *Christenheit*," thus mocking Luther's dedication of the *Letter* to the Elector Frederick and Duke John. The *Vindication* exegetes the gospel of John[92] to describe the ceaseless assault of the *Schriftgelehrten* on the Spirit throughout biblical and postbiblical history, just as Luther had described in the *Letter* the ceaseless assault of Satan and his spirits on the Word of salvation on account of Christ *extra nos*.[93] Central to the text is Müntzer's discussion of the Old Testament law. Müntzer argues that the law is not abolished by Christ and the gospel, but fully explained and fulfilled in Christ and in Christ's members. Through the Spirit, the law works inwardly in the elect to expose their unbelief and bring about the birth of true faith. Outwardly, the law is to be wielded by true believers for the benefit of all the elect. The law demands that the godless be cleared away, so that the elect have time and space to confront their unbelief and contemplate the will of God. According to Müntzer, mature, Spirit-led believers understand that God's mercy or goodness (*Gütigkeit*) is in harmony with and indeed executed through the law and severity. Punishment breaks the grips of delusion and creaturely fear and leads to salvation. Müntzer makes temporal authority not just subject to the church—as claimed, for example, by Boniface VIII in *Unam Sanctam* (1302)—but an instrument of the church. The Christian community holds the power of both the sword and the keys—both punishment and forgiveness, law and gospel, God the Father and God the Son. Rulers serve the community through the execution of these two powers, while remaining subject to the community's authority. Müntzer's doctrine of the law teaches that pain (*Pein*) and punishments (*Strafe*) are the means by which God mercifully rescues the elect, in part directly and inwardly, in part through the co-agency or instrumental agency of other elect who reshape the sphere of outward human existence. Müntzer's law doctrine is thus a comprehensive doctrine of suffering, and its detractors—Luther first and foremost—are revealed as pleasure seeking enemies of divinely appointed suffering.

In the *Vindication*, Müntzer depicts Luther as the epitome of the *Schriftgelehrten*, using scripture against Müntzer's proclamation of the Spirit just as the scholars of John appealed to scripture against Christ. Müntzer sees himself, accordingly, as the true, persecuted disciple of Christ—his self-conception mirroring Luther's on this point.[94] When Luther calls him a devil, Müntzer says, he experiences the fulfillment of Christ's prediction, "The pupil will not have it any better than the master" (Matt. 10:24).[95] Müntzer explains that all elect must undergo the suffering of the crucified, for this suffering is the message of all scripture, including the law and the prophets, and is reflected in all creatures. The willingness to endure suffering separates the "godless" and the "just":

> The whole of Holy Scripture is about the crucified son of God and nothing else (as is evidenced, too, by all creatures) which is why he [Christ] himself explained his ministry [*ampt*] by beginning with Moses and going on to all the prophets, showing how he had to suffer and enter into the glory of his father. . . . Paul, too, having searched the law of God more penetratingly than all his companions, Gal. 1, says that he can only preach Christ, the crucified, I Cor. 1. For he was unable to find in it anything else than the suffering son of God, of whom Matthew 5 says that he did not come to abolish the law or to tear up the covenant of God, but on the contrary to complete, explain and fulfill it. The hate-filled biblical scholars were unable to recognise any of this, for they did not search Scripture with their whole heart and spirit . . . . [T]hey wanted the comfort of the holy spirit but never once reached the ground [of their soul] through sadness of heart, as one must if

the true light is to shine out in the darkness and empower us to be children of God.[96]

Similar to Karlstadt's mature position is Müntzer's insistence that Christ completes the law by giving the Holy Spirit, who enables believers to grasp the law's true meaning and to fulfill it, thereby becoming children of God. The two reformers commonly accused Luther of a simplistic understanding of Paul,[97] through which Luther supposedly wanted to cover up his self-willed, cross-shirking faith. Yet Müntzer, unlike Karlstadt, expected a deification and transformation of the elect, whose certitude about their own and others' eternal status made possible the gathering of a true, pure church, through violence if necessary.

According to Müntzer, the pure teaching of the law must begin with "the beginning of the Bible and the order of its first chapter"[98]—that means, with God's ownership and due possession of souls. Through this divine law, the Holy Spirit punishes unbelief, inscribing the law on hearts so that beginners can "follow its instructions to discover the right ways to the source [ursprung] of faith."[99] Far from arguing for the literal application of every dictate of the Old Testament, as Luther had charged, Müntzer champions the law as God's means to reveal unbelief and create space for the Holy Spirit. Christ fulfills the law as its explicator, as the giver of the Spirit, and as the corporate body in which the elect participate.[100] Müntzer invokes the story of the adulterous woman brought to Christ in John 8; casting Luther in the role of the accusers, he argues that Christ "clarified his father's sternness by his own goodness [gu[e]tigkeyt]." This Gütigkeit encompasses every divine work and is "not annulled by the penalty [peyn] of the law." Instead, the elect person "wants to be chastised justly but not in wrath." Wrath does not belong to the eternal essence of God, but characterizes the human experience and misperception of God's remedy for human sin. Müntzer writes, "[T]he wrath was not with God in eternity, but springs from the perverse fear men have of God. They shrink from the pain and do not see how God is leading them out of their fear-provoking delusions and, after every penalty, into his eternity."[101] Human beings ought to have a pious fear of God, but instead, they fear creatures, including other human beings, and God's work to free them from this fear. This divine work takes the form of punishment, which is the infliction of suffering. Thus, when Müntzer writes that Christ's Gütigkeit "clarifies [erklert]" the Father's "sternness," he does not mean simply that the severity of God becomes apparent through contrast.[102] Rather, all creation is infused by goodness, and the penalties of God serve God's good ends of bringing the elect back to God and punishing the wicked.

Luther thus speaks falsely, according to Müntzer, when he appeals to the *Gütigkeit* of the Son to reproach Müntzer's teaching on the law. Rather, the law is established to "persecute" all those who "combat and try to subvert sound teaching," and the requisite power of the sword, like the keys of forgiveness, belongs to an "entire community [*gemayn*]." Rulers are "servants of the sword," but the sword can be taken from them if they do not "do right." The uprising that Luther accuses Müntzer of inciting will be prevented, Müntzer argues, only if rulers use the sword to its proper ends, against both the great and the small.[103]

The law thus works in two loci in Müntzer's view: *within* the soul of each elect person to expose unbelief and create room for the Spirit, and *outwardly*, through the elect as God's instruments, to punish the wicked and to create social and temporal space for other elect persons to receive and pursue the Spirit-filled life. Müntzer explains, "All perpetrators of original sin among the Christian community must, as Paul says, be justified by the law, so that the godless Christians who resist the wholesome teaching of Christ can be swept out of the way by the sternness of the Father, and so that the just can have time and space to learn the will of God." The godless, conversely, have no right to punish according to the law, "[f]or then the innocent person would have to let himself be afflicted," and the tyrant would excuse himself with the words, "I have to make a martyr of you, for Christ too suffered and you should not resist me." Müntzer cautions, "Very precise distinctions have to be drawn, now that the persecutors claim to be the best Christians."[104]

The *Vindication* labels as demonic deception both the "flattering *gu[e]tigkeyt*" that Luther allegedly used to defend godless, exploitative rulers, and the rulers' own "terrible severity [*grymmigem ernst*]" in applying a "ruined justice" to amass temporal goods. God is good, but God does not excuse evil-doing. God is severely just, but only against wickedness. The *Ernst* of the godless, Müntzer says, has not been "imbued [*einbildet*] by the finger of Christ, the Holy Spirit, 2 Cor. 3, with the friendly severity of the law and the crucified son of God. For the Holy Spirit leads those who seek the divine will to understand its most severe mercy in the light of both of these, I Cor. 2." Rejecting the "judgment" or "distinction" (*undterschayd*) of the Holy Spirit, Luther uses the Son's *Gütigkeit* and "patience" to dispense with the Father's law and "severity," to the extent that many now think "that Christ was patient only so that godless Christians could afflict their brethren." Christians are to judge and punish severely—not "according to appearances," but "according to the spirit of the law." At the same time, they are to "forgive according to the spirit of Christ, in light of the gospel."[105] The name of God, which Müntzer seeks to proclaim through his "office," is "comfort to the sad but to the healthy illness and ruin."[106]

Alongside its theoretical discussion of divine *Ernst* and *Gütigkeit*, the *Vindication* seeks to dismantle Luther's biographical claim to prophetic status and truth evidenced by suffering; in turn, Müntzer defends his own, kindred claim by describing Luther's persecution of him.[107] In his *Letter*, Luther noted that he had risked life and limb for the Gospel, while the "evil spirits" simply enjoyed his accomplishments—for example by getting married, as both Müntzer and Karlstadt had now done. In response, Müntzer ridicules Luther's claim "that the great persecution his teaching has to bear proves that it is the true word of God." "It surprises me very much," Müntzer scorns, "that the shameless monk can bear to be so atrociously persecuted, used as he is to good malmsey and whorish fare."[108] Luther "makes himself out to be a new Christ, one who has purchased so many good things for the Christian people by his blood and striven well for this noble cause: that priests may take wives."[109] Luther's *Letter* boasted of his many appearances before hostile authorities and opponents, contrasting his willingness to suffer with Müntzer's supposed penchant for flight. Müntzer now retorts:

> You never tire of prattling about how you stood up before a very threatening assembly at Leipzig . . . You had such a good time at Leipzig that you drove out of the city gate with a wreath of carnations on your head and you drank good wine at Melchior Lotter's. And when you were at Augsburg you were immune from danger there too, for you could lean on Staupitz as an oracle to help you . . . That you stood up at Worms before the Empire is to the credit of the German nobility, whose mouths you smeared with honey . . . You let yourself be captured [and taken to the Wartburg] at your own suggestion and then pretended it was against your will.[110]

On both a theoretical and personal level, the entire debate between Luther and Müntzer hinged on notions of true and false suffering. Luther argued that true believers would accept their God-given lot within the order of government and economy ordained by God. Faith yielded self-trust in favor of trust in God, and faith's bearers did not need to seek supra-ordinary vocations, freedom from suffering, or pride-driven, self-chosen suffering. If oppressed by wicked rulers, faithful subjects should and could only profess truth and abide by the Word, accepting persecution as God's alien work. Thus, Luther himself had stood before pope and emperor without making personal claims and without concern for himself; the Word had flowed and worked through him. In Müntzer's understanding, conversely, true faith was born in the elect person's discovery of inner unbelief—a discovery that required and demanded separation from creaturely attachments based on desire and fear. Rooted in the fear of God, as the possession of God, the elect became instruments for the execution of divine *Ernst* and *Gütigkeit* throughout the ecclesial and social order. They would face boldly all persecution intended to suppress their action on behalf of God's will, but they would not passively embrace martyrdom to preserve the easy life of the godless.

Both Luther and Müntzer recognized the need for careful distinctions in equating suffering and truth. Both accepted that suffering could be genuine but nonetheless demonic—that is, in the service of the devil. Both saw the eternal punishment of the damned and bliss of the godly as the end of history.[111] However, both also bound true faith to true suffering. One's own experiences of suffering, others' accounts of such experiences, and the visible suffering of Christians and Christian communities could all be markers of truth for these reformers. The problem was that Satanic forces could imitate "true suffering." Consequently, the successful navigation of religious confusion required a careful discernment of false accounts and false appearances of suffering. One had to see with eyes of faith (Luther) or with divine discernment springing from within (Müntzer). For Müntzer, Luther's apparently humble disposition and readiness for martyrdom and Christlike suffering concealed his unwillingness to risk his neck or even his comfort in defiance of human authorities. Likewise his teachings about simple faith in Christ, the authority of scripture alone, and obedience to temporal authorities—although presented as repudiations of fallen reason and will— actually concealed and supported his own and his followers' preference for easy, lust-filled living over the endurance of God's inward work and the risk of executing God's will. The peasants reaped continued poverty and struggle from the triumph of Luther's teaching, yet many embraced it, just as they had embraced papal doctrines, in order to remain complacent and spiritually unchallenged. For Luther, conversely, the aspirations of Müntzer and others like him to be emptied, receive the divine Spirit, and execute God's judgments revealed a haughty disposition and demonic spirit, whose outward mortifications and trials were a cover for a self- and Satan-directed attempt at storming heaven.[112] We find these arguments especially in Luther's master treatise, *Against the Heavenly Prophets*, in which Karlstadt was the chief target of his ire.

Suffering and the Main Points of Christian Teaching: Luther's Critique of the "Heavenly Prophets," 1524–1525

Due to its length, *Against the Heavenly Prophets in the Matter of Images and Sacraments* was released in two parts, the first appearing in December 1524, the second in January 1525. The text was Luther's answer to Karlstadt's publications on the Lord's Supper after their August 1524 meeting. Throughout, Luther accuses Karlstadt and the "heavenly prophets"—Müntzer included—of lodging salvation entirely in external acts; however, the crux of Luther's argument is that the so-called prophets reverse the external and the spiritual. Where God has ordained an external means for grace, in the preached Word, baptism, and the Lord's Supper, the prophets reject the external and look to an inward, spiritual Word, baptism, and Supper. Conversely, where external practices are merely *adiaphora* ("inessentials"), which can be adopted or omitted in Christian freedom and with regard for the needs of others, the prophets create laws and bind consciences. They deceive people into believing that the destruction of images is necessary for salvation, and thus lead people away from the truth of salvation by faith alone. According to Luther, this confusion springs from fallen human reason manipulated by Satan. Karlstadt is said to confuse the proper order of salvation by placing works and mortifications before faith; his position is always the "rational" one—namely, that human beings must earn salvation and that Christ's body and blood cannot be in the bread and wine. The glitter of rationality deepens Satan's hold on the soul.

At the deepest level, Luther's response to Karlstadt and Müntzer was shaped by his fundamental conviction that God's manner of giving salvation—by grace through faith in Christ—is opposed to fallen reason and will. Fallen reason wants to understand God on its own terms, and driven by profound distrust in God's promises, reason concludes that winning salvation requires an exercise of the will of which human beings are capable. Accordingly, the receipt of salvation inevitably involves spiritual suffering, as fallen nature is thwarted in its hopes and expectations; certitude of salvation requires despair of self, which is produced by God's alien work. Despair of self and trust in Christ, however, set the Christian in opposition to the world of sinners offended by the cross, unable and unwilling to see God at work *sub contrariis*.

Because Karlstadt and Müntzer shared the essential conviction that God's manner of conferring salvation confounds and crushes the pretensions of fallen human beings, while subjecting Christians to the world's hatred—in other words, because they shared a paradigm of the Christian as sufferer—Luther had to carry out and guide readers through an exercise of careful definition and discernment. In *Against the Heavenly Prophets*, Luther elaborated his core doctrine that Christian salvation lies *extra nos*, in Christ, and requires no contribution from human beings' inward, natural resources for salvation; there is no reserve of reason or will, no synteresis or ground, capable of activity or assent. Luther thus relied on the radicalization of the late-medieval mystical orientation toward Christ that helped him to his theological breakthrough in the first place. For Luther, the hearing of the Word empties the soul of self-trust and gives trust in God, with all its consolation and peace of conscience; the "heavenly prophets" claim to have emptied themselves and received God, but in so doing, they only veil their self-reliance and works-righteousness; they know that the soul needs to be reduced to nothingness, but they make this humbling into a human work, failing to see that true nothingness can claim no capacity to earn salvation.

Luther's short preface to *Against the Heavenly Prophets* sets the framework for the debate, depicting two possible directions for human life: one led by reason and Satan along a path of idolatry, which entirely inverts the divinely ordained order of salvation and the disposition of the inward and outward; the other led by faith in the Word.[113] Luther describes Karlstadt as "the Satan who here pretends to vindicate the sacrament"—thus, like Müntzer, Karlstadt is treated not as a wayward individual but as the mouthpiece and arm of Christ's implacable enemy.[114] Unable to keep the gospel down by force this Satan turns to the "cunning interpretation of Scripture," like the archheretic Arius, and finds a ready hearing among the reason-bound world. Crucial for our purposes is Luther's description of the way of reason as the easy, sweet way:

> Likewise, it was easy and pleasant for the Jews and Pelagians to believe [*thet es sanfft, und war leichtlich zu gleuben*] that works without grace made one pious; and under the papacy it sounded sweet [*lautet es susse*] that the

free will also contributes something toward grace. So, since it is in accord with reason, it sounds altogether pleasant [*gefellt es wol*] to say that there is simply bread and wine in the sacrament. Who cannot believe that? If one only today would grant the Jews that Christ was simply a man, I think it would be easy to convert them.[115]

Luther's delineation of things that were easy to believe over and against divine truths impossible to reason reminds of Müntzer's discussion in the *Manifest Exposé*. Faced with sweet-sounding deceit, Christians can protect themselves, Luther says, only by distinguishing the "main articles [*heubtstuecken*]" of the faith, which "govern the conscience in the spirit before God," and "things external or works." Salvation depends on faith and a good conscience—on the *Hauptstücke*—which produce works in turn. Works without faith, however holy they may appear, only lead to the glorification of the self and the neglect of God's glory. In Luther's assessment, the so-called prophets committed just this error. He charges that they "break images, destroy churches, manhandle the sacrament, and seek a new kind of mortification, that is, a self-chosen putting to death of flesh," but they do not teach how the conscience is to be "set aright," to be "absolve[d] and comfort[ed]" so that a person can do works from faith rather than self-trust. In all his books, Luther alleges, Karlstadt has never taught "what faith and love are" but only "external works"; he wants to slay "the conscience with laws, sin, and works."[116]

Luther lists five "main articles" of the Christian faith,[117] describing a salvation that is received and lived out in suffering, but sustained by joyous trust in God that despairs of self. The first article is the divine law, "which is to be preached so that one thereby reveals and teaches how to recognize sin." The prophets do not understand this article, Luther says, for it demands "a truly spiritual preaching . . . and a right use of the law."[118] The prophets do not properly cast down human pride and self-focus—human beings' *incurvatus in se*—with the law. Instead, they set up the law as a standard that can be attained by morally earnest Christians, and thus give the sinner occasion to exalt. Only when sin is "recognized and the law is so preached that the conscience is terrified and humbled [*erschreckt und gedemuetigt*] before God's wrath" is the Christian ready to learn the second article of faith, "the comforting word of the gospel and the forgiveness of sins," which anchors the conscience "in the grace of God." Repentance must be preached before forgiveness, law before Gospel. Having failed to frighten, the prophets fail to console; they only strengthen a pride that will fail, at the latest, in the face of death and judgment.[119]

The oppositions between Luther and the "radicals" usually emphasized by scholars—such as between Luther's outer Word and the radicals' inner Word, or between Luther's concern for forgiveness and the radicals' focus on rebirth and obedience to the law—do not capture the full richness of the argument. Luther complains often in *Against the Heavenly Prophets* that the radicals torment would-be pious consciences with their demand for works. Here, however, he charges that they neither afflict nor console sinful consciences. They do not terrify with the law and thus cannot comfort with the gospel. The status of the conscience determines the appropriate medicine, and the conscience cannot seek God until it has been cast down.[120]

Luther's third article is "judgment [*gericht*]," the "work of putting to death the old man," and Luther attributes this mortification to works as well as "suffering and affliction [*leyden und marter*], as we through our own discipline and fasting, watching, labor, etc., or through other persecution and disgrace put to death our flesh." Ascetic self-discipline can serve the same function as unchosen trials, but only for the person who uses it in faith to mortify the old self and its self-trust. Because the prophets, in Luther's view, remain inwardly exalted and self-directed, they cannot discipline themselves or embrace unchosen crosses and suffering correctly. Mocking Karlstadt's attempt to live off the sweat of his own brow, Luther writes, "They do not accept what God gives them, but what they themselves choose. They wear gray garb, would be peasants and carry on with similar foolish nonsense."[121]

Like a right disposition toward self-discipline and suffering, then, "works of love toward the neighbor" (Luther's fourth main article) also flow from faith; these works of love are done "free[ly] and for nothing." Luther's fifth and final article is the application of the law upon the "crude and unbelieving," to compel outward piety and ensure "external peace." Outward peace and piety are the responsibility of temporal government, Luther argues, but external "laws and works" must not to be imposed on Christian consciences, that is, upheld as necessary for salvation. Whether Christians should break or tolerate images and how they should handle "foods, clothing, places, persons, and all such external things" are questions to be decided in freedom and with an eye toward the needs of neighbors. Luther's point is that "Dr. Karlstadt and his spirits replace the highest with the lowest," trying to accomplish by force right away what can only be done in faith—the ordering of Christian ecclesial and social life in a manner that serves rather than undermines trust in God.

Despite this mistake, Karlstadt wants to "be considered the greatest spirit of all, he who has devoured the Holy Spirit feathers and all." Luther enjoins the reader not to get lost in trivial externals. The devil trumps up "minor matters" in order to distract Christians from the "truly important matters."[122]

As in the *Invocavit Sermons*, Luther argues in *Against the Heavenly Prophets* that images must be rooted "out of the heart through God's Word and making them worthless and despised" before any outward action is taken.[123] Luther charges that Karlstadt proceeds only outwardly and with compulsion, thus upholding *Bildersturm* as a work necessary for salvation. Karlstadt thus erects new idols in people's hearts, namely "false confidence and pride and works."[124]

Character assassination was the order of the day in sixteenth-century theological controversy—a way of undermining claims to teaching authority and simultaneously expressing or illustrating by contrast key principles of theology, doctrine, spirituality, and reform. As in the debate between Luther and Müntzer, in the debate between Luther and Karlstadt personal claims and attacks were prominent and gave concrete expression to a larger debate about true and false suffering. In a section of *On the Heavenly Prophets* devoted to Karlstadt's published complaint about his expulsion from Saxony,[125] Luther opens with the telling lines, "Thus far we have seen what kind of Word of God Dr. Karlstadt has, for the sake of which he exalts himself and makes himself a holy martyr." Luther chose his phrasing carefully. Karlstadt *makes himself* a martyr and is not made one by God, revealing his misplacement of "judgment" before law and gospel. Luther strains to show that Karlstadt's political action—publication of a supposedly "slanderous book" against the Saxon princes—does not reflect the patient suffering of persecution of which Karlstadt boasts. Karlstadt "should first humbly have asked the reason [for his expulsion] and set forth what was right, and thereafter suffered in silence." Luther adds, "It could not be expected of me, who am made out of simply flesh[126] ... But the high spirit of Karlstadt cannot do wrong nor err."[127] Luther claims to have played no role in Karlstadt's expulsion,[128] but he is happy for it, he says, because Karlstadt places the Law of Moses, improperly understood and applied, in the hands of the masses. In Deuteronomy 7, Luther reminds readers, Moses commanded the people not only to destroy images but also to slay the idolaters. Thus, Karlstadt's teaching can only incite rebellion and bloodshed in the manner of Müntzer's teaching.[129]

Luther accuses Karlstadt of neglecting his appointed post and duties as Archdeacon of All Saints' in Wittenberg and forcing himself "uncalled" and as a wolf upon the Orlamünders. However fair or unfair,[130] these charges carried significant theological weight as Luther aimed to shape readers' views and conduct with respect to Christian social life and work. According to Luther, Karlstadt's duties in Wittenberg were commanded by God, and as long as Karlstadt had remained in his post—to which he had also bound himself—he worked "usefully and with honor, and was liked and cherished." But "the murderous prophets came and made the man wild and restless, so that he wanted to learn something better and more unusual than God teaches in the Bible."[131] Luther implies here that Karlstadt fell under the sway of the Zwickau prophets, and perhaps also of Müntzer himself; the deeper point is that Karlstadt is driven by himself and Satan rather than faith, which inspires neither flight from a God-given vocation nor rebellion against God's order, but trust in God's will and ordinance come what may.

Luther piles complaint upon complaint: Karlstadt rushed to Orlamünde, he says, both to accumulate financial gain and to find a corner from which the rodent-like prophets might spread their poison. Karlstadt serves only "the spirit and the belly," per Philippians 3; thus, he sought out a comfortable position, not the place where preaching of the Word was most needed, and despite his claims to an inner call, he fled when the going got tough.[132] Karlstadt bowled over the Orlamünders with his "humble bearing and high-sounding words," so that they now act against their princes.[133] The princes had the right to expel Karlstadt without explanation, Luther argues, and Karlstadt's public complaint shows that he wants to be lord of the land.[134] Karlstadt's vaunted humility, finally, was a false front, adopted through unmortified self-will to conceal Karlstadt's unwillingness to be God's obedient instrument in daily work and suffering. Here, Luther derides Karlstadt's specialized mystical vocabulary as proof of his grasping for holier-than-Christian things. Luther writes:

> Is it not a fine new spiritual humility? Wearing a felt hat and a gray garb, not wanting to be called doctor, but Brother Andrew and dear neighbor, as another peasant, subject to the magistrate of Orlamünde and obedient as an ordinary citizen. Thus with self-chosen humility and servility, which God does not command, he wants to be seen and praised as a remarkable Christian, as though Christian behavior consisted in such external hocus-pocus. At the same time he strives and runs counter to duty, honor, obedience, and the power and right of the reigning prince and the governing authority, which God has instituted. This is God's new sublime art, taught

by the heavenly voice, which we at Wittenberg, who teach faith and love, do not understand and cannot know. This is the nice "turning from the material," the "concentration," the "adoration," the "self-abstraction," and similar devil's nonsense.[135]

Much of *Against the Heavenly Prophets* works to undress the apparent humility and suffering taught and practiced by Karlstadt and to expose the thriving self-will beneath. In Luther's depiction, the bulk of Karlstadt's supposed suffering was a self-chosen cloak, harmonious with and intended to conceal the desires and machinations of fallen nature—not really suffering at all. Luther's critique of self-chosen suffering connected with key teachings of Tauler and Suso: the former had cautioned against self-imposed sufferings that sprung from an unyielded will, the latter had described the servant's self-mortification as an arduous beginning stage in the journey toward union—an elementary training that was followed by a period of unchosen suffering that truly broke the servant's self-will. For these mystics, pious suffering could be "self-imposed" only to the extent that the created will had become God's instrument, united to God; for Luther, conversely, the faithful carried out self-discipline in order to exercise their trust in God. Union with Christ through faith preceded the work of *Gelassenheit*, which always remained incomplete. Thus, Luther situated the mystics' critique of self-willed suffering in a trust-centered framework that eschewed claims to perfect volitional union. Luther encouraged the self-discipline of the faithful, but he recognized the preeminent power of unchosen sufferings to try and strengthen trust in God rather than self. He refused to acknowledge or failed to recognize Karlstadt's insistence that volitional union was a postmortem attainment; yet his spirituality and Karlstadt's were fundamentally opposed—Luther's was oriented toward trust in God's grace, even and especially when experienced *sub contrariis*; Karlstadt's was oriented toward ever-deepening detachment from self and union with God's will. Luther demanded a different form of detachment—namely, detachment from ordinary (i.e., fallen) rational and emotional responses to earthly experiences— made possible by faith.

In Karlstadt's case, Luther admitted that his foe underwent both unwanted and self-chosen trials; but he saw Karlstadt's unwanted trials as a due consequence of his alliance with the devil. Toward the end of his discussion of images, Luther writes, "I wanted to show what lies behind Dr. Karlstadt's brash boast that he has God's Word and must suffer so much on its account.

Indeed, the devil, too, must suffer on account of it—not that he uses it rightly, but rather perverts it and thereby increases his wickedness and lies, as Dr. Karlstadt also does due to the same vexation [*anfechtung*]."[136] In short, Luther argues that, just as Karlstadt's self-chosen sufferings reveal his intact self-will, Karlstadt's unchosen sufferings are a result of his willful rejection of the Word—of his seeking to be something rather than to accept salvation and live Christian life on God's terms, within his appointed vocation and the social order as ordained by God for human well-being.

According to Luther, Karlstadt was seeking to attain exalted spiritual states and earn heaven itself through self-contrived human works; he strove for experience of and union with God through human ascent, rejecting God's descent through the means of Word and sacrament.[137] Indeed, Karlstadt and other prophets made God's means of grace into human works—no less than Roman clergy who upheld the sacrament as a sacrifice—while "forc[ing] all external words and Scriptures belonging to the inward life of faith into new forms of putting to death the old man." Luther attacks especially Karlstadt's teaching that true partaking of the Lord's Supper consists of passionate remembrance of the crucifixion and mortification of self-will and the old Adam:

> What Christ has said and referred to the inner life of faith, this man applies
> to outward, self-contrived works, even to the point of making the Lord's
> Supper and the recognition and remembrance of Christ a human work,
> whereby we in like manner, in "passionate ardor" and . . . with "outstretched
> desire," put ourselves to death. . . . [H]e obscures the clear words of Christ,
> "My blood poured out for you . . ." Their meaning is undoubtedly grasped,
> received, and retained only by faith, and by no kind of work.[138]

Christ must be received as a sacrament before Christ is adopted as an example; faith must be received from God before works or suffering pleasing to God can occur. The prophets "place the mortification of the flesh prior to faith, even prior to the Word," but the "order of God" dictates that "no one can mortify the flesh, bear the cross, and follow the example of Christ before he is a Christian and has Christ through faith in his heart as an eternal treasure." Christ comes into the heart through hearing first the law and then the gospel rightly preached.[139] Not to be missed here is Luther's affirmation of Christ's presence in the heart that has been emptied of self-trust (if incompletely) by the law; the prophets miss the means and hence the realization of their own goals of self-destruction and union with God. Karlstadt and the prophets will hear neither law nor gospel, but want to speak themselves, making even the accusation for sin into a human work; Tauler had rejected self-chosen suffering and commended waiting for God in silence.

Thus, finally, Karlstadt refuses to accept the real presence because he twists and tortures scripture according to "his own darkness instead of letting his stupid mind be broken and directed by the word and the Scripture of God." Every article of faith is "beyond the reach of reason," indeed offensive to reason. But, Luther charges, Karlstadt imagines that "reason happily and willingly accepts" faith and the Word of God.[140] Karlstadt, of course, had agreed that reason must be subjected and receptive to a higher light. The debate focused on the means by which the breaking of reason and the revelation of light came. Did Karlstadt's and Müntzer's intent to avoid false teachings— and the corruption of knowledge received from outside when processed by fallen reason and will—in fact secure Christians from deceit or merely leave them in the grips of their own inward resources? In Luther's view, Karlstadt had dreamed up the humblest works that reason could imagine—passionate remembrance of the crucifixion and rigorous self-accusation for sin—but he refused to hear God's far more severe accusation of human sin. Karlstadt afflicted consciences with petty, human demands, but left fallen nature intact and thriving. *Against the Heavenly Prophets* thus makes a final, fundamental assault on Karlstadt's conception of faith as knowledge, contending that Karlstadt failed to uphold the divine source of true knowledge and human passivity before the same:

> [Karlstadt] does not make such knowledge spiritual as it ought to be. For Isaiah [Isa. 53:11] speaks of a spirit and of spiritual knowledge which the Holy Spirit works in us, not we ourselves. I know and am convinced beyond doubt that this is the same as, Christ is given for me. But Dr. Karlstadt makes of it a human, carnal devotion and a passionate, ardent work in the heart, though not higher than the knowledge and recognition that Christ is given for us, which the devil and the hypocrites also know. He can teach knowledge, but not the use of knowledge. He spews out much about knowledge, but does not develop or rightly apply it, but permits it to remain a mere human work. That is to make it a carnal instead of a spiritual knowledge. For his spirit will not tolerate anything less than making carnal what is spiritual.[141]

To secure themselves from deceit in matters of images, sacraments, and salvation, Christians in Luther's view had to see the self-will and self-trust behind the humble garb of Karlstadt's self-chosen peasant's life, behind the prophets' claim to suffer persecution for truth, behind talk of extraordinary spiritual trials—behind even a vocabulary that sought to impress with its obscurity. Trust in Christ alone for salvation required a true recognition of one's own nothingness *coram deo* and instilled a true readiness to suffer the hatred of the world and all the trials of embodied social life. Those who trust in God do not need to speak of exalted spiritual states beyond faith itself, or to seek better ways of life than the humble exercise of vocation. Annihilation and union with God (Christ in the heart) were part of the universal Christian experience of faith; consequently, one could no longer claim higher kinds of self-loss and intimacy with the divine, although the strength of one's faith might be greater or lesser.

Karlstadt between Luther and Müntzer

From mid-1524 through early 1525, Karlstadt distanced himself from Müntzer and Luther alike. Together with his Orlamünde congregation, Karlstadt on his one flank rejected a defensive *Bund* as the product of self-will rather than yielding to the divine will, which forbids rebellion. Karlstadt cautioned Müntzer that he had not accused himself or faced his sin sufficiently. Thus, he had not been inwardly conformed to the crucified. On his other flank, in response to Luther's *Against the Heavenly Prophets*, Karlstadt quickly penned his *Several Main Points of Christian Teaching regarding which Dr. Luther brings Andreas Carlstadt under suspicion through false accusation and slander* (henceforth *Anzeige*, after the modernized German title).[142] Published in Augsburg in January 1525, the treatise answered Luther's charge that Karlstadt ignored or reversed the *Hauptstücke* of Christian teaching. Karlstadt relies throughout the work on his central conception of faith as loving knowledge of God, which provokes hatred of self and denial of the self-will. He argues that faith so defined frees Christians from bondage to sin and human opinion and rebirths them into conformity with the will of God and a free bondage to God's law, revealed in scripture. In his self-definition vis-à-vis Müntzer and Luther, Karlstadt like his competitors developed independently a shared mystical heritage and the shared assumption that God's truth and manner of conferring salvation are entirely contrary to fallen human reason and desire. Unmasking his opponents' self-will and cross-shirking, Karlstadt sought to show what true suffering involved for Christians as recipients of salvation and God's children in a fallen world.

Karlstadt and Müntzer

Although they first became acquainted during Müntzer's time as a student in Wittenberg from 1517 to 1519,[143] our primary insight into the inter-relationship of Karlstadt and Müntzer comes from four letters penned between late 1522 and mid-1524.[144] The letters between Karlstadt and Müntzer contain expressions both of common cause against Luther and his circle and of friendship grounded in a shared spirituality of accusation for sin: the sinner was to accuse himself for sin, and to accept his friend's accusations as a work of love. Also expressed is a shared striving for receptivity to God's teaching, indeed for prophetic status as a vehicle of God's truth.[145] We have no reason to doubt the veracity of the two reformers' professions of friendship; yet the friendship was neither naïve nor untroubled. An attentive reading of their letters reveals careful maneuvering for the upper hand. Each man wanted to enlist the other for his own vision of reform. Also noteworthy is that Müntzer criticized Karlstadt in various semi-public settings not only after the latter's repudiation of the Bund in July 1524, but also several times in 1522. When Müntzer complained in his March 1522 letter to Melanchthon about the lustful embrace of marriage by Wittenberg clerics, he certainly had Karlstadt's highly publicized nuptials in mind, and in the November 1522 colloquy with Wolfgang Stein at Weimar, Müntzer reportedly lumped Karlstadt together with other "fatuous" Wittenbergers.[146] Karlstadt's alienation from Luther's inner circle likely endeared him to Müntzer, possibly rekindling an earlier friendship.

The first extant letter between Müntzer and Karlstadt followed shortly after Müntzer's critical remarks of November 1522. In a lost letter of December 20 or 21, Müntzer wrote to Karlstadt from a location near Wittenberg.[147] On the basis of Karlstadt's surviving response, we can infer that Müntzer lamented his exile after the model of Jeremiah 20, disavowed the Zwickau prophets,[148] and sought Karlstadt's assistance to obtain a new position.[149] Karlstadt answered Müntzer hastily[150] with a letter addressed "to the servant of Christ, Thomas Müntzer, most dear brother." Karlstadt did not approve of Müntzer's Jeremiah-like "cursing." "In Jeremiah, too," Karlstadt writes, "I can see a grain of wheat fallen into the earth but not yet dead. For just like him you seem to me to feel something of the bitterness of mustard, but not yet to feel that you have become the least of all men." If Müntzer truly felt himself "the least of all," Karlstadt writes, he would "declare [himself] unworthy of the glory and honour with which Christ of Nazarath was crowned by that woman." Likely, Karlstadt refers to the woman who in Matthew 26 and Mark 14 anointed Christ with perfume in advance of his death.[151] Müntzer complains of persecution and the threats around him, but if he had truly died to his self-will and pride through inward bitterness, he would rejoice at suffering and impending martyrdom.

Karlstadt's letter acknowledges the genuineness of Müntzer's spiritual trials, and Karlstadt credits Müntzer with having made a good beginning toward the death of self-will in and through these trials. To guide Müntzer to the end, Karlstadt invokes the central themes of his own thought. Sin is separation from the will of God—a definition from the *German Theology*—while suffering is punishment for that separation and God's means to bring the human will back into precreated unity with the divine. Karlstadt insists that suffering comes from God, not the devil; thus, he continues to express the point about God's eternal ordination of suffering that he received from Tauler. He commends the effort to sink into God's will, while denying the accomplishment of union until after death:

> Your letter alerted me to the heavy seas in which you are swimming. Believe me: the Lord chastises his elect with judgment. But though it may for the moment seem to you, too, that you have been struck by a visitation of the enemy, this, too, has been sent by [God's] judgment, namely because of sin. You know how easy it is for us to cast off the will of God [*quam facile non sumus cum Dei uoluntate coniuncti*] since we are separated from it as often and to the extent to which our desires triumph. It is in the land of death that we exist, so the righteousness of Christ does not triumph in us until the life of the flesh is over [*vita carnis super est*] . . . Should it not please me, however, when you strive with such zeal to clamber into the abyss of the divine will, when you strain to be reborn there, where you were the life of God.[152]

Karlstadt instructs Müntzer to come to Wittenberg so that they can meet "face to face" and Karlstadt can "say the things which I am unwilling to commit to writing."[153] The ideas to be kept under wraps surely included God's direct communication with believers, for Karlstadt adds, "God is the master of my heart; I have learnt his power and his strong hand by experience. Hence I have said more about visions and dreams than any of the professors."[154] Yet Karlstadt—however much he accepted that visions and dreams might be divine in origin—did not ground salvation and reform in inward experience in the same manner as Müntzer. Müntzer esteemed scripture as a witness to the work of the inner Word and as a proving ground for dreams and visions, which he regarded as less reliable than the inner Word; but he did not finally consider scripture necessary. Karlstadt's reform program and spirituality held inner illumination and scriptural study inseparably together. The Spirit enables worship to take the form of a communal Bible study.[155]

Müntzer apparently did seek out Karlstadt in Wittenberg, for in the next surviving correspondence between the two men—a July 29, 1523 letter of Müntzer to Karlstadt—Müntzer sends his greetings to Anna Bodenstein.[156] This letter was carried by Nicholas Rucker, who was to seek Karlstadt's advice on the Allstedters' decision to withhold tithes from the Naundorf cloister and use the money instead for the care of the poor.[157] Seemingly desperate for an alliance, Müntzer complains that Karlstadt had broken a promise to write often, and he pleads—using substantially the same language as in his July 9, 1523, letter to Luther—"Tell me why you have not even brought about some small renewal of our old love." Müntzer dismisses Karlstadt's anxiety about the possible interception of letters as a lack of trust in God's leadership of their cause.[158] A shared piety of self- and mutual accusation for sin is reflected in Müntzer's final words to Karlstadt, "It may be that the Lord wants you as his procurator, so that you may expiate what you have perpetrated under the pompous regime of Antichrist. I talk to you, most beloved, as I do to myself."[159] In other words, Karlstadt's assistance in the Allstedters' legal affairs would make up for his prior academic and administrative service to the papal church.

The decisive break between Karlstadt and Müntzer followed the latter's efforts to bring Karlstadt and his Orlamünde community into the *Bund* in defense of the gospel.[160] Letters from Müntzer to Karlstadt and from Allstedt to Orlamünde were dispatched around July 17, 1524.[161] In the former, Müntzer asked Karlstadt to urge Schneeberg and fifteen other villages to join the alliance. Müntzer also sought Karlstadt's opinion on his liturgical reforms, probably relating the defensive "covenant" to the "new covenant" of Christ's blood (I Cor. 11:25), symbolized in the Eucharist.[162] Karlstadt quickly dispatched a reply in Latin to "my dearest brother in Christ, Thomas Müntzer, bishop of Allstedt."[163] Karlstadt declares himself still a correcting, loving friend, in line with the piety of mutual accusation. "The wounds inflicted by someone who loves you are better than the fraudulent kisses of an enemy," he writes.[164] Substantively, Karlstadt opens with a statement on signs: "I will scarcely be persuaded that the sheep of Christ are to be gathered more happily by another sign than the speaking of truth." Müntzer evidently had defended the elevation of the host as a sign of the gathering of the elect; rejecting that interpretation, Karlstadt urges Müntzer to abolish elevation as "blasphemy against Christ crucified."[165] Karlstadt describes the league, in turn, as a transgression against sole trust in God and as the fruit of spiritual uncircumcision. The league too is an attempt to "gather" the sheep by human power, rather than the power of God's truth. Pacts of human with human pollute the heart with the fear of human beings rather than the fear of God. They drown out the voice of God—and are thus contrary to the repeatedly asserted aims of Müntzer's own preaching. It is a mark of the spiritually circumcised that they proclaim truth without regard for the consequences. Karlstadt writes:

> It seems to me that leagues of this kind are altogether contrary to the divine will and cause incalculable harm to souls which have been sprinkled with the spirit of fear; for it is like replacing a walking-stick with a reed—trust [*fiducia*] in blessing, in the living God, with trust in cursing, in man [an allusion to Jeremiah 17:5–7] . . . The whole of Scripture testifies how much [this] alienates fearful minds from God, so that they become feckless, unable to hear the voice of the Lord; and even if Scripture were silent, experience would cry out in the streets that to cast one's trust and heart [*fiduciam et animum*] on man is to have a large, thick foreskin of the heart . . . I can hardly think of any sharper sword to dispatch us than having to die because our eyes are fixed on the conjectures and rumours of the mob.[166]

Briefly stated, the worst suffering would be a false martyrdom for human ends, and Karlstadt advises Müntzer to "rest [his] hope in the one God who is able to confound your adversaries," as Christ and the prophets teach. Karlstadt would have helped Müntzer, he says, had the latter's request been based on "contemplation of the judgments of God," for "you know that I owe you my life as in turn you owe me yours." Karlstadt also expresses his willingness to suffer martyrdom with Müntzer for the proclamation of God's truth.[167]

Along with Karlstadt's Latin letter to Müntzer, the Orlamünde community penned a vernacular letter to Allstedt, with an eye toward future publication—that is, to wash their hands of the scheme. Like Karlstadt's letter, the community's letter testifies strongly to the use of themes of right suffering to define religious boundaries and shape ecclesial-political action at the time. Karlstadt claimed in his 1525 *Apology* to have "added one or two lines" to the community's letter, which was likely produced by a circle of his more educated and devoted followers.[168] Karlstadt carried the letter to Wittenberg and had it printed by Hans Luft, with a title describing it as a statement "on the Christian way to fight."[169] For their part, the Orlamünders argue that Christians may not use "worldly weapons" in the face of persecution, for Christ ordered Peter to put away the sword when the crowd came to arrest him in Gethsemane. Echoing Karlstadt's central concern for harmony with the divine will, in fulfillment of the Lord's Prayer, they state, "when the time and hour is at hand in which we too [like Christ] have to suffer something for the sake of divine righteousness let us not run for knives and spears and drive out the eternal will of the father by our own violence [*den ewigen willen des vaters aus eygener gewalt zu veriagen*]. After all, we pray every day, 'Your will be done.' "[170] Where Müntzer saw in the *Bund* the surrender of the fear of creatures in favor of the fear of God and courage against the enemies of God, Karlstadt and his followers saw mere self-assertion.

The Orlamünders seek to answer the Allstedters' justification of the *Bund* through 2 Kings 23,[171] where Josiah "convenant[ed] himself to God, and to the people." In fact, they contend, Josiah promised to "give his whole-hearted and entire obedience to [God's] law, commandments and ceremonies, and . . . the people obeyed this covenant. . . . [T]he king and the people bound themselves at the same time to God." Josiah could not have simultaneously bound himself to God and the people, or "his heart would have been divided" in the service of two masters, contrary to Matthew 6:24.[172] Neither can the Orlamünders bind themselves to the Allstedters, for this would rob them of Christian freedom. Bondage to God's law is freedom, but bondage to human beings is slavery, the Orlamünders explain. If Christians choose the latter, the tyrants will justly mock them for their distrust in God's defense of the righteous and accuse and punish them for creating unrest. "Then it would be for this, and not for the sake of the stern righteousness of God, that we would have to die," the Orlamünders write, echoing their pastor.[173]

The Orlamünders underline, finally, that Christians should, like Christ, "only hear and accept the true speech of God," profess divine truth, and willingly endure the persecution that comes. Such is the godly way to "give account" according to 1 Peter 3:15.[174] The letter's closing admonition evinces the heart of Karlstadt's piety. The Orlamünders enjoin the Allstedters, "Learn to do the eternal will of God alone, our heavenly father, which he has revealed to us through his only son, Christ, in the Holy Spirit. Then you will be able to find peace for your hearts in God from all trials and temptations."[175] Learning the will of God—sinking into the divine will—does not bring freedom from suffering and persecution, only acceptance (*Gelassenheit*) that trials have a purpose in God's will.

Karlstadt Responds to Luther

Karlstadt introduces himself in the dedicatory epistle of the *Anzeige* as one "exiled on account of the truth without a hearing, yet called and chosen by God the Father to the true proclamation of the cross of Christ." The text is addressed to "his brothers on the River Saale and to all who seek or would like to seek God the true way." Aligning himself with Paul as the suffering proclaimer of Christ crucified and with the prophets, Karlstadt seeks to draw authority not only from the endurance of holy exile but also from his experience with inner tribulation, and he depicts Luther as unable to come through tribulation to salvation and truth. "I can accept it when Luther calls me unlearned," Karlstadt declares, "for I know that he himself is unable to pass the great sea which we all have to cross, to gain health and understanding."[176] Karlstadt promises in *Anzeige* to defend his understanding of the "main articles of Christian teaching" and the order among them—and to show that Luther failed to describe sufficient articles for Christian salvation.[177]

The main body of the *Anzeige* addresses in turn each of the five main articles of Christian teaching offered by Luther in *Against the Heavenly Prophets*. The text is loosely structured as a dialogue in which Luther states and defends each article, and Karlstadt replies. On the preaching of the law to reveal sin, Karlstadt underlines that the law must not merely be preached outwardly, but be written by God upon hearts, "so that sin is then rightly known and fled as an evil." Hatred of sin follows recognition of the grace of Christ "shown on the cross," which "liberates from the external law." The law then ceases to be a source of terror or an object of hypocritical, unwilling obedience; it is willingly obeyed.[178] In all this, Karlstadt expresses primarily an Augustinian outlook on the law, and he refers readers to his printed lectures on *The Spirit and the Letter* and his other books. He declares that he has known the "spiritual nature" of the law—that it "reveals God's justice and the injustice of

creatures"—longer than Luther, and that he understands Paul "more fundamentally" than Luther. Karlstadt argues that Luther's ordering of his five main
articles calls for the law to be preached and "known through . . . reason"; but
this manner of preaching and knowing the law produces in the "knower"
only "lust to sin" and "wrath against God's justice."[179] Karlstadt thus accuses
Luther of misunderstanding Augustine's fundamental anti-Pelagian views,
and he aligns Luther with the "Pelagians" who held that reason's grasp of the
law provided sufficient guidance for the attainment of eternal life by human
will and effort. Luther's ordering of the "main articles" is incorrect, because
the law is placed before faith—and hence the spirit and true knowledge.

According to Karlstadt, Luther's light regard for the Lord's Supper, baptism, and images follows from his failure to understand sin or even how sin
comes to be understood. Faith is a "loving knowledge of the crucified" that
does not look for "forgiveness . . . or salvation anywhere else but with Christ";
but to grow in loving knowledge of God revealed through Christ is also to
grow in conformity to God's will revealed through Christ.[180] Practices revealed in the New Testament cannot be *adiophora*.[181] Karlstadt argues forcefully that any true knowledge of sin will result in hatred of sin; such true
knowledge of sin is the "fear of God" and is worked by the Spirit within, not
preaching the law to reason. Moreover, just as knowledge of sin produces
hatred of sin, true knowledge of Christ transforms the heart into Christ. The
law is a testimony to sin, and scripture a testimony to Christ, but the Spirit
must reveal both within.[182]

Karlstadt adds here that sin is revealed not only by the Spirit's inward
teaching of the law, but also when God uses "plagues and great suffering
[*tru[o]bsal*]" to produce shame and improvement of life. In fact, Karlstadt
claims that persecution reveals and "create[s] dissatisfaction" with sin more
effectively than the law. Thus, Karlstadt alleges that Luther not only misorders
the first two articles of faith—putting law before faith—but wrongly
subordinates mortification and suffering as the third article. Preaching the
law in Luther's manner, "according to lines taken out of context and not . . . its
true content," does not "cast . . . down and destroy" consciences, but only
"confort[s]" and confirms them "in their wickedness," increasing delight in
sin and hatred of the law. Karlstadt addresses preachers in Luther's camp, "I
dare stake my life on whether you are capable of finding the really frightening
parts of the law, let alone that you are able to preach them."[183]

In key respects, Karlstadt's core arguments in the *Anzeige* sounded like
Müntzer's. Both charged Luther with a piecemeal approach to scripture

that failed to grasp the whole of Paul and shattered the continuity of the Old and New Testaments—of Moses, the prophets, and Christ. Both lambasted Luther for teaching an easy message of forgiveness, without regard for inward appropriation of the law: lust-driven, reason-bound beings could only misuse that message to harden their opposition to the will of God. Luther only pretended, in the view of both Müntzer and Karlstadt, to acknowledge the opposition of God's will for salvation and Christian life to the fallen reason and will of human beings. At the same time, despite their shared sources (including Tauler, Suso, and the *German Theology*) and their interrelated development, Karlstadt and Müntzer advanced very different theologies, spiritualities, and reform programs, crystalized around their divergent understandings of and responses to suffering. Müntzer looked to spiritual suffering—primarily defined as an inward confrontation with *Unglauben* following and enabling ascetic separation from creaturely lusts and fears—as a passing experience at the beginning of faith; thereafter, true believers would resist the oppression and persecution of the ungodly, ready to suffer in the fight to implement God's order. Conversely, Karlstadt upheld *Gelassenheit* as a continuous and ever-incomplete exercise of sinking into the divine will; faith became a central category in his thought and writing, no less than for Müntzer or Luther, but he offered yet a third definition of faith—as love-rich knowledge of the divine will that provoked self-hatred—and he spoke little of a promise to which faith was related. For Karlstadt, God's will was to be studied in scripture and learned in experience, including in the experience of persecution; rebellion was excluded as a rejection of God's will to use persecution to spur Christians' self-accusation and growth in union with God. Karlstadt's refusal to see union with God as an earthly attainment made all the difference for his view of the Christian as an ecclesial and political actor.

Karlstadt's *Anzeige* does connect the Wittenbergers' allegedly faulty doctrine of salvation to their economic exploitation of the poor, echoing Müntzer's own polemic. "However unlearned and foolish you are," Karlstadt says directly to evangelical preachers, "you demand the appropriate interest and tenth. You gather in rents and moneys and thus put under great pressure the poor—whom you cannot teach but whom you know how to cheat." Karlstadt will "pray to God," he says, "that he send into his harvest apostolic workers, for you are wolflike preachers. Whom will you frighten off from sins when you as pigs wallow and delight in your sins and preach delight in sins?" The preachers should lead God's "little flock" into the "right pasture" through the "articles of law" taught by Moses and Christ, but instead they offer the people "chaff and sugar-coated poison to eat."[184] The references to the harvest, to wolf- and swine-like preachers, and to "sugar-coated poison" especially remind of Müntzer. Karlstadt also joined Müntzer in mocking Luther's views of the last judgment as childish, deriding Luther as "one of the false prophets who frightened and scared us for a whole year with the coming of the last judgment. But now we see that he proclaimed lies and visions of his own heart."[185]

Karlstadt demands that true preachers reproach the world and contradict the false evaluations of reason. They should, he writes,

> come down from the broad realm and lofty heights of the law into the valley, which is to speak of sin in small portions [stuckweyß verzelen] and then not only of coarse sins which the world also considers to be sin. Rather, they must present those things which the wisdom of the world considers to be good and not sinful at all—sins in which the Pharisees remained and which they defined as right. Of such sins there are so many that I do not know one single prophet, evangelist, or apostle who spoke of each particular sin [alle sünd stuckweyß erzelt]. But it is true that we can speak of the unnamed sins on the basis of the named ones.[186]

Karlstadt's remarks here build to a critique of temporal as well as spiritual authority. He notes the failure of the biblical prophets to convince the "supreme princes, kings, and priests of the Jews of their sins," and he adds, likely with reference to the Saxon princes, "it would be good if the poor Christian man could understand such secret and treacherous sin, for there are several who have such good appearance in the eyes of the world that Dr. Luther himself refuses to acknowledge them as sinful and wicked, though God is truthful and Luther a liar."[187]

Turning to Luther's central theological concern, faith (the second article),[188] Karlstadt concedes that sin "must be quickly discredited" and the "grace of the cross" preached, so the "abject sinner" learns to "esteem the grace of Christ more highly and run after it the more." He counters, however, that the gospel "does not consist in the proclamation of the grace of Christ alone which has been proffered for the forgiveness of sins." The gospel includes as well the "immeasurable goods and treasures in Christ which Christ has obtained for us and desires to communicate to us if we believe in him." The marginal citations here to Ephesians 3 (see verses 16–21) and Titus 2 (see verses 11–14) highlight the reformer's interest in sanctification.

Christians receive from Christ power to become "sons of God" (John 1:17) and will become through Christ much more.[189]

According to Karlstadt, because Luther's article on law leaves reason intact and fallen nature unbroken, Luther's doctrine of faith becomes nothing more than a word of easy forgiveness, an excuse for the unrepentant sinner. Where salvation begins with the "knowledge of Christ," however, true knowledge of sin and an inward delight in the law follow inseparably and become ever deeper. Again, grace and faith precede any use of the law beneficial for salvation; the law cannot be the beginning of salvation. "What tears the heart away from itself and its sin?" Karlstadt asks amid a flurry of rhetorical questions. "The law? No. The knowledge of Christ? Yes, truly yes." Penance flows from grace and faith defined as knowledge of Christ, not law; repentance in the name of Christ means to grasp "the extent and severity" of one's sins "through Christ's suffering." One thousand years of reflection on the law could not work such repentance; indeed, no one truly understands sin "as sin and as something evil, without comprehending the suffering of Christ . . . Who can believe that any sin kindles [verschuldt] the wrath of God when he does not comprehend the reasons for Christ's death?"[190] Thus, baptism in the name of Jesus—that is, "in the knowledge of or faith in Christ" (Rom. 6)—means that one "leaves the old life and all its desires, lusts, and works and comes to stand in a new life." Karlstadt explains:

> In this new life, sin and the old life are not simply abhorred and hated, but a person actually crucifies his life through the known crucified Christ. Thus we do not simply live in the world as those who are dead or who have died. Rather, we choke lusts and desires through affliction and persecution which befall us and by living daily according to the will of God. All who have the spirit of Christ do this . . . Faith which recognizes [erkennt] Christ does all this . . . Their life is the life of Christ . . . But such repentance [in the name of Jesus] is above the law and accountable to the spirit of God only. For to be freed from the clutches of the lusts of the flesh or to die does not belong to nature or to the law, but to the spirit of God alone.[191]

Karlstadt's Christians do not become perfect instruments for the implementation of God's order (as in Müntzer's thinking), but people struggling through individual and communal study and self-accusation to make progress, driven by the Spirit of Christ. In Karlstadt's view, Luther wanted to blunt the law's accusation by first preaching it in a way that conformed to reason and creaturely desire, and then quickly leaving it behind. Furthermore, ignorance regarding the meaning of "baptism in the name of Jesus" led Luther and his followers to take baptism lightly—thus baptizing "children who do not understand their desires, let alone the death of their desires through Christ."[192]

In response to Luther's third article, judgment, Karlstadt faced the charge that he found salvation in a freely willed imitation of Christ's deeds of suffering, rather than in a freely received gift on account of Christ's own suffering. In agreement with Luther, Karlstadt accepts that self-mortification and patient suffering are good deeds only insofar as they flow from faith and grace. For Karlstadt, however, faith is a knowledge of God's will that requires loving attachment to that will and separation from any contrary will. Through suffering, Karlstadt says, Christians need to "subdue, break, and subordinate to the spirit" their "untamed flesh," thus growing in their faith, love, and grasp of the Word.[193]

Suffering is useless unless one suffers in knowledge of the truth and love of God, just as Christ defeated Satan "not so much through suffering and death as by professing the truth and love of God." The warfare of a Christian is against "all attacks and all obstacles which rise up against the knowledge of God." The inward struggle precedes the outward and is a struggle of truth against the unholy alliance of reason, flesh, and the devil, the master liar. Karlstadt explains, "We hold captive all reason in the obedience of Christ, and we must overcome devil, reason, and flesh through the truth which we know, and we must suffer tribulation in love and understanding, otherwise suffering is of no use to righteousness."[194]

According to Karlstadt, Luther imposes a false order when he teaches that suffering and the cross necessarily follow law and gospel. Already in his preface to *Anzeige*, Karlstadt explains that "some mortification comes before faith, but . . . some—and this is the best—comes with faith, while some follows in its wake."[195] The mortification that precedes faith in this three-fold scheme is self-castigation produced by the Spirit's inner prompting, as we will presently see; Karlstadt likely also included in the category all the suffering that God, in his view, used to produce hatred of sin.[196] Most important for our purposes is Karlstadt's argument that Luther's doctrine of faith ignores inward mortification, the second of the three types, which is the heaviest of crosses. Consequently, the outward sufferings of those who follow Luther can only be cause for the exaltation of unmortified nature, which still trusts in and presumes upon itself and its reason. Karlstadt deflected back toward

Luther the charges that Luther had made against him and Müntzer: Luther taught self-chosen suffering and made even unwanted suffering an occasion for self-exaltation. The attack here became personal, as Karlstadt traced Luther's doctrinal errors to a lack of inward experience. Implicitly, Luther's vaunted *Anfechtungen* cannot have been real. Karlstadt, in turn, was ready to give an account of his own experience.[197] He writes:

> The internal mortification of the flesh is much quicker and more unbearable than the external—by as much more as internal righteousness surpasses the external. I also know fully well that we must undergo external castigations with a great deal of caution, and I also know that Dr. Luther proffers some shaky arguments concerning the internal cross and invisible mortification. [I know] also that there is no one who can properly understand the yielding of one's soul [*übergebung eygner seele*]—which Christ teaches—unless he has himself endured [*erlitten*] it. One must begin the outward cross such as fasting and castigation when moved by the spirit [*mu[o]st du auß bewegligkeit des geystes anfahen*]. Blessed is the person who follows the spirit. Woe to the person who disregards such movement. Anyone who desires to benefit from such control of the flesh must subdue himself as the spirit of God leads him, whether this results in rejoicing or sadness . . . For hypocrisy [*gleychßnerey*] and pride creep in before one becomes aware of them. *If Dr. Luther is of a good spirit, let him write me how he felt in his heart when he suffered the loss and destruction of his great wisdom of which Mt 15 and Isa 29 spoke. . . . I would, God willing, write something for Christians from my own experience.* I do not believe that God leaves a person untested in accepting [*anzenemen*] inner mortification. However, few there are who understand this and fewer still who accept it.[198]

Similar to Müntzer, Karlstadt demands an account of an inward process.[199]

Karlstadt directly rebuffs the accusation that he upholds and practices a self-chosen suffering. "I have always written that we must accept persecution when God sends it to us,"[200] he writes, adding, "I know fully well that we must not desire any change in the cross that befalls us." To pursue a "self-appointed and chosen mortification and service" is to follow not God but a human evaluation of appearances. Karlstadt claims that he "especially" taught the people of Orlamünde about "the hidden danger of a self-appointed cross and, by contrast, the precious benefits that come from acceptance of the tribulation that may befall one." He also "directed them to the exercise of this," he says.

Finally, Karlstadt defends his "gray coat" because it gives no "sign of sup-posed holiness," unlike Luther's "sanctimonious cowl."[201]

In the dialogue form, Karlstadt has Luther explain the harm of the gray coat, namely that Karlstadt seeks to impose the wearing of it and other externals on others.[202] Karlstadt rebuffs the accusation that he had ever attrib-uted salvation to a coat. He maintains here previously formulated positions on "externals"—although they cannot save the soul, they can harm it,[203] and they can reveal the "inward disposition."[204] Monastic and academic garb are legitimately rejected because they deceive the "simple people," who judge "learning [kunst]" and "holiness" according to clothing. It is better to preach in simple clothing, for preachers who do this "do not create an offense or obstacle for the word, and entice no one to come to the word through costly pomp—to its dishonor." Karlstadt claims the finery he once wore brought him to sin, and that "a proud cloak encourages the proud flesh."[205]

If Luther, finally, wants to berate Karlstadt's pursuit of manual labor, he mocks God's commands in scripture. Manual labor is not self-chosen but a "genuine mortification of the flesh." Here, Karlstadt distinguishes unchosen and self-chosen suffering according to whether the will acts from union with God, whereas Luther's question was whether the will's action in imposing self-discipline flowed from and fostered self-trust. Karlstadt charges that is it Luther who follows his reason and will and refuses to be an instrument in God's hands, including when he permits an excess in living to clergy. "Christ permits evangelists and apostles to take food," Karlstadt writes, "but you go beyond Christ in granting to some a lordly and abundant table and two hun-dred guilders in addition." Paul orders Christians to avoid "inordinate beer bellies [vnordige schmeer Bewch]," but Luther encourages them. The refer-ence to Philippians 3:18 is clear, and Karlstadt again follows Müntzer in con-necting false, cross-shirking religion and economic exploitation: "Dr. Luther not only lines his own bastard nest with silver and gold, etc., but desires the poor man's sweat and blood and extracts it by force."[206]

Concerning the matter of regard for the weak in introducing religious reforms and the application of Biblical law to social life (Luther's fifth main article), Karlstadt's argument is that only those who have true faith—that is, loving knowledge of God and hatred of self—can properly discern a course of action. To rightly love their neighbors as themselves, Christians must un-derstand the need to hate and accuse themselves and their neighbors with respect to sin. Otherwise, the command to love neighbor and self would be in contradiction to the greatest command, to love God above all things.

Accusation and action against others' sin can be an expression of divine love, although it looks like hatred from the perspective of carnal love. These two types of love must be distinguished. Luther's stance reflects the reasoning of someone in the grips of carnal love—someone who does not yet understand love of God, self-accusation, and truly loving regard for the neighbor through the inward instruction of the Spirit.[207]

Concluding Remarks

From the beginning, Luther, Karlstadt, and Müntzer worked to reshape Christians' emotional and mental dispositions—to subject these dispositions to God's truth and discipline. The goal was not only to teach true doctrine, but also to inculcate forms of spirituality and life in accordance with that doctrine. The reformers needed, moreover, to offer compelling guidance to secure Christians from the deceit that had supposedly befallen previous generations. Christians needed criteria to evaluate their own spiritual experiences and lives and to evaluate doctrine, teachers, and communities. From the fundamental conviction that God's manner of conveying salvation was entirely contrary to the expectations of fallen reason and will, the reformers studied in this book offered suffering as inseparable from the receipt of salvation on God's terms and from life in the world on the basis of that salvation. In so doing, they drew deeply from the well of post-Eckhartian mystical teachings on annihilation and union. With the aid of Tauler and the German Theology, they divided the world into true and false doctrines and teachers, indeed true and false Christians, and they guided their reformed followers in careful discernment surrounding what became the highest form of deceit—false suffering.

For a time, Luther, Karlstadt, and Müntzer made common cause against the Roman church and scholastic theology, seeking to summon Christians away from allegedly self-willed and self-deceived religion back to the foot of the cross. Under the pressure of unsettling and violent events, however, their views and paths diverged dramatically. As they warned readers and hearers about each other, each relied on the still-shared conviction that a right doctrine of salvation and life had to uphold true suffering—no Christian could expect salvation, or respond rightly to the tumult of reform, on the basis of an unbroken self-will and fallen reason. At the same time, the three reformers defined differently the nature both of humans' sinful self-assertion, which needed to be humiliated and destroyed, and of the union with God or Christ attained in the wake of this destruction. Their democratization of mysticism in this respect was also delimitation—mysticism became a hammer to identify and malign the unannihilated, as well as a tool for self-critique and self-discipline. On the social plane, the democratization and delimitation of mysticism had major implications for the constitution of Christians as ecclesial-political actors.

From his trust-centered paradigm, Luther argued that Christians united to Christ by faith would accept that God works *sub contrariis*—even amid the persecution of the true church. According to Luther, God ordained and preserved a good social order and promised to care for Christians in all matters temporal and eternal; Christian faith clung to that promise in the face of every assault of conscience, sin, the devil, or the world. Müntzer, conversely, saw spiritual annihilation as an experience that marked the beginning of faith, when elect souls willingly confronted and broke through their unbelief; thereafter, God entered the empty space and souls again became the possession of God according to the created order. Unambiguously led and instructed by God, redeemed souls for Müntzer represented God's instruments to reorder church and society, casting down and separating the godless from the godly. Karlstadt, finally, was focused no less than Müntzer on conformity to the divine will and law; but he rejected the possibility of complete self-abnegation and union with God in the here and now. For Karlstadt, faith was neither trust in God's promise of salvation through Christ alone (as for Luther), nor the fear of God alone and expectation of God's possession and instruction of souls in a Spirit-led church (as for Müntzer). For Karlstadt, faith was a love-rich knowledge that could become ever deeper through inner illumination and study of scripture, as well as through consequent self-accusation and reformation of self and community. The process of immersion into God's will and growth in active conformity was individual and corporate. Karlstadt expected neither sinless Christians nor pure communities, and he interpreted persecution, like all suffering, as God's salutary rod of discipline, to be embraced in self-hatred.

Epilogue

What was the significance of the Reformation for the people who lived through it? How did it change the course of history? What does it still mean for us? Good historical scholarship is never disinterested excavation of the past, and the recent 500th Anniversary of the Reformation—or of the *95 Theses*, at any rate—gave impetus to sustained reflection on the meaning of the event, as well as to no small amount of hand-wringing about the vitality of the field of Reformation scholarship in the academy today. Stories of unintended consequences and even failure loomed large in published works: scholars described how the universalizing hopes of reformers on all sides produced only particular churches,[1] and how the aspiration to Christianize populations achieved little and cost a great deal. Clergy participated in social disciplining and religious oppression, serving political centralization. In the long run, confessional conflict encouraged skepticism and ushered in secularization.[2] From these perspectives, the Reformation represents a turning point from the medieval past to the modern world, but the achievements of the latter are ambiguous—limited political freedom threatened by fanaticism on the one side and despair of meaning on the other. Meanwhile, other streams of Reformation scholarship have downgraded the significance and questioned the coherence of the Reformation; the Reformation appears as a maelstrom of diverse medieval reforming currents—a series of disconnected reformations put to varied religious and political agendas.[3]

Reformers themselves were aware of their failures. Thomas Müntzer traced the collapse of the peasants' cause to the rebels' seeking of their own interests rather than God's will.[4] Martin Luther's later sermons are replete with expressions of concern over the misunderstanding and abuse of evangelical teachings—here, the same old anxiety about God's graciousness; there, smug assurance of salvation on the part of those who evidence little Christian devotion or charity.[5] For his part, Andreas Bodenstein von Karlstadt cannot

Enemies of the Cross. Vincent Evener, Oxford University Press (2021). © Oxford University Press.
DOI: 10.1093/oso/9780190073183.001.0001.

have judged his published recantation in exchange for bodily survival as the obedience to God's will whatever the consequences required by his own thought and teaching. All that said, it is suspect to indict a large and complex historical event for ushering in all that ails us, just as it was suspect for previous generations of scholars to find in the Reformation all that the modern world has cause to celebrate.[6] In an era of global Christianity, moreover, any story that arches from Reformation to secularization remains a European and North American story.

Such large-scale historical narratives cannot be rebuffed on the basis of the preceding study, which focused on how three reformers aligned suffering and truth, and on how they used and further developed a daring mystical tradition. That said, the reformers studied here were of particular significance to the unfolding of the Lutheran and radical traditions. Further, the first question to be asked and answered when it comes to determining the success, failure, or coherence of the Reformation remains: What did reformers want to achieve—the removal of the psychological, ritual, and social burdens of late-medieval Christianity?[7] the (re)Christianization of church and society?[8] genuinely Christian and effective consolation?[9] certitude of salvation and doctrine?[10] Each possible answer is compelling as a description of the aspirations of some or even most Reformation-era theologians and clergy—yet the deepest, all-encompassing question of the era was the question of truth. Reformers sought the truth about salvation and the orientation of life around that truth, in an era when fiercely competing versions divided the continent, when the enemy was understood to be very near and profoundly hidden. In light of truth, burdens might be removed or imposed; in light of truth, Christianization, consolation, and certitude were to be judged. The devil too instilled certitude, the devil too had his consolation, the devil and his agents could make falsehood look pious.[11] The solution discovered by Luther, Karlstadt, and Müntzer was to get the human being out of the way, to let God speak in ways that could not be manipulated by self-focused desire and imagination. God was to be the agent of reform through human beings, yet God first had to remake and teach God's instruments. In the reformers' view, no divine teaching tool was more effective than suffering, which taught that the self-will had no capacity to challenge the divine will. Likewise, no crucible for discernment was more effective than suffering, for here the self-will and all reasoning in its service could be exposed—in oneself and in others. One needed eyes to see, however, for pride hid itself under humility and suffering.

Careful discernment was essential to Christian salvation and life, and careful discernment needed to be taught. For Luther, Karlstadt, and Müntzer, post-Eckhartian mysticism was an inspiration and an ally for this endeavor. It is no surprise that true and false suffering continued to be themes in Luther's preaching well after the period studied here. Preaching at Coburg on the eve of the diet of Augsburg (1530), Luther denounced the "stinking, self-chosen suffering" of the "fanatics." They would not submit to the "true" suffering that "honestly grips and hurts"; instead, they wanted to choose their own crosses and to win merit from this feigned suffering before God. In the face of true suffering, they could only despair as Karlstadt had done in the Peasants' War. True believers, conversely, would "suffer willingly and joyfully," knowing that "Christ and his suffering" was given to them amid their own trials, trusting that God was at work underneath contraries, and above all, clinging to the promise of salvation through Christ rather than their own merits.[12] In Luther's *House Postils* (1544) one finds a sermon (written by Veit Dietrich) distinguishing the cross of Christians, inflicted primarily by the world and the devil, from others' mere suffering on account of sin. Under Luther's name, Dietrich echoed Luther's attack on self-chosen suffering, which does not truly hurt because it is desired; only Christ's cross saves, not the self-willed cross of monks, nuns, and Anabaptists.[13] The Dietrich sermon reflects Eckhartian ideas about self-surrender and joy in suffering as an experience that opens humans up to conformity with God's will—indeed, union with God. The *House Postils* became by far the most successful manual for preaching among Lutherans of the later sixteenth century and after.[14]

Luther's universalizing hopes were never naïve; Müntzer's may have been, but his expectation of a "full and final reformation" was hardly impervious to revision. Müntzer was not a static thinker unable to adjust after disappointment. Luther, Karlstadt, and Müntzer all had categories to interpret opposition and failure—including failure masquerading as success. Their democratization of mysticism involved a corresponding delimitation, distinguishing false teachings and Christians from true; and their accounts of the annihilation of the sinner and union with God inspired forms of dissent that acknowledged and sought to confront hard realities. Through it all, the goal was first and foremost to equip Christians to discern truth and to discipline themselves accordingly. That work continued long after the death of the first reformers in sermons and devotional literature[15]—for centuries the most eagerly consumed forms of printed literature. There is need for caution in assuming that this work had little effect in the long run. Reformers themselves were neither narrow in their goals nor naïve in their expectations nor shallow enough to assume that formal mechanisms of discipline and bare conformity mattered more than the transformation of minds and hearts.

Abbreviations

ABvK	*Andreas Bodenstein von Karlstadt (1486–1541): Ein Theologe der frühen Reformation.* Edited by Sigrid Looß and Markus Matthias. Wittenberg: Hans Luft, 1998.
AL	*The Annotated Luther.* Edited by Timothy J. Wengert, Kirsi I. Stjerna, Paul W. Robinson, Mary Jane Haemig, Hans J. Hillerbrand, and Euan K. Cameron. 6 vols. Minneapolis: Fortress Press, 2015–2017.
ARG	*Archiv für Reformationsgeschichte/Archive for Reformation History*
AWA	*Archiv zur Weimarer Ausgabe der Werke Martin Luthers.* Vienna, Cologne, and Weimar: Böhlau, 1991–2011.
CAS	*A Companion to Anabaptism and Spiritualism, 1521–1700.* Edited by John D. Roth and James M. Stayer. Leiden: Brill, 2007.
CH	*Church History*
CHRC	*Church History and Religious Culture*
CWTM	*The Collected Works of Thomas Müntzer.* Translated and edited by Peter Matheson. Edinburgh: T&T Clark, 1998.
DKdM	*Die Kirchenkritik der Mystiker: Prophetie aus Gotteserfahrung.* Edited by Mariano Delgado and Gotthard Fuchs. 3 vols. Fribourg: Academic Press Fribourg, 2005.
DTRG	*Eyn Deutsch Theologia. Das ist Eyn edles Bu[e]chleyn von rechtem vorstandt was Adam vnd Christus sey vnd wie Adam yn vns sterben vn[d] Christ[us] ersteen sall.* Wittenberg: Johann Rhau-Grunenberg, 1520.
EC	*The Essential Carlstadt: Fifteen Tracts by Andreas Bodenstein (Carlstadt) from Karlstadt.* Translated and edited by E. J. Furcha. Scottdale, PA: Herald Press, 1995.
GN	*Gottes Nähe unmittelbar erfahren: Mystik im Mittelalter und bei Martin Luther.* Edited by Berndt Hamm and Volker Leppin. Tübingen: Mohr Siebeck, 2007.
HAB	Herzog August Bibliothek, Wolfenbüttel
Hamm, DfL	Berndt Hamm. *Der frühe Luther: Etappen reformatorischer Neuorientierung.* Tübingen: Mohr Siebeck, 2010.

Hamm, EL	Berndt Hamm. *The Early Luther: Stages in a Reformation Reorientation.* Translated by Martin J. Lohrmann. Minneapolis: Fortress, 2017.
Hamm, RF	Berndt Hamm. *The Reformation of Faith in the Context of Late Medieval Theology and Piety.* Edited by Robert J. Bast. Leiden: Brill, 2004.
HTG	*The Theologia Germanica of Martin Luther.* Translated and edited by Bengt Hoffman. Mahwah, NJ: Paulist Press, 1980.
HvB	*Hildegard von Bingen in ihrem Umfeld: Mystik und Visionsformen in Mittelalter und früher Neuzeit.* Edited by Änne Bäumer-Schleinkofer. Würzburg: Religion & Kultur Verlag, 2001.
JEH	*Journal of Ecclesiastical History*
LH	*Luther Handbuch.* 2d Edition. Edited by Albrecht Beutel. Tübingen: Mohr Siebeck, 2010.
LJ	*Luther Jahrbuch*
LQ	*Lutheran Quarterly*
LW	*Luther's Works. American Edition.* 82 vols. Vols. 1–30: Edited by Jaroslav Pelikan. St. Louis: Concordia, 1955–76. Vols. 31–55: Edited by Helmut Lehmann. Philadelphia/Minneapolis: Muhlenberg/Fortress, 1957–1986. Vols. 56–82 ("new series" in progress): Edited by Christopher Boyd Brown. St. Louis: Concordia, 2009–.
McGinn, Presence, 1–6	Bernard McGinn. *The Presence of God: A History of Western Christian Mysticism,* 6 vols. New York: Crossroad, 1991–.
MQR	*Mennonite Quarterly Review*
MSB	*Thomas Müntzer. Schriften und Briefe: kritische Gesamtausgabe.* Edited by Günther Franz. Gütersloh: Gütersloher Verlagshaus Gerd Mohn, 1968.
MTD	*Theologia Deutsch.* Edited by Hermann Mandel. Leipzig: A. Deichert'sche Verlagsbuch Nachfolger (Georg Böhme), 1908.
OEML	*The Oxford Encyclopedia of Martin Luther.* Edited by Paul Hinlicky and Derek Nelson. 3 vols. New York: Oxford University Press, 2017.
PMRE	*Protestants and Mysticism in Reformation Europe.* Edited by Ronald K. Rittgers and Vincent Evener. Leiden: Brill, 2019.
QdR	*Querdenker der Reformation: Andreas Bodenstein von Karlstadt und seine frühe Wirkung.* Edited by Ulrich Bubenheimer and Stefan Oehmig. Würzburg: Religion & Kultur Verlag, 2001.
SCJ	*Sixteenth Century Journal*
STA	*Sermones des ho[e]chgeleerten in gnaden erleüchten doctoris Johannis Thaulerii sannt dominici ordens die da weißend auff*

den na[e]chesten waren weg im gaist zu[o] wanderen durch überswebendenn syn. von latein in teütsch gewendt manchem menschenn zu[o] sa[e]liger fruchtbarkaitt. Augsburg: Johann Otmar, 1508.

ThMA 1–3   *Thomas-Müntzer-Ausgabe. Kritische Gesamtausgabe.* Edited by Helmar Junghans and Armin Kohnle. 3 vols. Leipzig: Sächsische Akademie der Wissenschaften, 2004–2017. Vol. 1: *Thomas Müntzer. Schriften, Manuskripte und Notizen.* Edited by Armin Kohnle and Eike Wolgast. Vol. 2: *Thomas Müntzer. Briefwechsel.* Edited by Siegfried Bräuer and Manfred Kobuch. Vol. 3: *Quellen zu Thomas Müntzer.* Edited by Wieland Held and Siegfried Hoyer.

TRE   *Theologische Realenzyklopädie.* Edited by Gerhard Krause and Gerhard Müller. Berlin and New York: Walter de Gruyter, 1977–2004.

V   *Die Predigten Taulers: Aus der Engelberger und der Freiburger Handschrift sowie aus Schmidts Abschriften der ehemaligen Straßburger Handschriften.* Edited by Ferdinand Vetter. Berlin: Weidmann, 1910.

VD 16   *Verzeichnis der im deutschen Sprachbereich erschienenen Drucke des 16. Jahrhunderts.* Edited by Irmgard Bezzel. 25 vols. Stuttgart: Anton Hiersemann, 1983–2000. http://vd16.de

WA   *D. Martin Luthers Werke: Kritische Gesamtausgabe.* 73 vols. Weimar: H. Böhlau, 1883–.

WAB   *D. Martin Luthers Werke: Briefwechsel.* 18 vols. Weimar: H. Böhlau, 1930–1948.

WATR   *D. Martin Luthers Werke: Tischreden.* 6 vols. Wiemar: Böhlau, 1912–1921.

ZSSRK   *Zeitschrift der Savigny-Stiftung für Rechtsgeschichte.* Kanonistische Abteilung.

Notes

Acknowledgments

1. *The Book of Concord: The Confessions of the Evangelical Lutheran Church*, ed. Robert Kolb and Timothy J. Wengert (Minneapolis: Fortress, 2000), 389 (Luther's "Large Catechism").

Introduction

1. WA 51: 157.40–158.8.
2. ThMA 2: 271.1–15; CWTM 89.
3. On scripture and tradition, see Heiko A. Oberman, *The Dawn of the Reformation: Essays in Late Medieval and Early Reformation Thought* (Grand Rapids, MI: William B. Eerdmans), 269–96; on direct experience, Steven E. Ozment, *Mysticism and Dissent: Religious Ideology and Social Protest in the Sixteenth Century* (New Haven, CT: Yale University Press, 1973); on the quest for certitude of salvation and doctrine, and the decisive role played by the Holy Spirit as guarantor of certainty, see Susan E. Schreiner, *Are You Alone Wise? The Search for Certainty in the Early Modern Era* (Oxford: Oxford University Press, 2011).
4. Susan C. Karant-Nunn, *The Reformation of Feeling: Shaping the Religious Emotions in Early Modern Germany* (Oxford: Oxford University Press, 2010), has situated the efforts of early modern clergy to discipline emotions within the context of broader historical processes of confessionalization and social discipline that marked the sixteenth and seventeenth centuries. The present book attends to efforts to shape discernment, which required the proper disposition of the mind and heart. In response to Karant-Nunn and others, Ronald K. Rittgers, "The Age of Reform as an Age of Consolation," *Church History* 86, no. 3 (September 2017): 607–42, has challenged the predominant interpretation of the "Age of Reform" (c. 1050– c. 1650) through the "discipline paradigm." He describes a flourishing of verbal consolation and argues that the "age of discipline" was also an "age of consolation." I see consolation itself as a practice of discipline that prevented an unrestrained response to suffering transgressing boundaries of expected belief and behavior—a possible interpretation acknowledged by Rittgers, who aims to criticize "narrow and largely negative" views of discipline defined by "coercion or even punishment" (see Rittgers, "The Age of Reform," 617–18). Rittgers's essay grew out of his detailed study of the ministry of consolation in the sixteenth century, which focuses primarily on Lutherans; Ronald

K. Rittgers, *The Reformation of Suffering: Pastoral Theology and Lay Piety in Late Medieval and Early Modern Germany* (Oxford: Oxford University Press, 2012).

5. WA 50: 641.35–642.32; LW 41: 164–65.

6. For further analysis of this (printed) sermon, see Vincent Evener, "The 'Enemies of God' in Luther's Final Sermons: Jews, Papists, and the Problem of Blindness to Scripture," *Dialog* 55, no. 3 (Fall 2016): 229–38.

7. On Eckhart, see esp. Bernard McGinn, *The Mystical Thought of Meister Eckhart: The Man from Whom God Hid Nothing* (New York: Crossroad, 2003); McGinn, *Presence*, 4: 94–194; and (for comparison to Luther et al.) "Vere tu es Deus absconditus: the hidden God in Luther and some mystics," in *Silence and the Word: Negative Theology and Incarnation*, ed. Oliver Davies and Denys Turner (Cambridge: Cambridge University Press, 2002), 94–114; here, 104–105.

8. Luther likely owed his own interest to Johann von Staupitz (c. 1460–1524), who also inspired Karlstadt: see Volker Leppin, "Mystische Erbe auf getrennten Wegen: Überlegungen zu Karlstadt und Luther," in *Luther und das monastische Erbe*, ed. Christoph Bultmann, Volker Leppin, and Andreas Lindner (Tübingen: Mohr Siebeck, 2007), 154–62; for a broader study of Tauler-reception in Wittenberg in the 1510s, see Henrik Otto, *Vor- und frühreformatorische Tauler-Rezeption: Annotationen in Drucken des späten 15. und frühen 16. Jahrhunderts* (Gütersloh: Gütersloher Verlagshaus, 2003), 175f. I use the term "post-Eckhartian" to underline that it was particularly Eckhart's disciples who influenced Wittenberg reformers, although some genuine Eckhart sermons were included (pseudonymously) within Tauler's sermons; elsewhere, I use the term "Eckhartian"—without unnecessary repetition of "post"—to denote this tradition and form of mysticism.

9. The title itself comes from Luther's editions; the modern critical edition is Wolfgang von Hinten, ed., *'Der Franckforter' ('Theologia Deutsch'): Kritische Textausgabe* (München: Artemis Verlag, 1982).

10. For an overview of scholarship, discussed in detail later in this chapter, see Rittgers, "Martin Luther," in PMRE: 34–55; here, 40–51.

11. Relevant scholarship will be discussed in detail later in this chapter. For another detailed overview of scholarly views on the Protestant reception of mysticism, see Vincent Evener and Ronald K. Rittgers, "Introduction," in PMRE: 1–16; see also the individual chapters on Luther, Müntzer, and Karlstadt by Rittgers, Hans-Jürgen Goertz, and Evener, respectively: ibid., 34–99.

12. See Volker Leppin, *Die fremde Reformation: Luthers mystische Wurzeln* (München: C. H. Beck, 2016), esp. 187–207; and the relevant studies in Leppin, *Transformationen: Studien zu Wandlungsprozessen in Theologie und Frömmigkeit zwischen Spätmittelalter und Reformation* (Tübingen: Mohr Siebeck, 2015), esp. chapter 20; Leppin's arguments are discussed and critiqued later in this chapter. McGinn, *Presence* 6.1: 21–47, is more measured in the assessment of the mystical influence on Luther; he follows Oberman (*Dawn of the Reformation*, 131f.) in depicting Luther's relationship to medieval mysticism as a "*sic et non* relationship." For a summary and critique of McGinn's evaluation, see Rittgers, "Martin Luther," 49–51.

13. Studies of the influence of mystical authors on Luther have attended little to these uses of mysticism around the pervasive question of truth.

14. As discussed later in this chapter, Leppin attributes to Karlstadt and Müntzer a competing "transformation" of medieval mysticism over and against Luther's own transformation; yet he primarily sees transformation in the way Karlstadt and Müntzer applied mysticism on social-historical planes. I will argue that Müntzer especially transformed the post-Eckhartian inheritance in his soteriological and epistemological views, and that Karlstadt radically revalued and relocated the idea of union with God. The terms "revaluation and relocation" describe ways that Protestants resituated mystical ideas and aspirations within new frameworks, in light of the Protestant rejection of spiritual hierarchy; see Evener, "Epilogue," in PMRE, 431–34.

15. On the concept of democratization, see Heiko A. Oberman, *The Harvest of Medieval Theology: Gabriel Biel and Late Medieval Nominalism* (Grand Rapids, MI: Baker, 2000 [1963]); 341–43; Oberman, *Dawn*, 140; Hamm, EL, 197–98; Evener, "Epilogue," 431; Rittgers, "Martin Luther," 40. For democratization and secularization as processes beginning in the thirteenth century, see McGinn, *Presence* 3: 12–13. The seeming contradiction between Müntzer's democratization of mysticism and his attention to the elect discerned by Ute Gause, " 'auff daß der ernst des vatters die gottloßen christen aus dem wege rawme': Müntzers mystische Kirchenkritik," in DKdM, 2: 131–48; here, 136, resolves if we see that democratization and delimitation went hand-in-hand, as some Christians inevitably did not manifest faith defined in mystical terms.

16. For the concept of "competing theologies," see Günter Vogler, "Thomas Müntzer: Irrweg oder Alternative? Plädoyer für eine andere Sicht," ARG 103 (2012): 11–40, which informs the recent biography by Vogler and Siegfried Bräuer, *Thomas Müntzer: Neu Ordnung machen in der Welt, Eine Biographie* (Gütersloh: Gütersloher Verlagshaus, 2016), esp. 391–98.

17. The term "radical" does not adequately distinguish Karlstadt, Müntzer, or others (Anabaptists and spiritualists) from the early Luther and his followers: all were radical in crucial parts of their theology, in their stance toward existing institutions, and in their desire to return Christianity to its "roots" (Christ and scripture). Nonetheless, Luther did forge an alliance with the princes of Saxony, and the term "radical" will be used here to denote the marginalized position of Karlstadt, Müntzer, and their followers vis-à-vis this new ecclesial-political alliance. For justified criticism of the term radical, see Hans-Jürgen Goertz, *Radikalität der Reformation: Aufsätze und Abhandlungen* (Göttingen: Vandenhoeck & Ruprecht, 2007): 11–53; and Goertz, "Radikale—an der Peripherie oder im Zentrum der Reformation? Fünf Thesen zum 'reformatorischen Aufbruch' im 16. Jahrhundert," in *Thomas Müntzer, Zeitgenossen, Nachwelt: Siegfried Bräuer zum 80. Geburtstag*, ed. Hartmut Kühne, Hans-Jürgen Goertz, Thomas T. Müller, and Günter Vogler. (Mühlhausen: Thomas-Müntzer-Gesellschaft, 2010), 23–38; Goertz's contention that the entire Reformation was radical informs my view of Luther as dissenter here. The term "radical reformation" came into use through the work of George H. Williams; see George H. Williams, *The Radical Reformation*, 3rd ed. (Kirksville, MO: Truman State University Press, 2000); and his introduction to *Spiritual and Anabaptist Writers* (Louisville, KY: Westminster

John Knox, 1957), 19–35; esp. 22, where Williams defines radical in terms of cutting to the roots (Latin: *radix*).

18. On the factors determining the success or failure of reform agendas, see Vogler, "Thomas Müntzer," 33–39. Although most studies approach either Karlstadt or Müntzer in relation to Luther, it is necessary also to describe the interrelationship of Karlstadt and Müntzer; the latter has been undertaken by Siegfried Bräuer, "Der Briefwechsel zwischen Andreas Bodenstein von Karlstadt und Thomas Müntzer," in QdR: 187–209; William Wallace McNiel, "Andreas von Karlstadt and Thomas Müntzer: Relatives in Theology and Reformation," PhD diss., Queens University, 1998. Ulrich Bubenheimer, *Thomas Müntzer und Wittenberg* (Mühlhausen: Thomas-Müntzer-Gesellschaft, 2014), examines Müntzer's connections to various figures in Wittenberg.

19. For Müntzer and Anabaptism, see Gottfried Seebaß, *Müntzers Erbe: Werk, Leben und Theologie des Hans Hut* (Göttingen: Gütersloher Verlagshaus, 2002), and Werner Packull, *Mysticism and the Early South-German Austrian Anabaptist Movement, 1525–31* (Scottdale, PA: Herald Press, 1977). For Karlstadt and the Reformed, see Amy Nelson Burnett, *Karlstadt and the Origins of the Eucharistic Controversy* (Oxford: Oxford University Press, 2011), esp. 91–114. For Karlstadt's influence on both Reformed and Anabaptist figures (esp. Melchior Hoffman), see Calvin Augustine Pater, *Karlstadt as the Father of the Baptist Movements: The Emergence of Lay Protestantism* (Toronto: University of Toronto Press, 1984), 117f.; Pater's work must be consulted with caution, however, as he distorts Karlstadt's demonstrable views in order to depict the reformer as the "father of Baptist movements," and he overtaxes the evidence of Karlstadt's influence on others.

20. For Karlstadt's reception among Wegelians, spiritualists, and Pietists into the seventeenth century, see Ulrich Bubenheimer, "Karlstadtrezeption von der Reformation bis zum Pietismus im Spiegel der Schriften Karlstadts zur Gelassenheit," in ABvK: 25–71; Bubenheimer, "Andreas Bodenstein genannt Karlstadt (1486–1541)," *Fränkische Lebensbilder* 14 (1991): 47–64; here, 62–63; Bubenheimer, "Karlstadt, Andreas Rudolff Bodenstein von (1486–1541)," in TRE 17 (1988): 649–57; here, 655. On Pietism, see the introductory surveys of Johannes Wallmann, *Der Pietismus* (Göttingen: Vandenhoeck & Ruprecht, 2005), and Douglas H. Shantz, *An Introduction to German Pietism: Protestant Renewal at the Dawn of Modern Europe* (Baltimore: Johns Hopkins, 2013).

21. On Luther's own self-identification with Christ and expectation of martyrdom, see recently Lyndal Roper, *Martin Luther: Renegade and Prophet* (London: The Bodley Head, 2016), 121–23, 189–93, 314–18, 325.

22. See Brad S. Gregory, *Salvation at Stake: Christian Martyrdom in Early Modern Europe* (Cambridge, MA: Harvard University Press, 1999), 31–62, on the medieval memory of martyrs and the expectation of patient suffering and a good death in *imitatio Christi*.

23. Ibid. represents a magisterial study of martyrological literature in the Catholic, Protestant, and radical traditions.

24. On the pervasive sixteenth-century anxiety over false appearances, see Susan E. Schreiner, *Are You Alone Wise?* xii–xiii, 323–90, which draws on her earlier article, "Appearances and Reality in Luther, Shakespeare and Montaigne," *Journal of Religion* 83 (2003): 345–80. The separation of appearances and reality was connected not only to religious anxiety, but also to broader developments in European intellectual culture; many of these developments were critical in the rise of modern science. See Karsten Harries, *Infinity and Perspective* (Cambridge, MA: MIT Press, 2001), cited often by Schreiner.

25. McGinn, *Presence of God*, 4: 157–60, 212–17, 271–75. On issues of passivity and agency in Tauler specifically, see Richard Kieckhefer, "The Notion of Passivity in the Sermons of John Tauler," *Recherches de théologie ancienne et médiévale* XLVIII (1981): 198–211.

26. On the quest to find the true church in late-medieval and Reformation Europe, see esp. Scott Hendrix, "In Quest of the Vera Ecclesia: The Crises of Late Medieval Ecclesiology," *Viator* 7 (January 1976): 347–78.

27. Of overriding importance was the reformers' shared concern with the noetic effect of sin; see Schreiner, *Are You Alone Wise?* 58.

28. This fact is little noted in scholarship. Ronald J. Sider, *Andreas Bodenstein von Karlstadt: The Development of his Thought, 1517–1525* (Leiden: Brill, 1974), 104–47, argues that Karlstadt in 1520–1521 held to a "mature Wittenberg theology"; for English-speaking scholars especially, Sider's book remains among the most-cited works on Karlstadt.

29. Janet K. Ruffing, ed., *Mysticism and Social Transformation* (Syracuse: Syracuse University Press, 2001), offers several insightful studies of medieval figures, as well as an introduction by Ruffing critiquing the separation of "contemplation and action, theory and practice, . . . mysticism and ethical behavior" assumed in most modern academic approaches to the topic (2). See also the studies collected in DKdM.

30. On Luther's redefinition of union, I have been influenced especially by Berndt Hamm's essay, "Wie mystisch war der Glaube Luthers?" in GN, 237–88, translated into English in Hamm, EL, 190–232. (This introduction will cite the latter.) For Hamm's response to the so-called Finnish school and its argument that Luther taught a real indwelling of Christ and deification by ontic participation, see Hamm, EL, 204. For a clear introduction to Finnish perspectives on justification, also acknowledging criticisms, see Risto Saarinen, "Justification by Faith: The View of the Mannermaa School," in OHMLT, 254–73. Tuomo Mannermaa's major work is now available in English: *Christ Present In Faith: Luther's View Of Justification*, trans. Kirsi I. Stjerna (Minneapolis: Fortress, 2005). On Luther's view of theosis, see esp. Simo Peura, *Mehr als ein Mensch? Die Vergöttlichung als Thema der Theologie Martin Luthers von 1513 bis 1519* (Mainz: Zabern, 1994). Mannermaa, Peura, and others contributed to *Union with Christ: the New Finnish Interpretation of Luther*, eds. Carl E. Braaten and Robert W. Jenson (Grand Rapids, MI: Eerdmans, 1998). The present study sees Luther's insistence on trust in Christ *extra nos*, in the absence of innate intellectual and moral resources, as central to how he used an account of union to address questions of truth. For a Finnish interpretation of the theme of "nothingness" in Luther, see

Sammeli Juntunen, *Der Begriff des Nichts bei Luther in den Jahren von 1510 bis 1523* (Helsinki: Luther-Agricola-Gesellschaft, 1996); major conclusions are summarized on p. 10.

31. In his major treatise on *Gelassenheit* from 1523, Karlstadt both uses Eckhartian language about precreated unity and describes a return to the created order, similar to Müntzer's views; for Karlstadt, both states entailed an absence of any human willing distinct from God's will.

32. For a review of scholarship on Karlstadt's use of mysticism and place in the mystical tradition, including recent assessments by Bernard McGinn and Volker Leppin, see Vincent Evener, "Andreas Bodenstein von Karlstadt," in PMRE, 80–86.

33. For Müntzer, the created order involved God's possession of human souls and human possession of creatures, but the fall reversed this order: human beings gave themselves over to be possessed by creatures through their fear of and desire for the same. The importance and mystical roots of this motif have been emphasized most recently by Bräuer and Vogler, *Thomas Müntzer*, 154–55; Hans-Jürgen Goertz, *Thomas Müntzer: Revolutionär am Ende der Zeiten, Eine Biographie* (München: C. H. Beck, 2015), 222–23; and Goertz, "Thomas Müntzer," in PMRE, 69–70.

34. Important work included Susan Karant-Nunn, "What was Preached in German Cities in the Early Years of the Reformation? *Wildwuchs* versus Lutheran Unity," in *The Process of Change in early Modern Europe: Essays in Honor of Miriam Usher Chrisman*, ed. Phillip N. Bebb and Sherrin Marshall (Athens: Ohio University Press, 1988), 81–96; and Miriam Usher Chrisman, *Conflicting Visions of Reform: German Lay Propaganda Pamphlets 1519–1530* (Atlantic Highlands, NJ: Humanities Press, 1996). This research and discussion led to debate over the coherence of the Reformation; see Berndt Hamm, Bernd Moeller, and Dorothea Wendebourg, *Reformations-theorien: Ein kirchenhistorischer Disput über Einheit und Vielfalt der Reformation* (Göttingen: Vandenhoeck & Ruprecht, 1998). I have been influenced especially by Hamm's approach, which identifies deep-seated common ground among reform advocates and sharp divergence within those frameworks; debate could be especially bitter because shared assumptions and goals were at stake. For Hamm, the deepest *Gemeinsamkeit* was reformers' "system-leaping" rejection of the gradualistic, hierarchical, and plural means to salvation upheld by the medieval church. See Hamm's contribution, "Einheit und Vielfalt der Reformation—oder: was die Reformation zur Reformation machte," in Hamm, Moeller, and Wendebourg, *Reformations-theorien*, 57–127.

35. On ecclesial and social discipline, see Ute Lotz-Heumann, "Imposing Church and Social Discipline," in *The Cambridge History of Christianity, Volume 6, Reform and Expansion 1500–1660*, ed. R. Po-Chia Hsia (Cambridge: Cambridge University Press, 2007), 244–60; R. Po-Chia Hsia, *Social Discipline in the Reformation: Central Europe 1550–1750* (London: Routledge, 1989); and Carlos M. N. Eire, *Reformations: The Early Modern World, 1450–1650* (New Haven, CT: Yale University Press, 2016), 586–617. For a critique of the "discipline paradigm," Rittgers, "Age of Reform," esp. 609–19. On the concept of Confessionalization, see as an introduction Thomas A. Brady Jr., "Confessionalization: The Career of a Concept," in *Confessionalization in*

Europe, 1550–1700, ed. John M. Headley, Hans J. Hillerbrand, and Anthony J. Papalas (Burlington, VT: Ashgate, 2004), 1–20; Karant-Nunn, *Reformation of Feeling*, 260n24, defends the concept and cites relevant scholarship.

36. For more on my theoretical perspective, see Vincent Evener, "The Future of Reformation Studies," *Church History and Religious Culture* 97, nos. 3–4 (December 2017): 310–21.

37. For a helpful overview, Eire, *Reformations*, 590–616.

38. For a fascinating study of constructions of the self and the role of memory around the Eucharist, see David Warren Sabean, "Production of the Self during the Age of Confessionalism," *Central European History* 29, no. 1 (1996): 1–18.

39. Ancient and medieval traditions of consolation are described in the first three chapters, one of which focuses on "suffering and consolation in late medieval mysticism." Rittgers, *The Reformation of Suffering*, 1–83. Ibid., 218–25, addresses interest in mystical sources among later sixteenth-century Lutherans.

40. For the term "Wittenberg circle," see ibid., 6; for comparative discussion of Conrad Grebel, Müntzer, and Karlstadt, ibid., 155–61.

41. The theology of the cross is the focus of the culminating chapter on Luther, ibid., 111–24, and Rittgers disagrees with Robert Kolb's assessment that Luther's followers largely failed to comprehend the deep epistemological teachings of the *theologia crucis*; see ibid., 139, 337n90.

42. The main arguments of the book are summarized at ibid., 5–8. On suffering's proof and refinement of faith, see ibid., 149–53. For the concern of Lutheran pastoral care to console, see esp. Chapter 7 on church ordinances (ibid., 163–84). Chapter 8 details the "confessionalization" of suffering in consolation literature of the later sixteenth century (ibid., 185–217), while insisting that consolation and discipline were not opposed goals and that scholars have given too little attention to the clergy's aspiration to console (see also ibid., 8). For the point about the practice of lay consolation according to Lutheran teachings, see chapter 10.

43. Rittgers, "Age of Reform."

44. Much of the literature examined in the following pages is controversial literature, although controversial literature that was deeply concerned with doctrine and daily devotion.

45. Thomas Müntzer regarded consolation as a primary task of right preaching and teaching: the elect needed to understand how to grapple with the disconcerting discovery of their inner *Unglauben*. He complained that the Wittenberg doctrine of scripture alone sought to console the elect via externals no less than Roman ritualism.

46. See Rittgers, "Age of Reform," 629.

47. See note 1.

48. For a nuanced discussion that also addresses the views of Ulrich Zwingli and John Calvin, see Schreiner, *Are You Alone Wise?* 19–129; for a classic discussion in the context of Luther's views on the Holy Spirit, Regin Prenter, *Spiritus Creator: Luther's Concept of the Holy Spirit*, trans. John M. Jensen (Philadelphia: Fortress, 1953), 205f.

49. For a recent account focused on the three reformers' diverse transformations of mysticism, see Leppin, *Die fremde Reformation*, 192–207.

50. On Müntzer's view of scripture, see Ozment, *Mysticism and Dissent*, esp. 87–88.

51. For a summary statement of these points, see Schreiner, *Are You Alone Wise?*, 255–59; Catholic teaching denied the possibility of subjective certitude of salvation, but one could be certain of its objective availability. On Schreiner's use of the term "subjective," see ibid., 258.

52. Ibid., 83f., citing David C. Steinmetz's discussion of "exegetical optimism" in *Luther in Context*, 2nd ed. (Grand Rapids, MI: Baker, 2002): 96–97.

53. Schreiner, *Are You Alone Wise?*, 79–208.

54. Ibid., 258–59 (in conversation with Joseph Lortz), 261–62.

55. Schreiner investigates answers to these first two questions, focusing on the criterion of certitude and the role of the Spirit.

56. On the date of Luther's reading of Tauler, possibly already in the earlier phases of his lectures on Romans that began in November 1515, see Leppin, "Omnen vitam fidelium penitentiam esse voluit': Zur Aufnahme mystischer Traditionen in Luthers erster Ablaßthese," ARG 93 (2002): 7–25; here, 14, including Note 28.

57. McGinn, *Presence*, 1: xvi–xvii. For reflections on this paradigm in the study of Protestantism, see Evener and Rittgers, "Introduction," 7–10; Evener, "Epilogue," 429–35.

58. This scholarship, of course, did not consider Karlstadt or Müntzer as "Protestant." For an overview see Leppin, *Transformationen*, 399–400; Karl Dienst, "Mystik und Protestantismus—ein Widerspruch?" in HvB: 227–48; here, 227–29; and with particular concern for how this paradigm of opposition still shapes Reformation scholarship, Evener and Rittgers, "Introduction," 1–14. For overviews focused on Luther studies in particular, see Rittgers, "Martin Luther," in PMRE: 34–55; here, 40–42; Markus Wriedt, "Martin Luther und die Mystik," in HvB: 249–73; here, 249–52; Volker Leppin, "Luther's Roots in Monastic-Mystical Piety," in OHMLT: 49–61; here, 49–50; and Leppin, "Mystik," in LH, 57–61; here, 57–58.

59. Quoted from Rittgers, "Martin Luther," 42. The studies by Oberman, Iserloh, and Hägglund are found in Ivar Asheim, ed., *Kirche, Mystik, Heiligung und das Natürliche bei Luther* (Göttingen: Vandenhoeck & Ruprecht, 1967); Oberman's is reprinted in *Dawn*, 126–54. Regarding the diversity of the medieval tradition, already in the 1930s, Erich Vogelsang argued that Luther received differently various strands of the medieval mystical tradition; he said "yes" to the "German mysticism" of Tauler and the *German Theology*, "yes" and "no" to the "Roman mysticism" of Bernard and Gerson, and an early and unequivocal "no" to Dionysian mysticism. See Vogelsang, "Luther und die Mystik," LJ 19 (1937): 32–54; here 32–33. This conclusion has stood the test of time, although the term "German mysticism" has been duly criticized for its historical inaccuracy and its roots in Vogelsang's National Socialist agenda; see Leppin, "Mystik," 28.

60. An important statement of this position can be found in Leif Grane, *Modus Loquendi Theologicus: Luthers Kampf um die Erneuerung der Theologie (1515–1518)* (Leiden: E. J. Brill, 1975), 121–27; Grane here rejects the argument of Ozment, *Homo Spiritualis*, 1–3, that Luther came to his theological "master idea" through polemical self-differentiation from the mystical anthropology of Jean Gerson and

Tauler. Ozment himself also stressed the clefts between Luther's theology and medieval mysticism—including Luther's refusal to see the synteresis or Seelengrund as "soteriologically significant" (Ozment, *Homo Spiritualis*, 214–15; see also Steven Ozment, "*Homo Viator*: Luther and Late Medieval Theology," in *The Reformation in Medieval Perspective*, ed. Steven Ozment [Chicago: Quadrangle Books, 1971], 142–54). In *Mysticism and Dissent*, 21–25, Ozment argued that Luther was interested only in the non-mystical themes of the *German Theology*; in *The Age of Reform 1250-1550: An Intellectual and Religious History of Late Medieval and Reformation Europe* (New Haven, CT: Yale University Press, 1980), 240–44, Ozment summarized that Luther was more influenced by William of Ockham than by "mysticism," because the former related God and humanity "by will and words," while mysticism related God and humanity by ontology. The view that Luther found only confirmation and language in the mystics has been argued by many prominent Luther scholars, including: Bernd Moeller, "Tauler und Luther," in *La Mystique Rhénane: Colloque de Strasbourg 16-19 mai 1961* (Paris: Presses Universitaires de France, 1963), 157–68; Heinrich Bornkamm, *Luther: Gestalt und Wirkungen, Gesammelte Aufsätze* (Gütersloh: Gütersloher Verlagshaus [Gerd Mohn], 1975), 130–146; and Martin Brecht, *Martin Luther*, 3 volumes (Philadelphia: Fortress, 1985-1993), I: 137–44. Also noteworthy is the work of Karl-Heinz zur Mühlen, *Nos extra nos: Luthers Theologie zwischen Mystik und Scholastik* (Tübingen: J. C. B. Mohr-Paul Siebeck, 1972), summarized by Rittgers, "Martin Luther," 43–44. Vogelsang argued that while Luther used mystical language, his meaning was "entirely un-mystical," and that Luther read Tauler with "productive misunderstanding," failing or refusing to see the difference between himself and the mystic ("Luther und die Mystik," 32–33, 43, 52–53).

61. Summary and citations in Rittgers, "Martin Luther," 44–45.

62. See McGinn, *Presence*, 1: xix–xx; for further discussion of this point, see Evener and Rittgers, "Introduction," 9–10.

63. McGinn, *Presence*, 6.1: viii, 169. For McGinn's assessment of Luther, see ibid., 21–47; for a summary and evaluation of this assessment, see Rittgers, "Martin Luther," 49–51.

64. See the critique of McGinn's use of "immediacy" in Dennis E. Tamburello, "The Protestant Reformers on Mysticism," in *The Wiley-Blackwell Companion to Christian Mysticism*, ed. Julia Lamm (Malden, MA: Wiley-Blackwell, 2013), 407–21; here, 420n4.

65. Hamm, EL, 191, 194.

66. Ibid., 195–96. Hamm offers his definition as an alternative to McGinn's heuristic; the latter is broader, recognizing (helpfully, I think) more variety in expressions of mystical consciousness.

67. Ibid., 197–98.

68. Ibid., 205.

69. Ibid., 213–14.

70. Ibid., 222–23.

71. For these three, see Leppin, *Transformationen*, 408–20.

72. Leppin, *Die fremde Reformation*, 13, 30, 119. For my review of this book, see Vincent Evener, "From the Universal to the Particular: Luther and the Reformation after Five Hundred Years," JEH 69, no. 4 (October 2018): 806–20; here, 815–17.

73. Leppin, *Die fremde Reformation*, 15, 19, 24–26, 45–46.

74. Ibid., 41. The argument resonates with the core conclusion in Ozment, *Homo Spiritualis*, and with Hamm's argument that Luther found a new immediacy to God in the removal of moral-spiritual preconditions on the part of the human. According to Volker Leppin, "Passionsmystik bei Luther," LJ 84 (2017): 51–81; here, 70–73, 80, Luther received the dialectic of identification and contra-identification with Christ found in late-medieval passion mysticism, but he accentuated the contra-identification.

75. Again, this is a view shared by Hamm, EL, 27–30.

76. See esp. Leppin, "Omnen vitam," 8–13, 24; *Die fremde Reformation*, 25–29, 42, 52, 122–23.

77. Leppin, "Omnen vitam," 20–22; *Die fremde Reformation*, 27–31, 60; "Passionsmystik," 73.

78. Leppin, *Transformationen*, 411–12; *Die fremde Reformation*, 117–35. In "Passionsmystik," 78, Leppin argues that Luther's "Word-theological turn" did not entirely displace the "existential" and "experiential" dimensions of his understanding of faith, including in relation to suffering. Luther's passion sermons in the 1530s could still employ the language of passion mysticism, but "daneben trat eine stark distanzierende historisierende, lehrhafte Passionsbetrachtung" (ibid., 80–81).

79. Leppin, *Die fremde Reformation*, 156–58.

80. Ibid., 204–206.

81. Including Oberman, Ozment, and McGinn; for a summary, see Rittgers, "Martin Luther," 40.

82. Leppin, *Die fremde Reformation*, 192–99; for further analysis of Karlstadt in relation to Luther, see idem, "Mystisches Erbe auf getrennten Wegen: Überlegungen zu Karlstadt und Luther," in *Luther und das monastische Erbe*, ed. Christoph Bultmann, Volker Leppin, and Andreas Lindner (Tübingen: Mohr Siebeck, 2007), 153–69.

83. One can trace very precisely a similar transformation accomplished by Müntzer's compatriot in Allstedt, Simon Haferitz. Haferitz's published sermon for Epiphany frequently quotes from Tauler directly, but redirects and repurposes Tauler's ideas by adding concepts of "election" and "faith" shared with Müntzer. Haferitz also quotes but alters Luther's postils! See Vincent Evener, Vincent Evener, "*Mysticism*, Christianization, and Dissent: The Appropriation of Johannes Tauler in Simon *Haferitz's Sermon on the Feast of the Three Holy Kings* (1524)," ARG 106 (2015): 67–91; esp. 75-84.

84. Evener, "Epilogue," 433. Müntzer too relocated and revalued union as part of Christian life, but he also transformed the concept itself more fundamentally than Karlstadt.

85. Ozment, *Mysticism and Dissent*, 12.

86. Ibid., 59–60. Ozment's views remain influential and largely uncontested: see, e.g., R. Emmet McLaughlin, "Radicals," in *Reformation and Early Modern Europe: A Guide*

to Research, ed. David M. Whitford (Kirksville, MO: Sixteenth Century Society Press, 2008), 80–120; here, 104; Ruffing, *Mysticism and Social Transformation*, 16, 104–105.

87. Ozment, *Mysticism and Dissent*, 68–97. The individualism discerned by Ozment seems overstated, however. Müntzer was interested in God's leadership of the church through tried and tested preachers; the vision was corporate, and teaching and prophesy were to be subject to scriptural confirmation. For his part, Karlstadt envisioned a process of communal Bible study.

88. See ibid., 58–59.

89. Hans-Jürgen Goertz, *Innere und äußere Ordnung in der Theologie Thomas Müntzers* (Leiden: Brill, 1967); Goertz, "The Mystic with the Hammer: Thomas Müntzer's Theological Basis for Revolution," MQR 50 (1976): 83–113; and Goertz, "Thomas Müntzer," in PMRE, 60, 72.

90. Goertz, "Thomas Müntzer," 72–74; *Thomas Müntzer: Revolutionär*, 221–36; and "Karlstadt, Müntzer and the Reformation of the Commoners, 1521–1525," in CAS, 1–44; here, 20–34. For another perspective indebted (sometimes indirectly) to Goertz's earlier paradigms, see Gause, " 'auff daß der ernst.' " Gause adopts Siegfried Bräuer's view (influenced by Goertz) that Müntzer's reforms to worship in Allstedt sought to bring the laity into the mystical "Heilsprozess" (139–41). Thus, he argues that Müntzer had a *Volksmystik* that shaped his view of the *Volkskirche* (132–33, 136–37). Gause's argument that Müntzer lacked a positive or concrete account of unio mystica (137–38) is difficult to understand. Müntzer repeatedly describes union in terms of God's possession of the soul according to the created order; the *Ankunft* of certain faith (with fundamental doubt left behind); receptivity to dreams and visions that can be judged by the inner Word; etc. For Bräuer's work on Müntzer's liturgical reforms, see "Thomas Müntzers Liedschaffen: Die theologischen Intentionen der Hymenübertragungen im Allstedter Gottesdienst von 1523/24 und im Abendmahlslied Müntzer," LJ 41 (1974): 45–102; and recently, Bräuer and Vogler, *Thomas Müntzer*, 190–98.

91. Hermann Barge, *Andreas Bodenstein von Karlstadt*, 2 vols. (Leipzig: Friedrich Brandstetter, 1905 [Nieuwkoop: B. De Graaf, 1968]), 1: 94–95, 103, depicted Karlstadt as an independent pioneer of "lay-Christian puritanism"; however, Karl Müller, *Luther und Karlstadt: Stücke aus ihrem gegenseitigen Verhältnis* (Tübingen: J. C. B. Mohr [Paul Siebeck], 1907), quickly sought to repudiate the claim for Karlstadt's independence and importance. For a summary of the Barge-Müller debate, and scholarship flowing from it, see Looß, "Andreas Bodenstein von Karlstadt (1486–1541) in der modernen Forschung," in ABvK, 9–23; here, 10–11. The view of Müntzer as a *Schüler Luthers* was first advanced by Karl Holl, *Gesammelte Aufsätze zur Kirchengeschichte*, 3 vols. (Tübingen: J. C. B. Mohr, 1921–1928), 1: 425–34. Subsequent proponents of the view of Müntzer as a *Schüler Luthers* include Hayo Gerdes, "Der Weg des Glaubens bei Müntzer und Luther," *Luther* 26 (1955): 152–65; Franz Lau, "Die Prophetische Apokalyptik Thomas Müntzers und Luthers Absage an die Bauernrevolution," in *Beiträge zur historischen und systematischen Theologie: Gedenkschrift für D. Werner Elert*, ed. Friedrich Hübner (Berlin: Lutherisches Verlagshaus Herbert Renner, 1955), 163–70; Thomas Nipperdey, "Theologie und Revolution bei Thomas Müntzer," ARG 54 (1963): 145–81; and Walter Elliger, *Thomas Müntzer: Leben und Werk*

(Göttingen: Vandenhoeck & Ruprecht, 1975), see 93. Both Gerdes and Nipperdey set out to explain the crushing legalism they found in Müntzer's later writings. Their question was how Müntzer, despite beginning with Luther's ideas, finally destroyed Christian freedom. Gerdes pointed to deficiencies in Müntzer's character and religious experiences, Nipperdey to Müntzer's misunderstanding. For a helpful summary of research on Müntzer, see Bernhard Lohse, *Thomas Müntzer in neuer Sicht: Müntzer im Licht der neueren Forschung und die Frage nach dem Ansatz seiner Theologie* (Hamburg: Joachim Jungius-Gesellschaft der Wissenschaften, 1991).

92. Leif Grane, "Thomas Müntzer und Martin Luther," in *Bauernkriegs-Studien*, ed. Bernd Moeller (Gütersloh: G. Mohn, 1975), 69–98; 71, appropriately cautions against "naïve genetic explanation" and the forcing of "eine historische Person in einen von einer bestimmten Denkstruktur geprägten Typ." Like Grane (ibid., 88–89), I strive to reconstruct Müntzer's views inductively from the sources.

93. See chapter 5.

94. Ernst Kähler was the first to argue that Karlstadt found his roots in Augustine rather than Luther; see his *Karlstadt und Augustin: Der Kommentar des Andreas Bodenstein von Karlstadt zu Augustins Schrift* de Spiritu et Litera (Halle a.d. Saale: Max Niemeyer, 1952), 3*; Sider, *Andreas Bodenstein*, subsequently depicted Augustine as the decisive influence on Karlstadt, who developed a mature "theology of regeneration" after a period of genuine agreement with Luther. More recent work often assumes an overriding mystical influence; see, e.g., Sigrid Looß, "Radical Views of the Early Andreas Karlstadt (1520–25)," in *Radical Tendencies in the Reformation: Divergent Perspectives*, ed. Hans J. Hillerbrand (Kirksville, MO: Sixteenth Century Journal Publishers, 1988), 43f.; Looß, "Karlstadts Bild vom Menschen in seiner Wittenberger Zeit (1520–1523)," in *700 Jahre Wittenberg: Stadt, Universität, Reformation*, ed. Stefan Oehmig (Weimar: Verlag Hermann Böhlaus Nachfolger, 1995), 275–87; Goertz, "Karlstadt," 5–20; Leppin, "Mystisches Erbe," 153–69; and *Die fremde Reformation*, 192–95. For a further overview of relevant scholarship, Evener, "Andreas Bodenstein," 80–86. Groundbreaking work on Karlstadt's sources has been done by Ulrich Bubenheimer; see Bubenheimer, "Karlstadt, Andreas Ruldolff Bodenstein von (1486–1541)," 649–50, as well as his further work cited in chapter 4 and in Evener, "Andreas Bodenstein," 82–83. Resisting the temptation to characterize Karlstadt's theology *in toto*, Hans-Peter Hasse has offered excellent studies including *Karlstadt und Tauler: Untersuchungen zur Kreuzestheologie* (Gütersloh: Gütersloher Verlagshaus Gerd Mohn, 1993), which analyzes Karlstadt's reception of Tauler while also attending to the influence of other sources (Augustine, Bernard of Clairvaux, scripture itself); and "Tauler und Augustin als Quelle Karlstadts," in ABvK: 247–82.

95. Most recently, Goertz, "Thomas Müntzer," continues to focus on this question. On Müntzer as driven by apocalypticism, see Reinhard Schwarz, *Die apokalyptische Theologie Thomas Müntzers und der Taboriten* (Tübingen: J. C. B. Mohr/Paul Siebeck, 1977); and Gottfried Seebaß, "Reich Gottes und Apokalyptik bei Thomas Müntzer," LJ 58 (1991): 75–99. R. Emmet McLaughlin, "Apocalypticism and Thomas Müntzer," ARG 95 (2004): 98–131, criticizes the application of the term "apocalyptic" to Müntzer. For a broad review of Müntzer scholarship, see Lohse, *Thomas Müntzer in neuer Sicht*,

and Peter Matheson, "Recent German Research on Thomas Müntzer," MQR 86, no. 1 (2012): 97–109.

Chapter 1

1. For broad treatments of this mysticism, see McGinn, *Presence*, 4; Kurt Ruh, *Geschichte der abendländischen Mystik*, 4 vols. (München: Beck, 1990–1999), Volume 3; and Alois M. Haas, *Gottleiden—Gottlieben: zur volkssprachlichen Mystik im Mittelalter* (Frankfurt am Main: Insel, 1989).

2. On Luther and Bernard of Clairvaux, see Theo Bell, *Divus Bernhardus: Bernhard von Clairvaux in Martin Luthers Schriften* (Mainz: Zabern, 1993); Bernhard Lohse, "Luther und Bernhard von Clairvaux," in *Bernhard von Clairvaux: Rezeption und Wirkung im Mittelalter und in der Neuzeit*, ed. Kaspar Elm (Wiesbaden: Harrasowitz, 1994), 271–301; Franz Posset, *Pater Bernhardus: Martin Luther and Bernard of Clairvaux* (Kalamazoo, MI: Cistercian Publications, 1999); and Franz Posset, *The Real Luther: A Friar at Erfurt and Wittenberg* (St. Louis: Concordia, 2011). Posset, *The Real Luther*, situates the Wittenberg Reformation within a late-medieval "Bernard Renaissance," and he sees Bernard as the decisive influence on Luther's theology; according to Posset, Luther's theology of justification was a rediscovery of Bernard's: "Luther emerged as the Bernardus *Redivivus*" (127). More convincing by far is Lohse's delineation of discontinuities between Luther's theology and Bernard's monastic outlook; see Lohse, "Luther und Bernhard," 300. That said, attention to Luther's transformations, relocations, and revaluations of Bernard's themes may yield a more nuanced assessment. Karlstadt's reception of Bernard is treated briefly by Hans-Peter Hasse, *Karlstadt und Tauler: Untersuchungen zur Kreuzestheologie* (Gütersloh: Gütersloher Verlagshaus Gerd Mohn, 1993), 76–84.

3. Bernd Moeller, "Tauler und Luther," in *La Mystique Rhénane: Colloque de Strasbourg 16–19 mai 1961* (Paris: Presses Universitaires de France, 1963), 157–68; 158–59, esp. 158n3.

4. See Luther's prefaces to the *Theologia Deutsch* at WA 1: 153, 378–79; Steven E. Ozment, *Mysticism and Dissent: Religious Ideology and Social Protest in the Sixteenth Century* (New Haven, CT: Yale University Press, 1973), 17–25; and recently, Lydia Wegener, *Der 'Frankfurter'/'Theologia Deutsch': Spielräume und Grenzen des Sagbaren* (Berlin: De Gruyter, 2016), esp. 387–435 (discussing Wittenberg editions). The translation here is from *The Theologia Germanica of Martin Luther*, trans. Bengt Hoffman (Mahwah, NJ: Paulist, 1980), 54.

5. McGinn, *Presence*, 4: 239. Little has been published on Karlstadt's relationship to Suso; for some brief references, see Ronald J. Sider, *Andreas Bodenstein von Karlstadt: The Development of his Thought, 1517–1525* (Leiden: Brill, 1974), 181n29; Hasse, *Karlstadt und Tauler*, 104n19, 180–81.

6. On Müntzer's period of study in Wittenberg and the evidence for his study of Tauler, possibly in connection with Karlstadt, see Ulrich Bubenheimer, *Thomas Müntzer: Herkunft und Bildung* (Leiden: E. J. Brill, 1989), 145–93, esp. 181–86.

Müntzer also had ties to Christian Döring, a bookseller who facilitated the circulation of Tauler; see ibid., 173–75. If ThMA 2:12–14, dates Letter 10 correctly (see esp. 13n1), Müntzer may have read Tauler and Suso already in 1515 or 1516, before his contact with the Wittenbergers.

7. A few prior studies have made use of these marginalia: Henrik Otto, *Vor- und frühreformatorische Tauler-Rezeption: Annotationen in Drucken des späten 15. und frühen 16. Jahrhunderts* (Gütersloh: Gütersloher Verlagshaus, 2003), 183–214, 241–54, attends to Luther's and Karlstadt's annotations within a broad study of marginalia extant in late fifteenth- and early sixteenth-century editions. He concludes that Luther's apparent disinterest in mystical union and the ground of the soul was typical for contemporary readers, while Karlstadt's attraction to these themes was unusual. Two earlier studies address Karlstadt's Tauler-reception specifically: Hasse, *Karlstadt und Tauler*, 23–89; Ulrich Bubenheimer, "Karlstadt liest Tauler: Sein reformatorischer Weg im Spiegel seines Taulerbandes in der Bibliothek des Predigerseminars Wittenberg," Lecture to the Evangelisches Predigerseminar Wittenberg, June 16, 1987. Bubenheimer's lecture is preserved in a typed manuscript, held by the Predigerseminar; I thank Dr. Hans-Peter Hasse for placing his copy at my disposal. Steven Ozment, *Homo Spiritualis: A Comparative Study of the Anthropology of Johannes Tauler, Jean Gerson, and Martin Luther (1509–16) in the Context of their Theological Thought* (Leiden: E. J. Brill, 1969), devoted significant attention to Luther's marginal remarks to Tauler.

8. While at the Wartburg, Luther asked Philip Melanchton to purchase and send him a copy of the Basel 1521 edition of Tauler's *Sermons;* see Otto, *Tauler-Rezeption,* 176n8. The postils are found in WA 10/1.1: 1–728, 10/1.2: 1–208; LW 75–76. For a helpful introduction, see LW 75: xiii–xxxii; and John M. Frymire, "Works: Sermons and Postils," in OEML 3:561–89. For a broader study of the scope and significance of Reformation-era postil production, see John M. Frymire, *The Primacy of the Postils: Catholics, Protestants, and the Dissemination of Ideas in Early Modern Germany* (Leiden: Brill, 2010). Themes related to Luther's reception of Tauler surface even in the later *House Postils,* for instance in the following advice (in a sermon that was in fact authored by Veit Dietrich) that Christians humble themselves and yield their will in suffering: "Vnd dennoch solt du dich demu[e]tigen / auff deinen willen so hart nicht dringen / sonder in Gottes willen setzen / ob er dich wolte lenger im solcher not lassen stecken / das du es gedultig wo[e]llest tragen vnd leyden / wie du sihest das Christus hie thut." *Haußpostil D. Martin Luthers vber die Sontags vnd der fu[e]rnembsten Fest Evangelia durch das gantze Jar* (Nürnberg: Johann Vom Berg and Ulrich Neuber, 1545), 126v.

9. Reinhard Schwarz, "Thomas Müntzer und die Mystik," in *Der Theologe Thomas Müntzer,* ed. Siegfried Bräuer and Helmar Junghans (Göttingen: Vandenhoeck & Ruprecht, 1989), 283–301; 283–84.

10. DTRG.

11. For Arndt's edition, see *Die teutsche Theologia . . .* (Halberstadt: Georg Roten, 1597). VD 16 T 918. Arndt included most of the original marginalia, but he did add, omit, or alter some annotations—possibly influenced by another edition.

12. Martin Brecht, "Randbemerkungen in Luthers Ausgaben der 'Deutsch Theologia,'" LJ 47 (1980): 10–32; Wegener, Der 'Frankfurter', 430–34, weighs evidence for both Luther's and Karlstadt's possible authorship, leaving the question unresolved.

13. Wegner, Der 'Frankfurter', 385–86, argues that Luther was attracted to the German Theology because it contained strong anti-Pelagian themes that broke with Eckhart's assumption of "natural intimacy between God and human."

14. For Karlstadt, see esp. Hans-Peter Hasse, "Tauler und Augustin als Quelle Karlstadts: am Beispiel von Karlstadts Marginalien zu Taulers Predigt zum Johannistag über Lk 1, 5–23," in ABvK: 247–82; here, 260; Bubenheimer, "Karlstadt liest," 24.

15. WA 1: 611.8–9; LW 31: 221; see also Susan E. Schreiner, Are You Alone Wise? The Search for Certainty in the Early Modern Era (Oxford: Oxford University Press).

16. McGinn, Presence, 4: 198.

17. Ibid., 241, notes that Tauler "went through the normal theological education for a Dominican preacher, which would have lasted about eight years, but he did not do advanced studies."

18. This point will be demonstrated fully in ensuing chapters; for Luther, see for instance his reference to Tauler in the Explanations, WA 1: 557.29–32; LW 31: 129.

19. McGinn, Presence, 4: 94–100.

20. Ibid., 4: 137: "[A]nalogy does not indicate some kind of participation by God and creature in a particular predicate (e.g., esse), but rather denotes the fact that God alone really possesses that attribute. As Dietmar Mieth [Die Einheit von Vita Activa und Vita Contemplativa in den deutschen Predigten und Traktaten Meister Eckharts und bei Johannes Tauler (Regensburg: Pustet, 1969), 136] puts it: 'Analogy is not, as with Thomas, a connective relationship, but a relationship of dependence.'"

21. McGinn, Presence, 4: 101, 104. Eckhart describes this principle at the beginning of the Book of Divine Consolation; I have consulted the parallel Middle High and Modern German text of Kurt Flasch, ed., Das Buch der Göttlichen Tröstung (München: C. H. Beck, 2007); here, 8–13. This section was excerpted for the condemnation of Eckhart's teachings.

22. McGinn, Presence, 4: 125–36.

23. God, for Eckhart, is completely incomparable to anything and no predicate of God properly applies; ibid., 4: 123–24.

24. Ibid., 4: 144–45. Eckhart made the realization of this union with God in the passive (leidender) intellect the central theme of a sermon cycle that found its way pseudonymously into the first printed editions of Tauler's sermons, including the 1508 edition used by Luther and Karlstadt; Karlstadt annotated these four sermons extensively. On the sermons themselves, see Bernard McGinn, The Mystical Thought of Meister Eckhart: The Man from Whom God Hid Nothing (New York: Crossroad, 2003), 53–70; for references to further scholarship on the sermon cycle and for an analysis of Karlstadt's annotations, see Vincent Evener, "'Enemies of the Cross': Suffering, Salvation, and Truth in Sixteenth-Century Religious Controversy," PhD diss. (University of Chicago, 2014), 100–14; Karlstadt's later definition of faith as love-rich knowledge passively received may owe much to Eckhart himself. Evener, "Enemies of

the Cross" (91–100), discusses Luther's and Karlstadt's annotations to STA Sermon 1, the authorship of which is debated (Eckhart or Tauler).

25. McGinn, *Presence*, 4: 145–50.

26. Ibid., 4: 151–60: "What is essential is to appropriate the inner attitude that Jesus revealed in his suffering and death by becoming totally fixed on God, no matter what the external situations in which we find ourselves. Suffering . . . is not a *way* to God, but is actually identical with the goal" (159–60). On Christ in Eckhart's mysticism, ibid., 122–24.

27. Eckhart, *Das Buch der Göttlichen Tröstung*, 26–31, which discusses volitional unity with God, even if God wills that one suffer, be damned, or sin. The last point was condemned. Ibid., 30–33, cites Matthew 19:29, a verse beloved by Karlstadt. See also ibid., 64–65, "Daran soll der Mensch erkennen, daß er auf dem richtigen Weg is, wenn er beglückt und mit Freuden seinen naturhaften Willen läßt und verleugnet, wenn er sich selbst völlig entäußert, um alles zu leiden, was Gott will, dass er leide. . . . 'Wer zu mir kommen will, der muß aus sich selbst herausgehen, muß sich selbst verleugnen und sein Kreuz auf sich nehmen.' Das heißt: Er soll alles ablegen und abtun, was Kreuz und Leid ist. Denn gewiß: Wer sich selbst verleugnete und ganz aus sich herausginge, für den gäbe es kein Kreuz, kein Leid und kein Leiden."

28. Ibid., 72–79: God suffers "mit uns . . . auf seine Weise eher und ungleich mehr als der, der um Gottes willen leidet. . . . Gott leidet gern mit uns und um unsertwillen, wenn wir allein um seinetwillen leiden: Dann leidet er ohne Leiden. Leiden ist ihm so lustvoll, daß Leiden für ihn kein Leiden ist. Würden wir recht leben, dann wäre auch für uns Leiden kein Leiden, sondern Lust und Trost." The theme of "Leid ohne Leiden" is analyzed by Haas, *Gottleiden—Gottlieben*: 127–52 ("'Trage Leiden geduldiglich': Die Einstellung der deutschen Mystik zum Leiden"); on Eckhart, see 132–38.

29. McGinn, *Presence*, 4: 166–70.

30. Ibid., 4: 188–93.

31. Ibid., 4: 197–99; also helpful regarding Suso's life and works is Frank Tobin, "Introduction," in Henry Suso, *The Exemplar, with Two German Sermons*, ed. Frank Tobin (New York: Paulist, 1989), 13–51; here, 19–26.

32. McGinn, *Presence*, 4: 199–201; for fuller information, Karl Bihlmeyer, "Einleitung," in *Heinrich Seuse. Deutsche Schriften* (Stuttgart: W. Kohlhammer, 1907 [Frankfurt a.M.: Minerva, 1961; henceforth cited as SDS]), 1*–163*; 3*–62*.

33. Bihlmeyer, "Einleitung," 159*.

34. *Diss buch das da gedicht hat der erleücht vater Amandus genan[t] Seüß* (Augsburg: Hans Othmar, 1512); VD 16 S 6097; Augsburg Staats- und Stadtbibliothek, 2 Th Sch 218.

35. McGinn, *Presence*, 4: 220–21, 230, 235–36, 238.

36. Ibid., 4: 226.

37. Suso, *Exemplar*, 87–89. For the original, see SDS, 39.1–42.7.

38. Suso, *Exemplar*, 97; SDS, 52.6–53.3.

39. Suso, *Exemplar*, 98; SDS, 53.5–54.8.

40. Suso, *Exemplar*, 98; SDS 54.16–22.

41. Mcginn, *Presence*, 4: 215–17.

42. See my discussion of this image in chapter 3.

43. Suso, *Diss buch*, 58v; on this connection, see Hasse, *Karlstadt und Tauler*, 104n19, 226.

44. Suso, *Diss buch*, 123v, as first noted by Ronald J. Sider, *Andreas Bodenstein von Karlstadt: The Development of his Thought 1517–1525* (Leiden: Brill, 1974), 181n29.

45. Suso, *Diss buch*, 122v–125r (English: Suso, *Exemplar*, 308–16).

46. ThMA 2: 153.5–7.

47. Müntzer's regard for visions may also have been nourished by Jacques Lefèvre d' Étaples's *Liber trium virorum et trium spiritualium virginum* (Paris: Henricus Stephanie, 1513), which included the visions of Hermas and Hildegard von Bingen, among others. For a discussion, see Dieter Fauth, "Mystik bei Thomas Müntzer— historische Analyse, Wirkungsgeschichte und gegenwärtige Bedeutung," in HvB: 275–92; here, 276–81.

48. For Karlstadt, see Bubenheimer, "Karlstadt liest," 8–11; see also Hans-Peter Hasse, "Karlstadts Predigt am 29. September 1522 in Joachimsthal: Ein unbekannter Text aus Stephan Roths Sammlung von Predigten des Johannes Sylvius Egranus," ARG 81 (1990): 97–119. For Luther, see my discussion of the postils in chapter 3.

49. Vincent Evener, "Mysticism, Christianization, and Dissent: The Appropriation of Johannes Tauler in Simon Haferitz's *Sermon on the Feast of the Three Holy Kings* (1524)," ARG 106 (2015): 67–91.

50. On Tauler's intellectual sources and influences, see McGinn, *Presence*, 4: 244–48. For Tauler's biography, the foundational work is Louise Gnädinger, *Johannes Tauler: Lebenswelt und mystische Lehre* (München: C. H. Beck, 1993), 9–103.

51. Ruh, *Geschichte*, 3: 479; McGinn, *Presence*, 4: 241.

52. Gnädinger, *Johannes Tauler*, 117–19. Ruh, *Geschichte*, 3: 478, argues that for Tauler, in distinction from Eckhart and Suso, "das Seelenheil der städtischen Bevölkerung [war] ein wesentliches Anliegen." See also Alois M. Haas, "'Die Arbeit der Nacht': Mystische Leiderfahrung nach Johannes Tauler," in *Die Dunkle Nacht der Sinne: Leiderfahrung und christliche Mystik*, ed. Gotthard Fuchs (Düsseldorf: Patmos, 1989), 9–40; 24–25 ("Tauler spricht von der konkreten menschlichen Existenz her und entwirft nicht Programme asketischer Leidzufügung"), 31.

53. This compilation work apparently occured mostly after Tauler's return to Straßburg from Basel in 1343. See McGinn, *Presence*, 4: 243. Important questions about the sermons remain unanswered, e.g., regarding the relationship of the written sermons to preaching events and the extent of Tauler's involvement in the organization and editing of the sermons.

54. McGinn, *Presence*, 4: 254, 257–59. Tauler used the term "ground" more than 400 times, compared to the 140 uses in Eckhart's work. McGinn notes, "Like Eckhart, Tauler also insists that the *grunt* is the source and goal of all things in the most basic sense. . . . [This] means that the ground is nothing other than God. . . . The majority of the Straßburg preacher's uses of the ground language, however, deal with the *grunt* as the core of the human."

55. For Tauler's repudiation of the debate, see V 45, 196.28–32. (V is cited by sermon, page number, and line, if appropriate.) As McGinn, *Presence*, 4: 600n196, summarizes, Tauler in this sermon declared "that there is no question that love is more meritorious and useful than knowledge (*bekentnisse*) in this life, because 'love goes in where reason must remain without.'"

56. Gnädinger, *Johannes Tauler*, 125, notes that the Middle High German word *gemu[e]t* corresponds "nur ganz mangelhaft" to the New High German *Gemüt*. Tauler's term refers to an "alle sinnenhaften und geistigen Fähigkeiten und Kräfte zusammenfassendes Organ" or to the "Bezogenheit der Seele auf den eigenen Seelengrund, als inneren Ort, der den Blick in die eigene Tiefe und in den Abgrund Gottes freigibt"; see ibid., 125–26n31, citing the important study, Alois M. Haas, *Nim din selbes war: Studien zur Lehre von der Selbsterkenntnis bei Meister Eckhart, Johannes Tauler und Heinrich Seuse* (Freiburg: Universitätsverlag Freiburg Schweiz, 1971), 140f. See further Gnädinger, *Johannes Tauler*, 241–51.

57. McGinn, *Presence*, 4: 254–57; McGinn notes that the *gemu[e]t* and *ground* are not identical in Tauler. On Tauler's anthropology, see also Gnädinger, *Johannes Tauler*, 129–36, 241–51; Ruh, *Geschichte*, 3: 496–97.

58. McGinn, *Presence*, 4: 266–67; Gnädinger, *Johannes Tauler*, 136–47.

59. Gnädinger, *Johannes Tauler*, 121–29, whose discussion of Tauler's concept of human double-nothingness (*gebrestlich nicht* and *natúrlich nicht*) depends on Haas, *Nim din selbes war*, esp. 121–31.

60. On *Gelassenheit*, see esp. V 23, cited by Haas, *Gottleiden—Gottlieben*, 144; and Haas, "'Die Arbeit der Nacht,'" 38.

61. Tauler described this filling and union sometimes as a pouring-in of the Holy Spirit, sometimes as the birth of God in the ground of the soul; see McGinn, *Presence*, 4: 280–95, who notes that Tauler used the concept of birth less often than Eckhart. The motif "appears in about twenty of his sermons, though usually not as the main theme." The "birth of God" theme is central, however, to the Eckhart sermons included in STA—namely Sermons 2, 6, 8, 9 and possibly 1.

62. Ibid., 4: 268–70. The *lidikeit* that human beings must attain before God is described by McGinn as a "receiving in empty passivity"; this receptivity is awareness of the human condition: "Because God is essential activity (*wúrcken*), our ontological relation to him is always one of empty reception, or passivity (*liden*), whether we recognize it our not."

63. V 60, 327f., cited by Haas, *Gottleiden—Gottlieben*, 138–39.

64. Haas, *Gottleiden—Gottlieben*, 138–40; see also "'Die Arbeit der Nacht,'" 21–24. Gnädinger, *Johannes Tauler*, 123, describes the goal of asceticism and self-knowledge in Tauler as "eine unverfälschte, den gesamten Menschen erfassende Gottesbeziehung, die keinerlei Ersatzbefriedigung sucht."

65. See Haas, *Gottleiden—Gottlieben*, 141–43. Vis-à-vis Eckhart, Haas writes, Tauler "weiß . . . schärfer um die erbsündige Verfaßtheit des Menschen und um dessen Neigung zur Sünde."

66. Ibid., 140, which depends on Christine Pleuser, *Die Benennungen und der Begriff des Leides bei J. Tauler* (Berlin: Erich Schmidt, 1967). The original terms recounted and

glossed by Haas are, "*getrenge* (Bedrängnis) . . . *riuwe, bitterkeit, vorchte, trurecheit, lidunge, pinlicheit, bancheit* (Bangigkeit)."

67. Haas, *Gottleiden—Gottlieben*, 139; "'Die Arbeit der Nacht,'" 25. At V 75, 405 (cited in Haas, "'Die Arbeit der Nacht,'" 25), Tauler criticizes ascetic praxis that assails and destroys the flesh but not "die böse Sippschaft." See also Gnädinger, *Johannes Tauler*, 120.

68. McGinn, *Presence*, 4: 271–75.

69. Haas, *Gottleiden—Gottlieben*, 141.

70. The remark (discussed later in this chapter) is in reference to Sermon 61 of STA (corresponding to V 56); for a discussion of Karlstadt's note, see Otto, *Tauler-Rezeption*, 252.

71. Richard Kieckhefer, "The Notion of Passivity in the Sermons of John Tauler," *Recherches de théologie ancienne et médiévale* XLVIII (1981): 198–211. Ruh, *Geschichte*, 3: 491–93, lists "moral rigor" as the first of the chief themes of Tauler's *Sermons*; see also Ruh, *Geschichte*, 3: 508.

72. Kieckherer, "Notion," 199–200, summarizing the position of Ozment, *Homo Spiritualis*. "In his anti-Pelagian utterances, Tauler is explicitly referring to God's involvement at every stage in one's spiritual progress. In his apparently Pelagian statements, Tauler is taking an external viewpoint: It appears that man is in fact only the secondary cause of this striving, or the instrument for God's work in the soul" (Kieckhefer's summary).

73. Kieckhefer, "Notion," 200, summarizing Gösta Wrede, *Unio Mystica: Probleme der Erfahrung bei Johannes Tauler* (Uppsala: Universitet, 1974).

74. Kieckhefer, "Notion," 201: "Ozment's and Wrede's solutions . . . are not mutually exclusive, but complimentary. Wrede defines the active and passive phases in the mystic's behavior; Ozment points to a passive dimension present even within behavior which, from an external viewpoint, is active."

75. Kieckhefer, "Notion," 209; see also Haas, "'Die Arbeit der Nacht,'" 35–40, which describes the varied meanings of the "work of the night" in Tauler's sermon on Luke 5:1f. (V 63, 341–46) and endorses Kieckhefer's argument (see notes 75 and 86): "Und so hat die 'Arbeit der Nacht' für Tauler letztlich einen passiven Sinn als eine Reinigung, der sich der Mensch auszusetzen hat, ohne darüber zu verfügen."

76. Kieckhefer, "Notion," 201–203, 210.

77. See Otto, *Tauler-Rezeption*, 183–241, for an overview of Luther's, Lang's, and Jonas's notations.

78. For this paragraph, see Otto, *Tauler-Rezeption*, 175–80.

79. Moeller, "Tauler und Luther," 158n3.

80. Schwartz, "Thomas Müntzer und die Mystik," 284–85.

81. See note 6.

82. For a summary in the context of the development of Eckhartian mysticism, see Wegener, *Der 'Frankfurter'*, 91–109. Pioneering work has been done by Eric L. Saak; among his works, see esp. *High Way to Heaven: The Augustinian Platform between Reform and Reformation, 1292-1524* (Leiden: Brill, 2002); *Creating Augustine: Interpreting Augustine and Augustinianism in the Later Middle Ages* (Oxford: Oxford University Press, 2012); and "The Augustinian Renaissance: Textual

Scholarship and Religious Identity in the Later Middle Ages," in *The Oxford Guide to the Historical Reception of Augustine*, ed. Karla Pollmann and Willemien Otten (Oxford: Oxford University Press, 2013), 58–68.

83. Lohse, "Luther und Bernhard," 273.

84. Extant are Luther's marginal annotations from 1509–1510 to several of Augustine's writings, including *Confessions*, *City of God*, and *On the Trinity*. See WA 9, 5f.; Bernhard Lohse, *Evangelium in der Geschichte: Studien zu Luther und der Reformation*, ed. Leif Grane, Bernd Moeller, und Otto Hermann Pesch (Göttingen: Vandenhoeck & Ruprecht, 1988), 11–30 ("Die Bedeutung Augustins für den jungen Luther"); here, 13–14. For a comprehensive account of Augustine's influence on Luther's early academic theological work, see Adolf Hamel, *Der Junge Luther und Augustin: ihre Beziehungen in der Rechtfertigungslehre nach Luthers ersten Vorlesungen 1509–18 untersucht*, 2 Volumes (Gütersloh: C. Bertelsmann, 1934); Hamel's results are summarized and critiqued by Lohse, *Evangelium*, 14–15, 29.

85. Lohse, *Evangelium*, 14n10, 17n18, 22n34. In Luther's 1545 account of his theological "breakthrough," he states that he turned to *The Spirit and the Letter* after receiving his new understanding of the *iustitia Dei*, and that he found his new insight confirmed— unexpectedly—in Augustine; see WA 54.186.16–20; Lohse, *Evangelium*, 17.

86. On the date of Luther's encounter with Tauler, see Otto, *Tauler-Rezeption*, 183. For Luther's citations of *The Spirit and the Letter* in his lectures on *Romans*, see Lohse, *Evangelium*, 22–26.

87. Lohse, *Evangelium*, 22–23; he also cited other anti-Pelagian writings.

88. See Markus Matthias, "Die Anfänge der reformatorischen Theologie des Andreas Bodenstein von Karlstadt," in QdR: 87–109, who analyzes Karlstadt's depiction of his own conversion in the letter to Johann von Staupitz that prefaced Karlstadt's published lectures on *The Spirit and the Letter*.

89. Karlstadt published his commentary on *The Spirit and the Letter* for students, under the title *Pro divinae gratiae defensione*; four installments were printed between late 1517 and early 1519, reaching chapter 12 of Augustine's writing. The text of Karlstadt's commentary is now available in the *Kritische Gesamtausgabe der Schriften und Briefe Andreas Bodensteins von Karlstadt*, ed. Thomas Kaufmann (Göttingen: Gütersloher Verlagshaus, 2017), 1.2: 537–724; I have primarily relied on the foundational edition of Ernst Kähler, *Karlstadt und Augustin: Der Kommentar des Andreas Bodenstein von Karlstadt zu Augustins Schrift* De Spiritu et Litera (Halle [Saale]: Max Niemeyer, 1952). In late 1518, Karlstadt turned his attention to lectures on justification, publishing a summary as the *Epitome Andree Carolostadii De impii iustificatione*; these lectures were grounded in copious scriptural citations—Augustine is cited only twice—signaling a new turn in Karlstadt's method. On all this, see Kähler, *Karlstadt und Augustin*, 3*–37*, 45*–53*, as well as Bubenheimer, "Karlstadt liest Tauler," 1–11.

90. J. Patout Burns, ed., *Theological Anthropology* (Philadelphia: Fortress, 1981), 39–55; 61–96; Henry Chadwick, *Augustine of Hippo: A Life* (New York: Oxford University Press, 2009), 145–68.

91. See Vincent Evener, "Divine Pedagogy and Self-Accusation: Reassessing the Theology of Andreas Bodenstein von Karlstadt," MQR 87, no. 3 (July 2013): 335–67.

92. David C. Steinmetz, *Luther in Context*, 2nd ed. (Grand Rapids, MI: Baker Academic, 2002), 21, remarks on Luther's exegesis of Romans 9:10–29: "He embraces the most severe statement of Augustine's position on predestination (a position from which Augustine himself at times attempted to retreat) and states it as a conclusion which is indisputable." For a passage of *The Spirit and the Letter* that shows Augustine's reticence, see Augustine of Hippo, *Answer to the Pelagians* I, ed. John E. Rotelle, trans., intro. and notes Roland J. Teske (Hyde Park, NY: New City Press, 1997), 140–202; here, 192. Augustine's treatise will henceforth be cited in this edition as SL.

93. Abraham Friesen, *Thomas Müntzer, a Destroyer of the Godless: The Making of a Sixteenth-Century Religious Revolutionary* (Berkeley: University of California Press, 1990), 57–58. Friesen claims (53–72) that Müntzer was influenced chiefly by the young Augustine and his Neo-Platonism, rather than the older anti-Pelagian Augustine; as noted here, Müntzer received Augustine's anti-Pelagian views at least indirectly, and Augustinian views on salvation and the law clearly helped Müntzer to the formulation of his "mature" views, even if he developed Augustine's ideas in his own way and with a critical eye. For the evidence concerning Müntzer's reading of Augustine, see ThMA 2: 27–37, and esp. 30n7.

94. He may have read Augustine's works, like Karlstadt, in the Basel reprint (1515–1516) of the 1508 Amerbach edition. Luther used the Amerbach edition. See ThMA 2: 30n7, 35n14.

95. Proposition 20, MSB 515.3–6; CWTM 382.

96. See chapter 5.

97. MSB 339.11–19; CWTM 345. See the discussion of this treatise in chapter 6.

98. SL, 150–51.

99. SL, 152–53.

100. On this point, see Lohse, *Evangelium*, 28.

101. SL, 157; see also SL, 167.

102. At SL, 159, Augustine describes the law as a "schoolmaster" for the unrighteous, and he argues that the righteous use the law rightly when they "impose[] it upon the unrighteous to terrify them." This argument resonates with Müntzer's in the *Highly-Provoked Vindication*; see chapter 6.

103. SL, 154.

104. SL 155.

105. SL 158.

106. SL, 160–61, 164.

107. See esp. SL, 160–62.

108. Augustine could describe faith as "the beginning of salvation or of this chain leading to salvation" (SL, 185), and he associates faith with a good will (SL, 190).

109. Lohse, *Evangelium*, 19, notes that the nature of divine justice and human justification for Augustine depends on the Letter and the Spirit, not Luther's Law and Gospel; see also ibid., 28–29.

110. SL, 157, 180.

111. SL, 167–69, 172, 177.

112. SL, 181.

113. SL, 152.

114. Hasse, "Tauler und Augustin," 260, shows that Karlstadt "konzentrierte sich auf bestimmte Parallelen zwischen Tauler und Augustin, die ihm ins Auge fielen . . .: das Angewiesensein auf die Gnade Gottes; das Unvermögen des Menschen, von sich aus das Heil zu erlangen; die Notwendigkeit der Selbstverurteilung als Sünder; die Nutzlosigkeit von Werken und äusseren Übungen; die Bedeutung von Leiden, Demut und Schweigen für den Heilsweg."

115. One marker to Karlstadt's interest in sermons is the number of marginal remarks that he made; Hasse, *Karlstadt und Tauler*, 26–30, provides a count for each sermon. Hasse's "statistical overview" has informed my selection of sermons for discussion; at the same time, I have also made selections based on the themes of the sermons themselves, the quality of the marginalia, and the opportunity for comparison with Luther. In 2012–2013, Dr. Hasse assisted me with deciphering the marginalia; mistakes are my own.

116. Moeller, "Tauler und Luther," 160f.; Otto, *Tauler-Rezeption*, 188–201, 241–54.

117. See Gnädinger, *Johannes Tauler*, 121–29.

118. Haas, *Gottleiden—Gottlieben*, 138–46.

119. WA 9.103.20–21: "Hoc nota: quia hoc dicit omnis scriptura, omnis figura, omnis natura."

120. STA 126r. Karlstadt left only two remarks to this sermon, both here. The first consists of citations to Augustine's works, *The Spirit and the Letter* and *Grace and Free Will*; the second, "novu[m] testamentum." To be noted is that Tauler's exegesis is both historical and related to the present experience of the believer.

121. STA 126v., beginning, "Lieben kinder sehet für euch dem ding mu[o]ß vil anders sein dan[n] yr wo[e]llet wenen." Karlstadt left some light underlining in this section, and marked with a cross Tauler's exhortation to enduring the inward and outward cross of Christ.

122. Tauler's ensuing discussion is of confession and true penance—central concerns of the *95 Theses*.

123. STA 126v–127v.

124. STA 129v–130r. According to Tauler, Christ's agony during the passion was caused by the unwillingness of human beings to recognize their nothingngess—humans forsake the one thing that is necessary, "das ain (dz not ist)."

125. STA 130r; Karlstadt glosses, "vnum est necessarium," "nicht," and "Maria optimam partem."

126. STA 130r: "Omnia contra hominem" and "Romans 7."

127. STA 130v.

128. STA 130v. Karlstadt also wrote "nicht" at the bottom of this column. In all, the word "nicht" is written by Karlstadt three times on this page, and the Latin "ad nihilum" twice. He detected a theme.

129. STA 130v. Karlstadt wrote "nicht" next to the remark about God becoming nothing.

130. STA 130v ("erloschner blinder liebe"). In response to ensuing lines, Karlstadt wrote, "aller dieng vnwirdig."

131. WA 9.103.17–30.
132. 131r. He also wrote in response to the following, "Infernus," "usus rerum," and (at the bottom of the page), "cibus cum pavore sumendus."
133. STA 130v–131r.
134. STA 131r.
135. STA 131r. This was a response to the lines, "Dise verklainu[n]g sol nit bringen ain verzweifelte forcht. als die verzweifeler. sunder sy sol wircken ainen demu[e]tigen vnderfal. vnder got vnd vnder alle creatur in rechter gelassenhait." Karlstadt also wrote, "desperans timor non suboriatur ex nihilo." The final lines of Sermon 53, STA 131r–v, contain one of Tauler's characteristic invocations of the union of the human and divine abysses. Karlstadt made note of the theme of *divine* nothingness here, although the theme found no expression in his later work. Karlstadt also underlined the statement, "This true abasement (verklainunge) sinks into the divine inward abyss." Marginalia to the ensuing passage highlight the ideas "verlorenhait [of self]," "abgrund," and "nicht duplex."
136. Karlstadt also referenced "Augustinus contra Iulianum" and "Bernhard de diligendo deo" in reference to the lines "vo[n] ijm selber nichts haldt" See Hans-Peter Hasse, "'Von mir selbs nicht halden': Beobachtungen zum Selbstverständnis des Andreas Bodenstein von Karlstadt," in QdR: 49–73; here, 71n82.
137. STA 132r–STA 132v.
138. See Hasse, "'Von mir selbs,'" 70; "Tauler und Augustin," 259–60, 281–82.
139. Hasse, "'Von mir selbs,'" 72. For a comparative study of Luther's and Müntzer's self-understanding, see Siegfried Bräuer, "Selbstverständnis und Feindbild bei Martin Luther und Thomas Müntzer: Ihre Flugschriftenkontroverse von 1524," in *Wegscheiden der Reformation: Alternatives Denken vom 16. bis zum 18. Jahrhundert*, ed. Günter Vogler (Weimar: Hermann Böhlaus Nachfolger, 1994), 56–84. Recent studies of Luther emphasize his self-understanding as a prophet, but with little explanation of his understanding of prophethood; see my review of several works, "From the Universal to the Particular: Luther and the Reformation after Five Hundred Years," *Journal of Ecclesiastical History* 69, no. 4 (October 2018): 806–20; for explicit discussion of how Luther understood the category of "prophet," see Ronald K. Rittgers, "The Word Prophet Martin Luther," SCJ 48, no. 4 (Winter 2017): 951–76. Lyndal Roper, *Martin Luther: Renegade and Prophet* (London: Bodley Head, 2016), 121–23, 189–93, 314–18, 325, offers a compelling description of Luther's self-identification with Christ in the face of persecution and potential martyrdom. For a classic account of Luther's self-understanding vis-à-vis the "false brethren," see Mark U. Edwards Jr., *Luther and the False Brethren* (Stanford, CA: Stanford University Press, 1975). For Müntzer's self-understanding, see Bernhard Lohse, *Thomas Müntzer in neuer Sicht: Müntzer im Licht der neueren Forschung und die Frage nach dem Ansatz seiner Theologie* (Hamburg: Joachim Jungius-Gesellschaft der Wissenschaften, 1991), 103–12.
140. For an image, QDR, 103.
141. See Matthias, "Die Anfänge"; Kähler, *Karlstadt und Augustin*, 3–6.

142. STA 132v. Karlstadt glossed these lines with "Gelassenheit," and he noted the essential point of the preceding passage, "ym willen leit der schad." Another gloss of Karlstadt on this page reads, "aigen wol."

143. WA 9: 103.31–37 (my emphasis). On Luther's responsiveness to the theme of nothingness, see also Otto, *Tauler-Rezeption*, 186, analyzing Sermon 78 and Luther's marginalia. Tauler warns here against too frequent confession. Sins lead the person to "nützlichen Erkenntnis seines 'Nichts.' . . . Die angemessene Reaktion ist zwar *verschmehunge* seiner selbst, aber nicht in Schwermut, sondern in Gelassenheit." Rather than rush to confession, it is better (Tauler advises) "sich innerlich an Gott zu wenden und das eigene 'Nichts' zu betrachten." At "verschmehunge" Luther wrote, "hoc nota tibi," and to Tauler's advice against rushing to confession, he added, "utilissimum consilium." See WA 9: 104.11–14.

144. Scholars have noted Karlstadt's struggles with this anthropology; see esp. Bubenheimer, "Karlstadt liest Tauler," 17–20. Here Karlstadt only notes the threefold division (with the remark, "tres homines / vnus homo," and the numbers 1, 2, and 3), while responding to the essential point that the multitiered human has accordingly multiple wills, each of which must be entirely set aside.

145. *Homo Spiritualis*, 215; Ozment's conclusion is based upon reading this remark together with Luther's contemporary commentary on *Romans* (see 186–97). Otto, *Tauler-Rezeption*, 210–11, sees in Luther's remarks not a conscious repudiation of Tauler's position, but nevertheless the reflection of "eine letztlich unüberbrückbare Differenz. . . . Wer Tauler ohne den 'Grund' rezipiert, rezipiert eigentlich eben nicht Tauler."

146. Otto, *Tauler-Rezeption*, notes both reformers' uses of Sermon 13; see 181, 197, 197nn118–19. Luther's reference in the *Explanations* comes in his discussion of the 29th Thesis. Karlstadt's lecture text is *Epitome Andree Carolostadii De impii iustificatione, quam non male ad inferos deductu[m]que reductu[m]que vocaueris* (Leipzig: Melchior Lötter, d.Ä, 1519), and the copy in question is held by the Universitätsbibliothek München, Signature 4° Theol. 5464, 4; see Hasse, *Karlstadt und Tauler*, 44 and n48. This discovery was made by Ulrich Bubenheimer.

147. STA 31v. Karlstadt makes dutiful notes of the biblical passages: "ro 7 et gala 5 signat"; "caro contra spiritum gal 5"; "ro 8 qui aguntur spiritu dei." I follow Hasse, *Karlstadt und Tauler*, 38–46, in my rendering of most marginalia to Sermon 13.

148. STA 32r. "signu[m] graciae." Other glosses here included "tentationes" and "caro quo abstrahit."

149. STA 32r–v. See also STA 33r (where "abnegatio" is written twice, once in red and once in black) and 34r (once in red). Hasse, *Karlstadt und Tauler*, 45, argues—based on the numerous entries in Register A pointing to Sermon 13—that Karlstadt read the sermon as an explication of "abnegatio." For his complete analysis of Sermon 13, see ibid., 38–46.

150. As Hasse, *Karlstadt und Tauler*, 41–42, notes, Karlstadt critiqued Tauler's dependence on the faulty Vulgate text, recently corrected by Erasmus on the basis of the Greek.

151. 32r–v. "In veritate nihil sum. Bern in dedicatione Ecclesiae sermo 5 et Canticum sermo 54." The gloss is in red ink through "Bern," then supplemented with the full citation in black. Karlstadt also glosses "vernichten," "confidencia" and "einschlag." On the ensuing remark, "mansit voluntas contra Aug de fide et operibus capitulo 16," see Hasse, *Karlstadt und Tauler*, 43.

152. With a connecting line, Karlstadt connects this appearance of "vernichten" to one on the previous page, which in turn he connected to "getrawen."

153. STA 32v–33r.

154. STA 33r; Karlstadt writes, "außgen ym gaist vnd natur."

155. STA 33r–v. Tauler indicates that the still-living sister experienced a divine rapture at least once daily "in das go[e]tlich abgrunt gottes."

156. STA 33r–v. The marginalia and underlining on 33r, column 2 is in black, that on 33v is in red. 33r: "soror vidit deum," "vidit seipsam," "hellisch pein," "poena inferni," "ita Christus sus[ten]ta[t]us," "sancti non exaudiunt." 33v: "conversio ad passionem Christi," "non colunt sanctos," "Iudicium dei," "iudicium volo Luce xi," "subit penam inferni," "de persona," "non magna peccata," "quod petendum a domino."

157. STA 34r (several marginal remarks).

158. 34v. Although we shift attention now to Luther, Karlstadt's marginalia demonstrate continued interest in these themes, including especially in the nature of "Pharisees." See Hasse, *Karlstadt und Tauler*, 46.

159. STA, 35r. Karlstadt glosses here, in sequence, "denial" (i.e. of self), "the glory of God," "to receive from God alone," "perfection," "he discerns" (i.e. between the true friends of God and the "possessed grounds"), "they seek their own," and "true friends of God." All of these marginalia are in red, except "Gloria dei," which appears in black with a cross-reference to Sermon 13.

160. WA 9: 100.16–18. The sentence is incomplete. Luther also read with interest the next section, where Tauler cautions that the "false ground" often is "in a hidden way so intricately and harmfully mixed with the divine light" that it becomes difficult to distinguish them; one often follows nature when he believes himself to be serving God alone. Here, Luther corrected and explained the printed sentence. WA 9: 100.19–21.

161. STA 35v: "wissen sy nitt recht wo sy hyn lauffen so[e]llen. vnd su[o]chen der jn hilfet vnd rat vnd trost vn[d] ergetzlichkait tha[e]t. vnd wo[e]len in jn selbs verzweifelen vnd erbrechen. Vn[d] wißt das große angst vnd sorg darauff zu[o] haben ist. das es disen menschen sorgklich an jrem tode geen werde. Wan[n] sy haben got nit leüterlich gesu[o]cht vnd gemainet vnnd geliebet."

162. STA 35v.

163. This is not an uncontested interpretation; see my discussion and proposal in chapter 5.

164. Both Luther and Karlstadt followed the argument by noting the progression from the first to the second to the third type of myrrh. Luther gives longer descriptions of the myrrh than Karlstadt, describing the first as "Myrrha primo est aversio a bonis male delectantibus." WA 9: 99.1–2.

165. WA 9: 99.5–12; for analysis: Otto, *Tauler-Rezeption*, 188–89.

166. WA 9: 99.13–16.

167. STA 9r.

168. STA 9v. Karlstadt responds to the discussion here with extensive underlining. The cited marginal remark reads, "Got hat das leiden ewiglich geliebt," and there is a cross-reference to Sermon 34.

169. Underlined at STA 9v is "<u>das berait dich alles vnd</u> <u>dienet dir</u> <u>zu[o]</u> <u>warem</u> <u>frid,</u> <u>kündestu es nur genemen</u>."

170. WA 9: 99.17–20.

171. WA 9: 99.21; STA 9v.

172. STA 10r.

173. WA 99: 99.22–28. I have translated "saepius" as "rather," i.e. as "satius."

174. STA 10r.

175. STA 10r.

176. WA 9: 99.29–30.

177. STA 10r–v. The passage reads, "Such people want to be knowing and think they can avoid myrrh with their wisdom, and [they] ascribe this outer fate to fortune and misfortune, and think they should have avoided the suffering better. . . . They want to be too wise for God and teach him and master him and cannot accept the thing from him [Luther glosses: "accept with patience"]. They have great suffering and their myrrh becomes very bitter in them." Karlstadt marks the beginning of this section, "Mirra quomodo cognoscire" and at the appropriate point, "dependant fortunae."

178. WA 9: 99.31–34.

179. STA 110v–111r.

180. STA 110v–111v.

181. WA 9: 101.15–102.2. On the removal of God's gifts, Luther at STA 111r wrote: "And this sometimes ought to happen *effectualiter*, but always *affectualiter*, that you should be unaware, i.e., you should not think that you have or have done something." WA 9: 102.3–5.

182. STA 99r–v. Karlstadt follows this discussion with short marginalia that indicate little about his actual response: "drachma," "mulier," "pondus," "materia."

183. WA 9: 100.31–33.

184. STA 99v. Karlstadt glosses here, "Charitas quid"; Luther, "Quid sit amor vere."

185. STA 99v. Tauler finally employs the parable of the woman searching for the penny to uphold an active passivity. The "search that happens in the person" could happen "in a working way," that is, the person searches or helps to search, or "in a suffering way," that is, the person is sought by God. The active search is outward, the passive inward. Luther follows this discussion with brief marginalia, WA 9: 101.6–10. The outward search, according to Tauler, occurs "in outward exercises of good works . . . as one is admonished and driven by God and instructed by God's friends, and most of all with the exercise of virtues, such as humility, meekness, stillness, yieldedness and all other virtues." Far superior, however, is to enter into one's "most inward ground," where one can find God "in God's self, essence and nature," where God is "much nearer and more inward to the soul than the soul is to itself." Here, one leaves behind

everything pertaining to the senses and reason. Tauler declares that if one enters the ground and seeks God, God enters and seeks the seeker. Like Luther, Karlstadt also follow this discussion with brief remarks: "auswendig suchung"; "inwendig suchung"; "innerst grund," "domus," "sinnlich weiss," "vernunfftig weiss," "evertit domum." STA 99v–101r.

186. WA 9: 100.35–101.2. Luther also provides (at WA 9: 101.3) some Latin translations for Tauler's terms here: "fervorem" for "brinnen"; "carentia" for "mangel."

187. WA 9: 102.6–9.

188. STA 111v.

189. For an analysis, and another translation, see Ozment, *Homo Spiritualis*, 200–203.

190. This is a rather enigmatic citation of Matthew 25:5.

191. WA 9: 102.10–103.11. Luther continues here to criticize self-imposed and self-willed suffering, especially in imitation of the saints. His remarks conclude with the statement that one must "have an indifferent and naked will toward whatever must be borne, when, where, in what way, according to that which God should wish.... God seeks to destroy nothing in us, i.e. in the old man, than our own sense and will: when these so great heads and fonts are cut back, and the root drained, the members and powers of sin dry up just as rivers and branches." A separate remark of Luther's on page 111v reads, "Just as when material begins to suffer, begins to be led to another form, if it should oppose the agent, it both loses its prior and does not attain the following [form]. Thus here, because we are God's matter and clay." WA 9: 103.12–15. Tauler argues that one advances further in yielding to suffering than through "all the outer exercises that the entire world together could do" (STA 111v). Luther responds, "The reason is, because these are all works of men, that however is the work of God." WA 9: 103.15–17. Luther left only one more noteworthy comment to Sermon 45, at the point where Tauler confesses that he has not personally experienced God's indwelling. Luther writes, "He confesses that he teaches what he has not experienced." Unmarked by Luther are the sermon's descriptions of God's intercourse with God's self in and through the God-formed person, and of the sinking of "the created nothing into the uncreated nothing," so that the human spirit becomes "ain ainig ain. ain lauter go[e]tlich wesen," per the Psalm, "Abyssus abyssum inuocat." See Gnädinger, *Johannes Tauler*, 181–93; and her article, "Der Abgrund ruft dem Abgrund: Taulers Predigt *Beati oculi* (V45)," in *Das 'einig Ein': Studien zu Theorie und Sprache der deutschen Mystik*, ed. Alois M. Haas and Heinrich Stirnimann (Freiburg: Universitätsverlag Freiburg Schweiz, 1980), 167–207.

192. Themes of humility and human nothingness are prominent in the *Dictata super Psalterium* (1513–1515); for some analysis and citations, see Hamm, EL, 71–77.

193. On how Luther might have obtained this partial and the later, full copy of the text, see Andreas Zecherle, "Die 'Theologia Deutsch,'" in GN:1–96: 9–11; on the origins of the text itself, ibid., 7–8. The *terminus ad quem* for the original work is 1465, the date of the oldest complete manuscript—a manuscript of chapters 7–9 is dated to 1453—and the *terminus a quo* is established by the sermons of Tauler (d. 1361), whom the author of the *Theologia Deutsch* cites.

194. WA 1: 153. An image of the crucified Christ appeared on the cover page. This version of the *Theologia Deutsch* was printed twice, in Wittenberg in 1516 and in Leipzig in 1518.

195. On the authority of Luther's printed versions vis-à-vis the various manuscripts discovered since 1843, see Zecherle, "Die 'Theologia Deutsch,'" 11–13. Wolfgang von Hinten included the Luther editions in his critical edition, *'Der Franckforter' ('Theologia Deutsch'): Kritische Textausgabe* (München: Artemis Verlag, 1982). Because my concern is specifically with the Luther edition, I will refer to Hermann Mandel's edition of the same, MTD, and to the English translation by Bengt Hoffman, HTG. Hoffman did not translate Mandel directly, but his own copy of the 1518 edition. The correspondence of HTG to MTD is sometimes sufficient for our present purposes; I have provided my own translation where HTG does not correspond adequately to MTD.

196. WA 1: 378.2f.; HTG 53–54.

197. Brecht, "Randbemerkungen," attributed the marginalia to Luther in order to challenge Ozment's argument in *Mysticism and Dissent*, 17–25, that Luther was not interested in the "actually mystical" elements of the *German Theology*. Indeed, attention to Luther's reception of Eckhartian motifs shows his transformation and relocation of core themes surrounding the passive imitation of Christ (i.e. the endurance of foresakenness), the annihilation of the sinful soul (which Luther related to self-trust), and union with God. Yet the opposition of *Gelassenheit* to *Annehmlichkeit* was not—in these specific terms at least—central to Luther's message; Karlstadt expressly and repeatedly focused on this opposition. As mentioned earlier, Wegener, *'Der Frankfurter'*, 430–34, declines to make a definitive judgment between Luther and Karlstadt as possible authors; I argue here that the content of the marginalia corresponds to core themes of Karlstadt's *later-articulated* theology.

198. Ozment, *Mysticism and Dissent*, 20–21, 24–25, 61–97; disagreeing with Ozment's assessment of Luther's interest is Brecht, "Randbemerkungen," 29–32 (see previous note). Brecht agrees—as do I—that Luther had little interest in the theme of "deification"; this disinterest does not square with the centrality afforded to that theme by the so-called Finnish school of Luther studies, discussed in the Introduction.

199. Bubenheimer, "Karlstadt liest Tauler," 27–28; Hasse, *Karlstadt und Tauler*, 183n40.

200. DTRG, F2r.

201. Although I focus on different themes, I agree with Wegener's analysis that the *German Theology* constitutes not an unoriginal summary of Eckhartian mysticism (she uses the term "German mysticism") but rather a text with distinct themes that proved attractive in the context of the Reformation. See Wegener, *'Der Frankfurter'*, 1–68. As will become immediately apparent, I think the unique value of the *German Theology* for reformers was enhanced by the subsequently added prologue.

202. Along with the prologue, the register and the final two chapters appear to have come from subsequent editors. The terms "falscher freier Geist" and "Gottesfreund," which appear frequently in the prologue and register, are found only one time each in the text itself. Zecherle, "Die 'Theologia Deutsch,'" 14–18.

203. The author is said to be a "ein Teutscher herr, ein Priester und ein Custos in der Deutschen herren hauss zu Franckfurt"; MTD 1; HTG 55. The identity of the author remains a mystery to scholars. Zecherle, "Die 'Theologia Deutsch,'" 2–5.

204. MTD, 1; HTG 55 (translation altered).

205. There is no evidence that a unified sect of "free spirits" ever existed, but ideas recognizable in the condemnations at Vienne and in later proceedings did circulate; sometimes, daringly formulated teachings were misunderstood or misconstrued by opponents of the "free spirits," as happened in the case of Marguerite Porète. See Zecherle, "Die 'Theologia Deutsch,'" 69–75; McGinn, *Presence*, 4: 48–79; and Robert E. Lerner, *The Heresy of the Free Spirit in the later Middle Ages* (Berkeley: University of California Press, 1992).

206. Haas's description of the significance of the free-spirit controversy to the *German Theology* (followed by Zecherle, "Die 'Theologia Deutsch,'" 69) obfuscates more than it clarifies: he argues that the controversy is "peripheral" to the mystagogical aspect, but not "nebensächlich: Er ist der Anlaß, der erlaubt von der Sache, der *unio mystica*, zu reden." Alois M. Haas, "Die 'Theologia Deutsch': Konstitution eines mystologischen Texts," in *Das 'einig Ein': Studien zu Theorie und Sprache der deutschen Mystik*, ed. Alois M. Haas and Heinrich Stirnimann (Freiburg: Universitätsverlag Freiburg Schweiz, 1980): 369–415; here, 380–81.

207. In his *Operationes in Psalmos* (1519–1521), Luther criticized "mystical theology" for trying to bypass the incarnate and crucified Word in order to obtain union with the eternal, divine word; see chapter 2.

208. Haas, "Die 'Theologia Deutsch,'" 369–70, writes that the text contains "eine ausgebreitete Fülle von inhaltlich varierten Betrachtungen um letztlich ein und dasselbe Thema: die gnadenhafte Vergottung des Menschen im Lichte der vermittelnden Vorbildlichkeit des Lebens Christi." See also Zecherle, "Die 'Theologia Deutsch,'" 19–21.

209. Chapter 1, MTD 7.1f.; HTG, 60. The author equates knowing with the direct coming of the complete to the imperfect; it comes "wenn es [the whole], als ferre als muglich ist, bekant und enpfunden unnd geschmeckt wirt yn der seel."

210. Chapter 2, MTD 10.3f.; HTG 61–62; also Chapter 3, MTD 11.2–9; HTG 62.

211. Chapter 4, MTD 12.11–18; HTG 63–64; Chapter 5, MTD 13.15–14.9; HTG 64–65. In the incarnation, according to the Frankfurter, Christ's humanity "was nothing but a house or a habitation for God. His humanity belonged to God." See Chapter 13, MTD 32.12–23; HTG 76–77.

212. Chapters 13–14, MTD 31.1f.; HTG 76–77.

213. Chapter 34, MTD 66.4f.; HTG, 108–109. The discussion here concludes (MTD 66.24–25): "Adam, icheit und selbheit, eigenwillickeit, sünd oder der alt, (sic.) mensch und abkeren und abgscheiden von got, daz ist alles eins." See also Chapter 41, MTD 85.10–14; HTG, 129–30; Chapter 42, MTD 85.15f; HTG 130; and Chapter 45, MTD 89.7f.; HTG, 134–35. On the "doing or suffering," see Chapter 45, MTD 90.3–9; HTG 135.

214. Chapter 5, MTD 14.10–11: "Das ich mich icht gutes an nem, das kumpt von wone [Meinung] es sey mein ader ich sey es"; the truth is not "ynn myr bekant."

215. See, e.g., Chapter 29, MTD 59.3–12; HTG, 101; Chapter 30, MTD 60.12f.; HTG 102–103; and Chapter 48, MTD 91.28f.; HTG 137.

216. The eternal will "originally and essentially" in God is without work or actuality; but will *qua* will is compelled to activity. For the human person, the goal is for God's will to be "purely and fully present" in him, so that "God would do the willing there, not man, and the will would be one with and flow into the eternal will." Chapter 49, MTD 92.32f.; HTG 138–39. For a detailed analysis of the text's teaching concerning God's dependence on creation, see Wegener, '*Der Frankfurter*', 313–83.

217. Chapters 48–49, MTD 92.14–94.3; HTG, 137–39. Chapter 48 explains that human knowing ("bekentnus und vernunft"), which is "mit dem willen geschaffen und gegeben," should instruct the will and itself "das weder bekentnus oder wille von ym selber ist, oder das ir keins sein selbs ist oder sein sol, [etc.] . . .; sunder von dem sie sind, des sind sie auch, und dem sollen sie gelassen sein und wider dar yn fliessen, und werden yn selber zu nichte, das ist an ir selbheit."

218. Chapter 3, MTD 11f.; HTG 62–63; on the divinized life, see, e.g., Chapter 14, MTD 36.14–37.6; HTG 80; Chapter 30, MTD 60.27–61.21; HTG 103–104; and Chapter 31, MTD 61.22–62.4; HTG 104.

219. Chapter 3, MTD 12.1–8 (my translation; aided by HTG 63).

220. Chapter 10, MTD 23.5–6 (my translation; see also HTG 71). See also chapter 9, MTD 21.14f.; and chapter 56, MTD 102.15–103.3.

221. On the true versus false light, see esp. Chapter 29, MTD 57.15–20; HTG 101, which notes that "true light is the eternal light, which is the same as God. It also manifests itself as created light, godly or divine, termed grace. . . . [T]he false light is nature or of nature." In Chapter 38, 71.12–76.26; HTG 114–20, we read, "It is an essential quality of the true Light that It does not know deceit, is not inspired by the will to deceive, and that It cannot be deceived." The false light serves the striving of created nature for "special gain" or a "particular good," rather than the Good for the sake of the Good; the false light pleases and deceives "the I, the Me, and its outgrowths." Nature's self-seeking is the "first and basic deception." The Frankfurter writes, "Man fancies himself to be what he is not. He fancies himself to be God, yet he is only na-ture, a created being. From within that illusion he begins to claim for himself the traits that are marks of God. He does not claim only what is God's insofar as God becomes man or dwells in a divinized person. No, he claims what is the innermost of God, God's prime mark, namely the uncreated, eternal being" (MTD 71.15–72.15; HTG 115–16).

222. Chapter 10, MTD 24.1–9; HTG, 72: "Wir wollen als gestrichen [gestreichelt] seyn, alßo das wier yn uns großen smack und sußickeyt und lust yn uns finden. . . . Wan ein war liebhabender mensch hat got oder das ewig gut gleich lieb yn haben und yn darben, yn suß und yn saur und des gleich."

223. Chapter 11, MTD 25.1f. (my translation; see also HTG 72–74).

224. Chapter 14, MTD 36.14–37.6; HTG 80. According to chapter 36, MTD 68.5f.; HTG 111–12, the divinized life "is so deep that it can never be quite abandoned and rejected," despite the unavoidable "divine sorrow." Only those who presume falsely

to live the Christ life—driven by use or desire for reward—would ever abandon that (presumed) divine life or sorrow.

225. Chapter 22, MTD 45.12–46.16; HTG 89–90. On God's grieving over sin in and through the person, see chapter 35, MTD 67.14–68.4; HTG 109–10. On the free spirits' claim to "live in an un-suffering way," see Chapter 15, MTD 37.7f.; HTG 81–82.

226. Chapter 12, MTD 28.15–29.10; HTG 74–75. According to the Frankfurter, even the devil has "peace (*frid*)" when things "go according to his will and pleasure," but Christ's peace is inward, so that "all chosen friends of God and true followers (*nachvolger*) of Christ" remain "joyful and patient (*frölich und gedultig*)" in every kind of suffering.

227. Chapter 16, MTD 38.6–13; HTG 82 (translation altered).

228. Chapter 18, MTD 40.10–26; HTG 84 (translation altered).

229. Chapters 16–17, MTD 38.13–40.9; HTG 82–84. The knowledge that enables one to see the best in what is contrary to nature (the Christ life) is a seeing from the perspective of the whole. This knowledge must be given directly by God and cannot be attained through "much questioning or secondhand information or by way of reading and studying, or with high skills and academic mastery, or with high natural reasoning."

230. According to chapter 40, MTD 79.18f.; HTG 123–25, the false light loves knowledge more than its proper object; but it cannot know God or the Good, only the self, because it does not love God. The false light imagines itself to have transcended the Christ life, "wan es will nit Christus sein, sunder es wil got sein in ewigkeit. Das ist davon: Wan Christus und sein leben ist aller natur wider und schwer. Darumb wil die natur nit dar an, sunder wil got sein yn ewigkeit und nit mensch, oder wil Christus sein nach der urstend, das ist alles liecht, lustig, und gemachsam der natur. Darum hat sie es fu[o]r das peste, wan sie meynt, es sey ir pestes" (MTD 80.14–21).

231. On this phrasing, see also Chapter 24, MTD 49.2–3 (HTG 92); Chapter 26, MTD 54.7–8 (HTG 97); and Chapter 33, MTD, 65.1–4 (HTG 107). I deviate in my translation from HTG's rendering of "leidender" as "compassion."

232. Chapter 21, MTD 44.9–45.1 (my translation; aided by HTG 88–89). The suffering of God and non-retaliation for the harms inflicted by others marks the Christ life; see, e.g., Chapter 41, MTD 82.21f.; HTG 127f.; Chapter 44, MTD 88.12–25; HTG 133f.; and Chapter 51, MTD 95.15–96.12; HTG 141f. Note the distinction in the last-cited section between true and false freedom.

233. Chapter 23, MTD 47.1f.; HTG 90–91.

234. Chapter 24, MTD 48.24–52.15 (my translation). The spiritually poor person "finds" that he is unworthy of anything done to him by God or creatures, that he is "schuldig" before God and thus before all creatures "an gots stat yn leydender weiß und auch etwan yn tu[o]nder weis." Here the person feels, "Es ist billich und recht, das gott und all creaturen wider mich seien und recht uber mich und zu myr haben und ich wider niemantz sey and zu nicht recht hab."

235. Chapter 25–26, MTD 53.8–54.26 (my translation; aided by HTG, 96–97).

236. Chapter 40, MTD 78.26f.; HTG 122–26.

237. Chapter 27, MTD 54.27f.; HTG 98–99.
238. Chapter 38, MTD 72.16f.; HTG 116–17. The text claims here that God in God's self is not moved and does not suffer, "but wherever God is human and in a deified person, there things are different" (my translation).
239. See also the discussion in Schreiner, *Are You Alone Wise?*, 236–37.
240. Chapter 38, MTD 73.30f. (my translation; see also HTG 117–18). Like the preface, .the final chapters of the *German Theology* that appeared in Luther's editions were added to the original text by a later author. This author interprets the Frankfurter's teachings on the Christ-life and their application against the free spirits through Christ's command in Matthew 10:38 to take up the cross and through John 14:6 ("No one comes to the Father except through me"), writing, "Auch wer ym volgen will, der sol das creutz an sich nemen, und daz creutz ist anders nit denn Christus leben, wan das ist ein pitter creutz aller nature.... Aber die frey, falsch natur meynt, sie hab alles gelassen: sie will aber des creutzes nit und spricht, sie hab sein genug gehaben und durff sein nymer, und ist betrogen." MTD 96.32f.
241. DTRG, G3r, does contain the note, "Ein v[er]gotter mensch."
242. DTRG, B1v. Only this gloss uses the term, "Annemlickeyt"; at C4v a gloss reads, "Des guten soll sich nemands annhemen." Many annotations, nonetheless, point to discussions of the sinner's appropriation of divine good for the self: B1v, "Mercke wz hatt Ada[m]s sunde groß gemacht"; B2r, "wo durch gott gehindert wirt"; annotations on B2r, B3r, and C1r explain that all good belongs to God. Here, I focus on the annotations themselves; for relevant cross-references to Karlstadt's writings, see chapter 4.
243. DTRG, F3r. Later in the text, the gloss, "Was do sunde sey," appears next to the explanation, "[S]und ist anders wo[e]llen oder begeren oder lieb haben den got." DTRG, H4v.
244. DTRG, H3r.
245. DTRG, C2v–C4v; a gloss on F3r reads, "Sund ist gruntlicher vngehorsam."
246. DTRG, C1v–C2r.
247. In addition to the passage discussed here, see DTRG, G4v, "Christus leben ist aller natur wider"; I3v, "Die natur vnd Chr[ist]us leben seynn wider eyna[n]der. Chr[ist]us lebe[n] ist ei[n] creutz der natur."
248. DTRG, D1r–v. Glosses at D1v–D2r pick up on the Frankfurter's critique of natural reason; on faith and knowledge, note also the gloss at I1r, "Wyssen kumpt auß glauben."
249. DTRG, D2v. See also H4r, "Christe[n]thu[m] steet in warer gelassenheyt."
250. DTRG, D4v; on "humility" and "spiritual poverty," see also E1v, F2r–v.
251. DTRG, E2r. On self-will versus union with the divine will, see also I1r–I3v.
252. DTRG, F2r.

Chapter 2

1. WA 1: 614.28–29; LW 31: 226–27.
2. See esp. Ernst Kähler, "Die 95 Thesen:Inhalt und Bedeutung," Luther 38, no. 3 (1967): 114–24.

3. For an account of the controversy, see Scott Hendrix, *Martin Luther: Visionary Reformer* (New Haven, CT: Yale University Press, 2015), 55–67; Martin Brecht, *Martin Luther*, trans. James L. Schaaf, 3 vols. (Minneapolis: Fortress, 1985–1993), 1: 175–221.

4. Luther's rhetoric frequently implies a monolithic view of scholastic theology and theologians; it is not my purpose to endorse that view. Luther himself knew not all scholastic theologians were the same!

5. Hendrix, *Martin Luther*, 56, 71.

6. See Luther's *Disputation Against Scholastic Theology*, WA 1: 224.1–228.37, LW 31: 1–16.

7. On scholastic theologies of justification and Luther's critique of them, see Heiko A. Oberman, *The Harvest of Medieval Theology: Gabriel Biel and Late Medieval Nominalism* (Grand Rapids, MI: Baker, 2000 [1963]); Oberman, *Dawn of the Reformation: Essays in Late Medieval and Early Reformation Thought* (Grand Rapids, MI: William B. Eerdmans, 1992), 52–125; and Steven Ozment, *The Age of Reform 1250–1550: An Intellectual and Religious History of Late Medieval and Reformation Europe* (New Haven, CT: Yale University Press, 1980), 22–42, 231–39. Ockham was a foundational figure for the *via moderna*, whose followers held to a nominalist epistemology, employed the dialectic of God's absolute and ordained power, and saw salvation as governed by a free divine covenant with humanity. Ockham and Biel appealed to these views in defending their perspective on salvation, but other *moderni*, including Gregory of Rimini (d. 1358), drew different soteriological conclusions. Accordingly, I refer specifically to Ockham, Biel, and their use of the phrase, "facere quod in se est." I will avoid the term "nominalism"; see Alister E. McGrath, *Luther's Theology of the Cross: Martin Luther's Theological Breakthrough*, 2nd ed. (Oxford: Wiley-Blackwell, 2011).

8. On Luther's transformation of mysticism, see Volker Leppin, *Die fremde Reformation: Luthers mystische Wurzeln* (München: C. H. Beck, 2016), esp. 117–38. On Luther as the representative of an evangelical mysticism, see Berndt Hamm, "Wie mystisch war der Glaube Luthers?" in GN, 237–88; Hamm argues that Luther's democratization and intensification of mysticism involved the removal of preconditions for the experience of divine nearness. For an English version of the essay see Hamm, EL, 190–232, which is a translation of Hamm, DfL, 200–50. For the concept of "democratization," see McGinn, *Presence*, 3: 12–13 (also discussing the accompanying process of "secularization"); Oberman, *Dawn*, 126–54; here, 140; and Oberman, *Harvest*, 341–43.

9. Ronald K. Rittgers, *The Reformation of the Keys: Confession, Conscience, and Authority in Sixteenth-Century Germany* (Cambridge, MA: Harvard University Press, 2004), 29–30.

10. Despite this scriptural foundation, "the doctrine of absolution remained unorganized to the scholastic age." See John T. McNeill and Helena M. Gamer, *Medieval Handbooks of Penance: A Translation of the Principal Libri Poenitentiales* (New York: Columbia University Press, 1938), 7; quoted in Rittgers, *Reformation of the Keys*, 30.

11. Rittgers, *Reformation of the Keys*, 30, notes, "By the seventh and eighth centuries theologians had devised precise formulas for calculating how much payment (that is, penance) God was due for every kind of human moral transgression." Hamm, RF, 129, notes that "the ecclesiastical penitential system of the period made pivotal the external works of contrition—i.e. the satisfaction (*satisfactio*), not the soul's inner pangs of remorse for its transgression. The Irish penitential manuals . . . regard fasting as the most important form of penance."

12. Anselm of Canterbury, "Why God Became Man," in *Anselm of Canterbury: The Major Works*, ed. Brian Davies and G.R. Evans (Oxford: Oxford University Press, 1998), 260–356; here, 283. On Anselm: R. W. Southern, *Saint Anselm: A Portrait in a Landscape* (Cambridge: Cambridge University Press, 1990).

13. Rittgers, *Reformation of the Keys*, 31–33, 39.

14. For a classic, detailed discussion of the development of the idea of purgatory, see Jacques Le Goff, *The Birth of Purgatory*, trans. Arthur Goldhammer (Chicago: University of Chicago Press, 1984), 4–7, 131, 227.

15. Thomas N. Tentler, *Sin and Confession on the Eve of the Reformation* (Princeton, NJ: Princeton University Press, 1977), argues that the focus of theologians on inward contrition was itself a response to the lenient imposition of satisfactions. See also Rittgers, *Reformation of the Keys*, 39; and Berndt Hamm, *Frömmigkeitstheologie am Anfang des 16. Jahrhunderts: Studien zu Johannes von Paltz und seinem Umkreis* (Tübingen: J. C. B. Mohr [Paul Siebeck], 1982), 3.

16. Hamm, RF, 131–34.

17. Ibid., 134–36.

18. According to ibid., 135–36, such contritionism represented a "consensus" among twelfth- and thirteenth-century scholastic theologians: "inner reconciliation with God" becomes the decisive aspect of penance and precedes participation in the outward sacrament.

19. Rittgers, *The Reformation of the Keys*, 39–40.

20. Hamm, *Frömmigkeitstheologie*, esp. 3–8, 247–303.

21. Rittgers, *The Reformation of the Keys*, 40–44. On Luther's relationship to the varied schools of thought, see David C. Steinmetz, *Luther in Context*, 2nd ed. (Grand Rapids, MI: Baker Academic, 2002), 1–11. The three schools of thought on penance corresponded to three kinds of preaching according to Anne T. Thayer, *Penitence, Preaching, and the Coming of the Reformation* (Aldershot: Ashgate, 2002); see also Hamm, RF, 50–87 ("Between Severity and Mercy: Three Models of Pre-Reformation Urban Reform Preaching: Savonarola—Staupitz—Geiler").

22. According to Hamm, RF, 138–39, mystical literature now often excluded the ascent above devotion to the suffering humanity to higher stages of spiritual love described by Bernard of Clairvaux, among others; ascendant instead was a mysticism that bound the "grace of love . . . to the inner relationship of the painful, contrite heart to the suffering Christ and to a lifelong existence of identification with the tortured Son of Man."

23. Hamm, RF, 138–41, argues that "compared with the 12th century, the emphasis swings again more heavily to the external dimension of penitence, to the sacrament of

penance with confession and absolution by the priest and the works of satisfaction by the sinner."

24. John Bossy, *Christianity in the West, 1400–1700* (Oxford: Oxford University Press, 1985), 55; see also Bernd Moeller, "Piety in Germany Around 1500," in *The Reformation in Medieval Perspective*, ed. Steven E. Ozment (Chicago: Quadrangle Books, 1971), 50–75.

25. Moeller, "Piety in Germany," 52–56. Moeller argues as well that fifteenth-century Christians little questioned the legitimacy and authority of the church: "The willingness and indeed the desire to sanctify worldly life within the framework of the institutions created by the Church and with the help of the treasures of grace she offered were hardly as generally widespread at any other time in the Middle Ages and have never been more clearly visible." The laity "presupposed the competence and capacity of the Church for the achievement of salvation just as naturally as they did the value and necessity of good works for the same purpose."

26. Ozment arguesd in *The Reformation in the Cities: The Appeal of Protestantism to Sixteenth-Century Germany and Switzerland* (New Haven, CT: Yale University Press, 1975), 21–22, 78, and in *The Age of Reform 1250–1550: An Intellectual and Religious History of Late Medieval and Reformation Europe* (New Haven, CT: Yale University Press, 1980), 219, that late-medieval religion involved the "imposition" of monastic and clerical ideals, especially obedience and celibacy, upon the laity. Ozment's perspective remained constant through his more popular work, *Protestants: The Birth of a Revolution* (New York: Doubleday, 1991).

27. Ozment, *Reformation in the Cities*, 50, 77, 118.

28. For a summary of the relevant scholarship, see Ronald K. Rittgers, "Anxious Penitents and the Appeal of the Reformation: Ozment and the Historiography of Confession," in *Piety and Family in Early Modern Europe: Essays in Honour of Steven Ozment*, ed. Marc R. Forstor and Benjamin J. Kaplan (Aldershot: Ashgate, 2005), 50–69. For a broad summary and balanced assessment of whether fear and anxiety marked late-medieval religion, see Susan E. Schreiner, *Are You Alone Wise? The Search for Certainty in the Early Modern Era* (Oxford: Oxford University Press, 2011), 41–48. A significant challenge to Ozment's thesis was offered by Lawrence G. Duggan, "Fear and Confession on the Eve of the Reformation," ARG 75 (1984): 153–75; Duggan noted (p. 155) that Protestants frequently protested the laxity of confession rather than the severity. It is most helpful, in my view, to see Protestants as imposing or removing burdens according to whatever they believed aligned with the truth of salvation by grace, faith, and Christ alone; Luther summoned Christians to true suffering contrary to self-will, while he cautioned about false suffering.

29. Carter Lindberg, *The European Reformations*, 2nd ed. (Malden, MA: Wiley-Blackwell, 2010), 56–60.

30. Rittgers, "Anxious Penitents," 68–69; see also *Reformation of the Keys*, 29, 45–46, 57.

31. Schreiner, *Are You Alone Wise?*, 48–62.

32. Richard Kieckhefer, "The Notion of Passivity in the Sermons of John Tauler." Recherches de théologie ancienne et médiévale XLVIII (1981), 198–211; Lydia Wegener, *Der 'Frankfurter'/'Theologia Deutsch': Spielräume und Grenzen des Sagbaren* (Berlin: De Gruyter, 2016), here esp. 302–12.

33. Brecht, *Martin Luther*, 1: 176–78; Ozment, *The Age of Reform*, 216–17.
34. On the aspects of medieval devotion discussed in this paragraph, see esp. Kevin Madigan, *Medieval Christianity: A New History* (New Haven, CT: Yale University Press, 2015), 320–39, 430–33.
35. See WA 54: 179f., esp. 185.12–186.24.
36. For this perspective, see Berndt Hamm, "Naher Zorn und nahe Gnade: Luthers frühe Klosterjahre als Beginn seiner reformatorischen Neuorientierung," in *Reformation und Mönchtum: Aspekte eines Verhältnisses über Luther hinaus*, ed. Athina Lexutt, Volker Mantey, and Volkmar Ortmann (Tübingen: Mohr Siebeck, 2008), 103–43; here, 105–107; this essay is available in Hamm, EL, 26–58 (=Hamm, DfL, 25–64). Volker Leppin has also underlined the gradualism of Luther's theological development; in addition to the work cited elsewhere in this book, see his *Martin Luther*, 2nd ed. (Darmstadt: WBG, 2010).
37. On Luther's relationship and debts to the *via moderna*, see Ozment, *Age of Reform*, 231–39; and Steinmetz, *Luther in Context*, 18. McGrath, *Luther's Theology of the Cross*, discussed later in this chapter, argues that Luther's primary theological formation came through *via moderna* theologians. Hamm, RF, 153–78, argues that Luther's theology was shaped by the medieval scholastic definition of faith as receptive (it "receives and accepts" the absolute truth) and a "relationship ad extra."
38. For one concise summary of the varied influences, see Bernhard Lohse, "Luther und Bernhard von Clairvaux," in *Bernhard von Clairvaux: Rezeption und Wirkung im Mittelalter und in der Neuzeit*, ed. Kaspar Elm (Wiesbaden: Harrassowitz, 1994), 271–302; here, 272–76.
39. Hamm, "Naher Zorn," esp. 142–43, "Auch theologisch, insbesondere kreuzestheologisch ist schwer zu begründen, weshalb man eigentlich nur in der getrosten und befreiten Freude der Heilsgewissheit die Wende zu einer reformatorischen Gottesbeziehung sehen soll, nicht aber auch bereits in einer neuen Dimension von Dunkelheit und Bitterkeit, Schmerz und Seufzen, in einer angsterfüllten Verzweiflung an Gott und sich selbst. Für Luther jedenfalls gehörten die zwei Seiten der Heilsweges untrennbar zusammen, sowohl in seinen autobiographischen Rückblicken als auch in der Architektur seiner Theologie: das erschreckende Gesetz und das beseligende Evangelium. Die erschütternde Anfechtung verstand er als notwendige Voraussetzung des glaubenden Vertrauens auf Gotes Verheißung allein. In Gottes gütiger Führung sah er beides miteinander verklammert: die Nähe des richtenden Zorns und die Nähe der rettenden Gnade." Hamm notes Luther's 1532 statement, "Ich hab mein theologiam nit auff ein mal gelernt, sonder hab ymmer tieffer und tieffer grubeln mussen, da haben mich meine tentationes hin bracht, quia sine usu non potest disci." Ibid., 105n6, citing WATR 1: 146.12–14. See also WA 18: 719.9–12 (*De servo arbitrio* [1525], quoted in Hamm, "Naher Zorn," 111n26).
40. There was controversy in the medieval period over whether the infusion of *caritas* was to be understood as a created *habitus* or as the "direct, personal act of God" through the Holy Spirit; Luther in his marginalia to Lombard's sentences (1509–1510)

accepted the latter position, standing in continuity with his predecessor in the Augustinian eremites, Gregory of Rimini (d. 1358). See McGrath, *Luther's Theology of the Cross*, 88, 109–12.

41. For this and the next paragraph, see: Oberman, *Dawn*, 104–25; Oberman, *Forerunners of the Reformation: The Shape of Late Medieval Thought Illustrated by Key Documents* (Philadelphia: Fortress, 1981 [1966]), 123–41; and Ozment, *The Age of Reform*, 22–42.

42. Aquinas's views developed on this point, resulting in a conflict of interpretation. See Oberman, *Harvest*, 141–45.

43. This was not, as Luther and anti-Pelagians before him charged, a simple reassertion of the heresy of Pelagius; in the view of Ockham and Biel, grace in the form of the covenant precedes human action for salvation. God unchangeably binds God's self to accept imperfect moral acts as the condition for special grace and the forgiveness of sins, and subsequent cooperation with grace is necessary to the performance of condign merits. See McGrath, *Luther's Theology of the Cross*, 80–83. Pelagius did not hold this theology of the covenant, nor could he have anticipated the medieval scholastic distinctions between "congruous" and "condign" merits.

44. See my discussion of the late-medieval reception of Augustine in the preceding chapter, and the scholarship cited there.

45. On these points, see esp. Hamm, *Frömmigkeitstheologie*, 216f.

46. Hamm, "Naher Zorn," 114, 119–20.

47. Already in his first Psalm lectures (the *Dictata super Psalterium*), Luther criticized the notion that grace instills an inward habit or virtue by which one can will good works or earn salvation: "Das Einzige, was dem Menschen zu tun bleibt, ist das Eingeständnis, nichts tun zu können, und das flehentliche Bittgebet zu Gott." Ibid., 123–25, 141.

48. For a recent, balanced analysis of Luther's view in the *Dictata*, see Rittgers, *The Reformation of Suffering*, 87–94.

49. McGrath, *Luther's Theology of the Cross*, 171–72, 193, contends that Luther came already in the course of the *Dictata* to regard the *iustitia fidei* or *humilitas*—the two terms are at this time nearly identical, says McGrath—as a divine gift, rather than a human achievement. This was a decisive break with the notion of "facere quod in se est," even as Luther's humility theology held to the covenant idea of the *via moderni*: God freely establishes a *pactum* to give grace to those who humble themselves. But if God gives the humility, God's "involvement in human justification" now exceeds the "establishment of a generalized covenantal framework within which justification takes place." Taking Luther's new conception of *iustitia* as decisive, McGrath argues that Luther gradually reoriented his thought around it—a process completed only in the 1519 *Operationes*.

50. Debate was unleashed by Ernst Bizer, *Fides ex auditu: Eine Untersuchung über die Entdeckung der Gerechtigkeit Gottes durch Martin Luther* (Verlag der Buchhandlung des Erziehungsvereins Neukirchen Kreis Moers, 1958), 110f., who saw a clear break with humility theology and a clear expression of evangelical theology first in Luther's

defense before Cajetan, published as the *Acta Augustana* in November 1518. See also the discussion of McGrath's views, centered on the concept of *iustitia*, in the preceding note.

51. For the latter question, see the discussion and scholarship cited by Rittgers, *The Reformation of Suffering*, 115–16.

52. For the view that the *95 Theses* express Luther's early "humility theology," see Brecht, *Martin Luther*, I: 198; and Bizer, *Fides ex auditu*, 76–96, who includes the *Explanations* in this assessment but does not discuss the *Heidelberg Disputation* specifically. Regarding the *Heidelberg Disputation*, Brecht, *Martin Luther*, I: 234, argues that Luther's "genuinely new position," appears only in the final three theses; the first 24 represent "really only another summary of the critical theology of humility." See also Brecht, *Martin Luther*, I: 224, on the *Explanations*.

53. Volker Leppin, "Omnen vitam fidelium penitentiam esse voluit'—Zur Aufnahme mystischer Traditionen in Luthers erster Ablaßthese," ARG 93 (2002), 7–25; 22–25.

54. Hamm, DfL, 90–114 ("Die 95 Thesen—ein reformatorischer Text im Zusammenhang der frühen Bußtheologie Martin Luthers"); here, 109–11; now translated in Hamm, EL, 85–109. See also Hamm, RF, 149: "after 1516, faith and contrition drift further apart in [Luther's] writings. Faith remains connected to contrition—there is no faith in Christ without pain of repentance, but faith itself now loses its characteristic note of pain and takes on for Luther the characteristic of the undoubting, joyful confidence which clings to the word of promise in the Gospel, to that biblical promise which assures the sinner personally: your sins are forgiven."

55. See the next chapter.

56. Hamm, RF, 149–52.

57. On Luther's turn to the word of forgiveness in the sacrament, see Jared Wicks, "*Fides sacramenti—fides specialis*: Luther's Development in 1518," in *Luther's Reform: Studies on Conversion and the Church* (Mainz: Philipp von Zabern, 1992), 117–48; see also *Man Yearning for Grace: Luther's Early Spiritual Teaching* (Washington: Corpus Books, 1968), 216–64; Rittgers, *The Reformation of Suffering*, 107–108; and Schreiner, *Are You Alone Wise?*, 55, who writes, "Luther's purpose was to replace trust in anything subjectively human, including the experience of one's own disposition, with the certainty of the *fides sacramenti*."

58. On the oft-discussed question of whether Luther posted the theses on the Castle Church door, see Hendrix, *Martin Luther*, 59–61; either way, the theses became a matter of ecclesial and public concern because Luther sent them to Albert of Brandenburg, who forwarded them to Rome for judgment.

59. This point is made by Rittgers, *The Reformation of Suffering*, 105, citing Mark U. Edwards Jr, *Printing, Propaganda, and Martin Luther* (Berkeley: University of California Press, 1994), 163, 169. Rittgers points out that *95 Theses* were "rather complicated" and their "impact, though significant, was limited to humanists, theologians, and other elites."

60. Kähler, "Die 95 Thesen," 123; for the organization and argument of the *95 Theses*, see also Wicks, *Man Yearning*, 232–38.

61. I quote the theses as they appear in the *Resolutiones/Explanations*, WA 1: 525–628, LW 31: 83–252; there are small differences between the theses here and in their separate earlier printing (WA 1: 233–38).

62. Thus, if the analysis in this chapter presents a snapshot of Luther's theological development, that snapshot pertains to early 1518, not the fall of 1517.

63. Kähler, "Die 95 Thesen," 118, 124. According to Bizer, *Fides ex auditu*, 92–94, forgiveness in the *Resolutiones* is still given for contrition, not faith; Hamm, DfL, 111n82, rejects this interpretation because Luther had already broken with the notion of contrition as a virtue. Still, Luther in this transitional phase seems to attribute salvific significance to the sense of nothingness before God; this sense is the other side of faith's coin.

64. WA 1: 531.15–18; LW 31: 84–85.

65. WA 1: 530.26–531.3; LW 31: 84.

66. WA 1: 531.29–38; LW 31: 85. For Thesis 36, see WA 1: 592.34–37; LW 31: 189.

67. WA 1: 532.1–32; LW 31: 86–87.

68. WA 1: 533.35–534.4; LW 31: 88–89.

69. WA 1: 534.11–534.18; LW 31: 89. On death as the "greatest punishment" and voluntary death as the pinnacle of holiness, see WA 1: 547.4f.; LW 31: 110–11.

70. WA 1: 554.32–33; LW 31: 124.

71. WA 1: 554.27–555.25; LW 31: 124–25.

72. For a discussion, see Hamm, DfL, 91–92. Luther adds that the pope himself does not want to remit these *poenae*.

73. WA 1: 534.24–30; LW 31: 90.

74. WA 1: 554.26–567.24; LW 31: 123–145 (Theses 14–19). For further discussion of Luther's (and Karlstadt's) developing views around purgatory and ghosts, see Vincent Evener, "Wittenberg's Wandering Spirits: Discipline and the Dead in the Reformation," CH 84, no. 3 (September 2015), 531–55.

75. WA 1: 557.25–558.8; LW 31: 129.

76. WA 1: 557.29–32; LW 31: 129.

77. WA 1: 534.31–535.7; LW 31: 90. The translation of "Haec est crux illa et mortificatio passionum" is my own; LW has "the cross of mortification and suffering."

78. WA 1: 535.8–39; LW 31: 91–92.

79. WA 1: 535.40–536.LW 31: 92–93.

80. WA 1: 537.7–11; LW 31: 94.

81. See Scott H. Hendrix, *Luther and the Papacy: Stages in a Reformation Conflict* (Philadelphia: Fortress, 1981).

82. WA 1: 540.8–34; LW 31: 99–100.

83. WA 1: 540.34–41; LW 31: 100.

84. On this move, and Cajetan's repudiation of it, see Wicks, "*Fides sacramenti*."

85. WA 1: 540.41–541.11; LW 31: 100–101; see also WA 1: 596.19–23; LW 31: 196.

86. WA 1: 541.16–20; LW 31: 101 (translation altered).

87. WA 1: 541.20–24, 542.7–12; LW 31: 101–102.

88. See also the discussion of Thesis 40, WA 1: 597.2–23; LW 31: 197.

89. For all these themes in Tauler, see the preceding chapter.

90. WA 1: 542.24-34; LW 31: 103.

91. WA 1: 542.34-543.2; LW 31: 103.

92. WA 1: 543.3-544.8; LW 31: 103-105. The explication of Thesis 37, WA 1: 593.4f.; LW 31: 190-91, offers some of the strongest statements about the centrality of faith and union with Christ in Christian life. See esp. WA 1: 594.37-595.5 (LW 31: 193), "Ideo fide ubique opus est. Tantum habes quantum credis."

93. WA 1: 544.40-545.6; LW 31: 107.

94. Leppin, *Die fremde Reformation*, 41.

95. See Schreiner, *Are You Alone Wise?*, 79-129.

96. Only the explanation to Thesis 26 is of similar length.

97. WA 1: 605.27-29; LW 31: 212.

98. WA 1: 606.12-30, 607.18-21; LW 31: 213, 215. Here, Luther was certain, "Speaking boldly, I declare that I have no doubt about those things I have just now said, rather I am prepared to endure death by fire for them, and I maintain that everyone who holds the contrary is a heretic."

99. WA 1: 607.22-27; LW 31: 215.

100. WA 1: 608.17-609.8; LW 31: 216-18.

101. WA 1: 611.8-9; LW 31: 221.

102. WA 1: 611.21f.; LW 31: 222.

103. WA 1: 612.40-613.2; LW 31: 224.

104. WA 1: 613.12-20; LW 31: 225.

105. On the theology of the cross as a "principle of Luther's entire theology" that "may not be confined to a special period in his theological development," see classically, Walther von Loewenich, *Luther's Theology of the Cross*, trans. Herbert J.A. Bouman (Minneapolis: Augsburg, 1976 [a translation of the 5th German edition of 1967]), 12-13. Robert Kolb, "Luther's Theology of the Cross Fifteen Years after Heidelberg: Lectures on the Psalms of Ascent," JEH 60, no. 1 (January 2010), 69-85, shows that the theology of the cross continued to shape Luther's teaching long after 1518; see also Kolb's earlier essay, "Luther on the Theology of the Cross," LQ 16 (2002), 443-66. Rittgers, *The Reformation of Suffering*, 111-24, sees the "theology of the cross" as central to the consolation for suffering that Luther developed.

106. See Ronald K. Rittgers, "Embracing the 'True Relic' of Christ: Suffering, Penance, and Private Confession in the Thought of Martin Luther," in *A New History of Penance*, ed. Abigail Firey (Leiden: Brill, 2008), 377-94.

107. WA 1: 613.11-33; LW 31: 225-26. On the alleged deceitfulness of Scholastic theology, see Luther's strong words at WA 1: 620.35-37; LW 31: 238: "[W]ith what severity do we feel they should be punished who offer weapons, not to the Turks, but to demons, and supply them, not with any kind of weapons but our own, that is the Word of God, while they contaminate that Word with their fancies and, as Isaiah used to say, melt it down into an idol by their spirit [Cf. Isa. 40:19], so that it is no longer an instrument by which the soul is attracted to God but rather seduced into false opinions? . . . They 'have taken away the key of knowledge; they do not enter themselves and they hinder those who are entering' [Cf. Luke 11:52]."

108. WA 1: 614.18-27; LW 31: 227.

109. WA 1: 614.28–30; LW 31: 227.

110. On Luther's assessment of pilgrimages in 1518, see also WA 1: 597.29–598.17; LW 31: 198–99. Regarding the valorization of everyday life in its connection to God-pleasing suffering, see also WA 1: 531.4–13; LW 31: 84.

111. WA 1: 613.33–614.14; LW 31: 226–27.

112. Luther had previously, in Thesis 60, identified the power of the keys as the treasure of the church.

113. WA 1: 616.20–617.3; LW 31: 230–31.

114. WA 1: 617.5–15; LW 31: 232 (emphasis added).

115. WA 1: 617.26–27 ("verbum enim dulce trahit voluntatem, immo facit voluntatem hominis in Christum"); LW 31: 232–33.

116. WA 1: 622.2–25; LW 31: 241.

117. Especially helpful concering the Hidelberg Disputation is Karl-Heinz Zur Mühlen, *Reformatorisches Profil: Studien zum Weg Martin Luthers und der Reformation*, ed. Johannes Brosseder and Athina Lexutt (Göttingen: Vandenhoeck und Ruprecht, 1995), 174–98 ("Die Heidelberger Disputation Martin Luthers vom 26. April 1518: Programm und Wirkung"); here, 174–77. Zur Mühlen posits that the Eremites wanted "a learned clarification of the Luther affair." See also Heinrich Bornkamm, *Luther: Gestalt und Wirkungen, Gesammelte Aufsätze* (Gütersloh: Gütersloher Verlagshaus Gerd Mohn, 1975), 130–46 ("Die theologischen Thesen Luthers bei der Heidelberger Disputation 1518 und seine theologia crucis"). For a recent account in the context of a Luther biography: Hendrix, *Martin Luther*, 68–71.

118. Zur Mühlen, *Reformatorisches Profil*, 178.

119. Bornkamm, *Luther: Gestalt*, 131–33; repeated by Jos E. Vercruysse, "Gesetz und Liebe: Die Struktur der 'Heidelberger Disputation' Luthers (1518)." LJ (1981), 7–43.

120. Vercruysse, "Gesetz und Liebe," 8–10, 42–43.

121. Theses 3–4, WA 1: 353.19–22; LW 31: 39.

122. WA 1.356.37–358.17; LW 31.44 (translation slightly altered). The lines immediately following these quoted remarks can be read to say that human self-accusation constitutes salvific humility; indeed, the *Heidelberg Disputation*, like the *Explanations*, often relates salvation not to faith alone but to self-hatred and accusation. Rittgers, *The Reformation of Suffering*, 113, explains that for Luther in 1518 the sole agency is divine: "The crucial difference between the nascent theology of the cross of the *Dictata* and the mature theology of the cross in the *Explanations* and the *Heidelberg Disputation* is that in the later works, there is no room for human agency in producing humility, as Luther has come to believe in the complete bondage of the human will to sin, something he did not believe in the early lectures on the Psalms." The self-accusation described may be understood in the manner of the "voluntary" self-mortification Luther describes in the *Explanations*; the will is involved but driven entirely by God.

123. WA 1: 359.33–360.4; LW 31: 48–49; for Luther's attack on the soteriology of "facere quod in se est" and his insistence on the need to despair of trust in one's own works, see the further argumentation for Theses 16–18, WA 1: 360.25–361.18; LW

31: 50–52. Luther talks of "trust in creatures" at WA 1: 359.20–29; LW 31: 48 (explanation to Thesis 11).

124. WA 1: 357.15–16, 36–38; LW 31: 44–45 (Theses 4 and 6). LW translates "deformia" as unattractive. Thesis 6 is discussed further at WA 1.365.21f.; LW 31.58f.

125. WA 1: 360.16–22; LW 31: 50–51.

126. WA 1: 354.17–27; LW 31: 52–55: 19.

127. Bornkamm, *Luther: Gestalt*, 133–34.

128. WA 1: 361.34f.; LW 31: 52.

129. See Loewenich, *Luther's Theology of the Cross*, 27–49.

130. For the theme of divine hiddenness in Luther, Tauler, Eckhart, et al., see Bernard McGinn, "Vere tu es Deus absconditus: The Hidden God in Luther and Some Mystics," in *Silence and the Word: Negative Theology and Incarnation*, ed. Oliver Davies and Denys Turner (Cambridge: Cambridge University Press, 2002), 94–114, who concludes, "The mystics embraced the God who absents himself and condemns to hell, seeking ever-deeper contact with his absent presence. Luther fled *from* the God who hides himself in the mystery of predestination in order to take refuge in the God hidden *sub contrario* on the cross" (113–14). Also helpful on Luther's view of the hidden God is Steinmetz, *Luther in Context*, 23–31; and Loewenich, *Luther's Theology of the Cross*, 27–49.

131. WA 1: 362.11–19; LW 31: 52–53.

132. Addressing his own order, Luther would have been addressing both those who accepted that human beings could dispose themselves for saving grace through efforts springing *ex puris naturalibus* and believers in the prevenience of grace; see McGrath, *Luther's Theology of the Cross*, 34–95. The attack here is not only on supposed "Pelagianism," but on scholastic methodology and its stance toward reason. See also WA 1: 362.35–363.14; LW 31: 53–54 (Thesis 22).

133. WA 1: 362.23–33; LW 31: 53. For Aristotle, one becomes inherently good by doing good deeds; for Luther, one only remains and hardens inherent evil by presuming to do "good" deeds.

134. Noteworthy here is the critical response of Rittgers, *The Reformation of Suffering*, 323n10, to Gerhard O. Forde's contention (in *On Being a Theologian of the Cross: Reflections on Luther's Heidelberg Disputation, 1518* [Grand Rapids, MI: Eerdmans, 1997], 86) that Luther in the Heidelberg Disputation "limits the suffering caused by the cross to spiritual adversity; bodily trials are not in view."

135. WA 9: 101.5, discussed in chapter 1.

136. WA 1: 363.28–37; LW 31: 54–55 (my emphases).

137. WA 1: 364.16; LW 31: 56.

138. On the theme of "Christ present in faith," the arguments of the Finnish school should be noted. See my discussion in the introduction.

139. WA 1: 364.23–26; LW 31: 56; see also Thesis 27 and its discussion, WA 1: 364.27–38; LW 31: 56–57.

140. WA 1.365.9–20; LW 31.55–58.

Chapter 3

1. Andrew Pettegree, *Brand Luther: 1517, Printing, and the Making of the Reformation* (New York: Penguin, 2015), 80–81. The sermon had been preached in October 1517.
2. See Alejandro Zorzin, *Karlstadt als Flugschriftenautor* (Göttingen: Vandenhoeck & Ruprecht, 1990), 91, 91n21. According to Zorzin, only Luther, Karlstadt, and Thomas Murner had resolved by that point to write for people who could not read Latin.
3. See the introduction and chapter 4 for a discussion of scholars' assessment of the common ground and differences between the two reformers before 1522.
4. See Ulrich Bubenheimer, "Karlstadt, Andreas Ruldolff Bodenstein von (1486–1541)," in TRE 17: 649–57; here, 649–50; and Heiko A. Oberman, *The Reformation: Roots and Ramifications*, trans. Andrew Colin Gow (Grand Rapids, MI: Eerdmans, 1994), 117–48 ("Wittenberg's War on Two Fronts: What Happened in 1518 and Why").
5. As discussed in the Introduction, the notion that Müntzer initiated a mystical revolt against the non-mystical Luther is found in Steven E. Ozment, *Mysticism and Dissent: Religious Ideology and Social Protest in the Sixteenth Century* (New Haven, CT: Yale University Press, 1973); Siegfried Bräuer and Günter Vogler, *Thomas Müntzer: Neu Ordnung machen in der Welt, Eine Biographie* (Gütersloh: Gütersloher Verlagshaus, 2016), 217–19; and Hans-Jürgen Goertz, "Karlstadt, Müntzer and the Reformation of the Commoners, 1521–1525," in CAS, 1–44; here, 20–34.
6. On Luther's view of the "happy exchange" between the sinner and Christ, see Hamm, EL, 200–3.
7. As discussed in chapter 1.
8. This analysis is informed by Hans-Peter Hasse, *Karlstadt und Tauler: Untersuchungen zur Kreuzestheologie* (Gütersloh: Gütersloher Verlagshaus Gerd Mohn, 1993), 56–75, who argues that Karlstadt developed the concept of *Gelassenheit* in and after the "Wagons" image on the basis of his belief that *Gelassenheit* was a scriptural teaching, corresponding to the First Commandment ("You shall have no other gods before me") and Christ's exhortation in Luke 9:23, "Whoever wants to be my disciple must deny themselves and take up their cross daily and follow me" (NRSV). For this argument, see ibid., 178–85, 195–97, and the analysis of Karlstadt's published theses of 1540, *de abnegatione*, at 189–94.
9. On the importance of postils to the "dissemination of ideas" in the Reformation era, see John M. Frymire, *The Primacy of the Postils: Catholics, Protestants, and the Dissemination of Ideas in Early Modern Germany* (Leiden: Brill, 2009).
10. Pride of place here belongs to the *Sermon on Indulgence and Grace*, which saw 25 editions before 1520. See Pettegree, *Brand Luther*, 80–81. In other *Flugschriften*, Luther addressed the meditation on the passion so central to late-medieval devotion (*A Meditation on Christ's Passion*, 1519; 29 editions before 1525), addressed core themes of Christian catechesis (*A Short Explanation of the Ten Commandments*, 1518, which saw 10 editions before 1522; *An Exposition of the Lord's Prayer for Simple Laymen*, 1519, which saw 16 editions before 1525), and counseled Christians in relation to life's end (*A Sermon on Preparing to Die*, 1519; 25 editions before 1525). Many of these works were translated into Latin. The data here should be regarded as

approximate and is taken from Josef Benzing and Helmut Claus, *Lutherbibliographie: Verzeichnis der gedruckten Schriften Martin Luthers bis zu dessen Tod*, 2nd ed. (Baden-Baden: Valentin Koerner, 1989).

11. See the data in Zorzin, *Karlstadt als Flugschriftenautor*, 24, 26–29.

12. *A Sermon on the Sacrament of Penance* was published in 17 editions before 1521 (one low-German); *A Sermon on the Holy and Blessed Sacrament of Baptism* was published in 17 editions before 1523 (one low-German); *A Sermon on the Blessed Sacrament of the Holy, True Body of Christ and on the Brotherhoods* was published in 19 editions before 1523 (one low-German, one Latin, one Dutch, and two Czech).

13. A discussion may be found in John Bossy, *Christianity in the West, 1400–1700* (Oxford: Oxford University Press, 1985), 14–56.

14. Ronald K. Rittgers, *The Reformation of Suffering: Pastoral Theology and Lay Piety in Late Medieval and Early Modern Germany* (Oxford: Oxford University Press, 2012), 113; see also Pettegree, *Brand Luther*, 101, 120, 254–55.

15. Luther's relationship to monastic traditions is a rich area of research. I have found especially helpful Dorothea Wendebourg, "Luther on Monasticism," in *The Pastoral Luther: Essays on Martin Luther's Practical Theology*, ed. Timothy J. Wengert (Grand Rapids, MI: Wm. B. Eerdmans, 2009), 327–54. See also the handbook entry by Ulrich Köpf, "Mönchtum," in LH, 50–57.

16. *The Sacrament of Penance* cites Isaiah 40:1. WA 2: 720.8–9; LW 35: 18–19.

17. WA 2: 719.34–720.14; LW 35: 17–18.

18. Rittgers, *The Reformation of Suffering*, 107.

19. WA 2: 714.3–715.9; LW 35: 9–10.

20. See WA 2: 715.10–39; LW 35: 10–11; for Luther's breakthrough to this position, see Jared Wicks, "*Fides sacramenti—fides specialis*: Luther's Development in 1518," in *Luther's Reform: Studies on Conversion and the Church* (Mainz: Verlag Philipp von Zabern, 1992), 117–48.

21. WA 2: 716.1–717.40; LW 35: 12–14.

22. WA 2: 718.1–37; LW 35: 14–16.

23. WA 2: 720.31–721.6; LW 35: 19.

24. WA 2: 727.4–730.17; LW 35: 28–33. On these points, which are essential for understanding Luther's views of incipient and imputed righteousness, and of the Christian's simultaneous righteousness and sinfulness, see also LW 35: 35–36, WA 2: 732.9–15: "Alßo vorstehstu wie eyn mensch unschuldig, reyn, an sund wirt yn der tauff, und doch bleybit voll vill poßer neygung, das er nit anderß reyn heyst, dan das er angefangen ist reyn tzu werden, und der selben reynickeit eyn zeichen und bund hatt, und yhe mehr reyn werden soll, umb wilchs willen yhm gott seyn nachstelligen unreynickeyt nit rechnen will, unnd alßo mehr durch gottis gnediges rechnen dann seyns weßens halben [Ps. 32, 1 f.] reyn ist."

25. WA 2: 730.18–731.2; LW 35: 33.

26. See esp. WA 2: 731.3–732.24; LW 35: 34–36.

27. WA 2: 732.33–733.26; LW 35: 36–37: "Sin, evil inclination (*boeßneygung*), must be recognized as truly sin. That it does not harm us, however, is to be ascribed to the grace of God. He will not count sin against us if only we keep striving against it with

many trials, tasks, and sufferings, and at last slay it at death. To them who do this
not, God will not forgive their sins. For they do not live according to their baptism
and covenant, and they hinder the work of God and of their baptism which has been
begun." See also the ensuing section, WA 2: 733.27–39; LW 35: 38: "Believe, and you
have it. Doubt, and you are lost. So we find that through sin baptism is indeed hindered in its work, in the forgiveness and the slaying of sin. Yet only by lack of faith in
its operation is baptism canceled out. Faith, in turn, removes the hindrance to the operation of baptism. Thus everything depends on faith."

28. WA 2: 734.1–24; LW 35: 38–39.

29. WA 2: 734.14–735.7; LW 35: 39–40.

30. WA 2: 735.7–736.32; LW 35: 40–41. Luther still argues here that the monastic and
clerical estates, if properly constituted—that is, if "full of suffering and torment
(*marter*)"—prepare one more quickly for death than the married estate. Within a few
years, he will locate true suffering almost exclusively in the married estate.

31. WA 2: 754.1–8; LW 35: 67: "We have, therefore, two principal sacraments in the
church, baptism and the bread. Baptism leads us into a new life on earth; the bread
guides us through death into eternal life."

32. WA 2: 742.5–744.18; LW 35: 49–52. See also WA 2: 749.10–22; LW 35: 59–60.

33. WA 2: 744.19–30; LW 35: 53.

34. WA 2: 744.34–745.18; LW 35: 53: "Whoever is in despair, distressed by a sin-stricken
conscience or terrified by death or carrying some other burden upon his heart, if he
would be rid of them all, let him go joyfully to the sacrament of the altar and lay down
his woe in the midst of the community [of saints] and seek help from the entire company of the spiritual body." In several passages, Luther might be interpreted as allowing
Christ in heaven to suffer; see WA 2: 744.25–30, 745.19–746.5; LW 35: 53–54. On
Luther's views of divine suffering, see Dennis Ngien, *The Suffering of God according
to Martin Luther's "Theologia Crucis"* (New York: Peter Lang, 1995); Rittgers, *The
Reformation of Suffering*, 116–17; and recently David J. Luy, *Dominus Morti: Martin
Luther on the Incorruptibility of God in Christ* (Minneapolis: Fortress, 2014).

35. WA 2: 746.6–34; LW 35: 55–56.

36. WA 2: 747.4–25; LW 35: 56, where Luther is critical of private masses occurring
without fellowship. On receiving Christ as a sacrament before receiving Christ as an
example, see Rittgers, *The Reformation of Suffering*, 158.

37. WA 2: 746.34–747.3; LW 35: 56.

38. WA 2: 747.26–748.5; LW 35: 57–58.

39. See the discussion beginning at WA 2: 749.23–31; LW 35: 60. Luther proceeds here
to address "abominable abuses and misbeliefs" about the sacrament, including suspicion and speculation about the real presence, any devotion to the real presence
that neglects the exercise of faith and fellowship, and reliance on the mass as "a work
which of itself pleases God" (*opus gratum opere operato*) and which should accordingly be repeated as often as possible, regardless of the "change of love and faith" in
the communicants. This last belief is said to offer a "false security," forgetting that the
sacrament must be "used in faith." WA 2: 749.23–752.25; LW 35: 60–65.

40. WA 2: 752.36–753.24; LW 35: 65–66.

41. McGinn, *Presence,* 1: xv–xvi; see the Introduction.
42. For citation, I use AWA 2. There is no acceptable, complete translation of the *Operationes* in English, although such a translation is planned for the New Series of Luther's Works, published by Concordia. In 1826, Henry Cole produced a translation, *Martin Luther's Complete Commentary on the First Twenty-Two Psalms* (London: W. Simpkin and R. Marshall); one volume of an updated version of Cole's translation was offered by John Nicholas Lenker, *Luther's Commentary on the First Twenty-Two Psalms* (Sunbury, PA: Lutherans in All Lands, 1903) [henceforth LAL]. Unfortunately, the Cole version preceded even the first Weimar edition of the *Operationes,* WA 5 (1892). Only Luther's commentary on the first and second *Psalms* has been translated from the Weimar for LW; see LW 14: 279–349. Translations from the *Operationes* will be my own, unless a citation to Lenker (LAL) is indicated. In all translations, I have been aided by the Lenker volume.
43. For a discussion around the theme of suffering, see Rittgers, *The Reformation of Suffering,* 115–118; 326n36.
44. Information from Benzing and Claus, *Lutherbibliographie,* 63–64.
45. My translation of the Vulgate.
46. For a detailed discussion of Dionysius's views: McGinn, *Presence,* 2:157–82. The introductions by Jaroslav Pelikan, Jean Leclercq, and Karlfried Froehlich in *Pseudo-Dionysius: The Complete Works,* trans. Colm Luibheid (Mahwah, NJ: Paulist, 1987), 11–46, cover Pseudo-Dionysius's spirituality and his influence into the sixteenth century.
47. See Bernard McGinn, "Vere tu es Deus absconditus: The Hidden God in Luther and Some Mystics," in *Silence and the Word: Negative Theology and Incarnation,* ed. Oliver Davies and Denys Turner (Cambridge: Cambridge University Press, 2002), 94–114; esp. 113–14: "The mystics embraced the God who absents himself and condemns to hell, seeking ever-deeper contact with his absent presence. Luther fled *from* the God who hides himself in the mystery of predestination in order to take refuge in the God hidden *sub contrario* on the cross."
48. Luther recognized "mystical theology" in Tauler, as well, and responded by asserting the priority and singular necessity of the "proper theology" that focuses on the incarnate Christ: "Unde totus iste sermo procedit ex theologia mystica, quae est sapientia experimentalis et non doctrinalis. Quia nemo novit nisi qui accipit hoc negotium absconditum. Loquitur enim de nativitate spirituali verbi increati. Theologia autem propria de spirituali nativitate verbi incarnati habet unum necessarium et optimam partem." WA 9: 98.14–27. With regard to Dionysius, it must be remembered that Tauler and the *German Theology* both cite Dionysius, and Dionysius's influence (both direct and indirect) throughout the broader mystical tradition was extensive; Luther's extensive use of the motif of "darkness" in the *Magnificat Commentary* should caution us against positing an exclusively negative relationship to the Dionysian tradition. On Luther's rejection of Dionysius by 1519–20, see Erich Vogelsang, "Luther und die Mystik," LJ *19* (1937), 32–54; here, 33–37; Volker Leppin, "Mystik," in LH, 57–61; here, 58 (Leppin is duly critical of Vogelsang in other respects).
49. AWA 2: 284.1–3; LAL 256.

50. AWA 2: 284.4–10; LAL 256–57. "Just as impatience, dejection, and confusion do not properly and primarily proceed from the multitude and magnitude of the afflictions, adversities, or evils, of whatever kind they may be, but rather from the feelings of the person who is alarmed at them and who is in an unwise way thirsting after the contrary, prosperity, happiness, and honor; so despair, spiritual dejection, and the confusion of a restless conscience do not properly and primarily arise from the multitude and magnitude of sins, but rather from the feelings of the person who is alarmed at them and who is in an unwise way seeking after an abundance of good works and righteousness and salvation." See further AWA 2: 286.1–8; LAL 258.

51. See here, AWA 2: 293.2–13; 310.12f.

52. The despair of the works-righteous person at death "probat enim se non in deum sperare, sed in opera praesumare, quia, si vellet sperare, deum haberet adhuc praesentem, in quem posset sperare." AWA 2: 286.20–287.2.

53. AWA 2: 287.7–12.

54. AWA 2: 288.3–21, 290.13–21; see also AWA 2: 289.3–15, which sheds light on Luther's refusal to allow union with God apart from or above the incarnate Christ: "Ita descendit salus a Christo deo adusque peccatum, et nos a peccato ascendimus ad salutem usque in Christo homine." According to AWA 2: 289.16–290.12, temporal gifts are given that "we might learn to worship, hope in and love God more," but because of our fallen affect (*vitio nostri affectus*), the opposite result occurs. Fallen affect likewise becomes presumptuous in the receipt of God-given spiritual "gifts and merits," "ut divinae bonitati necessarium visum fuerit erigere crucem et per eius praedicationem salvos facere credentes, stultos et peccatores, reprobare vero sapientes et sanctos, ut I Cor 1[:23] dicit: 'Nos praedicamus Christum crucifixum, Graecis quidem' (id est, sapientibus) 'stultitiam, Iudaeis vero' (id est, sanctis) 'scandalum, ipsis autem vocatis Iudaeis et Graecis' (id est, peccatoribus et stultis) 'virtutem dei et sapientiam.'"

55. AWA 2: 294.1–10.

56. The other Dionysian categories, also mentioned by Luther, are "proper" and "symbolic" theology.

57. AWA 2: 294.19–296.11.

58. AWA 2: 305.18–25; see also AWA 2: 306.4–7.

59. On God as "No-thing" in Eckhart, see McGinn, *Presence*, 4:132; for Eckhart's understanding of union with God, ibid., 181–87.

60. Luther names only Peter Lombard specifically here; Luther had criticized this definition of hope in Thesis 25 of the *Disputation Against Scholastic Theology*: "Spes non venit ex meritis, sed ex passionibus merita destruentibus. Contra usum multorum." WA 1: 225.15–16; LW 31:10.

61. AWA 2: 296.12–298.5. According to Luther, AWA 2: 299.1–19, tribulation cannot produce patience, probation or hope unless hope has already been given; without hope, tribulation produces despair. At AWA 2: 316.14–21, Luther argues that if hope proceeds from merit, only the just can hope, and therefore no one will flee to God's mercy.

62. AWA 2: 299.20–301.10. See also AWA 2: 304.9–12, where Luther describes tribulation as an "officina spei," adding that works righteousness yields despair.

63. AWA 2: 301.21–302.2.

64. See AWA 2: 304.17–25, where Luther notes that God tries Christians with "despair or storms of conscience" so that they might be summoned from works, "quia spiritualissima, etsi acerbissima, haec pugna est intra te solum cum solo deo consummanda, sola spe sustinente et exspectante deoque causam totam commendante deumque contra deum vincente, sicut Iacob (Gen 32[:24–30])."

65. See the discussion in Chapter 1 of the view of Eckhart, Suso, and Tauler on true *imitatio Christi* versus outward and active self-mortification.

66. AWA 2: 302.23–303.19. Note here Luther's distinction of patience as pertaining to the loss of temporal goods from hope, which pertains to the loss of spiritual goods. Hope may be called "patientiam spiritualem seu patientiam in culpis sustinendis"; while patience may be called "spem corporalem seu spem in ferendis poenis" (AWA 2: 303.25–27).

67. AWA 2: 304.3–6, and 304 note x.

68. These *tentationes* mount to hatred of God. AWA 2: 309.17–310.4.

69. AWA 2: 307.11–17. See also Luther's approbation, near the end of the *digressio*, of the scriptural tropes "exitus" and "egressus" to describe the "purgationem et spei operationem." AWA 2: 320.8–14. The ideal of purity here applies not to human nature or lusts, but to the relationship to God in trust. Mortification and purgation remain essential concepts, as in the monastic-mystical triad of purgation-illumination-perfection, but the purgation now comes with the infusion of faith, hope, and love. The purgation, illumination, and perfection *sub contrario* are simultaneous.

70. AWA 2: 307.18–308.7.

71. On the theme of rapture as a reflection of Luther's debt to medieval mysticism, see Heiko A. Oberman, *Dawn of the Reformation: Essays in Late Medieval and Reformation Thought* (Grand Rapids, MI: Eerdmans, 1992), 142–54 (part of the essay, "*Simul Gemitus et Raptus*: Luther and Mysticism").

72. AWA 2: 317.7–319.3.

73. On the vase analogy, see AWA 2: 320.1–7. The remaining points come from AWA 2: 320.15–321.5.

74. On events leading to the Leipzig Disputation, see Oberman, *Reformation: Roots*, 117–48. For recent analyses of the Disputation from the perspective of Luther's biography, see Heinz Schilling, *Martin Luther: Rebel in an Age of Upheaval*, trans. Rona Johnston (Oxford: Oxford University Press, 2017 [2013]), 152–55; and Hendrix, *Martin Luther*, 77–81. For particular attention to Karlstadt's role in events, see Hermann Barge, *Andreas Bodenstein von Karlstadt* (Nieuwkoop: B. De Graaf, 1968 [Leipzig: Friedrich Brandstetter, 1905]), I: 114–180. For Karlstadt's view of "poenitentia passiva" against Eck, see Hasse, *Karlstadt und Tauler*, 93–96.

75. For studies of the image, see Hasse, *Karlstadt und Tauler*, 100–13; Ulrich Bubenheimer, "Andreas Rudolff Bodenstein von Karlstadt: Sein Leben, seine Herkunft und seine innere Entwicklung," in *Andreas Bodenstein von Karlstadt 1480–1541: Festschrift der Stadt Karlstadt zum Jubiläumsjahr 1980*, ed. Wolfgang Merklein

(Karlstadt: Michel-Druck, 1980), 5–58; here, 19–28; Bubenheimer, "Andreas Bodenstein von Karlstadt und seine fränkische Heimat," in QdR: 15–48; here, 28–37; and Erwin Mühlhaupt, "Karlstadts 'Fuhrwagen': Eine frühreformatorische 'Bildzeitung' von 1519," Luther 50 no. 2 (1979), 60–76. Most recently, there is Lyndal Roper and Jennifer Spinks, "Karlstadt's *Wagen*: The First Visual Propaganda for the Reformation," *Art History* 40, no. 2 (April 2017): 256–85, which contains fine reproductions of the image; for a critique of this essay's handling of Karlstadt's theology and reception of mysticism, see Vincent Evener, "Andreas Bodenstein von Karlstadt," in PMRE: 78–99; here, 79n6. A modern German translation is provided by Ulrich Bubenheimer in "Interpretation und Konfrontation: Medien und Verfahren im kirchengeschichtlichen Unterricht," *Entwurf: Religionspädagogische Mitteilungen* 4 (1976), 55–57+3. Bubenheimer provides an image with numbering; I will cite the text fields via parenthetical reference and according to this numbering. Karlstadt created first a Latin version of the "Wagons," which survives only in fragmentary form; according to Hasse, *Karlstadt und Tauler*, 101, Karlstadt translated some of the Latin sayings into German, but replaced others. Evidently, the German sayings created by Karlstadt for the image had to be shortened because of space limitations. Fuller sayings appear in the explanatory tract that Karlsatdt subsequently issued.

76. On Eck's complaint to the Elector about the image, see Bubenheimer, "Andreas Rudolff Bodenstein von Karlstadt," 25–26.

77. In this same text field, Karlstadt promises that he can support every saying through "heylige schrifften vn[d] lerern." His explanatory treatise was entitled, *Auszlegung vnnd Lewterung etzlicher heyligenn geschrifften So dem menschen dienstlich vnd erschieszlich seint zu Christlichem lebe[n]. Kurtzlich berurth vnd angetzeich[n]et in den figurn vnd schrifften der wagen. In sonderheit. Des creutzes tzu welchem vnser goth vnd herr den menschen berufft* (Leipzig: Melchior Lotter, d.Ä, 1519); VD 16 B 6113; henceforth cited as AuL. The tract is number 12 the "Chronologisch geordnetes Verzeichnis der gedruckten Schriften des Andreas Bodenstein von Karlstadt," provided by Zorzin, *Karlstadt als Flugschriftenautor*, 273–307. It was printed only once.

78. WABr 1: 369.63–66 (my translation).

79. The assertion of Mühlhaupt, "Karlstadts 'Fuhrwagen,'" 62, that the second figure represents the laity, given a halo to indicate Karlstadt's high regard for their religious capacity, has little basis. I follow Bubenheimer, "Karlstadt und seine fränkische Heimat," 33.

80. Bubenheimer, "Karlstadt und seine fränkische Heimat," 31; Bubenheimer also states that an unoccupied saddle on one of the lower-frame horses represents Karlstadt's "conversion to Luther's new anti-scholastic theology" (37).

81. It is not clear why Karlstadt ascribes to scripture as a whole the killing function that Augustine and Luther had attributed to the Law. Hasse, *Karlstadt und Tauler*, 101–2, notes that the Latin text on the wagon read, "Lex Dei currus ad Christum," so Karlstadt may mean to imply law with his use of "Schrift." The corresponding German caption only reads, "der wag zu Christo." Yet Karlstadt's poem uses the word "Schrift," as does his exegesis in AuL.

82. AuL, D1r–D3v. As Bernhard Lohse, *Evangelium in der Geschichte: Studien zu Luther und der Reformation* (Göttingen: Vandenhoeck & Ruprecht, 1988), 19–22, argues, Luther found his center in the dialectic of Law and Gospel rather than Spirit and letter. For a discussion of Karlstadt's reception of Augustine's views on law and the Spirit and the letter, see Ernst Kähler, *Karlstadt und Augustin: Der Kommentar des Andreas Bodenstein von Karlstadt zu Augustins Schrift* de spiritu et litera (Halle [Saale]: Max Niemeyer: 1952), 37*–42*; and Ronald J. Sider, *Andreas Bodenstein von Karlstadt: The Development of His Thought 1517–1525* (Leiden: Brill, 1974), esp. 21–44. Sider downplays the mystical influence on Karlstadt and characterizes Karlstadt's mature theology as Augustinian—points with which I disagree throughout this book.

83. Karlstadt attributes this position to Augustine and Bernard of Clairvaux.

84. Field 16 reads, "keiner ist gotlicher gabe[n]. an glaube[n]. begreiflich."; Text 15, "Giß vor got dein hertz. glaub im er hilft an schertz."

85. Translation here and elsewhere based on consultation of Bubenheimer, "Interpretation und Konfrontation."

86. Initially, Karlstadt intended to indict a specific Franciscan with this figure, but at the request of Spalatin, the distinctive cap on the figure was altered: "Die Kappe sieht jetzt aus wie ein Zwittergebilde zwischen Mönchskappe und Doktorhut." Bubenheimer, "Andreas Rudolff Bodenstein von Karlstadt," 19. Ultimately, Domincans in Leipzig interpreted the figure as one of their own. Ibid., 24.

87. Bubenheimer, "Interpretation und Konfrontation," explanation to Caption 37.

88. For an analysis: Hasse, *Karlstadt und Tauler*, 106–113, who notes Karlstadt's reception of the cross allegories of Bernard of Clairvaux, Augustine, and Tauler.

89. AuL, A2v.

90. AuL, C4v, "[D]u must dir vnd deynem willen absterben / wiltu anders dein creutz ertragen / vnd fruchtbar werden / als geschribe[n] / es sterb dan ein korn / so bleibst allein vnd an frucht." Christ's command to take up the cross is to be understood as if Christ said, "[D]ein creutz das ich dir in ewiger lieb bereit vnd tzu geteylt hab / das nym tzu dir /vnnd volg mir."

91. AuL, A2r.

92. AuL, A3r, "in recht vernichtigkeit dein selbst alhie ko[m]men."

93. AuL, A3v–A4r. Karlstadt continues: "[The kingdom of heaven] consists not in rewards and our own desires (außwircku[n]g vnd eygem lust), but in the hearing, perceiving and bringing about of God's will. In sum, if God becomes everything in all our thinking, willing, speaking, seeing, hearing, doing and working, so that we earnestly seek only God himself, as Paul wrote, then God has his kingdom in us."

94. AuL, A3v–A4r.

95. AuL, A4r–v; see also D2v–D3.

96. AuL, A4v–B1r ("Der handel dieser nacht heyst nemlich / anne[m]lickeit / wolgeuollickeit / ankleblickeit / genugde vn[d] lust in guten wercken"). At B1v, Karlstadt equates Gelassenheit to "Verlassenheit"; on this, see Hasse, *Karlstadt und Tauler*, 106n27.

97. See Chapter 1.

98. AuL, A4v–B2r. Karlstadt attribued the teaching, "Vnser wil macht guter werck substa[n]sz," to the Thomist Johannes Capreolus, whom he had cited in his own scholastic works; see Bubenheimer, "Andreas Rudolff Bodenstein von Karlstadt," 24.

99. AuL, E1r–E2r.

100. AuL, B2v, B3v–B4r. On true trials as un-chosen, B6r.

101. This view was indebted to Augustine's understanding of fallen nature as born *incurvatus in se*. Augustine and Karlstadt focused on human inability to control evil desire, Luther on inborn self-trust. For Karlstadt's discussion, which cites Augustine extensively, see AuL, C1v–C2r. Karlstadt refers to the anger of the insulted person, noting that one may refrain from acting upon anger, but not from becoming angry.

102. See AuL, B6r.

103. AuL, B4r–v, also citing James 1:2.

104. AuL, B4v–B5r. Job 9 is here cited: "[G]ot erhort mich schreyhenden / aber ich glaub nit das er mich erhort hab / Dan[n] er vberschut vnd erfuldt mich mit bitterkeyt / vnd lest meinen geyst nicht ruhen. Das ist vil heilige[n] alhie begegnet / das sie von der grossen verr wegen / welche sie tzu got gehabt / nit gewist habe[n] ob yn got gnedig gewest oder nit."

105. AuL, B5v–B6r. "Aber nymants sal vertzweyffeln / wan ym / yn lettzten tzugen / anfechter der hell antasten / vnd vmbgeben yn mit schmertzen des todts / dan got furt den menschen yn die hell / vmb sein aufzfure[n]."

106. AuL, B6r–v: "Ich bedarff keyner kunst / dan des creutz Christi dz mir Christ[us] aufflegt."

107. AuL, B6v.

108. Cf. McGinn, *Presence*, 6: 79–80.

109. AuL, C1r: "Gotliche lieb ist ein anfaherin vn[d] ha[n]dt haberin / aller obertzelter gots gabe[n]. wu sie nicht ist / do ist kein lebendig glawb. Keyn bestendig hoffnung / keyn lawtere demutigkeit vn[d] gelassenheit / kein warhafftig gedult / vn[d] kein ernstlich vrteyl." Love belongs to the *Gelassenheit* enjoined by the saying in Christ's right hand, and to the patience enjoined by the exhortation to cross-bearing in Christ's left hand; love holds the person constantly in self-condemnation (Caption 28).

110. On self-accusation and *odium sui*, see also AuL, C3v–C4r, D4v, and E2r–E3r.

111. AuL, C4v. "Got hat durch seinen willen vns geordent vnd gesetzt in ewigkeit zu allem dem das wir von ym haben / vnd macht alle werck yn vns / vn[d] furt vns / durch alle anfechtu[n]g / also macht er dz creutz."

112. AuL, D1r.

113. AuL, D1v–D2v. On the notion that Christ alone, not Scripture, comforts and saves the sinner, see also D4r–v.

114. AuL, D3v, D4r.

115. Caption 11, explicated AuL, D6v.

116. AuL, D2v–D3r. On God's work here as grace, see D4v, explicating Caption 9. Karlstadt's rejection of the possibility of self-produced contrition was expressed in Caption 34, explicated at D4v–D5r.

117. AuL, D5v. The discussion here reflects Augustine's famous lines in the *Confessions*, "You command continence. Give what you command!"

118. AuL, D6r.

119. AuL, D5v–D6r, E2v (discussing Text Field 23).

120. AuL, E3r–v. Karlstadt presents his position as opposed to "mein schulmeistere."

121. AuL, E4r. Karlstadt's discussion of the upper wagon concludes here, with the saying "Nymants ist oberster gaben vehig // Er sey dan in goth glewbig" (E4v).

122. Caption 34; AuL, E5v.

123. Karlstadt found little space in the *Interpretation* to discuss the images and captions surrounding the lower wagon—a mere 3 pages (E4v–E5v), compared to 56 for the upper wagon. He notes the subtlety of the scholastics' supposed deception: they acknowledge sin and the necessity of grace, but they minimize both and relegate sin to an action in order to amplify the role of human willing. On reason, Karlstadt cites from Augustine the saying that "one does not live blessedly after human reason, but after God, who is the highest good."

124. In advance of the Leipzig disputation in February 1519, Karlstadt tried to dissuade Luther from his intended attack on Papal primacy. See Bubenheimer, "Andreas Rudolff Bodenstein von Karlstadt," 28–29.

125. See Zorzin, "Verzeichnis," 24. I use here the first edition: *Missive vonn der aller hochste tugent gelassenheyt. Endres Bodensteyn von Carolstat Doctor* (Wittenberg: Johann Rhau-Grunenberg, 1520), which is VD 16 B 6173. I use the copy provided online by the Sächsische Landesbibliothek—Staats- und Universitätsbibliothek, Dresden, Signature Hist.eccl.E.242,23.y.

126. *Missive*, A2r–v; EC, 28–29.

127. *Missive*, A3r, B2r–v; EC 30, 35. Karlstadt likens the friends who counsel him to look after his well-being to Peter when he said, "Lord, far be it from you that you should be captured, beaten, and killed by the Jews at Jerusalem" (Matt. 26). Karlstadt writes, "Although Peter had a sound, worldly, natural opinion, as he and other Christians might have, Christ, nonetheless, said to Peter, 'Get away from me, Satan, you devil, you obstructer. For you do not understand what God wills, but only what is human' [Matt 16:23]."

128. *Missive*, A3r–v; EC 30–31. Numerous lines express Karlstadt's conviction that God works through suffering as a contrary to fallen reason, will, and perception, "I know that he is my gracious lord when he makes me anxious" (*Missive*, A4v; EC 32) and, "[God] wills my good, even though it may appear to me like bitter and acrid gall and pus" (*Missive*, B3r; EC 37). Karlstadt delineates five comforts for suffering: that "Christ on the cross also had to hear and suffer such robbers of God's word"; that "each tribulation washes away sin, if its pain is endured in faith [Tob. 3:5] and has been accepted through hope in God [Jas. 1:2ff.]"; that "God tests and proves our faith through temptation"; that "all suffering is a punishing rod with which the heavenly Father visits, cleanses, and beautifies his children"; and that the word teaches that Christ had to descend into hell before his resurrection, showing that God always "castigates so that he might show mercy" (*Missive*, A3r; EC 30). Patient suffering is not, however, meritorious *coram deo*, as in the late-medieval penitential system.

129. *Missive*, A3v; EC 31. Karlstadt's use of Psalm 118 is highlighted by marginal annotations reproducing the phrases, "Auerte oculos" and "Et respo[n]debo exprobra[n]tibus mihi verbum."

130. *Missive*, A4r–B1r; EC 32–33. Karlstadt's argument depends on a claim about the clarity of scripture—"not only a scholar, but also a layperson who hears it read, is able to understand it"—and the charge that the pope "understands scripture according to his own lights."

131. Karlstadt appeals to Deuteronomy 33:9 and Luke 14:26–27, among other passages, to insist that God and Christ are to be preferred to family. B1r–B2v; EC 34–36. See Chapter 1 for his attraction to relevant passages in Tauler.

132. *Missive*, B1v; EC 34 (translation altered). If Karlstadt errs, he says, the pope must prove him wrong from scripture.

133. *Missive*, B1v–B2v; EC 34–36 (translation altered). Sigrid Looß's contention that Karlstadt viewed the work of Christ's sword as "largely an intellectual process" neglects both text and context. See "Radical Views of the Early Andreas Karlstadt (1520–25)," in *Radical Tendencies in the Reformation: Divergent Perspectives*, ed. Hans J. Hillerbrand, (Kirksville, MO: Sixteenth Century Journal Publishers, 1988), 48.

134. *Missive*, B2v–C1r; EC 36–37.

135. *Missive*, B3r; EC 36–37.

136. *Missive*, B3v; EC, 37–38 (translation altered; I have inserted a sentence found in *Missive* but not EC; I have added emphasis to highlight Karlstadt's addition to I Cor. 13).

137. *Missive*, B4r; EC, 38 (translation altered).

138. Hendrix, *Luther and the Papacy*, 95–120.

139. Lyndal Roper, *Martin Luther: Renegade and Prophet* (London: Bodley Head, 2016), 232, is refreshingly skeptical about the Elector Frederick's supposed resistance to Luther's return.

140. See Henrik Otto, *Vor- und frühreformatorische Tauler-Rezeption: Annotationen in Drucken des späten 15. Und frühen 16. Jahrhunderts* (Gütersloh: Gütersloher Verlagshaus, 2003), 176n8.

141. The *Magnificat Explained* is dedicated to John Frederick, the nephew of the Elector Frederick the Wise, who is said to have expressed anxiety to Luther over Luke 1:52, "He has brought down the powerful from their thrones." Luther writes in the dedicatory epistle that all human beings and rulers especially must learn the "fear of God," which comes from a right understanding of how God works among human beings. WA 7: 545.5–22; LW 31: 298. In her introduction and annotations to the treatise for the new *Annotated Luther* series, Beth Kreitzer underlines the influence of late-medieval mysticism, especially Tauler; see AL 4: 307–84; esp. 311–12. For a helpful analysis of mystical motifs, see Karl-Heinz zur Mühlen, *Reformatorisches Profil: Studien zum Weg Martin Luthers und der Reformation*, ed. Johannes Brosseder and Athina Lexutt (Göttingen: Vandenhoeck & Ruprecht, 1995), 86–100 ("Luthers Frömmigkeit und die Mystik: Seine Auslegung des 'Magnificat' von 1521"); esp. 89–94. Zur Mühlen identifies three themes of Luther's *Frömmigkeit* in the Magnificat commentary: *Kreuzeserfahrung, Heilsvertrauen,* and *Freiheit zu humaner Aktivität*.

Under *Kreuzeserfahrung* he notes Luther's use of the dialectic of *Erfahrbarkeit und Nichterfahrbarkeit Gottes*. It is worth noting that Luther does not clearly or consistently express the mediated character of God's presence in the commentary, even though his understanding of the Word coming from outside was well established by 1521. On this last point, zur Mühlen's article is misleading. For another account of mystical influences on and mystical themes in the commentary, see George H. Tavard, "Medieval Piety in Luther's Commentary on the Magnificat," in *Ad Fontes Lutheri: Toward the Recovery of the Real Luther*, ed. Timothy Maschke, Franz Posset, and Joan Skocir (Milwaukee: Marquette University Press, 2001), 281–301; Tavard's analysis will be discussed in the following notes. Christoph Burger, *Marias Lied in Luthers Deutung: Der Kommentar zum Magnifikat (Lk 1, 46b-55) aus den Jahren 1520/21* (Tübingen: Mohr Siebeck, 2007) offers a discussion of Luther's translation. Burger's introduction notes that Luther's commentary is likely to offend post-Enlightenment readers: Luther describes God and human beings as "competitors," rejects any human self-regard, and democratizes mysticism in a way that overtaxes ordinary believers (4–5); however that may be, all this stands at the heart of what Luther wants to convey and accomplish. Burger offers a brief comparison of Luther's and Müntzer's exegesis of the Magnificat (18–19), but he concludes with a statement that misses the centrality of promise and faith to Müntzer's views, and the centrality of suffering to Luther's own understanding of faith. Müntzer's interest in inward processes of salvation is downplayed, and he is said to have read the text "in erster Linie als einen sozialkritischen Text."

142. The text was printed three times in Wittenberg, and twice each in Augsburg and Basel. It was subsequently printed in numerous translations: Latin (1525 and 1526 in Straßburg), low German (1526, Wittenberg), French (1528, Paris); Dutch (1534) and English (1538).

143. WA 7: 546.21–34; LW 21: 299; see also WA 7: 571.24–27; LW 21: 325.

144. Tavard "Medieval Piety," 292–96, pointed to the "the binary and trinary structure of Luther's presentation" in *The Magnificat Explained*. He thereby tried to connect Luther's text to the Victorines, to Bonaventure's *Itinerarium mentis in Deum* and, more broadly, to the "medieval conception of the ascent to God." Yet the connection to Bonaventure's *Itinerarium* is unpersuasive, based on a generic account of the structure of the text rather than on any direct textual reference. More importantly, Luther's argument excludes any possibility of a human ascent to the divine, such as that described by Bonaventure; there is instead only divine descent.

145. WA 7: 547.8–34; LW 21: 299–300.

146. WA 7: 548.12f.; LW 21: 301. See also WA 7: 593.30–594.4; LW 21: 347.

147. WA 7: 550, 1–18; LW 21: 302-3; on the rapture, love, and joy of the soul that experiences God's regard for the "poor, despised, afflicted, miserable, forsaken, and those who are nothing," see also WA 7: 548.2–11; LW 21: 300.

148. WA 7: 557.10f.; LW 21: 310–11(my emphasis).

149. WA 7: 550.35–551.11; LW 21: 303. Like Luther, Karlstadt could not accept without modification Tauler's three-fold anthropology; dividing the person primarily into inner and outer, Karlstadt was unwilling to align reason with the inner person, and he

worried that a three-fold anthropology might imply an unfallen orientation to God and hence human capacity to initiate salvation. Ulrich Bubenheimer, "Karlstadt liest Tauler: Sein reformatorischer Weg im Spiegel seines Taulerbandes in der Bibliothek des Predigerseminars Wittenberg," Lecture to the Evangelisches Predigerseminar Wittenberg, June 16, 1987 (typescript held by the Predigerseminar), 17–20.

150. Zur Mühlen, *Reformatorisches Profil*, 91; see also Steven Ozment, *Homo Spiritualis: A Comparative Study of the Anthropology of Johannes Tauler, Jean Gerson, and Martin Luther (1509–16) in the Context of their Theological Thought* (Leiden: E.J. Brill, 1969), 214–15; Ozment, *"Homo Viator: Luther and Late Medieval Theology,"* in *The Reformation in Medieval Perspective*, ed. Steven Ozment (Chicago: Quadrangle Books, 1971), 142–54.

151. On Bonaventure's reception and use of the Dionysian motif, influenced by Thomas Gallus (d. 1246), see McGinn, *Presence*, 3:78–87 (on Gallus), 109–12.

152. WA 7: 551.19–552.9; LW 21: 304–5.

153. WA 7: 554.30–555.20; LW 21: 307–8.

154. WA 7: 551.21–556.10; LW 21: 308–9; on *Annehmlichkeit* and its converse, see also WA 7: 564.26–32; LW 21: 318.

155. WA 7: 556.12–557.5; LW 21: 309, including Luther's description of "impure and perverted lovers . . . unable to love and praise the bare, unfelt goodness that is hidden in God." See also Luther's subsequent account of the vision of "three virgins" had by "a certain godly woman." WA 7: 557.11–36; LW 21: 310.

156. See Louise Gnädinger, *Johannes Tauler: Lebenswelt und mystische Lehre* (München: C. H. Beck, 1993), 251–61.

157. WA 7: 560.13–27; LW 21: 313–14.

158. WA 7: 561.21–562.25; LW 21: 314–15.

159. WA 7: 562.32–563.2; LW 21: 316.

160. WA 7: 563.31–564.5; LW 21: 317.

161. WA 7: 563.5–9, 564.6–17; LW 21: 316–17.

162. WA 7: 564.18–22 ("das sich der mensch yhm willig ergibt und folget"); LW 21: 317.

163. The discussion is outlined at WA 7: 577.29–578.28; LW 21: 331–332.

164. See WA 7: 585.23–586.28, 588.8–10; LW 21: 339–342.

165. Luther clearly references his own situation, assailed from his perspective by an alliance of the "spiritually proud" and mighty, at WA 7: 578.30f.; LW 21: 332–34. See also WA 7: 588.16–589.12; LW 21: 342–43, where Luther writes about the outward humility of the spiritually proud *Gelehrten*. Although Luther assumes in *The Magnificat Explained* that the endurance of poverty and oppression can be a salutary exercise of one's faith—one's trust in God—he also says that pride can misappropriate these experiences; the poor and oppressed are not de facto faithful Christians. Conversely, wealth and power frequently tempt to self-trust, although biblical figures like Abraham, Isaac, Jacob, David, and Daniel prove that faith and poverty of spirit can endure the trial of prosperity. When Mary sings of God's help to the oppressed and the hungry, she refers to those who are "willing to be nothing and lowly of heart, . . . especially if they have been forced into it for the sake of the right." She does not sing about those who suffer unwillingly, "but of those who are one with

God and God with them, and who believe and trust in Him." WA 7: 591.27–592.6; LW 21: 345–46. Not to be overlooked here is the explicit endorsement of union with God.

166. WA 7: 587.8–18; LW 21: 341.

167. See the discussion by Beth Kreitzer in AL 4: 309. AL still groups the treatise as a "pastoral writing"—a sensible arrangement, so long as one realizes (a) that texts could serve multiple functions and mix genres, and (b) that pastoral writing was not done in a vacuum apart from academic theology, theological and ecclesial-political controversy, and ecclesial-political life.

168. See Roper, *Martin Luther*, 17f.

169. WA 7: 575.17–20, 24–27; LW 21: 329.

170. WA 7: 582.8–10, 17–18; LW 21: 336.

171. WA 7: 585.3–5; LW 21: 339 (slightly corrected).

172. WA 7: 556.13f., 585.3–6; LW 21: 309, 339.

173. The discussion here focuses on the model sermons for Advent and Christmas that Luther penned at the Wartburg—the *Wartburg Postil*. For the distinction of this postil collection from others, see the Benjamin T. G. Hayes's excellent introduction in LW 75: xiii–xxxii. The Wartburg postils, as incorporated into the 1525 *Winter Postil*, were given new centrality in the Lutheran tradition through the 1700 edition of Philip Jakob Spener.

174. See Rittgers, *The Reformation of Suffering*, 115–16, 326n36.

175. WA 10/1.1: 2.13–4.5 (concluding, "Auch das Euangelium ist gantz nit mehr denn eyn historia von dem kleynisten ßon gotis und von seyner vorkleynung"); LW 75: 4. On the need to receive Christ as a "gift" before holding Christ as an "example," see WA 10/1.1: 11.12–13.18; LW 75: 8–10. Christ in the prefatory epistle is upheld not, in the first order, as a model for behavior that needs to be imitated (i.e. through self-humbling) but as an "example" of the way that every Christian must come to faith (i.e. by being humbled).

176. WA 10/1.1: 5.10–6.2; LW 75: 5.

177. On the Catholic response to the Reformation regarding issues of certitude, see Susan E. Schreiner, *Are You Alone Wise? The Search for Certainty in the Early Modern Era* (Oxford: Oxford University Press, 2011), 131–207.

178. WA 10/1.2: 25.15–26.4; LW 75: 30–31 (Gospel Sermon for Advent I).

179. WA 10/1.2: 75.16–76.5; LW 75: 75.

180. WA 10/1.2: 147.9–14; LW 75: 136.

181. See e.g. WA 10/1.2: 92.15–93.4; LW 75: 90.

182. WA 10/1.2: 197.2–198.6; LW 75: 178–180.

183. WA 10/1.1: 40.18–41.10; LW 75: 198. Many more citations could be added for each of these themes. On trials as salutary for preachers, WA 10/1.1: 301.18–303.7; LW 75: 349–50. At WA 10/1.1: 317.12–14; LW 75: 359, Luther says that "boredom and disgust with one's vocation" is "a definite sign that you are in a truly God pleasing estate."

184. WA 10/1.2: 159.20–162.12 (including 160.19–21, "Alßo auch wirtt fur aller welt gotis gnaden predigt den demutigen, auff das sie alle demutig wurden, aber sie wollten nicht"); LW 75: 146–49.

185. WA 10/1.2: 198.19–32 (concluding, "das heyst recht demutigen und allen menschen die vermessenheytt ausschneyden und tzu nichte machen. Das heyst nu warhafftig den weg des herrn richten, rawm geben, und platz machen"); LW 75: 179 (translation altered).

186. WA 10/1.2: 198.33–199.14 (concluding, "Eyn solch hertz, yhe mehr es ßo gesynnet ist, yhe baß dem herrn den weg bereyttet, obs auch dieweyl eyttel malmasier truncke, und auff roßen gienge und nicht eyn wortt bettet"); LW 75: 179.

187. WA 10/1.1: 45.21–46.4; LW 75: 201 (Sermon on Titus 2:11–15; Christmas Day).

188. WA 10/1.2: 29.27–30.12; LW 75: 34. The editors of LW 75 track carefully changes between the sixteenth-century editions; I use the 1522 text here, omitting additions made in 1540.

189. WA 10/1.1: 88.19–89.9 (concluding, "Die Ehre hatt Christus gott erwidder bracht, damit das er unß geleret, wie alle unßer *ding nichts sey denn eyttel tzorn und ungnad fur gott*, das wyr unß ynn keynen weg rhumen noch unß selb drynnen wolgefallenn mugen, ßondernn furchten unnd schemen mussen, alß ynn der grossisten far und schande, das alßo unßer ehre und selbgefallen tzu poden gestossen und *gantz nichts werde*, unnd wyr fro werden, das wyr yhr ßo loß werden, das wyr yn Christo mugen erfunden und behallten werden, wie gesagt ist"); LW 75: 225–26.

190. WA 10/1.1: 89.10–91.11; my translation deviates from LW 75: 226–27, which does not translate "feyn gelassen" from the passage "stehen feyn gelassen und willig ynn gottis willen."

191. WA 10/1.1.325.14–352.5; 370.18–374.20; LW 75: 364–81, 392–95.

192. On Luther's concept of the noetic fall, and on the broader early modern anxiety about the deceptiveness of appearances, see Schreiner, *Are You Alone Wise?*, 324–90.

Chapter 4

1. Andreas Karlstadt, *Von Mannigfaltigkeit des einfältigen, einigen Willen Gottes. Was Sünde sei* (Köln: Arnd von Aich, March 1523), E4r. This text was printed twice, in Köln by Arnd von Aich (VD 16 B 6251) and in Augsburg by Silvan Otmar (VD 16 B 6252); I use the former. The English translation is from EC, 209. In the original, the passage reads, "Das yst eyn antzeig vnnd tzeichen / des gotlysche[n] ewigenn / vnnd bestendigen willens / das er vnser natur vnd vnserm willenn saur vnnd herb ist / da bey kann eyn Christ verstehen / waßerley willen gottis ym eynfall / dann ist er mit vnserm aigen willen vereyndt sueß vnnd mildt / so schat er vns." *Von Mannigfaltigkeit* is publication number 53 in Alejandro Zorzin's "Chronologisch geordnetes Verzeichnis der gedruckten Schriften des Andreas Bodenstein von Karlstadt," which is an appendix to his *Karlstadt als Flugschriftenautor* (Göttingen: Vandenhoeck & Ruprecht, 1990), 273–307. In this chapter, I adopt Zorzin's modernized spelling for all titles; the specific edition consulted will be noted with VD number and (as appropriate) a signature referencing the collection of the Herzog August Bibliothek (HAB). Initial research for this chapter was conducted with the support of a doctoral fellowship from the Rolf und Ursula Schneider Stiftung of HAB in 2012.

2. Parts of this chapter, in an earlier version, appeared in my essay, "Divine Pedagogy and Self-Accusation: Reassessing the Theology of Andreas Bodenstein von Karlstadt," MQR 87 (July 2013): 335–367.

3. The account of the Wittenberg movement in this chapter is especially informed by: Amy Nelson Burnett, *Karlstadt and the Origins of the Eucharistic Controversy: A Study in the Circulation of Ideas* (Oxford: Oxford University Press, 2011), 10–35, which focuses on developments and publications surrounding the mass; Jens-Martin Kruse, *Universitätstheologie und Kirchenreform: Die Anfänge der Reformation in Wittenberg, 1516–1522* (Mainz: Philipp von Zabern, 2002), 279–389; Ulrich Bubenheimer, "Martin Luthers Invocavit Predigten und die Entstehung religiöser Devianz im Luthertum: Die Prediger der Wittenberger Bewegung 1521/1522 und Karlstadts Entwicklung zum Kryptoradikalen," in *Kryptoradikalität in der Frühneuzeit*, ed. Günter Mühlpfordt and Ulman Weiß (Stuttgart: Steiner, 2009), 17–38; and Bubenheimer, "Andreas Rudolff Bodenstein von Karlstadt: Sein Leben, seine Herkunft und seine innere Entwicklung," in *Andreas Bodenstein von Karlstadt 1480–1541: Festschrift der Stadt Karlstadt zum Jubiläumsjahr 1980*, ed. Wolfgang Merklein (Karlstadt: Michel-Druck, 1980), 5–58, esp. 31–44. I have also consulted the accounts of Mark U. Edwards Jr., *Luther and the False Brethren* (Stanford, CA: Stanford University Press, 1975), 6–33; Volkmar Joestel, *Andreas Bodenstein genannt Karlstadt: Schwärmer und Aufrührer* (Wittenberg: Drei-Kastanien Verlag, 2000), 24–33; James S. Preus, *Carlstadt's Ordinaciones and Luther's Liberty: A Study of the Wittenberg Movement, 1521–22* (Cambridge, MA: Harvard University Press, 1974); and Ronald J. Sider, *Andreas Bodenstein von Karlstadt: The Development of his Thought, 1517–1525* (Leiden: Brill, 1974), 148–201. All accounts rely on the sources in Nikolaus Müller, *Die Wittenberger Bewegung 1521 und 1522* (Leipzig: M. Hensius Nachfolger, 1911).

4. See Burnett, *Karlstadt,* 24–25, esp. note 60.

5. Karlstadt seems to have added the celebration of the mass to a "vespers or preaching service," much to the surprise of attendees; he had previously announced his intention to celebrate an evangelical mass on New Year's Day. We do not know if that announcement was in defiance of the elector's wishes that "traditional usages be retained until agreement had been reached through preaching, lecturing, writing, and disputations." On all this, see Burnett, *Karlstadt,* 27–28, esp. notes 74 and 76.

6. For this argument, see Sider, *Andreas Bodenstein,* and Preus, *Carlstadt's* Ordinaciones. Others have argued that there were substantial theological differences between Luther and Karlstadt even before their public break, although these did not prevent common cause: see Ulrich Bubenheimer, "Karlstadt, Andreas Ruldolff Bodenstein von (1486–1541)," in TRE 17: 649–57; here, 650; Sigrid Looß, "Karlstadts Bild vom Menschen in seiner Wittenberger Zeit (1520–1523)," in *700 Jahre Wittenberg: Stadt, Universität, Reformation,* ed. Stefan Oehmig (Weimar: Verlag Hermann Böhlaus Nachfolger, 1995), 275–87; here, 276; and Looß, "Andreas Bodenstein von Karlstadt (1486–1541) in der modernen Forschung," in ABvK: 9–23; here, 12–13. Amy Nelson Burnett's analysis surrounding the mass yields a complex understanding of common ground and divergence between Luther and Karlstadt in 1521–1522. Karlstadt largely adopted Luther's understanding of the mass: he defined the sacrament as a sign of

the promise, found its purpose in the assurance of forgiveness, and argued that faith alone made a person worthy to receive. He continued to assume the corporeal presence of Christ in the bread and wine, and the two men agreed on numerous reforms to practice, such as the ending of private masses. In fact, Karlstadt's relevant publications in the fall of 1521 reflected a larger consensus of "all members of the reform party in Wittenberg." Still, disputes between Luther and Karlstadt over whether it was a sin to commune in one kind only and over external ritual forms—above all, elevation of the host—reflected a deeper rift concerning "whether one should give priority to divine law or to Christian freedom." The question also concerned "the relationship between external actions and internal disposition." Burnett explains that "for Karlstadt, external ceremonies had to conform to what was preached, both amplifying and confirming the message of the gospel and reflecting the form of worship that God had commanded in Scripture." Karlstadt relied on both a literal exegesis of scripture and a dualism of spirit and matter learned from Augustine's Neo-Platonism and Erasmus. Burnett, *Karlstadt*, 11, 14, 23, 31–35.

7. These are the poles of *Gelassenheit* and rebirth so often emphasized by recent scholarship; for an effort to describe Karlstadt's unique theological position, see Evener, "Divine Pedagogy," esp. 338.

8. See Ulrich Bubenheimer, "Scandalum et ius divinum: Theologische und rechtstheologische Probleme der ersten reformatorischen Innovationem in Wittenberg 1521/22," ZSSRK 90 (1973): 263–342.

9. Kruse, *Universitätstheologie*, 383; on Melanchthon's positions, see ibid., 320–21, 323–27. See also Bubenheimer, "Luthers Invocavitpredigten," 19–30.

10. Students had engaged in various anti-clerical acts since the summer of 1521, but the December incidents involved the citizenry as well. Kruse, *Universitätstheologie*, 319, 337–39.

11. Quoted from Edwards, *Luther and the False Brethren*, 8; see also Kruse, *Universitätstheologie*, 339–40; Burnett, *Karlstadt*, 27; Bubenheimer, "Luthers Invocavitpredigten," 24. The *Six Articles* were presented to the *Rat* after an earlier and more unruly presentation of articles was rebuked by the Elector. The Elector forbade implementation of the articles.

12. Burnett, *Karlstadt*, 27–28. On the alliance of direct inspiration and dissent, see Steven E. Ozment, *Mysticism and Dissent: Religious Ideology and Social Protest in the Sixteenth Century* (New Haven, CT: Yale University Press, 1973).

13. Kruse, *Universitätstheologie*, 354, writes, "Über den bisherigen Wittenberger Konsens ging Karlstadt allein mit der von ihm vertretenen vollständigen Ablehnung der Beichte hinaus"; see also Burnett, *Karlstadt*, 23.

14. Spurred on by Gabriel Zwilling's preaching, monks in the Augustinian cloister refused to celebrate private masses and communed in both kinds in October 1521. In September, Melanchthon and a group of his students received communion in both kinds. In November, Justus Jonas distributed communion in both kinds ("als erster") in the *Schloßkirche*. See Bubenheimer, "Luthers Invocavitpredigten," 19–23; Kruse, *Universitätstheologie*, 317–18. For Karlstadt's act, see Kruse, *Universitätstheologie*, 349f.; Bubenheimer, "Luthers Invocavitpredigten," 27; Sider, *Andreas Bodenstein*, 159.

15. Burnett, *Karlstadt*, 28; Bubenheimer, "Luthers Invocavitpredigten," 27; Kruse, *Universitätstheologie*, 354–55.

16. On these writings and their publication, see Bubenheimer, "Andreas Rudolff Bodenstein von Karlstadt," 31–32.

17. For Karlstadt's summary of the *Rat's* decision, see his *Von Abtun der Bilder. Und daß kein Bettler unter den Christen sein soll* (Wittenberg: Nickel Schirlentz, 1522 [VD 16 B6214]), A1v–A2r; EC, 101–2. Karlstadt notes, "the eyes of all the world are upon us, observing our deeds and life."

18. *Ein löbliche Ordnung der fürstlichen Stadt Wittenberg*, published 4 times in 1522. I have consulted the Augsburg edition of Melchior Ramminger, VD 16 W 3697. For summary and analysis, see Kruse, *Universitätstheologie*, 362–66 (note 512 addresses Karlstadt's involvement in writing the *Ordnung*).

19. According to Kruse, *Universitätstheologie*, 370, the incident may not have been as large or tumultuous as it is sometimes depicted; its significance lay in the Elector's response, which placed the blame on "individual preachers."

20. Bubenheimer, "Luthers Invocavitpredigten," 21–23, 26; Kruse, *Universitätstheologie*, 332–36. After covertly visiting Wittenberg in early December 1521, for example, Luther remarked to Spalatin, "Omnia vehementer placent, que video et audio" (WAB 2, 410.18–22).

21. Kruse, *Universitätstheologie*, 334.

22. Bubenheimer, "Luthers Invocavitpredigten," 26; Bubenheimer, "Luthers Stellung zum Aufruhr in Wittenberg 1520–1522 und die frühreformatorischen Würzeln des landesherrlichen Kirchenregiments," ZSSRK 102 (1985): 147–214; here, 187–201; Kruse, *Universitätstheologie*, 344–47.

23. Edwards, *Luther and the False Brethren*, 10–13. Even before Luther's return, Electoral representatives had identified Karlstadt's preaching as a source of "Aufruhr" and attempted to stop or curtail his preaching activity; see Bubenheimer, "Luthers Invocavitpredigten," 29; Kruse, *Universitätstheologie*, 370. At this time, according to Bubenheimer, "Karlstadt verwies auf sein Predigtamt an der Schloßkirche, machte aber auch eine innere Berufung geltend, der er folgen müsse, womit er wohl die über seine Amtspflichten hinausgehenden Predigten rechtfertigen wollte."

24. On the motivations for Luther's return, see the assessment of Kruse, *Universitätstheologie*, 377–78.

25. The arguments advanced were anticipated by the *Sincere Admonition*. See Bubenheimer, "Luthers Invocavitpredigten," 26. One analysis of the sermons may be found in Kruse, *Universitätstheologie*, 378–82. Kruse objects to the notion that only Luther's return re-established order and moderation; unrest was not widespread, and a moderated *Ordnung* had already been created in negotiations with the Elector's representatives. See ibid., 373n556.

26. LW 51: 69–100; WA 10/3: 1–64.

27. Kruse, *Universitätstheologie*, 387–89. Here Kruse notes, "Luthers Kritik an der Entwicklung in Wittenberg [konzentrierte sich] vor allem auf den Bereich der gottesdienstlichen Reformen. . . . Hier kam es nach seiner Rückkehr zu Veränderungen. Dagegen wurden wichtige Bestimmungen der Stadtordnung bereits

in der ersten Hälfte des Jahres 1522 in die Praxis überführt. So stellte der 'Gemeine Kasten' die Armenfürsorge auf eine neue Grundlage, traten die Ausführungen über die Besoldung der Priester in Kraft, lösten sich die Bruderschaften auf und wurde das Frauenhaus geschlossen sowie unter der Aufsicht des Rates Bilder und Altäre aus den Kirchen entfernt."

28. This treatise (*Von Abtun*) was printed twice in Wittenberg and once in Straßburg; see Zorzin, "Verzeichnis," 48. As indicated in note 17, I consult the first Wittenberg edition, printed by Nikel Schirlentz.

29. *Von Abtun*, A1v–A2r; EC 101–2.

30. *Von Abtun*, A4r; EC, 105; see also Bubenheimer, "Karlstadt, Andreas Rudolff," 654.

31. *Von Abtun*, C4r–v; EC, 117.

32. *Von Abtun*, A2v–A4r, B4r; EC, 102–5, 111.

33. *Von Abtun*, B1r–B2r; EC, 107–8.

34. *Von Abtun*, C2v; EC, 114.

35. *Von Abtun*, C2v; EC, 114–15 (rendering of Biblical citations slightly altered). See also *Antwort Andres Bodenstein von Carolstad Doctor geweihtes Wasser belangend. Wider einen Bruder Johann Fritzhans genannt, (vom) Holzschuher Orden* (Wittenberg: Melchior Lotter, d.J., 1521), B1r: "Ich geschweyg / das des ausserlichen menschen heyligkeit / allein odder sunderlich / ym leyden stehet vnnd volbracht wurt / als geschriben / Corrumpitur autem homo zc. ii.Corint.iiij. der alt mensch wurt teglich tzerbrochen." HAB, A: 359 Theol. (8); Zorzin, "Verzeichnis," 30.

36. Karlstadt polemicizes against contrived papal or scholarly evasions of the scriptural prohibition of images, and he warns those who follow such evasions because of the status of the contrivers. See for instance *Von Abtun*, A4r, C1v–C2r; EC, 105, 113: "[I]f you should follow someone on account of his status, appearance, pleasant words, and friendly disposition, thus coming in conflict with a divine prohibition, you will surely die."

37. See the *Predigt oder Homilie über den Propheten Malachiam genannt*, printed in Wittenberg by Nickel Shirlentz and in Augsburg by Sigmund Grimm and Marx Wirsung; Zorzin, "Verzeichnis," 49. The sermon was published with a dedicatory letter dated February 18, 1522, indicating that Karlsadt had preached on *Malachi* over several days. I quote from the Augsburg edition, VD 16 6180; HAB, A 131.2 (39).

38. Karlstadt never claimed to be a prophet, but a "called and chosen preacher of the cross of Christ"; see Hans-Peter Hasse, " 'Von mir selbs nicht halden': Beobachtungen zum Selbstverständnis des Andreas Bodenstein von Karlstadt," in QdR: 49–73; 55–56, 70. However, through the analogy between prophetic speech and the speech of an evangelical preacher, Karlstadt's understanding of prophets could shape his activity and self-understanding as a Christian preacher and teacher. Karlstadt's commitment to the ideal of complete self-surrender—to Tauler's injunction, "Von mir selbs nicht halden" (see ibid., 70–73)—allowed him to see himself as an empty vessel through which divine teaching flowed.

39. *Predigt über Malachiam*, B1v–B3r.

40. *Predigt über Malachiam*, B3v–B4r. The model of the evangelical preacher is not only the prophet, but Christ who says, "[M]ein ler ist nit mein ler / sonder des der mich

geschickt hat . . . Die Euangelisten gotis sollen offenlich bekennen / das ire leer / wort / vnd kunst gotis ist / vnd nichts ir eygen."

41. Bubenheimer, "Luthers Invocavitpredigten," 30–37. For the letter from Karlstadt to Pömer, see Ulrich Bubenheimer, "Andreas Bodenstein von Karlstadt und seine fränkische Heimat," in QdR: 15–48; 45–47.

42. Scholars disagree on the extent of the *Predigtverbot* against Karlstadt. Bubenheimer, "Luthers Invocavitpredigten," 36, and Zorzin, *Karlstadt als Flugschriftenautor*, 110n41, think that Karlstadt was completely silenced, whereas Kruse, *Universitätstheologie*, 383n617, contends he was only banned from the pulpit of the city church—thus forced to constrain his preaching to the castle church, where he was deacon.

43. On the phases and pauses of Karlstadt's publication activity, see esp. Zorzin, *Karlstadt als Flugschriftenautor*, 110–30; concerning this pause, 119.

44. *Ein Sermon vom Stand der christgläubigen Seelen; von Abrahams Schoß und Fegefeuer der abgeschiedenen Seelen*, printed seven times according to Zorzin, "Verzeichnis," 52. I have consulted the Augsburg 1523 edition published by Sigmund Grimm, HAB, A: 156 Theol. (6), and the first edition published by Philipp Ulhart in Augsburg, possibly at the end of December 1522. I quote from the latter, VD 16 B 6197.

45. See Evener, "Wittenberg's Wandering Dead," 531–34.

46. See the discussion of the late-medieval penitential system in chapter 2.

47. *Sermon vom Stand*, A2r–A4v. The improvement of departed souls does not happen through intercessory prayer, Karlstadt says.

48. *Sermon vom Stand*, A4v–B1v.

49. Although Gansfort was the source of the analogy, the main contours of the argument come from Karlstadt's take on scripture and Eckhartian mysticism. On Gansfort's influence, see Craig M. Koslofsky, *The Reformation of the Dead: Death and Ritual in Early Modern Germany, 1450–1700* (London: Macmillan Press, Ltd., 2000), 31–34.

50. *Sermon vom Stand*, B1v.

51. *Sermon vom Stand*, B2r.

52. See *Sermon vom Stand*, B2r–B4r. See especially B2v, where Karlstadt argues forcefully that the souls of those who die in Christ are not, as the priests say, "vnselig / in jamer / in elend in sünden," yet they also are not "aller sünde . . . ledig." Rather, "Sy sein in starcker vnd hitziger senligkait oder verlangen / vnnd sein gern drinn. Warumb wolt ir sy küelen? Ye hitziger vnd hefftiger jr leben ist / ye neher sy zü dem aller lautterstem ewigem leben nahen / gleichsam das liecht des auffgangs / wie vil meer es dem mittag nahet / ye liechter vn[d] klarer es wirt."

53. *Sermon vom Stand*, B3r–C1r: "It is indeed correct that true Christians have here a toilsome and burdensome life, for because God loves them, God punishes them with his rod. Prov. 3. Heb. 12. All who rightly desire to live in Christ must suffer persecution; also, they must bear their cross all day long, from which is manifoldly understood that every Christian in this life suffers evil, harm, pain, affliction or oppression. However, when he departs from this life, he then goes into the state and life of comfort . . . or into rest . . . and feels trouble and work no longer, but has complete comfort (*vollen trost*) . . . Abraham says indeed that Lazarus here received evil, but in the life and state of souls he is comforted."

54. *Sermon vom Stand*, C1r.

55. *Sermon vom Stand*, C1r–v: "Nun wolten die seelen ... gern am liechten tag sehen / vnd mit vollem hertzen lieben / vnd das sy got allenthalben erfült / Senen sich darnach vnd haben schmertzlichen verlangen darnach vnd steend also in gelassenheit / vnd geschwinder lanckweyligkait." No one can see God "ehr alle creaturische ding / vnd die vmstendige finsternuß / oder grobhait vom aug abgeryben vnd abgewüscht werden." *Erkenntnis* and *Sehnlichkeit* are bound: since human beings on earth know Christ only in darkness, no more than "ain klaine senligkait" is possible; but the *Sehnlichkeit* of the departed is "in vnzelicher weyß / hefftiger vnd geschwinder / dann vnnsere verlangligkait" (C1r-C2r).

56. *Sermon vom Stand*, C1v.

57. *Sermon vom Stand*, C2r–v. The term "abyss (*Abgrund*)" appears here. "Demnach mu[o]ß das fegfewer ain klar aug / das ist / rayn vrtayl vnd erkantnuß machen / vnd zu[o] voller lieb vnd gerechtigkait fieren / das ist ain auffgekaimdt erdtrich / das on wasser ist / vnd wan[n] sich die erden / das ist / der gayst durch solche bewegnuß aufthu[o]t / vnd ist gantz dürz / so kompt got vn[d] verleßt es mit nichte / sonder er erfült es mit seiner maiestat vnd glorien / vnnd macht es im abgrundt sath vnd vol" (C2r).

58. Karlstadt draws from the notion in I Peter 4:6 that Christ must have preached to the dead, or otherwise he could not judge them. *Sermon vom Stand*, C2v.

59. *Sermon vom Stand*, C3r. On Karlstadt's argument that such ignorant but saved souls constitute the "wandering dead," see Evener, "Wittenberg's Wandering Dead," 550–54.

60. *Sermon vom Stand*, C3v.

61. See Joestel, *Andreas Bodenstein*, 31.

62. In February 1523, Karlstadt renounced further participation in academic promotions; and he already had begun to try his hand at farming. Sider, *Andreas Bodenstein*, 176–78.

63. See note 1. I translate the title more literally than EC.

64. *Was gesagt ist: Sich gelassen, and was das Wort Gelassenheit bedeutet, und wo es in heiliger Schrift begriffen [ist]*. The tract was printed twice in Augsburg in 1523, by Philipp Ulhart and Silvan Otmar respectively; see Zorzin, "Verzeichnis," 54. I consulted a copy of the Ulhart edition, HAB, A: 156 Theol. (7), VD 16 B 6257.

65. Sider, *Andreas Bodenstein*, 179–80, esp. n24, notes that Karlstadt avoids harsh polemic and a direct attack on Luther in these two tracts and in all his tracts before Luther's direct challenge at the Black Bear Inn. Nonetheless, the work of self-distancing from Luther and Wittenberg is unmistakable and definitive of Karlstadt's work in this period.

66. DTRG, F3r.

67. *Von Mannigfaltigkeit*, A2r; EC 186 (translation altered), continuing, "If we do not follow God's will directly and do not will as God wills, or omit that which God does not will, we must not think ourselves God's friend or capable of thinking, committing, or omitting anything that pleases God."

68. *Von Mannigfaltigkeit*, B1r–B3r; EC 190–92 (translation partly my own), citing DTRG, B1v, C3v, F3r, H4v; see also H3r. At B3r, EC 192, Karlstadt announces a shift

in his topic to the divine will, although he enters that topic through a discussion of disobedience.

69. *Von Mannigfaltigkeit*, A2r, EC 186: "whoever learns the hidden will of God and does what God wants done is a friend of god. And whoever does not immerse (*eynsenckt*) his will in God's will or does not lose his own will in God's must not ever think himself a friend of God."

70. *Von Mannigfaltigkeit*, A2r–A3r; EC 186–187: "So da[nn] Christus eine[n] willen mit got gehabt / vn[d] sich im aller hochsten mit got seynem vater v[er]eynwilligt hat / magk keiner ey[n] freund Christi seyn / er sey dan tzu[o]uor eines willes mit got / vn[d] well / beger / thu[o]n / vn[d] lasse nicht / dan das got wil / begert tzu[o]thu[o] n oder lassen. . . . ich [werd] ein angeborner freund gotis vn[d] volgend Christi . . . / wann ich leuterlich / on alles vmbsehen / vn[d] an diß oder genes / oder on annemung eines andern dings / gots willen annemen / vn[d] das ich also mit got vereyndt / ein geist / vn[d] eyn dingk werd." In *Von Mannigfaltigkeit*, *Annehmlichkeit* can describe both a sinful regard for the self or creatures (D1v; EC 201) and a necessary stance of receptivity to God.

71. EC 187–88. These last lines were omitted from the original I consulted, but see broadly *Von Mannigfaltigkeit*, A2r–B1r; EC 186–90.

72. The transition reads, unexpectedly, "Nu solt ich sagen / dz dannest tzeite[n] die nit sunde[n] so gotlichen willen nit stracks erfullen." *Von Mannigfaltigkeit*, B3r; EC, 192.

73. "God-fearing" follows EC; the phrase in the version consulted by me is "gotfruchtsamer."

74. *Von Mannigfaltigkeit*, B3r–v; EC 193.

75. *Von Mannigfaltigkeit*, B3v–B4r (my translation); EC, 193.

76. *Von Mannigfaltigkeit*, C1r–v; EC 195–96. Karlstadt continues with a critique of self-willed, self-inflicted suffering, associating such suffering with the Jews in Isaiah, "die sich mager mit fasten machten vnd kasteyhten sich / vnd krumpten iren halß vor qualu[n]g / als einen ryng oder reyff / das alles nicht was das sy teten / drumb das sy iren willen suchtenn." In a section entitled, "Es mus aigen willen in anderen stucken auch vergehen," C2r–C3v, EC 196–98, Karlstadt outlines a broad definition of fasting and castigation that includes the care of the rich for the poor. The analogy to the seed that dies, much liked by Karlstadt, continues to appear in the section, "In gottis willen wirt der mensch new," where baptism is offered as a symbol of the "gründliche[n] absterben vnsers aigen willens." *Von Mannigfaltigkeit*, C3v–C4r; EC, 198–99. Rebirth is the "absterben aigens willens. dann wu[o] lieb tzu[o] vns / vnd vnserheyt tzu[o] meyn vnnd meynheit ist. vnnd wu[o] ich byn / vnnd wu[o] meyn will steet / da ist vnnd steit meyn verderben vnnd helle [etc.]."

77. *Von Mannigfaltigkeit*, C4r–D1r; EC 199–200 (translations slightly altered); see also D2r–v; EC 202.

78. *Von Mannigfaltigkeit*, D1v–D2r; EC 201; the relevant sections are entitled "Annemlikeit eyn[en] grewlich thier tragt nach dem menschen" and "Got lesset gut vnd boes ym menschen bleyben."

79. In his 1524 tract, *Ob Gott eine Ursache sei des teuflischen Falles* (Jena: Michael Buchfürer), Karlstadt discusses a disputation on this topic that occurred during his

time in Wittenberg. The text is VD 16 B 6176; Zorzin "Verzeichnis," 59. I've consulted HAB, A 156 Theol. (5).

80. *Von Mannigfaltigkeit*, D3v. Karlstadt ultimately *defends* this scholastic distinction—evidence of a softening stance toward that tradition—on which, see also *Ob Gott eine Ursache*, B3v-B4r. EC 409n20 incorrectly states that Karlstadt repudiated the "distinction" because it sought to evade "the vexing problem of God's responsibility in sinful human actions."

81. See *Von Mannigfaltigkeit*, E2r-v ("Weil nu got dz boeß schaffet / vnd lyferet einen sunder seynen bosen begirden / vnnd thut das durch syne[n] v[er]henckliche[n] willen / wil ich nit widerspreche[n] dz gots will / der verhenget vnnd nachlesset / ein wirckende krafft sey. Ich weisz wol / das der wirket / der ein ruden vnd stecken bewegt vnd schlecht ymand. vnd das thut gottis verhencklicher will. er schlegt mit dem Assur gleich als mit einer ruden / stecken. Esa.x"); EC 205–6.

82. See *Von Mannigfaltigkeit*, E2v; EC 207. According to Karlstadt, all Christians suffer persecution, which God permits—"jedoch ist es got ent/kegen vnd wider / das ein mensch eine[n] *vergotten knecht gottis* veruolgen magk" (my emphasis). EC translates "junger Christi" as "young Christian." In this paragraph, "must be fulfilled" and "bring its work into reality" are my own translations.

83. See the sect., "Es ist nit eyn dingk zeitlicher vnd verhencklicher / oder tzorniger will gots, " *Von Mannigfaltigkeit*, G1v-G2r; EC 216–17.

84. The entire discussion in this paragraph covers *Von Mannigfaltigkeit* D3r-E4r; EC 203–8.

85. *Von Mannigfaltigkeit*, E3v-E4r; EC 208–9.

86. DTRG, F2r: "Der me[n]sch hatt keynen freyen wille[n] sonder eyn aygen willenn[n]" and "gottis wille vn[d] menschen wille ist wydder eynander."

87. Karlstadt does not seem to arrive at a distinct position vis-à-vis the assertion he imputes to his opponents, i.e. that God's will alone causes all things, including evil. God's will is still all-defining for Karlstadt in a way that leaves no space for human freedom. Karlstadt has argued that in some supra-rational way God's permissive will brings about things contrary to God's eternal will, although the two wills are the truly one. He then says that God's will seems multiple only from the perspective of human beings who do not have access to full knowledge of the singular will. His opponents must have made similar assumptions, unless they thought God was also the devil!

88. Later in the treatise, Karlstadt describes the prohibition of images as a divine command that—like the prohibition of coveting, or of reliance upon military might for one's defense—stands beyond human comprehension and must accordingly be accepted in humble surrender; see *Von Mannigfaltigkeit*, H1r-H2r; EC 220–22. When faced with obscurity regarding God's will, Karlstadt concludes, Christians can cast lots—such is the degree to which Karlstadt prefers instrumentality to human assertion. *Von Mannigfaltigkeit*, J1r; EC 225.

89. Of note here is the return to the theme of kingship: a king's will is expressed in his law, and God as the source of kingship is to be obeyed above human kings. *Von Mannigfaltigkeit*, D3r.; EC 202–3.

90. *Von Mannigfaltigkeit*, E4r–v; EC 209. I have used but substantially altered Furcha's translation.

91. DTRG, F2r, G4v, I3v.

92. *Von Mannigfaltigkeit*, E4v; EC 209–10. This section concludes, E4v–F1r, with lines that read: "Dar auß magk einer erkennen / ob er gots willen hab / oder seynen willen befynd. ob er dem ewigen / oder verhencklichem willen gotis geuolgig sey. fuelet einer gotis ewigen willen / also das go[e]tlicher will in ym lebet / vnd gewaltig ist / so muesz er gewyß fuelen / das er willenloß werde vnd seynem aignem willen absterbe." In a short ensuing section, "Tauff der Christen," Karlstadt interprets the baptism of Christians as this dying to self and becoming will-less, so that one can say "ich lebe nit. sonder Christus der lebt in mir. Ro. vi."

93. *Von Mannigfaltigkeit*, F1r ("mu[o]ß man nyt yn vernunfftiger / sond[er] in synlicher weiß lernen vnd smecken"); EC 210.

94. *Von Mannigfaltigkeit*, F2r; EC 211. See also F3v; EC 213: "Vnser natur vnnd gotis tzorniger oder verhencklicher will tragen vber eyns. aber der ewig gotis wyll ist wyder vnsern willen."

95. See here the entire section, "Sele fynden," *Von Mannigfaltigkeit*, F3r–4v; EC 212–15.

96. *Von Mannigfaltigkeit*, G1v, G3r; EC 216–18.

97. *Von Mannigfaltigkeit*, G2r–H1r; EC 216–20. "Wie wol dye beschneydungh vnnd tauff/ vnnd andere eusserlyche tzeychenn / we/der frum / weder bo[e]ß machenn. vereinen auch gott nycht / als der ewygh gottis wyll / myt hertzen angenommen/ denn menschenn got vereynt vnnd anleymbt / dannest mu[o]stenn dye gleubyghe solyche eusserlich dyng yn irer weyß annemen / vnnd als tzeychen der ynnerlichen gerechtikeit vnd eynikeit gebrauchen."

98. See esp. DTRG, E2r.

99. To shorten this quotation, I have omitted biblical references, including to Job 13:15, a favorite of Karlstadt's.

100. *Von Mannigfaltigkeit*, G4v–H1r; EC 220. For other descriptions of union with God, see especially *Von Mannigfaltigkeit*, E1v–E2r; EC 206; F2v, EC 212; and G3r–G4r, EC 218.

101. See Vincent Evener, "Epilogue," in PMRE, 429–39; here, 431–34.

102. *Was Gesagt ist*, E3v; EC, 162.

103. *Was gesagt ist*, D3v; EC 156, advises that no one should be troubled by the terminology of the *German Theology*, because it describes no more than Christ commands in Luke 9:23. For analyses of this treatise: Hasse, *Karlstadt und Tauler*, 173–185; McGinn, *Presence*, 6.1: 77–82.

104. *Was Gesagt ist*, A1v, F1v; EC, 134, 164. Unlike the other two, the question arising from the *Missive* appears not in the dedicatory epistle, but later in the text. Karlstadt's initial discussion of meaning (A2v; 135) declares that he wants to have *Gelassenheit* understood in an active sense; it is not "being forsaken (*verlassen*)," but the movement of "forsaking." This does not mean that the human is self-moving, as we will see.

105. *Was gesagt ist*, C2v–D3v; EC 148–56: *Gelassenheit* appropriates "noch wesen / noch leben / noch wachsen / noch verstentnuß vnd weyßhait / noch sein aygne seele." The

highest *Gelassenheit* is attained when "du dich deiner aygner person vertzygen hast / so bistu von allen dingen letig" (C3r). However, note the statement, "Ich will mitt disen Graden weder zyl noch regel geben habe[n] [/] rede vnd schreyb ain yeder die warhait gottes nach seiner eingetruckte vermanu[n]g. Das ich solt sagen das alle obuermelte grad flayschlich vn[d] den flayschlichen menschen anhangen / so wayß ich nit ob ichs mo[e]cht erhalten" (D3v).

106. See especially *Was gesagt ist*, B1v ("Darumb hayst sy billich vngelassenhait weyl sy nichts gu[o]tts will verlassen / vnd Annemligkait das sy sich / aller tugent fast annympt vnd in sich mit lüsten zeücht vnd für das jr achtet"); EC 140.

107. *Was gesagt ist*, B3v, D2v, D3v, D4r, and F3r; EC, 143–44, 154–55, 157, 167. At D2v, Karlstadt argues that the supposedly yielded soul, if he suffers "for God's sake," often "has an eye on his suffering and stands there, enjoying and loving it when he should have fled this, too, for God's sake" (trans. per EC). At D4r, he writes, "Jedoch das des selben gelaß icheit oder sicheit ernstlich verurtaylt vnnd auffgeben werd / darauff mu[o]st du vnablaßlich wachen / dan[n] der Teüffel wartet auff den vngelaß der vngelassenhait / als ain fuchs auff hüener / der sy fressen will."

108. *Was Gesagt ist*, A3r; EC, 136. On the negative side, Karlstadt writes, "Su[o]chen wir aber das vnser / oder scho[e]pffen lust auß gottes gaben / vn[d] zyehen sy in das vnser / so verlasen wir got / . . . vnd vberfaren eeliche gelübdte / vnd werden stinckende hu[e]ren vnd vngelasasse secke" (A3v; EC, 136–37).

109. *Was gesagt ist*, A4r ("Dan[n] gelassenhait dringet vn[d] fleüßt durch auß / vber alles das geschaffen ist / vn[d] kumpt in jr vngeschaffen nicht / das sy vngeschaffen vnnd nicht gewest / das ist in jren vrsprung vnd scho[e]pffer / wan[n] als du nichts gewest bist / da bistu in erkantnuß vnd willen gottes gantz mit ainander gestanden / vnd ist auff erden vnd hymel nichts geweßt / des du dich hettest mo[e]gen mit recht annemen"), B4r–v (the yielded soul must be "form loß . . . / das ist bloß vnnd wüest seyn aller Creaturen / wann sy Gott soll einnemen vnnd gechehen lassen / das sy Gott besytzet / herzschet vnnd zyeret / als in der ersten schaffung was (hymels vnd erden)"), D3r–v ("Der mensch ist anfencklich nicht gewest / weyler sein icht vnd ettwas oder sich vnd sicheit gelassen / vnd ordenlich vbergeben / so mu[o]ß er es dem vbergen [/] der in ettwas icht oder sich hatt gemacht / das ist. Er mu[o]ß sich / vnd alles das etwas in jm ist / mit seinem sich vnd icheit / Gott auffgeben / vnd in seinem willen nider tauchen / wan[n] ainer das thet / er wer in leyden vnd wercken gelassen"); EC, 138, 144, 155.

110. See esp. *Was gesagt ist*, D3r–D4r; EC 155–56: "Darauß ist zu[o] mercken / was das wo[e]rtlin sich bedeüt / vn[d] wie ain warhafftiger vnd gelaßner dienst Gottes / der seelen augen auff schwinget / in den abgründigen willen gottes / vnd in das grundloß gu[o]tt kreücht / wo[e]lches gott selber ist / da kain sich oder ich sein mag. Alle dieweyl ain seele auff nicht anders sicht dan[n] auff gotes wille[n] / vn[d] dz ewig gu[o]t / dz got ist / so fu[o]sset auch jr hertz an kayner creatur / Ja sy dringt auch durch jr auffschwingung vnd sencket sich in gottes willen / vnd stirbt dar jr selber ab von grund an / vnd verleürt / sich / vnd ir sicheit gantz zu[o] mal / vn[d] das mu[o]ß sein vnd geschehen. Darumb mo[e]cht ich wol sagen mit andern leüten / wo[e]lcher sein ich vnd icheit / oder sich vn[d] sein sicheit recht

geließ der hett wol gelassen. . . . Ein gelassen Ich oder Icheit / ist wann ich mich veracht vnd vbergeb vnd geb dem alles das gu[o]t / der mirs geben hat / dan[n] die flüßlin myessen in jren brun[n] vnd jr mo[e]re wider flyessen vnd keren / wan[n] sy ordenlich widerkeren wo[e]llen. Dieße Ich oder Sich werde[n] dan[n] nützlich gelassen / wan[n] aygner will gelassen wirt / wan[n] aygner wil verschmiltzt vnnd gottes will sein werck in der creatur bekompt [this is a key theme of the *German Theology*] / vn[d] wurd nicht anders gewolt / dan[n] das / vnd wie gott will / al dan[n] werden Ich vnd sich vbereben / vn[d] alles das dem geschaffen will nachvolgt oder auß jme entspreüsset / dz wirt alles samptlich recht gelassen."

111. *Was gesagt ist*, D3v–D4r ("Wo[e]lcher von grund will gelassen sein / vnd der sein / der sich gelassen hat / der mu[o]ß jm vnwidernemlich entwerden / vnd sein icheit oder sicheit frey außgeben / so wirt diß gelassen sich oder sicheit / ain Christfo[e] rmigs ich"); EC 154–57. The prayer of the person with the "new life of Christ" is "your will be done." See also the final remarks on "hymelischer gelassenhait" (*Was gesagt ist*, F3r–v; EC 167–68), which relate to the divine filling of the soul that has become "lere vnnd letig." This divine *Erfüllung* renders the soul impervious to creatures and lusts, "nach dem der mensch in der gantzen sele ist / vnd die seele in ainem vollen frid vnd gehorsam füert."

112. *Was Gesagt ist*, A4r; EC 137–38. See also *Was gesagt ist*, B1r–v; EC 139–40, where Karlstadt's language is strongly reminiscent of the *German Theology*: "Derwegen dringt gelassenhait durch alles das mein / vnd vrtaylet mich vnd alles das mein ist / aller gu[o]thait vnwirdig vnd spricht. Mir gebür nicht g[o]tes vo[n] recht das gott oder ain creaturen geben kan / das ich auch sollt in allain dem meinen gestrafft werden / vnd das ich der straff ku[m]met wirdig bin. Also fleüget gelassenhait vberauß / vn[d] würffet den menschen in ain gestreng verachtung vnd grawhen seyn selber vnd macht das der mensch dencket / es ist zimlich vnd recht / das gott vnd alle seyn creaturen wider mich seynd. . . . Gelassenhait hat alle lieb vnd lust on mittel / in Got lautter vnd liebet gott nicht als das oder jhenes / sonder als ain wesenlich gu[o]tt. Vngelassenhait hatt lust vnd lieb in dem / das geschaffen ist / vnnd liebet diß oder jhenes gu[o]t / als jr aygen gu[o]tt."

113. *Was gesagt ist*, D3v ("würdest du dich in disem gelaß teglich brauchen"); EC 155. Karlstadt writes here, "Anyone who desires to be wholly and truly yielded must irrevocably deny and divest (*vnwidernemlich abgeen vnd entwerden*) himself (and all that is his and which means anything to him). He must become one with the divine will, so that he does not see, hear, taste, desire, understand, or will anything other than what God wills. Whatever prevents or diverts him from accepting God's will must become his martyrdom. This is the cross which we must carry daily, Lk. 9:23."

114. See esp. *Was gesagt ist*, B3v; EC 143: "Also syhestu das gelassenhait ain anfang Christlichs leben ist / vnd mu[o]ß alle go[e]ttliche tugent erhalten / wa sy nitt wachet da so[e]lt der leeriung von der Schu[o]el Christi."

115. *Was gesagt ist*, B2v ("Christus fordert von seynen leerjungen ain soliche geschickligkait / wo[e]lche vber alle natürliche krefften ist. Er will das wir alles gelasen sollen das wir besitzen / vnd das wir kain creaturisch ding in vnser seele lassen eingeen / vnd das die seele alle ding vberwündt. Aber das ist aller vernunfft

vnmüglich / als Christus beken[n]t / sagend. Das bey den menschen vnmüglich ist / das ist müglich bey gott. Das ain mensch sein güetter verlaß vmb Gottes willen / das vermag er nitt / es sey dan[n] das jms gott in sonderhait vnd wunderbarlich ain sollichen gelaß verleych"); EC 141–42. Describing *Gelassenheit* as spiritual circumcision, Karlstadt points out that "nyemandt kan sich selber beschneyden . . . Gott mu[o]ß alle ding in seinem hauß oder tempel selber schaffen vnd ordenen / die er darein haben will"; *Was gesagt ist*, C2r; EC 147

116. Ulrich Bubenheimer, *Thomas Müntzer: Herkunft und Bildung* (Leiden: E. J. Brill, 1989),164–70.

117. *Was gesagt ist*, B2v; EC 142.

118. *Was gesagt* ist, B4v; EC 144 (my emphasis).

119. *Was gesagt ist*, F3r; EC 167 (the penultimate section, "Vngelassenhait ist hoffart"). Karlstadt writes,"Dise verleügnung mu[o]ß nit laubig vnd küel sein / sonder hertzlich vn[d] hytzig / Nicht aine[n] tag / sonder ewig weren. Auch soll er alletag auff die vngelassenhait vnd annemligkait wachen vnd warten gleych als ain zorniger Beer vnd grymmiger lo[e]w offt jre feynde warten / so jre jungen fressen vnnd verschlinden / vnnd mu[o]ß der mensch sein creütz des zorns / hassz vnd neydes wider seine seel teglich ertragen vnd nymmer ablegen so er Christo nachvolget vnd ain leeriung Gottes vnd Christi will werden. "

120. Cf. DTRG, F3v, specifically the annotation, "Merck wie hoch gott durch sunde entzurnet wirt."

121. For Karlstadt, the soul deceives itself, preferring to avoid the cross of self-accusation. See *Was gesagt ist*, E2r–v; EC 159–60: "The soul appears as if it is easy and dear to nature and as if it always wishes and desires God's will. But if one could know oneself properly and sincerely for even an hour, one would sense in oneself the cross and a thousand mortal sins, and hate, avoid, and flee oneself as one flees a hostile person and look upon oneself as one looks upon one's worst enemy."

122. See Volkmar Joestel, *Ostthüringen und Karlstadt: Soziale Bewegung und Reformation im mittleren Saaletal am Vorabend des Bauernkrieges (1522–1524)* (Berlin: Schelzky & Jeep, 1996), 80–83.

123. Ibid., 83–84, correcting the argument of Sider, *Andreas Bodenstein*, 27.

124. Joestel, *Ostthüringen*, 87–103, gathers the available evidence for the reforms untertaken in Orlamünde under Karlstadt's leadership. Notworthy are the conclusions, "So wird bei Karlstadt der Gottesdienst zum Diskussionspodium über das rechte Glaubensverständnis," and, "Über soziale Reformen wie etwa die Einrichtung eines gemeinen Kastens oder auch nur die Verabschiedung einer solchen Ordnung durch den Rat gibt es jedoch weder für Orlamünde noch für Kahla einen Hinweis."

125. On the legality of Karlstadt's move to Orlamünde and of the University's recalling of Karlstadt, see Sider, *Andreas Bodenstein*, 188–90; Sider also discusses (190–94) the subsequent exchanges between the University and Chapter in Wittenberg, the *Orlamünde* Rat, the Elector, and Karlstadt. See additions and corrections by Joestel, *Ostthüringen*, 136–39.

126. Martin Reinhart, *Wes sich Doctor Andreas Bodenstein von Karlstadt mit Doctor Martino Luther beredet zu Jena, und wie sie wider einander zu schreiben sich entschlossen haben*, published three times in 1524 in Wertheim, Leipzig and Augusburg, respectively. HAB, Signature A: 156 Theol. (8).

127. Joestel, *Ostthüringen*, 136–40.

128. See the tracts from this period translated in Amy Nelson Burnett, *The Eucharistic Pamphlets of Andreas Bodenstein von Karlstadt* (Kirksville, MO: Truman State University Press, 2011), which correspond to Zorzin, "Verzeichnis," 57, 65–69. Burnett, *Karlstadt*, 54–76, 91–114, analyzes Karlstadt's developing arguments and his influence within Zwinglianism, concluding "Zwinglian eucharistic theology owed a great deal to Karlstadt as pathbreaker, catalyst, and source of some of its arguments."

129. *Ursachen, daß Andreas Karlstadt eine Zeit stillschwieg. Von rechter, unbetrüglicher Berufung*, printed first in Jena, then again the next year in Augsburg (Zorzin, "Verzeichnis," 56); this text is available in the modern German edition of Erich Hertzsch, ed., *Karlstadts Schriften aus den Jahren 1523–25*, 2 vols. (Halle: Veb Max Niemeyer Verlag, 1956) [henceforth simply Hertzsch], 1: 1–19, and it is translated in EC, 169–84, as *Reasons Why Andreas Carlstadt Remained Silent for a Time and On the True, Unfailing Calling*. I translate *unbetrüglicher* differently. Karlstadt reflected on the danger and distraction of public teaching earlier in *Was gesagt ist*; see B2r–v, EC 140–41, where he argues that a truly yielded person would not teach publicly—"Ich erfrew mich in innerliche[n] ho[e]ren / solt ich leeren oder predigen vnd mich beflecken?" citing Song of Songs 5—unless driven by "obedience to God, brotherly love, or Christian fidelity."

130. Karlstadt addresses the Orlamünders as "Euch brüdern / die yr mich berufft."

131. Hertzsch 1: 3; EC 170. "[B]etter work of teaching" and "outward bodily labor" are my translations.

132. Hertzsch 1: 3–5; EC 170–72.

133. Hertzsch 1: 6–10; EC 172–76.

134. Hertzsch 1: 11–14; EC 177–79: "die Christus geyst erliden oder geschmeckt."

135. Hertzsch 1: 9; EC 175.

136. Hertzsch 1: 15; EC 180: "Ich weis das der priester seynen finger ym blut one vrsach nit teufft / vnd darnach siebenmal kegen dem furhanck / mit dem eingetunckten finger sprenget. Dann wir mussen auch die besprengung des bluttes Christi / siebenfeltigklich verstehn / vnd erleyden / ehe vnsere fürhenge allenthalben abfallen/ vnnd ehe wir auch ein rein vnd weiß wolgefegt silber werden/ welchs sibenmal durch fegt ist. Wir mussen ym fewer gefegt werden / als silber / denn got furet sein volck durchs fewr [Jer. 6:27]. Der im ersten oder dritten fewer nit besser wirt / der ist ein verworffen silber [Zech 13:9]." The references to purgation remind of Müntzer, but neither Zech. 13:9 nor Jer. 6:27 appears in the register of Müntzer's biblical citations in ThMA 1 or 2. Conversely, EC (the best available index at this time) registers no reference by Karlstadt to Num. 19 and its seven-day rite of purification after contact with a corpse—a passage Müntzer cited often. In this present treatise, Karlstadt mentions another theme that will be significant for Müntzer—the

separation and gathering of the elect (Hertzsch 1: 4; EC 171)—but again, the Bible passages deemed relevant by Karlstadt (Mark 13:27; Matt. 24:31) do not appear in ThMA 1 or 2.

137. Hertzsch 1: 16–17; EC 180–81.

138. Hertzsch 1: 16–17; EC 180–81 (translation altered).

139. Hertzsch 1: 16–17 (my translation; see EC 181–82).

140. Hertzsch 1: 18; EC 182 (translation altered).

141. Hertzsch 1: 19; EC 182. See also: Hertzsch 1: 19; EC 183 "Auch ist es Christlicher / das ich den schaden gutter werck erkenn vnd klag / dan dz ich gottis gebot gewaltigklich durch forchte vnd ein böß werck willigklich versprech."

142. *Verstand des Wortes Pauli: "Ich begehrte ein Verbannter [zu] sein von Christo für meine Brüder" Röm 9[:3]. Was Bann und Act [ist]*, printed January 1524 in Jena by Michel Buchfürer, then again in 1524 in Augsburg; see Zorzin, "Verzeichnis," 58. I have consulted a copy of the Jena printing, VD 16 B 6212; HAB, A: 258.74 Quod. (2).

143. *Ob man gemach fahren und des Ärgernisses [wegen] die Schwachen verschonen soll in Sachen so Gottes Willen angehen* (Basel: Thomas Wolff, 1524); Zorzin, "Verzeichnis," 70; available in Hertzsch 1: 73–97; EC 247–68.

144. Karlstadt claims to have been asked about this passage "in einer collacion." *Verstand*; A2r. On this, see Zorzin, *Karlstadt als Flugschriftenautor*, 123, 123n63, 156, 156n104.

145. In *Whether We Should Go Slowly*, Karlstadt compares such a stance to permitting a child to play with a sharp knife, in the belief that it would be contrary to love to take the knife away. Hertzsch 1: 87–89; EC, 260–61.

146. *Verstand*, A2r. Karlstadt raises immediate objections based on Christ's command of separation from evil doers ("Christus hat ein schwert bracht / vn[d] wil vns / in sonderheit von solchen bru[o]dern abschneiden / vn[d] teylen / die ein gotloses wesen vn[d] leben fu[e]ren") and on the Biblical injunction to obey God rather than humans. Karlstadt notes that Adam was expelled from Paradise for listening to Eve, and that Paul said, "So ich selbst oder ein Engel vom hymel heraber khem / vnd leret anders / so sol er ein vorbannter sein" (A2v).

147. *Verstand*, A3r–A4r: "Ich weis nicht / ab ein creutze / ho[e]cher vnnd bitterer sey / denn das / das der gleubige / der gotlosen wesen / vor seinen augen sehen muß. Und das sie alle wolmeynung vnnd gu[o]theytten Gotis / vorlachen / vnnd vorspotten. Nu[o] / ap gleych ein teil vnsers creutzes ho[e]cher wa[e]r / dan[n] diss creutze / das die liebe wircket / so weis ich dannest / das kein creutze lautterer ist. Vnd das kein außgestrackter schmertze / dem menschen fu[e]rkomen kan / den[n] der / der auß go[e]tlicher liebe / kegen Got vnnd dem nechsten außfleusset. Ey was kan den liebreiche[n] glauben / oder glaubreiche liebe / schmertzlicher anfechten / vn[d] bitterlicher mit lauterer wermu[o]t trinken/ dann das sich die welt / go[e]tlicher gunst / so schentlich vortzeyht / vnd thut iren eygen nu[o]tz vorachten?"

148. See, e.g., DTRG, C4v, F3v, H2r; such passages were likely at the root of Karlstadt's similar remarks at *Was gesagt ist*, D4r; EC 156: "Jm gegentayl der lieb gottes / wann yemandt sein ich oder sich lautterlich gelassen hatt / mu[o]ß jm nicht layd sein oder werden / dan[n] das wider Gott ist / mo[e]rcket er das ain creatur wider

gottes willen will oder thu[o]t / so so[e]lt er in hefftigen schmertzen / vn[d] hat layd / vnlust trawrigkait / angst / todt / hell vnd ewig fewer bey der selben widerwilligen creatur."

149. *Verstand*, A4v–B2v: Paul wants to be like Christ in bearing the sins of the world "bey Got oder vor got" and not "wider Got"; thus, Paul "durch Gottis geyst / begert / ein verbanter oder bann von Christo zu[o] sein / das er / den hon vnd spott / warhafftiglich fu[e]r seine bru[e]der leyden wolt / den ein verbanter leyden sol. Aber one schuldt / als Christus / one abdritt vonn dem vater / als Christus. In fester eynigkeit / mit Got / als Christus. . . . Nicht das er dem bann vrsach gebe / oder etwas thu[o]n wo[e]lde / das wider Gottis willen were" (B2r–v). Paul's goal was not to please his brothers, but that his brothers would turn to God.

150. *Verstand*, B2r (my emphasis). Karlstadt shifts at B3r–v to a discussion of how Christians are to apply the *Bann* and *Acht*—namely, only for the sins against which God speaks the ban. The tract ends with Karlstadt's personal declaration, "Wolte Got / das ich ein verbanter wer von Christo fu[e]r die welt / oder fu[e]r meyne bru[e]der / als ich den inhalt Pauli / von got gelernet / vnd yetzt angezeygt hab" (B4v).

151. See also *Whether We Should Go Slowly*, Hertzsch I: 80; EC 253.

152. See esp. *Ob Gott eine Ursache*, A2r, which describes a debate that occurred in Wittenberg, probably between 1520 and 1522.

153. Karlstadt's most extended reflection on these themes came in *Wie sich der Glaube und Unglaube gegen das Licht und Finsternis, gegen Wahrheit und Lügen, gegen Gott und den Teufel halten. Was der freie Wille vermag*—a tract that was printed twice, in Basel in 1524 by Thomas Wolff and in Straßurg in 1525. See Zorzin, "Verzeichnis," 71. I have consulted the Basel edition, VD 16 B 6464. The treatise distinguishes from "final," saving faith both the "small" faith that must and will grow in knowledge and love, and the "rootless" or "middle" faith that will falter in trials. Karlstadt also distinguishes "foolish unbelief" (such as Paul's before his conversion) from "condemned unbelief." Rootless faith and foolish unbelief reflect knowledge of Christ without final acceptance or rejection, and rootless faith may be replaced by the gift of small faith or culminate in condemned unbelief. These remarks are exegetical; explicitly rejecting his earlier beliefs, Karlstadt concludes that scripture describes faith and unbelief in various ways. On all this, see A3v–A4v. For Karlstadt, small faith provides the certitude of salvation prized by Luther's soteriology, but in a manner joined to self-accusation and the confession of nothingness. See the section, "Der mittelglaub machet nit selig: vnnd leiret auch nit zu[o] gotte[s] reich / als d[er] recht klein glaub," B2r–B3r: "Der recht klein glaub / machet nicht selig / ehe er vnser hertz in die aller kleinste kleinheit / vnd tieffste niderkeit füret / vnnd vns als ein klein kindlein machet." Those who die in middle or rootless faith, conversely, die in uncertainty and will continue to receive teaching after death, until their knowledge without commitment becomes loving acceptance or rejection. "Got würt nyemants one erkantnüs seyner herligkeit / vrteylen." Human beings are prepared to receive—and choose or reject—truth only through a period of "verwunderung vnd bewegligkeit," which for most extends beyond the grave.

154. See *Ayn scho[e]ner Sermonn vonn Spalttung der gu[o]tten vnnd bo[e]ßen Engelischen gaystern jm himel* (Augsburg: Heinrich Steiner, 1524), B2v–C1r: "Syhe Gott pflegt durch seine krefften in grunndt vnserer hertzen absteygen / vnnd sich selbs nach seyner abgeen / der krafft offenbaren / vnnd außsprechen. Alles durch seynen lebendtigen mund / der eyn eynplickendt liecht ist vnnd lasset sein werck im grunde der seelen / vnnd das selb werck haysset d[er] glawb / wo[e]llicher eyn erkanndtnis Gottes ist / vnd verheyrattet das hertz mitt Gott / vnd das hertz würdt alls bald starck [/] Wun[n]sam / vnnd voller frewden / es versteet / vnnd liebet Gottes abgeende krafft die es verstanden hatt / vnd thu[o]t im eere / vnnd schetzet die erkanntte krafft vber alles das sein hertz erkennen kan / vnd fasset das berlin / vnd gibet alles das er besitzet darumb vnd verlaßet alle seine habe für das / vnd darin[n] hat Gott wolgefallen / vnd in dem selben wirt Gottes namen hailig / seyn eere groß vnd vol." This sermon, preached on September 29, 1523 in Orlamünde, was printed three times; see Zorzin, "Verzeichnis," 55 (under the title, *Von Engeln und Teufeln ein Sermon*); the edition I consulted is VD 16 B 6187; HAB A: 151.24 Theol. (23).

155. *Wie sich*, B3v. "Ein yeglicher würt nach seinem pfund vffs ho[e]chst vnnd hertest bewegt werden / ehe er bereyt würt / das werck der seligkeyt zü leiden." Karlstadt attributes movement of the soul especially to God's Word, noting that the be-liever must be united with God's sharp "righteousness," in departure from created (*angeschaffen*) wisdom. Yet such a departure is accomplished only in final faith.

156. *Wie sich*, A3r–v, B4r–v, C1v–C2v (on truth and lies as the respective origins of faith and unbelief); *Ob Gott eine Ursache*, B3r–B4r. On the fear of creatures, including the devil and demons, *Ayn scho[e]ner Sermonn*, C1r–v.

157. *Ob Gott eine Ursache*, A4r–v: "Auß dem aber ku[o]mbt der schad vnd falh her / das die vornunfftigen creaturen genu[e]gde / an yren natu[e]rlichen krefften / haben . . . Man predig yhnen was man wil / so wo[e]llen sie bey yrer natu[e]rliche vernunfft bleyben. Vnnd ir geschaffen licht / fu[e]rs beste vnd genugsam schatzen. Vnnd vorsprechen das lichte / vnd Gotis einreden. . . . Got / hat die vornunfftige krefften / nicht derhalben geschaffen / das wir genu[e]gde dran hetten. Sondern / das wir ein vorlangu[n]g entpfiengenn nach seynem geyste. Vnd in rechte gelassenheit kemen / vnsers eigenthumbs / vnd Gottis wu[e]rden / vnnd begereten / das vns Got selb leeren / weyßen vnd erfu[e]llen wo[e]lt. Demnach solte[n] vnsere krefften von vns außgehn / als vnsere arm vnnd hende / vo[n] vnserm leip außgen / vn[d] solte[n] sich nach gotis werk außstreke[n] / als sich die arme vn[d] hende / nach d[er] spies austrecke[n]. Die aber ire krefften / nicht außbreytten nach gottis wirckung / die achtens dafu[e]r / das sie etwas vermo[e]gen / one den geist Christi / außrichten oder thun. Darumb fallen sie durch ire krefften / welche got wol vn[d] gut schuff / vnnd verlassen den Got / der sie / vnd ire eygen krefften gemacht / vnd ins wesen außgefu[e]rt hat. // Also hat der teuffel than."

158. Karlstadt continued to exhort readers to *Gelassenheit*. On the title page of *Wie sich*, immediately following the title, one reads the lines: "Die rouhen Christen seind in dem kleinen vngetrew vnd vngelassen / wie mo[e]chten sie in dem grossen gelassen vnd getrew sein?" See also ibid., A4r, C2r.

159. *Wie sich*, C1v–C2r.: "Wenn mich got wil glaubhafftig mache[n] / vnd seinen glauben in mein hungerichte vnnd dürstige krefften giessen. So geht got ab / inn mein / arm / begyrigs hertz / mit seyner vngeschaffner vnnd liechter warheyt / vnnd offenbaret sich meinem hertzen / das er ein warhafftiger vnnd getrewer gott ist / vnnd versicheret meynen geyst / das er eygentlich weiß / das gott warbafftig (sic.) vnnd getrew ist . . . das selb werck heysset der glaub / welcher ein liebreiches erka[e]ntnüß gottes ist / vnd die kunst gottes / oder ein offenbarung gottes genent ist"; this same faith brings the Christian "in die kleynste nidrigkeyt," for God reveals to children that which is hidden from the wise. "Dann bücher / bustaben / bapier / vnd dinten / vernufft vnd weyßheit / hindern vnd fürdern gar nichts / es were denn das ein mensch in hoher gelassenheyt schrifft lesen oder ho[e]ren thet." At C3v, Karlstadt argues with reference to Abraham that only God's "inward address and promise" can assure the Chrisitan of the truth of God's "outward speach and action" and of forgiveness itself: "Denn es ist ye gantz vnmüglich das einer gottes freund oder sone werd / ohne die inwendige vnd heimliche offenbarung gottes / als wenig auch das geschehen mag / das einer gottes eüsserlich wort annem / vnd für ein wort des preütgamß / der fro[e]lickeyt / des trostes vn[d] außgestreckten lustes halt / wenn sich got nit zu[o]uor / oder gleich im eüsserlichen geho[e]r mit seinem hellen vn[d] lichten abgehenden stral offenbaret / so vil das er ho[e]re[n] kan / wer gott ist / was er ist / was er will / alles nach den teylen." See also *Wie sich*, D1v–D3r.

160. In *Ob Gott eine Ursache*, A4r, Karlstadt depicts the dictum, "do what is within you," as an expression of *Ungelassenheit* and the appropriation of the soul's powers for the self: "Got hat mir einen freyen willen / vnd geystliche krefften / eygenthu[e]mblich geben / vnd er hat mich vnd alle meine krefften / gu[o]t / recht / vnd wolgeschaffen. Drumb wil ich bey meinem willen vnd krefften bleyben / vnd zu[e] friden sein / vnd so vil thun als ich sol. [margin: facere q(uo)d in se est] Das aber ist ein teuffelische vngelaßenheit." See also *Wie sich der Glaube*, D4r.

161. *Wie sich*, C4r–v. Sons of the devil are exactly like their father, Karlstadt says. They want to take their "natural powers," created good in them by God, and set these powers "über alle ding . . . / got gleich werden / vnd genügd dran haben." They hate God's justice and have "lust vnd annemligkeyt zu[o] irer geschaffen natur." In the final section of this treatise, D3r–D4v, Karlstadt explains that *Unglauben* arises in those "die mit jren natürlichen kreffte[n] genügig seind / vnd wo[e]llen nit dürre oder lehr stehn / biß sie durch gottes geyst / die warheyt gottes verstehn. Als die hochsinnige ko[e]pff thu[o]n / so den verstand der warheit / auß eygner vernufft / fassen." Yet these do not immediately fall into "den eüssersten verthümpten vnglauben / wenn sie irem finstern licht nachfolgen / vnd alles für recht halten das sie dadurch verstehn. Neyn. Sie stehend ein zeytlang / eyner doch lenger denn der ander / vff dem mittel verstandt (welchen in das finster liecht / das ist ir eygen krafft / geben hat) in bewegligkeyt / vnd wissen nitt waran sie seine. Das sie so lang leyden / als die warheyt mit parabolen vnd vorhengken fürschwebet."

162. See esp. *Wie sich*, D3v–D4v, where Karlstadt explains that just like the damned, the chosen abide in darkness in their natural powers, "ehe sie der geyst go[e]tlicher forcht einwesseret." But the chosen "verachte[n] vnnd verlassen jre finsternüß

/ . . . sie fliehen von jren näturlichen krefften / als von jrer vernufft / weißheyt / vnnd von jrem liecht in jnen / das die finsternüß selbert ist / vnnd verstehn nicht von sich selbert"; conversely, when the uncreated light illuminates and reveals human darkness, "die got verachter lieben sich vnnd ir angeschaffens liecht / vnd eygen kreften." To hate the self as the faithful do is to stand in God's "warhafftige vnd gerechte vrteyln. Sie wo[e]llen vo[n] dem vrsprung leren / der die warheyt selber ist / vnnd nit von jrem finstern liecht."

163. *Wie sich*, D1r. Unbelief is blind during that time alotted to souls for growth; in the end, it must confess and fear God's truth, justice, and power—although with angst, chagrin, revulsion, and gnashing of teeth.

164. *Von dem widerchristlichen Mißbrauch des Herren Brot und Kelch*, published for the first time between mid-October and mid-December, 1524. The work saw three printings that year; see Zorzin, "Verzeichnis," 65. I have used HAB, A: 156 Theol. (9) a copy of the edition printed in Nürnberg by Hieronymus Höltzel (VD 16 B6234). I take the title from Burnett, *The Eucharistic Pamphlets*, but all translations of the text are my own. Burnett's careful reconstruction of the date of writing (versus publication) establishes that this particular treatise was written to be "the opening volley in his [Karlstadt's] public campaign against Luther" after the confrontation at the Black Bear Inn; see Burnett, *Karlstadt*, 67. On the problem of dating Karlstadt's eucharistic writings published in Basel in 1524, Burnett, *Karlstadt*, 54–56.

165. *Mißbrauch*, A2v–A3r. "Das ist ain gemayner vnd grewlicher schad / daß vnnsere Christen vergebung der sünden im[m] Sacrament suchen. // Nemlich / wen[n] sy jre gewissen / als sy reden / a[e]ngstet oder betru[e]bet / jrer sünde halbe[n] / so schicken sy sich / das hochwirdig sacrament zu[e]empfahen / vnd wen[n] sy es empfangen / werden sy zu[o] friden / durch ainen falschen won vnnd glawben." Karlstadt calls self-invented faith here "magical" and a "false light," which ends up with an "invented image (ertichts bild)" of Christ.

166. *Mißbrauch*, A3r–v. The translation of I Corinthians 11:26 follows Karlstadt's version. Karlstadt at B2r underlines the order of knowledge, memory, and proclamation. That is, if proclamation is not grounded in the memory of God-given knowledge, one speaks only human wisdom. Noteworthy here is the conclusion that bread and wine cannot touch, let alone instruct the ground of the soul; ibid., C2v–C3r.

167. See the section, "Was Gedechtnuß sey"; *Mißbrauch*, A4r.

168. *Mißbrauch*, B1v, C2v.

169. *Mißbrauch*, A4v–B1r: "Welche das rechte erkantnuß Christi haben / die haben die gerechtigkayt in jrem grundt . . . Ja das ist war / wen[n]s nit ain gefroren oder todte erkantnuß ist / sonder eyn inprünstige hytzige geschefftige vnnd krefftige kunst Christi / die den erkenner in das erkan[n]t leben / vnd todt Christi verwandelt / vnd vmb Christus willen mo[e]cht alles th[o]n oder lassen / das Christus habe[n] will. "

170. *Mißbrauch*, B1v. The second part of this treatise, beginning B3r, deals with question of who it is that eats and drinks "unworthily" and thus acquires guilt for the body and blood of Christ (per I Cor. 2). Karlstadt argues for self-examination with respect to one's possession of "love-rich" knowledge. This self-examination occurs in "the inward person and sees directly into the ground of the soul, where God is active and

creates God's gifts." No one would need to test themselves per Paul's injunction if the sacrament itself conveyed assurance, Karlstadt argues; assurance must precede reception, contrary to Luther's position. Ibid., B3r–C2r.

171. *Mißbrauch*, C3r–v ("in etlich hündert Jaren noch kayns recht gepredigt ist").

Chapter 5

1. See Siegfried Bräuer and Günter Vogler, *Thomas Müntzer: Neu Ordnung machen in der Welt, Eine Biographie* (Gütersloh: Gütersloher Verlagshaus, 2016), 92.

2. Ibid., 133.

3. Ulrich Bubenheimer, *Thomas Müntzer: Herkunft und Bildung* (Leiden: Brill, 1989), 175–86. On Müntzer's acquaintance with mystical sources, see Reinhard Schwarz, "Thomas Müntzer und die Mystik," in *Der Theologe Thomas Müntzer*, ed. Siegfried Bräuer and Helmar Junghans (Göttingen: Vandenhoeck & Ruprecht, 1989 [henceforth cited as DTTM]), 283–301; here, 283–85.

4. Hans-Jürgen Goertz, "Thomas Müntzer," in PMRE, 56–77 (see specifically 63–71), argues that God alone is the first and only agent of salvation for Müntzer; but Müntzer often appears to describe self-mortification as a precondition for God's work and to demand a response to God's work that may be withheld—without it, the elect will be damned. Müntzer most consistently represents an active passivity of the sort that Richard Kieckhefer describes in relation to Johannes Tauler; see "The Notion of Passivity in the Sermons of John Tauler," *Recherches de théologie ancienne et médiévale* XLVIII (1981), 198–211.

5. See Susan E. Schreiner, *Are You Alone Wise? The Search for Certainty in the Early Modern Era* (Oxford: Oxford University Press, 2011), 92–97; 238–41.

6. See Ludwig Fischer, ed., *Die Lutherischen Pamphlete gegen Thomas Müntzer* (Tübingen: Max Niemeyer, 1976).

7. See Thomas Albert Howard, *Remembering the Reformation: An Inquiry into the Meanings of Protestantism* (Oxford: Oxford University Press, 2016), 110–22.

8. A particularly helpful review of scholarship up to c. 1990 can be found in Bernhard Lohse, *Thomas Müntzer in neuer Sicht: Müntzer im Licht der neueren Forschung und die Frage nach dem Ansatz seiner Theologie* (Hamburg: Joachim Jungius-Gesellschaft der Wissenschaften, 1991); more recent scholarship is summarized by Peter Matheson, "Recent German Research on Thomas Müntzer," MQR 86, no 1 (2012), 97–109. The thesis that Müntzer was a *Schüler Luthers* began with Karl Holl, *Gesammelte Aufsätze zur Kirchengeschichte* (Tübingen: J. C. B. Mohr, 1921), 1: 420–67, and was followed by numerous leading scholars in the 1950s–1970s (see the introduction, note 87). Challenges to this perspective found Müntzer's roots in medieval mysticism or apocalypticism; on the latter view, see the Introduction, note 91. The assertion that Müntzer found his roots in medieval mysticism rather than Luther was advanced by Hans-Jürgen Goertz, *Innere und äussere Ordnung in der Theologie Thomas Müntzers* (Leiden: E.J. Brill, 1967). Goertz's more recent work has stressed that Müntzer's reception of mysticism was shaped by his

anti-clerical milieu and by his apocalypticism, leading to the development of a rev-
olutionary theology that sought the renewal of the world. See Hans-Jürgen Goertz,
Thomas Müntzer: Revolutionär am Ende der Zeiten, Eine Biographie (München: C.
H. Beck, 2015), 221–36; see also his "Thomas Müntzer" (PMRE), 72–74; and
"Karlstadt, Müntzer and the Reformation of the Commoners," in CAS, 1–44; here,
20–34. *Revolutionär am Ende der Zeiten* is an updated version of Goertz's *Thomas
Müntzer: Mystiker, Apokalyptiker, Revolutionar* (München: C. H. Beck, 1989), one
of several biographies published on the supposed 500th Anniversary of Müntzer's
birth; this biography was translated into English as *Thomas Müntzer: Apocalyptic,
Mystic and Revolutionary*, trans. Jocelyn Jaquiery (Edinburgh: T&T Clark, 1993).
Goertz's 2015 biography of Müntzer maintains the primary positions of the older
work; see Goertz, *Revolutionär*, 11. The flurry of biographical sketches produced for
the 1989 anniversary lacked any notable contribution asserting that Müntzer was a
Schüler Luthers; see James M. Stayer, "Thomas Müntzer in 1989: A Review Article,"
SCJ 21 no. 4 (1990), 655–70. In an original (if flawed) analysis, Abraham Friesen,
*Thomas Müntzer: A Destroyer of the Godless, The Making of a Sixteenth-Century
Religious Revolutionary* (Berkeley: University of California Press, 1990), argued that
the early Augustine, Eusebius and Tauler were decisive influences on Müntzer. For a
source-grounded study of Müntzer's relationship to Wittenberg theological circles,
see Ulrich Bubenheimer, *Thomas Müntzer und Wittenberg* (Mühlhausen: Thomas-
Müntzer-Gesellschaft, 2014). For Müntzer's theology, see DTTM, which was a response to (Marxist) accounts that downplayed Müntzer's theological interests.
9. Lohse, *Thomas Müntzer in neuer Sicht*, 81f., and Leif Grane, "Thomas Müntzer
und Martin Luther," in *Bauernkriegs-Studien*, ed. Bernd Moeller (Gütersloh: G.
Mohn, 1975), 69–98; here, 71, 88–89, have both emphasized Müntzer's occupation as a preacher and exegete, rather than a systematic theologian. See also Tom
Scott, *The Early Reformation in Germany: Between Secular Impact and Radical Vision*
(Surrey: Ashgate, 2013), 247–56 ("Müntzer and the Mustard-Seed: A Parable as
Paradox?"), calling attention to Müntzer's "pastoral experience" in Allstedt to elu-
cidate the reformer's development and use of the "mustard seed allegory." Against
Goertz and others, Grane, "Thomas Müntzer," 71, warned against "naive genetic explanation" and the forcing of "eine historische Person in einen von einer bestimmten
Denkstruktur geprägten Typ."
10. See Günter Vogler, "Thomas Müntzer—Irrweg oder Alternative? Plädoyer für
eine andere Sicht," ARG 103 (2013), 11–40, adapted to be part of the conclusion to
Bräuer and Vogler, *Thomas Müntzer*, 391–98.
11. Bräuer and Volger, *Thomas Müntzer*, 217–19, argue that Müntzer conceived of faith
as a process involving the whole person, whereas for Luther faith involves the ears
and saves in a moment; such a depiction does little justice to Luther's rich doctrine
of faith, which looked to humility as the divinely worked precursor and confirmation of faith, and which was indebted to mystical ideas of annihilation and union.
12. In addition to Goertz's work, cited in note 8, see Volker Leppin, *Die fremde
Reformation: Luthers mystische Wurzeln* (München: C. H. Beck, 2016), 195–99.
13. This section depends esp. on Bubenheimer, *Herkunft*.

14. See ThMA 2, 82.1–2, and 82n7;Bubenheimer, *Herkunft*, 95. For Thomas Müntzer's correspondence, I use the newer critical edition of the Sächsische Akademie der Wissenschaften zu Leipzig (ThMA 2). The new critical edition of Müntzer's writings (ThMA 1) was released after the completion of this chapter, which employs MSB. I have consulted ThMA 1, especially its introduction to sources. Unless otherwise noted, translations are provided per CWTM, a translation of MSB.

15. Müntzer held his Braunschweig prebend for about 7 years. He expressed his desire to resign in a letter to Hans Pelt dated March 31, 1521 (ThMA 2, 82); his replacement was appointed February 22, 1522. Bubenheimer, *Herkunft*, 90–91.

16. Bubenheimer, *Herkunft*, 94–96; ThMA 2, 9.4. The phrase, "castigator of unrighteousness," is from a letter written by Klaus Winkeler, Han's Pelt's servant, to Müntzer, dated just before July 25, 1515. Unknown is whether Müntzer's "castigation" was a matter of public or private criticism. The same letter exhorts Müntzer to live in "the fiery love of purity" (ThMA 2, 10.11–12). In addition to or in conjunction with his mystical interests, Müntzer may have participated in humanist circles in Braunschweig; see Bubenheimer, *Herkunft*, 108–10; 141; 194–228.

17. Bubenheimer, *Herkunft*, 102–6, citing studies by himself and Siegfried Bräuer; for the relevant correspondence, see ThMA 2, 14–18; CWTM 9–12.

18. See Manfred Bensing and Winfried Trillitzsch, "Bernhard Dappens 'Articuli ... contra Lutheranos': Zur Auseinandersetzung der Jüterboger Franziskaner mit Thomas Müntzer und Franz Günther 1519," in *Jahrbuch für Regionalgeschichte* 2 (Weimar: Hermann Böhlaus Nachfolger, 1967), 113–47; here, 136–37. Dappen's text is now also available in ThMA 3, 39–53. For a discussion, see Bubenheimer, *Herkunft*, 106–8.

19. ThMA 2, 100–114; CWTM 35–38, 40–41. Pelt's devotion to Luther must have predated the events in Worms, on which he reports, for he claimed to have "almost all of [Luther's] writings." On Pelt and this letter, see Bubenheimer, *Herkunft*, 116–124. As Bubenheimer observes, Pelt's letter assumes Müntzer's approval of the zeal of Hans Hornburg, a brewer who had broken the Easter fast in 1521. Pelt writes of Hornburg, "I know no one in this town who is a more fervent follower *in actual practice* of the said Martin than Hans Hornburg who does not want to be a merchant and will not take anything on apart from his brewery, for he only wants enough to live on; he puts his trust in God and has no great concern for temporal goods. I am, I swear by God, still raring to go. I, too, hope to let go, but it will be a bitter pill; this does not seem to be possible, so pray God on my behalf that he will give me his grace" (my emphasis). According to Bubenheimer, *Herkunft*, 119, Hornburg's attitude reflects Müntzer's demand "nach einer 'Entgröberung' von den weltlichen Gütern als einer Voraussetzung für das Hören des lebendig Stimme Gottes."

20. Bubenheimer, *Herkunft*, 110–13.

21. Ibid., 170–186.

22. Ibid., 144–153.

23. Ibid., 153, cautions against reading the later break between Luther and Erasmus of Rotterdam back into 1517: "Der 'Wittenberger Lager' und die sogenannte 'Wittenberger Universitätstheologie' waren in den Jahren 1517–1519 ein

komplexes und keineswegs geschlossenes Gebilde. In jenen Jahren differenzierten selbst Wittenberger Zeitgenossen nicht zwischen den Humanismus und der frühreformatorischen Theologie an der Universität Wittenberg, sondern konnten beides als Einheit sehen und demgemäß Erasumus und Luther auf eine Ebene stellen." Timothy J. Wengert, "Martin Luther, Philip Melanchthon, and their Wittenberg Colleagues," in OEML, 2: 518–41, sees the humanist methodology of "returning to the sources" as definitive of Wittenberg theology; Wengert rejects broader definitions of humanism that equate it with a particular "philosophy or anthropology" (i.e., Erasmus's). On Müntzer and Wittenberg's biblical humanism, see Helmar Junghans, "Thomas Müntzer als Wittenberger Theologe," in DTM: 258–282. For excellent studies of the fate of humanism in the Reformation, proceeding from a substantive rather than methodological definition of humanism, see Erika Rummel, *The Confessionalization of Humanism in Reformation Germany* (New York: Oxford University Press, 2000), and *The Humanist-Scholastic Debate in the Renaissance and Reformation* (Cambridge, MA: Harvard University Press, 1995), 126–52.

24. Bubenheimer, *Herkunft*, 153–170, citing several of his own earlier studies.

25. Ibid., 175–186. On the study of Tauler in Wittenberg, see Henrik Otto, *Vor- und frühreformatorische Tauler-Rezeption: Annotationen in Drucken des späten 15. und frühen 16. Jahrhunderts* (Gütersloh: Gütersloher Verlagshaus, 2003), 175–82.

26. This is the case if ThMA 2, 12–13, 13n1, correctly dates the letter of Sister Ursula to Müntzer.

27. Bensing and Trillitzsch, "Bernhard Dappens 'Articuli,'" 115–24, 134–41. See also Bubenheimer, *Herkunft*, 186–193.

28. These arguments evidence knowledge of conciliar positions, for instance the decrees *Haec Sancta* and *Frequens* of the Council of Constance (1414–18).

29. Bubenheimer, *Herkunft*, 186–93, finds in Dappen's report evidence of both Müntzer's connnection to Wittenberg theologians and "eigenständige Akzente." Müntzer's unique accents represent, however, "keinen Widerspruch zur frühreformatorischen Wittenberger Universitätstheologie." As unique accents, Bubehenheimer identifies Müntzer's view of authority in the church as flowing from the ground up—a view he later extended to the relationship of rulers and ruled—and his expectation of martyrdom. For Müntzer, the imitation of Christ involved "a repetition of Christ's passion in all its aspects," including death.

30. Bensing and Trillitzsch, "Bernhard Dappens 'Articuli,'" 138–41. Luther had made a kindred complaint against the "universities" in his preface to the 1518 edition of the *Theologia Deutsch*: WA 1: 379.2–5.

31. For Karlstadt's understanding of the necessity of an inward call, see chapter 4.

32. Bubenheimer, *Herkunft*, 192–93.

33. Bräuer and Vogler, *Thomas Müntzer*, 92. For Müntzer's time in Zwickau, see Helmar Junghans, "Thomas Müntzer in Zwickau, 1520/21," in *Thomas Müntzer— Zeitgenossen—Nachwelt: Siegfried Bräuer zum 80. Geburtstag*, ed. Hartmut Kühne, Hans-Jürgen Goertz, Thomas T. Müller, and Günter Vogler (Mühlhausen: Thomas-Müntzer-Gesellschaft, 2010), 163–88. Junghans notes that the Müntzer who came

to Zwickau—at the time around 30 years old—stood under the influence of Biblical humanists, Wittenberg reformers, and late-medieval mystical authors. Yet he developed "eine eigene Theologie zunehmend situationsbezogen" (171).

34. Hans Pelt also believed that the necessity of suffering on behalf of the truth was an important part of Luther's message. See his June 25, 1521 letter to Müntzer, ThMA 2, 100–14; CWTM 35–38.

35. Luther did not receive the surviving letter but may have received a final version based upon it. Junghans, "Thomas Müntzer in Zwickau," 174; ThMA 2, 45n2.

36. Elliger, *Thomas Müntzer*, 82–93, argues that Müntzer's letter betrays the influence of Luther's *Ein Sermon von der Betrachtung des heiligen Leidens Christi* from April 1519.

37. ThMA 2, 45.2–47.10; CWTM 18–19. He calls ceremonies "monstrosities wearing the helmets and shields of faith."

38. ThMA 2, 47.10–48.6; CWTM 19. In 1520, Müntzer was unbothered by the question of God's responsibility for evil, noting that the wicked "cannot design or decide on anything unless it has been planted in their hearts."

39. This statement, ThMA 2, 48.9–11; CWTM 19, is curiously juxtaposed to the ensuing indication that he has the support of the entire *Rat* and almost the entire town.

40. ThMA 2, 48.9–50.3; CWTM 19–21. The possibility of writing against Tiburtius is repeated at the end of the letter, TMA 2, 52.13–54.1.

41. I discuss later in the chapter and notes whether Müntzer intended to emulate Luther with his *Prague Manifesto*.

42. Junghans, "Thomas Müntzer in Zwickau," 174–75, notes that Müntzer described Tiburtius as attacking the "new preachers"—thus, the entirety of evangelical preaching. On the accuracy of the Müntzer's depiction of Tiburtius's views, see Elliger, *Thomas Müntzer*, 81–93.

43. ThMA 2, 50.5–7; CWTM 20.

44. See for instance WA 10/1.1:10.20–13.1; LW 75:8–9; WA 2:141.12–13; LW 42:13.

45. ThMA 2, 50.8–20; CWTM 20: Tiburtius is supposed to have said, "The new preachers preach nothing but the gospel but this is deplorable: for they contravene the commands of men which need to be observed most. Many things have to be added to the gospel. One does not need to live according to the gospel all the time. If poverty were evangelical, kings etc. would not be permitted to own the riches of the world." Müntzer also reports that Tiburtius rejected Christ's injunction to turn the other cheek on the grounds that it would allow heretics to "persecute the church with impunity, by inhibiting us from invoking the secular arm." Müntzer later argued that true Christians must not passively suffer martyrdom. For Luther's exegesis of the Sermon on the Mount, see Susan Schreiner, "Martin Luther," in *The Sermon on the Mount through the Centuries*, ed. Jeffrey P. Greenman, Timothy Larsen, and Stephen R. Spencer (Grand Rapids, MI: Brazos, 2007), 109–28.

46. See the essay by Schreiner cited in the preceding note.

47. ThMA 2, 51.1–5; CWTM 20–21.

48. ThMA 2, 52.8–13; CWTM 21.

49. ThMA 2, 54.1–3; CWTM 21. Müntzer viewed consolation as essential to the office of the priest; see also ThMA 2, 69.3–11; CWTM 27.

50. On the "friends of God," see McGinn, *Presence*, 4: 407–31.

51. ThMA 2, 54.3–11; CWTM 22. There is also, near the end of the letter, a fascinating reference to earlier dangers (possibly in Braunschweig) from which God is supposed to have saved Müntzer "for other struggles with this world." Müntzer expresses confidence that God will provide continued protection and "the voice and the wisdom which none of our adversaries will be able to resist"—a reference to Luke 21:15.

52. See ThMA 2, 57.4–8, 57n3; CWTM 23; Junghans, "Thomas Müntzer in Zwickau," 179. In a letter of late January or early February 1521, Agricola conceded that Egranus had "no understanding of sacred Scriptures" and that he was "an infant in true theology"; ThMA 2, 74.1–4; CWTM 29–30. On Egranus's lack of sympathy for core Wittenberg teachings, see also Elliger, *Thomas Müntzer*, 105–6. Agricola's November 2 letter offers a view of Müntzer's engagement with Luther's works: Müntzer had evidently requested that Agricola send him copies of Luther's *Operationes in psalmos*. In late December, he received a copy of *Why the Pope's Books and those of his Disciples have been burnt by Dr. Martin Luther* and print sheets of parts of the *Operationes*. See ThMA 2, 60–62; CWTM 24. On Müntzer's reading of Luther, see Erwin Mülhaupt, "Welche Schriften Luthers hat Müntzer gekannt?" LJ 46 (1975), 125–37.

53. See Egranus's letter to Müntzer, ThMA 2, 76–78; CWTM 28–39, showing that Müntzer already was claiming the inspiration of the Spirit in his teachings and polemic.

54. See the reconstructed letters 24, 27 and 29 in ThMA 2.

55. ThMA 2, 73–74; CWTM 29–31.

56. For the course of the conflict, see recently Bräuer and Vogler, *Thomas Müntzer*, 105–19.

57. "Propositiones probi viri d. Egranus," in MSB 513–15, CWTM 380–83; in the main text, the propositions will be referred to parenthetically by number.

58. See Bräuer and Vogler, *Thomas Müntzer*, 111–12. Elliger, *Thomas Müntzer*, 132–66, offers a detailed assessment of the extent to which the *Propositions* corresponded to Egranus's actual teachings. According to Elliger, Egranus wanted a balanced appeal to human moral and mental exertion aided by grace. It is not my purpose here to evaluate the accuracy or fairness of Müntzer's summary, only to show Müntzer's understanding that suffering was central to the message he shared with Luther and the "Martinians."

59. MSB 515.15–16; CWTM 383.

60. See also Propositions 3 and 19.

61. CWTM 380 translates "amaritudine" as "affliction." The original phrase is "ut nos securissimi simus sine omni amaritudine"; in the margin Müntzer referred to "Locus sancti Petri Cristus passus." MSB 514.6–8.

62. CWTM 380n3; WA 1: 238.19–21; LW 31: 251–52.

63. Elliger, *Thomas Müntzer*, 141.

64. Ibid., 148.

65. Ibid., 154–55.

66. Müntzer may not have read the anti-Pelagian Augustine directly (see ThMA 2, 30.2–3, 30n7, 34.1, 35n14–n15, 36.9–10, 36n10), but this statement undermines the

argument of Friesen, *Thomas Muentzer*, 54, that Müntzer was influenced solely by the pre-*Confessions* Augustine, not by the later Augustine.

67. Elliger, *Thomas Müntzer*, 124–26, links Müntzer's teaching on the Spirit to the influence of the cloth-maker Nikolaus Storch; Müntzer is said to have understood Storch's conception of the Spirit as a Reformation teaching. The evidence of Storch's influence is rather slight. Better is the analysis of Junghans, "Thomas Müntzer in Zwickau," 182–83, who notes the similarity of Müntzer's "theology of the Spirit" to that of Johann Agricola.

68. Junghans, "Thomas Müntzer in Zwickau," 187. Junghans also argues that Biblical humanists and Wittenberg reformers were the primary influences on Müntzer at this time—not Storch. Müntzer was perceived by Zwickauers and presented himself as a "Lutherschüler."

69. On the circumstances of his departure from Zwickau, see Bräuer and Vogler, *Thomas Müntzer*, 118–19; on his planning to visit Prague, 127–30. For the Prague mission, he enlisted the support of two of the future so-called Zwickau prophets, Markus Thoma (Stübner) and Nikolaus Storch, both laymen. See esp. Letters 35, 36 and 38 in ThMA 2, 82–89 (CWTM 31–33, with different numbering).

70. ThMA 2, 91.3–92.9; CWTM 34–35. "Breath forth the entire crucified Christ" is my translation of "totum spirent crucifixum."

71. ThMA 2, 92.10–12; CWTM 35. This claim is oddly juxtaposed with Müntzer's indication that he could not enter the parish in Zwickau because "traps were being set for me there day and night, which finally came out into the open." See Junghans, "Thomas Müntzer in Zwickau," 183. In the letter to Luther discussed earlier, Müntzer expressed his anticipation of great suffering, while simultaneously claiming to have widespread support from the people and the Rat. There is a disconnect between the self-image of active flirtation with martyrdom, and what we can reconstruct of events. Luther will call upon just this disconnect to mock Müntzer's refusal to appear before a harmful or biased tribunal.

72. ThMA 2, 92.13–94.2; CWTM, 35. In a letter to Michael Gans, also of June 15, Müntzer entrusted Gans with his papers and promised to send a will in case he met death in Bohemia. He wrote as well, "Velim ego, si possem, omnib[us] om[ni]a fieri, donec cognoscant crucifixum co[n]formita[te] suae abrenunctiationis." ThMA 2, 88.5–6; CWTM 33.

73. Bubenheimer, *Herkunft*, 144–53.

74. For this paragraph, Elliger, *Thomas Müntzer*, 184–88.

75. Bräuer and Vogler, *Thomas Müntzer*, 144, reject the term "manifesto" as the invention of later editors; absent evidence that Müntzer attempted to post or publish the work, they prefer the term "Sendbrief." This is the term applied in ThMA 1. The editors of ThMA 1 note (p. 413) that although Müntzer penned versions A and D on poster-sized paper (for the letter designations, A-B-C-D, see note 77), it would have been absurd to post a single handwritten sheet in a city the size of Prague; Müntzer also wrote on both sides! Nevertheless, the unusual choice of paper—also for C—may have corresponded to plans to print a broadsheet. In this case, the term "Sendbrief"

proves not quite accurate; for that reason, I have maintained the more usual designation of Manifesto.

76. See the preceding note; if Müntzer intended to post the single sheet on November 1, that would have been a futile exercise—but he may have wished to print the theses as dated.

77. Friedrich de Boor, "Zur Textgeschichte des Prager Manifests," in Max Steinmetz, Winfried Trillitzsch, and Hans-Joachim Rockar, *Prager Manifest*, (Leipzig: Zentralantiquariat der DDR, 1975), 7–15; here, 8–13. In addition to the versions discussed here, there is also an incomplete Czech translation, in a hand other than Müntzer's. My notes will adopt the letter designations provided by de Boor for the various versions of the *Manifesto*: A = short German; B = longer German; C = Czech; D = Latin. These designations correspond to those used in ThMA 1, 411–440, while MSB and CWTM use C for the Latin and D for the Czech. De Boor's analysis, including the proposed sequence, is by no means proven fact; it is offered here as a well-argued case showing insights that may be won by attending to audience.

78. De Boor, "Textgeschichte," 9.

79. On the prominence of mystical language, especially in B, see Bräuer and Vogler, *Thomas Müntzer*, 151, 155.

80. Ibid., 154.

81. MSB 491.6–492.4; CWTM 357–58.

82. For the origin of Müntzer's views concerning the *Ordnung Gottes*, see the recent assessment of Bräuer and Vogler, *Thomas Müntzer*, 142; they are cautious about the identification of Tertullian as a primary source for Müntzer's concept—for which see, Wolfgang Ullmann, *Ordo rerum: Die Thomas Müntzer-Studien*, ed. Jakob Ullmann (Berlin: Kontext Verlag, 2006), 53–84. Ulrich Bubenheimer has shown that Müntzer encountered the concept of "ordo" in Quintilian; see Bubenheimer, *Herkunft*, 210–16. For an overview of scholarly discussion up to c. 1990, see CWTM 357n6; Lohse, *Thomas Müntzer in neuer Sicht*, 66f.

83. See MSB 492.4–17; CWTM 358: "the hearts of men are the paper or parchment on which God's finger inscribes his unchangeable will and his eternal wisdom . . . a writing which any man can read, providing his mind (*vornunfft*) has been opened to it. . . . God has done this for his elect from the beginning, so that the testimony they are given is not uncertain, but an invincible one from the holy spirit . . . For anyone who does not feel the spirit of Christ within him, or is not quite sure of having it, is not a member of Christ, but of the devil, Romans 8[:9]." See also MSB 502.4–5; CWTM 368 (Version B) and MSB 508.10–13, 26–27; CWTM 375 (D). On written scripture as a witness to "dye rechte heilige schrifft," see MSB 498.24–27; CWTM 365 (B); compare MSB 507.7–8; CWTM 374 (D). Conviction regarding the truth of Scripture is best confirmed by inward instruction, a point B alone makes: "Und es ist auch kein gewisser gezceugnisse, das die biblie warmacht, dan dye lebendige rede Gots, do der vater den szon anspricht im hertzen des menschen. Disse schrift künnen alle ausserwelten menschen lesen." Yet it is easier—B continues—to abide with scripture than endure the trials of direct instruction: "Sie leiden auch keine anfechtunge

des glaubens im geist der forcht Gots . . . Sie wollen auch vom geist der frocht (sic.) Gots nit geengstet seyn. Dorümb vorspotten sie die anfechtunge des glaubens in ewigkeyt . . . Dan Goth redt alleine in die leidligkeyt der creatüren, welche dye hertzen der ungleubigen nicht habn . . . [S]ie kunnen und wollen nit leherwerden, dan sie haben einen schlipperlichen grundt, es ehkelt yhn vor orem besitzer. Darumb fallen sie abe in der zceyt der anfectunge . . . Der ungleubige wil durch keinen wegk mit seinem leiden Cristo gleichformick werden, er wils nur mit honigsussen gedancken ausrichten. Dorumb sein solche vortumpte pfaffen, dy den rechten slussel wegknemen . . . nit besprenget mit dem geist der forcht Gots am dritten tage, wie mugen sie den am sibenden tage geluttert werden, Numeri am XVIIII." MSB 498.27–500.2; CWTM 363–66. See also MSB 507.10 –27 (D).

84. MSB 492.17–20; CWTM 358; see also MSB 500.3–9; CWTM 366–67 (B; "niemandt oder ghar wenig wissen, was sie holten sollen oder welchem houffen sie zcufallen sollen"); MSB 508.2–6; CWTM 375 (D).

85. MSB 492.20–26 ("unvorruckliche kinder Gots"); CWTM 358. MSB 500.16–501.7; CWTM 367 (B), expounds on the clerics' failure in consolation, "The end-result is that no one is sure of his soul's salvation. For these same Beelzebub-like fellows bring a single piece of Holy Scripture to market. Hey, a man doesn't know if he deserves God's hate or love! (Ecclesiastes 9:1)." Consequently, the good and the wicked have not been separated, an important theme for Müntzer. See also MSB 508.24–26; CWTM 375 (D).

86. MSB 492.20–34; CWTM 358–59. See too MSB 500.25–28; CWTM 367 (B).

87. See Bräuer and Vogler, *Thomas Müntzer*, 143.

88. In the German, the phrase is "dorch untrechtliche unde warhafftige drucknüsse beswert." As CWTM 362n8 notes, "drucknüsse" may be read as a reference to *Betrüge* (deceptions) or *Bedrücknis* (oppression) based on the differing translations in the Czech and Latin versions; CWTM proposes that Müntzer had both meanings in mind.

89. MSB 495.14–496, 1; CWTM 362.

90. In 1517–18, both Karlstadt and Luther published stories of *Anfechtung* and conversion expressing their debt to Johann von Stauptiz. For comparative analysis, see Volker Leppin, "Die Wittenbergische Bulle: Andreas Karlstadts Kritik am Luther," in DKdM: 117–30; here, 123–27; and Leppin, "Mystische Erbe auf getrennten Wegen: Überlegungen zu Karlstadt und Luther," in *Luther und das monastische Erbe*, ed. Christoph Bultmann, Volker Leppin, and Andreas Lindner (Tübingen: Mohr Siebeck, 2007), 154–62; here, 158–62. For detailed analysis of Karlstadt's long-neglected account, see Markus Matthias, "Die Anfänge der reformatorischen Theologie des Andreas Bodenstein von Karlstadt," in QdR, 87–110.

91. MSB 493.4–14; CWTM 359. I return here to analysis centered on version A.

92. MSB 493.16–17; CWTM 359.

93. MSB 494.2–4; CWTM 360. The reproach of scholars belongs to A alone. In B, Müntzer directs the same statement to "pfaffen," MSB 504.3; CWTM 370, and in D to *sacrificuli* (Matheson: "priestlings"), MSB 509.34; CWTM 377.

94. MSB 494.15-24; CWTM 360-61.

95. MSB 493.26-30; CWTM 361. This reference is unique to A, and Müntzer may have thought it particularly appropriate for public posting (as de Boor argues). Müntzer invokes in B the language of imminent harvest and separation, professing to have been "hired" by God and to have "sharpened [his] sickle"; he asks the Bohemians "das yr fleyß sollet thun, das lebendige worth Gots auß Gots munde selbern solt studiren." MSB 504, 12f.; CWTM 370-71. See also MSB 510.4f.; CWTM 377 (D).

96. Documentation of Müntzer's contact with Wittenberg circles comes from the pen of Günther. In a letter dated January 25, 1522, Günther reports having learned—evidently through Markus Stübner—of the resistance to Müntzer's activity in Zwickau. He writes to Müntzer, "I desire that you would desire to be embraced by me and that I should hear your spirit in full flow. On the other hand see that the light which is in you be not darkness. Different men mutter different things about you; the devil is not dead but prowls around like a roaring lion looking for someone to devour. I hope that you have proved the spirit, not fantasizing in the name of Christ but being zealous in his spirit." Günther is unsure of Müntzer's whereabouts, having heard that Müntzer was "put to flight" from Prague and might now be in Thuringia. ThMA 2, 125-27; CWTM 42-43.

97. For a short summary, Bräuer and Vogler, *Thomas Müntzer*, 155. For the evidence that Müntzer may have been put to flight, see ThMA 2, 125-26n3.

98. Letters of late 1522 through March 1523, including a December 1522 letter from Karlstadt to Müntzer, evidence Müntzer's desperate search for a position; see ThMA 2, 141-157.

99. ThMA 2, 127n1, discusses the evidence for a location near Wittenberg, as well as the possibility that Müntzer was in Wittenberg in March 1522. TMA 2, 127-28n2 discusses Müntzer's acquaintance with Melanchthon and the origins of this correspondence.

100. I have corrected CWTM 43 per ThMA 2, 130.3.

101. Bartholomäus Bernhardi had married in early 1521, followed by Günther, Karlstadt and others. An *Apologia* of December 13, 1521, written in Bernhardi's name by Karlstadt, had been widely misattributed to Melanchthon. Such a misattribution may have motivated Müntzer's rebuke of Melanchthon. ThMA 2, 130n6.

102. ThMA 2, 130.2-133.4; CWTM 43-45 (my emphasis). The key lines surrounding the emptying and possession of the soul read, "Nullam preceptum . . . angustius stringit christianum qua[m] sanctificatio nostra. Nam illa primum ex voluntate Dei animam euacuat, dum delectationes anima inferiores nequaqua[m] in falsum possessorem sumere possit." ThMA 2, 132.11-133.1.

103. ThMA 2, 133.4f.; CWTM 45. Müntzer proceeds here to condemn the petty quarrels over the mass in Wittenberg; it still has not been restored to the "apostolic rite." Preachers ought to examine hearers and administer bread and wine only to those who demonstrate "fructum intelligentie sue," "quod hij verum possessorem [Ps. 119:25] habeant, quibus intellectus testimoniorum Dei largitus sit non mortuarum ex chartis sed viuarum promissionum."

104. It is not clear to what extent, if any, the *Invocavit* sermons provoked Müntzer's response here. Bräuer and Kobuch point rather to *De abroganda missa privata M. Lutheri sententia*. See ThMA 2, 127n1, 134nn37–39, and 135n43.

105. Compare to the undated fragment, CWTM 48; ThMA 2, 222–24.

106. Reflecting his urgency, Müntzer writes this line in German rather than Latin: "Lieben bruder, last ewer merhen, es ist zeyt!"

107. ThMA 2, 135.3–136.3; CWTM 45.

108. ThMA 2, 136.3–137.3; CWTM 45 (translation altered). In March 1522, Luther was still open to the possibility that something akin to purgatory might await some souls after death; by November 1522 (when he preached the sermon published as *Sermon vom Stand*), Karlstadt had reinterpreted purgatory as a life-long *and* postmortem experience of God's pedagogy, which produces desire for God and hatred of self. See Vincent Evener, "Wittenberg's Wandering Dead: Discipline and the Dead in the Reformation," CH 84, no. 3 (September 2015), 531–555. Müntzer's reinterpretation of purgatory related primarily to the spiritual experiences of the living; but see the reference to postmortem discipline at ThMA 2, 221.6–8; CWTM 73. For discussion of Müntzer's correspondence with Christoph Meinhard, see Bräuer and Vogler, *Thomas Müntzer*, 220–21.

109. ThMA 2, 140.13–141.2; CWTM 51 (July 14, 1522): "Müntzer flees from the scribes and pharisees and hypocrites Mt. 23; for their houses are deserted, lacking a heavenly owner (*posessorem supernum*). For they seek their own ends, not those of Jesus Christ. At first, of course, they blabbed on about the need to abandon the sacrifice [the mass]. But now they would dearly like to deny that, just as the whole populace cries out: Great, great! why did they begin something which they were quite unable to keep up with?" Another source is provided by notes that George Spalatin took in a late-November or early December 1522 colloquy between Müntzer and Wolfgang Stein at Weimer. See ThMA 3, 113–14. The (quite circular) progression of the notes reflects the place of suffering as Müntzer's truth-bedrock: "Scientia Dei opus esse. / Quid esset scientia Dei? / Non posse haberi, nisi ex fide et experientia fidei. / Quid fides? / Non posse doceri, nisi habentem experientiam fidei. / Quid experientia fidei, aut quomodo posset acquiri? / Ex scientia Dei. / Non posse doceri, nisi habentem spiritum et scientiam Dei. / Quommodo possit haberi scientia et spiritus Dei? / Non posse doceri, nisi periculis et laboribus / Du must dir es gar sauer lassenn werdenn, dann es it mir gar sauer wordenn. / Fidem non esse nisi Christum et experientiam fidei vera opera fidei. Et eam credo haberi ex scriptura et Evangelio et Christi. / Ha lieber gesell, ich schißß dir eyn dreck in die schrifft, in das ewangelium und in Christum, wenn du nicht hettest die kunst und geist Gottes. / De Wittenbergensibus male sentit et loquitur, nominans fatuos Doctor Martinum, Doctor Carlostadium, Philippum Melanchthonem atque adeo Doctor Langum."

110. On his marriage and the birth of his son, see Bräuer and Vogler, *Thomas Müntzer*, 198–99.

111. This idea was aptly formulated by Carl Hinrichs, *Luther und Müntzer: ihre Auseinandersetzung über Obrigkeit und Widerstandsrecht* (Berlin: W. De Gruyter, 1952), 1.

112. See Siegfried Bräuer, "Die Vorgeschichte von Luthers 'Ein Brief an die Fürsten zu Sachsen von dem aufrührerischen Geist,'" LJ 47 (1980): 4–70; here, 52–54; and "Thomas Müntzers Liedschaffen: Die theologischen Intentionen der Hymnenübertragungen im Allstedter Gottesdienst von 1523/24 und im Abendmahlslied Müntzers," LJ 41 (1974), 45–102, which is wedded to Goertz's thesis regarding Müntzer's mystical thought-form; and for Bräuer's most recent account, citing an array of relevant scholarship, Bräuer and Vogler, *Thomas Müntzer*, 187–98.

113. See my essay, "Mysticism, Christianization, and Dissent: The Appropriation of Johannes Tauler in Simon Haferitz's *Sermon on the Feast of the Three Holy Kings* (1524)," ARG 106 (2015): 67–91.

114. Bräuer, "Die Vorgeschichte," 42; Bräuer and Vogler, *Thomas Müntzer*, 199–201.

115. ThMA 2, 162.1–165.2; CWTM 55–56. Regarding the Zwickau tumult, Müntzer claims, "nisi obstitissem, nocte crastina tot[us] senatus fuisset interfectus."

116. ThMA 2, 168.14–170.3; CWTM 58. For Luther's critique of mystical terms, see his August 3, 1523 letter to Spalatin, WAB 3, 120.30–32, and the sources cited by ThMA 2, 170n71; CWTM 59n430. Relevant passages from Luther's *Against the Heavenly Prophets* (WA 18:70.37–71.8, 101.8–10, 137.5–138.26; LW 40:88, 117, 147–48) will be discussed in chapter 6. ThMA 2, 150 (reconstructed letter 53) infers from Karlstadt's December 1522 letter to Müntzer that Müntzer had distanced himself from the Zwickau prophets also in correspondence with Karlstadt.

117. ThMA 2, 162.3–164.3; CWTM 56.

118. TMA 2, 165.2–167.7; CWTM 56–58. See also TMA 2, 155.2–10 (March 19, 1523), which is a letter of Müntzer to followers in Halle regarding his expulsion from there, after a brief stint as chaplain to the Cistercian cloister St. George in Glaucha: "Ich bitte euch, das yr euch meyns vortreybens nicht ergeren wollet, dan yn solcher anfechtunge wyrt der selen abgrunt gereumeth, auff das er meher vnde mehr erleutet, erkant werde, das vnuberwintliche geczeugnuß des heyligen geysts czu schepffen. Es kan nymant Gots barmhertzykeit entfinden, er muß vorlassen seyn . . . das ist auch, do Christus, vnser heyland, von saget: 'Wan ich wegghee, so kump der troster, der heylige geyst,' der kan nymant gegebe[n] werden dan dem trostlosen."

119. ThMA 2, 168.1–12; CWTM 58.

120. ThMA 2, 168.12–170.6; CWTM 58–59. In a July 29, 1523 letter, Müntzer pled with Karlstadt, "Quare nec paruam veteris charitatis renouationem impartitus sis, refer"; see ThMA 2, 188.5–189.1, and 187n1; and CWTM 65. This correspondence is discussed in chapter 6.

121. Michael G. Baylor, "Thomas Müntzer's First Publication," SCJ 17, 4 (1986): 451–458, provides an introduction and translation. Müntzer may have visited Stolberg in April 1522, "renewing contacts and perhaps preaching a sermon." The letter is based on a loose translation of Psalm 93; see CWTM 60n438. A handwritten draft survives along with the printed version, *Ein ernster sendebrieff an seine lieben bruder zu Stolberg, vnfuglichen auffrur zu meiden* (Eilenburg: Nikolaus Widemar, 1523).

ThMA 2, 175–84 provides the versions side-by-side; I discuss the draft in note 124, but focus my analysis on the longer printed text.

122. ThMA 2, 182.14–183.3; CWTM 64. The term "memmen" was also used in the *Prague Manifesto*.

123. See also Müntzer's letter to Frederick the Wise of October 4, 1523, which relates to his conflict with Ernest of Mansfeld. ThMA 2, 205.5f.; CWTM 69–70.

124. Differences between Müntzer's handwritten draft of the letter to the Stolberg brethren and the published version may show that Müntzer responded constructively or at least strategically to Luther's concerns about high-flown, non-biblical (mystical) terminology. The draft explicitly invokes terms like *Entblößung*, *Gelassenheit*, and *Verwunderung*. But these are absent from the printed version. The draft reads, "Christ's true reign comes to pass only after the splendor of the world has been completely discarded (*nach aller entplossung der czyrde der werlt*). It is then that the Lord comes and casts down the tyrants to the ground. After the weakness experienced by the members of the elect in complete self-surrender (*gelassenheit*) he supports and endows them with strength which flows from him. He girds them around with his power; the man whose loins are crushed waits on the Lord prior to the wedding. He who has not discovered anything about such waiting (*erharru[n]g*) has no God, either, for his feet are not planted on the rock. For all true, godly men must know what to do, so that they cannot be moved; for one's heart becomes a throne for God by realising that it has surely been chosen by God as his possession (*besitczu[n]ge*). But before one can be sure of salvation torrents of water come again and again with thundering so fearsome that one loses the will to live … [T]he Lord only gives his holy testimony to someone who has first made his way through perplexity (*vorwunderunge*). That is why the hearts of men are so seldom touched with the true spirit of Christ, the true possessor of souls (*warhafftigen besitczer der selen*); they [want] a foretaste of life eternal before the heart is prepared by the pains of hell for the endless days of eternity." The "vainglorious" Stolbergers "wolt vil außrichten unde dye anfegtu[n]g des außr[ic]htens nicht außleyden. Wer seyne helle nicht myt gute leyden wyl, der leyde sye mit knyrsenden czene[n], so wirt er belac[h]et." ThMA 2, 177.8–184.2; CWTM 60–61 (translation altered).

125. Baylor, "Müntzer's First Publication," 453, argues that Müntzer's warning against "vnfuglichen auffrur" implied only that the time was "not yet ripe"; thus, he "urged his associates to prepare themselves inwardly." However, Müntzer's focus was on the Stolbergers themselves—how they could be emptied of themselves in order to act for God in the world—not on the times. Regardless, Müntzer certainly accepts a justified uprising.

126. Louise Gnädinger, *Johannes Tauler: Lebenswelt und mystische Lehre* (München: C. H. Beck, 1993), 272–86.

127. ThMA 2, 175.6–177.6; CWTM 62. The statement, "Dieweil aber sich die außerwelte[n] Gottes wercks in achtung zu habe[n] nicht vntterwinte[n], ist es nicht mo[e]glich, das Gott etwas darbey thun solle," shows a demand for active passivity, rather than a rooting of salvation in grace alone. See note 4.

128. ThMA 2, 177.7–15; CWTM 62.

129. ThMA 2, 177.16–178.9 (Müntzer exclaims: "Ach, des grossen, hochuerstockten vnglaube[n]s, der sich mit dem tote[n] buchstabe behelffen wil vnde leugnet de[n] finger, der in d[as] hertze schreibet, 2. Cor. 3"); CWTM 62.

130. ThMA 2, 178.9–179.1; CWTM 62–63.

131. ThMA 2, 179.1–182.10; CWTM 63.

132. Bräuer, "Die Vorgeschichte," 43–44. The attempt was made through Hans Zeiß, who may have personally handed Müntzer's July letter to Luther. For Luther's account of his meeting with Zeiß, see WAB 3: 120.27–34.

133. Bräuer and Vogler, *Thomas Müntzer*, 207–8.

134. For this analysis, see Bräuer, "Die Vorgeschichte," 47–50. The editors of ThMA 1, 267–68, 288, express substantial reservations about the evidence for the *Lehrgespräch*, concluding: "Mithin bleibt die Genese von 'Protestation oder Entbietung' weithin ungeklärt." The same can be said for the 11 questions sent by Spalatin to Müntzer and for the treatise *On Counterfeit Faith*, which does not clearly represent a response to the questions.

135. MSB 569.1–12; CWTM 224–25 (see especially n146 there).

136. MSB 225 (*Protestation odder empietung Tome / Mu[e]ntzers vö Stolberg am Hartzs seelwarters zu / Alstedt seine lere betreffende / vnnd tzum anfang von dem / rechten Christen glawben / vnnd der tawffe.*); CWTM 188. On the title itself, see CWTM 188n1; Bräuer and Vogler, *Thomas Müntzer*, 209. On Müntzer's aims in the publication, see MSB 239.27–240.4; CWTM 207–8: "In diser entpietung und bedingung habe ich in einer summa gesagt von dem schaden der kirchen, welcher durch die unvorstandene tauffe und getichten glauben uns uberfallen hat. . . . Durch mein vornemen wil ich der evangelischen prediger lere in ein besser weßen furen und unser hinderstellige, langsame Ro[e]mischen brudere auch nicht verachten."

137. Müntzer refers to an unnamed "he" or "you (du)" who has failed to produce any evidence from the church fathers or scripture for his view of baptism; there is no scriptural evidence that the apostles or Mary were baptized with water, he says. MSB 227.32–228.11; CWTM 191.

138. MSB 226.4–21 ("unvorru[e]gklich der einige unbetriegliche fußstapffen der apostolischen warhafftigen christenheit ist"); CWTM 188–89.

139. MSB 227.29–32; CWTM 191. Müntzer linked the long history of ecclesial and doctrinal strife to this trust in "meaningless externals."

140. MSB 228.13–229.13; CWTM 191–93. Note the exegetical statement here: "Dann es muß die kunst Gotis betzeugt werden aus der heyligen biblien in einer starcken vorgleichung aller wort, die in beyden testamenten clerlich beschriben stehn, I. Cho. 2."

141. MSB 231.6–21; CWTM 195–96. See also MSB 218.17–21; CWTM 214–15, "Was ein mensch ho[e]rt ader siht, das Cristum weiset, nympt er an zum wunderbarlichen gezeugnis, seinen unglauben dadurch zu voriagen, zu to[e]dten und zu malmen."

142. MSB 231.21–232.8; CWTM 196–97.

143. Sects. 10–12, MSB 232.9–234.18; CWTM 197–98.

144. MSB 233.19–23; CWTM 198.

145. MSB 233.27–234.12; CWTM 198–99.

146. MSB 234.14–18; CWTM 199–200 (translation altered).

147. MSB 234.20–29; CWTM 200.

148. MSB 234.30–235.7; CWTM 200.

149. MSB 235.7–18; CWTM 200–201.

150. MSB 235.19–27; CWTM 201. Possibly a play on "liecht" and "leicht."

151. MSB 236.9–26; CWTM 202–3; here, Müntzer addresses the elect, just as at the outset he says he writes for the "elect friends of God" (MSB 226.2; CWTM 188). On the discussion of easy faith, see also Sect. 4, MSB 227.9–23; CWTM 190. 4: Christians have made their faith "zum solchen leichtfertigen dinge . . . one alle uberkommung [Gewinn]," and they are "rumreytig, hoch zu schreiben, ja auch grosse bucher vol, vol klicken, sagende: Ich glewbe, ich glewbe, so wir doch mit eyttelm getzanck und sorgen der zeitlichen guther teglich umbgehn, und noch von tag zu tag wuchersuchtiger werden und sagen, ich glewb und halte den gantzen christenglawben, das er recht sey und habe eine feste starcke hoffnung zu Gotte etc. Du lieber mensche, du weist nicht, wo du ja oder nein zu sagst. Du hast Got deine dornen und disteln im geringsten nicht lassen außrewthen."

152. MSB 235.28–236.7; CWTM 201–2 (my emphasis).

153. MSB, 502.11–15; CWTM 369 (B). See also *Counterfeit Faith*, MSB 221.15–16; CWTM 219.

154. Kieckhefer, "Notion of Passivity," 209; see note 4 in this chapter.

155. MSB 236.20–26; CWTM 202–3.

156. CWTM 203 omits the "etc." of MSB 237.2; Müntzer means to attack the entirety of ascetic and penitential praxis in its underlying motivation.

157. MSB 236.27–237.19; CWTM 203–4. Cited is John 4.

158. MSB 237.21–238.2; CWTM 204–5.

159. MSB 238.3–20; CWTM 205. Instead of "creature," CWTM has "man"; I have followed MSB. See also Müntzer's remarks in Section 3, MSB 226.32–227.8; CWTM 190, concluding, "Der einige trost der ellenden kirchen erwarttet das, das die außerwelten sollen und mussen christformig werden und mit mancherley leyden und zucht Gottis werck in achtung haben."

160. MSB 238.21–239.3; CWTM 205–6. The *Schriftgelehrten* argue that one should not cast pearls before swine, but Peter (2 Pet. 2:22) teaches who the "mastsewen" are—namely "alle ungetrewe, falsche gelerten, sie seint von welcher secten sie wollen, die fressen und sauffen vor gut nemen und treiben alle yre luste in wolleben und greynen mit scharpffen tzehnen wie die hunde, wenn man yn ein wort widderspricht." Among numerous other texts cited marginally by Müntzer is Phil. 3, which describes "enemies of the cross of Christ" whose "god is their stomach."

161. MSB 239.5–16; CWTM 206–7, concluding, "thun nicht wie die Gergesener bothen dem Herrn, er solt von yrem lande abweichen, so er doch alleine dohin kam, sein wort dartzu entpiethen den dorfftigen, do wolten sie das one schaden yrer luste uberkommen. Ist unmoglich."

162. Sects. 20–22, MSB 239.26–240.21; CWTM 207–9.

163. MSB 218.5–15; CWTM 214.

164. MSB 218.17–219.2; CWTM 214–15.

165. MSB 219.4–17, CWTM 215–16.

166. MSB 219.19–28; CWTM 216–17. Sect. 5 refers to "alle vether, die patriarchen, propheten, und sunderlich die aposteln," setting their tribulations against the "wansynnigen, wollustigen schweyne" who want to barge into faith ("hyneynplatzen"), but who "sich vorm stormwyndt, prawßenden bulgen und vorm gantzen wasser der weyßheyt entsetzen. Dann yre gewissen mergken wol, das sie zuletzt in solchem ungewitter werden vorderben. Darumb seint sie mit allen yren vorheischungen gleich einem nerrischen manne, der auff den sandt bawbet." Sect. 6 takes up the apostles and especially Peter; MSB 220.1–33; CWTM 217–18.

167. MSB 220.19–28; CWTM 218. To use scripture rightly, one must be "led by the teaching of the spirit."

168. MSB 222.6–19; CWTM 220: "Das man einem sußen Cristum der fleischlichen werlt predigt, ist das ho[e]chste vorgift, die von anbeginne den scheflin Cristi gegeben ist. Dan durch sulchs annhemen, will der mensch gotformig sein, so er nymmermer wil, auch gantz nicht begert, cristformig zu werden." On the whole Christ, see also Sect. 11, MSB 222.20–223.4, CWTM 220–21; on Christ as "foundation-stone" (Eph. 2:20) and "stone of stumbling" (Rom. 9:32), see Sect. 13, MSB 223.24–32; CWTM 222, including note 120; on right proclamation, see Sects. 7–9, MSB 221.1–222.5; CWTM 218–19.

169. MSB 223.5–23; CWTM 221–22.

170. We may number elements picked up by Müntzer from Matthew 16 as follows: (1) Jesus scolding the Pharisees and Sadducees for demanding a sign, to which he replies, "this evil and adulterous generation seeks a sign, and no sign will be given to it except the sign of Jonah"; (2) Jesus warning the disciples against the "yeast" of the Pharisees and Sadducees; (3) Peter's profession of Jesus as the Messiah; (4) Jesus foretelling his suffering and death at the hands of "the elders and scribes and chief priests"; and (5) after Peter's objection ("God forbid!"), the dramatic rebuke, "get behind me Satan; you are a stumbling block to me because you do not understand God's things but human things." (6) Jesus pronounces, "If anyone wishes to come after me, let him deny himself and take up his cross and follow me." These are my translations, from the Vulgate. Correspondingly, Müntzer wants the elect to learn (1) that "no one can believe in Christ until he has first conformed himself to him. Through experiencing unbelief the elect leaves behind him all the counterfeit faith he has learnt, heard or read from Scripture; for he sees, that an outward testimony cannot create an inward reality (wesen), but can only do what it was created to do." The elect person will (2) reject the "inexperienced" as potential teachers, and seek revelation, professing with Peter (3), "I know full well that Christ is the son of the living God." But to seek revelation is (5) to confront unbelief and (4) to go "through despair and the most extreme reverses. Hell has to be endured before one can take due precautions against its engulfing gates." Finally (6), the true faith of the suffering elect and the false faith of the damned is distinguished by the former's willingness to take up Christ's cross. MSB 224.1–36; CWTM 223–24.

171. MSB 224.17–36; CWTM 223–24.

172. ThMA 2, 212.4–214.1; CWTM 70–71.

173. ThMA 2, 214.1–215.3; CWTM 70–71; Müntzer concludes, "They are still neophytes . . . who still have to be put to the test; they should not be in charge of souls, but for a long time yet should remain catechumens, that is, diligent students of his divine work; they should not teach until they themselves have been taught by God."

174. My point is not that these themes can only have come through post-Eckhartian mysticism, but that Müntzer clearly found them there and developed them by thinking with and through Eckhartian texts.

Chapter 6

1. On the debate over Word and Spirit between Luther, on the one hand, and Karlstadt and Müntzer, on the other, see Susan E. Schreiner, *Are You Alone Wise? The Search for Certainty in the Early Modern Era* (Oxford: Oxford University Press, 2011), 87–100.

2. See Volker Leppin, *Die fremde Reformation: Luthers mystische Wurzeln* (München: C. H. Beck, 2016), 117–38.

3. As throughout this book, there is no intent here to be reductionist by either claiming sole derivation of these views from Eckhartian mysticism or denying the significance of political circumstances and calculation to the positions taken by Luther, Karlstadt, and Müntzer in the Peasants' War.

4. Siegfried Bräuer, "Die Vorgeschichte von Luthers 'Ein Brief an die Fürsten zu Sachsen von dem aufrührerischen Geist,'" LJ 47 (1980): 41–70; 47–55. Evidence may be found at ThMA 3: 132–33.

5. In this conflict, thirty Allstedters formed a secret "covenant (*Bund*)," swearing "to stand by the gospel, to give no more tithes to monks and nuns and to help destroy and drive the same [monks and nuns] away." The evidence for this secret *Bund* comes from later interrogation protocols; see Siegfried Bräuer, *Spottgedichte, Träume und Polemik in den frühen Jahren der Reformation: Abhandlungen und Aufsätze*, ed. Hans-Jürgen Goertz and Eike Wolgast (Leipzig: Evangelische Verlagsanstalt, 2000), 91–121 ("Thomas Müntzer und der Allstedter Bund"); 94, 98f.

6. Bräuer, "Die Vorgeschichte," 55–62. Zeiß arrested Ciliax Knauth, a member of the *Rat*. His plan to arrest other members met with armed resistance from the citizenry, and the *Rat* dispatched to Duke John a defiant letter betraying Müntzer's strong influence. See ThMA 2: 252–56; CWTM 80–81. The letter argues that, if John and Frederick yield to the nuns' demands, they will be protecting the godless against the injunctions of Romans 13 and Exodus 23. The Allstedters declare their willingness to suffer in resisting the "devil at Mallerbach" on behalf of their "brothers," because in so doing, they will grow in conformity to Christ: "Das wir aber weiter denn teufel zcu Mallerbach solt[en] anbethen, gestaten, das vnser bruder ym vberantwort[e]t werden zcum oppffer, wollen wir gleich so wenig thun, wie dem Turgken vnterthanig zu sein. Geschicht vns dorvber etwan gewalt, so weis doch die welt vnd sonderlich die frum[m]en auserwelt[en] Got[es], woru[m]b wir leiden vnd das wir Christo Jhesu gleichformig werden, der ew[e]r gnaden beware in der recht[en] forcht Got[es]." The weak are not to be spared, and Romans 13 is not to be understood as commanding submission to authorities that fail in their divinely appointed purpose.

7. For a recent account of Allstedt's various conflicts and the involvement of the Ernestine princes, see Siegfried Bräuer and Günter Vogler, *Thomas Müntzer: Neu Ordnung machen in der Welt. Eine Biographie* (Gütersloh: Gütersloher Verlagshaus, 2016), 202–8, 225–249.

8. See Bräuer, "Die Vorgeschichte," 65–67. Bräuer argues that Müntzer must have requested the opporutnity to preach, since John and John Frederick regarded the task of judging preaching as outside the competence of secular rulers. See also Bräuer and Vogler, *Thomas Müntzer*, 448–49n112. ThMA 1: 300–1, summarizes arguments for placing initiative on the princes' side, but does not argue either way. See ThMA 1 on the relation between the preached sermon and the published text, and on the response—or lack thereof—of the court to the preached and published version.

9. Siegfried Bräuer, "Selbstverständnis und Feindbild bei Martin Luther und Thomas Müntzer: Ihre Flugschriftenkontroverse von 1524," in *Wegscheiden der Reformation: Alternatives Denken vom 16. bis zum 18. Jahrhundert*, ed. Günter Vogler (Weimar: Hermann Böhlaus Nachfolger, 1994), 57–84; here, 62, correcting Bräuer, "Die Vorgeschichte," 67.

10. Bräuer, "Die Vorgeschichte," 67–70; "Selbstverständnis und Feindbild," 58–65. Notably, Luther regarded not only armed defense but also *Bilderstürme* as undue force. Thus, Luther readily grouped Karlstadt with Müntzer as belonging to the same "spirit." On possible reasons for Luther's hesitation to attack Müntzer publicly, see Bräuer, "Die Vorgeschichte," 64.

11. See MSB 262.23–26; CWTM 251, "In den letzten tagen werden die liebhaber der lu[e]ste wol ein gestalt der gu[e]ttickeit haben, aber sie werden vorleucknen ire krafft. Es hat kein ding auff erden ein besser gestalt und larve dann die getichte gu[e]te." According to Müntzer, clemency is meaningless apart from severity, but false clemency is supremely deceptive.

12. Müntzer speaks of "eine treffliche unuberwintliche zuku[e]nfftige reformation" (MSB 255.24–25; CWTM 244), but also imagines the continued existence of the godless, for whom he intercedes "mit dem frumen Daniel, wo sie Gottis offenbarung nicht widder sein" (MSB 261.23–24; CWTM 250). For diverse scholarly views concerning Müntzer's apocalypticism, see R. Emmet McLaughlin, "Apocalypticism and Thomas Müntzer," ARG 95 (2004): 98–131, who argues that that the term "apocalyptic" does not illuminate Müntzer's thought; and Gottfried Seebaß, "Reich Gottes und Apokalyptik bei Thomas Müntzer," LJ 58 (1991): 75–99, who argues that Müntzer's concern is with penultimate and not ultimate events. Hans-Jürgen Goertz sees apocalypticism as shaping the direction of Müntzer's mystical views toward alteration of the world; see the discussions in the introduction and chapter 5.

13. MSB 254.9–14; CWTM 242–43.

14. MSB 252.10–253.11; CWTM 240–41. The argument is replete with Eckhartian terminology (*gemu[e]th, abgeschiden sein, einkehr, abgrundt*) applied to the elect: "[E]in außerwelter mensch, der do wissen wil, wilch gesicht oder trawm von Gott, natur oder teuffel sey, der muß mit seynem gemu[e]th und hertzen, auch mit seynem naturlichem vorstande abgeschiden sein von allem zeitlichen trost seines fleisches . . . [E]s wirt kein wollustiger mensch annemen, Luce 7, dann die disteln und

dornen—das seynt die wolluste diser welt . . . —vordrucken alle wirckung des worts, das Gott in die selen redet. Drumb, wann Got scho[e]n sein heiliges wort in die selen spricht, so kan es der mensch nicht ho[e]ren, so er ungeu[e]bt ist, dan er thut keinen einkehr oder einsehn in sich selber und in abgrundt seiner selen, Psal. 48 [49]. Der mensch wil sein leben nit kreutzigen." When the lusts have been crucified, "Dann wirt der mensch erst gewar, das er Gotis und des heiligen geists wonung sey in der lenge seiner tage. Ja, das er warhafftig geschaffen sey allein der ursach, das er Gottis gezeugnis in seinem leben erforschen sol, Ps. 92 [93] und 118 [119]. Desselbigen wirt er itzt gewar in den teilen durch bildreiche weyse, itzt auch im gantzen im abgrund des hertzen, 1. Corint. 13." Müntzer also offers other means for the discernment of dreams and visions. They must "in der heiligen biblien bezeuget seint" and, further-more, not "rausser quelle durch menschliche anschlege, sonder einfaltig herfliesse nach Gottis unvorru[e]cklichem willen." True visions are usually given in tribula-tion. On Simon Hafertiz's transformation of Eckhartian mysticism around themes of faith and election, see Vincent Evener, "Mysticism, Christianization, and Dissent: The Appropriation of Johannes Tauler in Simon Haferitz's *Sermon on the Feast of the Three Holy Kings* (1524)," ARG 106 (2015): 67–91.

15. MSB 259.3–260.4; CWTM 247–48: "Treibt seyne feynde von den außerwelten, dann yhr seyt die mitler dozu. Lieber, gebt uns keyne schale fratzen vor, das die krafft Gotis es thun sol an ewr zuthun des schwerts . . . Er wirdt ewre hende leufftigk machen zcum streytte und wirdt euch auch erhalten. Aber yhr werdet daru[e]ber ein grosses creutz und anfechtung mu[e]ssen leyden, auff das euch die forcht Gottis erkleret werde. Das mag on leyden nicht gescheen, aber es kost euch nichts mehr dann die ferligkeyt umb Gots willen gewoget und das unnu[e]tz geplauder der widdersacher." MSB 261.6–16; CWTM 249–50 offers the example of Joshua and the Israelites con-quering the promised land.

16. MSB 250.9–252.1; CWTM 238–40 (translation altered). My translation of the second part of the sentence beginning, "But if a man," deviates significantly from CWTM; I intend to capture the stance of active passivity required by Müntzer, as well as the possible echoing of the *German Theology*'s teaching that God needs creatures for God's work to find effect. On the latter point, see the discussion in chapter 1; I argue in chapter 5 that Müntzer's view of human agency vis-à-vis grace is best understood as requiring humans to adopt a stance of passivity in response to God's work.

17. MSB 246.4–247.5, 259.19–260.4, 263.4–6; CWTM 234–35, 248, 251.

18. See ThMA 2: 261.3–5; CWTM 82.

19. MSB 249.7–10; CWTM 237. "Und seint doch yrer eygen seligkeit nit vorsichert, wilchs doch nothalben sein solt, Roma. 8. Sie ku[e]nnen hu[e]bsch vom glauben schwatzen und einen truncken glauben einbrawen den armen vorwirreten gewissen."

20. MSB 244.15–18; CWTM 232 ("Nothing is so scorned and despised as the spirit of Christ. And yet no one can be saved until the holy spirit has assured him of his salva-tion"); for a brief swipe at Catholic views, MSB 243.1–3; CWTM 231.

21. See Mark U. Edwards Jr., *Luther and the False Brethren* (Stanford, CA: Stanford University Press, 1975). Müntzer also uses the category of "false prophets" here (MSB 244.13–15; CWTM 232).

22. MSB 245.2–246.16; CWTM 232–35.

23. MSB 245.22–25; CWTM 234. See also MSB 258.32–33; CWTM 247.

24. MSB 248.17–32; CWTM 237.

25. Similar language is found in Müntzer's letter to the "God-fearing people of Sangerhausen," written around July 15, 1524; see TMA 2: 279.2–5; CWTM 93.

26. MSB 263.2–8; CWTM 251–52 (biblical citations omitted).

27. WA 15: 210.8–211.17; LW 40: 48–50, citing I Cor. 11:19.

28. Bräuer, "Die Vorgeschichte," 52n53, against Carl Hinrichs, *Luther und Müntzer: Ihre Auseinandersetzung über Obrigkeit und Widerstandsrecht* (Berlin: W. De Gruyter, 1961), 145.

29. WA 15: 211.LW 40: 50 (my emphases). LW maintains the variety of Luther's use of singular and plural third person. I have altered the LW translation of "der Satan" as "this devil" to be more literal.

30. WA 15: 211.22–212.7; LW 40: 50–51 (translation altered significantly).

31. Luther claims to have "wol erkennet und geurteylt" the spirits' teaching on two prior occasions; WA 15: 212.8–9. WA takes this as a reference to the *Invocavit Sermons* and Luther's 1522 tract, *Von beider Gestalt des Sacraments*.

32. WA 15: 212.10–22; LW 40: 51. Luther continues here, "I have already heard earlier from the spirit himself here in Wittenberg, that he thinks it necessary to use the sword to carry out his undertaking. At that time I had a hunch that they would go so far as to overthrow civil authority and make themselves lords of the world. . . . He [Müntzer] has been once or twice in my cloister at Wittenberg and had his nose punched." See also WA 15: 215.11–13; LW 40: 54. Müntzer denied this claim in the *Highly-Provoked Vindication*: "pin ich doch in sechs oder syben jaren nit bey dir gewesen." MSB 341.8–11.

33. WA 15: 213.11–214.18; LW 40: 52–53. On humble submission to others' judgment as belonging to the Christian spirit, see WA 15: 215.31–216.8; LW 40: 54–55.

34. WA 15: 214.19–215.3; LW 40: 53 (my emphasis).

35. WA 15: 215.11–30; LW 40: 54.

36. WA 15: 216.21–217.2; LW 40: 55.

37. WA 15: 217.10–218.16; LW 40: 56–57.

38. WA 15: 212.23–213.10, 218.17–219.10; LW 40: 51–52, 57.

39. WA 15: 219.10–18; LW 40: 57–58; see also WA 15: 220.25–33; LW 40: 59.

40. WA 15: 219.19–34; LW 40: 58.

41. WA 15: 220.34–221.8; LW 40: 59 (translation altered).

42. See ThMA 2: 284.1–4; CWTM 85–86; and for discussion, ThMA 2: 265–66n2. Friedrich von Witzleben also impeded his subjects from coming to Allstedt. On these events, see also Bräuer and Vogler, *Thomas Müntzer*, 238–40.

43. ThMA 2: 271.1–17; CWTM 89. Müntzer wrote two letters to the people of Sangerhausen; see ThMA 2: 265–74, 277–81; CWTM 83–91 (ThMA 2 and CWTM differ on the dating and order of these letters).

44. For Müntzer's letters to Zeiß, see ThMA 2: 297–307, 311–22; CWTM 95–103.

45. A *Geheimbund* may have been grounded in Allstedt already in the summer of 1523; see Bräuer, *Spottgedichte*, 94. Some 300 persons from outside Allstedt belonged to

the group that walked directly from the sermon to the town hall to enlist the *Rat*. On Müntzer's sermon and the formation of the *Bund*, see Bräuer and Vogler, *Thomas Müntzer*, 241–43.

46. See ThMA 2: 279.11–280.1; CWTM 84 (c. July 15, 1524), where Müntzer reports to followers in Sangerhausen, "more than thirty leagues and covenants of the elect (*anschlege und vorbundtnis*) have been formed."

47. For Müntzer's conception of covenants and true martyrdom, see his letter to Zeiß of July 25, 1524, ThMA 2: 316–22; CWTM 101–3. Zeiß is exhorted to report on the *Bund* to the princes and encourage them to covenant with their people, before an uprising became unavoidable.

48. Thus, Müntzer's hope of answering Luther's *Letter* via a text printed in Allstedt was frustrated. Müntzer lodged a protest with Frederick the Wise via a letter of August 3, 1524, ThMA 2: 330–35, CWTM 110–13; here he writes, "The Christian faith which I preach may not be in accord with that of Luther but it is identical with that in the hearts of the elect throughout the earth, Psalm 67. For even if someone were born a Turk he still has the beginning of that same faith, that is, the movement of the holy spirit." Müntzer rejects the claim that "Christians should suffer and let themselves be martyred [by tyrants]."

49. Bräuer and Vogler, *Thomas Müntzer*, 249.

50. ThMA 2: 342.2–344.8; CWTM 116–17 (translation altered). "Nothing will be able to stop" translates "vnuberwintlichen," which reminds on the *Prague Manifesto*. In the *Sermon to the Princes*, Müntzer cited Job 28 when describing the distress (*betru[e]bnis*) that comes with visions and Luther's consequent rejection of visions. MSB 254.9–13; CWTM 242.

51. Bräuer, "Die Vorgeschichte, " 65; Bräuer and Vogler, *Thomas Müntzer*, 258.

52. WA 15: 238.1–240.3.

53. Müntzer was already in Mühlhausen when Luther wrote his letter (dated August 21, 1524), and the letter may never have arrived. WAB 3: 328n1; Bräuer and Vogler, *Thomas Müntzer*, 258–60.

54. ThMA 2: 374.1–382.13; for the dating of the Articles, 371n1; for a translation, CWTM 455–59. Walter Elliger, *Thomas Müntzer: Leben und Werk* (Göttingen: Vandenhoeck & Ruprecht, 1975), 581f., sees Pfeiffer as the chief author; CWTM 455n1 rightly notes that "Müntzer's language and ideas also surface unmistakably."

55. On the events of this paragraph, see Bräuer and Vogler, *Thomas Müntzer*, 262–77. Bräuer and Vogler describe the military character of the *Bund* (273); Pfeiffer was enrolled as chaplain, but Müntzer's name does not appear on the rolls.

56. ThMA 1: 323.

57. A surviving, handwritten copy from the Electoral Archives, entitled *Testimony of the First Chapter of the Gospel of Luke*, may represent a copy submitted for censorship; see however Bräuer and Vogler, *Thomas Müntzer*, 289. The relationship between the handwritten *Testimony* and the published *Manifest Exposé* is unclear, and two alternatives have been proposed: "Parallele Entstehung mit Entschärfung des umfangreicheren Textes im 'Gezeugnis' als Zensurexemplar zur Vorlage bei den

Weimarer Behörden oder aber Erweiterung des Textes des 'Gezeugnis' nachdem Müntzer erkannt hatte, dass sich seine Landesherren für seine theologischen Vorstellungen und deren praktische Auswirkungen nicht gewinnen lassen würden." ThMA 1: 322. The editors support the latter position on the grounds that Müntzer would not have attempted to deceive authorities with a tamer text only to publish the fiercer one; see their reconstruction of events, ibid., 322–23. A thorough evaluation need not be attempted here. Our present purpose is best served by attention to the *Exposé*, which is more thorough in its critique of Wittenberg positions and more detailed overall. The printed title is: *Außgetrückte emplössung des falschen Glaubens der ungetrewen welt durchs gezeu[e]gnus des Euangelions Luce vorgetragen der elenden, erbermlichen Christenheyt zur innerung jres irsals.* Several citations from Jeremiah (23:29; 1:9; 1:18) align Müntzer with the prophetic tradition. MSB 267; CWTM 260.

58. Müntzer refers more to clerics than rulers in the *Exposé*.

59. This reference is also contained in the *Testimony*, MSB 268.2; CWTM 263, and could have been penned before Müntzer knew of Luther's *Letter*.

60. MSB 268.6–23; CWTM 262. True *Meisterschaft* can be "ero[e]fnet" according to Müntzer only "mit außlegung der heyligen schrifft in der lere des geystes Christi durch die vergleychung aller geheymnus und urteyl Gottes. Dann es haben alle urteyl das ho[e]chst gegenteyl bey in selber. Wo sie aber nit zusammen verfast werden, mag keyns gantz und gar verstanden werden (wie helle oder klar es ist) on des andern unaußsprechlichen schaden. Das ist die grundtsupp aller bo[e]ßwichtischen zurtrennung."

61. At MSB 268.30–269.8, CWTM 262–63, the *Testimony*'s clear reference to Roman faith, "der sich rhumet seiner prechtigen gewonheit und herkommen," parallels a complaint about the biblical scholars' "bu[o]chstabischen glauben" and "gedichten wort und glauben," which only hardened people in old ways.

62. MSB 269.27–32; CWTM 264.

63. MSB 270.7–27; CWTM 264.

64. MSB 271.9–272.33; CWTM 266–268 (translations altered). Müntzer also cites as examples Moses, Jacob and Gideon; see MSB 272.33–273.25.

65. MSB 273.25–38; CWTM 268–70. "Ein ungeu[e]bter glaub zur ersten ankunfft hat keyn ander urteyl, denn sich an allen orten fo[e]rchten und schwerlich allem singen und sagen stadt zu[o] geben. Wer do leychtlich glaubt, ist eyns leychtfertigen hertzens."

66. MSB 273.39–278.22; CWTM 270–74.

67. For the parallel concern with certitude of salvation and certitude of doctrine, see Schreiner, *Are You alone Wise?*

68. MSB 278.23–280.34; CWTM 274–78 (translation slightly altered). Müntzer here addresses Luther's depiction of him as a "false prophet" and Luther's personal claim, "ich habs gethon"; he associates Luther with the New Testament *Schriftgelehrten* who "Christon anß creu[e]tz brachten."

69. MSB 280.35–281.36; CWTM 278 (translation slightly altered).

70. MSB 282.8–283.2; CWTM 278–80.

71. MSB 283.3–30, CWTM 280, concluding "auch Got nach dem ringen der außerwelten den yammer nit lenger wirt ku[e]nnen und mu[e]gen ansehen, und die tag mu[o]ß er seynen außerwelten verku[e]rtzen, Mat. am 24."

72. MSB 283.31–285.37; CWTM 280–284. "Since man has fallen from God to serve the creatures it is only just that he has (to his cost) to fear the creature more than God." Romans 13 teaches, according to Müntzer, that the sole function of princes is to punish evildoers. "Gott hat die herren und fu[e]rsten in seynem grymm der welt gegeben, und er wil sie in der erbitterung wider weg thu[o]n [citing Hosea 13]."

73. MSB 287.18–288.5; CWTM 284–86. Although Mary and Zechariah "feared God above all things," they couldn't distinguish "the possible from the impossible" without the revelation of the "spirit of the fear of God at the beginning of faith."

74. MSB 288.17–290.13; CWTM 286–88. The scholars ignore Matthew 13 and "haben daselbst imaginirt, auß eynem alten balcken visiert, die engel mit langen spiessen, die sollen absu[e]ndern die gu[o]tten von den bo[e]sen zum ju[e]ngsten tage."

75. MSB 292.33–293.16; CWTM 292.

76. MSB 293.17–295.23; CWTM 292–96.

77. MSB 296.20–298.7; CWTM 296. For Müntzer, scripture itself "exhorts us in the most emphatic manner possible that it is by God alone that we should and must be taught."

78. MSB 298.8–299.8; CWTM 298.

79. MSB 298.8–300.12; CWTM 298–300.

80. MSB 300.13–301.2; CWTM 300. With the aid of mystical vocabulary, MSB 301.2–302.35; CWTM 302–4, describes the experience of God's work in an agonizing discovery of unbelief, which in turn yields true faith and certitude of salvation. The Holy Spirit drives the elect to these outcomes. Faith gains the victory "after it has overcome the world, whose existence within the heart is a thousand-fold more varied than outside it. After coming to this earnest recognition faith overflows; nothing can stop it from growing in the believer, from increasing its capital."

81. MSB 303.34–304.35; CWTM 304–6.

82. MSB 305.8–307.13; CWTM 306–8. "Self-denial" translates "im untergang seyns willens." For further polemic against belly-preachers: MSB 301.28–308.30; CWTM 310.

83. MSB 307.17–309.9; CWTM 308–10 (translation substantially altered).

84. On Luther's apocalyptic horizon, see above all Heiko A. Oberman, *Luther: Man between God and the Devil*, trans. Eileen Walliser-Schwarzbart (New Haven, CT: Yale University Press, 1982). Conversely, Bernhard Lohse, *Martin Luther's Theology: Its Historical and Systematic Development*, trans. Roy A. Harrisville (Minneapolis: Fortress, 1999), 332–35, emphasizes Luther's concern for continuing historical development.

85. MSB 310.17–27; CWTM 312.

86. MSB 311.3–16; CWTM 312–14. My analysis here is influenced by Seebaß, "Reich Gottes," 75–99.

87. MSB 312.6–22; CWTM 314–18.

88. MSB 312.22–314.36; CWTM 314–18.

89. MSB 316.14–317.17; CWTM 318–20 (translation altered). Müntzer continues, "Ach, allerliebsten, da ist die weßheyt (sic.) des creu[e]tzes, mit wellcher Gott seyne außerwelten gru[e]sset. Da mu[o]ß eyner sich an der gantzen welt nit ergern und sihet in keynem winckel etwas gu[o]ts, und die gantz welt ergert sich an der wirckung des besten gu[o]ts und sagt, es sey teu[o]fflisch gespenst."

90. MSB 317.30–318.21; CWTM 320–22. "Genuine" translates "ungetichte," that central concern of Müntzer's evident in the title *Von dem gedichteten Glauben*. See Schreiner, *Are You Alone Wise?* 238–41.

91. On the genesis, printing, and possible circulation of the treatise, ThMA 1: 376–78, assesses the limited evidence.

92. Especially John 8. See MSB 341.1–4; CWTM 347.

93. MSB 322.11–323.3, 322n8; CWTM 327–28, 327n8, 328n13.

94. Luther's readiness to put himself in the place of Christ is a key emphasis in Lyndal Roper, *Martin Luther: Renegade and Prophet* (London: Bodley Head, 2016), 121–23, 189–93, 314–18, 325.

95. MSB 323.4–324.11; CWTM 328–29.

96. MSB 324.12–325.2; CWTM 329–30 (translation altered). MSB 325.3–21; CWTM 330–31 derides the scholars as driven by money, reward, ease, and reputation.

97. See MSB 325.28–29; CWTM 331.

98. MSB 326.25–27.3; CWTM 332 (translation altered). I follow ThMA 1: 383n127 in rendering *undterschaydts* as "chapter," although other interpretations are possible. Compare MSB327n102–103 and n106, CWTM 332n79.

99. MSB 325.24–27; CWTM 331.

100. See MSB 326.12–327.17; CWTM 332–33.

101. MSB 330.6–13; CWTM 336 (translation altered); CWTM translates *gu[e]tigkeyt* as "clemency," but Müntzer's expansion of the discussion to "all God's works" requires a broader translation.

102. As implied by MSB 330n175.

103. MSB 328.7–329.4; CWTM 334. See also MSB 329.13–29, CWTM 335 (where Müntzer blames "all usury, theft and robbery" as well as rebellion on the "lords and princes" who "nemen alle creaturen zum aygenthumb"); and MSB 335.24–28; CWTM 341 (where Müntzer answers the charge of inciting rebellion, arguing that a person with "pure judgment" will not "love rebellion" or oppose a "fu[e]glicher empo[e]rung"). On Luther's alleged "getichter gu[e]tigkeit," see MSB 329.12–13; CWTM 335.

104. MSB 330.14–25; CWTM 336 (translation slightly altered).

105. MSB 330.26–331.24; CWTM 336–37 (translation altered).

106. MSB 332.5–7; CWTM 338.

107. See MSB 337.11f.; CWTM 343–44. Rebuffing Luther's assertion that Müntzer fights against him while enjoying his protection, Müntzer declares, "Undter deinem schirm und schutz pin ich gewesen wie das schaff undterm wolff." Müntzer buttresses his personal claims and rejects Luther's in several ways, not only through appeal to suffering. For one, Müntzer notes the enthusiasm of "das arme dürstige volck" for his work in Allstedt, arguing that Luther had accomplished nothing of

the sort in Wittenberg; consequently, Luther needed to rely on the princes to stop Müntzer; see MSB 333.2–20; CWTM 339. Müntzer also mocks Luther's learning (see, e.g., MSB 333.21–26, CWTM 339), and he repudiates Luther's charge that he (Müntzer) hears and teaches according to a "heavenly voice." His teaching is confirmed by scripture: "Was der almechtig got mit mir machet oder redet, kann ich nit vill ru[e]mens von; dann allayn was ich durchs gezeügnuß Gottes dem volck auß der heyligen schrifft vorsage, und will, ob Got will, meinen dunckel nit predigen." (MSB 338.19–22; CWTM 344). Finally, Müntzer attacks Luther's self-professed humility with theological argumentation and personal polemic. Müntzer accuses Luther of making God the cause of evil and blaming God "daß du ein armer sünder und ein gifftiges würmlein pist mit deiner beschissen demu[e]th. Das hast du mit deinem fantastischen verstandt angericht auß deinem Augustino, warlich ein lesterliche sach, von freyem willen die menschen frech zu[o] verachten." MSB 339.11–19; CWTM 345.

108. MSB 334.2–6; CWTM 339.
109. MSB 335.31f.; CWTM 341–42. Müntzer sharply criticizes Luther for subsequently surrendering married priests "to the chopping block" in his response to the emperor's mandate that "secular authorities should not hinder the punishment of married clergy, as laid down by Canon Law" (see CWTM 341–42n178). At MSB 336.11–24 CWTM 342, Müntzer mocks Luther's conduct at Orlamünde: "Christus gibt den preyß seynem vatter" but Luther demanded "einen grossen titel" from the Orlamünders. Luther also lavishes exalted titles on the princes, Müntzer complains.
110. MSB 340.21–342.2; CWTM 346–48. Müntzer asserts that the German princes would have slain Luther, if he had not stood up at Worms.
111. See especially the correspondence cited in ThMA 2: 338n29.
112. See Luther's 1529 *Lectures on Isaiah*, WA 31/2: 265.9–32; 284.21–285.6; LW 17: 8–9, 31. Discussing Isaiah 40:3, "The voice of one crying in the wilderness," Luther declares, "Away with our schismatics, who spurn the Word while they sit in corners waiting for the Spirit's revelation, but apart from the voice of the Word [i.e. public preaching]! They say one must sit still in a corner and empty the mind of all speculations, and then the Holy Spirit will fill it. The sophists also taught this. In vain, however, do we rely on this, and that for two reasons. In the first place, because we are not able to empty our soul of speculations. The devil will provide you with many thoughts. In the second place, because the flesh has not yet been killed in you. When you have heard the Word, you earnestly kill the flesh and empty your soul." Concerning Isaiah 40:29 ("He gives power to the faint"), Luther says, "It is as if God were saying: 'You must be weary and emptied, so that there is no way out for you. Then I will give you strength. First you must become nothing, then consolation and strength will come.' This happened to me, Martin Luther, who against my will came up against the whole world, and then God helped me. . . . Here you see what a difficult thing faith is, and yet our people spurn it and say, 'Faith must be preached to the Turk, not to the Christians,' as if faith were such a small matter that all had it in common. Our Enthusiasts have not yet experienced the strength of this faith, and I myself am still struggling with it." Note worthy is Luther's continued argument

that his understanding of salvation—with its orientation to Christ and the preached Word *extra nos*—involved a true reduction of the person to nothingness over and against the fanatics' self-willed efforts. Luther derides Müntzer's notion of a faith supposedly shared by the elect among the Turks as shallow, easy, and pleasing to fallen nature.

113. My discussion here addresses the framework of the treatise and cannot involve detailed engagement with points of sacramental theology and exegesis; for a recent discussion of the treatise and Karlstadt's response to it focused on sacramental teachings, see Burnett, *Karlstadt*, 69–76.

114. See WA 18: 139.7–12; LW 40: 149: " Das ich yhn nu eynen teuffel nenne, soll sich niemand verwundern, Denn an D. Carlstad ligt myr nichts, Ich sehe auff yhn nicht, sondern auff den, der yhn besessen hat und durch yhn redet."

115. WA 18: 62.6–63.20; LW 40: 79–81 (translation altered).

116. WA 18: 63.21–65.2; LW 40: 81–82.

117. See also Luther's *Letter to the Christians at Strassburg in Opposition to the Fanatic Spirit,* esp. WA 15: 393.6–394.11; LW 40: 67f.

118. WA 18: 65.9–13; LW 40: 82. See also LW 40: 135–36.

119. WA 18: 65.14–23; LW 40: 84 (translation altered).

120. On the evolution of Luther's conception of the conscience, see Michael G. Baylor, *Action and Person: Conscience in Late Scholasticism and the Young Luther* (Leiden: E. J. Brill, 1977), 1–19, 119–272. Randall C. Zachman, *The Assurance of Faith: Conscience in the Theology of Martin Luther and John Calvin* (Minneapolis: Fortress Press, 1993), argues that for Luther, conscience can confirm God's judgment over sin but not God's forgiveness, of which the sinner finds assurance only by believing the Word *extra nos*.

121. WA 18: 65.24–30; LW 40: 83.

122. WA 18: 65.31–67.2; LW 40: 83. The opposition is between "geringe stueck[en]" and "die rechten furnemesten stuecken"—that is, the five *Hauptstücke* under discussion, and especially the first two, law and gospel.

123. On arguments about images and iconoclasm, see Joseph Leo Koerner, *The Reformation of the Image* (Chicago: University of Chicago Press, 2004), 153–70 (discussing Luther); and Carlos M. N. Eire, *War Against the Idols: The Reformation of Worship from Erasmus to Calvin* (Cambridge: Cambridge University Press, 1986), 54–73.

124. WA 18: 67.9–68.60; LW 40: 84–85. See also WA 18: 71.17–72.2, 78.21–24; LW 40: 89, 94.

125. *Ursachen derhalben Andreas Karlstadt aus den Landen zu Sachsen vetrieben* (Strassburg: Johann Prüss d.J., 1524); Zorzin, "Verzeichnis," 72.

126. A reference to the title of Müntzer's *Highly Provoked Vindication,* as WA and LW note.

127. WA 18: 85.1–86.5; LW 40: 102–3. See also WA 18: 100.3–6; LW 40: 116.

128. See Luther's description of his communication with John Frederick after the meeting with Karlstadt in Jena, WA 18: 99.10–13; LW 40: 115.

129. WA 18: 86.6–88.30; LW 40: 103–106. Luther denies that Karlstadt can be vindicated on the basis of the Orlamünde community's letter to Allstedt, which is discussed later in this chapter; Karlstadt may not intend "murder and rebellion," but he has a "rebellious and murderous spirit" just like Müntzer. See also WA 18: 92.5–30; LW 40: 108–9.

130. For a discussion, see Ronald J. Sider, *Andreas Bodenstein von Karlstadt: The Development of his Thought, 1517–1525* (Leiden: Brill, 1974), 188–90.

131. WA 18: 94.13f.; LW 40: 111f. Note the question, "Solt nicht eyn guter geyst Gotts ordnung eyn wenig bas furchten" (WA 18: 95.16–17; LW 40: 112)?

132. WA 18: 95.26–97.5, 99.20–23 ("Were er nů gewiss gewesen, das er zum pfarrer beruffen were, solt er sie nicht ubergeben haben und ehe das leben drueber lassen, wie er bis daher hatte gestritten und sich geweret, Denn von goettlichem beruff sol man nicht lassen, wie sie sich rhumen eyttel Gottes gemeynschafft zu haben"); LW 40: 112–13, 116. Luther also argues here that no one may appeal to an inner calling in acting against God's "usual order" unless he proves the calling with miracles.

133. WA 18: 98.9; LW 40: 114.

134. WA 18: 100.6–26; LW 40: 116–17.

135. WA 18: 100.27–101.10; LW 40: 117. The terms cited by Luther are "entgrobung," "studirung," "verwunderung," and "langweyl.'" On the use of mystical terminology, see also WA 18: 70.37–71.8, 137.5–138.26; LW 40: 88, 147–48.

136. WA 18: 83.21–25; LW 40: 100.

137. WA 18: 136.9–137.19; LW 40: 146–47: "[W]ie er dyr mit den worten geyst, geyst, geyst das maul auff sperret und doch die weyl, beyde brucken, steg und weg, leytter und alles umbreysst, dadurch der geyst zu dyr kommen soll, nemlich, die eusserlichen ordnung Gotts ynn der leyplichen tauffe zeychen und muendlichen wort Gottes und will dich leren, nicht wie der geyst zu dyr, sondern wie du zum geyst komen sollt." "The inward experience follows and is effected by the outward." See also WA 18: 185.8–28; LW 40: 195.

138. WA 18: 138.10–26; LW 40: 148. See also WA 18: 168.25–180.7, 193.26–194.15, 195.23–197.7; LW 40: 178–90, 203–207.

139. WA 18: 139.5–26; LW 40: 149.

140. WA 18: 143.1–144.1; LW 40: 153–54 (translation altered). WA 18: 182.22–23; LW 40: 192. See also WA 18: 186.1–187.13; LW 40: 195–97.

141. WA 18: 198.7–17; LW 40: 208.

142. *Anzeyg etlicher Hauptartickeln Christlicher leere. In wo[e]lchen Doct. Luther den Andresen Carolstat durch falsche zusag vnd nachred verdechtig macht* (Augsburg: Philipp Ulhart, 1525). See Zorzin, "Verzeichnis," 73; VD 16 B 6099.

143. Bubenheimer, *Thomas Müntzer*, 145–70.

144. There are three surviving letters between Karlstadt and Müntzer themselves, along with the letter of the Orlamünders to Allstedt, which was published and manifests Karlstadt's authorial hand. For a study: Siegfried Bräuer, "Der Briefwechsel zwischen Andreas Bodenstein von Karlstadt und Thomas Müntzer," in QdR: 187–209; esp. 208.

145. This is not to say that they had identical conceptions of what it meant to be a prophet. As discussed in chapter 4, Karlstadt did not identify himself as a prophet, but he depicted true preaching as prophetic—the preacher was "nothing" and hence a vehicle for divine speech. See also Hans-Peter Hasse, "'Von mir selbs nicht halden': Beobachtungen zum Selbstverständnis des Andreas Bodenstein von Karlstdt," in QdR: 49–73.

146. As noted by TMA 2: 151n2. Müntzer's criticism of the Wittenbergers' denial of the doctrine of purgatory, however, may not have been in contradiction to Karlstadt: see Evener, "Wittenberg's Wandering Spirits," 549.

147. See ThMA 2: 151n1. On the contents of Müntzer's correspondence, see Bräuer, "Der Briefwechsel," 191–92.

148. This does not appear from the translation of CWTM 53; but see ThMA 2: 152–53.

149. ThMA 2: 150 (conjectural letter 53). Karlstadt may have helped Müntzer obtain a briefly held post in Glaucha; see Bräuer, "Der Briefwechsel," 194.

150. To be noted is the refrain, "But we can return to this another time," repeated three times, and the concluding admonition, "Come as soon as possible." ThMA 2: 152.3, 10, 13; 154.1; CWTM 53.

151. ThMA 2: 151.3–152.3; CWTM 52–53. See Hans-Peter Hasse, "Karlstadts Predigt am 29. September 1522 in Joachimsthal: Ein unbekannter Text aus Stephan Roths Sammlung von Predigten des Johannes Sylvius Egranus," ARG 81 (1990): 97–119, 113–14n81, cited by ThMA 2: 152n5–7. The reference to the grain of wheat is from John 12:24.

152. ThMA 2: 152.4–13; CWTM 53 (translation slightly altered following ThMA; CWTM translates MSB).

153. ThMA 2: 152.14–153.4; CWTM 53. The passage is revealing, as Karlstadt commends Müntzer for seeking *only* his counsel—the counsel of someone now excluded from Luther's circle.

154. ThMA 2: 153.5–7; CWTM 53. On Karlstadt's view of dreams and visions, see ThMA 2: 153–54n19, which cites Sider, *Andreas Bodenstein von Karlstadt*, 261, and *Von Mannigfaltigkeit*, D3v, where Karlstadt writes, "Aber wie dem sey, so ist dannest gotlicher will in H. geschryfft klerlicher tzu[o] mercken dan in dreymen, in gesichten unde verwickelte[n] geleychniß."

155. See Volkmar Joestel, *Ostthüringen und Karlstadt: Soziale Bewegung und Reformation im mittleren Saaletal am Vorabend des Bauernkrieges (1522–1524)* (Berlin: Schelzky & Jeep, 1996), 87.

156. The letter is addressed "to his dearest brother Andrew Karlstadt, farmer in Wörlitz." ThMA 2: 188.1; CWTM 65. Karlstadt had already given up his land in Wörlitz and resettled in Orlamünde. Rucker could not deliver the letter and returned it to Müntzer. See ThMA 2: 188–89nn3, 7.

157. ThMA 2: 189.8–190.3; CWTM 65. Karlstadt was a doctor of both laws and had participated in a similar measure in Wittenberg in early 1522. See ThMA 2: 190n10.

158. ThMA 2: 188.2–189.2; CWTM 65. On Karlstadt's promise and failure to correspond, see ThMA 2: 188n5, 187n1.

159. ThMA 2: 190.3–5; CWTM 65–66.

160. See Bräuer, "Der Briefwechsel," 199, 208. In Bräuer's account, the exchange over the *Bund* decisively ended for Müntzer any hope of common cause with Karlstadt and the Orlamünde *Gemeinde*. Karlstadt, conversely, hoped to correct Müntzer in his letter, and he later remained gentler in his assessment of Müntzer than others. For Karlstadt's account of the receipt of the letters, see EC 381; Bräuer, "Der Briefwechsel," 201.

161. On the expectation that the Orlamünders would support Allstedt, see ThMA 2: 337.6–8.

162. See ThMA 2: 289n11; Bräuer, "Der Briefwechsel," 202.

163. Translation of CWTM 91, reordered per the Latin ThMA 2: 287.1. On the use of the title "bishop" among reformers, see Bräuer, "Der Briefwechsel," 201.

164. ThMA 2: 287.2–88.4; CWTM 91. The reference is to Proverbs 27:6 (see ThMA 2: 288n4).

165. ThMA 2: 288.5–289.4; CWTM 91 (translation of the first sentence my own, aided by CWTM).

166. ThMA 2: 289.6–290.9; CWTM 92.

167. ThMA 2: 290.9–20; CWTM 92.

168. Bräuer supposes that Müntzer and Allstedt had turned to this circle specifically, with an expectation of support built up through previous, now lost exchanges. See also ThMA 2: 292–3n2.

169. On the printing of the text and the title, which may have been created by Karlstadt or the printer Luft, see Bräuer, "Der Briefwechsel," 204–5.

170. ThMA 2: 293.1–294.11; CWTM 93.

171. Müntzer had preached about the *Bund* on the basis of this text.

172. As ThMA 2: 295n25 notes, "[Diese] Stelle spielt bei Müntzer gleichfalls eine große Rolle, vor allem als Kriterium für die Gottesfurcht."

173. ThMA 2: 294.16–296.9; CWTM 94.

174. ThMA 2: 296.19–18; CWTM 94 (my translation). On the interpretation of the "Pfund" and the question of "account" in both Karlstadt and Müntzer, see the sources cited by Bräuer, "Der Briefwechsel," 206n90–91.

175. ThMA 2: 296; CWTM 94 (translation altered). As Bräuer, "Der Briefwechsel," 207, notes, Müntzer interpreted the response of Karlstadt and Orlamünde as the result of "kreatürliche Menschenfurcht, also elementare Glaubensschwäche."

176. *Anzeige*, A2r–v; EC 342–43 (commas removed). The line is a reference to Ezekiel 47; Karlstadt references Jeremiah and Zechariah throughout. Karlstadt seeks an open hearing before a Christian *Gemeinde*—but not, like Müntzer, before all nations.

177. *Anzeige*, B1r–v; EC 346–7. Karlstadt insists that he places faith and love first; see *Anzeige*, C1r; EC 351. On the insufficiency of Luther's articles as they pertain to the treasures of Christ that come to Christians through faith, see *Anzeige*, D4r–E1r; EC 362–63.

178. *Anzeige*, A2v–A3r; EC 343 (translation altered).

179. *Anzeige*, A3r–v; EC 343–44 (my translation); these arguments are repeated at *Anzeige*, C4v–D1r; EC 357: "Anyone . . . who understands sin through reason alone,

with the aid of the law only, without knowledge and illumination of the Holy Spirit, understands sin . . . in such a way as to have more delight in sin than ever before"; this person also comes to hate the law, which is a worse sin than any mere carnal sin. Karlstadt attributes a "rational knowledge of sin [gained] through the law" to Jews, Pelagians, and non-Christians—categories that Luther himself applied to Karlstadt, Müntzer, and like "spirits."

180. *Anzeige*, A3v–4r; EC 344–45.
181. The practices of concern to Karlstadt were the celebration of the Lord's Supper as a remembrance of Christ's sacrifice, believers' baptism, and the removal of images; *Anzeige*, B3r–v; EC 348–49.
182. *Anzeige*, C1v–C3r; EC 352–55.
183. *Anzeige*, D1v–D2v; EC 358–59.
184. *Anzeige*, D2v–D3r; EC 359–60 (translation altered). Karlstadt names specific preachers here.
185. *Anzeige*, D3r; EC 360. The reference, not noted in the marginalia or text, is to Jeremiah.
186. *Anzeige*, D3v; EC 361. The translation of the last line, obscured by EC, is my own. I also have rendered "groben" as "coarse" rather than "grave."
187. *Anzeige*, D3v; EC 361 (translation altered).
188. At *Anzeige*, D4r, EC 362, Karlstadt states that he has addressed the topic extensively in another book, likely *Wie sich der Glaube*, as Furcha proposes (see EC 414n24).
189. *Anzeige*, D4r–E1r; EC 362–63.
190. *Anzeige*, E1r–v; EC 363–64 (translation extensively altered).
191. *Anzeige*, E2v; EC 365–66.
192. *Anzeige*, E3r; EC 366.
193. *Anzeige*, E3r–v; EC 366–67 (translation altered).
194. *Anzeige*, E3v; EC 367.
195. *Anzeige*, A4v–B1r; EC 345–46 (translation altered). Karlstadt refers to several books he has written "von der to[e]dtung des fleysch vnd des Alten Adams." These books cannot be Karlstadt's two tracts on *Gelassenheit*, as Furcha (EC 413n8) proposes, for Karlstadt states that he was presently (in January 1525) seeking to publish the works. Likely, the reference is to lost works.
196. *Anzeige*, E3v; EC 367.
197. On the failure of scholarship to take Karlstadt's reported *Anfechtungen* seriously, see Markus Matthias, "Die Anfänge der reformatorischen Theologie des Andreas Bodenstein von Karlstadt," in QdR: 87–110; here, 87–89. On the competing accounts of *Anfechtung* and conversion authored by Karlstadt and Luther in 1517–1518, see Volker Leppin, "Die Wittenbergische Bulle: Andreas Karlstadts Kritik anm Luther," in DKdM: 117–30; here, 123–27; and Leppin, "Mystische Erbe auf getrennten Wegen: Überlegungen zu Karlstadt und Luther," in *Luther und das monastische Erbe*, ed. Christoph Bultmann, Volker Leppin, and Andreas Lindner (Tübingen: Mohr Siebeck, 2007), 154–62; here, 158–62.
198. *Anzeige*, E4r; EC 367–68 (translation altered; my emphasis).

199. *Anzeige*, E4r; EC 368: "Das ist war / wo[e]llicher einen rechten warhafftigen glauben hatt / Der mu[o]ß mir ettwas sagen künden / vom absterben weltlicher weißheit oder mu[o]ß ho[e]ren / das ich jm sag / Du glaubest nit recht / den[n] das Euangelium Christi scheüsset nit feel."

200. Luther is said to be well aware of this fact, because he received a copy of a letter that Karlstadt wrote to the "men of Orlamünde." *Anzeige*, E4v; EC 368.

201. *Anzeige*, E4v–F1r; EC 368–69. The translation of the phrase, "kein anzeyg verdechtlicher heyligkeit," is my own.

202. *Anzeige*, F1r; EC 369.

203. See Ulrich Bubenheimer, "Karlstadt, Andreas Rudolff Bodenstein von (1486–1541)," TRE 17: 649–57; 654.

204. *Anzeige*, F1v: ". . . gibt bo[e]ß anzeygen des innerlichen gemu[e]ets." Cf. EC 370.

205. *Anzeige*, F1v–F2r; EC 369–70 (translation altered).

206. *Anzeige*, F2r–v; EC 370–71.

207. *Anzeige*, F3r–v; EC 372. For Karlstadt's defense of his understanding of Christian freedom, see *Anzeige*, F4v; EC 374.

Epilogue

1. For a review of six significant books reflecting this narrative, see Vincent Evener, "From the Universal to the Particular: Luther and the Reformation after Five Hundred Years," JEH 69, no. 4 (October 2018): 806–20. None of the narratives mentioned in this paragraph emerged for the first time in 2017; each has been informed by long research and each accounts for important fields of available data.

2. The narrative of failed Christianization structures Carlos M. N. Eire, *Reformations: The Early Modern World, 1450–1650* (New Haven, CT: Yale University Press, 2016). Eire describes Christianization as the effort to "lessen the gap between the ideal and the actual" (691; see also 588–90; 616–17), and he tells how competing visions of Christianization in the early modern era produced conflict and eventually gave rise to skepticism, rational thought, and toleration (561, 585, 661–62). The end result of the drive for Christianization was de-Christianization; religious division meant that religion could no longer be the "marrow of all social, economic, political, and cultural exchanges" (viii, 717–18). Religion became a "private concern" (756). An earlier work focusing on Christianization and the unintended consequence of Confessionalization was Scott Hendrix, *Recultivating the Vineyard: The Reformation Agendas of Christianization* (Louisville, KY: Westminster John Knox, 2004); Hendrix sought to affirm the coherence of the Reformation, over and against other scholars' emphasis on plurality and diversity, by identifying a shared goal of Christianization behind competing agendas. See also Scott Hendrix, "Re-Rooting the Faith: The Reformation as Re-Christianization," CH 69 (2000): 558–77; as well as the essays responding to *Recultivating the Vineyard* found in Anna Marie Johnson and John A. Maxfield, eds., *The Reformation as Christianization: Essays on Scott Hendrix's Christianization Thesis* (Tübingen: Mohr Siebeck, 2012). Both

Eire and Hendrix take the concept of "Christianization" from Jean Delumeau, *Catholicism Between Luther and Voltaire: A New View of the Counter-Reformation* (London: Burns & Oates, 1977), but they define the term differently than Delumeau. For another account of the Reformation's universal aspirations ending in secularization, see Brad S. Gregory, *The Unintended Reformation: How a Religious Revolution Secularized Society* (Cambridge, MA: Belknap, 2012).

3. See my discussion in "The Future of Reformation Studies," CHRC 97, no. 3–4 (2017): 310–21.

4. ThMA 2: 496–504; CWTM 160–61.

5. Particularly influential were Luther's House Postils. See Martin Luther, *Hauβpostil D. Martin Luthers vber die Sontags vnd der fu[e]rnembsten Fest Evangelia durch das gantze Jar* (Nürnberg: Johann Vom Berg and Ulrich Neuber, 1545). VD 16 ZV 10044.

6. See the remarks of Thomas Albert Howard, *Remembering the Reformation: An Inquiry into the Meanings of Protestantism* (Oxford: Oxford University Press, 2016), 2.

7. As argued by Steven Ozment, *The Reformation in the Cities: The Appeal of Protestantism to Sixteenth Century Germany and Switzerland* (New Haven, CT: Yale University Press, 1980), e.g., 50, 77–78, 118; for this view in a popular textbook, see Carter Lindberg, *The European Reformations*, 2nd ed. (Malden, MA: Wiley-Blackwell, 2010), 56–60; for a defense of Ozment's perspective, see Ronald K. Rittgers, "Anxious Penitents and the Appeal of the Reformation: Ozment and the Historiography of Confession," in *Piety and Family in Early Modern Europe: Essays in Honour of Steven Ozment*, ed. Marc R. Forster and Benjamin J. Kaplan (Aldershot: Ashgate, 2005), 50–69.

8. See the discussion of Eire and Hendrix in note 2.

9. Ronald K. Rittgers, *The Reformation of Suffering: Pastoral Theology and Lay Piety in Late Medieval and Early Modern Germany* (Oxford: Oxford Unviersity Press, 2012); "The Age of Reform as an Age of Consolation," CH 86, no. 3 (September 2017): 607–42.

10. Susan E. Schreiner, *Are You Alone Wise? The Search for Certainty in the Early Modern Era* (Oxford: Oxford University Press, 2012).

11. Anxiety about deceit (false certitude) is a central theme in Schreiner, *Are You Alone Wise?*, 261f., and Rittgers discusses false consolation (see "Age of Reform," 629).

12. WA 32: 29.18–32.17; LW 51: 199–201. Luther's concern with Karlstadt in this sermon was undoubtedly a response to the latter's resurfacing in Reformed circles; in response to suffering, Karlstadt and his ilk are said to become "gar erschlagen und verzagt, mehr denn kein weib."

13. *Hauβpostil*, 152b–54b. The sermon argues that Christians willingly embrace suffering as deserved punishment for sin; but their suffering is not primarily punishment—rather the devil and the world assail them because of their faith.

14. See John M. Frymire, "Works: Sermons and Postils," in OEML: 3:561–89.

15. Cf. Gregory, *Unintended Reformation*, 372.

Index

For the benefit of digital users, indexed terms that span two pages (e.g., 52–53) may, on occasion, appear on only one of those pages.